B. P. Pratten

The King and the Kingdom

A study of the four Gospels. Second Series

B. P. Pratten

The King and the Kingdom
A study of the four Gospels. Second Series

ISBN/EAN: 9783337183578

Printed in Europe, USA, Canada, Australia, Japan

Cover: Foto ©Lupo / pixelio.de

More available books at **www.hansebooks.com**

THE KING

AND

THE KINGDOM.

AND

THE KINGDOM:

A STUDY OF THE FOUR GOSPELS.

'To the present age is ascribed productiveness and changeableness of opinions, and at the same time indifference to opinions. But that cannot arise from this: no man in all corrupted Europe can be indifferent to truth as such, for it, in the last resort, decides upon his life; but every one is at last become cold and shy towards the erring teachers and preachers of truth. Take the hardest heart and brain which withers away in any capital city, and only give him the certainty that the spirit which approaches him brings down from eternity the key which opens and shuts the so weighty gates of his life-prison, of death, and of heaven,—and the dried-up worldly man, so long as he has a care or a wish, must seek for a truth which can reveal to him that spirit.'—RICHTER's *Levana*.

'Hasten the time when, unfettered by sectarian intolerance, and unawed by the authority of men, the Bible shall make its rightful impression upon all; the simple and obedient readers thereof calling no man Master, but Christ only.'—Dr. CHALMERS.

'I speak as to wise men; judge ye what I say.'—1 Cor. x. 15.

SECOND SERIES.

NEW YORK: G. P. PUTNAM'S SONS.
LONDON: WILLIAMS AND NORGATE.
1893.

PREFACE.

MANY thoughtful and honest minds cannot but feel that under the pressure of a systematised theology the gospel of Christ has lost much of its freshness and power. The very reverence paid outwardly to Scripture has tended towards this result. By every generation, throughout eighteen centuries, the divine Truth has been expounded, weighed, measured, attacked, defended. This ceaseless handling could scarcely fail to soil and dim its native brightness. The atmosphere of Christian thought, necessary and life-giving though it be, is always more or less weighted with foreign particles, emanations of the human mind, which have settled into a thick film of dogmatic teaching, blurring in no small degree the truth which lies beneath. There is surely no irreverence in the touch which would brush away these accretions of centuries.

Probably they whose profession it is to preach the gospel are of all men least likely, in the ordinary course of theological study, to accept it in its simplicity. This involves no disparagement of their learning or sincerity. It arises from the fact that they are bound down to creeds and articles of religion, and that their minds have been nourished and developed by the ideas of spiritual fathers and doctors of the Church. So it comes to pass that their interpretations of Scripture are tinged unconsciously with traditional beliefs. Their expositions of the New Testament have a definiteness which did not exist in the teaching of Jesus, and almost every parable he spoke has had impressed upon it some settled, orthodox meaning.

There is indeed much in the present aspect of Christianity to occasion sorrow and perplexity. On the one side are clashing creeds and sects, seeming but to rend and disfigure the

Truth at which they clutch; on the other side is a band of honest, fearless sceptics, acute in the exercise of criticism, and so self-confident that they scruple not to adopt unhesitatingly the conclusions of their own minds, to the utter rejection of whatever appears miraculous in the gospel narratives. Yet surely the compilers, who wrote in apostolic times, were not destitute of common sense and powers of judgment, and they must have had infinitely better means of arriving at the facts than can be claimed by any investigator after the lapse of eighteen centuries.

Disregarding alike dogmatic interpretations and hostile criticisms, it is no small comfort to turn to the narratives themselves, seeking with patient study their true import. Independent and unprejudiced enquiry is the best preservative against the two extremes of believing too easily or doubting too much. To do full justice to the authors of the Gospels we must take their work as it were fresh from their own hands. If the gospel histories are worth anything, they will be self-luminous, and by their own light alone should they be interpreted. If in the main points and circumstances they are held to be not reliable, they can scarcely be deemed worthy of serious study.

In this spirit the following investigation has been conducted. Everything is sought to be taken as it stands, without abatement and without addition, the simple object being to arrive at the facts intended to be conveyed by the evangelists, and to grasp the truths and doctrines taught by Jesus.

Not scholarship, as may easily be seen, but only earnestness of thought and sincerity of purpose, can be urged in favour of this work. It is the outcome of many years of painstaking, loving labour, the foundation having previously been laid by a similar methodical and careful review of each of the four gospels separately. Not until that apprenticeship to the subject was ended, did the author venture to undertake the more important task of combining the four narratives, pondering them as before verse by verse, phrase by phrase, and when necessary word by word. No preconceived ideas, his own or of others, were voluntarily allowed to influence the investigation; no theories or doctrines had to be upheld, no reasonable conclusions needed to be shrunk from or evaded, no fear of adverse judgment or criticism, no dread of blame, no hope of praise or profit have been at work to interfere with the expression of free and honest thought. That fact may serve, it is hoped, to extenuate any apparently undue boldness of utterance: if the writer seems, as may often be the case, to undervalue the opinions of other men, it is not out of disrespect, but simply because truth is to be prized above everything; whenever the conclusions arrived at are strongly stated, it is because they have been as strongly felt. A careful reader will note the gradual growth of opinion from first to last. The true nature of Christ's gospel, of the kingdom of heaven, and of real discipleship to Jesus, must needs dawn more and more, here a little and there a little, on the mind which sets itself to the study of his divine teaching.

All Scriptural quotations are from the Revised Version, unless otherwise stated.

Frequent references will be found to the following works:

THE HOLY BIBLE. Literally and idiomatically translated out of the original languages. By Robert Young, D.D. A. Fullarton & Co., Edinburgh, Dublin and London.

THE NEW TESTAMENT. With various readings from the most celebrated manuscripts of the original Greek Text. By Constantine Tischendorf. Tauchnitz Edition. Volume 1000. Sampson Low, Son & Marston, London.

THE NEW TESTAMENT. Translated from the critical text of Von Tischendorf. By Samuel Davidson, D.D. Henry King & Son, London. (*All readings and renderings mentioned as being those of Von Tischendorf are from this work, the renderings, of course, being by Dr. Davidson.*)

THE NEW TESTAMENT FOR ENGLISH READERS. By Henry Alford, D.D. Rivingtons, London.

THE HOLY BIBLE. Translated by Samuel Sharpe. Williams & Norgate, London.

THE ENGLISHMAN'S GREEK NEW TESTAMENT, together with an interlinear Translation. S. Bagster & Sons, Limited, London.

THE ENGLISHMAN'S CONCORDANCE OF THE GREEK NEW TESTAMENT. S. Bagster & Sons, Limited, London.

THE
KING AND THE KINGDOM:

A STUDY OF THE FOUR GOSPELS.

PART II.

THE enforced sojourn of Jesus in Galilee was now drawing to its close. The fourth evangelist states plainly the reasons which led to it. 'And after these things Jesus walked in Galilee; for he would [John] not walk in Judæa, because the Jews sought to kill him.' From the other evangelists we have learnt what happened during this period, which was full of incidents; and we know that the mind of Jesus was then busy with respect to the establishment and practical working of that 'assembly' which he designed to found. Alas! that his ideal plan should never yet have been realised. John's narrative passes over in silence this eventful portion of the career of Jesus, but records the fact that his prolonged absence from Judæa at length occasioned comment, and that some officious advice was offered to him by his relatives. 'Now the feast of the Jews, the feast of tabernacles, was at hand. His brethren therefore said unto him, Depart hence, and go into Judæa, that thy disciples also may behold the works which thou doest.' He had previously gained a number of adherents in the south: why should he remain in the north so long away from them? There could be no better opportunity than the coming feast for a display of his miraculous powers. It was time, and the proper course, that any claims he had to make, should be made as publicly as possible. 'For no man doeth anything in secret, and himself seeketh to be known openly.' Why should he work in a corner, when he could do so before the eyes of all men? 'If thou doest these things, manifest thyself to the world.' This disclosure for a moment of the family life of Jesus is somewhat startling. He was surrounded by grown-up brothers and sisters, who seem to have been quite unable to comprehend his claims and his powers. It is evident that his mother preserved silence with respect to his birth, leaving the divine purposes to accomplish themselves without explanation or interference on her part. Her husband is never mentioned; possibly he had passed away from this life. We must not attribute the advice now tendered, to sarcasm or unkindness. A serious argument seems to have been intended, to which Jesus replied with equal seriousness. The advisers do not seem to have troubled themselves to ascertain whether the reported works of

B

Jesus were actually true. Supposing them to be so, he could not do a wiser thing than submit them to the test of public criticism. His brethren themselves were not only unsympathetic, but unbelieving. 'For even his brethren did not believe on him.' There is nothing wonderful in that. None believed in him, who did not care to listen to him, who were not moved by his words, or who had not enough of faith to accept facts vouched by others, or of interest to go and see and judge for themselves.

To the counsel given him Jesus replied that the fitting time for his departure to Judæa had not arrived. In that respect his brethren were freer than himself, for at any moment they could go without attracting observation, or dread of consequences. With him it was far otherwise: he was not only widely known, but, outside the circle of his own disciples, intensely hated on account of his uncompromising denunciations of evil. 'Jesus therefore said unto them. My time is not yet come; but your time is always ready. The world cannot hate you; but me it hateth, because I testify of it, that its works are evil.' Whenever he went, it would be, he knew, at peril of his life. His brethren must go up without him, for he was not prepared to go during festival time. 'Go ye up unto the feast: I go not up yet unto this feast.' The Revisers note that 'many ancient copies omit *yet:*' the Sinaitic, which is the most ancient, does so. The author of 'Gospel Difficulties' remarks as follows: 'In his Commentary on Tatian's Harmony, Ephrem Syrus has the following: "He said not, I do not ascend *to* this feast but *in* this feast (Non dixit, non ascendo ad festum hoc sed in festo hoc)." Tatian therefore early in the second century apparently knew nothing of the reading of the Received Text of the present day in this passage. It is of course very easy to understand how likely it would be that a copyist might think that "to this feast" was required by the sense of the passage, and how therefore, if Tatian's reading was correct, the spurious reading crept in.' Tischendorf adopts the Sinaitic reading: 'I go not up unto this feast.' Jesus repeated as his reason : 'because my time is not yet fulfilled.' The words seem to indicate a fixed time during which Jesus was debarred from undertaking the journey, although the period of restraint was near its close. He had confined his ministrations to Galilee owing to some threat against his life. The fact that 'the Jews sought to kill him' is alluded to as a matter within public knowledge. He may have been under legal penalties: possibly one of them was to the effect that if within a certain time he revisited Jerusalem his life would be forfeit. The expression used by Jesus seems to point to something of that kind. That is but a supposition, and it may be considered more probable that Jesus referred to the fulfilment of an appointed period in his destiny, as in another passage where the same verb, *sumpleroō*, 'to fill completely,' is used: 'And it came to pass when the days were well-nigh come (Gr., were being fulfilled) that he should be received up, he steadfastly set his face to go to Jerusalem.' Jesus was able to forecast his own destiny. Elijah and Moses had been with him on the mount 'and spake of his decease (or, departure) which he was about to accomplish at Jerusalem.' Must not the mind of Jesus have been constantly looking towards that final crisis? Though he might rarely care to talk about it, yet what more natural than that some reference to it should be made when his plans and course of action were alluded to?

Having resisted his brethren's importunity, and arranged for their prior departure, Jesus was free to follow the course dictated by his own judgment. He gave no further hint of his intentions, and continued his residence in Galilee. 'And having said these things unto them, he abode *still* in Galilee.' The Revisers have retained the italicised word 'still,' which is dispensed with by Tischendorf and Young. The Revised Version continues as follows: 'But when his brethren were gone up unto the feast, then went he also up:' the Revisers retain the expression 'were gone up,' as it stands in the Authorised Version; but Alford, Young and Tischendorf replace it by 'went up.' This alters the sense. The Authorised and Revised Versions represent the departure of Jesus as deferred until his brethren had left, which accords with Luther's version; the three other translators represent the departure of Jesus as simultaneous with that of his brethren, if even he did not go with them: 'But when his brethren went up unto the feast, then he also went up.' It would seem that instead of preceding Jesus they chose to delay their departure. That is on the supposition that the word 'yet' is to be retained. If, however, it is omitted, it seems necessary to fall back upon Tatian's reading: 'I do not ascend in this feast.' The verb here used, *anabainō*, will bear that sense also, as in the passages: 'No man hath ascended into heaven,' 'I ascend unto my Father,' and in various other passages.

7 John 9

„ 10

3 John 13
20 John 17

Jesus in his journey sought to avoid publicity, for it is added: 'not publicly, but as it were in secret.' The oldest MS. omits 'as it were,' and Tischendorf's version stands: 'not openly, but in secret.' There was no attempt at concealment, only Jesus travelled incognito, as a private traveller, not preaching and healing on his way. But when he reached the borders of Judæa, his incognito was dropped perforce; crowds resorted to him, and he recommenced his work of healing and teaching. Matthew and Mark here take up the narrative. 'And it came to pass when Jesus had finished these words, he departed from Galilee, and came into the borders of Judæa beyond Jordan; and great multitudes followed him; and he healed them there.' Mark does not allude to the cures, but notifies the fact that Jesus resumed a course of teaching. 'And he arose from thence, and cometh into the borders of Judæa and beyond Jordan: and multitudes come together unto him again; and, as he was wont, he taught them again.'

7 John 10

19 Mat. 1. 2

10 Mark 1

Meantime the celebration of the feast of tabernacles had begun in Jerusalem, and enquiries were being made as to his whereabouts. 'The Jews therefore sought him at the feast, and said, Where is he?' Young renders, 'Where is that one?' Alford, 'Where is that man?' and observes: 'The *Jews* are, as usual, the rulers, as distinguished from the multitudes. Their question itself (*that man*) shews a hostile spirit.' The public mind was excited, and there was much discussion and difference of opinion about Jesus, some upholding his character, and others denouncing him as a demagogue. 'And there was much murmuring among the multitudes concerning him: some said, He is a good man; others said, Not so, but he leadeth the multitude

7 John 11

„ 12

astray.' No one ventured to espouse his cause in public, for the vengeance of his enemies was to be dreaded. 'Howbeit no man spake openly (publicly—Young) of him for fear of the Jews.' Alford says: 'Here again *the Jews* are distinguished from the *multitudes*.' This distinction drawn by Alford will not bear investigation. 'The Jews' are constantly referred to throughout John's gospel, but not in the sense of 'the rulers, as distinguished from the multitudes.' The allusions to 'the Jews' are very frequent: in chapter 2, three times, ch. 3, twice, ch. 4, twice, ch. 5, four times, ch. 6, twice, ch. 7, five times, ch. 8, four times, ch. 9, twice, ch. 10, four times, ch. 11, eight times, ch. 12, twice, ch. 13, once, ch. 18, six times, ch. 19, ten times, and ch. 20, once. Under ordinary circumstances, an author describing events happening in his own country does not speak of his countrymen as 'the English,' 'the French,' and so on. But throughout Judæa there was a mixed population, Romans, Jews, Galileans, Samaritans. The fact brought out clearly in John's gospel is that the persecutions, the accusations, the injustice directed against Jesus, which culminated in his death, all proceeded from 'the Jews.' Writing long after the events had happened, at a distance from Palestine, probably for foreigners, there was no better or more natural way of showing by whom these things were done, than that adopted in the fourth gospel. The hostility to Jesus was not on the part of Romans, Samaritans or Galileans, but of the Jews.

For two or three days the appearance of Jesus at the feast of tabernacles was delayed, but in the midst of the week he entered the temple and taught in public. 'But when it was now the midst of the feast Jesus went up into the temple, and taught.' The ability displayed in his teaching excited astonishment, especially as he had received no training after the orthodox fashion. 'The Jews therefore marvelled, saying, How knoweth this man letters, having never learned?' Alford says: 'It appears to have been the first time that he *taught* publicly at Jerusalem.' The question as to the source of his knowledge appears to have been in derogation of his authority, for Jesus replied to the criticism by assuring them that he stood forth as a teacher not in his own name but as directly commissioned from another. 'Jesus therefore answered them, and said, My teaching is not mine, but his that sent me.' Those among his listeners who were anxious to learn and do the will of God, would be in no doubt as to the character of his teaching. 'If any man willeth to do his will, he shall know of the teaching, whether it be of God, or *whether* I speak from myself.' A teacher having his own ends to serve would be careful about his own reputation. 'He that speaketh from himself seeketh his own glory.' But the teacher who could throw aside self-interest, caring only to deliver the message entrusted to him, without regard to consequences, gave thereby unmistakable evidence of truth and rectitude. 'But he that seeketh the glory of him that sent him, the same is true, and no unrighteousness is in him.' There was need for some bold expounder of the divine will; for although they had the law of Moses, there was a universal disregard of that law. 'Did not Moses give you the law, and *yet* none of you doeth the law? What was their justification for aiming at his life? 'Why seek ye to kill me?' That question seems to have astounded the listening crowd. They knew nothing of any such attempt, not being in the counsel of those who had plotted the death of Jesus. His assertion was attributed (what enemy among the crowd first broached the idea?) to morbid self-deception. 'The multitude answered, Thou hast a devil (Gr. demon): who seeketh to kill thee?' Jesus referred to the miracle of healing performed by him when last at Jerusalem, which had caused the hostility and persecution, as explained previously by this evangelist: 'Therefore did the Jews persecute Jesus, and sought to slay him, because he had done these things on the sabbath day.' Taking up this charge of sabbath-breaking which had been made against him, Jesus now argued the question. There is some uncertainty here as to the correct rendering. The Authorised Version is as follows: 'Jesus answered and said unto them, I have done one work, and ye all marvel. Moses therefore gave unto you circumcision; (not because it is of Moses, but of the fathers).' Alford explains: 'The argument seems to be, Moses *on this account* gave you circumcision, not because it was of Moses, but of the fathers; *i.e.*, it is no part of the law of Moses properly so called.' That would apply equally to the Revised Version: 'Jesus answered and said unto them, I did one work, and ye all marvel. For this cause hath Moses given you circumcision (not that it is of Moses but of the fathers).' But the Revisers have given as an alternative reading: 'I did one work and ye all marvel because of this. Moses hath given you circumcision.' This alters the sense. Tischendorf inserts neither 'for this cause,' nor 'because of this,' following the oldest MS., which omits the word rendered in the Authorised Version 'therefore:' 'I did one work, and ye all marvel. Moses hath given you circumcision.' The general astonishment at the fact of Jesus having chosen or ventured to heal on the sabbath-day, induced him to argue out the question. They themselves did not scruple to circumcise children on the sabbath. Why? Because they found themselves in the dilemma of either breaking the law which 'ordains circumcision on the eighth day' (Alford), or of breaking the sabbath to the extent of then performing the ceremony whenever the occasion demanded. Why then should they blame Jesus for having exercised a similar freedom of judgment? His act was, to say the least, as necessary and beneficent as theirs. They did it for the child's sake; he did it for the man's sake; theirs was a mere ceremonial observance; his was an actual, visible, tangible, perfect gift of healing: 'and on the sabbath ye circumcise a man. If a man receiveth circumcision on the sabbath, that the law of Moses may not be broken; are ye wroth with me, because I made a man every whit whole on the sabbath?' If they presumed to claim the right of judging him with respect to that matter, let them not regard the action from a superficial point of view, but enter into the merits of the question, and decide upon it impartially and righteously. 'Judge not according to appearance, but judge righteous judgement.'

In proportion to the boldness of Jesus was the timidity of his adversaries. They had launched forth their sentence of condemnation and death, but now they seemed to shrink from doing anything against him. Their evident vacillation of purpose was the subject of comment and wonder among some of the inhabitants of Jerusalem. Here was Jesus speaking in public, and his enemies keeping an unaccountable silence. 'Some therefore of them of Jerusalem said, Is not this he whom they seek to kill? And lo, he speaketh openly, and they say nothing unto him.' Was this only as the ominous hush before the outburst of a storm? Or might it not be possible that the opposing rulers had after all become convinced that Jesus was in truth the expected Messiah of their nation? 'Can it be that the rulers indeed know that this is the Christ?' The popular opinion, having no authoritative guidance from the upper classes, swayed hither and thither, as one view or another of the subject presented itself. Some argued that because they knew the origin of Jesus, he could not be the Messiah, whom they expected to come in some sudden and mysterious way. 'Howbeit we know this man whence he is: but when the Christ cometh, no one knoweth whence he is.' Alford states that Justin Martyr represents Trypho the Jew saying, 'Even if Christ has been born and exists somewhere, he is unknown, and is not even conscious of his own identity, until Elias shall come and anoint him and make him manifest to all.' The discussion of this idea being notorious, Jesus alluded to it in the course of his teachings in the temple. He told the multitude that they were taking up only a half-truth: it was true that they knew him and his home; but it was equally true that he had been sent by One having a real existence, of whom, however, they were ignorant. 'Jesus therefore cried in the temple, teaching and saying, Ye both know me, and know whence I am; and I am not come of myself, but he that sent me is true, whom ye know not.' On the word 'true' Alford observes: 'The nearest English word would be *real*: but this would not convey the meaning perspicuously to the ordinary mind; perhaps the A. V. *true* is better, provided it be explained to mean *really existent*, not *truthful*.' Probably Luther's version conveys the sense of the original: 'Es ist ein Wahrhaftiger, der mich gesandt hat.'

Their uncertainty and unbelief could not disturb the knowledge and assurance of Jesus. 'I know him; because I am from him, and he sent me.' These words must not be pressed unduly. The evangelist wrote of the Baptist: 'There came a man, sent from God, whose name was John.' When Jesus used the same expression about himself, it should carry the same meaning. Yet the saying, 'I know him, because I am from him,' may bear on the lips of Jesus a significance higher and deeper than the same words uttered by another. Both the ambassador of a king and the son of a king might be entitled to say, 'I know him, because I am from him,' but the assertion would mean much more in the case of the son than of the ambassador.

The claim thus made by Jesus to a direct commission from God, was deemed sufficient to justify his apprehension, and his enemies took steps with that object. 'They sought therefore to take him.' Yet no result followed: his capture was not effected, and the evangelist does not scruple to attribute this immunity to the fact that his destiny was foreordained and overruled. 'And no man laid his hand on him, because his hour was not yet come.' So among the people Jesus gained many adherents. 'But of the multitude many believed on him.' That they became professed disciples, we are not told: the question with them was argumentative, a matter of opinion and judgment rather than of life and action. 'And they said, When the Christ shall come, will he do more signs than those which this man hath done?' These expressions of popular approval were noted by the Pharisees, and they in conjunction with the chief priests decided to seize Jesus, and sent out officers for that purpose. 'The Pharisees heard the multitude murmuring these things concerning him; and the chief priests and the Pharisees sent officers to take him.' Having knowledge of this, Jesus warned the people that his time with them would be short. He would not speak of his death as death, but would have them regard it with him as simply his going back to Him from whom he came, whom Jesus knew, but whom they knew not. 'Jesus therefore said, Yet a little while am I with you, and I go unto him that sent me.' A time would come when they would be anxious for his presence, and would search for him without success. 'Ye shall seek me, and shall not find me.' Between him and them there must be an impassable gulf of separation: 'and where I am, ye cannot come.' In connection with the earthly life of Jesus, we know of nothing to explain these words. His mind was dwelling on his return to his heavenly Father, and his saying must refer to coming experiences in the life beyond the present. To the Jews it was altogether enigmatical: he was about to go somewhere away from them. Whither? 'The Jews therefore said among themselves, Whither will this man go that we shall not find him?' Was he about to transfer himself and his teaching to a heathen land and people? 'Will he go unto the Dispersion among (Gr. of) the Greeks, and teach the Greeks?' Did he intend to quit Judæa, and in some foreign country indoctrinate all who would listen to him, both Jews and Gentiles? Alford says: 'Their interest in this hypothesis, that He was going to the dispersed among the Greeks, is, to convey contempt and mockery.' Of that we can scarcely feel sure, inasmuch as the suggestion was made 'among themselves,' not addressed to Jesus, and the idea was at once dismissed as improbable, so that his saying still remained inexplicable. 'What is this word that he said, Ye shall seek me, and shall not find me: and where I am, ye cannot come?'

On the third or fourth day after his arrival at Jerusalem, Jesus adopted a very decided course of action, challenging attention by the utterance in public of most emphatic declarations respecting himself and his influence upon others. It was the last and great day of the feast, and Jesus stood forth before the assembled crowds, proclaiming in their ears the nature of the gift he was able to promise to his followers. 'Now on the last day, the great *day* of the feast, Jesus stood and cried, saying, If any man thirst, let him come unto me and drink. He that believeth on me, as the scripture hath said, out of his belly shall flow rivers of living water.' Here is the same figure of speech as was adopted in the discourse with the woman of Samaria, the same tone of thought, method of persuasion, and promised benefit. Standing forward as the Messiah of his people, Jesus utters no call to arms, no word about political rights or national freedom. His promises are not general, but only to individual and willing hearers, to such as possessed a burning thirst, were conscious of an inward want, and were disposed to come to him for teaching and relief: 'If any man thirst, let him come unto me, and drink.' In such an invitation there was nothing revolutionary, no 'leading astray' of the multitude: the promise is a grand one, but symbolical, and would sound to many far-fetched and visionary. This is no demagogue inciting the multitude, but an earnest high-minded Teacher seeking to impart spiritual blessings. And his promise is conditional: 'He that believeth on me.' He claims unreserved confidence, boundless trust; and to such disciples he guarantees an inward, self-evolved satisfaction of their highest aspirations; nothing of worldly glory, no gratification of earthly ambition, no shout of victory, no song of triumph: simply the personal realisation of a figurative prophecy: 'as the scripture hath said, out of his belly shall flow rivers of living water.' Alford says: 'We look in vain for such a text in the Old Testament.' But in several places the flowing out of water is alluded to, as: 'And it shall come to pass in that day, that living water shall go out from Jerusalem.' Jesus seems to have chosen a similar expression as best suited to convey his idea of a pure and perpetual supply of that for which human nature thirsts.

The evangelist here inserts the following explanation: 'But this spake he of the Spirit, which they that believed on him were to receive: for the Spirit was not yet *given*: because Jesus was not yet glorified.' The Revisers, following the oldest MS., have omitted 'Holy' before 'Spirit,' but they have retained the italicised word 'given' after 'yet.' The word 'given' appears in the text of the Vatican MS. Alford observes: 'The additions "given," "upon them," as some authorities read, and the like, are all put in by way of explanation, to avoid a misunderstanding which no intelligent reader could fall into. Chrysostom writes: "The evangelist says, For the Holy Ghost was not yet, *i.e.*, was not yet given, because Jesus was not yet glorified: meaning by the Glory, the Cross."' Tischendorf has: 'But this spake he of the Spirit, which they that believe on him were about to receive; for the Spirit was not yet, because Jesus was not yet glorified.' Young is to the same effect: 'But this he said concerning the Spirit, which those believing in him were about to receive; for as yet the Holy Spirit was not, because Jesus was not yet glorified.' Jesus alluded to a spiritual influence about to be imparted to his disciples; it had not yet been bestowed, nor could it be until a further point had been reached in the career of Jesus. We must wait for more light on this subject, observing only that Chrysostom's idea that the 'glory' means the 'cross' cannot be accepted without evidence. Alford remarks: 'It is obvious that the word 'was' cannot refer to the *essential existence* of the Holy Spirit. . . The word implied is not exactly "given," but rather "working," or some similar word: was not—had not come in: the dispensation of the Spirit was not yet.' It is easier to understand the words of Jesus than the explanation of the evangelist, although his interpretation of them must be accepted as authoritative.

The effect of this declaration of Jesus varied according to the dispositions of the hearers. Some of them expressed the conviction that he was the long-expected prophet. '*Some* of the multitude therefore, when they heard these words, said, This is of a truth the prophet.' The Revisers, following the oldest MS., have altered 'many' to 'some' and 'this saying' to 'these words.' Alford explains: 'From the prophecy of Moses, Deut. xviii. 15, 18, the Jews expected some particular prophet to arise, distinct from the Messiah, whose coming was, like that of Elias, intimately connected with that of the Messiah Himself.' Others discerned in Jesus sufficient to warrant the belief that he was actually the Messiah. 'Others said, This is the Christ.' But against the possibility of that, some raised the argument that the Messiah could not be expected to come from a place so far outside of Judæa as Galilee. 'But some said, What, doth the Christ come out of Galilee?' On the contrary, the Scriptures had foretold that he would be a descendant of David, and from Bethlehem, David's native village. 'Hath not the scripture said that the Christ cometh of the seed of David, and from Bethlehem, the village where David was?' This question shows a total ignorance of the opening history of Jesus as recorded by Luke. Even if the events which happened thirty years ago were not entirely forgotten, there was nothing within public knowledge to identify Jesus in connection with them. In face of Herod's slaughter, the object had been concealment. That had been secured by the flight to Egypt. Even after Herod's death Joseph had feared to revisit Judæa, and, as a matter of course, in Galilee no hint would be given likely to lead to the identification of Jesus. It is quite possible, nay, it is most reasonable to suppose that his Mother's mind must have been haunted by a constant dread lest their secret should be exposed, and the life of Jesus thereby jeopardised. The enemies who were now seeking his life would have been only too glad to know that he was the child whom Herod had sought to slay because he had been worshipped by the Magi as the King of the Jews. How wonderful had been the workings of divine Providence! Notwithstanding the entire silence which had been maintained respecting the high origin and destiny of Jesus, the question of his Messiahship was now coming to the front. It was earnestly debated by the multitude. Doubtless the leisure of the festival time afforded a fit opportunity for considering such a matter. Two parties were formed, one in favour of Jesus and one against him. 'So there arose a division in the multitude because of him.' Some of his opponents were desirous to seize him, although they did not actually venture to do so. 'And some of them would have taken him; but no man laid hands on him.' Although Jesus stood in great danger, the very officers who had been sent to apprehend him held their hands; they returned without the expected prisoner, to the astonishment of the Pharisees, and in reply to the enquiry why they had failed to fulfil their mission, the officers could only say that the discourses of Jesus were not like those of any other man: he was no ordinary haranguer of a mob, nor could they venture upon the profanation of attempting to silence a teacher so unparalleled. 'The officers therefore came to the chief priests and Pharisees; and they said unto them, Why did ye not bring him? The officers answered, Never man so spake.' So the Pharisees were forced to argue against the scruples of their own emissaries. This they did in a tone of angry, bitter scorn. 'The Pharisees therefore answered them, Are ye also led astray?' Could they point to a single man of reputation or learning who had become a disciple of Jesus? 'Hath any of the rulers believed on him, or of the Pharisees?' Tischendorf renders,* 'any one of the rulers,' and the Revisers have replaced 'have'

---

* The 'renderings' alluded to as of Tischendorf are those of Dr. Davidson.

by 'hath.' The verdict of the populace in favour of Jesus was to be attributed to a judicial blindness due to their ignorance of the law. 'But this multitude which knoweth not the law are accursed.' Alford notes: '*multitude* is here a word of contempt—*rabble*.' One voice among the Pharisees, however, was raised on behalf of Jesus. In the Authorised Version we read: 'Nicodemus saith unto them. (he that came to Jesus by night, being one of them.)' Tischendorf has simply: 'Nicodemus said unto them, being one of them,' which is the reading of the oldest MS. Alford notes: 'The reading here varies very much: some ancient copies omitting " by night," others inserting it in different positions.' The Revisers omit 'by night,' but for some unexplained reason insert instead thereof the word 'before.' 'Nicodemus saith unto them (he that came to him before, being one of them).' If the multitude did not know the law, let the Pharisees beware of disregarding it. Did the law justify the passing of judgment upon Jesus, without first hearing his defence and taking evidence with respect to his actions? 'Doth our law judge a man, except it first hear from himself and know what he doeth?' Young and Tischendorf render literally 'the man,' not 'a man.' This pertinent and searching question was answered only by a contemptuous sarcasm. 'They answered and said unto him, Art thou also of Galilee?' Did he expect the light and learning of Jerusalem to be overborne by the uncultured ideas of a Galilean? Let Nicodemus take up the investigation of that question, and he would soon become convinced that no Teacher worthy of the name could spring out of such a locality and such surroundings. 'Search and see that out of Galilee ariseth no prophet.'

This feast of tabernacles was not the first occasion on which the public voice in Jerusalem had made itself heard in favour of Jesus. At a previous passover-festival many disciples had been gained, and an enthusiasm manifested of which Jesus declined to avail himself. The incident is recorded only by the fourth evangelist, and, although it occurs in the earlier portion of the narrative, he gives no indication to what period of the career of Jesus it refers, simply placing together the events of two passovers and giving precedence to the last on account of 'the cleansing of the temple.' The other evangelists place that event towards the end of the ministry of Jesus, and as John does not specify the time there is no justification for assuming that the cleansing of the temple occurred twice, especially in face of the obvious similarity in the details. Neither does the evangelist specify any time in what follows, but simply states that it was at Jerusalem during a passover. 'Now when he was at Jerusalem at the passover, during the feast, many believed on his name, beholding his signs which he did.' The Authorised Version continues: 'but Jesus did not commit himself unto them.' This conveys the idea of a willingness on their part to espouse and promote the cause of Jesus in some fashion of their own choosing, but from which he held aloof. The Revised Version (agreeing with Tischendorf, Young and Alford) reads: 'But Jesus did not trust himself unto them.' Alford explains that 'in the original, the same verb is used for *believed* in verse 23, and for *trust* in this verse.' So the meaning must be that he did not feel that confidence in them which they showed in him. The evangelist explains that he possessed a perfect intuition in judging the characters of men generally, which made him independent of private information: he was able to gauge the disposition of every man he met: 'for that he knew all men, and because he needed not that any one should bear witness concerning man (or, a man); for he himself knew what was in man (or, the man).' It is most reasonable to suppose that the opinion thus expressed was based upon the evangelist's own observation. Jesus frequently exhibited this power: as when he saw Nathanael coming to him and pronounced him an Israelite indeed without guile; when he surnamed Peter, 'Rock'; when he termed him 'Satan'; when he surnamed two disciples 'Sons of thunder'; when he said to Judas, 'That thou doest, do quickly'; when he perceived the craftiness and hardness of heart of scribes and Pharisees. But Alford argues: 'Nothing less than *divine knowledge* is here set forth; the words are even stronger than if the reference had been to the persons here mentioned: as the text now stands, it asserts an entire knowledge of all that is in all men.' If such an assertion be intended, it is simply made by the evangelist, and can be worth no more than the opinion of any other man. How could the writer of this gospel know that Jesus knew all that was in the heart of every man living? The supposition is monstrous, incredible.

The visit of Nicodemus already alluded to would seem to have been made at that passover-time when the minds of the multitude were inclined towards Jesus, for the account of the visit immediately follows. Nicodemus was not only a Pharisee, but a leading man among the Jews. 'Now there was a man of the Pharisees, named Nicodemus, a ruler of the Jews.' Under cover of the night he paid a visit to Jesus. 'The same came unto him by night.' Following the three oldest MSS. the Revisers have replaced the word 'Jesus' by 'him.' This alteration makes more apparent the connection with the preceding account of the passover. We can only conjecture the reason for choosing the night time. Probably one motive was secrecy; probably the whole of the day was occupied by Jesus in teaching or otherwise, and the private conference sought by Nicodemus was deemed important enough to require a fixed appointment when there would be ample leisure and no fear of interruption. Nicodemus opened the conversation with courtesy and candour. He addressed Jesus by the recognised title 'Teacher,' and he scrupled not to admit that the conviction of Jesus' divine mission had been forced upon the minds of himself and others of his class: 'and said to him, Rabbi, we know that thou art a teacher come from God: for no man can do these signs that thou doest, except God be with him.' Young's rendering in the past tense, 'Rabbi, we have known' seems to bring out the fact that the matter had been considered and decided. It may be inferred from the use of the word 'we' that Nicodemus came as a delegate: had this been merely his private opinion, he would not so have expressed it as to compromise others of his class. The Pharisees were constrained to admit the reality of the miracles wrought by Jesus, and that they could only be performed by the favour and power of God; therefore his teaching must be divinely authorised. Either the conversation turned naturally to questions relating to the kingdom of God, and the record is fragmentary, or Jesus at once deliberately directed his discourse to that subject. He startled Nicodemus by making a very solemn and emphatic assertion.

S. John 3

'Jesus answered and said unto him, Verily, verily, I say unto thee, Except a man be born anew (or. from above), he cannot see the kingdom of God.' The Revisers have replaced the word 'again' by 'anew,' with the alternative rendering 'from above,' which is adopted by Tischendorf. Young renders: 'If any one be not born from above, he is unable to see the reign of God.' There must be a fresh, super-mundane, heavenly birth, before any man can see the reign of God, discern the mode and manner of the divine rulership. Nicodemus was staggered by this declaration. It was too positive and earnest to be regarded as a mere figure of speech. It was evident to his mind that Jesus was describing some natural fact of human existence, which was as much a reality as being born into the world. But how could anything of that kind happen to a man a second time? 'Nicodemus saith unto him, How can a man be born when he is old? can he enter a second time into his mother's womb, and be born?' Jesus explained that the birth he alluded to was by the combination of the element of water with spirit. 'Jesus answered, Verily, verily, I say unto thee, Except a man be born of water and the Spirit, he cannot enter into the kingdom of God.' The Sinaitic MS. reads, 'he cannot see the kingdom of heaven.' Tischendorf has, 'he cannot enter into the kingdom of heaven,' and he substitutes 'one' for the words 'a man.' The English translators by beginning the word 'spirit' with a capital letter, and introducing before it the definite article, incorporate into the text an idea of their own. The true meaning seems to be that the birth alluded to is by a compounding of water with spirit. This is confirmed by the words which follow, in which Jesus contrasts the nature of the first birth and of the second birth, and distinguishes between the two. 'That which is born of the flesh is flesh; and that which is born of the spirit is spirit.' How can translators be justified in placing a capital to the first word 'Spirit,' and not to the second word 'spirit,' which follows immediately? The Authorised Version led the way, and the Revisers, Tischendorf, Young and Alford have followed suit. Luther's version does not give the idea of a person to the word spirit. 'Was vom Fleisch geboren wird, das ist Fleisch; und was vom Geist geboren wird, das ist Geist.' The translation of Samuel Sharpe brings the true meaning of the original clearly to our view: 'Unless a man be born of water and spirit, he cannot enter the kingdom of God. What is born of the flesh, is flesh, and what is born of the spirit is spirit.' The earthly life is a fleshly life; the heavenly life is a spiritual life; the lower nature is flesh and blood, the higher nature is water and spirit. The apostle Paul was cognizant of this truth. He wrote: 'If there is a natural body, there is also a spiritual body. So also it is written, The first man Adam became a living soul. The last Adam became a life-giving spirit. Howbeit that is not first which is spiritual, but that which is natural: then that which is spiritual. The first man is of (out of—Young) the earth, earthy: the second man is of (out of—Young) heaven. As is the earthy, such are they also that are earthy: and as is the heavenly, such are they also that are heavenly. And as we have borne the image of the earthy, we shall (or, let us) also bear the image of the heavenly. Now this I say, brethren, that flesh and blood cannot inherit the kingdom of God.' Is not that precisely to the same effect as what Jesus said to

Nicodemus? The fact must not be rejected or even wondered at because it is inscrutable. 'Marvel not that I said unto thee, Ye must be born anew (or, from above).' None can trace the course of wind or spirit, though our ears catch the sound and we are certain of the unseen reality. Those who have attained the new, spiritual birth, are equally invisible, intangible, untraceable. 'The wind bloweth (or, the Spirit breatheth) where it listeth, and thou hearest the voice thereof, but knowest not whence it cometh, and whither it goeth: so is every one that is born of the Spirit.' Alford explains that 'in both languages, that in which Jesus spoke, as well as that in which this speech is reported,' the word is the same, '*Pneuma* being both *wind* and *spirit*.' Unfortunately our translators have here again taken upon themselves to supply a capital letter to Spirit, thereby introducing a personality which could not otherwise be inferred. Young renders: 'Thou mayest not wonder, that I said to thee, It behoveth you to be born from above; the Spirit where he willeth doth breathe, and his voice thou hearest, but thou hast not known whence he cometh, and whither he goeth: thus is every one who is born of the Spirit.' This interpretation is adopted by some others, neither 'it' nor 'he' being expressed in the original. Alford says: 'Bengel, after Origen and Augustine, takes the word *pneuma* with which this word opens, and which we have rendered *wind*, of the Holy Spirit exclusively: but this can hardly be. The form of the sentence, as well as its import, is against it. The words (*bloweth, hearest, knowest*) are all said of well-known facts.' Tischendorf renders the verse: 'The wind blows where it will, and thou hearest the sound thereof, but knowest not whence it comes and whither it goes: so is every one that has been born of the Spirit.' The 'Englishman's Greek New Testament' gives as the literal translation, 'everyone that has been born of the Spirit.' This last clause of the verse makes it evident that the comparison is not to be taken, as seems generally to have been assumed, as illustrating the mysterious manner in which the new spiritual birth is accomplished, but the incomprehensible, invisible existence of those who have been born anew.

Nicodemus was lost in wonder, if not in doubt. Such a mystery was too deep for him to comprehend, or feel at all certain about. 'Nicodemus answered and said unto him, How can these things be?' Whatever his profession, this reply was conceived in the spirit of a Sadducee. Jesus reminded him that such uncertainty and want of assurance with respect to the future life were ill suited to his high position as a Jewish teacher. 'Jesus answered and said unto him, Art thou the teacher of Israel, and understandest not these things?' It was in vain for Jesus, 'a teacher sent from God,' and others like him, to speak out what they knew and testify to what had come under their own observation, if their declarations were to be met with incredulity. 'Verily, verily, I say unto thee, We speak that we do know, and bear witness of that we have seen; and ye receive not our witness.' This seems to refer to a prevalent scepticism of all scriptural and divine teaching. On the words, 'We speak that we do know...' Alford has the note: 'Why these plurals? Various interpretations have been given: "Either He speaks concerning Himself and the Father, or concerning Himself alone" (Euthymius): "He speaks of Himself and the Spirit (Bengel); of Himself and the

Prophets (Beza, Tholuck) ; of Himself and John the Baptist (Knapp); of Teachers like himself (Meyer); of all the born of the Spirit (Lange, Wesley); of the three Persons in the Holy Trinity (Stier); or, the plural is only rhetorical (Lücke, De Wette)."' Alford adds: 'I had rather take it as a proverbial saying; q.d., "I am one of those who," &c. Our Lord thereby brings out the unreasonableness of that unbelief which would not receive His witness, but made it an exception to the general proverbial rule.' Most probably Nicodemus would understand the word 'we' to include Jesus and John the Baptist. The Pharisees had refused to accept the testimony of the latter, and Nicodemus now hesitates to believe a positive statement made by the former. If the teaching of Jesus on earthly matters was disregarded, as it had been, what expectation could there be of faith in his assurances relating to heavenly matters? 'If I told you earthly things, and ye believe not, how shall ye believe, if I tell you heavenly things?' No other teacher than himself was familiar with the heavenly world. 'And no man hath ascended into heaven, but he that descended out of heaven, *even* the Son of man, which is in heaven.' Young's literal rendering agrees exactly with that in the 'Englishman's Greek New Testament:' 'And no one hath gone up into the heaven, except he who out of the heaven came down—the Son of man who is in the heaven.' Here are four statements: (1) Only one person had gone up into the heavenly world. (2) That one had come down out of the heavenly world. (3) He was a man, the representative or Messiah of men, 'the Son of man.' (4) And he was in heaven. Let us consider these statements seriatim. (1) 'No man hath ascended into heaven.' Luther uses the present tense: 'Und niemand fährt gen Himmel. And no one goes to heaven:' but other translators agree in using the past tense, 'hath ascended.' So clear was this to Alford that he argues: 'He is here speaking by anticipation. He regards therefore throughout the passage, the great facts of redemption *as accomplished*, and makes announcements which could not be literally acted upon till they had been so accomplished.' Any mind unwarped by theological dogmas must at once dismiss such attempted explanations. The assertion of Jesus is a very simple one, requiring no rectification or amplification: no man had gone up into heaven except (2) one who had come down out of heaven. We know that one to be Jesus. Luke has told his miraculous birth, John has declared his lofty, ancient, divine origin: he was an inhabitant of heaven born into our world, to sojourn here and pass his human life among us, for the teaching and salvation of mankind, being (3) 'the Son of man,' in all things made like unto his brethren. The last statement, (4) 'which is in heaven,' requires consideration. The Revisers note that 'many ancient authorities omit' the words. The two oldest MSS. omit them, notwithstanding which Tischendorf retains them. Alford regards them as asserting 'the being in heaven of the *time then present*,' but he explains or qualifies this by saying, '(heaven about Him, heaven dwelling on earth) *while here*,' which transforms the words either into a mere figure of speech or into a contradiction of terms. Alford says also: 'Doubtless the meaning involves, *whose place is in heaven*.' That commends itself as a reasonable interpretation, the distinction being between 'the Son of man which is in heaven,' conversant with 'heavenly things,' and 'the Son of man which is on earth,' conversant only with 'earthly things.' 'No man hath ascended,' obviously means 'no man living on earth.' The passage asserts the existence of humanity in heaven; but as there is a doubt whether the words 'which is in heaven' were actually spoken by Jesus, it would not be satisfactory to attempt any development of the doctrine they may be taken to convey.

The influence of this Son of man descended out of heaven was designed to be exerted widely and beneficially upon mankind, and would resemble that of the brazen serpent made and raised on high by Moses at the command of God for the healing of the dying Israelites. 'And as Moses lifted up the serpent in the wilderness, even so must the Son of man be lifted up: that whosoever believeth may in him have eternal life.' The Authorised Version stands as follows: 'that whosoever believeth in him should not perish, but have eternal life.' The Revisers and Tischendorf, on the authority of the two oldest MSS., have omitted the words, 'not perish, but.' The Revisers have also made the words 'believeth in him may have,' a marginal reading, and have altered the sense by putting in the text, 'believeth, may in him have eternal life.' This alteration differs from the rendering of Tischendorf, Luther and Young, that of the last being, 'so it behoveth the Son of man to be lifted up, that every one who believeth in him may not perish, but may have life age-during.' Taking the proper rendering of the word 'eternal' to be 'age-during,' the question presents itself whether that term is not here applicable equally to the serpent-bitten and serpent-healed Israelites and to the believers on the uplifted Son of man? Otherwise the simile is not exact, but defective in an important particular, standing in fact as follows: As the serpent uplifted in the wilderness gave a life which was *not* eternal, even so the uplifted Son of man will give a life which is eternal. But if we take the natural sense of the word 'age-during' this inconsistency disappears. The Israelites were dying before completing the full term or age of their earthly existence: the act of healing restored to them their proper 'age-during' life, which, however it might vary according to differences of constitutions and surroundings, would not be prematurely cut short by the serpent-poison. Even so the Son of man is held forth as conveying a virtue sufficient to antidote everything which threatens to bring to a premature end the heavenly existence of which he had been speaking. The idea is scriptural. Messiah's life-prolonging influence is not for this world, but for the next. 'In Adam all die . . . Even so in Christ shall all be made alive' . . . 'As we have borne the image of the earthy, we shall also bear the image of the heavenly.' The nature of the promise of 'eternal life' depends upon the meaning of those two words. There can be no doubt as to the sense of the word 'life;' the word translated 'eternal' or 'everlasting' must be brought to assume in our minds its proper import—'age-during;' then comes the question as to the significance of 'age:' is it a period absolutely endless? or is it a period of vast duration? or is it a period fixed by the constitution of our nature, which the influence of the Son of man will maintain to its utmost limit?

God, in his love to mankind, had devoted his only begotten Son to the work of securing that supreme boon to all who placed their confidence in him. 'For God so loved the world, that he gave his only begotten Son, that whosoever believeth on him should not perish, but have eternal life.' Tischendorf, on the authority of the two oldest MSS., has replaced 'his' by 'the.' The introduction of the words 'should not perish' clearly points to the impending catastrophe of Death. This cannot be the death which all who are born on earth must undergo: no faith in Jesus saves from that. But he is speaking of 'heavenly things,' and the corollary to be drawn from his words is this: (1) either the seeds of dissolution implanted in our nature will survive in our resurrection-life, and develop in the world to come the same inevitable premature mortality as in this; or, (2) in the next stage of our existence there will be a liability and inclination towards transgression of some divine law, entailing the same fatal consequences as those which overtook the first Adam and his posterity, and which will need to be avoided or counteracted by faith in Jesus. The Mosaic account of the fall of man involves the idea of his premature death: 'In the day that thou eatest thereof thou shalt surely die;' growth and development would stop, and dissolution would begin. That is the only rational interpretation, seeing that Adam did not forthwith expire. The nine hundred and thirty years which Adam lived, and even the nine hundred and sixty nine of Methuselah, completed not the full age to which the perfect man would have attained but for his transgression; and the elements of decay matured rapidly and fatally in his posterity, cutting short the term of human life by centuries, so that Shem the son of Noah lived 600 years, the son of Shem 438 years, the next descendants respectively 433, 464, 239, 239, 230, 148 and 205 years, the last named being Terah the father of Abraham. Still the age of man steadily declined, until 80 years was held to be its extreme limit. The mind of the patriarch Jacob was profoundly impressed by the rapid and constant decline, for in telling his age to Pharaoh he said: 'The days of the years of my pilgrimage are an hundred and thirty years: few and evil have been the days of the years of my life, and they have not attained unto the days of the years of the life of my fathers in the days of their pilgrimage.' The period of our earthly existence has not been enlarged by the work of Christ: his salvation extends not in that direction; his repeated promises of 'life age-during' are for the world to come, for that heavenly life and kingdom which can only be revealed and realised through being 'born anew of water and the Spirit.' Dropping the ecclesiastical and symbolical ideas attached to that second birth, regarding it not as restricted to a few but as the universal privilege of mankind, it is a solemn, inevitable, merciful reality, a phase and crisis of our destiny as important, probably far more important than our birth into this world. In the 'heavenly things' appertaining to that new sphere of existence, the Son of man must still be taken for our Guide and Saviour; he will preserve his adherents from the sins and evils which threaten that life, as they have here marred and shortened this, and as our 'second Adam' he will become to us 'a life-giving spirit.'

Let none deem this view of the divine mercy too bold or too wide. The Christ came not for judgment, but for salvation; not to save particular persons, but the world. 'For God sent not the Son into the world to judge the world, but that the world should be saved through him.' The Revisers, following the two oldest MSS., have altered 'his Son' to 'the Son.' They have also replaced in this and the two next verses the word 'condemn' by 'judge,' therein agreeing with Tischendorf, Young and Alford. The office of the Son is not to make inquisition into the errors and sins of mankind, but to deliver them from their condition of disease and death. Those who trust themselves to him are not arraigned as criminals, or called upon to answer for past misdeeds. 'He that believeth on him is not judged.' Nor does the advent of the Son involve any such judicial procedure towards those who withhold from him their confidence: the rejection of him by them leaves them in their former evil and perilous condition. 'He that believeth not hath been judged already, because he hath not believed on the name of the only begotten Son of God.' There can be no excuse for those who, when light has come into the world, deliberately prefer the darkness. 'And this is the judgement, that the light is come into the world, and men loved the darkness rather than the light.' Only evil deeds could have sought the cover of the night: 'for their works were evil.' Every wrongdoer hates light and avoids it, because it must disclose his iniquity. 'For every one that doeth (or, practiseth) ill hateth the light, and cometh not to the light, lest his works should be reproved (or, convicted).' But he who truly works, and works truly, comes forward to where the light shines most, that it may be thrown upon his work and show that it has been wrought out honestly as in the sight of God. 'But he that doeth the truth cometh to the light, that his works may be made manifest, that (or, because) they have been wrought in God.'

Alford alludes to the fact that 'many Commentators, since the time of Erasmus, who first suggested the notion, have maintained that the discourse of our Lord breaks off at verse 16, and the rest to verse 21 consists of the remarks of the Evangelist.' The principal grounds for that idea are (a) that all allusion to Nicodemus is henceforth dropped. (b) That henceforth past tenses are used. (c) On account of the use of *only begotten*, verses 16, 18, which is peculiar to John. Alford argues vigorously against all this, and concludes 'that the words following, to verse 21, cannot be otherwise regarded than as uttered by our Lord in continuation of his discourse.' With respect to the use of the term 'only begotten' 'Stier well enquires, Whence did John get this word but from the lips of his divine Master? Would he have ventured on such an expression, except by an authorization from Him?' Certainly it is inconceivable that any honest historian could present such a combination of assertions relating to the subject on which Jesus discoursed with Nicodemus, unless warranted by express words of Jesus spoken either then or at some other time.

A more important question is as to the meaning of the solemn and positive declarations of Jesus respecting the new birth. The conclusions already arrived at have been based on the natural interpretation of the words employed, without reference to anything apart from them. The discourse has been taken as conveying its own meaning, as complete in itself, not needing to be supplemented by a reference to something found elsewhere, and not to be understood figuratively for the mere purpose of its assumed connection with a Church ordinance. But by many persons that mode of dealing with the discourse has been set aside; they have rushed to the conclusion that

Jesus spoke symbolically; that to be born 'again' or 'anew' or 'from above,' means to be baptized; that the 'water' is the water of baptism; that the 'spirit' is the Holy Spirit, who comes with or through the rite of baptism. But surely if Jesus wished to impress upon Nicodemus the absolute necessity of baptism, he could and would have used plainer words, as he did on another occasion: 'He that believeth and is baptized shall be saved.' From first to last Nicodemus gathered no such meaning, but was lost in doubt and wonderment at the strangeness, the depth and the breadth, of these statements of Jesus: 'How can a man be born when he is old .. How can these things be?' Luther's figurative interpretation, quoted by Alford, we can appreciate and respect: 'My teaching is not of *doing* and *leaving undone*, but of *a change in the man*; so that it is, not *new works* done, but a *new man* to do them; not another *life* only, but *another birth*.' From the first there has been a difference of opinion. Alford quotes Chrysostom: 'Some say, from heaven, some, from the beginning,' and adds that 'he and Euthymius explain it by *regeneration*: Origen, Cyril, and Theophylact taking the other meaning.' Of course the 'new birth' means 'regeneration,' but not necessarily by baptism. Alford takes upon himself to say: 'It is impossible that Nicodemus can have so entirely and stupidly *misunderstood* our Lord's words, as his question here would seem to imply.' It is much more natural and probable to assume that Nicodemus detected no reference to baptism in the words of Jesus, notwithstanding the fact that 'the idea of a new birth was by no means alien from the Rabbinical views. They described a proselyte when baptized as "like an infant just born," Lightfoot.' If we suppose Jesus to have been anxious to impress upon his hearer the importance of baptism, would it not have been wise and right to speak with the utmost plainness, to avoid all possibility of doubt or misapprehension? Why should we either attribute obscurity to the speaker or perversity to the listener? If Dean Alford had not started with the foregone conclusion that the 'water and spirit' must as a matter of course refer to the water administered and the Spirit received in baptism, and if, instead of doing so, he had bent his mind to an unprejudiced investigation of the discourse of Jesus, probably he would not have accused Nicodemus, nor have penned the following passage: 'There can be no doubt, on any honest interpretation of the words, that to be born of water refers to the token or outward sign of baptism, to be born of the Spirit the thing signified, or inward grace of the Holy Spirit. All attempts to get rid of *these two plain facts* have sprung from doctrinal prejudices, by which the views of expositors have been warped. Such we have in Calvin: who explains the words to mean, "the Spirit who cleanses us, and by diffusing His influence in us inspires the vigour of heavenly life:" Grotius, "the Spirit, who cleanses like water;" Cocceius, "the grace of God, washing away our uncleanness and sins;" Tholuck, who holds that not Baptism itself, but only its *idea*, that of *cleansing* is referred to; and others, who endeavour to resolve water and the Spirit into a figure, so as to make it mean "the cleansing or purifying Spirit." All the better and deeper expositors have recognized the coexistence of the two, water and the Spirit.' 'Doctrinal prejudices!' Alford applied the expression to prejudices against the doctrine of baptismal regeneration: his opponents would say it applies equally to prejudices in favour of that doctrine. Apart from that question, Alford contends that a real meaning, instead of a bare figurative meaning, should be attached to the statements of Jesus. To that extent we are in agreement: under that conviction and in that direction, the foregoing independent investigation has been carried out.

We have now to return to the feast of tabernacles. After the incidents connected with it, the observation follows: 'And they went 7 John 53 every man unto his own house.' This may be understood to denote the completion of the festival, during which 'the people lived for a week in booths, to remind them of their desert wanderings.'* Jesus retired to the mount of Olives, on the outskirts of Jerusalem. 'But 8 John 1 Jesus went unto the mount of Olives.' Early in the morning he returned to the city, seated himself in the temple, and there began discoursing to the crowd which came to hear him. 'And early in the „ 2 morning' (literally, at dawn—Young) 'he came again into the temple, and all the people came unto him, and he sat down, and taught them.' Although the temple was the recognised place for religious worship, it bore small resemblance to our consecrated cathedrals and churches. The people seem to have wandered at their will within its precincts, and went even to the length of buying and selling, making it a market place for doves, sheep and oxen, which were probably, at least ostensibly, required for sacrifice. After a time, the discourse being either ended or interrupted, the scribes and Pharisees made their appearance, bringing with them a woman who had been detected in her sin. They placed her in the midst of those present, and told Jesus what was the charge against her. 'And the „ 3, 4 scribes and the Pharisees bring a woman taken in adultery; and having set her in the midst, they say unto him, Master (or, Teacher), this woman hath been taken in adultery, in the very act.' The only question to be decided was as to what ought to be done to her. The Mosaic law doomed the offender to death, which was to be brought about, not by a single executioner, but by the combined action of the congregation, each casting a stone or stones at the criminal. Alford explains: 'The command here mentioned is not to be found, unless "putting to death" generally, is to be interpreted as stoning.' It would seem, however, to have been necessarily and clearly inferred, as Alford admits, from 22 Deu. 23, 24, and the command was so understood. 'Now in the law Moses commanded us to stone such.' Alford „ 5 renders 'such' as 'such women.' The accusers invited Jesus to express his views as to the proper mode of dealing with the woman. 'What then sayest thou of her?' The Revisers, adopting the reading „ 5 of Wordsworth, have added 'of her.' The narrator explains that the question was not put in good faith, but with the express object of founding upon the reply of Jesus an accusation against him. 'And „ 6 this they said, tempting (or, trying) him, that they might have *whereof* to accuse him.' We can only conjecture the grounds on which they could have done so. Jesus had already been reproached as 'a friend of publicans and sinners.' If on this occasion he 11 Mat. 19 inclined towards mercy, his leniency would expose him to further

---

* " Helps to the Study of the Bible."

misinterpretation and calumny. He had also been charged with breaking the law of Moses by infringing the sabbath: if in this case he were to advocate the remission of capital punishment, he would be laying himself open to a similar reproach. Yet the fate of this erring woman seemed to be left in his hands; a word from him justifying the view expressed by these scribes and Pharisees might be equivalent to a sentence of death against her. Moreover, the punishment of death for such an offence was probably opposed to Roman law, and the enemies of Jesus would have been only too ready to denounce him as the instigator of the deed if, having been appealed to on the subject, he made no protest against the proposed death by stoning. Alford quotes Lücke on this point: 'Some kind of civil or political collision the question certainly was calculated to provoke: but from the brevity of the narration, and our want of more accurate knowledge of criminal proceedings at the time, it is impossible to lay down definitely, wherein the collision would have consisted.' Jesus did not feel himself called upon to answer the question put to him. Wisely and discreetly he maintained an entire silence. Criminals should be brought by their accusers to a proper tribunal of justice. Why should Jesus be appealed to publicly on a point of law in this particular case? He practically refused to discuss the matter; they had no right to question him, and he certainly had the right to remain silent. He chose to do so, and by his attitude and gesture plainly intimated his determination. 'But Jesus stooped down, and with his finger wrote on the ground.' Under the peculiar circumstances, this method of refusing to be entangled into a discussion, was wise and dignified. Probably a feeling of indignation may have had to do with it. All they cared about was to trump up an accusation against himself, and they were not ashamed to make this poor, guilty, trembling creature the occasion of it! He will baffle their designs; not a word shall they extract from him. Let them go their way, leaving him to his work, or at least to his meditations. His mind is busy with some other train of thought: better anything than to take or give counsel with such men on such a subject! It were useless to show the anger which, we know, could flash on occasion from his eye; it were cruel to look towards the crushed, shame-laden woman: better to fix his gaze on the ground at his feet. Those apparently idle, aimless tracings of his fingers on the floor are signs, not of vacancy, but of a mind at work, full to overflowing with who can say what blended thoughts of scorn, grief, pity. What words, if any, were written by the nervous workings of his fingers during that deep absorption, none can tell, though some have tried to guess. 'One of our MSS. reads: "He wrote on the ground the sins of each of them,"' (Alford). When would the divine law come to be written as easily on human hearts? When would it cease to be as light, as fleeting, as well-nigh invisible there, as though traced on unyielding stone or on the wind-blown, feet-trodden dust of the earth? When would the two great laws of love to God and man be recognised as binding and supreme? Many and deep the problems Jesus might then be pondering. They scrupled not, however, to interrupt his reverie, pestering him with repetitions of their question, 'What then sayest thou of her?' At last he raised himself to meet their supercilious gaze and give an answer to their mocking words. It was their matter, not his; they had raised the question about their duty; let them act according to their light and conscience. 'But when they continued asking him, he lifted up himself, and said unto them, He that is without sin among you, let him first cast a stone at her.' If, knowing well the infirmities, degradation, and sinful propensities of human nature, they judged it right, wise, expedient, and their duty, to insist upon the rigorous exaction of the stern penalty decreed by Moses so many centuries ago, let them proceed to carry out the sentence. Let any one of them who knew himself to be pure in mind, in heart, in conduct, cast the first stone at her, and then all would be free to follow his example. That was the first and last word of Jesus on the subject. Again he hid his face from everyone, stooped down, and began afresh that mysterious writing on the ground. 'And again he stooped down, and with his finger wrote on the ground.' Not one of them dared now to lift his hand first against the woman. When the eldest was seen to rise, it was not to cast a stone, but to leave the place. The next in age and honour followed his example. With every departure, the responsibility laid upon those remaining was felt the more; one by one each man slunk away, until Jesus and the woman alone were left. 'And they, when they heard it, went out one by one, beginning from the eldest, *even unto the last*: and Jesus was left alone, and the woman where she was, in the midst.' Then Jesus rose from his stooping posture: had he done so sooner, or had he not stooped at all, probably his adversaries would have met his gaze defiantly, and have braved out the matter to the end. It was far better settled thus. Better, it would seem, than Jesus himself anticipated; for his first question indicated unconsciousness and surprise. 'And Jesus lifted up himself, and said unto her, Woman, where are they?' His last look at them had discerned a general determination to convict her. Was it possible that not one out of all of them had formulated the sentence of condemnation? 'Did no man condemn thee?' Yes! it had turned out even so. 'And she said, No man, Lord (Sir—Young).' Then she might dismiss all fear: Jesus would be the last man to raise hand or voice against her. 'And Jesus said, Neither do I condemn thee.' She was free to go, uncondemned, but not unwarned. Let her ever henceforth avoid the sin which had placed her life in peril. 'Go thy way; from henceforth sin no more.'

To this narrative the Revisers have appended the note: 'Most of the ancient authorities omit John vii. 53—viii. 11. Those which contain it vary much from each other.' Alford explains: 'This passage is to be treated very differently from the rest of the sacred text. In the Alexandrine, Vatican, Paris, and Sinaitic MSS., the ancient Syriac Versions, and all the early fathers, it is omitted: the Cambridge MS., alone of our most ancient authorities contains it. Augustine states, that certain expunged it from their MSS., because they thought it might encourage sin. But this will not account for the very general omission of it, nor for the fact that Ch. vii. 53 is included in the omitted portion. Eusebius assigns it apparently to the apocryphal "Gospel according to the Hebrews." . . In the MSS. which contain it, the *number of variations* is very much greater than in any other equal portion of Scripture: so much is this the case, that there are in fact three separate texts, it being hardly possible to unite them into one.' The passage was rejected by Tischendorf, as no part of the original gospel. But he gives it in two forms, one from the text of D, or the Cambridge MS.; the other according to the received text, or the Elzevir of 1624. Comparing these, the differences are unimportant. The narrative carries on the face of it the stamp of authenticity. The minute details and touches are such as could have been given only by an eye-witness. As in a picture a great artist is revealed by his manner and style, so in this narrative we discern certain inimitable characteristics of Jesus, his wisdom, his caution, his self-restraint, his deep insight, his mastery in argument, his loving gentleness, his broad compassion.

S John 12

The evangelist now introduces a new subject with the words, 'Again therefore Jesus spake unto them, saying, I am the light of the world.' The expression 'again therefore' seems to indicate the recommencement of an address: possibly Jesus had been interrupted, and his congregation dispersed, by the entrance of the priests with the woman; and possibly the rising sun,—the people having assembled at early dawn,—suggested the metaphor. It was very bold, suggestive, self-laudatory,—deliberately chosen on that account,

,, 12

—for Jesus added: 'He that followeth me shall not walk in the darkness, but shall have the light of life.' No ordinary man could dare to speak such words; only one who knew himself to be above all others of mankind, in his person, attributes, office, could claim a pre-eminence so exalted, so superhuman. In this and similar assertions made by Jesus with respect to himself, we find the justification of this evangelist for those astounding statements about the origin, nature and influence of Jesus, which are placed in the forefront of

I John 4

the narrative. When the writer asserted: 'In him was light, and

,, 5

the light was the life of men. And the light shineth in the darkness:

,, 9

and the darkness overcame it not ... The true light, which lighteth every man, was coming into the world,'—the authority for such statements was the express declaration of Jesus. The evangelist was not giving us his own notions, but the actual claims and assurances of Jesus himself.

In opposition to the solemn asseveration now made by Jesus that he was the light and life of the world, the Pharisees brought two objections: (1) it was an uncorroborated statement; (2) it was

S John 13

false. 'The Pharisees therefore said unto him, Thou bearest witness of thyself; thy witness is not true.' Jesus took up the question. Even though his statement rested only upon his own word, it was none the less true; for he knew his origin and his destiny, his abode prior to his entrance into this world, and the place which would

,, 14

receive him on his departure hence. 'Jesus answered and said unto them, Even if I bear witness of myself, my witness is true; for I know whence I came, and whither I go.' On those points they were entirely ignorant, and could exercise only a judgment based upon the

,, 14, 15

ordinary experiences of humanity. 'But ye know not whence I come, or whither I go. Ye judge after the flesh.' Not so did Jesus judge any man; but any judgment he might form would be based upon higher knowledge than that of mankind generally, for it would not be merely human, he being aided by the presence and guidance

,, 15, 16

of Him who had sent him hither. 'I judge no man. Yea and if I judge, my judgment is true: for I am not alone, but I and the Father that sent me.' In verse 16 Tischendorf, following the Sinaitic MS., reads 'he' instead of 'the Father.' These sayings of Jesus possess an actuality, reality, which it is well for us to grasp and hold. Others can give us, with respect to God and things unseen, only abstract reasonings, abstruse speculations; Jesus gives us positive statements of facts within his own experience. In some other portion of the universe he had a prior existence; there he had submitted himself to the will of One who had sent him on a mission to mankind: while here, he was conscious of the presence and guidance of him who had sent him; when his earthly career should end he knew whither he would depart out of the world. All this is as clear and positive as it is startling and profoundly interesting. There is no incongruity between it and our comparatively small experiences of things material and spiritual. In the mind of Jesus there was no shadow of doubt, hesitation or uncertainty. He was as sure of the personal existence of the Father who had sent him, as of his own. If the unsupported testimony of Jesus was not enough for these Pharisees, let them know that there were actually two persons certifying, Jesus and his Father. 'Yea and in your law it is written, that the witness of two men is true. I am he that beareth witness of myself, and the Father that sent me beareth witness of me.' Thereupon they challenged him, apparently in derision, to produce his Father. 'They said therefore unto him, Where is thy Father?' To this Jesus replied, that they were as unable to recognise himself as his Father: no knowledge of him 'after the flesh' was a true revelation, and if they had possessed any spiritual perception of himself, they would have discerned his Father also. 'Jesus answered, Ye know neither me, nor my Father: if ye knew me, ye would know my Father also.' The essential idea of Fatherhood is likeness of nature, and the failure to know, appreciate, comprehend, the Son must extend also to their apprehension of the Father.

These sayings of Jesus were recorded by one who heard them, and who was able to state the exact place of their delivery. 'These words spake he in the Treasury, as he taught in the temple.' And still his enemies failed to carry out their design of apprehending him; not from want of will or opportunity, but owing to some divine overruling of their plans. That seems to be the meaning of the evangelist's statement: 'And no man took him, because his hour was not yet come.' Being still free, Jesus shrank not from speaking. He addressed to the Pharisees some bold, plain, parting words, amounting to repudiation if not denunciation. 'He said therefore again unto them, I go away, and ye shall seek me, and shall die in your sin: whither I go, ye cannot come.' Jesus seems here to foretell a time when the present circumstances would be reversed: he would be absent, and they anxious to find him, yet doomed to perish in their sin, it being impossible for them to gain his presence. The Revisers in this verse have altered 'my way' into 'away,' and 'sins' into 'sin,' agreeing with Young and other modern translators. Tischendorf inserts the word 'away' a second time: 'Whither I go away:' the verb, *hupagō*, is the same in both places. The saying sounded mysterious: to go whither none of them could follow, might signify going out of the world altogether. Was he then, thinking of suicide? 'The Jews therefore said, Will he kill himself, that he saith, Whither I go, ye cannot come?' The question was not so harsh and offensive as it would have been had they known, as we know, the prescience of Jesus with respect to his approaching death. In repelling their suggestion, he explained the precise import of his words. His origin was different from theirs: he belonged to another world than this. 'And he said unto them, Ye are from beneath; I am from above: ye are of this world: I am not of this world.' That fact justified the assertion he had made: this was a world of perishing sinners, and if they believed not that One had come from another world with the offer of life age-during, there could be no escape from death. 'I said therefore unto you, that ye shall die in your sins: for except ye believe that I am he (or, I am), ye shall die in your sins.' Tischendorf renders: 'ye will die in your sins:' it was no threat, but a pure statement of the fact that without a deliverer bringing life from above, there can be no hope of salvation from death. Alford calls attention to the fact that the italicised word 'he' is not in the original. The remark of Jesus gave rise to a further question. 'They said therefore unto him, Who art thou?' In the Revised Version the answer of Jesus stands as follows: 'Jesus said unto them, Even that which I have also spoken unto you from the beginning (or, How is it that I even speak to you at all?)' An alternative rendering so peculiar indicates considerable doubt as to the meaning. Alford explains: 'Our Lord's reply has been found very difficult, from reasons which can hardly be explained to the English reader. The A. V. "even *the same* that I said unto you from the beginning," cannot well be right. The verb rather means to *speak* or *discourse*, than to *say*: the connecting particle cannot well be rendered *even*; and the word rendered "from the beginning" far more probably means "essentially," or "in very deed." This being premised, the sentence may be rendered (literally) thus: "Essentially that which I also discourse unto you:" or, "In very deed, that same which I speak unto you." He is the word—His *discourses* are the *revelation of Himself*.' Tischendorf renders: 'Altogether that which I am telling you;' Young: 'Even what I speak to you at the beginning.' The alternative rendering: 'That I even speak to you at all,' differs from all the above, especially as the Revisers have prefaced it with the three italicised—imaginary—words, '*How is it*,' and have inserted a note of interrogation. That would have been no answer to the question, but sounds like an expression of petulant impatience, which it is not likely would have been uttered by Jesus. Putting that aside, the other renderings agree in one point: in reply to the enquiry *Who* he was, Jesus told *what* he was: 'that same which I speak to you;' 'that which I am also telling you;' 'that I speak to you;' 'what I said to you;' 'that which I have altogether spoken unto you;' and 'altogether that which also I say to you,' the last being the translation given in the 'Englishman's Greek New Testament.' The only doubt is as to whether the word rendered by the Revisers 'from the beginning,' by Young and Sharpe, 'at the beginning,' is not better rendered by 'essentially,' or 'in very deed,' or 'altogether.' In either case we need go back no further than the 'beginning' of this discourse and the saying of Jesus, 'I am the light of the world.' He would have them know him only under the aspect in which he had presented himself: not as a Person merely, but as a Power and Influence, dispersing 'darkness' and imparting 'the light of life.'

The meaning of what follows is not apparent on the surface. 'I have many things to speak and to judge concerning you.' The Revisers have replaced 'say' by 'speak,' and 'of you' by 'concerning you.' Young renders : 'Many things I have to speak, and to judge concerning you.' The English idiom leaves us in doubt whether the 'speaking' as well as the 'judging' is 'concerning you,' or whether two distinct statements are made : (1) 'I have many things to speak,' and (2) 'I have many things to judge of you.' Luther's translation is clear : 'Ich habe viel von euch zu reden und zu richten.' 'I have much of you to speak and to judge,' which agrees with the order of the words in the original : 'Many things I have concerning you to say and to judge.'

'Howbeit he that sent me is true.' The connection between this and what precedes is not clear. The word *alēthēs*, rendered 'true,' is defined : *of persons*, true, sincere ; truthful, frank, honest : *of things*, real, actual. Samuel Sharpe brings out the meaning clearly and boldly : 'Moreover he that sent me is to be trusted,' which answers to Luther's 'wahrhaftig,' 'truthful or reliable.' That makes evident the sense of the following words : 'And the things which I heard from him, these speak I unto (Gr. into) the world.' The 'Englishman's Greek New Testament' renders verbatim : 'And I what I heard from him, these things I say to the world.' The oldest MS. reads, 'heard with him.'

The evangelist states that the listeners did not understand the allusion. 'They perceived not that he spake to them of the Father.' The Revisers have replaced 'understood' by 'perceived.' The 'Englishman's G. N. T.' renders : 'They knew not that the Father to them he spoke of.' In verse 26 the Sinaitic MS. reads, instead of 'he that sent me,' 'the Father that sent me,' and in this verse : 'they perceived not that he spake to them of the Father God.' That reading obviates the following comment of Alford : 'However improbable this may be, after the plain words, "the Father that sent me," in verse 18, it is stated as a fact.' According to the Sinaitic MS., they understood that he spoke of his father, but at once asked, 'Where is thy father?' because they did not realise the fact that he meant the Divine Father.

Perceiving their obtuseness, Jesus foretold the way in which they would come to know him, and that his acts and words were by the power and teaching of the Father. 'Jesus therefore said, When ye have lifted up the Son of man, then shall ye know that I am *he* (or, I am); and *that* I do nothing (or, and I do nothing) of myself, but as the Father taught me, I speak these things.' Let us try to grasp the meaning of this. The plain, natural sense of 'lifted up' is 'exalted.' The verb is *hupsoō*, the same as in the passage, 'he that humbleth himself shall be exalted.' That sense is not to be considered as interfered with or displaced because the evangelist, on a subsequent occasion, attached an additional interpretation to the word : 'And I, if I be lifted up from (or, out of) the earth, will draw all men unto myself. But this he said, signifying by what manner of death he should die.' On the words 'by what manner of death' Alford has the note : 'The words here can hardly point to more than the external circumstances of his death .. St. John does not say that this was *all* that the lifting up meant, but that it was its first and obvious reference.' Nor need we be concerned about the interpretation which the evangelist or any other man may have seen fit to attach to words of Jesus used on another occasion; the only question is as to the sense which the words themselves will here warrant. That death by crucifixion involved a lifting up from or out of the earth was a mere collateral fact, which might be indicated by a passing reference, but which cannot be accepted as a reason for attaching the idea of crucifixion to the term 'lifted up' wherever and whenever it may occur. Dismissing any doubt or difficulty which might arise on that point, we have simply to ponder the expression as it stands, 'When ye have lifted up the Son of man.' The title 'Son of man' is applied by Jesus to himself, and to the Messiah; to himself therefore as the representative of humanity. 'When ye have exalted me as your Messiah, then you will know what I am to you, that what I do is not personal to myself, that what I teach you, I have learned from the heavenly Father:' that would seem to be the natural and proper sense of this saying of Jesus.

But though his own people as yet knew and received him not, Jesus had no feeling of loneliness or failure. 'And he that sent me is with me; he hath not left me alone.' Rejected, opposed, scoffed at by men, Jesus was doing in the world the work which God had appointed him. 'For I do always the things that are pleasing to him.'

These words of Jesus were not without effect, but produced conviction and faith in the minds of many of those present. 'As he spake these things, many believed on him.' To these new converts Jesus addressed himself specially. He told them that the test of real discipleship consisted in a constant adherence to his teaching. 'Jesus said therefore to those Jews which had believed him, If ye abide in my word, *then* are ye truly my disciples.' Then they would gain a knowledge of the truth, and the truth would give them freedom. 'And ye shall know the truth, and the truth shall make you free.' The freedom of which he spoke was spiritual; but they did not take his words in that sense. They prided themselves on descent from Abraham; they had never been slaves to any man: what, then, did this offer of freedom signify? 'They answered unto him, We be Abraham's seed, and have never yet been in bondage to any man: how sayest thou, Ye shall be made free?' Jesus solemnly reminded them that there was a moral slavery, and that every sinner had made himself the slave of sin. 'Jesus answered them, Verily, verily, I say unto you, Every one that committeth sin is the bondservant of sin.' The seed of Abraham was of two kinds: the son of the bondwoman, and the son of the freewoman; the former had no permanent inheritance in common with the latter, who alone could claim the paternal home. 'And the bondservant abideth not in the house for ever: the son abideth for ever.' Alford says: 'I believe, with Stier and Bengel, the reference to be to Hagar and Ishmael, and Isaac: the *bond*, and the *free*. They had spoken of themselves as *the seed of Abraham*. The Lord shews them that there may be, of that seed, *two kinds*; the *son* properly so called, and the *slave*. The latter does not abide in the house for ever: it is not his right nor his position—"Cast out the bondwoman and her son." "But the *son* abideth ever."' Young's literal rendering is as follows: 'But the servant remaineth not in the house to the age, the Son remaineth to the age.' *Eis ton aiōna*, ' to the age,' although translated ' ever,' signifies no more than the full term of life. We must not venture to give it, here or elsewhere, a more extended meaning. Although bondslaves, there was a way to freedom: if the acknowledged son and heir released them from servitude, no one could entangle them again in the yoke of bondage. 'If therefore the Son shall make you free, ye shall be free indeed.' The fact was undeniable that they were children of Abraham, yet none the less they were seeking the life of Jesus, not for any act of wrong or injustice on his part, but simply because his expressed opinions differed from their own. 'I know that ye are Abraham's seed; yet ye seek to kill me, because my word hath not free course in you (or, hath no place in you).' Inasmuch as Jesus spoke only from actual observation and knowledge of his Father, they, in opposing him, revealed an antagonistic parentage. 'I speak the things which I have seen with *my* Father (or, the Father); and ye also do (or, do ye also therefore) the things which ye heard from *your* (or, the) Father.' By words and acts alone could true sonship be demonstrated; be they whose sons they might, their deeds proved them to be aliens from Jesus and his Father. The force and spirit of this saying touched them not: they only reiterated the old, parrot cry, that they claimed descent from Abraham. 'They answered and said unto him, Our Father is Abraham.' Jesus would admit only one kind and one evidence of sonship,—identity of spirit and of action. 'Jesus saith unto them, If ye were (Gr. are) Abraham's children, ye would do the works of Abraham.' The Revisers note that some ancient authorities read 'ye do' for 'ye would do.' They were not now manifesting the patriarch's spirit or fulfilling the patriarch's will. 'But now ye seek to kill me, a man that hath told you the truth, which I heard from God: this did not Abraham.' Let us learn to cherish this description of Jesus by himself: 'a man that hath told you the truth, which I heard from God.' There are many still who are ready to accept and believe in him under that aspect, and they have here the justification of his own words for doing so. Let not those who are able to take a higher view of Jesus, and who can rise to a loftier flight of faith, condemn or despise those who simply look up to him with reverence as 'a teacher sent from God.' The remembrance of this saying of Jesus, his own portrait of himself held forth for these men's regard, would have sufficed to stifle many an anathema in the act of utterance, and quench many a fire kindled by religious bigotry. Jesus, in this very passage, is protesting against the spirit of persecution. Abraham had never been guilty of it; and they who now sought to suppress the truth by killing the speaker, proved themselves of a different stock. 'Ye do the works of your father.' They sought to evade the argument by going behind the obvious meaning, as though Jesus were attempting either to impute the stain of illegality to their natural birth, or to intimate that they were in no sense children of the God and common Father of mankind. 'They said unto him, We were not born of fornication; we have one Father, *even* God.' Jesus was not seeking to make them out different from other men, but he would have them deal with realities instead of words. The fatherhood of God was no meaningless expression, but denoted community of will and spirit. If God were their Father, their minds would coincide with His, and they would love instead of hating his messenger. 'Jesus said unto them, If God were your Father, ye would love me: for I came forth and am come from God.' Young renders literally: 'If God were your Father, ye would have been loving me, for I came out from God, and am come.' The verb *exerchomai*, rendered in the Authorised Version 'proceed forth' and by the Revisers 'come out,' must not be strained to any theological sense. It was a word in common use, applied to any ordinary departure from one place to another, as in the passage: 'But they *having gone out*.' Its import here is clear from the following words: 'For neither have I come of myself, but he sent me.' Taking the verse in its entirety, no mere man could ever dare to say such things of himself. Here again we find the declaration of Jesus harmonising with the opening statement of the evangelist: 'And the Word became flesh, and tabernacled among us (and we beheld his glory, glory as of the only-begotten from the Father).' If Jesus then came as God's messenger, why were those he addressed unable to comprehend his words? 'Why do ye not understand (or, know) my speech?' They claimed to be of the household of God, but could not grasp the sense of the divine language. '*Even* because ye cannot hear my word.' Alford explains: 'To understand a man's speech,—as here used, is literally to *understand the idiom or dialect* in which a man speaks, his *manner of speech*; see Matt. xxvi. 73, where the same word is used in the original.' Tischendorf and Young do not insert the italicised word 'even,' which may convey a wrong idea. Luther's version gives a clear meaning: 'Warum kennet ihr denn meine Sprache nicht? Denn ihr könnet ja mein Wort nicht hören.' 'Why then do ye not know my speech? For indeed ye cannot hear my word.' The verb *akouō*, rendered 'hear,' signifies in this place, and often elsewhere, to 'listen to,' as in the passage: 'If he shall hear thee.' Their inability to comprehend him was as gross as though he spoke an unknown foreign tongue; and it was evidence of the fact that they were of a far different parentage and mode of life. 'Ye are of *your* father the devil, and the lusts of your father it is your will to do.' Instead of 'it is your will to do' the Authorised Version has 'ye will do,' which Alford condemns as 'wholly inadequate and misleading . . . The original means, your will is to do, you love, or, are inclined to do.' Tischendorf renders, 'ye desire to do'; Young, 'ye wish to do.' Having named the devil, Jesus went on to speak of him as of one whose origin, history and character were well known. 'He was a murderer from the beginning, and stood not in the truth, because there is no truth in him.' To the word 'stood' the Revisers have appended the note: 'Some ancient authorities read *standeth*.' Apart from that fact, Alford renders the word as 'standeth.' He says: 'The A. V. *abode* is ungrammatical, the original word being *present* in sense.' Young renders: 'In the truth he hath not stood.' Tischendorf has, 'and stands not in the truth': but there is nothing to indicate whether his adoption of the word 'stands' arises from difference of translation or of version. The following sentence also is open to uncertainty in translation: 'When he speaketh a lie, he speaketh of his own: for he is a liar, and the father thereof.' This agrees with the Authorised Version, the Revisers having simply altered 'of it' to 'thereof.' But they give as an alternative rendering: 'When one speaketh a lie, he speaketh of his own: for his father also is a liar.' Alford does not touch upon this difference of translation; his note simply broaches the question whether the devil is said to be the father of *lies* or of *liars*. Young renders: 'When one may speak falsehood, of his own he speaketh, because he is a liar—his father also.' Tischendorf renders: 'When he speaks lies, he speaks from his own nature; for he is a liar, and so is his father.' Samuel Sharpe renders: 'When any one speaketh a lie, he speaketh after the manner of his kindred, for his father also is a liar.' We have here the explanation of Jesus himself as to the sense in which he used the term 'father.' The word conveys two ideas: descent and likeness. Jesus dwells chiefly on the latter; indeed, he assumes that the former can exist only in connection with the latter. 'Adam .. begat *a son* in his own likeness, after his image.' That is the essential idea of parentage; however great and numerous the differences in body and mind between father and child, they are overborne, put out of sight, are as nothing, compared with the manifold and far greater similarities of nature. That like begets its like is the universal law, with man, brute, bird, fish, trees, plants: any great and sudden divergence from the parental type is a physical impossibility. Ascending to the higher platform of spiritual life, Jesus insists upon this obvious and irrefragable law. No bodily diversities have then to be taken into account; there is absolutely nothing to modify the law that like must beget its like. Jesus speaks as having cognizance of spiritualities beyond our ken, and he seems to recognise an action of spirit upon spirit, and powers of transformation and identification between spirits, of which our limited earthly experience is ignorant if not wholly unconscious. But we shall not err in taking the lower ground of metaphor and analogy, and tracing out the meaning Jesus sought to convey to our minds by the figurative term 'father.' 'When any one speaketh a lie, he speaketh after the manner of his kindred; for his father also is a liar.' These Jews had claimed kindred with Abraham: 'We be Abraham's seed . . . Our father is Abraham.' In the natural sense that was true: 'I know that ye are Abraham's seed': but in the spiritual sense it was false: they had not the spirit of Abraham, but the spirit which stooped to actions Abraham would have scorned to do. The truth held good: 'Ye do the works of your father': only the spirit which had begotten their murderous desires, was not the spirit by which Abraham was animated. Let us not overlook the fact, that in seeking the life of Jesus these men had no personal quarrel against him; they were resolved to close his career at any price, simply because they could not otherwise close his mouth, and they deemed his teaching heretical and dangerous. What Jesus and every right-minded, unprejudiced person could only denounce as a crime, they probably regarded as a sacred duty, for the apostles were taught to anticipate the time when 'whosoever killeth you will think that he offereth service unto God.' On that point of the discussion there could be no agreement; these Jews shifted the ground of argument, and urged that at all events Jesus could not deny them the common claim of humanity to be children of one heavenly Father. 'We have one Father—God.' This application of the word 'father' both to Abraham and to God, indicates that the term was understood to be used in a sense not strictly literal. Jesus took up their challenge, and contended that they had no right to the title of God's children, inasmuch as their spirit was hostile to His will. On the contrary, they were doing the devil's work, they had his spirit, they were his children, he was their father: to say any one of these things was to imply the whole of them. The act manifests the spirit, and the spirit denotes the parentage. Jesus spoke from the first to the same effect. In the sermon on the mount he had said : 'Love your enemies, and pray for them that persecute you ; that ye may be sons of your Father which is in heaven.' The likeness would constitute the sonship: 'for he maketh his sun to rise on the evil and the good, and sendeth rain on the just and the unjust.' The evangelist also presents the matter in the same light : 'But as many as received him, to them gave he the right to become children of God'; the submissive, obedient, trustful spirit transforms the natural man into the man divine : '*even* to them that believe in his name: which were begotten, not of bloods, nor of the will of the flesh, nor of the will of man, but of God.' The new birth, which theologians have shown an inclination to make dependent upon and mysteriously connected with the rite of baptism, Jesus and the evangelist have declared to be contingent upon character. On the other hand, instead of this God-like transformation and uprising, there may be a course of devil-worship and degradation ; the actions of the life are the evidences of the Spirit who rules : 'Ye do the works of your father.'

These Jews had reached a state of mind altogether alien from the truth. They might believe a lie, but they would not believe the truth. 'But because I say the truth, ye believe me not.' Could any one of them point to any crime in the life of Jesus which made his evidence untrustworthy ? 'Which of you convicteth me of sin ?' The alteration by the Revisers of 'convinceth' into 'convicteth' was anticipated by Young, who renders : 'Who of you convicteth me of sin ?' Tischendorf renders : 'Which of you convicts me for sin ?' Alford says : 'The question is an appeal to his *sinlessness of life* as evident to them all, as a pledge for his truthfulness of word.' To what could their rejection of unimpeachable evidence be attributed ? 'If I say the truth, why do ye not believe me ?' It must be admitted that relationship to God involved reception of a divine message. 'He that is of God heareth the words of God.' And from the fact that they refused to hear, the conclusion must be drawn that they could claim no relationship to God. 'For this cause ye hear *them* not, because ye are not of God.'

In proportion to the solemn earnestness of Jesus, was the obtuseness and indifference of the listeners. They answered him now with a scoffing insinuation. Was he not, in all he was saying, justifying their previous assumption, that he was a heretic from the Jewish faith, and impelled to his teaching by some misleading demon ? 'The Jews answered and said unto him, Say we not well that thou art a Samaritan, and hast a devil (Gr. demon) ?' To this grave charge Jesus gave a dignified and calm denial. 'Jesus answered, I have not a devil (Gr. demon).' On the contrary, by word and deed he was doing honour to his Father, in spite of the dishonour they were casting on himself: 'but I honour my Father, and ye dishonour me.' Jesus was actuated by no personal ambition. 'But I seek not mine own glory.' There was One who desired to see him honoured, and who took judicial oversight of the words and acts of all. 'There is one that seeketh and judgeth.' rendered by Young, 'There is one who is seeking and judging.' Acceptance of the teaching of Jesus involved momentous consequences. In his accustomed solemn and emphatic manner he declared that obedience to his instructions would ward off death. 'Verily, verily, I say unto you, If a man keep my word, he shall never see death.' It is important here to take the literal rendering of Dr. Young, 'If any one may keep my word, death he may not see—to the age.' The sense of the original is bound up with the word 'age,' and there can be no right conception of the passage apart from that term. Even in the translations there is no escaping from it, the words 'ever, everlasting, eternal,' being obviously derived from the Latin form of 'age,'—*ævum, ætas.* We are bound to take the words of Jesus in their natural sense, without either underestimating or overstraining their significance. It cannot be denied that the word 'age' conveys the idea of limitation; it denotes a certain period, however indefinite or prolonged that period may be. On the other hand, it appears from the answer of the Jews in the context (v. 52), that the popular notion of the expression 'age' was that it signified a vast stretch of time, amounting in fact to perpetuity, just as we are now accustomed to interpret the words 'ever' and 'never.' But in construing this solemn promise of Jesus, we must not take up the random, hasty, haphazard interpretation of his words which happens to be the popular one. We must seek to grasp accurately the real import of every phrase and word he used. Let us be sure that his form of expression in dealing with so weighty a matter was wisely and deliberately chosen. The statement, 'he shall never (in no wise— 'Englishman's Greek Testament') see death,' is at once defined, enlarged and restricted by the addition—'to the age.' What is an age? The word denotes a fixed period of human existence.

'Thou shalt come to thy grave in a full age,
Like as a shock of corn cometh in in its season.'

'Behold, thou hast made my days *as* handbreadths;
And mine age is as nothing before thee.'

When Jesus assures life 'to the age,' immunity from death 'to the age,' he is simply promising that nothing shall cut short the allotted term of existence. This does not amount to a declaration of immortality. The apostle Paul realised a far more extended stretch of time than an 'age,' and he gave expression to his idea by using the word in the plural 'ages.' 'That in the ages to come he might shew the exceeding riches of his grace in kindness toward us in Christ Jesus.' 'Unto him *be* the glory in the church and in Christ Jesus unto all the generations of the age of the ages.' 'The mystery which hath been hid from the ages and from the generations.' There is obviously a gradation of time in the words 'generations,' 'age,' 'ages.' Jesus did not see fit to employ the plural form. His promise was personal, applicable to each individual: 'If any one may keep my word, death he may not see—to the age.' Obedience to the precepts of Jesus will ensure the prolongation of human life to its utmost limit. More than that can scarcely be insisted on from these words of his. And never yet in the world's history has such an experience been granted to a child of Adam. Human life was cut short by the first transgression; the centuries of Methuselah were but a shortened career, and to what a span has man's life dwindled down since then! When our second Adam, the Man from heaven, works his will within us, the law of the spirit of life will completely rule and enormously prolong our existence. Is not such a promise enough for us? It is too much for this world, and we wait its realisation in the world to come. If Jesus had intended to promise absolute immortality, no linguistic difficulty stood in the way of doing so. He could have conveyed that idea as easily as the apostle Paul did subsequently. This is a suitable opportunity for considering the apostle's teaching on this subject. 'To them that by patience in well-doing seek for glory and honour and incorruption, eternal life,' rendered by Young: 'To them, indeed, who in patient continuance of a good work, seek glory, and honour, and incorruptibility—life age-during.' The aim is the highest possible,—incorruptibility or immortality, but its antecedent and preparative is 'life age-during.' Again: 'For this corruptible must put on incorruption, and this mortal must put on immortality.' This the apostle speaks of as a far-off and final change, which will be granted alike to the dead and the living 'at the last trump:' the dead (that is, the pre-deceased) and the living (that is, survivors in this world) will simultaneously, instantaneously be transformed. 'We shall all be changed, in a moment, in the twinkling of an eye, at the last trump: for the trumpet shall sound, and the dead shall be raised incorruptible, and we shall be changed.' The figure of 'the last trump' implies previous preparation, all arrangements made, every individual watching in his place, the innumerable host of the redeemed duly instructed how and when to act, having gone through prior evolutions, and waiting but the signal from the Captain of their salvation to attain their ultimate perfection.

Take another passage. 'Our Saviour Christ Jesus, who abolished death, and brought life and incorruption to light through the gospel,' rendered by Young, 'who abolished death, but who enlightened life and immortality through the good news.' Here is an evident distinction between life and immortality: the latter is more than the former, though it be life age-during. Jesus has revealed both, but the life age-during must come before the life immortal.

In the following passage the sense of 'age' and 'age-during,' and the higher significance of 'incorruptibility' or 'immortality,' come out clearly. 'Now unto the king eternal (Gr. of the ages), incorruptible, invisible, the only God, be honour and glory for ever and ever (Gr. unto the ages of the ages).' In the following passage also, 'immortality' is held to be a divine prerogative. 'Until the appearing of our Lord Jesus Christ: which in its (or, his) own times he shall shew, who is the blessed and only Potentate, the King of kings (Gr. them that reign as kings) and Lord of lords (Gr. them that rule as lords): who only hath immortality, dwelling in light unapproachable, whom no man hath seen, nor can see: to whom be honour and power eternal.' The last word is rendered by Young 'age-during:' the ascription of praise to the immortal king, by creatures having their appointed 'age,' is properly described by the term 'age-during.'

Another form of expression has been used to convey the idea of immortality: 'after the power of an endless (Gr. indissoluble) life.' Jesus, however, does not speak of incorruptibility, immortality, endless or indissoluble life, but of 'life age-during,' and it behoves us to weigh his words with care, to insist to the utmost upon their proper meaning, but not presume to go beyond it.

The solemn asseveration of Jesus was regarded by the opposing Jews as evidence of madness, or worse. 'The Jews said unto him, Now we know that thou hast a devil (Gr. demon).' They proved it, to their own satisfaction, thus: The best and greatest men had died, yet here was one who said that he could save from death. Was he, this carpenter's son, a greater man than Abraham and all the prophets of the past? Was he not arrogating to himself an unheard-of power and name? 'Abraham is dead, and the prophets: and thou sayest, If a man keep my word, he shall never taste of death. Art thou greater than our father Abraham, which is dead? and the prophets are dead: whom makest thou thyself?' We must again take Dr. Young's literal rendering. 'Now have we known that thou hast a demon: Abraham died, and the prophets, and thou sayest, If any one may keep my word, he shall not taste of death to the age! Art thou greater than our father Abraham, who died? the prophets also died; whom dost thou make thyself?' The words of Jesus were 'death he may not see to the age;' the Jews quote them as 'he shall not taste of death to the age.' Alford explains that the expressions were synonymous; '*To behold death* as to *taste of death*, is a Hebrew way of speaking for *to die*, and must not be pressed to mean, "shall not *feel* (the bitterness of) death," in a temporal sense, as Stier has done.' Alford observes further: 'The *death of the body* is not reckoned as *death*, any more than the *life of the body* is *life*, in our Lord's discourses; see ch. xi. 25, 26, and notes. Both words have a deeper meaning.' That is only another way of saying that Jesus' promise of 'life age-during' is to be interpreted figuratively, and not according to the natural sense of the words. The other passage which Alford refers to, spoken with reference to the death and resurrection of Lazarus, assuredly does not bear out the idea of a figurative interpretation. It is evident from the comment of these Jews that the words of Jesus were taken literally, nor are we at liberty to assume that Jesus did not intend them to be so understood. In straining after 'a deeper meaning' the words become meaningless.

In reply to the criticism, 'Whom makest thou thyself?' Jesus admitted that any self-exaltation or self-praise would be worthless. 'Jesus answered, If I glorify myself, my glory is nothing.' His title to power and honour was his Father's gift: 'it is my Father that glorifieth me.' And that they might not repeat their question, 'Where is thy Father?' Jesus added: 'of whom ye say, that he is your God.' Tischendorf, following the Vatican MS., renders, 'our God.' Alford notes: 'Whom ye are in the habit of calling *your* God—*i.e.*, the God of Israel. A most important identification, from the mouth of our Lord himself, of *the Father* with the *God of Israel* in the Old Testament.' The God they professed to worship, they were, in truth, ignorant of. 'And ye have not known him.' The Authorized Version has, 'yet ye.' Alford explains: 'The sense is, of Whom ye say that he is our God, and (not *yet* nor *but*) know him not.' The improved rendering of the Revisers was anticipated here, as generally elsewhere, by Dr. Young. Jesus had the knowledge which they lacked, and it would be a moral impossibility for him to deny what he knew to be true. That being his justification for not yielding to their opinions and strenuously upholding his own, he puts the naked truth plainly and honestly before them. 'But I know him; and if I should say, I know him not, I shall be like unto you, a liar.' Young uses the past tense: 'But I have known him, and if I say that I have not known him, I shall be like you—a liar.' It must not be supposed that in making so positive and serious a charge there was anything approaching to passion in the utterance of Jesus. He must have been wholly incapable, even under the greatest provocation, of 'giving the lie' in any offensive sense. He spoke more in sorrow than in anger, and we may assume that his tone was neither vehement nor sarcastic. There must have been a ring of sadness and compassion in his accusing words. An inconsiderate reader is apt to give to such denunciations an emphasis which accords not with the gentle and loving spirit of Jesus. Try as we will to realise the scene, the occasion, and the surroundings of this or any other particular incident recorded by the evangelists, there must still ever be a risk of misconception and misrendering. Our own ideas and feelings mingle unconsciously with the narrative, and often, in repeating the sayings of Jesus, we express ourselves rather than him. The true and accurate reading of the gospels, and indeed of Scripture generally, depends far more upon the depth of the reader's insight than upon the clearness of his voice and the elegance of his delivery. It would follow, that the fullest and most appreciative mind would best interpret, by the living voice, the sense of Scripture, were it not for two reasons: (1) that too little care is given to the cultivation and management of the voice; and (2) that the reverence felt for Scripture deters many from rendering it artistically, as they would any other work of genius. Yet surely the public reading of the Bible not only justifies but claims the highest efforts of our best and most attractive faculties; in proportion to our appreciation of its pathos, simplicity, fulness, graphicness, sublime conceptions, magnificent imagery, and ennobling doctrine, should be our care to make the reading worthy of the writing. Why should all the power of expression which resides in the human voice be restricted to the singing? Why should the choristers do their utmost in the chanting, and the reader perform his task negligently, apparently with cool indifference, as though he were physically if not mentally incapable of throwing heart and soul into the reading? How often might depths and breadths of meaning be brought out by judicious inflections and pauses, by that natural, irrepressible vibration of the voice which accompanies the expression of whatever is deeply felt and realised! That is a vastly different thing from what is known and taught as the grace of elocution. No teaching can give the hidden fire, and no instruction should be imparted or allowed in Scripture reading. All about it must be natural, spontaneous; only let the mind of the reader be upstrung to the proper pitch of earnest and intensely reverential thought, and his reading will become naturally and spontaneously artistic. There must be no copying of others in manner or method, no straining for effect, but a hearty desire to apprehend the full significance of the narrative, the prophecy, the teaching, or the parable, and to bring out its meaning with force and clearness. The style should vary with the subject-matter. Many readers adopt one manner and one tone for everything, being always either too impassive or too intensely solemn. The first and foremost aim of a reader should be to feel as well as to understand: that will enable him to infuse into his delivery, and impart to the listeners, his own emotions and perceptions. Such an effectual reading of the Scriptures would convey more pleasure and profit, intellectual and moral, than any sermon; the well-known words which now fall barren on careless ears, would then become 'spirit and life,' and the interest and spirituality thereby generated would diffuse themselves over the other portions of the service of prayer and praise. Nothing of that can be hoped for so long as a negligent, unimpassioned style of reading prevails, such as would better befit the perusal of some old and tedious Act of Parliament.

Jesus repeated his assertion with respect to his knowledge of God. 'But I know him, and keep his word.' Young indicates a difference of tense: 'But I have known Him, and His word I keep.' The expression 'keep his word,' would seem to mean, as in verse 52, 'act according to his will.' Then, alluding to their question, 'Art thou greater than our father Abraham, which is dead?' Jesus tells them: 'Your father Abraham rejoiced to see (or, that he should see) my day; and he saw it, and was glad.' This is rendered by Tischendorf: 'Your father Abraham exulted that he might see my day: and he saw and was glad.' Young reverses the position of the words 'rejoiced' and 'was glad:' 'Abraham, your father, was glad that he might see my day; and he saw, and rejoiced.' The patriarch had rejoiced in being privileged both to anticipate and to behold the day of Jesus. Alford says: 'What is the meaning of *My day?* Certainly, the day of Christ's appearance in the flesh.' That seems to be the only possible interpretation. It agrees with the opening words of this discourse of Jesus: 'I am the light of the world.' It is corroborated by the revelation of Moses and Elijah upon the mount conferring with Jesus, who now declares that Abraham had manifested the same interest in his career. It is all very mysterious to us, 'who are but of yesterday, and know nothing, because our days upon earth are a shadow.' Jesus reveals matters which had come to his knowledge in a prior state of existence, in another world than ours: he claims acquaintance with the God of the Jews, and with the father of their nation. And in all this there is nothing intrinsically improbable: a life elsewhere is as credible as this life is certain; a life prolonged through centuries, in what respect is that more marvellous than a life prolonged through years? And that the loftiest Being in the universe should be known by Another claiming fellowship with Him, that our progenitor, translated to a higher sphere, should take an interest more or less active in mundane affairs, is a rational belief when based on revelation, although it could not be evolved from man's inner consciousness.

The criticising hearers of Jesus gave no credence to his assertion. He stood before them, walked among them, as an ordinary man. It was their humour to scoff at his words, rather than to ponder them.

8 John 57 'The Jews therefore said unto him, Thou art not yet fifty years old, and hast thou seen Abraham?' The conception of a prior, heavenly origin and existence did not enter into their minds. Jesus now
,, 58 solemnly, plainly and unmistakably declared the fact. 'Jesus said unto them, Verily, verily, I say unto you, Before Abraham was (Gr. was born), I am.' The Tauchnitz edition has the following exceptional note: '*Translate*, Before Abraham was born, I am.' That is the rendering of Tischendorf. Young, however, renders: 'Before Abraham came—I am.' Samuel Sharpe: 'I was before Abraham was born.' Luther: 'Ehe denn Abraham ward, bin ich.' 'Before Abraham was (or, became), am I.' Alford prefers: 'Before Abraham was made, I am.' The verb in the original is *ginomai*, which is defined: to become, to happen: to be born: to be.' Alford adds the note: 'As Lücke remarks, all unbiassed explanation of these words must recognise in them a declaration of the essential præ-existence of Christ.' That truth was a natural inference from the previous portion of the discourse, and the emphatic asseveration of Jesus places it beyond question. The word of Jesus himself stands in
1 John 1, 2 confirmation of the evangelist's opening of this gospel: 'In the beginning was the Word, and the Word was with God, and the Word was God. The same was in the beginning with God.'

The saying of Jesus found no place in the minds of the listeners. Exasperated beyond measure, they were on the point of pelting him with stones, and would have done so, had he not in some way
8 John 59 concealed himself. 'They took up stones therefore to cast at him: but Jesus hid himself (or, was hidden).' It must not be assumed that this attempt at stoning had a judicial character, or that the death of Jesus was the object of the would-be stone throwers. It was a sudden, unauthorised outburst of popular frenzy, not in any way resembling the stoning of Stephen, who, after arraignment, was
7 Acts 58 'cast out of the city' and deliberately put to death in the presence of
22 Acts 2) 'witnesses,' Saul 'standing by, and consenting, and keeping the garments of them that slew him.' The habit of throwing stones at earnest-minded preachers and reformers would seem to have been a favourite pastime of the intolerants of those days, who, on one
14 Acts 19 occasion, persuaded the multitude to stone Paul, and afterwards dragged him out of the city, supposing that he was dead. Jesus now stood in the same danger, and how he escaped is not clear, especially as there is much uncertainty in the various readings. The Autho-
8 John 59 rised Version stands: 'But Jesus hid himself, and went out of the temple, going through the midst of them, and so passed by.' The two oldest MSS. stop at the word 'temple,' and the Revisers have done the same, adding the footnote: 'Many ancient authorities add *and going through the midst of them went his way, and so passed by.*' Alford observes: 'There does not appear to be any miraculous escape intended here, although certainly the assumption of one is natural under the circumstances. Jesus was probably surrounded by His disciples, and might thus hide himself.' That is a fair interpretation of the words, 'hid himself, and went out of the temple, going through the midst of them, and so passed by.' The only way of hiding in a friendly crowd would be by stooping down, those about him making a passage, so that Jesus could reach the edge unrecognised, and walk away. Such a mode of retreat would not be dignified, but it was

better so than that his incensed enemies should resort to violence. In some way, at all events, Jesus either 'hid himself' or 'was hidden,' and so escaped.

In verse 31 it was stated that Jesus began his discourse to 'those Jews which had believed him.' Yet immediately upon his first observation we find them questioning, doubting, arguing, showing resentment at his teaching, and at last (verse 48) attacking his reputation. Jesus was accustomed to be treated, more or less, in that way. This may be taken to indicate the fact that it was no custom of the Jews to listen in silence to their religious teachers. Probably Jesus himself committed no innovation when, at the age of twelve years, he was found 'sitting in the midst of the teachers, both hearing them, and asking them questions.' The liberty he thus claimed for himself, he freely allowed to others. Indeed, he seems to have encouraged the fullest questioning, and often provoked criticism by his outspoken sentiments, always answering carefully and thoroughly any argument brought against him. The discourses to Nicodemus, to the Samaritan woman at the well, and to his twelve apostles at various times, show this custom under its most favourable aspect. Jesus never resented, but ever welcomed discussion of his teaching, although the criticisms were generally hostile. An example of this is to be found in the 6th chapter of John. The multitude is there represented as repeatedly putting questions, in fact carrying on an argument with Jesus. From the consecutiveness of the narrative it is evident that certain spokesmen of the multitude must have been selected, the discussion being carried on with a closeness and accuracy of reasoning not otherwise possible. This example is very striking when we bear in mind the social status of the multitude. It was composed of persons to whom a full and satisfying meal was a matter of consequence, a thing to be eagerly desired ; for Jesus told them : 'Ye seek me, not because ye saw signs, but because ye ate of the loaves, and were filled.' Moreover, the discourse was delivered in a place set apart for religious worship and teaching, 'in the synagogue,' which may be taken as fairly representative of our churches and chapels. All this is quite opposed to the mode of religious teaching which now prevails. Children are often taught theology at an early age, and through very rigid formulas, perhaps necessarily so, the subjects dealt with being above the competence and comprehension of the infant mind, so that catechisms must be learned by rote, the tremendous and supernatural character of the dogmas therein enunciated finding no foothold in a child's nature, and being only realisable, if remembered at all, in the maturity of manhood. Religious instruction is bestowed upon adults in the same authoritative, unchallenged manner. We are accustomed to listen in submissive silence to sermons from the pulpit : many preachers seem to have a conviction, not that they are divinely taught, but that they have been divinely appointed to teach. No sign of criticism or dissent must be betrayed by the hearers, who are sometimes warned against inattention, as though it were a sin, and forbidden even to discuss the sermon afterwards, as though all comment, unless it happens to be favourable, on the discourse, were a mocking of sacred subjects. What are the results ? We have form without spirit ;

doctrines which weak and plastic minds bow down before with reverence, but which hard-headed men, accustomed to free, honest, independent thought, treat either with scorn or indifference. The undemonstrative silence of a congregation would be a terrible thing to preachers, had they not become habituated to it. To go on preaching, sentence after sentence, for an hour at a time, and that week after week for years together, and never be able to glean, by word or look, the slightest intimation as to the effect produced on the great majority of the hearers, that, rightly viewed, must be no small trial to a Christian minister. No wonder he sometimes strives to break through that awful monotony, catches at signs of languor and mind-wandering, and rebukes his congregation sharply, finds fault with a smile here, a whisper there, a tendency to nod everywhere, and bewails occasionally the strange and startling fact that his most solemn exhortations and invitations produce apparently no effect on the majority of his flock. All men, clergymen among them, must reap as they have sown. The claim to authoritative teaching, which sets itself above criticism and practically denies the right of reply, is the surest way to estrange the sympathy of those to whom such teaching is addressed. There can be no bond of intellectual union between minister and people, on such conditions. He cannot expect to act the part of a potter, nor will they submit to be moulded as clay in his hands. Be his ideas and pretensions as an ordained minister of the gospel what they may, he stands none the less a mere man among fellow men, and should seek to submit his views to the judgments, the criticisms, the questionings, which are necessarily generated in the minds of intelligent hearers. They may, indeed, through custom or indifference, be content to listen in silence, but only in one way, by mutual argument and exchange of views, can their minds and hearts become satisfied, and the Truth prevail. As it is, there is a great gulf fixed between ministers and people, none the less formidable and deplorable because it is more real than apparent. The courtesies of social life conceal it partly; as does also the estrangement springing from opposed ideas. The more frequently such ideas are repeated by the pastor, and listened to in sullen or contemptuous silence by the flock, the wider grows the breach between them, albeit there may be nothing to indicate the sad and solemn fact. Some few among the hearers, who may be gifted with an uncommon share of intellectual energy, and who are led to turn it towards the study of the New Testament, may hammer out a theology for themselves, and find at the fountain-head the teaching and comfort their souls crave: but where can those persons turn, whose souls rebel against the preaching so pertinaciously and positively reiterated, but who either have not enough mental capacity to expose its fallacies, or who turn with disgust from theological doctrines so handled and enforced? They naturally take refuge in the realities of life, its business, its ambitions, in anything and everything except that patient and wrapt attention which to every religious teacher must be, as it was to Jesus, the 'one thing needful.' Undoubtedly there are exceptions: congregations reverential, submissive, interested, docile, swayed by a minister exercising real power. 'By their fruits ye shall know them.' Does the result amount to this: that church services are better attended, prayers more frequent, the Communion table crowded, the children catechised? Good, good, good, a thousand times good, if you will: religious fervour in any form is better than callousness of heart, and earnestness of belief and hope must help forward morality, down even to the vagaries of the Salvation Army. But what about the upgrowth of independent thought, the clash of mind with mind, the play of intellectual life and vigour, the spirit of enquiry, which are as essential to the continuance and development of Christianity as to everything else in the gradual progression of humanity? These are greater matters, though orthodoxy cares not for them, and ritualism aims at something different. The question is this: Shall adults continue to receive religious teaching, as well as children? If so, can it be wise and right that they should receive it in the same manner as children,—in absolute, submissive silence? Jesus did not so teach, neither was he so listened to. Well was it for his cause, though ill for him, well was it for the world to remotest ages, that the religious teaching of the Jews was thus fundamentally different from that prevailing throughout Christendom. Had Jesus been doomed to preach to congregations which never dared to criticise, to enquire, to express doubt, to speak out their own opinions, to cavil even, think you that his sermons would have produced the effect they did? There is reason to suppose that he gave no latitude to criticism beyond what was common in those days: we are told, on the contrary, that his tone was more positive than that to which the people had been accustomed: 'And it came to pass, when Jesus ended these words, the multitudes were astonished at his teaching: for he taught them as *one* having authority, and not as their scribes.' And as the apostles preached from synagogue to synagogue, the same measure was meted out to them as had been to their Master: their words found acceptance or rejection according to the impression they were able to produce on the minds of the hearers. There was no such thing in those days as passive listening in compulsory dumbness. Follow the career of the first preachers, as they went from place to place: the synagogues were always centres of intellect, of thought, of debate, albeit error and blind orthodoxy often gained the ultimate physical victory, as in the case of Stephen: ' But there arose certain of them that were of the synagogue called of the Libertines, and of the Cyrenians, and of the Alexandrians, and of them of Cilicia and Asia, disputing with Stephen. And they were not able to withstand the wisdom and the Spirit by which he spake.' 'They came to Thessalonica, where was a synagogue of the Jews: and Paul, as his custom was, went in unto them, and for three sabbath days reasoned with them from the scriptures.' The reasoning was not, in those days, all on one side, the pastor arguing from the pulpit, and the sheep forbidden to utter even one responsive bleat. 'They . . came to Antioch of Pisidia; and they went into the synagogue on the sabbath day, and sat down. And after the reading of the law and the prophets, the rulers of the synagogue sent unto them, saying, Brethren, if ye have any word of exhortation for the people, say on.' We have changed all that. But has the change been wise and beneficial? Is it well for the people? Is it well for the priest?

Opposition to the ministry of Jesus came from various quarters. We have seen that when he did begin to gain influence over men, it was sometimes lost immediately, on his continuing to address them. His trial took at one time a domestic turn. His 'friends' arrived at the conclusion that he was going, or had gone, out of his mind. His marvellous statements about himself, his influence over men as the giver of age-during life, and his pre-existence to Abraham, coupled with the slander about demoniacal possession circulated by his opponents, may have led to that conclusion. It was known that enormous crowds were attracted to him, and that Jesus and those with him were occupied without intermission. The result of a friendly council would seem to have been that some kind of restraint should be exercised over him. 'And the multitude cometh together again, so that they could not so much as eat bread. And when his friends heard it, they went out to lay hold on him: for they said, He is beside himself.' His supernatural power of exorcism was turned by his enemies into an argument which pointed in the same direction. 'And the scribes which came down from Jerusalem said, He hath Beelzebub, and, By (or, in) the prince of the devils (Gr. demons) casteth he out the devils (Gr. demons).' Matthew gives a detailed account of what led them to make the charge. A demoniac who was both blind and dumb was brought to be cured by Jesus. The cure extended to the infirmities of blindness and deafness, to the amazement of all beholders. 'Then was brought unto him one possessed with a devil (or, a demoniac), blind and dumb: and he healed him, insomuch that the dumb man spake and saw. And all the multitudes were amazed.' Luke appears not to have known about the blindness, for he does not mention it. 'And he was casting out a devil (Gr. demon) *which was* dumb. And it came to pass, when the devil (Gr. demon) was gone out, the dumb man spake: and the multitudes marvelled.' The recovery of speech would naturally be more manifest to the crowd than the recovery of sight. All could mark his previous silence, and hear his utterances after the cure, but those only who came near, and had an opportunity of close investigation, would ascertain the fact of his restored vision. The discrepancy in the narratives indicates an independent source of information.

The wonder of the multitude led them to debate the question whether the ability of Jesus to perform so great a miracle, did not prove him to be the expected Jewish Messiah, for Matthew adds: 'And said, Is this the Son of David?' When the Pharisees heard that idea expressed, they took upon themselves to counteract it, by asserting that the miracle should be regarded as evidence of a compact between Jesus and the ruling spirit of all demons. 'But when the Pharisees heard it, they said, This man doth not cast out devils (Gr. demons), but by (or, in) Beelzebub the prince of the devils (Gr. demons).' We have seen that Mark attributed that slanderous assertion to 'the scribes which came down from Jerusalem.' The scribes and Pharisees were constantly associated in opposition to Jesus. Luke appears not to have known who were the authors of the calumny, for he speaks vaguely, 'But some of them said, By (or, In) Beelzebub the prince of the devils (Gr. demons) casteth he out devils (Gr. demons).' Luke, however, records the fact, omitted by Matthew and Mark, that this suggestion led to another. Jesus was urged to disprove the accusation by giving some sign out of heaven. 'And others, tempting *him*, sought of him a sign from (out of—Young) heaven.' Jesus being cognizant of what was in their minds, endeavoured to convince them by argument. 'But he, knowing their thoughts, said unto them ...' This stands in Matthew: 'And knowing their thoughts he said unto them ...' It is to be inferred from the narrative that the charge of Satanic agency was not launched forth in the hearing of Jesus, but that he was intuitively, whether supernaturally or not we cannot venture to say, aware of it. The demand of a sign out of heaven was sufficient to show what was passing in their minds. From Mark's narrative it appears that Jesus and his accusers were not standing face to face, but were some distance apart, for we are told, 'And he called them unto him, and said unto them in parables ...' His usual figurative teaching had on this occasion a special application to what had just happened. Every community, large or small, be it a nation, a city, or a family, can only be held together by unity of purpose. National rebellion and social anarchy are synonymous; tumults among fellow citizens lead to destruction of property and business; and feuds in a family must disorganize and eventually break up the home. 'Every kingdom divided against itself is brought to desolation; and every city or house divided against itself shall not stand.' Luke does not mention 'every city,' but adds to the first clause of the verse, 'and a house *divided* against a house falleth (or, and house falleth upon house).' Mark's record is the same in sense, although differing somewhat in words. In the accounts of our Lord's sayings we constantly meet with such variations, which obviously must have arisen from defects in the memory or notes of the first or subsequent reporters. 'And if a kingdom be divided against itself, that kingdom cannot stand. And if a house be divided against itself, that house will not be able to stand.' Matthew and Luke apply to the 'kingdom' the expression 'brought to desolation.' Luke alone applies to the 'house' the word 'falleth.' Mark adopts both for the 'kingdom' and the 'house' the term 'stand.' He also prefaces the illustration with the question, 'How can Satan cast out Satan?' The drift of the argument is best apprehended by Young's translation of the word 'Satan' as 'adversary:' 'How is an adversary able to cast out an adversary?' Each evangelist continues the account in his own way, the agreement being substantial and the verbal discrepancies unimportant. 'And if Satan casteth out Satan, he is divided against himself: how then shall his kingdom stand?' 'And if Satan also is divided against himself, how shall his kingdom stand? because ye say that I cast out devils (Gr. demons) by (or, in) Beelzebub.' 'And if Satan hath risen up against himself, and is divided, he cannot stand, but hath an end.' It would be the height of absurdity for the Adversary thus to oppose himself, foil his own plans, weaken his own power, annihilate himself. And if the act of exorcism by Jesus involved complicity with Satan, how would these Pharisees account for the exercise of the same power by disciples of their own? 'And if I by (or, in) Beelzebub cast out devils (Gr. demons) by (or, in) whom do your sons cast them out? therefore shall they be your judges.' Luke records this verse in precisely the same words. The Authorised Version has 'children' in Matthew and 'sons' in Luke. The Revisers have brought the passages into harmony. Alford explains that the word 'sons' is equivalent to 'scholars—disciples,' and refers for one instance of such use of it to the passage, 'And the sons of the prophets that were at Beth-el came forth to Elisha.' Alford says: 'The interpretation of this verse has been much disputed: viz., as to whether the casting out by the sons of the Pharisees were real or pretended exorcisms ... In Josephus we read that Solomon "left forms of exorcism, by which they cast out demons, so that they never return. And this kind of cure is very common among us to this day."' It is clear that some kind of exorcism, real or imaginary, was practised by the Jews; and Jesus argued that the rule of judgment applied to him with reference thereto, must also apply to others. It could not be held that the power allowed and extolled in others, was evidence of Satanic agency when displayed by Jesus; nor would those sons of the Pharisees tamely submit to be branded, by implication, with so terrible a charge: 'therefore shall they be your judges.' On any fair and honest reasoning, the very opposite conclusion must be arrived at: the demon spirit must be held to be cast out by the divine spirit, and the fact admitted, that the divine power and rulership was being established among them. 'But if I by (or, in) the Spirit of God cast out the devils (Gr. demons), then is the kingdom of God come upon you.' Instead of the word 'Spirit' Luke introduces the word 'finger.' 'But if I by the finger of God cast out devils (Gr. demons), then is the kingdom of God come upon you.' The sense is the same; but did Jesus use both forms of expression? If not, which of the two? Who changed 'Spirit' into 'finger,' or the reverse? To a Jewish mind the difference would be immaterial, the latter being a proverbial way of expressing the former; so that a reporter of the discourse, being equally familiar with both forms, might unconsciously have adopted the one for the other. 'Then the magicians said unto Pharaoh, This is the finger of God,' that is, the working of God's power. 'Tables of stone, written with the finger of God:' probably a Jew would not take that literally, any more than the words of the Psalmist: 'When I consider thy heavens, the work of thy fingers, the moon and the stars which thou hast ordained.' The 'finger' of God is synonymous with the working, the Spirit, the ordainment of God.

Mark has not recorded the argument with respect to the sons of the Pharisees, but the additional illustration which follows is given by the three evangelists. In Mark it stands: 'But no one can enter into the house of the strong *man*, and spoil his goods, except he first bind the strong *man*; and then he will spoil his house.' In Matthew the only difference is in the opening words, which are, 'Or how can one enter,' instead of 'But no one can enter.' In Luke the illustration is more elaborated: 'When the strong *man* fully armed guardeth his own court, his goods are in peace: but when a stronger than he shall come upon him, and overcome him, he taketh from him his whole armour wherein he trusted, and divideth his spoils.' Jesus puts forward the parable as accurately representing the nature of the work in which he was engaged. So far from being in collusion with the adversary, he was his most strenuous and powerful opponent. The casting out of demons denoted victory over the prince of demons; and the imparting of the same power of exorcism to the disciples of Jesus might fitly be compared to the dividing of a conqueror's spoils among his followers. The idea of complicity with evil must be scouted. The strongest form of proverb was not too strong to denote the antagonism which exists between Jesus and evil, and the utter impossibility of any combination, truce, or agreement among those engaged in such a warfare. 'He that is not with me is against me; and he that gathereth not with me scattereth.' Luke gives precisely the same words. Mark omits them.

The scandalousness of the charge which had been brought against Jesus impelled him to utter a very solemn warning. 'Therefore I say unto you, Every sin and blasphemy shall be forgiven unto men : but the blasphemy against the Spirit shall not be forgiven.' Mark's account is fuller, and seems to give the exact words of Jesus. 'Verily I say unto you, All their sins shall be forgiven unto the sons of men, and their blasphemies wherewithsoever they shall blaspheme : but whosoever shall blaspheme against the Holy Spirit hath never forgiveness, but is guilty of an eternal sin : because they said, He hath an unclean spirit.' These last eight words, giving the reason why Jesus made the observation, agree in effect with Matthew's, 'Therefore I say unto you :' obviously there was some such preface to the remark, though Mark does not record it.

Let us first note the difference between the Authorised and Revised Versions of Matthew. 'All manner of sin and blasphemy' is now rendered 'Every sin and blasphemy,' which agrees with Tischendorf. Young renders, 'All sin and evil speaking.' The alteration is an important one. 'All manner' simply refers to the *kinds* of sin and blasphemy which shall be forgiven ; but the words 'every' and 'all' keep out of view the kinds, and relate to the entire catalogue, as a whole, of sin and blasphemy. The Revisers note that instead of 'unto men,' 'some ancient authorities read *unto you men*.' That is the reading of the Vatican MS., but Tischendorf does not adopt it. In the Authorised Version verse 31 ends with the words 'unto men,' but the Revisers have not repeated them, in deference to the reading of the two oldest MSS. In verse 31 the Authorised Version has '*against* the *Holy* Spirit,' the italics showing that the words 'against' and 'Holy' were added by the translators. The Revisers have not italicised the word 'against,' which is rendered 'of' by Young, but they have omitted 'Holy,' with Young and Tischendorf. Tischendorf renders 'will be forgiven' and 'will not be forgiven,' instead of 'shall be forgiven' and 'shall not be forgiven.' This may be regarded as more than a mere verbal difference. The word 'shall' is more restrictive, seeming to indicate rather the power and possibility of forgiveness than its certainty and universality ; the word 'will' is absolute, does not involve but rather excludes the idea of any uncertainty : 'all sin will be forgiven,' is simply the assertion of a fact ; 'all sin shall be forgiven,' raises in the mind a conception of one who says it shall or it shall not.

In Mark the Revisers have twice inserted the word 'their,' where it does not appear in the Authorised Version : 'All their sins shall be forgiven unto the sons of men, and their blasphemies.' Tischendorf renders : 'All things shall be forgiven unto the sons of men, the sins and the blasphemies.' The Revisers have replaced the words 'is in danger of eternal damnation,' by, 'is guilty of an eternal sin.' Alford gives the same reading. The Sinaitic MS. reads, 'shall be in danger.' The word 'damnation' (judgment—Young) has been altered to 'sin' on the authority of the two oldest MSS. Instead of 'is guilty,' Tischendorf renders 'will be guilty.' Young's rendering is as follows : 'All the sins shall be forgiven to the sons of men, and evil speakings with which they may speak evil ; but whoever may speak evil of the Holy Spirit hath not forgiveness—for the age, but is in danger of age-during judgment.'

Taking Matthew and Mark together, what is the doctrine here enunciated by Jesus ? ' Every sin and blasphemy shall be forgiven unto men.' 'All their sins shall be forgiven unto the sons of men, and their blasphemies wherewithsoever they shall blaspheme.' By introducing in Mark the word 'their,' the Revisers have brought out the fact that the allusion is to sins and evil speakings of man against man. In Matthew also only a slight pause is needed : 'shall be forgiven—unto men,' to indicate that the sin and evil speaking referred to are those 'unto men' or 'unto you men,' not 'unto the Spirit.' The 'Englishmen's Greek New Testament' gives the literal translation of Matthew thus : 'Every sin and blasphemy shall be forgiven to men ; but the concerning the spirit blasphemy shall not be forgiven.' Until the Revisers, following the two oldest MSS., excluded after 'forgiven' the words 'unto men,' which had stood for centuries as the last two words of this verse, it was not possible to adopt the view which is probably the correct one. 'Unto men' seemed bound to the previous word 'forgiven.' The passages can now be read as though they stood : 'All sins and evil speakings unto men shall be forgiven.' 'All their sins unto the sons of men shall be forgiven.' The 'Englishman's Greek New Testament' renders Mark literally thus : 'All the sins to the sons of men, and blasphemies whatsoever they shall have blasphemed shall be forgiven ; but whosoever shall blaspheme against the Spirit the Holy . . .'

And how must we understand the word 'forgiven ?' Forgiven by man, or forgiven by God ? That question has no bearing upon the matter, if we can only be persuaded that 'forgiveness' must be a fact and not a fiction, actual and not merely verbal, a reality in existence and not simply an intellectual conception : to the prisoner, freedom from confinement ; to the debtor, cancelment of the debt ; to the transgressor in any shape, deliverance from the penalty imposed. Nothing short of that can be real forgiveness. To the extent to which man can deliver man from the consequences due to or actually inflicted upon wrong doing, to that extent does the exercise of human forgiveness reach. And the divine forgiveness must surely reach as far and perform as much, unless it be a mere figment of the imagination, a theological idea, a belief in some assumed change in the mind and will of God towards us, of which, however, we can have no evidence apart from some corresponding change in ourselves and our surroundings. When Jesus asserted that all sin and evil speaking among men will be forgiven, must he not have meant, that in the onward progress of humanity a time will come when the sins and slanders of this life will have been sufficiently atoned for, leaving no resentment of past wrongs on the part of the injured, and no permanent stain upon the moral nature of the injurer, the renovation of society being perfected through the regeneration of each individual, with no punishment, human or divine, to be imposed or dreaded on account of past transgressions? Such a consummation can be brought about only through the working of 'the Holy Spirit of God, in whom we are sealed unto the day of redemption;' and if a man grieves, maligns, blasphemes, speaks evil of that Spirit whence can regeneration and forgiveness come to him? That sin, and its penalty, lie not within the range of human jurisdiction. They are bound up with the very existence of the transgressor, defiling and hardening the mind and conscience: he 'hath never forgiveness, but is guilty of an eternal sin,' literally, he 'hath not forgiveness—for the age, but is guilty of an age-during sin.' This is the one moral obliquity from which there can be no salvation: the transgressor must bear the burden of his infamy to his 'last day;' the guilt and condemnation are declared by the Saviour to be 'age-during:' we may neither take from nor add to that declaration. ^{1 Eph. 30}

Matthew has preserved a further saying of Jesus on this subject. 'And whosoever shall speak a word against the Son of man, it shall be forgiven him.' The evil speaking of mankind against the Messiah is pardonable, equally with that against men in general. 'But whosoever shall speak against the Holy Spirit, it shall not be forgiven him, neither in this world (or, age), nor in that which is to come.' Young renders: 'neither in this age, nor in that which is coming.' 'Neither in this age, nor in that to come,' is the rendering of Samuel Sharpe. Luther, however, used the word 'Welt,' 'world,' and it is surprising how tenaciously translators have clung to the word 'world.' Dr. Samuel Davidson, in his translation from the Latin critical text of Von Tischendorf, retains the word 'world:' yet in Beza's Latin Testament the passage stands, ' neque in hoc seculo, neque in futuro.' Alford admitted the true meaning of the word *aiōn*, but seems to have regarded as a matter of indifference the fact that it has been rendered in a variety of ways. He says: 'The expressions *this world*, (equivalent to *this present world*, Tit. ii. 12: 2 Tim. iv. 10; *this time*, Mark x. 30; *the course (age) of this world*, Eph. ii. 2; *this present evil world*, Gal. i. 4), and *the world to come* (see Mark x. 30; equivalent to *that world*, Luke xx. 35; *the ages to come*, Eph. ii. 7) were common among the Jews, and generally signified respectively the time before and after the coming of the Messiah.' In every passage here quoted by Alford, the word 'age' has been adopted by Young. The persistent use of a wrong word is no small matter. The Revisers have not discarded 'world,' but they have given the word 'age' in the margin. For that much let us be thankful. ^{12 Mat. 32}

Jesus added another illustration of the supreme folly of attributing good works to an evil origin. The suggestion was contrary to the course of nature. 'Either make the tree good, and its fruit good; or make the tree corrupt, and its fruit corrupt: for the tree is known by its fruit.' Adopting that simple rule of judgment, the abominable slander uttered against Jesus betrayed the natural depravity of the speakers. Jesus did not scruple now to endorse with his own authority the crushing sarcasm which the Baptist had applied to the Pharisees and Sadducees: 'Ye offspring of vipers.' That title might well designate them: their bitter hostility, their hissing calumnies, their tortuous insinuations, their crawling subtleties, the poisonous malice of their envenomed tongues,—all these things were as evident ^{12 Mat. 33} ^{3 Mat. 7}

as they were inimical and repulsive to good and earnest-minded teachers. Truth and charity were as strange to their lips as an unknown language. 'Ye offspring of vipers, how can ye, being evil, speak good things? for out of the abundance of the heart the mouth speaketh.' The thoughts, good or evil, treasured in the mind, and the desires cherished in the heart, must needs find utterance, and thereby manifest the disposition and character. 'The good man out of his good treasure bringeth forth good things: and the evil man out of his evil treasure bringeth forth evil things.' The conversation of a man, even his most casual talk, is as important as any other form of human action, and will be judged in the same way. 'And I say unto you, that every idle word that men shall speak, they shall give account thereof in the day of judgement.' How must we understand this allusion to 'the day of judgement?' Not, assuredly, according to the popular conception of it. The words of Jesus must be taken in their simplicity in the light of the context only. In the original there is no article before 'day:' it is simply 'in day of judgment,' which undoubtedly means 'in time of judgment.' He does not say judgment after death, or final judgment, or divine judgment, or universal judgment. Let us take a somewhat similar saying of Jesus: 'Agree with thine adversary quickly, whiles thou art with him in the way; lest haply the adversary deliver thee to the judge.' That would be a day, time, way of judgment. The idea in both passages is confined to that. We must not add to it what Jesus did not add. He does not assert, (how then can we presume to do so?) that judgment will be held in every case, but simply that when a judgment does take place, every casual remark brought before the tribunal will be investigated, and the responsibility attaching to its utterance brought home to the speaker. Jesus had just declared: 'All evil-speaking shall be forgiven unto men.' He seems now to be alluding to exceptional cases, in which there is not forgiveness but judgment. It is obvious that he could not at one and the same time have intended it to be understood that all our evil words would be forgiven and that all idle words would be judged. It is equally evident that his object was to inculcate the responsibility attaching to all speech, especially that which takes the form of criticism. The lesson he would have men learn was this: 'For by thy words thou shalt be justified, and by thy words thou shalt be condemned.'

At this point there is some uncertainty about the arrangement of the narrative. Following Luke's order, we should have to pass over five verses of Matthew. Verse 43 begins with the word 'but,' which indicates a sequence, yet the subject introduced appears, at first sight, to have no connection with what precedes, but to be more nearly related to the matter lately presented, for Jesus gives an explanation of the fact of demoniacal repossession after exorcism. On the other hand, the words in verse 45, 'Even so shall it be also unto this evil generation,' show the bearing of this on the previous discourse, and lead to the conclusion that Matthew's arrangement is correct. He tells us that some of the class of persons Jesus had been condemning, retorted by asking him for a sign in attestation of his authority. 'Then certain of the scribes and Pharisees answered him, saying, Master (or, Teacher), we would see a sign from thee.' Jesus replied that such a demand was in itself an indication of evil and immorality: only when the guidance of reason and conscience are set aside, and the sanctities of human nature violated, can there arise a craving for some other and external illumination to supply the want of that natural light which lighteth every man. 'But he answered and said unto them, An evil and adulterous generation seeketh after a sign.' Luke does not state who were the questioners, but tells us that these words of Jesus formed the opening of a discourse to a large congregation. 'And when the multitudes were gathering together unto him, he began to say, This generation is an evil generation: it seeketh after a sign.' Probably the scribes and Pharisees had chosen for their visit a time shortly previous to that fixed for the sermon to be delivered by Jesus, and he preferred to give his answer the greatest publicity possible. He told them that the arbitrary desire for a miracle would not be gratified, except after the same fashion as that in which Jonah became a sign to the Ninevites: 'and there shall no sign be given to it but the sign of Jonah. For even as Jonah became a sign unto the Ninevites, so shall also the Son of man be to this generation.' Matthew gives the words of Jesus more fully: 'and there shall no sign be given to it but the sign of Jonah the prophet: for as Jonah was three days and three nights in the belly of the whale (Gr. sea-monster), so shall the Son of man be three days and three nights in the heart of the earth.' The expression 'heart of the earth,' is peculiar. Alford constructed the following argument respecting it. 'Jonah himself calls the belly of the sea-monster "the belly of Hades," = *the heart of the earth* here. And observe, that the type is not of our Lord's body being deposited in the tomb of Joseph of Arimathea, for neither could that be called "the heart of the earth," nor could it be said that "the Son of man" was there during the time; but of our Lord's personal descent into the place of departed souls.' The argument outruns the subject of discourse. A descent 'into the place of departed souls' could be no sign to living men. Probably the expression 'heart of the earth' was a colloquial figure of speech, as we now speak of 'the bosom of the earth.' The meaning attachable to the words of Jesus seems to amount to this: The teacher himself must be the sign,—as Jonah to the Ninevites, so Jesus to his generation. But taking the word 'sign' as equivalent to 'wonder' or 'marvel,' the mysterious reappearance of Jonah after an absence from the world of three days would be paralleled in the history of Jesus by a similar supernatural resurrection, after an interment in the earth extending over the same period. He tells them here what he told his disciples privately, that after three days he would rise again.

If reformation did not follow upon the preaching of Jesus, it could be for no lack of a sign, for the example of the Ninevites proved the contrary. 'The men of Nineveh shall stand up in the judgement with this generation, and shall condemn it: for they repented at the preaching of Jonah; and behold, a greater than (Gr. more than) Jonah is here.' Young renders: 'for they reformed at the proclamation of Jonah, and lo, something greater than Jonah here:' Tischendorf: 'because they repented at the proclamation of Jonah, and behold, more than Jonah is here.' The omission by Dr. Young of the definite article at the beginning of the verse is not unimportant.

'The men of Nineveh shall stand up in the judgement,' may be taken by some persons to refer to a day of general, simultaneous judgment both of living and dead, but there is seen to be no ground for such an idea when the word 'the' before 'men' is struck out. Jesus is here simply contrasting the privileges and conduct of those who asked him for a sign, with those of men who reformed their lives at Jonah's warning: in that review, or judgment, the Jews would stand condemned by Ninevites. The judgment here spoken of is not that of God over his creatures, or of Messiah over mankind, but the silent, self-evident condemnation of one class of persons by comparison with others, Ninevites rising up out of ancient history to cast discredit on the men of the latest generation. That is the natural, unstrained sense of the assertion made by Jesus, harmonising with the context and developing his argument. It is a hasty and inconsiderate idea, to assume that the juxtaposition of the words 'the judgment' with the word 'rise' must needs refer to the resurrection of the dead at the last judgment. Against an interpretation of the passage so far-fetched and misleading, it is enough to point out that the condemnation proceeds from the Ninevites, not from the judge. The Revisers have helped forward the proper view of the passage by altering 'rise' into 'stand up.'

The drift of the argument is evident from the expression, 'more than Jonah is here.' In blind perverseness the scribes and Pharisees were asking for something they had not and could not have, some special 'sign.' Jesus replies that they had already more than was necessary: Jonah had sufficed for the reformation of the Ninevites, and here was more than Jonah. The allusion was indefinite, not restricted to the personality of Jesus: they had 'more' everyway: advanced knowledge, a purer creed, and, in place of a half-hearted, wavering prophet, unwillingly making proclamation of coming doom, an incomparable, earnest, loving Teacher, living, preaching, and working miracles among them.

12 Mat. 42   Precisely the same idea is conveyed by the next illustration. 'The queen of the south shall rise up in the judgement with this generation, and shall condemn it: for she came from the ends of the earth to hear the wisdom of Solomon; and behold, a greater than (Gr. more than) Solomon is here.' More, by as much as heaven exceeds earth, and the gospel of the kingdom of God the wisdom of the world.

Luke corresponds very nearly with Matthew, except that he places the reference to the Ninevites after that to the queen of the south.
11 Luke 31, 'The queen of the south shall rise up in the judgement with the men of this generation, and shall condemn them: for she came from the ends of the earth to hear the wisdom of Solomon; and behold, a greater than (Gr. more than) Solomon is here. The men of Nineveh shall stand up in the judgement with this generation, and shall condemn it: for they repented at the preaching of Jonah; and behold, a greater than (Gr. more than) Jonah is here.' In both narratives the words rendered respectively by the Revisers 'stand up' and 'rise up' represent the Greek verbs *anistēmi* and *egeirō*. This free interchange of two words is inconsistent with the idea that they carry a theological sense, in relation to the doctrine of a resurrection. In the original there is no definite article: it is simply, 'Men of Nineveh,' as in Matthew.

12 Mat. 43   Jesus continued: 'But the unclean spirit, when he (or, it) is gone

out of the man, passeth through waterless places, seeking rest, and findeth it not.' The word 'but,' which indicates a connection with what went before, is omitted in the Authorised Version; it is inserted by Young, Tischendorf and Alford. Here is the case of a man who has been under the dominion of spiritual evil, but is freed from it. Jesus speaks here, as often elsewhere, of the evil spirit as a real, living Being. That is a mystery which we cannot fathom; we must not feign to possess knowledge on a subject of which we are profoundly ignorant. We know absolutely nothing about spiritual Beings such as are here alluded to, and we can only follow, humbly and reverently, the words of our great Teacher on the subject. He pictures to us, in his expressive, figurative way, the restlessness and misery of the disembodied spirit—a weary traveller through a desert, with no water to appease thirst, and no place for shelter and repose. The resolution is therefore taken to return to the former dwelling-place. 'Then he (or, it) saith, I will return into my house, whence I came out.' Acting upon this determination, the prior abode is found to be, according to Young's literal translation, 'unoccupied, swept, and adorned.' 'And when he (or, it) is come, he (or, it) findeth it empty, swept, and garnished.' Luke's narration of the parable is from first to last almost word for word identical with Matthew, except that the first word, 'but,' is omitted, and also here the word 'empty.' But for that, we should be inclined to think that the chief point of the warning lay in this fact of the emptiness of the place—that there was nothing to hinder repossession. As it stands, no particular stress attaches to the word 'empty.' The old home now showed all the external signs of decency and refinement; but there had been no barring of the door against the possibility of re-entry. It stood invitingly open, and the former evil occupant sought the companionship of seven kindred spirits, worse in character than himself; all together they took possession of that living temple which should ever be kept sacred to the service of God and man, and the lordship of evil being now re-established over the man's body and mind, his condition became worse than before, and finally hopeless. 'Then goeth he (or, it), and taketh with himself (or, itself) seven other spirits more evil than himself (or, itself), and they enter in and dwell there: and the last state of that man becometh worse than the first.'

Matthew records the application given by Jesus himself to this parable. 'Even so shall it be also unto this evil generation.' The advances they had been able to make towards a better, purer, higher life, would be forfeited and lost. The fair show of social decorum and religious observances would be disorganised, trampled into confusion, and ruthlessly destroyed. Past history would repeat itself, with added marks of evil, of misery, of horror.

Luke here relates an incident not recorded by the other evangelists. Among the crowd of listeners was a woman, who was so enraptured by the discourse of Jesus that she gave vent to her feelings by a loudly-uttered cry of admiration. Her tribute of praise was conceived in true womanly fashion, amounting in fact to this, Happy the mother of such a son! 'And it came to pass, as he said these things, a certain woman out of the multitude lifted up her voice, and said unto him, Blessed is the womb that bare thee, and the breasts which thou did suck.' Even such an outburst as that Jesus would not suffer to pass unnoticed or unimproved. It is evident that on all occasions he manifested the utmost consideration for any arguments or sentiments expressed by those he was addressing. He left no objector without a fitting reply, and occasionally suffered repeated interruptions to the chain of his reasonings. He now takes up the woman's saying, and deals with it appreciatively and gently. The eulogy was based upon his preaching, and any blessing connected with that must fall primarily, chiefly, if not entirely, upon those who heard from him the word of God in a spirit of obedience. True, their happiness might reflect itself upon his mother, but what was that compared with the direct blessing resulting from his teaching?

11 Luke 28 — 'But he said, Yea rather, blessed are they that hear the word of God, and keep it.' It was as though one should exclaim, Happy the mother of so skilful a physician! and be answered, Yes, but how much happier the multitudes he has been able to cure!

Probably the observation of the woman was suggested by the fact that the mother of Jesus was then known to be standing at the edge

12 Mat. 46
3 Mark 31
8 Luke 19
3 Mark 21

of the crowd, waiting until his discourse should be finished. This is here stated both by Matthew and Mark, and the incident has already been considered in connection with Luke's narrative, the displacement in which probably extends to this portion also. Mark tells us, just before he relates the charge of the scribes of complicity with Beelzebub, that the friends of Jesus went out to lay hold on him, under the idea that he was beside himself. At the close of the reply

31 of Jesus, Mark reports that his brethren and mother were standing without, enquiring for him, and Matthew introduces them at the same point in the narrative. The inference is clear: at the very time when the woman, in her outspoken impetuosity, was assuming the mother of Jesus to be the happiest among women, Mary's heart must have been agitated with grief and anxiety. No one could realise her blessedness so fully as herself. The salutation of the angel Gabriel would even yet be sounding in her ears, as would the

1 Luke 42 congratulatory words of Elisabeth, 'Blessed *art* thou among women, and blessed *is* the fruit of thy womb.' But now, and for how long before we know not, her sublime joy had been turned to bitter misery. The problem of her life was not an easy one. From the time when Joseph her husband had been minded to put her away privily, she had been destined, owing to her unparalleled experiences and surroundings, to occupy a false position, not morally false, but outwardly so, on account of that strange secret in her history of which her betrothed husband knew nothing and judged wrongly, until he received a special revelation on the subject, and of which the world at large and probably Mary's own family knew absolutely nothing to her dying day. Her miraculous conception of the child Jesus was not a matter which could be entrusted to the four winds of idle rumour, subject to all the irreverence and scepticism which would have mingled with public discussion and criticism. Such a topic must needs have been far too sacred for the world's gaze and comments. The holy marvel doubtless remained a locked secret in Mary's bosom. She kept all these things, and pondered them in her heart, and must have watched her child's development and course of action with feelings of submissive, self-repressive awe and expectation.

So it came to pass, that her other children had no perception of the divine origin and heavenly work of Jesus; they judged of him according to the idea current with those who were older than themselves, men of learning and reputation, scribes and Pharisees, who had come in contact with him, tested him, and condemned him. Every glimpse we get of the family life confirms this natural conclusion. At one time we find Jesus admitting the fact that he was 'a prophet without honour in his own house,' and the neighbours persuaded that he was simply on an equality in all points with his brothers and sisters. At another time we are told that 'even his brethren did not believe on him,' and challenged him to take more active measures to convince the world, if he really believed in himself. Now we find his 'friends' criticising his public teachings and growing notoriety, and expressing their conviction that he was 'beside himself.' In their efforts to 'lay hold on him' they naturally enlisted the aid of his relatives, whose errand to Jesus seems to have been in connection with this attempt. His mother was perforce with them. How could she have stood aloof? She was but a weak woman, apparently a widow, for Joseph her husband is never alluded to. In that position, it would have been a moral impossibility for her to disclose now any of the miraculous events connected with the birth of her first-born son. There was no one to confirm her words. Who would have believed them? The apparent insanity of the mother in making such a statement would have corroborated the idea of insanity in Jesus. How must her heart have been pierced with grief, her soul bowed down by the weight of conflicting emotions! At such a moment, what an irony must it have seemed to extol her happiness as mother of Jesus! Doubtless the angel's words held true: 'Blessed *art* thou among women;' yet she could not now realise their truth, but was undergoing the terrible experience foretold to her by Simeon, that her son would be 'for a sign which is spoken against; yea, and a sword shall pierce through thine own soul.'

[margin: 13 Mat. 53; 7 John 5; 1 Luke 28; 2 Luke 35]

Immediately following the allusion to the queen of the south and the men of Nineveh, Luke gives a parable not reported by the other evangelists. It has an obvious bearing upon what precedes, and teaches that no attesting sign was necessary, nothing more, indeed, than what was already at hand, if only a rational use were made of the ample opportunities for light and knowledge. 'No man, when he hath lighted a lamp, putteth it in a cellar, neither under the bushel.' The Revisers have altered 'secret place' to 'cellar.' Alford agrees that the word *kruptos* is 'more properly a *crypt*, or covered passage.' It would be the act of a fool to place the lamp where its light cannot be seen, taking pains to smother its rays when kindled. As a matter of course, it must occupy a conspicuous position in sight of all comers: 'but on the stand, that they which enter in may see the light.' Now comes the application of the parable. 'The lamp of thy body is thine eye.' This stands in the Authorised Version, 'The light of the body is the eye.' The Revisers have altered 'light' to 'lamp,' the word being the same as that rendered 'lamp' in the previous verse. The three oldest MSS. have 'thine eye,' instead of 'the eye;' the Revisers have adopted that reading, but have gone beyond it, by putting 'thy body' for

[margin: 11 Luke 33; ,, 33; ,, 34]

'the body,' which Tischendorf has not done, but renders: 'The lamp of the body is thine eye.' A man's eyesight answers the same purpose as a lamp: by it he sees; without it, all is dark. The illumination of the entire man depends upon the point of vision; if that is unimpaired, he walks confidently, rejoicingly, in an atmosphere of light; but if that is defective, in proportion to the defect he must live in darkness,—absolute darkness if the eyes are wholly blind. 'When thine eye is single, thy whole body also is full of light; but when it is evil, thy body also is full of darkness.' Alford discards the expressions, 'full of light,' 'full of darkness,' translating literally 'light' and 'dark.' Luther does the same, and Young's rendering is: 'When thine eye may be simple, thy whole body also is lightened: but when it may be evil, thy body also is darkened.' From this Jesus draws (1) a warning, and (2) an encouragement. This is the warning: 'Look therefore whether the light that is in thee be not darkness.' This somewhat alters the sense of the Authorised Version, which stands: 'Take heed therefore that the light which is in thee be not darkness.' Young agrees with the Authorised Version. Tischendorf retains 'Take heed,' but instead of 'be not darkness' he puts 'is not darkness,' which admits the sense which the Revisers have introduced by using the word 'whether.' They represent Jesus as urging self-examination. Let those who desired a sign, and who could not perceive the truth of his doctrine, ask themselves whether this did not proceed from their own defect of vision. The purest light is darkness to the blind, and no amount of external illumination would avail for eyes that would not or could not see. The very opposite condition might, and in some cases did, exist. There were persons who saw all things clearly, and were conscious of no darkness, however much others might grope and stumble and complain of want of further evidence. This certainty of perception was attributable to the same internal cause: their moral vision was sound and true. Let men only rightly cherish and rationally use the faculties with which God has endowed them, and the clear light of truth will shine within them and around them. This was the encouragement. 'If therefore thy whole body be full of light, having no part dark, it shall be wholly full of light, as when the lamp with its bright shining doth give thee light.' As we can place the lamp where we will, so we can use our eyes in the way we choose, and find accordingly darkness or light. The most obvious truth does not reveal itself, unless contemplated by the judgment; assurance with respect to the deepest mysteries must spring from the exercise of our reasoning faculties. There is such a thing as wilful blindness: men cannot perceive, because they will not look; or they misjudge, because they look hastily and carelessly. And there is a partial blindness, a defect of vision, which calls for external aids and correctives; and a total blindness, where there is utter darkness. Jesus by this parable reminded his hearers that the reception or rejection of his teaching depended upon themselves.

Luke records a further incident which is not found elsewhere. Whilst addressing the people, Jesus was invited by a Pharisee to breakfast with him. 'Now as he spake, a Pharisee asketh him to dine (Gr. breakfast) with him.' We may assume that the words 'as he spake' do not import that Jesus was interrupted for the purpose of conveying the invitation, as though it came in the course of a sermon. Jesus did not generally deliver set harangues of that kind, and it is obvious that there were frequent breaks, when the hearers were at liberty to express their feelings and interpose remarks or questions. The word rendered 'dine,' and in the margin 'breakfast.' is explained by Alford to signify the first meal of the day. Jesus accepted the invitation, entered the house, and took his place at the table. 'And he went in, and sat down to meat,' rendered by Young, 'and having gone in, he reclined (at meat).' The astonishment of the Pharisee was excited, and in some way expressed, at the fact of Jesus neglecting the ablution which was customary before meals. 'And when the Pharisee saw it, he marvelled that he had not first washed before dinner (Gr. breakfast).' Young renders, 'that he did not first baptize himself before the dinner.' Doubtless Jesus deemed the act superfluous at that comparatively early hour, and what was not requisite for cleanliness he would not perform for the sake of a traditional superstition. He was in no mood to defer to the judgment and feelings of the class of men who had that very morning accused him of Satanic agency, and he now deliberately turned round upon his opponents, and exposed in plain, unmitigated terms a variety of errors and evils in their creed and life. Had Jesus made no stand, and uttered no reproof, his enemies might have been encouraged to persevere in their libellous criticisms. Their object was to weaken his hold and influence over the people, and not for an instant would he suffer that design to prevail by submitting in silence, either in public or private, to their unjust accusations and insinuations. He addressed himself to his host on the question now raised, and scrupled not to contrast the Pharisaic system of punctiliousness in external ceremonial trifles, with their utter debasement of character and disregard of moral principle. 'And the Lord said unto him, Now do ye Pharisees cleanse the outside of the cup and of the platter; but your inward part is full of extortion and wickedness.' The word 'extortion' takes the place of 'ravening' in the Authorised Version. Young renders it 'rapine;' Tischendorf, 'robbery.' The charge was a grave one, and could never have been made if it had not been notoriously and undeniably true. The Baptist and Jesus denounced with equal uncompromising vehemence the Pharisaic class, and never a word of protest came from the listening crowds; at least, we read of none, nor of any vindication attempted on behalf of the class thus publicly accused. Was there not consummate folly in all this hypocrisy? Was the outside only of man's nature moulded by God, and not the inward, spiritual qualities,—that they should so care for the former and fail to cultivate the latter? 'Ye foolish ones, did not he that made the outside make the inside also?' By altering 'fools' to 'foolish ones,' the Revisers make it evident that the term was not used in contempt. Young renders it 'unthinking!' There was a better way of making food 'clean' than by the scouring of cup and platter: let them share it with the poor, and they need have no scruples of conscience as to the correct way of eating their own portion. 'Howbeit give for alms those things which are within (or, ye can): and behold, all things are clean unto you.' Brotherly kindness ranked higher than ceremonial observances, and the broad, free spirit of liberality would replace the narrow punctiliousness of ritualism. The Authorised Version stands, 'But rather give alms of such things as ye have,' which Alford explains to be 'literally, the things inside.' Tischendorf renders, 'But give what is in them as alms;' Young, 'But the what ye have give *as* alms.'

It was a characteristic of the Pharisees, a reproach and evil to them, thus to prefer the little to the great, to care much about religious trifles, and nothing about justice towards men and heart-felt devotion to God. 'But woe unto you Pharisees! for ye tithe mint and rue and every herb, and pass over judgment and the love of God.' The giving of the tenth part of a man's property was regarded by them as a cardinal test of character, the surest way, and by no means a cheap one, of acceptance with the God they professed to worship. Elsewhere Jesus represents a Pharisee as enumerating this among his other virtues: 'I give tithes of all that I get.' What they thus gave, as they deemed, to God, was probably never devoted to the real service of humanity, for they were accused by Jesus of looking with complacent approval on the man who, on the plea of having given his property to God, withheld it from the support of his parents. 'Give for alms those things which ye can,' was the counsel of Jesus to them. The dedication of tithes to so-called divine uses, ranked far lower in his esteem. Then, as in later times, they went to the support of an ecclesiastical system, and its spirit of Pharisaic propagandism was denounced by Jesus as bringing about results the very reverse of beneficial: 'Woe unto you, scribes and Pharisees, hypocrites! for ye compass sea and land to make one proselyte; and when he is become so, ye make him twofold more a son of hell than yourselves.'

The sense of proportion was inverted in these men: in their eyes the little was held great and the great little; the first was put last, and the last first; the fundamental obligations of judgment and the love of God were ignored, and the faculties which should have been concentrated on the substantial realities of morality, were wrapped up in the skirts and fringes of ritualism and formality. Jesus sought to make this clear to them, saying, 'But these ought ye to have done, and not to leave the other undone.' The heart-work and the life-work should be expended on what was most important, and the leisure would suffice for the minor duties, which now had become, if not their all in all, at least their primary concern.

Another fault of character in them, was the love of precedence. Seated in synagogues, or passing through the public streets, they were accustomed to the first place and the most obsequious courtesy. Thus to lose the sense of fellowship and of equality, was an evil, a regrettable deprivation, albeit they felt it not, but rejoiced to be singled out and held aloof from the crowd of their fellow creatures. 'Woe unto you Pharisees! for ye love the chief seats in the synagogues, and the salutations in the market-places.'

The homage they craved and received was altogether undeserved. The world at large cared not to enquire into their true character. When a social gulf exists between class and class, it is surprising how indifferent and ignorant they are with respect to each other. That is the case now, in spite of a free press and the habit of public criticism.

Rank and wealth are worshipped apart from moral character. The toiling multitudes have nearer and more pressing concerns than to investigate nicely the habits and principles of their 'betters.' All have their faults, and all keep them out of sight as far as possible. That immunity the Pharisees enjoyed, in common with others, and it served but to perpetuate their unhappy, woeful condition. 'Woe unto you! for ye are as the tombs which appear not, and the men that walk over *them* know it not.' The Authorised Version stands: 'Woe unto you, scribes and Pharisees, hypocrites!' but these last four words are omitted by the Revisers, not being in the two oldest MSS.

At this point of the discourse a lawyer who was present interposed the remark, that this condemnation of the Pharisees reflected also upon those of his own profession. 'And one of the lawyers answering saith unto him, Master (or, Teacher), in saying this thou reproachest us also.' Tischendorf renders, 'illtreatest,' Young 'insultest.' Alford observes: 'This man appears to have been not a common Pharisee merely, but besides, a *lawyer*, whose duty it especially was to interpret the law. Perhaps he found himself involved in the censure of verse 42.' That explains why this lawyer applied this reproach to his own class. It was their duty to define the obligations of the Mosaic law, and to insist upon the due performance of all its requirements. It was they who taught the necessity of tithing 'mint and rue and every kind of herb.' Why should they be charged with that as though it were a crime? Why should it be assumed that they passed over weightier matters? Jesus replied that the curse, the error, the evil, the woe,—either term seems applicable,—attaching to their profession, was that of indifference to human weakness and to the stern necessities and facts of ordinary life. It was easy work for them to spin out interpretations of the Law, multiplying its obligations and enforcing the duty of obedience in every point; but when they had piled up that burden, so that it lay heavy upon the consciences of men, could or did these teachers of the Law give the slightest help towards fulfilling it? They could teach, but they could not give either the will or the power to practise. They were simply overloading human nature, overtasking human endurance, utterly heedless of the evil and misery resulting from their unwise teachings. 'And he said, Woe unto you lawyers also! for ye lade men with burdens grievous to be borne, and ye yourselves touch not the burdens with one of your fingers.' Is there nothing akin to this in these days? No similar unauthorised, injudicious teaching? Preachers are ever insisting upon a variety of duties which are performed half-heartedly, unwillingly, aye, hypocritically, by some, and deliberately disregarded by others. 'You should pray more, come to church to pray, pray in your closets and families,—God loves to be prayed to.' What? is prayer to be deemed a duty, so that man must pray verbally, apart from the sense of want and desire? Is our heavenly Father so strange a Being as to be angry with his children if they are not always asking him for the very things he is always, unasked, freely giving them? Surely some hideous blunder lies at the foundation of such a system of teaching. 'You should watch and pray in Advent, you should keep Lent, with fast and prayer for forty days, you should observe the holy Easter week, and ponder Christ upon the cross every Good Friday,' and so on, and so on.

Alas for the minds which can esteem this as Christianity, and persuade or be persuaded to submit to such a yearly routine, as though it had aught to do with the glorious gospel of our Lord and Saviour Jesus Christ! Erroneous teaching of that kind involves mental and spiritual evil all round. There is a perverted sense of duty, a mistaken idea of acceptableness to God, and of Christian virtue and perfection, in the teacher and his submissive devotees; and in those who listen to such exhortations, and obey them not, often, probably, an injury to the moral nature, a searing of the conscience, a feeling of wrong doing which they cannot away with, a haunting sense of alienation from that heavenly Father who must needs become nearer and dearer to every willing soul whenever the true gospel of salvation is rightly and wisely proclaimed. Not one in a thousand of a congregation may be sufficiently strong-minded, clear-headed, endowed, through earnest, independent, long-continued study of the New Testament, with the knowledge and spiritual discernment necessary to enable him to sift the chaff from the wheat, the false from the true, the thoughts of men from the words of Jesus, in the sermons to which it is our lot to listen. On behalf of those commonly denounced as neglectful hearers, it behoves us to raise this firm and emphatic protest. They stand before their spiritual teachers like sullen, obstinate, unhappy children, unwisely taught, unwisely threatened, unwisely dealt with from first to last by well-meaning but misguided and misguiding pedagogues. The children are deemed rebellious because they will not bow to a yoke against which their very nature revolts, nor stoop to lift the burden so carefully bound up by those who are persuaded that this load of man's devising was meant for every back, and that the duty exists of carrying it by an effort which must be personal and individual. 'Ye lade men with burdens grievous to be borne, and ye yourselves touch not the burdens with one of your fingers.' Regarded as a simple statement of fact, apart from any idea of condemnation or reproach, is not this true?

The scribes, devoting themselves to antiquarian and legal researches, were out of harmony with the times. They foolishly busied themselves in attempts to perpetuate the memory of events long past, and which it would have been better to veil, if not to forget. They had no sympathy with living prophets and reformers, with John the Baptist and Jesus, but they would fain have the old prophets kept in mind. Not content to 'let the dead Past bury its dead,' they had undertaken the task of searching out and renovating the martyrs' tombs. It was another mistake of judgment, another misapplication of the thought and energy which should be consecrated to 'the living Present.' 'Woe unto you! for ye build the tombs of the prophets, and your fathers killed them.' It may be doubted whether the expression 'woe unto you' conveys the sense of the original. Samuel Sharpe discarded it, using in each case the modern form of exclamation, 'alas!' 'Alas for you, for ye build the tombs of the prophets, and your fathers killed them.' That rendering does away with the idea that Jesus intended to denounce divine vengeance, immediate or remote, on those he was addressing. His reiterated 'woe' or 'alas' was a lamentation over their unhappy state of mind and heart. He now points out to them the startling fact, that their connection with the past was closer than they themselves would be disposed to admit. In honouring the martyred saints they were condemning themselves, for they were animated by the same spirit and walked in the steps of their forefathers who had slain the prophets. 'So ye are witnesses and consent unto the works of your fathers: for they killed them, and ye build *their* tombs.' The two last words are italicised by the Revisers, not being in the two oldest MSS. Tischendorf renders: 'For they indeed killed them, and ye build.' Imagine the descendants of a murderer subscribing to repair and renovate the grave of his victim! What an anomaly, what a perversion of the moral sense, what unblushing effrontery! the world would say. Surely the memory of such a deed should cause the cheek to burn with shame; it was a crime to be spoken of with horror, not thus dragged forth to the light of day. That it was part of a chapter in ecclesiastical history, one of those bloody pages which defile the records of theological strife,—that the authors of the deed escaped the punishment due to all murderers, this made no difference in the enormity of the guilt or the detestation in which it should be held. The Jews stood alone in this respect: the charge of killing heaven-sent prophets could not apply to heathen nations. God in his wisdom had decided to send from time to time to his chosen people teachers and special messengers. 'Therefore also said the wisdom of God, I will send unto them prophets and apostles.' Their divine commission could not exempt them from its foreseen consequences: some of them were doomed to death and persecution; but their blood would not remain unavenged. To this people, from the beginning of human history, had these prophets been sent, and from this people the innocent blood they had shed would be required: 'and *some* of them they shall kill and persecute: that the blood of all the prophets, which was shed from the foundation of the world, may be required of this generation.' What a catalogue of murdered religious teachers from first to last! 'From the blood of Abel unto the blood of Zachariah, who perished between the altar and the sanctuary (Gr. house).' It is uncertain who this Zachariah was, but the peculiar atrocity connected with his death is indicated by the circumstance of his having been butchered in the priests' court, probably whilst engaged in his priestly duties. All this bloodshed would have to be accounted for: 'yea, I say unto you, it shall be required of this generation.' Human life was still as sacred in the eyes of God as when he first declared: 'Surely your blood, *the blood* of your lives, will I require.' Divine Providence still worked to the same end as when, after long years of immunity, Reuben was constrained to remind his brethren: 'Spake I not unto you, saying, Do not sin against the child; and ye would not hear? therefore also, behold, his blood is required.' But how could the Jewish people be held responsible for the death of Abel? This opens out the wider question, How could that generation have to answer for the cumulative blood-guiltiness of past ages? By the slow, silent, inevitable, retributive workings of Divine Providence. It is not that one man answers for another man's sin, but that the law of natural descent transmits the habits and dispositions of ancestors to children. It is an indubitable fact that God has organised our existence on that basis, so that evil is thus perpetuated for a lengthened period, and good for a far longer period. The evil qualities have a tendency to die out in three or four generations, whereas the inherited effects of a virtuous life endure to the remotest posterity. This is the solemn truth enunciated in the declaration: 'For I the Lord thy God am a jealous God, visiting the iniquity of the fathers upon the children, upon the third and upon the fourth generation of them that hate me; and showing mercy unto a thousand generations of them that love me and keep my commandments.' The divine teaching by means of inspired prophets, and the divine interferences in the shape of defeats and captivities, were designed to bring the Jewish people to a better mind, to counteract the evil effects of the bad blood inherited from their sinning and rebellious forefathers; but the experience of many centuries was finally thus summed up by the martyr Stephen: 'Ye stiffnecked and uncircumcised in heart and ears, ye do always resist the Holy Ghost: as your fathers did, so do ye. Which of the prophets did not your fathers persecute? and they killed them which shewed before of the coming of the Righteous One; of whom ye have now become betrayers and murderers; ye who received the law as it was ordained by angels, and kept it not.' Jesus threw away his life and labours in efforts to bring them, as a nation, to a better mind. At the end, he could only say to the blind directors of the public conscience, 'Fill ye up then the measure of your fathers,' and with streaming eyes bewail the approaching doom of that fair metropolis of Judæa whose children he would have gathered together and protected, if only they would have deigned to listen and obey. Now they must be left to the consequences of their long-continued guilt and obstinacy: the conquering hosts of the unsparing Romans would seek by fire and blood to discipline the people to their sway, the nation would resist to the death, Jerusalem must be destroyed, the temple, the priesthood, and the whole system of religious worship be abolished, and the surviving Jews scattered to the four winds. On that generation would thus fall the terrible consummation of past transgressions, and in one huge catastrophe of bloody massacre all the innocent blood of past ages would 'be required of this generation.'

Alas! for these lawyers, for they stood as absolute stumbling-blocks in the path of intellectual progress. 'Woe unto you lawyers! for ye took away the key of knowledge.' Not content with turning their own backs upon mental, moral, spiritual advancement, they had barred the way of access against others. 'Ye entered not in yourselves, and them that were entering in ye hindered.' Is there not a warning here against all attempts to stereotype the religious ideas and convictions of one age, so they may be perpetuated to remote generations? The Reformers of the Church of England three centuries ago drew up 39 Articles, and from that day to this they stand unrepealed and unaltered. The object was to ensure uniformity of opinion, that vain, unrealisable dream of theologians. They were 'agreed upon by the Archbishops and Bishops of both Provinces, and the whole Clergy, in the Convocation holden at London in the year 1562, for the avoiding of Diversities of Opinions and for the establishing of Consent touching true Religion.' The Declaration of the King imposed upon all persons submission to the Articles 'in the plain and full meaning .. in the literal and grammatical sense,' and the Declaration ends thus: 'That if any Public Reader in either of Our Universities, or any Head or Master of a College, or any other person respectively in either of them, shall affix any new sense to any Article, or shall publicly read, determine, or hold any public Disputation, or suffer any such to be held either way, in either the Universities or Colleges respectively ; or if any Divine in the Universities shall preach or print anything either way, other than is already established in Convocation with our Royal Assent : he, or they the Offenders, shall be liable to Our displeasure, and the Church's censure in our Commission Ecclesiastical, as well as any other ; and We will see there shall be due Execution upon them.' What is that but an attempt to 'take away the key of knowledge?'

The outspoken condemnation of the Pharisees and lawyers by Jesus provoked them beyond measure. They retaliated to the utmost of their power. Upon his leaving the house they began to oppose him vigorously. 'And when he was come out from thence, the scribes and the Pharisees began to press upon *him* vehemently (or, set themselves vehemently against *him*), and to provoke him to speak of many (or, more) things.' The Authorised Version stands : 'And as he said these things unto them, the scribes and the Pharisees began to urge *him* vehemently.' The Revisers have altered 'As he said these things' into 'When he was come out from thence,' on the authority of the two oldest MSS. [11 Luke 53]

Instead of taking to heart the solemn condemnation of Jesus, those who were the objects of it now sought to browbeat him by a simultaneous attack. Young describes the scene in these words : 'The scribes and the Pharisees began fearfully to urge and to provoke him about many things.' The more he could be induced to say, the better for their purpose, for if only they could find ground to charge him with slander or libel, and bring him within the clutch of the law, they would thereby be able to silence him, and revenge his assault upon their reputation ; 'laying wait for him, to catch something out of his mouth.' The Authorised Version adds : 'that they might accuse him,' which is now omitted as not being found in the two oldest MSS.

Luke intimates that during the breakfast and discourse in the Pharisee's house an enormous crowd had assembled, and that Jesus, before addressing them, dropped a few words of warning to his disciples. 'In the mean time, when the many thousands of (Gr. myriads of) the multitude were gathered together, insomuch that they trode one upon another, he began to say unto his disciples first of all (or, First of all), Beware ye of the leaven of the Pharisees, which is hypocrisy.' Tischendorf renders : 'In the mean time, when the multitude was gathered together in tens of thousands, insomuch that they trode one upon another, he began to say unto his disciples first ..' The expression 'he began to say,' seems to indicate that his discourse was interrupted, probably owing to the crowd outside. The few words he uttered were 'unto his disciples first,' before he went out to face the multitude. He bade them avoid that cardinal vice of the Pharisees, that leaven which permeated their character and actions—hypocrisy. But now Luke goes on with a discourse of Jesus of some length, from verse 2 to 12. Those verses have already been considered in connection with the instructions given to the disciples before sending them out to preach, as recorded in the tenth chapter of Matthew. This part of Luke's narrative appears to have been [12 Luke 1] misplaced. A long address of that kind was not likely to be delivered to the disciples while the multitudes were elbowing and crushing each other. It is probable that Luke, having that part of the discourse without any indication as to its proper place, inserted it where he thought it would come in most appropriately, and the warning against hypocrisy seemed to be a fit introduction to the opening sentence, 'But there is nothing covered up that shall not be revealed.' This idea is somewhat strengthened by the fact that the connecting word 'but' is omitted in the oldest MS.

12 Luke 2

Among these 11 misplaced verses of Luke is one which does not even belong to the same group. Verse 10 is as follows: 'And every one who shall speak a word against the Son of man, it shall be forgiven him: but unto him that blasphemeth against the Holy Spirit it shall not be forgiven.' This is given by Matthew and Mark in connection with the charge of casting out demons by Beelzebub, and it should obviously have been inserted by Luke in his account of the same matter, that is, between verses 23 and 24 of chapter 11. It is a reasonable supposition that Luke, having a large mass of material before him in the shape of information and tradition from various sources, and exercising the greatest care in assorting and compiling it, may sometimes have been in doubt as to the proper position to be occupied by particular portions, and selected for them the place which seemed on the whole most appropriate. Had the narratives of Matthew and Mark been before him, they would have enabled him to fix the above-mentioned verse in its right position.

10

12 Mat. 32
3 Mark 28-30

Among the crowd gathered before Jesus was one who made himself conspicuous by requesting a special favour. He was smarting under a sense of injustice: the whole of an inheritance had fallen to his brother, and he begged Jesus to use his influence on his behalf, and urge upon this brother that he ought to consent to an equal division of the property. 'And one out of the multitude said unto him, Master (or, Teacher), bid my brother divide the inheritance with me.' Jesus showed no sympathy with the request. He sternly reminded the man that the performance of such a function lay altogether outside his appointed sphere of duty. 'But he said unto him, Man, who made me a judge or a divider over you?' Holding no official position, it was not for him to investigate complaints and apportion justice; nor could any friend attempt to arbitrate, or argue the merits of the question, having heard one party only. But whether any injustice existed or not, or on whichever side the wrong lay, this squabbling about property might well form the text for a sermon against covetousness. Here was a warning to shake one's self free from that vice in every shape. 'And he said unto them, Take heed, and keep yourselves from all covetousness.' The word 'all' has been introduced by the Revisers on the authority of the three oldest MSS. Whatever is superfluous to life is not essential: 'for a man's life consisteth not in the abundance of the things which he possesseth (Gr. for not in a man's abundance consisteth his life, for the things which he possesseth).' The literal translation in the 'Englishman's Greek New Testament' is: 'for not in the abundance to anyone his life is of that which he possesses.' The Greek word rendered 'abundance' really signifies 'superabundance,' the substantive *perisseuma* being so defined, and the verb *perisseuō*, which is here used, meaning: 'to be over and above; to be more than

12 Luke 13

14

15

15

enough.' Any superfluity is useless: it can neither nourish nor in any way benefit the person who has it. This very simple, yet almost universally forgotten truth, Jesus illustrated by a parable. He pictured a rich landowner rejoicing over unusually abundant harvests. The yield was so great, that he was somewhat perplexed about its storage. 'And he spake a parable unto them, saying, The ground of a certain rich man brought forth plentifully: and he reasoned within himself, saying, What shall I do, because I have not where to bestow my fruits?' He decided to improve and enlarge his homestead, pulling down the old barns and erecting larger ones, where there would be ample room for everything. 'And he said, This will I do: I will pull down my barns, and build greater; and there will I bestow all my corn and my goods.' The Authorised Version reads, 'all my fruits and my goods.' The Revisers have followed the Alexandrine MS. in replacing 'fruits' by 'corn.' The Sinaitic MS. omits 'and my goods.' That done, he would dismiss from his mind all anxiety. He need not trouble himself about the future, for henceforth he could take his business and his pleasure easily. He would rest and be thankful, enjoying during the many years to which he looked forward the good things of life freely and heartily. 'And I will say to my soul (or, life), Soul (or, life), thou hast much goods laid up for many years; take thine ease, eat, drink, be merry.' But in the midst of all this prosperity, self-satisfaction, and bright anticipations, there came to him a sudden summons to face —Death. That was one of the possibilities he had overlooked. All his wealth could not prolong his life, not even for a day. In all haste he must make his last will, and decide who should inherit the property he could enjoy no longer. 'But God said unto him, Thou foolish one, this night is thy soul (or, life) required of thee (or, they require thy soul); and the things which thou hast prepared, whose shall they be?' That is the case of every man who amasses wealth for the future, but whose trust is in uncertain riches rather than in God. 'So is he that layeth up treasure for himself, and is not rich toward God.' Man's only true wealth is confidence in God. His daily bread must nourish our lives, and to store up the bread as though it sufficed apart from the Giver, will lead to a sudden shock, a rough awakening from the dream of covetousness to the realities of life and death.

Commentators have carried this parable beyond its proper scope. Alford says: 'It was *by God's blessing* that he became thus rich, which might have been a *real* blessing, if he had known how to use it;' and he quotes Ambrose: 'Thou hast barns—the bosoms of the poor, the houses of widows, the mouths of infants .. these are the barns which will last for ever.' Jesus did not speak the parable to enforce the duty of almsgiving, but to show that life did not depend upon superabundance, and that whoever acted under the idea that it did, was a foolish person, and would be forced to recognise his folly at the last. If this rich man had given freely—perhaps he did —he could not thereby lengthen his life, nor could any amount of alms-giving wean him from the fond delusion that he had many years of healthy, happy, enjoyable life in reserve. He is represented as simply forgetting—it is a common and terrible forgetfulness— that 'the life is more than the food, and the body than the raiment.'

The next 10 verses in Luke are prefaced by the words 'And he said unto his disciples.' This indicates that they formed no portion of the address spoken at this time to the multitude. They have already been considered in connection with 6 Matthew 25—34, and they appear to have formed part of the sermon on the Mount, although placed apart by Luke. But what follows is recorded by Luke only, and is evidently part of an address to the disciples, not restricting that term to the apostles. Jesus sought to impart to them courage and hope. 'Fear not, little flock; for it is your Father's good pleasure to give you the kingdom.' Although few in number, they were a flock, held together and watched over. Their heavenly Father intended that they should rise to higher privileges and responsibilities. Young's literal rendering is striking: 'for your Father delighted to give you the reign.' Seeking things above, they could well afford, and Jesus counsels them, to disembarrass themselves of earthly possessions. 'Sell that ye have, and give alms.' Tischendorf renders: 'Sell your goods.' The advice is obviously for those who are called upon to give up worldly trading and affairs and devote their lives to the establishment of the new order of things, the reign of the heavens. They would be making a good exchange: providing a purse for the future which would never wear out, and an inexhaustible treasure for their use in a better world. 'Make for yourselves purses which wax not old, a treasure in the heavens that faileth not.' It would be beyond all risk of loss or damage: 'where no thief draweth near, neither moth destroyeth.' There was a need for these precepts, because the work in which they were to engage demanded their entire devotion, and as no worldly emolument could be hoped for, they must be animated by the thought of a heavenly recompense. 'For where your treasure is, there will your heart be also.' If they parted with their earthly possessions and ambitions, it was that they might be free, not to beg but to work, and that for a better final recompense. Jesus recognised the fact that 'the labourer is worthy of his hire,' but he led his apostles to expect no more than meat and drink, ordaining that 'they which proclaim the gospel should live of the gospel.' A bare livelihood on earth, in return for much labour and suffering, and a treasure unfailing in heaven,—that was what Jesus offered his disciples. He would have them maintain an attitude of watchfulness and expectation. 'Let your loins be girded about, and your lamps burning; and be ye yourselves like unto men looking for their lord, when he shall return from the marriage feast: that when he cometh and knocketh, they may straightway open unto him.' The simile must be looked at as a whole. The girding of the loins seems to signify the shortening and tightening of the loose outer garment, so that the wearer might be ready at any moment to walk swiftly and unimpeded; the lamps burning may denote the lights required by servants waiting to admit their lord on his return from a marriage feast. Alford observes: 'There is only a hint at the cause of his absence—He is gone to a wedding: the word used may mean almost any feast or entertainment.' The servants must keep on the alert, ready at the knock which may come at any time, to meet their lord at the outer gate. If the parable ended here, its import might be thus restricted. But Jesus continued it as follows, 'Blessed are those servants (Gr. bondservants), whom the lord when he cometh shall find watching : verily I say unto you, that he shall gird himself, and make them sit down to meat, and shall come and serve them.' That cannot apply to any ordinary occasion : obviously the marriage is that of the lord himself, and the servants are waiting and watching for the arrival of the bridegroom, with the bride and others, at his own house. This is made clear by the following description of a Jewish marriage extracted from 'Helps to the Study of the Bible.' 'This ceremony was performed in the "upper room" of private houses. The betrothed pair stood under a canopy, the bride being veiled, both wearing crowns, which were several times exchanged during the ceremony. The officiating minister was not a priest, nor necessarily a rabbi, but an elder, who, standing behind the canopy holding a cup of blessing, invoked a benediction on the assembly. He then gave a cup of wine to the betrothed, who pledged one another, the bridegroom draining his cup, dashing it to the ground, crushing it with his heel, swearing fidelity until its powdered fragments are re-united. The marriage contract was next read, and attested by each person present drinking a cup of wine. The friends next walk round the canopy, chanting psalms and showering rice upon the couple. The ceremony is concluded by the elder invoking the seven blessings upon them, drinking the benedictory cup, and passing it round the assembly. It was for this cup that our Saviour supplied the wine at Cana. After dark, the bridegroom led the bride to her house attended by the friends of each, while others joined the procession on its way, bearing hymeneal lamps in token of respect. Arrived at the bridegroom's house all were invited to a feast, which by the rich was repeated for seven nights, the festivities being prolonged to a late hour.'

The Revisers have replaced 'wedding' by 'marriage feast.' Alford retained the word 'wedding,' but spoke of it as a 'feast or entertainment.' Young and Tischendorf render 'marriage.' Sharpe 'wedding,' Luther 'Hochzeit,' and Beza's Latin version has 'nuptiis.' The word *gamos* is defined as 'wedding, marriage,' but 'in the plural, a marriage-feast ;' the plural is here used, and is rendered in the 'Englishman's Greek New Testament.' 'wedding feasts.' Still it may perhaps be open to question whether the plural form, like our word 'nuptials,' does not signify the actual marriage ceremony. The remark of Alford seems hardly correct : 'The main *thought* here only is that he is away at a feast, and will return. But in the background lies the *wedding* in all its truth.' In all translations except the Revised Version, the idea of the wedding is prominent ; what is kept in the background is the feast prepared for the bride and bridegroom and their guests. Jesus does not alluded to that, but to a subsequent feast given to the servants of the house, which might naturally be the case on one of the six festal nights succeeding the marriage. The lord on that occasion would manifest his appreciation of their faithful, efficient, watchful service, by superintending the arrangements for their comfort, and he would not scruple to break through the barriers of class and rank, and condescend to minister personally to their wants. 'Blessed are those servants (Gr. bondservants) whom the lord when he cometh shall find watching : verily I say unto you, that he shall gird himself, and make them sit down to meat, and shall come and serve them.' Tischendorf renders:

'he will gird himself about, and make them sit down at table, and coming near will minister unto them.' We see now the sense to be attached to the words, 'Let your loins be girded about:' assume the garb, the office, the service appointed to you in the Master's household; let everything about you be suited to the task you are called to do; learn to watch patiently, and to perform your life-work with earnestness and alacrity. The lesson Jesus was anxious to impress was the duty and necessity of vigilance. 'And if he shall come in the second watch, and if in the third, and find *them* so, blessed are those *servants*.' Tischendorf reads, 'blessed are they,' following the two oldest MSS. Instead of making that alteration the Revisers have indicated it by italicising the word 'servants.'

By another simile Jesus urged the consideration that our duty and our convenience cannot be made to correspond. It was obvious that if only the owner of a house could foretell the time when a burglary would be attempted, he would prefer to keep watch for that occasion only. As it is, he is always in uncertainty, and must be constantly on guard, knowing that the danger is imminent, and that if ever he leaves the house he does so at the peril of finding on his return that it has been broken into. 'But know this (Or, But this ye know), that if the master of the house had known in what hour the thief was coming, he would have watched, and not have left his house to be broken through (Gr. digged through).' As the necessity is laid upon the householder of being ever on the spot or on the alert, personally or by deputy, so it is incumbent upon the disciple of Jesus to keep at his post of duty, for he is exposed to similar uncertainty, and knows not—or rather should know—what irreparable injury and loss may ensue from any relaxation of that watchfulness, caution, self-restraint, and devotion to duty which are essential to our well-being, bodily and spiritual, temporal and eternal. 'Be ye also ready: for in an hour that ye think not the Son of man cometh.' It cannot be doubted that by 'the Son of Man' Jesus designated himself, as Messiah and Head of mankind: The nature and object of his 'coming' are evident from the context. It would not be for the purpose of executing judgment, either among those of his own household or upon his declared enemies, but in the natural course of events. He represents himself as participating in all the experiences of humanity, and on the most momentous and joyful occasion in his career he must needs rely upon the fidelity and devotion of those who are engaged in his service. If they should fail him, he will suffer shame and disappointment; if they carry out his wishes and are zealous in his service, he will make them sharers of his joy, will delight to show them honour, and even reciprocate their good offices. The 'coming' for which he would have us prepare ourselves is not that of a Deity, with vengeance in one hand and reward in the other, but the 'coming of the Son of man,' in the same nature as our own, with no greater difference between ourselves and him than that which exists between a master of exalted rank and the servants who live in his house and wait upon his bidding.

One of the apostles was in doubt whether the parable was to be considered applicable to them only, or extended to others also. 'And Peter said, Lord (Sir—Young), speakest thou this parable unto us, or even unto all?' The question was natural and necessary, for the servants in a ruler's household are few indeed compared with those persons scattered over his estates. The answer of Jesus went straight to the point. Whoever holds any position of responsibility or trust, to him the rule laid down in the parable as a matter of course applies. 'And the Lord said, Who then is the faithful and wise steward (or, the faithful steward, the wise *man*), whom his lord shall set over his household to give them their portion of food in due season?' The word *sitometrion*, rendered 'portion of food,' is defined as 'a measured allowance of corn,' and is translated in the 'Englishman's Greek New Testament' 'measure of corn.' The general lesson conveyed by the parable is demonstrated by altering the circumstances connected with it. Jesus drops the simile of domestics waiting for their lord's return, and takes the case of a man who by his character or wisdom has earned a superior position, throwing upon him the responsibility of seeing that all committed to his oversight are duly provided and cared for. Alford somewhat narrows the interpretation by saying: 'In its highest sense it applies to his Apostles and ministers, inasmuch as to them most has been given as the *stewards*—but its application is gradationally downwards through all those who know their Master's will, even to the lowest, whose measure both of responsibility and reward is more limited.' It is true that the apostle Paul wrote: 'Let a man so account of us, as of ministers of Christ, and stewards of the mysteries of God;' and again: 'The bishop (or, overseer) must be blameless as God's steward.' But the apostle Peter applies the term 'stewards' to the general body of Christians: 'According as each hath received a gift, ministering it among yourselves, as good stewards of the manifold grace of God.' It cannot be argued, therefore, that to the clergy 'most has been given as the stewards;' and although the apostles, dealing with spiritual gifts, used the word 'steward' in that connection only, Jesus in the parable itself does not. On the contrary, he takes up the ordinary office of a steward in a nobleman's establishment, and there is no hint that any class of teachers or any kind of teaching is designedly referred to. Moreover, the words 'steward' and 'servant' are used apparently as synonymous in the parable, and in the oldest MS., the Sinaitic, the original reading was 'servant,' not 'steward,' the word having been altered by a later hand. Adhering to the terms of the parable, we are bound to apply it to the affairs of ordinary life. The steward's duties are not to be taken as representing those of priests and pedagogues. The most prominent and universal feature in human history is—Labour; and the apportionment of a due reward to Labour is one of the most serious, and hitherto, alas! most difficult problems of society. We talk glibly about the struggle which ever exists between Capital and Labour. It is time we asked ourselves, in the name of morality and Christianity, Whether any such strife is natural and necessary? Whether, at least, its conditions ought not to be considerably modified? Every capitalist is a steward. Every employer is a steward. The superior position itself is evidence of faithfulness and wisdom, either in the man himself or his ancestors. Having regard to the grand truth of human brotherhood, it must be admitted that the status of a large manufacturer, for instance, is that of a faithful and wise steward, who has, under divine Providence, been set over a household, to give them their portion of food in due season. Such responsibility clearly attaches to him. How is it generally fulfilled? The answer is plainly recorded in the huge fortunes of the few and the degraded condition of the masses. Overlooking the teaching of Jesus, we have taken up the science of political economy in the same spirit and to the same ends as Macchiavelli handled the science of political government. His point of view was the interest of the governors, not of the governed, and the very idea of morality, of right and wrong in rulership, was excluded from his system. In dealing with human beings, any system which leaves out of account the principles of justice, of compassion, of brotherly love, becomes thereby earthly and devilish. The law of supply and demand regulates the tides of commerce, and human labour, being a saleable article, must fluctuate in value with other things. Of course, of course! that is, if you assume that a brother or a sister is to be considered simply as a chattel, bought and sold, used and worked, with as little regard to his or her bodily, mental, social welfare, as a plough or a steam engine. It rests with the great employers of labour, to what extent they will avail themselves of the power they possess to extort the largest amount of work for the smallest amount of pay. It would be difficult, and might be even dangerous, for an individual employer or firm voluntarily to pay more than the recognised market price of labour. One of the penalties attaching to a long-continued course of wrong-doing is the difficulty and risk of departing from it. Tyranny descends from one generation to another,—an inherited curse which it is hard to shake off. The first step towards amendment is to recognise and confess the evil; then the thought and energy which formerly were devoted to its maintenance and perpetuation will be free to set about the task of its eradication. It is not in human nature for one class deliberately and systematically to resolve upon oppressing and starving the class below them. The monstrous wrong has grown up gradually, like errors in politics, in finance, in theology, one side of the question being brought into undue prominence, and the other side wholly overlooked. The laws of political economy, when applied to human beings, must be blended with human sympathy, or they will produce misery instead of happiness, injustice and slavery instead of right and freedom. Where, between masters and servants, there is personal or direct intercourse, the system of 'starvation wages' has not come into operation. The treatment of domestics can scarcely be admitted as a case in point, they being unmarried and having no families to maintain. But take that branch of labour which is not manual but clerical: the stern law of supply and demand does not reduce salaries to the lowest *crushing* point. A merchant's or manufacturer's clerk grows up from youth to manhood, and often continues to his life's end, in the same service. As his necessities increase, when he marries, when his children need education, he states his case, and his employer manifests consideration and sympathy. The Christian law of brotherhood demands that the same consideration and sympathy should be extended to the very lowest manual labourer. This momentous question has been fully, eloquently, impartially faced and argued by Joseph Cook of

Boston. The ten lectures* delivered by him on the subject deserve the careful, earnest study of every Christian, and especially of Christian employers. Here are a few quotations from that work:—
"I went through Manchester, in England, carefully studying the poor. Sometimes I walked by open doors, where the filth inside the threshold was as deep as outside. I saw poultry picking up their living not oftener outside than inside these doors. One evening, on the top of an omnibus, I went out into the suburbs of Manchester, and came upon palaces, immense private establishments, with grounds kept in the best English styles. Whose houses are these? They are the masters' houses; manufacturers' houses. This is the country seat of Sir So-and-so, who owns such-and-such acres of factories in Manchester, under the soot yonder. Where do his workmen live? They must live close to their work, under the eaves of the factories: and I found I had been studying the houses of the operatives employed by these very princes and masters. Skilled operatives' houses in Manchester are often very comfortable, but I am speaking of the condition of the lowest paid labourers. There was before me in Manchester what does not yet exist in New England,—an hereditary class of operatives. Little by little men had gone down to the squalid condition in hovels where I saw children fight over a piece of fish dropped from a pedlar's cart. I have stood there myself, and peeled an orange, and the peel was picked up swiftly from the sidewalk, and eaten by hungry children. I could fire an arrow in the street over sixty or eighty children that looked as if they had been unwashed from birth. Within a cannon-shot stood these palaces of the manufacturers. That contrast is seen all through the Old World; and it results from these great principles, that subdivision of labour increases the skill of the operative, and that the larger the establishment the greater the profits. The man who manages the great establishment may become rich, and can take care of himself; the man who makes the pin-head loses capacity to do anything else. If he loses the opportunity to make that pin-head, he knows no other trade, and may suffer terribly before he can learn one, and find another place to work. What else did I see in Manchester? Near one of the great factories was a long brick building; and I saw women pass it, and hand their infants in at the gate. When six o'clock came in the afternoon, I saw these same women coming back, and receiving out of that gate their babes. What sort of housekeeping is that? . . . Even John Stuart Mill, using England as a lens, and putting behind that telescope the best eyes of political economy, writes a deliberate chapter (Political Economy, Book V., chapter VII.) on the Probable Future of the Labouring Classes, and goes so far as to say that he finds the prospects hopeful, only because he expects the entire system of wages to be superseded by that of co-operation. But the system of wages is woven with the whole structure of modern life, and does not show a tendency to vanish out of history like a morning cloud. The accumulation of wealth falls chiefly to employers, and not to operatives. The distance between the two classes is a result of deep causes arising from the two great laws of the manufacturing system. It is out of these laws that there

* "Labour." By Joseph Cook. Hodder and Stoughton. Price 1s. 6d.

inevitably originates what has been called in modern times a manufacturing aristocracy. De Tocqueville, using this phrase, compares the territorial aristocracy of former ages with the manufacturing aristocracy of to-day, and finds the former superior to the latter, because it was bound by law, or thought itself bound by usage, as the latter is not, to come to the relief of its serving-men, and to succour them in their distresses (Democracy in America, vol. II., Book II., chap. XX.; also vol. II., Book IV., chap. V.) . . . Advocating no socialistic proposition, and defending no communistic dream, I yet believe the day will come when the cost of its production will determine the pay of labour. The cost of production includes the support of a family. . . . There must be somewhere a lifting of the income of the lowest-paid class of labourers : otherwise we shall have monstrosity after monstrosity. . . . De Tocqueville ventures to affirm that the modern manufacturing aristocracy, which to a large extent has taken the place of the hereditary and territorial, differs from the old feudal aristocracy in that it feels no responsibility for the age of its dependants. Give us the best service of youth ; crush out the right of children to a fair education in primary branches; give us the strength of the girl before her powers have been fully confirmed ; give us the strength of mothers when their lives draw near to dangerous physical crises ; give us the strength of manhood up to the last hour in which it can labour remuneratively ; and then let the ruined girl, let the mother in her weakness, let old age in its dependence, shift for themselves. . . . I arrive at the conclusion that justice is not dangerous to capital. . . . 1. The cost of producing labour should determine the price of labour. 2. The cost of producing labour includes that of rearing a family. 3. The cost of rearing a family depends on the standard of comfort and decency, below which labourers will not go, or ought not to go. . . . Only the golden rule can bring the golden age. . . . On my study table there is a collection of treasure or rubbish—I hardly know which to call it—on political economy : ten or twelve feet of volumes representing the best discussions in social science for the last two hundred years. Gather and examine in chronological order any such collection of books, and you will find that down to about 1840 or 1850, they are full of the see-saw theory of wages and profits, and teach a godless science ; a series of propositions utterly without piety, and having in mind no Christian principles. About 1840 and 1850, after the reform-laws in Great Britain had come into force, you find this series of books changing position ; and God be praised that to-day political economy does not deserve to be called the dismal science. . . . 6. The rate of profit, therefore, depends on a variety of circumstances, of which the rate of wages is only one. 7. Ricardo's doctrine that the rate of profit depends on wages only, is therefore an inaccurate, because an inexhaustive, statement of the case. 8. When the efficiency of labour is increased by the improvement of machinery, or any other cause, profits may be increased, although wages may remain the same. 9. It may happen from the same causes that both the rate of wages and the rate of profit may be increased at the same time. There is no see-saw in the relation between labour and capital, if these propositions are true. . . . There has rarely been taught authoritatively a more mischievous falsehood in political economy than the assertion that wages and capital are of necessity an eternal see-saw, putting the labourer and the employer into a state of constant war. . . . Justice is no peril to capitalists, nor fair wages a diminution of fair profits.'

These extracts suffice to show the vastness and urgency of the subject. We have only to open our eyes and see for ourselves the degraded condition of the masses in our cities. Observe the crowd of the lower class poor in the eastern, southern, or northern streets of London,—their dress, their unhealthy faces, their language, their manners. Then think what must be their surroundings, where and how they live, and in what an atmosphere. Think of the hard straits they must be put to, their scanty and unwholesome food, their lack of all those decencies and conveniences which are prime necessaries of existence with the classes above them. The fact is undeniable and notorious, that many kinds of labour are terribly underpaid. Why should that be? How did such an unchristian system originate? How can it be first mitigated and eventually abolished? That is the grave problem which presses for solution. Let us no longer be deluded by a lying spirit in the garb of political economy. Let the fact be recognised and faced, that a fair amount of wage is part of the prime cost of an article, as much as if it were a part of the raw material. There is, after all, a certain starvation point below which the rate of wages cannot be pressed. Let that point be raised some few degrees. Let the human workman receive the same consideration as the machinery, which it is found necessary to keep in proper working order, whatever be the expenditure required to do so. Probably the additional cost will fall upon consumers, not upon the manufacturer. Be that as it may, let the responsibility of paying adequate wages rest henceforth on the right shoulders,—those of the master who employs the workman. If they are Christians, they must both act upon the principle laid down by Christ. The labourer must give honest, hearty work, and the master must offer sufficient pay,—sufficient to provide for the workman and his family, so that his children may not be defrauded of their right to education. Education by the State, either wholly or partly free, with compulsory attendance, is one mode of grappling with the evil which has grown up in our midst; and the introduction of this system will render easier the next step in advance. The spirit of liberality is not quenched among our wealthy manufacturers, as is evident from the princely sums given for people's parks, for schools, and in other ways. These things, however, are but palliatives, and the real reform must begin at the other end,—by putting the workmen into a position to do what is needful for themselves. In some effectual way that must be brought about,—probably by the combination of different methods, including among them the principle of co-operation. The 'kingdom of heaven' proclaimed by Jesus is based upon loftier maxims and principles of action than those current in the world. The obligations of the gospel are laid upon all men, and extend to every sphere of human duty. It is an idle pretext, an act of hypocrisy, to call Jesus ' Lord, Lord,' and fail to do the things he says. The whole life should be permeated, its every nook and cranny illuminated, swept, garnished by his Spirit. That is what he demands in this parable, which applies to all holding responsible positions. Jesus will judge every one by the way in which he performs his proper life-work. 'Who then is the faithful and wise steward, whom his lord shall set over his household, to give them their portion of food in due season?' Is not that precisely the appointed task of every parent and of every master? And with respect to our fulfilment of that task, the Son of man will judge us at the last. The patient, loving, anxious, long-suffering Mother, will rejoice in his approval when the burden of her life is laid aside. The Father, be his condition high or low, who has laboured and battled in the world for his children's sake, will be welcomed as a good soldier of Jesus Christ. The Master who has cared for his servants, who has not defrauded or oppressed them, who has been as careful 'to give them their portion of food in due season' as to secure his own gain and increase his own wealth,—his character and course of action will be stamped with our Lord's approval. 'Blessed is that servant (Gr. bondservant), whom his Lord when he cometh shall find so doing. Of a truth I say unto you, that he will set him over all that he hath.' The spirit of Christian brotherhood is that which will commend us to Christ and advance our interests in his coming kingdom, when the world's maxims and the mistakes of the science falsely so-called of political economy will be replaced by a judgment which is unerring and compassionate.

This is no new gospel, however much we may have overlooked and perverted the truths which Jesus preached. The apostles are at one with him in pressing home this duty. 'Masters, render unto your servants that which is just and equal: knowing that ye also have a Master in heaven.' Against the oppression of the poor by the rich in the matter of wages, James entered this emphatic protest: 'Behold, the hire of your labourers, who mowed your fields, which is of you kept back by fraud, crieth out: and the cries of them that reaped have entered into the ears of the Lord of Sabaoth.' The warning which Jesus uttered against this form of covetousness, this breach of trust, this neglect and perversion of duty, is very solemn. 'But if that servant (Gr. bondservant) shall say in his heart, My lord delayeth his coming: and shall begin to beat the menservants and the maidservants, and to eat and drink, and to be drunken: the lord of that servant (Gr. bondservant) shall come in a day when he expecteth not, and in an hour when he knoweth not, and shalt cut him asunder (or, severely scourge him), and appoint his portion with the unfaithful.' Looking round upon our country and our time in sober sadness, would it be easy, would it even be possible to assert that the worship of wealth does not prevail over the worship of Christ? Things must have come to a terrible pass to have evoked and justified Mrs. Browning's 'Cry of the Children' and Thomas Hood's 'Song of the Shirt.' The employers of labour must be regarded as primarily and directly responsible for evils such as those which when dragged to light shock the moral sense of the community. The greed of riches has been so keen, the race for wealth so eager, that the claims of humanity, the dictates of conscience, and the teaching of Jesus have been alike forgotten. How strangely, how startlingly, do his words apply: 'If that servant shall say in his heart, My Lord delayeth his coming!' The 'day of judgment' has been regarded as a remote event, destined to happen at some period in the dim and distant future: meantime, there was held to be no divine oversight with respect to the course of this world's trading; prices must rise or fall according to the stress of competition, and the wages of men, women and children must follow the same cast-iron law of political economy, the necessity for keeping them at the very lowest point being self-evident, on account of the largeness of the item and the fact that other charges were necessarily fixed, such as rent of premises and the cost, repair and maintenance of machinery: the reduction of workmen's wages was the readiest and most effectual economy practicable. If the master suffered with them, if he had been losing, were it only interest on his capital, at the same time, if the reduction had been temporary and exceptional, it might have been excusable. But there has been growing opulence among employers, whilst want, misery and degradation have become chronic among the working class. What is that but oppression, coupled with selfishness and self-indulgence? 'And shall begin to beat the menservants and the maidservants, and to eat and drink, and to be drunken.' Seeing extremest luxury on one side, and extremest poverty on the other, this simile can scarcely be deemed too strong. There has been a hideous misconception of Christian duty; somnolence if not searing of the conscience. Huge fortunes have been amassed under this system, with never a thought of any loss of Christian status. The so-called 'evangelization of the masses' may even have been a pet form of charity with some of these wealthy manufacturers. They have been looking forward to a heavenly life hereafter, have believed in Jesus as their Redeemer, and have been anticipating and preparing for his 'coming.' But not in the way he has appointed them. 'The lord of that servant shall come in a day when he expecteth not, and in an hour when he knoweth not.' Acceptance with Jesus is not to be found through any Church membership, or form of worship, or sacramental pledge, but in doing the work of this life on the principles and in the spirit he has inculcated. Were Jesus now to revisit earth, and to look round about upon all things, as when he espied the abuses in the temple, think you that he would look without shame and indignation on the slums in which the lowest class of labourers live, or with complacency upon the palaces of the masters who have risen to wealth, refinement, rank, notwithstanding the degradation of their operatives? Would he not quickly execute his threat; 'and shall cut him asunder, and appoint his portion with the unfaithful?' Such neglect and oppression of one's poorer brethren must lead to exclusion from the brotherhood of which Jesus is the head. Such a steward will find no permanent place in his Master's household. And because the judgment is not executed speedily, because the evil goes on from generation to generation, oppressor and oppressed alike hardening into indifference, and being even taught to look upon such a system as the natural ordering of divine Providence, are we to suppose that no account is taken of it, and that this parable uttered by Jesus will be the only token of his reprobation? He himself has intimated by another parable how sudden and complete may be the reversal in the world to come of the relative positions of rich and poor in this. He assures us that deliberate injustice, the sinning in this fashion against light and knowledge, will meet with a heavy punishment. 'And that¹ servant (Gr. bondservant), which knew his lord's will, and made not

¹ Luke 17

ready, nor did according to his will, shall be beaten with many stripes.' But Jesus assumes that the failure of Christian duty in this matter may not be deliberate or of set intention, but may arise from heedless ignorance; and in such cases, although the evil is none the less actual and deplorable, and cannot be perpetrated with impunity, yet the punishment with which it is avenged will be of a far lighter character. 'But he that knew not, and did things worthy of stripes, shall be beaten with few stripes.' Christian morality branches out in all directions and embraces every duty, personal, domestic and social. It is easy to understand how and why the last named has come to be least regarded and most neglected. The doctrine of repentance was proclaimed from the first. The necessity of personal reformation of character was strongly urged by the apostles, and ever has been in the Christian church. Family relationships have always stood, both by nature and grace, well within the sphere of Christian influence. Parental responsibility has been accepted as self-evident, scarcely needing any enforcement. 'But if any provideth not for his own, and specially his own household, he hath denied the faith, and is worse than an unbeliever.' But as the circle of duty widens outwards, the feeling of sympathy and obligation naturally becomes less intense: our individual wants and domestic trials must needs be realised more vividly by ourselves than those of others. It is open to question, also, whether our spiritual guides have not, in preaching the gospel, somewhat unwisely overshot the mark. They have been so earnest in exhortations to generosity, that they have forgotten to inculcate simple justice. The duty of almsgiving has seemed a nobler grace than the mere payment, in the ordinary way, of adequate if not liberal wages. And there have been so many objects of high and spiritual interest to be pleaded for: missions to the heathen, schools for religious education, Bible societies, tract societies, church building, hospitals, reformatories. Subscriptions to such objects have been supposed to constitute the first and foremost duty of the wealthy, whilst the injustice which has oppressed and degraded the poor has been eating like a canker into the social system, and left to extend and perpetuate itself, as though it were some heaven-sent scourge, which society must endure as it may, and palliate if possible, but can never hope to extirpate. We have been taught, moreover, that this world, with all that appertains to it, is of far less consequence than the world to come, where—by some process of divine judgment apart from human effort—it is assumed that the wrongs and inequalities of our present existence will right themselves, poor and rich alike being made happy or miserable for ever, according to their reception or rejection of the gospel message now, and their faith or unbelief with respect to those doctrines and mysteries which it is the appointed work of Christ's ministers to preach and elucidate. What wonder that under such a system of teaching the common, fundamental, reciprocal duties of man to man have been lost sight of and ignored? Let us revert to the pure and simple gospel of Jesus, and ponder well his warnings against all unjust stewardship. The recognition of Christianity in its social aspects comes late and last in the world's gradual development. It is the great want and work of the Church, and until that want is felt and that work is faced, the regeneration of society will be as far off as ever.

In Matthew's gospel this parable stands in another connection, as though delivered after the prophecy of the destruction of Jerusalem. Alford assumes that it was spoken twice. He says: 'How much more natural that our Lord should have preserved in his parabolic discourses the same leading ideas, and again and again gathered his precepts round them,—than that the Evangelists should have thrown into utter and inconsistent confusion, words which would have been treasured up so carefully by those that heard them; to say nothing of the promised help of the Spirit to bring to mind all that he had said to them.' To this it must be replied: (1) We repeatedly find in the gospel narratives similar instances of confusion. (2) This would naturally arise from the difficulty of constantly noting down long discourses at the time they were spoken. That would have been an impossible task, except on special occasions, or on the assumption that one of the apostles was an adept in reporting, and was always present, note book in hand. (3) The assumed need of the Spirit's aid to bring to their minds the things previously spoken, would be in itself an evidence that no regular, methodical record had been kept of them. (4) Alford seems to have overlooked the fact that not only this but the preceding parable must, on his view, have been delivered twice, and both together on the two occasions, which is somewhat improbable. The question when they were spoken is not material. As they fit smoothly and accurately in Luke's narrative, but rather incongruously in Matthew's, it seems likely that a misplacement at the time of compilation, or a displacement subsequently, has occurred in the latter. On comparing the following with Luke, it will be seen how nearly the words agree in both evangelists. 'But know this (or, But this ye know), that if the master of the house had known in what watch the thief was coming, he would have watched, and would not have suffered his house to be broken through (Gr. digged through). Therefore be ye also ready: for in an hour that ye think not the Son of man cometh. Who then is the faithful and wise servant (Gr. bondservant), whom his lord hath set over his household, to give them their food in due season? Blessed is that servant (Gr. bondservant) whom his lord when he cometh shall find so doing. Verily I say unto you, that he will set him over all that he hath. But if that evil servant (Gr. bondservant) shall say in his heart, My lord tarrieth: and shall begin to beat his fellow-servants, and shall eat and drink with the drunken; the lord of that servant (Gr. bondservant) shall come in a day when he expecteth not, and in an hour when he knoweth not, and shall cut him asunder (or, severely scourge him), and appoint his portion with the hypocrites: there shall be the weeping and gnashing of teeth.'

The marginal reading 'severely scourge him,' introduced by the Revisers, does not appear in other translations. The words in the text, 'shall cut him asunder,' are thus explained by Alford: 'The reference is to the punishment of cutting, or sawing asunder: see Dan. ii. 5; iii. 29: Sus. ver. 59; see also Heb. iv. 12; xi. 37.' Those passages contain nothing to confirm the interpretation of Alford. The idea of attributing such a simile to Jesus is repulsive. The verb in the original is *dichotomeō*, to cut in two, cut asunder. There is an analogous verb, *dichostateō*, to stand apart, disagree. If the servant is represented as 'cut apart,' it was in order that he might 'stand apart.' The expression seems plainly and naturally to signify exclusion from the Christian fellowship: the 'cutting asunder' is from the household in which the steward held a responsible position. That no form of capital punishment is implied, is obvious from the closing sentence in Matthew, which represents the mental anguish suffered by those who have been thus 'cut asunder.' The word 'hypocrites' is used by Matthew instead of 'unfaithful:' unfaithful servants are necessarily hypocrites.

In Luke's narrative immediately following upon this parable are 5 verses which have no traceable connection with the context. They agree with verses 34 to 36 of the 10th chapter of Matthew, which were spoken on the sending forth of the apostles, and these five verses in Luke have been already considered in relation to that event. The next 6 verses in this 12th chapter of Luke are recorded as having been spoken 'to the multitudes,' but without any indication as to the time. Four of them correspond nearly with 16 Mat. 1—4 and 8 Mark 10—13, which have been already dealt with, but the subject touched on may well bear reconsideration. Jesus intimated that the failure of the people to appreciate his mission and forecast its consequences, was not owing to any defect in their power of judgment. They were able and accustomed to observe for themselves, and to arrive at correct conclusions on other matters. 'And he said to the multitudes also, When ye see a cloud rising in the west, straightway ye say, There cometh a shower: and so it cometh to pass. And when *ye see* a south wind blowing, ye say, There will be a scorching heat (or, hot wind), and it cometh to pass.' The Revisers, following the oldest MS., have altered 'out of the west' to 'in the west.' The allusion here is not simply to the exercise of judgment, but rather to the insight of future events: how from one thing another thing might with certainty be anticipated. They did not want to be caught in a shower, or expose themselves to any sudden increase of temperature, so they watched the clouds and changing wind, and protected themselves in time. Were they not equally able to prognosticate the consequences of their own lives and actions? Was not the blindness wilful, hypocritical, when they shut their eyes to coming evils, living for the present regardless of the future? 'Ye hypocrites, ye know how how to interpret (Gr. prove) the face of the earth and the heaven: but how is it that ye know not how to interpret (Gr. prove) this time?' They were able, if they would, to deduce the future from the present. Why should they delay amendment until the time of final and irrevocable judgment? 'And why even of yourselves judge ye not what is right?' For they were like litigants on their way to the tribunal of justice, and the present moment gave the last chance of voluntary repentance. Let the debtor, the wrong doer, avail himself of the opportunity, and exert his utmost to escape the stern retribution which threatened him if unyielding and unrepentant. 'For as thou art going with thine adversary before the magistrate, on the way give diligence to be quit of him.' The omission of the connecting word 'for' in the Authorised Version marred the sense and force of the passage. This is not an alteration in the reading, but in the translation: Young also inserted the word 'for.' If the offender continued obdurate, so much the worse for him: the matter would be carried to the extremity, the adjudication would be made, the warrant of the judge would issue, and the prisoner would be handed over to the jailor. 'Lest he hale thee to the judge, and the judge shall deliver thee up to the exactor, and the exactor cast thee into prison.' That is Tischendorf's rendering. Young's is as follows: 'That he may not drag thee before the judge, and the judge may deliver thee to the officer, and the officer may cast thee into prison.' The Authorised Version begins: 'Lest he hale thee to the judge.' The Revisers have inserted the word 'haply,' which weakens the passage, making the punishment a mere possible contingency instead of an absolute certainty: 'lest haply he hale thee unto the judge, and the judge shall deliver thee to the officer (Gr. exactor), and the officer (Gr. exactor) shall cast thee into prison.' The imprisonment, however long continued, would not be held equivalent to the cancelment of the debt. 'I say unto thee, Thou shalt by no means come out thence, till thou have paid the very last mite.' All unfulfilled obligations will bring their penalty, and there can be no joy or freedom for any one who has failed in duty and scorned repentance, until through much suffering and effort he has retrieved the past. That seems to be the scope of this parable.

In the Authorised Version Luke's narrative continues thus: 'There were present at that season some that told him of the Galileans.' Alford remarks: 'The words *at that season* may mean *at that very time*, viz. as He finished the foregoing discourse: but it is not *necessary* to interpret thus; for, Matt. xii. 1; xiv. 1, the similar expression is certainly *indefinite*. The opening words do not mean, as A. V., that these persons *were in the crowd, and remarked to the Lord concerning these Galileans*, in consequence of what He had said ch. xii. 57: such a finding of connection is too fine-drawn. It is obvious that no connection is intended between this incident and the foregoing discourse.' Dr. Young renders: 'And there were present certain at that time, telling him about the Galileans.' This does not favour the view of Alford, neither does the course adopted by the Revisers. In the two other passages he alludes to they have left the expression indefinite, 'at that season,' but here they have inserted the word 'very.' 'Now there were some present at that very season which told him of the Galileans.' Tischendorf, however, does not indicate that the persons were present in the crowd, but the contrary. 'And there came some at that season telling him of the Galileans.' Still, the insertion by the Revisers of the omitted word 'for' in verse 58 of the last chapter and of the omitted word 'now' or 'and' at the beginning of this verse, denotes a connection which was not previously manifest. Jesus had been dealing with the subject of retributive justice, and to that he now again refers. The Roman governor had made a stern example in his treatment of certain Galileans. To express the abhorrence and infamy attaching to them, he had caused their blood to mingle with the sacrifices offered to the avenging deities of the Roman people. That would seem to be the meaning of the statement: 'whose blood Pilate had mingled with their sacrifices.' Alford, Tischendorf, Young, and the 'Englishman's Greek New Testament' omit the word 'had' before 'mingled.' Alford says: 'It must have occurred at some feast in Jerusalem, on which occasions riots often took place, and in the outer court of the temple. Such slaughters were frequent.' That interpretation of the expression seems far too weak. The act was judicial, striking, solemn, or it would not have been attributed to Pilate and spoken of as exceptional. Men were naturally impressed by the heinousness of the guilt which had been visited by so ignominious a death. Not so Jesus. 'And he answered and said unto them, Think ye that these Galileans were sinners above all the Galileans, because they have suffered these things?' It is obvious from the words 'suffered these things,' that there had been some form of public execution marked by unusual severity. Jesus, however, did not admit that the criminality of these men was as exceptional as their punishment. That may well have been doubtful, to say the least; for the enormity of guilt has often been defined by political rather than moral considerations, and the men called 'traitors' by their contemporaries and 'patriot martyrs' by historians, have expiated their 'treason' by executions attended by every possible mark of execration. The time was not far off,—and Jesus knew it,—when he himself would be delivered up to this same Pilate, and scourged and crucified as a malefactor. It would be unsafe, it might be uncharitable, to judge the characters of men according to the treatment they received from the rulers of this world. But the lesson which should come home to every man was twofold: the need of personal reformation, and the certainty of final retribution. 'I tell you, Nay: but except ye repent, ye shall all in like manner perish.'

Then Jesus referred to another event. Eighteen persons had lost their lives, not by way of law, but by an accident altogether exceptional. A tower had fallen, crushing them to death. Probably no one had apprehended the possibility of such a catastrophe. Any fatal occurrence which men cannot account for, they always have been disposed to ascribe to 'the visitation of God,' even deeming such a conclusion reverential. The phrase, properly understood, means only that human science, skill and foresight either cannot explain, or did not suffice to avert the calamity. But in some minds there is a tendency to carry the inference a step further, and to assume that some supernatural power has been exercised in the event, which therefore comes to be regarded in the light of a visitation of divine judgment. Against such an idea Jesus protested. 'Or those eighteen, upon whom the tower in Siloam fell, and killed them, think ye that they were offenders (Gr. debtors) above all the men that dwelt in Jerusalem? I tell you, Nay.' Comparative degrees of guilt in men are not to be measured by the mode of death which befalls them. The purest patriot may suffer like the vilest criminal, and fatal accidents may overtake alike the guilty and the innocent. The emphatic, 'I tell you, Nay,' of Jesus stands out against all rash judgments. But from instances of sudden, unexpected death, he would have us draw the same warning. 'But, except ye repent, ye shall all likewise perish.' 'If ye may not reform,' is Young's rendering, and it is preferable, on account of the theological ideas and definitions which have become attached to the word 'repent.'

The expression 'likewise perish' demands consideration. In the Authorised Version it so stands in both verses, but the Revisers have altered it in verse 3 to 'in like manner.' Tischendorf has 'in like manner' in verse 3, and 'in the same manner' in verse 5. Samuel Sharpe has 'thus perish' in verse 3 and 'perish in like manner' in verse 5. Young has 'even so' in verse 3 and 'in like manner' in verse 5. Alford suggests 'in like manner' for both verses. He says: 'The force of this is lost in the A. V. *likewise*. It is strictly *in like manner*.' That being the case, what is the significance of the expression? Here is Alford's comment on verse 3: 'as indeed the Jewish people did perish by the sword of the Romans.' And this is his comment on verse 5: 'Here, the similarity will be—in the ruin of your whole city. This does not render it necessary that these words should have been spoken to actual dwellers in Jerusalem: for nearly the whole nation was assembled there at the time of the siege.' To give this national and local restriction to the warning of Jesus is unsatisfactory: indeed, any such application of his words seems far-fetched and unreliable. It transforms the teaching into a prophecy, and assumes that the saying could be interpreted only by the light of a future event. On the contrary, by keeping close to the subject, the meaning naturally attaching to the statement of Jesus becomes obvious. He spoke first of a judicial execution by Pilate. That was no indication of exceptional guilt; but a similar judicial execution awaited all who remained impenitent. He spoke next of an unexpected, overwhelming catastrophe. That also gave no reason for assuming unusual criminality on the part of its victims; but a similar sudden, irresistible destruction would overtake all who failed to reform their lives. The imminence, certainty and universality of Divine judgment—that is the lesson here taught by Jesus. It applies not to the Jews only, but to men of all nations throughout all time.

In connection with this subject Jesus delivered a parable. He represents the owner of a vineyard inspecting a fig tree planted therein. For three years together he has found it unproductive, and at last he issues orders for its removal. 'And he spake this parable; [13 Luke 6. 7] A certain man had a fig tree planted in his vineyard; and he came seeking fruit thereon, and found none. And he said unto the vinedresser, Behold, these three years I come seeking fruit on this fig tree, and find none: cut it down; why doth it also cumber the ground?' Tischendorf renders, 'cut it out:' the object was not merely to get rid of the trunk and branches, but to free the soil for something better. But the vinedresser even yet did not despair. He thought the tree was worth another effort, and that if he bestowed upon it extra care, and manured it well, it might still become productive. 'And he answering saith unto him, Lord (Sir—Young and [,, 8] Alford), let it alone this year also, till I shall dig about it, and dung it.' That should in any case be the final effort; the year's respite was the tree's last chance. 'And if it bear fruit thenceforth, *well*; [,, 9] but if not, thou shalt cut it down.'

We are left to draw our own conclusions from the parable, and therefore cannot be too careful to keep within its prescribed limits. Its most prominent lesson seems to be this: Perseverance to the last in hope and effort, and that equally in the task of self-reform and of altruistic influence. This barren fig tree represents an exceptional case of obduracy and moral worthlessness. No other tree in the vineyard failed as this did. Yet he who was best able to judge, who watched it constantly, was anxious, in spite of his bitter disappointment, to save it from destruction. He resolved to make one persistent, final effort, admitting at the same time that if that failed all hope must be abandoned, and the axe must be left to do its work. Life and usefulness must go together. The fruit-producing tree is the proper symbol for humanity. We are called to something higher than a useless, aimless, selfish existence. Each soul's career is watched over, its worth or worthlessness duly appraised, and its ultimate destiny determined accordingly. In various ways Jesus enforces the grand truth of moral responsibility. The negligent steward is 'cut asunder' from the household, that he may no longer disorganize and disgrace it. The barren fig tree is 'cut out,' that it may no longer cumber the ground.

Alford observes: 'This Parable has perhaps been interpreted with hardly enough reference to its own peculiar context, or to the symbolic language of Scripture in other places. Ordinarily the owner of the vineyard is explained to be the *Eternal Father:* the dresser and intercessor, the *Son of God:* the fig tree, *the whole Jewish people:* the vineyard, the *world*.' Against that interpretation Alford argues, and then gives his own. He says: '*Now who is this intercessor?*' and he arrives at the conclusion, 'Clearly, it seems to me, *the Holy Spirit of God*.' Then he assumes that the 'three years' are an allusion 'to *the three years of our Lord's ministry*,' and he meets certain objections brought against that assumption. On what a sea of uncertainty and error do they set forth, who go beyond the primary and essential idea embodied in the parable! The lesson which the first hearers would naturally draw from it, is the lesson for us. All beyond that is a surplusage of guesswork, based upon conceptions which grew up subsequently in the minds of theologians. In proportion as the parables are construed mystically, after a recognized 'orthodox' fashion, they lose force and freshness, and instead of serving to illustrate the grand central truths on which Jesus would have us fix our thoughts, they become perplexing and unprofitable.

The following incident, recorded only by Luke, is described with much vividness, and was evidently derived from an eye-witness. It happened in a synagogue, on the sabbath. Jesus was teaching, and among the listeners was a deformed woman. For eighteen years she was known to have suffered from a spinal weakness, being bowed down and unable to stand erect. 'And he was teaching in one of the synagogues on the sabbath day. And behold, a woman which had a spirit of infirmity eighteen years; and she was bowed together, and could in no wise lift herself up.' The expression, 'had a spirit of infirmity,' may be taken as the idea entertained by the narrator and others. Alford says: 'The A. V. has here mistaken the position of the word which it renders *in no wise*. It means *altogether*, and belongs to the verb *lift herself*.' He renders it, 'could not lift herself upright.' Tischendorf, 'wholly unable to lift herself up.' Young, 'not able to bend back at all.' The 'Englishman's Greek New Testament' replaces 'in no wise' by 'wholly.' Her pitiable condition attracted the notice of Jesus, who called her to him. How must she have been astounded at his words! 'And when Jesus saw her, he called her, and said to her, Woman, thou art loosed from thine infirmity.' Then on her crippled form she felt the touch of those hands which never touched in vain. From his body to hers there passed a mysterious, invigorating power; as by some subtle magic her muscles shook off their hitherto unconquerable torpor, the vigour of her best days was instantaneously restored, and she was seen standing upright and heard uttering her thanksgiving to God. 'And he laid his hands upon her: and immediately she was made straight, and glorified God.'

The man whose office threw upon him the duty of maintaining order in the synagogue was so narrow-minded, prejudiced, bigoted, as to resent this marvellous exhibition of the healing power of Jesus. Without venturing to condemn the act or the actor, he expressed his displeasure, vented his petty criticism, by reminding those present of the sanctity of the day. His indignation was excited by what appeared to him a desecration of the sabbath, and he showed the courage of his convictions by reproving the people. He rose up and delivered his little sermon on the text, 'Remember the sabbath day to keep it holy.' He could argue the question verbally and technically, but how far off was he from the spirit of divine compassion which had made the sabbath for man! He urged the congregation to beware of encouraging sabbath work in any form; if people wanted to be healed, the synagogue should be kept open for them throughout the week. 'And the ruler of the synagogue, being moved with indignation because Jesus had healed on the sabbath, answered and said to the multitude, There are six days in which men ought to work: in them therefore come and be healed, and not on the day of the sabbath.' Jesus answered this conscientious, self-satisfied, zealous critic reproachfully, almost scornfully. 'But the Lord answered him, and said, Ye hypocrites.' The Revisers have altered the word from the singular to the plural, following the three oldest MSS. This man was one of a class, a fair representative of his sect. Jesus had affixed to the scribes and Pharisees generally the designation 'hypocrites.' It is obvious that the term was not deemed offensive, in the sense of implying open discourtesy. The word *hupokritēs*, had a wider application than our translation of it, the signification 'hypocrite' being subsidiary: 'one who answers: an interpreter or expounder. One who plays a part *on the stage*, a player, actor. A dissembler, pretender, hypocrite.' The indignation manifested by this ruler of the synagogue was not feigned, but real, and it impelled him to take the course he did. The lives of such dogmatists were full of incongruities and anomalies; wedded to an erroneous system of faith and morals, their most solemn convictions involved a kind of double-dealing; seeking to hold fast by the letter of the divine law, they opposed its spirit; going about to establish their own righteousness, they repudiated and opposed anything and everything which overstepped the limits of their authorised maxims and orthodox conventionalities. In proportion as men become unnatural they must needs develop inconsistency, and nothing tends so much in that direction as wrong notions in religion. It was so in the days of Jesus: is it less so now? He detected in these venerators of the divine revelation, these devout advocates and exemplars of constant prayer, these strict sabbatarians, a spirit and habit of conduct which was best described by the word actors or hypocrites. In the New Testament the term is never used except by Jesus, and whenever he affixed the stigma he was careful to give the reason for it. Probably unconscious hypocrisy is more common than that which is deliberate and intentional, and its effects may be quite as harmful. With loving, compassionate boldness Jesus dragged forth this lurking vice into open daylight. On this occasion it sufficed to show that this man and his co-religionists were in the habit of doing on the sabbath work of the same kind as that which had just been performed by Jesus. 'Doth not each one of you on the sabbath loose his ox or his ass from the stall (Gr. manger), and lead him away to watering?' Even their rigid creed admitted the necessity for that. And wherein did this action of Jesus differ? In two points only. The laying on of the hands by Jesus involved far less labour than a journey to the stable, the untying and retying of a halter, the leading out and home of an animal; and the need of this woman for the relief he was able to give,—how vastly was that in excess of the few hours' thirst of a dumb creature! Here was a suffering woman, one of Abraham's daughters, who by some malign power had been physically bound in ceaseless discomfort day after day, year after year, during eighteen long years. Ought she not to have been loosed from that bond on the sabbath day? 'And ought not this woman, being a daughter of Abraham, whom Satan had bound, lo, *these* eighteen years, to have been loosed from this bond on the day of the sabbath?' Who could dare to answer No, to such a question? His adversaries were dumbfounded by the argument. Not one word could they suggest in self-justification, especially as the crowd were enthusiastically on the side of Jesus, and were manifesting unbounded joy as they discussed the astounding and beneficent marvels wrought by him. 'And as he said these things, all his adversaries were put to shame: and all the multitude rejoiced for all the glorious things that were done by him.'

Young renders 'Satan' by 'Adversary.' The words of Jesus, 'whom the Adversary had bound,' carry far more weight than those which expressed the popular notion that the woman 'had a spirit of infirmity.' Jesus had superhuman knowledge, and he certainly attributed this physical deformity to the spiritual adversary of mankind. In some way, direct or indirect, it was his doing. If we believe that Jesus exercised his spiritual powers on behalf of mankind, it is equally credible that a hostile spiritual being may exercise his powers to the detriment of mankind. Why or how, we cannot tell. We only know that this mysterious antagonism of good and evil, of malice and beneficence, runs throughout the whole Bible history, from the first page to the last, and that it was admitted and endorsed by Jesus and his apostles.

The gift of prescience possessed by Jesus probably intensified his mental sufferings. Knowing that he was destined to end his life, under circumstances of ignominy, at Jerusalem, he now prepared to undertake what he knew would be his last journey thither. 'And it came to pass, when the days were well-nigh come (Gr. were being fulfilled) that he should be received up, he steadfastly set his face to go to Jerusalem.' The expression 'steadfastly set his face,' denotes the moral courage required and exercised. Not only did he resolve to go, but he attracted the utmost publicity, undertaking organised missionary work on the journey, and sending messengers to announce his coming to places on the road : 'and sent messengers before his [9 Luke 52] face.' That would be an absolute necessity, if he desired to find audiences ready to listen to his teaching. In places where the inhabitants were scattered, previous notice would have to be given, the approach of Jesus announced, and the times at which he would be prepared to address the people duly arranged beforehand. The messengers set about the performance of this task in a village inhabited by Samaritans. 'And they went, and entered into a village of the [„ 52] Samaritans, to make ready for him.' It was a recognised fact that the Jews had 'no dealings with Samaritans,' but the disciples of [4 John 9] Jesus were above any prejudice of that kind, and they seem to have assumed that the spirit of exclusiveness was on the side of their own nation only, and that the Samaritans would appreciate as a privilege the proposed visit to them of the great Jewish teacher. Had he not on a former occasion been acknowledged as Messiah by the Samaritans of Sychar? But the disciples were quickly undeceived : they found that Samaritans could be quite as haughty and bigoted as Jews. As soon as it was ascertained that Jesus was travelling towards Jerusalem, a peremptory refusal was given to his entering their village. 'And they did not receive him, because his face was [9 Luke 53] *as though he were* going to Jerusalem.' Two of the disciples were greatly incensed at this indignity being put upon their Master, and they were anxious to see his prophetic character vindicated by a summary act of judicial vengeance. His divine authority would be best shown by some sign from heaven, and knowing well the supernatural powers which could be wielded by Jesus, they waited but a word of permission from him to invoke in his name consuming fire from the sky on the heads of those who had thus scornfully rejected his presence and teaching. 'And when his disciples James and John saw [„ 54] this, they said, Lord, wilt thou that we bid fire to come down from heaven, and consume them?' The Revisers, following the two oldest MSS., have omitted 'even as Elias did.' The suggestion was indicative of their reverence and faith, and might well occur to these two who had lately been permitted the vision of their Master transfigured and glorified on the mountain-top. But such a purpose was far from the mind of Jesus, and the idea was instantly met by a stern rebuke. 'But he turned, and rebuked them.' The Revisers, following the [„ 55] three oldest MSS., have omitted: 'and said, Ye know not what manner of spirit ye are of. For the Son of man is not come to destroy men's lives, but to save *them*.'

Jesus and his disciples directed their steps elsewhere. 'And they [„ 56] went to another village.' On the way thither the following incident occurred. A man expressed a wish to become a follower of Jesus, no matter whether he was going to Jerusalem or elsewhere. 'And as [„ 57] they went in the way, a certain man said unto him, I will follow thee whithersoever thou goest.' He may have been a Samaritan, anxious to prove himself superior to the narrow mindedness which had been shown by his countrymen. The words 'whithersoever thou goest,' seemed to point to a fixed abode somewhere, but Jesus could not offer that to any follower. As he was at this moment, such he was always : a homeless wanderer. 'And Jesus said unto him, The foxes have [„ 58] holes, and the birds of the heaven *have* nests (Gr. lodging-places) ; but the Son of man hath not where to lay his head.'

The conclusions thus derived from Luke's narrative are somewhat disturbed on comparing it with Matthew. He inserts this incident at a much earlier period of the history. He tells us that the man was a scribe, but the conversation is almost word for word the same. 'And there came a scribe (Gr. one scribe), and said unto him, Master (or, Teacher), I will follow thee whithersoever thou goest. And Jesus saith unto him, The foxes have holes, and the birds of the heaven *have* nests (Gr. lodging-places); but the Son of Man hath not where to lay his head.' The position this occupies in Matthew leads to the inference that the offer was made and the reply of Jesus given when he was on the point of entering a boat to cross the lake of Gennesaret; that, however, is but an inference, whereas Luke says plainly that the incident happened 'as they went in the way.' With respect to Matthew's narrative generally, the Reverend J. J. Halcombe makes the following observations: 'We perceive at once that, whilst it shews a distinct chronological framework, upon which the whole narrative is built up, yet that the idea of chronological order, so far from being the paramount idea or controlling principle of narration, is altogether subordinated to the design of giving special prominence to the Oral Teaching of our Lord . . . . Thus it happens that throughout the first half of his Gospel, whilst grouping together, and so to speak classifying, discourses spoken on very different occasions, S. Matthew as a rule introduces Christ's actions, and even the actions of his enemies, not with reference to the time to which they properly belonged, but with reference to their suitability to illustrate His Oral Teaching, and so to complete a Portrait, rather than a Biography of the Divine Teacher.' * On the other hand, as it was the express intention of Luke to compile his narrative in due order, we must needs suppose that he endeavoured to do so in this instance, and that his words, 'as they went in the way,' were not inserted without warrant as a mere connecting link. But with respect to the two somewhat similar incidents immediately following, Luke does not give any clue as to time or sequence.

Jesus desired a person to become his follower. 'And he said unto another, Follow me.' The man pleaded for a slight delay on account of a domestic bereavement. 'But he said, Lord, suffer me first to go and bury my father.' No: the command was imperious, the necessity for immediate action urgent, the highest duty must stand first and foremost. 'But he said unto him, Leave the dead to bury their own dead; but go thou and publish abroad the kingdom of God.' Matthew omits the command and the concluding words recorded by Luke, but brings out the fact that the call to 'follow' Jesus was addressed to one of his acknowledged disciples. 'And another of the disciples said unto him, Lord, suffer me first to go and bury my father. But Jesus said unto him, Follow me; and leave the dead to bury their own dead.'

Luke records another saying of Jesus uttered under similar circumstances. Another volunteer presented himself, who, like the last, was not quite ready. 'And another also said, I will follow thee, Lord; but first suffer me to bid farewell to them that are at my house.' The cause of Jesus would brook no such delay: hesitation, indecision, half-heartedness of that kind, must be taken to indicate

---

* "Gospel Difficulties," pp. cxv., cxvii.

unfitness for the task. 'But Jesus said unto him, No man having put his *Luke 62
hand to the plough, and looking back, is fit for the kingdom of God.'

These three replies are strikingly characteristic of the mind and policy of Jesus. The call to follow him involved more than mere discipleship: it necessitated the relinquishment of life's comforts and conveniences; it interfered with the regard due to social customs and etiquette; it demanded the rupture of family ties, and an earnestness of purpose to make everything yield to the sacred cause in hand. The 'followers' of Jesus must feel themselves without an earthly home; as the only living men among a host of dead; as labourers tied to one plough and one furrow in the world's harvest-field. Jesus deemed it necessary to put all this in the most emphatic language possible. In proportion to the earnestness of his declarations should be our care not to misunderstand or misapply them. It would be a perversion of their true import to assume that they admit of universal application. Elevate the tone and aims of a Christian community to the highest conceivable degree, still it could never be desirable that all should become 'followers' of Jesus in this sense: any general adoption of such maxims would lead to social confusion and misery. All persons could not simultaneously choose a wandering, homeless life; they could not all delegate to others the duties of ordinary existence, shaking off from themselves the claims of family relationship and withholding customary observances of respect; they could not all go about proclaiming the kingdom of God, and holding fast to that as the one object of life. Obviously such precepts are not for all persons. Are they suitable for all times? That also may be open to question. We can conceive a condition of society when such sacrifices of the few will no longer be needed for the spiritual enfranchisement and elevation of the many. Rightly restricting the application of such a call to those who voluntarily dedicate themselves entirely to the worship of God and the service of humanity, the Romish Church has sought, with a laudable enthusiasm, to enforce the perpetual observance of these principles of action on all her ministers. Vows of celibacy are imposed on her clergy, and monks and nuns are encouraged to live apart from the world around them. We know what that system has led to; we can trace its workings; we can observe its effects. It was a grand experiment, founded on a sublime idea,—the very chivalry of Christianity. But its attendant evils have exceeded its benefits, its corruptions have overborne its purity, its doctrines of self-effacement and unquestioning obedience have sapped the foundations of moral freedom and hindered the growth of religious truth. Before attempting to build up any system on precepts enunciated by Jesus, it behoves us to be quite sure that we fully understand them, not only his words but his spirit, and that we do not erroneously extend their application beyond the persons for whom and the circumstances and times for which they were intended.

At first Jesus had restricted the number of his followers to twelve. Subsequently he invited others to 'follow' him, and we have seen how carefully he made his selection, and how rigid were the ideas of self-sacrifice and devotion he impressed upon them. After a time, he found himself the recognised leader of no less than eighty-two persons, and as he had formerly sent forth the twelve apostles he now appointed seventy others to undertake, under his directions, a similar mission. As on the previous occasion, he arranged that they should go forth not singly, nor all together, but in pairs; and they were sent as harbingers of himself, to certain towns and localities which he had decided to visit, probably in company with the twelve apostles. 'Now after these things the Lord appointed seventy others, and sent them two and two before his face into every city and place, whither he himself was about to come.' Tischendorf retains the word 'also' after 'others;' the Revisers, following the Vatican MS., have omitted it. Alford notes: 'The words should not be rendered, as in A.V., *other seventy also*, but *others also, seventy in number*. The *others* may refer, either to the Twelve, ch. ix. 1, or perhaps, from the similarity of their mission, to the *messengers* in ch. ix. 52.'

This missionary enterprise of Jesus was evidently conceived on a large scale. All that it was possible for him to attempt in the work of evangelisation, he did. But he was painfully impressed by the inadequacy of the means at his disposal. There was a plenteous harvest, but a scarcity of reapers. Jesus began by pointing out that fact to his followers, urging them to take the same view of the matter as himself, and to offer their own services in the emergency. 'And he said unto them, The harvest is plenteous, but the labourers are few: pray ye therefore the Lord of the harvest, that he send forth labourers into his harvest.' Dr. Young has gone beyond the Authorised and Revised Versions by inserting capitals: 'Beseech ye then the Lord of the harvest, so that He may put forth labourers into His harvest.' This is but an exemplification of the idea which has been commonly attached to this saying of Jesus. It is assumed, as a matter of course, to be an exhortation to prayer on behalf of that missionary enterprise in particular, and of missionary enterprises generally. That interpretation overlooks the nature of the simile, which is that of a harvest-field: the lord of the harvest is the owner or superintendent, whose business it is to arrange for the ingathering: these labourers are cognisant, like himself, of the need for immediate action, and it is expected of them that they will tender their services for the work which must be done at once. There must be a perfect understanding and readiness on both sides. The 'lord of the harvest' is there, waiting to employ; the 'labourers' go to him direct, and ask to be employed. As the labourers represent the disciples, so the lord of the harvest represents Jesus. He had used the same words before sending out the twelve apostles: 'The harvest truly is plenteous, but the labourers are few. Pray ye therefore the Lord of the harvest, that he send forth labourers into his harvest.' Then it is added: 'These twelve Jesus sent forth.' In so doing he acted the part of 'the lord of the harvest.' He would send forth only volunteers, men who were convinced that the right moment for action had come, who were anxious about the work, and hopeful as to its results. The same conclusion is forced upon us by Luke's narrative: for after saying, 'Pray ye therefore the Lord of the harvest, that he send forth labourers into his harvest,' it is added: 'Go your ways: behold I send you forth.' Jesus is the sender, 'the Lord of the harvest.' And he would have them conscious of the dangers to which they would be exposed, and of their utter helplessness. 'I send you forth as lambs in the midst of wolves.' No representative of Jesus must engage in strife, even in self-defence. There is nothing to indicate that by 'wolves' Jesus intended any particular religious opponents. Travellers in those days were in danger of attack from robbers, to whom possibly the allusion refers. These messengers of Jesus must carry with them nothing to invite attack, or which would be worth defending. 'Carry no purse, no wallet, no shoes.' Divested of all incumbrances, they would be recognised as simple messengers, and as such they would be at liberty also to dispense with those formal ceremonious greetings which were customary between travellers: 'and salute no man on the way.' Miss L. M. von Finkelstein, in one of her lectures, has explained this: 'You can observe the very same thing which was in Christ's mind every day of your life in Palestine. The ordinary salutation between strangers meeting on the road takes at least half-an-hour, and is a most ceremonious affair. All travellers greet each other in the same way, with one exception—the messenger who runs from place to place is allowed to pass on, and when people see him run along they merely call out to him, and if he answers that he is a messenger he passes unhindered. Now Christ's disciples were essentially messengers, and they would have had little time for preaching had they saluted every traveller on the road. It was for that reason that the command was given.'

Wherever the disciples took up their abode, Jesus would have them intimate, in a solemn and striking manner, that they came not for purposes of debate and strife. 'And into whatsoever house ye shall enter, first say (or, enter first, say) Peace *be* to this house.' If the owner of the dwelling were like-minded, that calmness of soul and temper which they had learnt from intercourse with Jesus would pervade the household. 'And if a son of peace be there, your peace shall rest upon him (or, it).' But if, unhappily, the spirit of contention reigned, they must still retain that quiet mind with which they had entered. 'But if not, it shall turn to you again.' Not for any expressed differences of opinion, nor for any other reason, might they reject or seem to disparage the hospitality freely tendered. 'And in that same house remain, eating and drinking such things as they give.' They would not be eating the bread of idleness, and their efforts for the general welfare might fairly claim a bare subsistence, without any forfeiture of independence: 'for the labourer is worthy of his hire.' No fickleness of purpose, no distaste of their surroundings, should induce them to change the abode to which they were at first welcomed. 'Go not from house to house.'

When they entered into a city, and were received as forerunners of Jesus, they were to put forth the same powers of healing as they had seen him exercise, taking no remuneration in money, but only such hospitality as might be offered them. 'And into whatsoever city ye enter, and they receive you, eat such things as are set before you: and heal the sick that are therein.' This simple, quiet declaration is of startling import. In sending out the twelve Jesus had invested them with the same—and greater—powers. Now to seventy disciples at once he attributes, as though it were a matter of course, the miraculous gift of healing. How great must be the mistake of those who would have us regard the miracles of Jesus as proofs of his divinity! He sought to make them the common heritage of humanity. There dwells in all of us a mysterious power of which we are unconscious, an influence for good which we have never learnt the secret how to exert, a phenomenal attribute lying on the border-land between matter and spirit, whereby the latter controls the former. To the most learned physicians disease is still a mystery: that it can be propagated by a touch, and without a touch, we all know ; Jesus disclosed the fact that there exists a similar contagion of healing, and if only we could put ourselves on his level, or be taught, guided, influenced by him as were the twelve and the seventy, we should realise the literal truth of his assertion. ' Verily, verily, I say unto you, He that believeth on me, the works that I do shall he do also.'

14 John 12

Conjointly with the exercise of their powers of healing, the disciples were to proclaim the nearness of God's kingdom. 'And say unto them, The kingdom of God is come nigh unto you.' These marvels of mercy were its manifestations : flashes of light and love from the heavenly realm of divine beneficence. The nearness was present, actual, a thing realised, not a promise of something about to be revealed. The reign of God has never been so near to men as in those days when Jesus and his apostles went about proclaiming its proximity and demonstrating its laws and powers.

10 Luke 9

But the messengers of Jesus must be prepared for rejection as well as acceptance. They must not allow themselves to be repelled without making a solemn protest. 'But into whatsoever city ye shall enter, and they receive you not, go out into the streets thereof and say, Even the dust from your city, that cleaveth to our feet, we do wipe off against you.' The Revisers have altered ' cleaveth on us ' to ' cleaveth to our feet,' the reading of the three oldest MSS. being, 'cleaveth on us on our feet.' This symbolical action was not uncommon. Alford explains : ' It was a custom of the Pharisees, when they entered Judæa from a Gentile land, to do this act, as renouncing all communion with Gentiles. Rejection, however disheartening and contemptuous, must in no wise shake the assurance of the disciples themselves, and they were to give proof of this by adding, ' Howbeit know this, that the kingdom of God is come nigh.' The proffered boon was none the less real and substantial because men, failing to appreciate it, thrust it from them. The folly, the wrong, the guilt of such conduct would be intolerable, more so even than that of Sodom.

10 Luke 10, 11

'' 11

'I say unto you, It shall be more tolerable in that day for Sodom, than for that city.' The reception of these messengers was equivalent to the reception of Jesus ; their rejection, to the rejection of himself ; and the rejection of him, to the rejection of God Himself. 'He that heareth you heareth me, and he that rejecteth you rejecteth me : and he that rejecteth me rejecteth him that sent me.'

,, 12

,, 16

,, 13 15

Between verses 12 and 16 Luke inserts the following. 'Woe unto thee, Chorazin ! woe unto thee Bethsaida ! for if the mighty works (Gr. powers) had been done in Tyre and Sidon, which were done in you, they would have repented long ago, sitting in sackcloth and ashes. Howbeit it shall be more tolerable for Tyre and Sidon in the judgment, than for you. And thou, Capernaum, shalt thou be exalted unto heaven ? thou shalt be brought down unto Hades.' In dealing with the mass of material at his command, Luke must occasionally have had to rely on his own judgment with respect to the position to be occupied by certain portions of the narrative. His object was to place all things in order, but the fitting place for various short traditional sayings of Jesus might not be obvious. These he would naturally insert at the most appropriate and convenient points. If, as seems probable, these verses 13, 14 and 15 comprised one of these scattered notes, the mention of 'Sodom' in connection with the word 'tolerable' would be sufficient to induce the compiler to place it where it now stands. That might seem preferable to either dropping it in at hap-hazard, without any regard to the context, or introducing it alone, as probably some passages of doubtful standing are introduced, by some such words as 'Jesus said.' These remarks apply, more or less, with equal force to Matthew's gospel. It is a mere tradition that he wrote it; to what extent it may have been compiled by others, we know not; and it does not make any claim to chronological accuracy. The Reverend J. J. Halcombe arrives at the following conclusion: 'A strict adherence to an exact historical order of events being manifestly inconsistent with the plan on which S. Matthew wrote, all transpositions of his text required in any attempt to shew what that order really was, provided only they are exactly regulated by the order vouched for by other Evangelists, are neither "arbitrary," nor in the slightest degree inconsistent with his absolute accuracy.'* Now in Matthew we find a parallel passage to that just quoted from Luke, but introduced at an earlier period. Alford has in this instance held, contrary to his usual practice, that the words were spoken twice by Jesus; but the Reverend J. J. Halcombe has not scrupled to place them in juxtaposition with the passage in Luke. In Matthew they are introduced with these words: 'Then began he to upbraid the cities wherein most of his mighty works (Gr. powers) were done, because they repented not.' That is a very unusual form of preface; whether by Matthew himself or by a subsequent compiler, it is simply the writer's way of introducing the subject. If we could be sure that Matthew not only wrote but arranged the narrative bearing his name, the words 'then began he' would denote a sequence, but not otherwise. Alford says: 'This expression betokens a change of subject, but not of locality or time:' he does not venture to argue that it signifies identity of time, although the 'close connexion of the whole chapter' leads him to that conclusion. He adds: 'I would rather regard the *then began he* as the token of the report of an ear-witness, and as pointing to a pause or change of manner on the part of our Lord.' The word 'upbraid' seems hardly consistent with the character of Jesus. Tischendorf renders it 'reproach.' Samuel Sharpe's rendering of 'woe' by 'alas,' gives to the utterance a sorrowful and compassionate tone. Young's version is: 'Then began he to reproach the cities in which most of his mighty works were done, because they reformed not.' Matthew's record of these reproaches or regrets of Jesus is as follows: 'Woe unto thee, Chorazin! woe unto thee Bethsaida! for if the mighty works (Gr. powers) had been done in Tyre and Sidon which were done in you, they would have repented long ago in sackcloth and ashes. Howbeit I say unto you, it shall be more tolerable for Tyre and Sidon in the day of judgement, than for you. And thou, Capernaum, shalt thou

[11 Mat. 20]
[21-24]

"Gospel Difficulties," p. cxx.

be exalted unto heaven? thou shalt go down unto Hades: for if the mighty works (Gr. powers) had been done in Sodom which were done in thee, it would have remained until this day. Howbeit I say unto you, that it shall be more tolerable for the land of Sodom in the day of judgement, than for thee.' Comparing this with Luke, there is great similarity. The woe of Chorazin and Bethsaida is word for word the same, except that Luke introduces 'sitting' and 'I say unto you.' Respecting Capernaum it seems doubtful whether the words were 'go down' or 'be brought down,' the authorities differing as to the MS. of Matthew. Luke omits all that follows in Matthew after 'Hades,' but he had just before quoted almost similar words concerning Sodom. Now comes the important question, What is the real import of the passages? Alford rushes unhesitatingly to this conclusion: 'That the reference here is to the *last great day* of judgment is evident, by the whole being spoken of in the future.' That is obviously an abbreviated form of the argument, for it does not follow that because the judgment is future it must therefore be the last great day of judgment. The argument fully stated amounts to this: The judgment applies to Tyre and Sidon as well as to Chorazin and Bethsaida, to Sodom as well as to Capernaum: therefore, the future tense only being used, the judgment of Tyre and Sidon and of Sodom must be future. But Sodom was judged and destroyed ages ago: therefore that past judgment is not referred to, but some other, which can only be the last great day of judgment. That this is fairly put, is evident from these words added by Alford: 'Had our Lord been speaking of the *outward* judgment on the rebellious cities, the future might have been used of *them*, but could not of Sodom, which was already destroyed.' It may be urged, on the contrary, that the word 'shall' cannot apply to Sodom, and that therefore the meaning of the sentence is not that which might appear from its literal, hard and fast grammatical construction. It would involve no change of meaning to put it thus: It shall be less tolerable for thee in the day of judgment than for the land of Sodom; or, It shall be less tolerable for thee than for the land of Sodom in the day of judgment. Any critical reader, apart from foregone conclusions and theological training, would understand that to be its meaning. Jesus was simply drawing a contrast between the guilt and doom of Sodom and of existing cities. He was not enunciating any new doctrine of final retribution, involving the resurrection not only of individuals but of cities and citizens in their corporate capacity. That is what the idea of Alford amounts to, and it is absurd on the face of it. Jesus draws a comparison and warning from ancient history, and men thrust into it their own conclusions drawn from other parts of Scripture! Are the customary elisions of speech which are common in all languages, and which are recognised intuitively by our judgment and common sense, to be disregarded when we deal with the utterances of Jesus? Every italicised passage is a standing protest against such a system of interpretation. We may surely claim the right of grasping an idea without that circumlocution which strict grammarians might insist on. Take the passage in Luke: 'It shall be more tolerable in that day for Sodom, than for that city.' The meaning is on the surface: That city is less to be borne with in that day, than was Sodom. If more tolerable for Sodom, surely less tolerable for that city; so the sense is unaltered if we put the sentence thus: It shall be less tolerable in that day for that city, than for Sodom. Now all is seen to depend on the position given to the words, which may be taken in this order: In that day for that city it shall be less tolerable than for Sodom. The future tense has no reference to Sodom, the judgment of which, being past, could be thus held up as an example. It is open to question whether the right sense is attached to the word 'tolerable.' Is it the conduct which is 'more tolerable' in the eyes of the judge, or the punishment inflicted by the judge which is 'more tolerable' to the criminal? The former, most probably; for although the latter is generally assumed, it involves the introduction of an extraneous idea, that of the state, condition, or punishment, so that in Beza's Latin version each of the six passages in which the word 'tolerable' occurs is amplified by the introduction of the word 'conditio:' 'tolerabilior erit *conditio* terræ Sodomorum et Gomorrhæorum,' although, strange to say, only in 6 Mark 11 is the word 'conditio' italicised.

The estimate Jesus was led to form of his countrymen is not a little startling. Driven from Judæa, he laboured in Galilee; but he was far from satisfied with the result of his efforts, even in the places where they had been most abundant. He had not succeeded in bringing about the moral reformation at which he aimed. He could preach to the people, he could work miracles among them, but he could not influence their hearts or transform their lives. They remained impenitent, unreformed; and he was forced to the conclusion that the Gentiles were more open to conviction and amendment than were the Jews. Even the heathen cities of Tyre and Sidon, against which Jewish prophets had been commissioned to launch forth divine threatenings, and which 'had been chastised by God's judgment under Nebuchadnezzar and Alexander' (Alford), were, in the opinion of Jesus, less obdurate than Chorazin and Bethsaida. So intense was the conviction of Jesus with respect to the moral obtuseness of those among whom he had laboured, that he declared Sodom itself would have been saved by such a revelation as Capernaum had received and despised. And yet, at this very time, Capernaum was regarding itself with complacency and self-glorification, dreaming of advancement heavenwards when her sins were dragging her down to death. There might be material prosperity, increasing commerce, growing wealth: what could all that profit when spiritual indifference prevailed, leading to hatred of the Truth and rejection of the Messiah?

No account is given of the labours of the seventy. After a time which may have been long or short, they returned to Jesus, delighted with the success of their mission, and enthusiastic about the gifts of healing which they had been able to exercise. 'And the seventy returned with joy, saying, Lord (Sir—Young), even the devils (Gr. demons) are subject unto us in thy name.' To this observation Jesus made a remarkable reply. 'And he said unto them, I beheld Satan fallen as lightning from heaven.' The Authorised Version has: 'as lightning fall from heaven.' In effect the sense is the same, the instantaneousness of the flash making it impossible to draw a distinction between 'fall' and 'fallen.' Tischendorf renders 'falling;' Young 'having fallen;' the 'Englishman's Greek New Testament;' 'I beheld Satan as lightning out of the heaven falling.'

10 Luke 17

„ 18

From fallen lightning no danger is to be dreaded; it has become powerless, extinct. The simile is full of meaning. To the mind of Jesus, the spiritual Adversary of himself and of mankind stood revealed, as real, as threatening, as irresistible, as demonstrable, as is the lightning which springs from its unseen source above, and which falls upon us, how, whence or why we know not. That there should exist a spiritual Being inimical to mankind, is no more incredible or mysterious than is the fact that lightning may consume us, or floods drown us, or malaria infect us. The constitution of the physical universe does not exclude these perils to the body, and the constitution of the moral universe may with equal reason be held to involve similar spiritual perils. The eye of Jesus discerned realities invisible to us, and he spoke with equal certainty of the ministrations of heavenly messengers and of attacks from a spiritual adversary. Modern scientists, accustoming themselves to withhold credence from what they cannot see, or feel, or in some way test and demonstrate by analysis, would laugh away all such ideas. Not so Jesus. He believed in them, promulgated them. Spiritual influences inimical to human welfare were as fully within his category of actually-existent dangers, as were serpents and scorpions with their offensive instincts and poisonous fangs. The former class of agents was as real and malevolent as the latter, and the one might be taken as representative of the other. The dangers from both were equal, and instead of bidding us shut our eyes to either, Jesus assured his disciples that through the power which he had given they could safely encounter and overcome them. 'Behold, I have given you authority to tread upon serpents and scorpions, and over all the power of the enemy: and nothing shall in any wise hurt you.'[10 Luke 19]

Let us keep to the similes which Jesus used as illustrations of Satanic agency,—the lightning-flash and the serpent-sting. Thunderstorms are comparatively rare, and injury from a thunderbolt rarer still. Moreover, the wit of man devised the lightning-rod to attract the flash and guide it harmless to the ground. Just so, the incursions of demoniacal agency were always fitful, and Jesus interposed a barrier between us and them, warding off in some simple but efficient way, as by some master-stroke of heavenly science, their evil influences. We can rejoice that these are now altogether exceptional. Our immunity may not be so complete as we flatter ourselves, but even were it perfect, it would ill-become us to misconstrue it as an evidence that the danger was always imaginary and the dread of it irrational. Take the other metaphor,—of serpents and scorpions. Between such poisonous reptiles and the human race there has ever been a deadly feud. As civilization has advanced, they have declined, the law of self-preservation impelling men to hunt out and extirpate them with remorseless energy. Abounding most in tropic heat, some parts of the world have never known these dangerous scourges; even from places where they most abounded they have slunk away, and the race must needs be finally crushed out. So has it been, and will be, with hostile spiritual influences. The Holy Spirit bestowed by Jesus on his disciples has supplied an antidote to the deadly venom of man's ghostly enemies, whose attacks may be sometimes insidious and sometimes direct. The apostle Paul wrote: 'Even Satan fashioneth himself into an angel of light. It is[11 ii. Cor. 14, 15] no great thing therefore if his ministers also fashion themselves as ministers of righteousness; whose end shall be according to their works.' Religious hypocrites were classed by John the Baptist and by Jesus as viperous. 'Ye offspring of vipers, who warned you to flee from the wrath to come?' 'Ye serpents, ye offspring of vipers, how shall ye escape the judgement of Gehenna?' Over such men, and over the spirit which animates them, Jesus promised his followers an easy and perfect triumph. 'Behold, I have given you authority to tread upon serpents and scorpions, and over all the power of the enemy; and nothing shall in any wise hurt you.'

Yet not in that triumph over spiritual foes would Jesus have his disciples exult, but in their own heavenly privileges. 'Howbeit in this rejoice not, that the spirits are subject unto you; but rejoice that your names are written in heaven.' The word 'rather,' before 'rejoice,' has been omitted by the Revisers. It is not in the three oldest MSS. Young renders: 'Your names were written in the heavens,' and Tischendorf, 'your names have been written in heaven.' The idea seems to be the same as is thus expressed elsewhere: 'Ye are come . . . to the general assembly and church of the firstborn who are enrolled in heaven.' Not strife and victory on earth, even in the noblest cause, is to be the limit of Christian expectation, but that heavenly citizenship from which all evil will be excluded, and in which the powers and prerogatives of redeemed humanity will find their free and fullest scope.

The Authorised Version continues as follows: 'In that hour Jesus rejoiced in spirit.' The Revisers have capitalised the last word, and placed 'Holy' before it, following the reading of the two oldest MSS. Tischendorf also renders: 'In that hour he exulted in the Holy Spirit.' Alford inserts this note: 'Read, with all the most ancient authorities, *the holy spirit:*' he does not venture to use capitals. By doing so, here and elsewhere, the text assumes in the eyes of ordinary readers a meaning beyond the sense contained in the original. The idea of a separate and divine personality inevitably springs up on seeing the words 'Holy Spirit' so printed, which idea does not necessarily arise when capital letters are not used. Samuel Sharpe renders: 'In that hour Jesus rejoiced in his spirit.' Avoiding both of these extremes, let us neither omit 'holy,'—for it is found in the oldest copies extant,—nor capitalise it, nor insert the word 'his.' What is the meaning of the expression, 'Jesus rejoiced in the holy spirit?' Apart from preconceived theological dogmas, no thought of any 'spirit' except that of Jesus himself would enter our minds. We have long since arrived at the conclusion that the term 'holy' is applied to any thing or any person specially devoted to the service of God. In his spirit of self-dedication to the divine will, Jesus now rejoiced. That this is the true sense becomes more evident from what follows. Jesus gives thanks to his Father, the supreme Ruler, humbly acquiescing in the unfolding of His purposes. 'In that same hour he rejoiced in (or, by) the Holy Spirit, and said, I thank (or, praise) thee, O Father, Lord of heaven and earth, that thou didst hide these things from the wise and understanding, and didst reveal them unto babes.' The seventy disciples had returned to Jesus, congratulating themselves and him on the effectual exercise of their miraculous powers, especially that of exorcism. He had discoursed with them on this matter, had assured them of perfect immunity from spiritual evil, and of victory over it, but had bidden them rejoice rather in the prospect opened out to them of the heavenly life. Surrounded by his band of earnest disciples, the heart of Jesus overflowed with thankfulness at the success which had been granted to his mission. But his disciples were men of humble rank in life; the ruling class of his countrymen held aloof from him; scribes and Pharisees ranged themselves in opposition. None more sensible,—more sensitive, indeed,—of this than Jesus himself. Looking round upon his disciples, comparing them with persons renowned for learning, 'the wise and understanding,' he was free to admit the fact that his adherents suffered by the comparison: the contrast was as great as that between men grown up and highly educated, and very 'babes.' Jesus was learning to submit to the inevitable. He had sought in vain to gain the ears and hearts of others. It was obviously the divine purpose that he should succeed in this direction only. His work had fallen short of his ideal. He now recognises the solemn fact that this apparent failure was of divine appointment. It was strange that those best qualified to judge should reject his teaching; but it was far more wonderful that these 'babes' should attain to the heavenly wisdom. God had chosen the weak things of the world to confound the wise. Convinced that it was so, Jesus bows to the divine will. 'Yea, Father, for (or, that) so it was well-pleasing in thy sight.' This view of the text is confirmed by Alford, who inserts the following note on the words 'I thank thee:' 'Not merely, *I praise thee*, but in the force of the Greek word *I confess to thee, I recognize the justice of thy doings*.' Young renders, 'I confess to thee, Father, Lord of the heaven and of the earth, that Thou didst hide these things from wise men and prudent, and didst reveal them to babes; yes, Father, for so it was good pleasure before thee.' The acquiescence of Jesus was complete, being based upon his conviction that all his experiences throughout life were divinely arranged. That seems to be the import of the words which follow: 'All things have been delivered unto me of my Father.' The 'all things' here alluded to must signify what had just been spoken of,—the works and teaching of Jesus with all the consequences resulting therefrom. He had been carrying out God's purposes, and if he could gain no greater measure of success, it was simply because in the divine wisdom men were left free to acknowledge or deny him, to accept or reject his salvation. His assurance sprang from the consciousness that he was doing God's work in the world. It ill becomes us to claim, or rather to parody his claim to a similar special divine direction. In one sense, of course, all that befalls ourselves is the Lord's doing: his laws cannot be broken, his retributions cannot be escaped. But to attribute the failure of our plans and hopes, springing often from our greed of wealth, our selfish ambitions, or brought about by errors of judgment or conduct, to providential interposition,—this is rather profanity than piety. Jesus, in all his plans and purposes, was one with the Father, supreme and alone among men in his knowledge of God, and himself, in his true character and nature, unrecognized by men and known to the Father only. 'And no one knoweth who the Son is, save the Father; and who the Father is save the Son.' But that knowledge of God which men possessed not, it was the office and life-work of Jesus to impart, therefore he added : ' and he to whomsoever the Son willeth to reveal *him*.' The Authorised Version stands : ' and *he* to whom the Son will reveal *him* ;' the alteration of ' will ' into ' willeth to,' is important. Young and Tischendorf bring out the same sense ; the former : ' and to whomsoever the Son may will to reveal *Him* ;' the latter : ' and he to whom the Son may wish to reveal him.' Jesus did not, would not, could not make the same revelation to all alike ; it was not the work of a moment, of a month, of a year, or even of a life : it depended not on the time employed in teaching, nor could any teaching avail unless the disciple himself were receptive of the truth. But to earnest disciples, such as those who now stood by him apart from ordinary listeners, Jesus did indeed disclose new truths. To these disciples he now turned aside, and addressed them privately, congratulating them on their opportunities and the use they made of them. ' And turning to the disciples, he said privately, Blessed *are* the eyes which see the things that ye see.' Tischendorf has, ' he said apart ;' Young, ' he said by themselves.' They saw the Father's love and goodwill to mankind manifested through the miracles of Jesus : disease and infirmity flying at his touch, mental and spiritual disorder banished, body, soul and spirit released from the trammels of evil, and placed once more in the path of true freedom and happiness. And the doctrine also of Jesus was equally new to the world : his works and words satisfied aspirations hitherto unfulfilled : ' For I say unto you, that many prophets and kings desired to see the things which ye see, and saw them not ; and to hear the things which ye hear, and heard them not.' On the words 'prophets and kings,' Alford has the note : ' David united both these, also Solomon.' That seems to miss the full significance of the allusion. Jesus does not limit it to those who combined both offices. His observation is general : ' *many* prophets and kings.' Prophets, teachers of morality, have longed for a revelation of pure and perfect truth, a system of ethics based on the wants of humanity and harmonising to the fullest extent with social requirements. Many kings have sought to promote the physical well-being of their subjects, to eradicate disease, to remove the evils attendant upon ignorance and vice, to abate misery, to augment happiness, to lengthen the span and brighten the monotony of our earthly existence. Jesus alone among mankind was able to demonstrate the feasibility, and inaugurate the era, of the moral and physical regeneration of mankind.

These remarks to the disciples are recorded by Luke only, but up to that point his account agrees very closely with that of Matthew, which is as follows : ' At that season Jesus answered and said, I thank (or, praise) thee, O Father, Lord of heaven and earth, that thou didst hide these things from the wise and understanding, and didst reveal them unto babes : yea, Father, for (or, that) so it was well pleasing in thy sight. All things have been delivered unto me of my Father : and no one knoweth the Son, save the Father ; neither doth any know the Father, save the Son, and he to whom the Son willeth to reveal him.' ' Knoweth the Son—knoweth who the Son is ; neither doth any know the Father—and who the Father is ;' these are the only discrepancies here between Matthew and Luke, the two narratives being otherwise word for word the same. Evidently both evangelists had the same or an equally reliable record: the slight divergence is just such as might naturally occur between two reporters, or be introduced by a compiler.

Matthew alone records the following sayings of Jesus. They appear to have been spoken to the multitude, forming no part of that private address to the disciples which is given by Luke but not alluded to by Matthew. The crowd which surrounded Jesus no doubt comprised all classes, the majority being of the toiling poor. That many of them were persons to whom a meal free of expense was a welcome boon, and the vain hope of living upon the bounty of Jesus an inducement to follow him, is evident from his telling them on one occasion, 'Ye seek me, not because ye saw signs, but because ye ate of the loaves and were filled.' Jesus could not but feel compassion for those engaged in the monotonous round of ceaseless and exhausting toil. He seems to have been struck by the outward signs of overwork apparent in many of those about him, and he had a word of consolation for them. He could encourage them by no socialistic theories, no promise of a more equal distribution of property, no immediate prospect of an ameliorated earthly lot: he was indeed trying to lay the groundwork for all that, but the reconstitution of society upon principles of Christian brotherhood was a far-off ideal, —alas! that it should be so still,—and until its realization, patient submission was the only attainable alleviation. He had a message for them, not of emancipation from their heavy toil, but of some easing and lightening of the burden. 'Come to me, all ye labouring and burdened ones, and I will give you rest.' The promise is not of entire immunity, but of partial repose from toil. The old English version, standing in the Communion service, is 'I will refresh you,' which corresponds with Luther's, 'Ich will euch erquicken.' How did Jesus propose to effect this? By supplying them with his own form of yoke, and teaching them his own method of burden-bearing. 'Take my yoke upon you, and learn of me.' He would have them imitate his own disposition of meekness and humility: 'for I am meek and lowly in heart.' That would ensure them spiritual repose, recruitment of their flagging energies, the sense of rest in the midst of toil: 'and ye shall find rest unto your souls.' He could assure them of this by his own experience. His yoke was comfortable to the shoulder, and it reduced the weight of the burden. 'For my yoke is easy, and my burden is light.' Alford defines the word 'easy' as '*not exacting*; answering to *kind*, spoken of persons.' Tischendorf renders, 'for my yoke is good;' Luther, 'denn mein Joch ist sanft—for my yoke is soft.' By the simile of a yoke, which is necessarily associated with the idea of a heavy burden, Jesus intimates that there can be no escape from the labours incident to our lot in life. He is not alluding to any burden which he himself places upon men's shoulders, nor does the yoke represent any restriction by him upon our freedom of action or will. Probably there is no passage of Scripture more commonly misread than this; the simile is constantly taken apart from its proper sense, the context being disregarded and the exhortation of Jesus misconstrued and misapplied. Alford, on the words 'learn of me,' speaks of 'the reception of the divine grace for the pardon of sin, and the breaking of the yoke of the corruption of our nature.' How far off are such ideas from these sayings of Jesus! He does not allude to the breaking of any yoke, nor to any kind of moral corruption. Alford says again: 'Doubtless, outward and bodily misery is not shut out; but the promise, *rest to your souls*, is only a spiritual promise. Our Lord does not promise to those who come to him *freedom from* toil or burden, but *rest in the soul*, which shall make all yokes easy, and all burdens light.' That accords with the simile, except that it is not intimated that 'all yokes' will be easy, but only the yoke of Jesus, which is his spirit of meekness and humility. Alford goes altogether outside the advice and assurance so lovingly given by Jesus, when he adds: 'The main invitation however is to those burdened with the yoke of sin, and of the law, which was added because of sin. All who feel that burden are invited.' What a perversion and confusion of the thought and metaphor! The yoke which eases a burden is spoken of as a burden; the 'yoke of sin' in connection with the divine law, either as though both were burdens, or as though the yoke of sin made the law a burden. Then: 'all who feel that burden are invited:' Jesus invites men who feel the burden of sin, and teaches them how to find rest to their souls under it! Is it not evident that such doctrines about sin and the law have no connection with these sayings of Jesus? The ideas and subjects are incongruous, and the attempt to amalgamate them leads to contradictions and absurdities. The application of the simile is sufficiently wide, without introducing matters on which it has no bearing. The labour and load of life represent far more than mere bodily toil. The nature of the burden varies: whatever constitutes a trial, an overtasking of the energies,—anxiety, grief, ill-health, disappointment, the failure of our projects, the strain and worry of business, injustice from others, unavoidable poverty, family responsibilities and sorrows,—there are burdens innumerable to be borne, and only this yoke of Jesus which can act as a lever to the lightening of the load and the easing of the weary shoulder. Jesus gave this counsel at a moment when his spirit rejoiced, not that events had turned out as he designed, but because he bowed to the Father's will and submitted to the decree of his supreme wisdom. He had 'learned obedience by the things which 5 Heb. 8 he suffered,' and out of the fulness of his own experience he eulogised the repose springing out of meekness and lowliness of heart. We need not seek to extend the broad and beautiful lesson here taught by Jesus; yet, so long as his words are not perverted from their true sense, we are not restricted in their use, and they have never been more touchingly applied than in the first verse of the well-known hymn:

   'I heard the voice of Jesus say,
   Come unto me and rest.
   Lay down, thou weary one, lay down,
   Thy head upon my breast:
   I came to Jesus as I was,
   Weary, and worn, and sad:
   I found in him a resting-place,
   And he has made me glad.

   'I heard the voice of Jesus say,
   Behold, I freely give
   The living water, thirsty one,
   Stoop down, and drink, and live:

> I came to Jesus, and I drank
> Of that life-giving stream;
> My thirst was quenched, my soul revived,
> And now I live in Him.

> 'I heard the voice of Jesus say,
> I am this dark world's Light:
> Look unto Me, thy morn shall rise,
> And all thy day be bright:
> I looked to Jesus, and I found
> In him my Star, my Sun;
> And in that Light of life I'll walk
> Till travelling days are done.'

Such ideas stand forth among the most perfect expressions of Christian faith, hope and joy. Believing souls apply them according to their individual moods and experiences. To one here and there, perchance, the singing of the hymn, excluding the last two lines, brings tender reminiscences of some dear one who has left this world to find in Jesus the rest, the water of life, and the light of the world to come. It peals forth as the rapturous death-bed song for the dying Christian, or rather as the resurrection hymn of the newly-departed. But the liberty we claim of thus using the sayings and promises of Jesus altogether apart from their primary connection, should make us only the more careful, in our expositions of Scripture, to adhere closely to their proper significance as shown by the context. The misinterpretation and misapplication of this declaration of Jesus can scarcely fail to act and react injuriously, involving not only the loss of the lesson he would have us learn, but also wrong judgments and estrangements of Christian sympathy with respect to our fellow men. Our poorer brethren, living hard lives of unremitting toil, lacking the refinements, the luxuries, alas! even the decencies of civilisation, herding in unsanitary dwellings, nourished on inferior food, its supply often scanty and always precarious, with no hope of amelioration on this side the grave,—yet admidst all their disadvantages active, energetic, industrious, cheerful, contented,—what splendid examples do they constitute of that meekness and lowliness of heart counselled by Jesus as the best panacea for the labouring classes throughout the world! What grand specimens of humanity exist among them! If we rail at their faults, let us at least discern and eulogise their virtues. In this matter they exhibit far more of the spirit of Jesus than we are accustomed to give them credit for. They have well learned their lesson of obedience, alike to the mysterious dispensations of Providence and the arbitrary and oppressive decrees of society. What a miserable, narrow, effete theology is that, which misreads, warps, distorts this simple precept of Jesus, overlays it with dogmas and mystical interpretations, blinds our eyes to living exemplifications of the spirit he inculcated and commended, and would, if it could, persuade those who through such meekness and lowliness of heart have found rest to their souls, that they are aliens from the Son of man, and can never approach him, or be acceptable in his sight, except through sacraments, priestly teaching and absolution, prayers and creeds and church-membership!

The following incident is recorded by Luke. One of those Jewish doctors 'whose especial office it was to teach the law' (Alford), took

upon him to put a question to Jesus. 'And behold, a certain lawyer 10 Luke 25
stood up and tempted him, saying, Master (or, Teacher), what shall I
do to inherit eternal life?' The question may be taken to assume a
connection between the mode of life here and its continuance in
another world, amounting in fact to this: How must I live, or what
must I do, on earth, in order to secure endless existence hereafter?
However generally that interpretation may be adopted, as though it
were a matter of course, open to no argument or question, the literal
rendering of Dr. Young puts us on the track of finding another and
and very different sense: 'Teacher, on doing what—shall I inherit
age-during life?' Death, considered as the penalty of transgression,
what is it but the premature ending of the natural 'age' of man?
The promise of the law was 'life,' not 'age-during life,' for that was
lost to mankind through the first transgression: and the law exacted
no penalty and conveyed no promise outside the limit of our earthly
existence. Therefore the question propounded by this Jewish
lawyer was natural and momentous, 'On doing what—shall I inherit
age-during life?' As far as can be ascertained from Scripture, the
doctrine of age-during life was first revealed by Jesus; it was the
peculiar feature of his teaching. The lawyer, consciously or unconsciously, was quoting the words and adopting the ideas of Jesus:
'and age-during life shall inherit.' 'Who may not receive back 19 Mat. 29
manifold more in this time, and in the coming age age-during life' 18 Luke 30
(Young). Jesus had, indeed, proclaimed this age-during life as the
gift of God granted to men through him. 'He who is hearing my 5 John 24
word, and believing Him who sent me, hath life age-during.'
'Verily, verily, I say to you, He who is believing in me, hath life 6 John 47
age-during.' Possibly the lawyer anticipated that his question would
lead to a repetition by Jesus of such declarations, for the words
'stood up and tempted him' imply an intention of entangling Jesus
in some argument or accusation. But Jesus simply answered the
question by putting another. What did this lawyer hold to be the
sum and substance of the law? 'And he said unto him, What is 10 Luke 26
written in the law? how readest thou?' The lawyer was ready
with his summary of human duties. 'And he answering said, Thou ,, 27
shalt love the Lord thy God with (Gr. from)* all thy heart, and
with all thy soul, and with all thy strength, and with all thy mind;
and thy neighbour as thyself.' Jesus accepted that as a true and
full epitome of the divine law. 'And he said unto him, Thou hast ,, 28
answered right.' And the connection between life and duty was of
the closest kind. 'This do, and thou shalt live.' The perpetuation ,, 28
of life must needs depend upon observance of God's decrees: therein
consists the harmony of our nature with his will and with the surroundings, physical and moral, individual and social, amidst which
he has placed us. This is the case both in this world and the next.
It applies equally to that broken span of life inherited from the first
Adam, who 'is of the earth, earthy,' and to that age-during life 15 i. Cor. 47
which comes to us through the second Adam, who is 'the Lord from
heaven' (A. V.). There must be an incorporation of our nature
with his: 'He who is eating my flesh, and drinking my blood, hath 6 John 54

* The note '(Gr. from)' should refer also to the following three instances of the
word 'with.'

life age-during.' (Young). His spirit of obedience is the spirit of life within us: his spirit of life within us is the spirit of obedience. There is no self-contradiction in Jesus when at one time he says, 'This do, and thou shalt live,' and at another time, 'Because I live, ye shall live also.' And the life he promises is *age-during*, not *endless*. God has given to every living creature an appointed time, or 'age.' All that can be hoped is, that each shall reach the utmost limit of existence. An immortality of this earthly life would be a curse, and not a blessing. An immortality of changeless being hereafter may be equally undesirable and unattainable. Having gained Christ, we trust to 'know him, and the power of his resurrection.' Our hope should not rest in the ceaseless perpetuation of one changeless mode of existence, but in the assured triumph over death, whenever and wherever it may come, that we 'may attain unto the resurrection from the dead.' Jesus was made our high priest, after the order of Melchizedek, 'after the power of an endless (Gr. indissoluble) life.' That did not save him from death upon the cross, but it ensured his resurrection: 'I lay down my life, that I may take it again.'

There was nothing in the reply of Jesus which the lawyer could lay hold upon to criticise and question; but that he might not appear abashed or foiled in his purpose, he broached another topic of enquiry. 'But he, desiring to justify himself, said unto Jesus, And who is my neighbour?' Alford supposes, 'that *to justify himself* may mean, to get himself out of the difficulty, viz.: by throwing on Jesus the definition of *one's neighbour*, which was very narrowly and technically interpreted among the Jews, excluding Samaritans and Gentiles.' Jesus entered upon no verbal or technical argument, but illustrated the matter by drawing a picture which exhibited the working of the spirit of exclusiveness and the spirit of neighbourliness. 'Jesus made answer and said, A certain man was going down from Jerusalem to Jericho; and he fell among robbers, who both stripped him and beat him, and departed, leaving him half dead.' If ever one human being stood in need of assistance from another, that poor traveller did. An opportunity for help soon arose. A priest happened to be going that road. He caught sight of the half-murdered man, and at once—what? Simply and deliberately avoided him. 'And by chance a certain priest was going down that way: and when he saw him, he passed by on the other side.' Afterwards a Levite came upon the scene, and he, all unconsciously, imitated the conduct of his spiritual superior: 'And in like manner a Levite also, when he came to the place, and saw him, passed by on the other side.' A passing glance was enough for both these men. Fortunately they were followed by a man whose brotherly sympathies were not extinct. 'But a certain Samaritan, as he journeyed, came where he was: and when he saw him, he was moved with compassion.' All the help within his power he hastened to render: 'and came to him, and bound up his wounds, pouring on *them* oil and wine.' The Revisers agree with Young in adopting the word 'on' instead of 'in,' but Tischendorf retains 'in.' Either word will suit, now the term 'beat' is used instead of 'wounded': they were surface-wounds, not sword-cuts. The difficulty now was how to remove the patient. His rescuer managed to place him on the saddle

of the animal he himself had been riding, led him to an inn, and
there saw that all his wants were provided for. 'And he set him on 10 Luke 34
his own beast, and brought him to an inn, and took care of him.'
After a night's rest the invalid was sufficiently restored to admit of
his kind friend pursuing his journey. Having bestowed what care
and time were requisite, he must needs provide money, and that he
did in the most delicate way, not troubling the sufferer about the
matter, but placing what he thought would be sufficient, or perchance
it was the utmost he could spare, in the hands of the innkeeper, whom
he begged to see to the stranger's wants, at the same time making
himself responsible for any further expenditure which might be found
necessary. 'And on the morrow he took out two pence (denaries—   „ 35
Young) and gave them to the host, and said, Take care of him; and
whatsoever thou spendest more, I, when I come back again, will repay
thee.' The Revisers, following the two oldest MSS., have omitted
after 'morrow' the words 'when he departed.'

Why did the Samaritan do so much, and those two others absolutely nothing? Were the priest and the Levite totally destitute of
the commonest feelings of humanity? The object of Jesus in delivering the parable was not to portray Jewish culpability, or to exalt
heathen benevolence. The question it dealt with was that of neigh-
bourship, and Jesus brought the lesson to bear on that one point.
He assumed that one of the travellers was a neighbour of the
wounded man, and he asked the lawyer to guess which one of them
it was. 'Which of these three, thinkest thou, proved neighbour   „ 36
unto him that fell among the robbers?' The Authorised Version
has 'was neighbour,' which Tischendorf retains. Young, agreeing
with the 'Englishman's Greek New Testament,' renders, 'to have
been neighbour.' Alford did not alter the text of the Authorised
Version, although he quoted this from Wordsworth: 'Observe, that
the *was* neighbour, is literally *became* neighbour.' Luther renders:
'Welcher dünkte dich, der unter diesen dreyen der Nächste sey
gewesen dem, der unter die Mörder gefallen war?' which may be
taken to correspond with Young. The Revisers' word 'proved,'
which is rather a gloss than a translation, and which is stronger than
Wordsworth's 'became,' may therefore be disregarded. The lawyer
expressed his opinion that the one who showed kindness to the
wounded man must have been his neighbour. 'And he said, He that   „ 37
shewed mercy on him,' which means that they were both Samaritans.
That explained everything, according to the teaching and spirit of
Jewish exclusiveness. The priest and Levite were not necessarily
callous to human suffering, but they were imbued with caste prejudices. So widespread and deep was the feeling of national aversion,
that the Samaritan woman at the well expressed astonishment that
Jesus, being a Jew, should have condescended to ask a drink of water
at her hands. A special vision from heaven was needed to teach
even the apostle Peter, after years of intercourse with Jesus, that he
'should not call any man common or unclean.' Those engaged in 10 Acts 28
sacerdotal functions would naturally be most punctilious in avoiding
any suspicion of ceremonial uncleanness. To have given any help to
the wounded man, would have brought the priest and Levite into
close personal contact with him. They could not venture to approach
and touch a Samaritan! Not until one of his own nation came up,

could any be found who would regard and help him as a 'neighbour.' The parable was a protest against the spirit of bigotry and intolerance, showing how hideous and hateful were self-righteousness and arrogance, how inimical to the best instincts and interests of humanity. There must be no narrow-mindedness in settling an answer to the question, 'Who is my neighbour?' Here was a Jewish lawyer exercising his intellect in verbalisms and quibblings about the import and bearing of the simple divine command, 'Thou shalt love thy neighbour as thyself.' It had been so expounded as to extinguish the spirit of brotherhood appertaining to our common nature, and a better and broader interpretation of the law was needed than the one in vogue. There may have been a touch of indignation and impatience in the words with which Jesus dismissed this lawyer, with his questioning and questionable subtleties. 'And Jesus said unto him, Go, and do thou likewise.' The light of nature was a sufficient guide to the meaning of the grand law of human brotherhood. There was no need to ask, 'Who is my neighbour?' A heart open to compassion, a soul overflowing with love, would answer unhesitatingly and peremptorily, Who is *not* my neighbour? The love of man to man must free itself from all cant of creeds, prejudices of caste, and national antipathies. On the common ground of humanity, Jew and Samaritan must not only meet but shake hands as 'neighbours.'

In the course of journeying with his disciples, Jesus reached a village, the name of which is not here recorded. The mention of it by Luke as 'a certain village' leads to the inference that the documents in his possession did not enable him to give the exact locality. 'Now as they went on their way, he entered into a certain village.' There he was hospitably lodged and entertained in a lady's house. 'And a certain woman named Martha received him into her house.' The expression seems to signify more than a visit of a few hours made in passing. A sister of Martha eagerly availed herself of the opportunity of listening to the discourse of Jesus. 'And she had a sister called Mary, which also sat at the Lord's feet, and heard his word.' The Revisers have followed 'many ancient authorities' (Alford) in replacing 'Jesus' by 'Lord.' The word is 'Lord' in the oldest MS., and in the Vatican MS. it had been altered to 'Lord' by a later hand. It would seem that Jesus was allowed to carry on his teaching in the house itself. But the mistress of the house was not at leisure to attend these gatherings. She was bent on honouring her guest with festal entertainments, and devoted herself with much energy and anxiety to the task. 'But Martha was cumbered (Gr. distracted) about much serving.' Herself overburdened, she disapproved of her sister's negligence. It must needs be supposed that Martha did not scruple to express herself freely on the point to Mary, before presuming to trouble Jesus with her domestic grievance. But Mary could not tear herself from the Teacher's feet, and her offended sister, overwrought by the pressure of her well-meant, hospitable cares, and sensitive upon the point even to petulance, ventured to lay her complaint before Jesus, and actually solicited his interference. 'And she came up to him (having stood by him—Young), and said, Lord (Sir—Young), dost thou not care that my sister did leave me to serve alone? bid her therefore that she help me.' Such a crisis, arising out of such sweet foibles of character in these two loving women, was not a little embarrassing. Jesus disposed of it with extreme delicacy and courtesy. Called upon to express his wish in the matter, he did so with friendly sincerity and candour. He must needs incline to one side or the other, and he did not hesitate to plead for freedom of judgment and action on behalf of Mary. The contention between the sisters was as to the most fitting and welcome mode of showing their esteem for him. Jesus was not unmindful of all that Martha had done and was doing for his comfort and entertainment, and he had perceived her anxiety and her efforts branching out in many directions. 'But the Lord answered and said unto her, Martha, Martha, thou art anxious and troubled about many things.' Here again the Revisers have altered 'Jesus' to 'Lord.' It stands 'Lord' in the Sinaitic, which is the oldest MS., and in the Vatican MS. the original reading was 'Lord,' the word having been altered by a later hand. So in the Vatican MS. in verse 39 'Lord' had been inserted, and in verse 41 erased. Such modifications are suggestive. On this particular point it must not be assumed that antiquity is an evidence of accuracy: a feeling of reverence might naturally seem to justify the copying of the word 'Lord' from an older MS., but few probably would have ventured to dispense with 'Lord' and insert 'Jesus,' except upon overwhelming evidence. [10 Luke 41]

That Jesus should have twice uttered the name of Martha, may be taken to indicate either that her impetuosity of speech and spirit needed that emphatic call upon her attention, or that Jesus dwelt upon the word for the purpose of emphasising its meaning, which is 'stirring up, bitter, provoking.' In either case the repetition was a kind of gentle reproof. Nor was Jesus able to say that he greatly appreciated everything his hostess, in her kindness and large-heartedness, was so busy and earnest about. On the contrary, his wants were few, and he would willingly have them considered all merged and summed up in one. 'But one thing is needful.' The two oldest MSS. read, 'But there is need of few things or of one,' and the Revisers note that many ancient authorities have, 'But few things are needful, or one.' And that one was the very thing which Mary had chosen to supply him with. 'For Mary hath chosen the good part.' The best mark of respect which could be shown to him, the service which above all else he desired and appreciated, was this simple and rapt attention to the truths he taught. To aught else he was comparatively indifferent. How then could he comply with Martha's request, and send away Mary from her seat at his feet to attend to mere household matters? It was due from him rather to justify her presence, and to forbid her absence: 'which shall not be taken away from her.' [42] [42] [42]

This charming episode in the gospel narrative carries its lesson on the face of it. If we must needs make a practical application of it to ourselves or others, let us not go beyond its plain significance and bearing. We can show Jesus no greater honour, we can give him no greater pleasure, than that of sitting at his feet to listen and ponder his teaching. Ten thousand instructors in Christ cannot improve the truths enfolded in his simplest sayings. But we must go him direct, hear him ourselves, exercise our own judgment on his doctrine, and seek to grasp the real import and spirit of his words. Translators, interpreters, commentators, there must needs be: let us recognise the value of their labours, and lean upon their learning, but only that we may through them 'learn Christ.' To do that effectually, we must shut out from our ears all other voices. He speaks to us as to men capable of judging what he says. We are surrounded by an atmosphere of so-called Christian thought, which was never generated by the breath of Jesus. Discordant sounds impinge upon our ears, and we are directed hither and thither for the right creed and the true faith. There are still teachers who presume to claim apostolical descent and authority, others who deem themselves divinely appointed through laying on of hands, others with lower pretensions based on congregational election, others self-elected, all perchance equally self-confident. What a Babel of tongues, what a diversity of notions, what a contrariety of dogmas, what a trampling of theological feet, what an opening and shutting, none too gently, of theological doors! It is all well meant, designed and carried out with a view to the Master's honour: but are we sure that he attaches any importance to the modes of serving him which have been devised according to the rules and precepts of men? We are bidden to meet him in this way and that way, through one sacrament or another sacrament, through prayers, through praises, through preachings, through fastings, through devout meditations, in church-goings, in Bible-readings, in creeds and confessions, in priestly counsel and absolution. If we are competent to exercise ourselves in such doctrines and rituals, surely we are equally competent to grasp the meaning of the teaching of Jesus by taking his own words direct from his own lips. Earnest, honest, independent thought, the exercise of a sound, unfettered judgment with respect to the gospel record,—that is the great want of the age, the one thing needed for a better knowledge of Jesus and of his salvation. His teachings have been not only examined under every possible light, but as it were—analysed, their component parts first separated and then worked up anew by preachers and commentators into an amalgam of their own, supposed to be his, and vaunted as the true essence of Christianity. Take, as an example of the confusion and error incident to this disregard of the plain, primary sense, the oft-quoted words, 'but one thing is needful.' Jesus used them with reference to the attention shown to himself and his words by Mary as compared with Martha's hospitable cares on his behalf. Dean Alford applies it to ourselves, saying: 'The *good portion* is the *one thing* which is needful—see John vi. 53—the *feeding on the bread of life by faith*.' The idea is reversed, and an extraneous idea inserted from another discourse of Jesus. And we know how generally preachers follow in the wake of Alford when dealing with this text.

As Jesus was walking with his disciples he caught sight in passing of a man who was blind and had been so from birth. 'And as he passed by, he saw a man blind from his birth.' The disciples, sharing the Jewish idea that every infirmity was the punishment of sin (Alford), asked Jesus with whom in this case the transgression rested. 'And his disciples asked him, saying, Rabbi, who did sin, this man or his parents, that he should be born blind?' We know, as a matter of fact, that the sins of parents are often visited upon their children; but whether to this extent, the disciples were in doubt, or whether even the blindness might not be a judgment upon the man himself. There are sins of ignorance, unconsciously committed, secret faults as well as presumptuous transgressions. Could the possibility of such involuntary sin extend to an unborn child? Alford's note is as follows: 'How could *he himself have sinned* before his birth? Beza and Grotius refer the question to the doctrine of the transmigration of souls, that he may have sinned in a former state of existence; this however is disproved by the consideration adduced by Lightfoot, that the Pharisees believed that the *good souls only* passed into other bodies, which would exclude this case. Lightfoot, Lücke and Meyer refer it to the possibility of sin *in the womb*; Tholuck to predestinated sin, punished by anticipation; De Wette to the general doctrine of the pre-existence of souls, which prevailed both among the Rabbis and Alexandrians: s e Wisdom viii. 19, 20.' How much, or how little, or whether anything at all of such ideas was in the minds of the disciples, we know not. They could have had no settled opinion upon the subject. Their question was a mere guess, and Jesus put it aside as being either false or inapplicable. 'Jesus answered, Neither did this man sin, nor his parents: but that the works of God should be made manifest in him.' Alford suggests that to get at the sense we must supply here after 'his parents,' *that he should be born blind;* and also after 'but,' *he was born blind.* Samuel Sharpe supplies the supposed omission by rendering: 'Neither did this man sin, nor his parents; but it was that the works of God should be shown in him.' But where he inserts a semi-colon, and the Revisers a colon, Tischendorf and Young place a comma. Much depends on punctuation and pause. If, instead of assuming a hiatus, we read the sentence without a break, the sense is modified: 'Neither did this man sin nor his parents but that the works of God should be made manifest in him:' that is, whether the sin lay with him or them, its only effect would be to render him an object of divine power and compassion. It seems more reasonable to take that as the proper sense of the passage, than to assume, as otherwise we must, that Jesus regarded the man as having been doomed to blindness from birth in order to give opportunity for a miraculous restoration of his sight at last. It was enough to know that wherever sin and infirmity were found to exist, there was a call and an occasion for the exercise of the power which had been divinely given. 'We must work the works of him that sent me.' Following the two oldest MSS. the Revisers have replaced 'I' by 'we.' Not only did Jesus humbly describe himself as the messenger of God, but he associated others with him in that capacity, having imparted to them the same miraculous powers. And equally as regarded himself and them, such works must be performed whenever the occasion presented itself: 'while it is day: the night cometh, when no man can work.' That Jesus was thinking of the brevity of life's term of labour, and of his approaching departure from the world, is evident from his next remark: 'When I am in the world, I am the light of the world.' The Authorised Version begins with the words 'As long as,' which the Revisers have replaced by 'when,' therein agreeing with Tischendorf, Alford and Young. Samuel Sharpe puts 'while.' The sense of the three forms appears to be identical. No ordinary man could have presumed to utter such words. We can but walk by the light which God vouchsafes us. 'Light, more light,' is the cry of the wisest. But Jesus declares himself the very sun of the firmament, the daylight of the world. And having made that astounding assertion, he proceeded to deal with the case of physical blindness which had suggested the saying. But not in the way we should have expected; not by a word, or a touch, as had been his habit in other instances. Once he had restored sight to two blind men who expressed belief in his power, by touching their eyes, saying, 'according to your faith be it done unto you.' The same method of cure was adopted with the two blind beggars of Jericho, who called upon him as 'son of David.' In another instance Jesus spat on the eyes, put his hands on them, and restored the sight gradually. In this case of blindness from birth, Jesus used other means. He spat on the ground, kneaded the moistened earth into clay, and with that as a plaster smeared the eyes. 'When he had thus spoken, he spat on the ground, and made clay of the spittle, and anointed his eyes with the clay (or, and with the clay thereof anointed *his* eyes).' The Revisers have followed the two oldest MSS. by reading 'his eyes' instead of 'the eyes of the blind man.' Having done that much, Jesus called the man's energy and faith into action by bidding him go to a certain pool and there wash off the clay: 'and said unto him, Go, wash in the pool of Siloam (which is by interpretation, Sent).' There is no ground for supposing that interpretation to have been mentioned by Jesus. The only doubt is as to whether the remark was thrown in by the evangelist or by a copyist. Alford says: 'The reason of this derivation being stated has been much doubted. Some consider the words to have been inserted as an early gloss of some allegorical interpreter. But there is no external authority for this supposition.' The man carried out the directions of Jesus, and thereupon received sight. 'He went away, therefore, and washed, and came seeing.' Alford comments thus on the miracle: 'The value especially of the *fasting* saliva, in cases of disorders of the eyes, was well known to antiquity. In the accounts of the restoring of a blind man to sight attributed to Vespasian, the use of this remedy occurs. The use of *clay* also for healing the eyes was not unknown. No rule can be laid down which our Lord may seem to have observed, as to using, or dispensing with, the ordinary human means of healing. He himself determined, by considerations which are hidden from us.' We cannot but wonder at the extremely low ground here taken by Alford. What proper analogy or comparison can there be between any common mode of dealing with diseases of the eye, and the astounding marvel of giving sight to one born blind? However, in the next sentence Alford sets aside his own idea, for he adds: 'Whatever the means used, the healing was not in *them*, but in Him alone.' That is going to the contrary extreme. We are not justified in assuming that any means adopted by Jesus were superfluous. Is it to be supposed that he would have acted as he did in this case, without any reason or necessity for so doing? His methods of cure are seen to vary: because we cannot say why or wherefore, are we at liberty to infer that they had nothing to do with the result, that 'the healing was not in *them*, but in him alone?' On the contrary, we may feel confident that Jesus did nothing in vain, and that he would not have condescended to make a parade of means which were not essential adjuncts to the cure.

The man's neighbours, and those who had been accustomed to see him seated to solicit alms, could not but enquire whether this was the same person. 'The neighbours therefore, and they which saw him aforetime, that he was a beggar, said, Is not this he that sat and begged?' The Revisers, following the three oldest MSS., have altered the word 'blind' to 'a beggar.' The transformation was so great, that considerable doubt existed as to the man's identity. 'Others said, It is he: others said, No, but he is like him.' The passage has been strengthened by inserting the words, 'No, but,' to agree with the two oldest MSS. The man's own assurance was forthcoming to convince his questioners. 'He said, I am he.' All this seems very natural, when we consider the marvellous change which had been wrought in his condition. Imagine what it must have been to him to open his eyes for the first time upon this wonderful world : to see the sky and clouds, the earth, the fields, the grass, the flowers, the glorious setting and rising of the sun, the moon 'walking in brightness,' and all the stars of the firmament, the running stream and the outspread lake, the trees and shrubs waving in the wind, the happy birds flying to and fro, the patient cattle, the domestic animals; to watch the faces, the movements, the bright and varied dresses of his fellow creatures, the smiles upon the children's faces, the play of passion and of character in adults : to gaze upon the houses, the streets, the shops, the bustle and business of mankind : what a changed world it was to him! What wonder that he himself should be changed, almost beyond recognition? The fixed, stolid gaze of the sightless eyes was gone: instead of groping with a stick, he walked self-confidently and nimbly ; the glow of happiness and hope was on his countenance : he was the same, yet not the same, so greatly changed that his own assertion might well be needed to convince those who stood in doubt of his identity. Then followed the natural question as to the means whereby he had received sight. 'They said therefore unto him, How then were thine eyes opened?' He answered that the man Jesus, whose name was so well known, had in a very simple way brought that about. 'He answered, The man that is called Jesus made clay, and anointed mine eyes, and said unto me, Go to Siloam, and wash : so I went away and washed, and I received sight.' Impelled by a feeling of curiosity, the hearers enquired where Jesus was to be found ; but the man himself did not know. 'And they said unto him, Where is he? He saith, I know not.'

The report of such a miracle could not fail to spread. Not only did it reach the ears of the Pharisees, but the man himself was produced to them in evidence. 'They bring to the Pharisees him that aforetime was blind.' Another fact came out in connection with it : that the miracle had been wrought on a sabbath. 'Now it was the sabbath on the day when Jesus made the clay, and opened his eyes.' We know the intense scrupulousness of the Pharisees with respect to the observance of the sabbath. Jesus had previously been charged with breaking the divine law by infringing the sacred rest of the day. Probably he anticipated a renewal of that charge, and deliberately resolved to set it at defiance, when he prefaced his labour of love with the words. 'We must work the works of him that sent me, while it is day.' The Pharisees questioned the man closely as to the manner in which the miracle had been performed. 'Again therefore the Pharisees also asked him how he received his sight. And he said unto them, He put clay upon mine eyes, and I washed, and do see.' That was sufficient, in the minds of some, to condemn Jesus as a sabbath-breaker, a man therefore who could not possibly be charged with a divine mission. 'Some therefore of the Pharisees said, This man is not from God, because he keepeth not the sabbath.' But others shrank from accepting and thus applying that form of argument: they were disposed rather to reverse it, and instead of saying, This man has broken the sabbath, and is therefore a transgressor, to say, This man has wrought beneficent miracles, and therefore cannot be a sinner. No agreement was possible between the holders of such opposite views. 'But others said, How can a man that is a sinner do such signs? And there was a division among them.' With the view of ascertaining what would be the natural and unbiassed opinion of the character of Jesus, apart from theological preconceptions and arguments, the man himself was questioned on the point. 'They say therefore unto the blind man again, What sayest thou of him, in that he opened thine eyes?' The answer was given unhesitatingly. 'And he said, He is a prophet.' Then the idea was broached—alas! for the baseless prejudices and false suspicions generated by partisanship—that the whole affair was pure deception from beginning to end, that the man had not been born blind, and had not received his sight, but was an emissary of Jesus, probably hired to cry him up as a prophet. Resolved to sift the matter to the bottom, the parents of the man were summoned, and not until their evidence had been taken did these doubters and traducers relinquish their theory about collusion and deception. 'The Jews therefore did not believe concerning him, that he had been blind, and had received his sight, until they called the parents of him that had received his sight, and asked them, saying, Is this your son, who ye say, was born blind? how then doth he now see?'

It will be observed that the evangelist attributes this incredulity to 'the Jews,' whereas he had previously spoken, in verses 13, 15 and 16, of 'the Pharisees.' Why does he make that distinction? This opens out an important question, which it is advisable to examine thoroughly and dispose of once for all. When we speak or read of the Jews or the Jewish people, we are accustomed to take it for granted that the term includes all Israelites. That is not always the case. The word 'Jews,' in strictness, denotes the inhabitants of Jewry or Judæa, and in every instance in which this evangelist uses the expression we find it bears that sense. 'The Jews sent unto him from Jerusalem priests and Levites.' Nathanael did not greet Jesus as king of the Jews, but said, 'Thou art the king of Israel.' The mention of 'the Jews' manner of purifying,' may signify that 'in Cana of Galilee' this traditional custom was observed as in Judæa. 'The passover of the Jews was at hand, and Jesus went up to Jerusalem,' the capital of Judæa. As the feast could only be kept there, it was natural to call it 'the passover of the Jews.' 'The Jews answered and said unto him.' 'The Jews therefore said, Forty and six years was this temple in building.' There is no mention or

thought of Gentiles, but naturally and as a matter of course the dwellers of Jerusalem and the neighbourhood are designated by the customary title of 'Jews.' 'A man of the Pharisees, named Nico-   3 John 1
demus, a ruler of the Jews.' At that time the land of Canaan was divided into four provinces, Galilee and Peræa, North Peræa, Samaria and Judæa, under four different Roman governors. The rulership of Nicodemus, whatever its character, must certainly have been restricted to the inhabitants of Judæa, that is to 'the Jews.' Jesus when speaking of the whole nation, irrespective of locality, uses the term 'Israel:' 'Art thou the teacher of Israel?' 'There arose therefore   ,, 10
a questioning on the part of John's disciples with a Jew about puri-   ,, 25
fying,'—not a Jew as distinguished from a Gentile, but in connection with the mention of 'the land of Judæa,' a Judæan, not one of those from 'beyond Jordan.' 'For Jews have no dealings with Samaritans.'   ,, 26
This passage is not in the oldest MS., and the Revisers note that 4 John 9
'some ancient authorities omit' it. If inserted by the evangelist we must take it in the same sense as elsewhere. Samaria lay between Judæa, the country of the Jews, and Galilee, which was also inhabited by men of the same nation and religion, although not 'Jews.' It is quite possible that the rancour was chiefly if not entirely between the Samaritans and the Judæans or 'Jews' only. This seems probable, from the fact that Jesus was once refused admittance into 'a village 9 Luke 52
of the Samaritans,' not because he and his disciples were recognised as Israelites, but because it was evident that they were journeying towards Jerusalem : the Samaritans would hold no intercourse with those who were about to associate with their enemies 'the Jews.' 'Salvation is from the Jews.' This follows immediately upon the 4 John 22
mention of Jerusalem, which the Samaritan woman understood to be the only place, according to Jewish ideas, in which God must be worshipped. 'He went forth from thence into Galilee. For Jesus   ,, 43-45
himself testified, that a prophet hath no honour in his own country. So when he came into Galilee, the Galileans received him, having seen all the things that he did in Jerusalem at the feast : for they also went unto the feast.' Here the distinction is plain between Jews and Galileans. Jesus was a Jew, having been 'born in Bethlehem of 2 Mat. 1
Judæa.' His own countrymen, the Jews, rejected him, but the Galileans received him. Jews and Galileans were of the same religion, both Israelites. 'There was a feast of the Jews ; and Jesus 5 John 1
went up to Jerusalem.' 'So the Jews said unto him that was cured,   ,, 10
It is the sabbath, it is not lawful for thee to take up thy bed.' 'For   ,, 16
this cause did the Jews persecute Jesus, because he did these things on the sabbath.' 'The Jews sought the more to kill him.' It is   ,, 18
now abundantly evident that the constant mention of 'the Jews' by the evangelist is altogether apart from any thought of heathens or Gentiles. By 'Jews' he means the inhabitants of Jerusalem and of Judæa generally, as distinguished from Galileans and other Israelites, and he shows how bitter and constant was the opposition of the Jews to Jesus, compelling him sometimes to fly from the south country of Judæa, and to confine his ministry chiefly to the north country of Galilee. 'Now the passover, the feast of the Jews, was at 6 John 4
hand.' 'The Jews therefore murmured concerning him.' 'The   ,, 41
Jews therefore strove one with another.' There is nothing in these   ,, 52
passages to modify the previous conclusions. The following passages

7 John 1-3	corroborate them. 'And after these things Jesus walked in Galilee: for he would not walk in Judæa (Jewry—Authorised Version), because the Jews sought to kill him. Now the feast of the Jews, the feast of tabernacles, was at hand. His brethren therefore said unto
,, 11	him, Depart hence, and go into Judæa.' 'The Jews therefore sought
,, 13	him at the feast.' 'No man spake openly of him for fear of the
,, 15	Jews.' 'The Jews therefore marvelled, saying, How knoweth this man letters, having never learned?' The evangelist now makes a still closer distinction. Inhabitants of Jerusalem were necessarily Jews, but all Jews would not be inhabitants of Jerusalem; so he explains, 'Some therefore of them of Jerusalem said, Is not this he whom they seek to kill?' And now the evangelist, referring for the
,, 35	first time to heathens, reports: 'The Jews therefore said among themselves, Whither will this man go that we shall not find him?' will he go unto the Dispersion among (Gr. of) the Greeks, and teach the Greeks?' He might go to those who were not Jews or Gentiles,
8 John 22	to the Galileans, but in Galilee they could find him. 'The Jews therefore said, Will he kill himself, that he saith, Whither I go, ye
,, 31	cannot come?' 'Jesus therefore said to those Jews which had
,, 48	believed him.' 'The Jews answered and said unto him, Say we not well that thou art a Samaritan, and hast a devil (Gr. demon)?'
,, 52	'The Jews said unto him, Now we know that thou hast a devil (Gr.
,, 57	demon).' 'The Jews therefore said unto him, Thou art not yet fifty
9 John 18	years old, and hast thou seen Abraham?' 'The Jews therefore did not believe concerning him, that he had been blind, and had received his sight.' That is the passage which suggested this investigation. Possibly all the Pharisees were not Jews: at all events, the evangelist here brings out the fact that these objectors were Jews, not from
,, 22	Galilee or elsewhere than Judæa. 'They feared the Jews: for the Jews had agreed already, that if any man should confess him *to be*
10 John 19	the Christ, he should be put out of the synagogue.' 'There arose
,, 23, 24	again a division among the Jews because of these words.' 'Jesus was walking in the temple, in Solomon's porch. The Jews therefore
,, 31	came round about him.' 'The Jews took up stones again to stone
,, 33	him.' 'The Jews answered him, For a good work we stone thee not.' It were absurd to suppose that in these passages the Jews are
11 John 7, 8	mentioned in contradistinction to Gentiles. 'He saith to the disciples, Let us go into Judæa again. The disciples say unto him, Rabbi, the Jews were but now seeking to stone thee; and goest thou thither again?' Nothing could be plainer than that the term 'Jews' is applied and restricted to the dwellers in Judæa, the countrymen
,, 19	and co-religionists of Jesus. 'Many of the Jews had come to Martha
,, 31	and Mary.' 'The Jews then which were with her in the house.' Of course Gentiles could not have been present: no thought of such a
,, 33	thing was in the writer's mind. 'And the Jews also weeping (Gr.
,, 36	wailing).' 'The Jews therefore said, Behold how he loved him.'
,, 45	'Many therefore of the Jews .. believed on him.' 'Jesus therefore
,, 54	walked no more openly among the Jews, but departed thence into the country near to the wilderness, into a city called Ephraim: and there he tarried with his disciples:' of course among men of their own
,, 55	nation. 'Now the passover of the Jews was at hand: and many
12 John 9	went up to Jerusalem.' 'The common people therefore of the Jews
,, 11	learned that he was there.' 'Many of the Jews went away, and

believed on Jesus.' 'As I said unto the Jews, Whither I go, ye | 13 John 33
cannot come; so now I say unto you.' The inference is plain: the disciples to whom Jesus spoke thus were not Jews, at least not all Jews. 'And the officers of the Jews seized Jesus.' 'Now Caiaphas | 18 John 12
was he which gave counsel to the Jews.' 'I ever taught in the | „ 14
synagogues (Gr. synagogue), and in the temple, where all the Jews | „ 20
come together.' 'The Jews said unto him, It is not lawful for us | „ 31
to put any man to death.' 'Art thou the king of the Jews?' | „ 33
'Pilate answered, Am I a Jew? Thine own nation and the chief | „ 35
priests delivered thee unto me.' It is obvious from this, that the term 'Jew' did not extend to Gentiles living in Judæa. 'That I should | „ 36
not be delivered to the Jews.' 'He went out again unto the Jews.' | „ 38
'Will ye therefore that I release unto you the king of the Jews?' | „ 39
'Hail King of the Jews.' 'The Jews answered him.' 'The Jews | 19 John 3, 12
cried out.' 'He said unto the Jews.' 'Jesus of Nazareth, the king | „ 14, 19
of the Jews.' 'This title therefore read many of the Jews.' 'The | „ 20
chief priests of the Jews.' 'Write not the king of the Jews, but, | „ 21
that he said, I am king of the Jews.' 'The Jews therefore, because | „ 31
it was the preparation.' 'Secretly for fear of the Jews.' 'As the | „ 38, 40
custom of the Jews is to bury:' probably it was not customary thus to embalm the dead in Galilee and elsewhere. 'Because of the Jews' | „ 42
Preparation.'

So much for John's gospel. Turning now to Matthew we find the following passages. 'Where is he that is born King of the Jews?' | 2 Mat. 2
was the question of the Magi, and under that title Jesus at last was crucified; but the prophecy quoted took a wider view: 'which shall | „ 6
be shepherd of my people Israel.' 'And came into the land of | „ 21, 22
Israel. But when he heard that Archelaus was reigning over Judæa .. he withdrew into the parts of Galilee.' The distinction between the land of Israel as a whole, and Judæa as a part of Israel, is here unmistakable. 'I have not found so great faith, no, not in | 8 Mat. 10
Israel.' 'It was never so seen in Israel.' 'Go rather to the lost | 9 Mat. 33
sheep of the house of Israel.' 'They glorified the God of Israel.' | 10 Mat. 6
'Judging the twelve tribes of Israel.' 'Tell ye the daughter of | 15 Mat. 31
Zion, Behold, thy King cometh unto thee:' but it was as 'Son of | 19 Mat. 18
David,' who ruled over Israel. 'Art thou the King of the Jews?' | 21 Mat. 5
Pilate was merely 'Governor of Judæa,' and therefore could only | 27 Mat. 12
take cognizance of a claim to kingship over 'Jews;' but the chief | 3 Luke 1
priests, the scribes and elders, mocking said: 'He is King of Israel.' | 27 Mat. 42

Mark, besides these titles affixed to Jesus by Pilate and the elders, | 15 Mark 2
supplies only one other passage bearing on the subject. 'For the | 10, 12, 18, 26, 32
Pharisees, and all the Jews, except they wash their hands diligently | 7 Mark 3
(or, up to the elbow) eat not.' This is preceded by the observation, 'And there are gathered together unto him the Pharisees, and certain | 7 Mark 1, 2
of the scribes, which had come from Jerusalem, and had seen that some of his disciples ate their bread with defiled, that is, unwashen, hands.' Obviously there was not the same strict observance of 'the tradition of the elders' among the Israelites generally, as prevailed among 'all the Jews.'

Luke contains the following passages. 'Many of the children of | 1 Luke 16
Israel shall he turn to the Lord their God.' 'The Lord God shall | „ 32, 33
give unto him the throne of his father David; and he shall reign over the house of Jacob for ever (Gr. unto the ages).' 'He hath | „ 54, 68

holpen Israel his servant.' 'Blessed *be* the Lord, the God of Israel.' 'And hath raised up a horn of salvation for us in the house of his servant David.' 'Till the day of his showing unto Israel.' 'Looking for the consolation of Israel.' 'The glory of thy people Israel.' 'For the falling and rising up of many in Israel.' 'I have not found so great faith, no, not in Israel.' Pilate's title is of course the same, but the hope of the disciples had embraced not Jews only but all Israelites: 'But we hoped that it was he which should redeem Israel.'

It was the more important to undertake this exhaustive examination of the Gospels, because throughout the Acts the term 'Jews' is used in a wider sense. We there read of 'Jews' at Jerusalem and Damascus, of Grecian Jews, Jews of Phœnicia, Cyprus, Antioch, Salamis, Antioch of Pisidia, Iconium, Philippi, Thessalonica, Berœa, Athens, Corinth, Ephesus, Achaia, in Greece, Asia, Rome, and 'throughout the world.' Nor can it be supposed that these are called Jews as being of the tribe of Judah, for in several passages 'Jews and Greeks' are spoken of, and in one place 'Jews among the Gentiles,' the title of 'Jews' being used then in the same broad sense as now. So we find the word 'Jews' used in two ways: throughout the Gospels generally, and in John's Gospel especially, as denoting the Judæans or Southern Israelites, as distinguished from the Israelites of Galilee and elsewhere; and throughout the Acts as embracing all Israelites in opposition to Gentiles. Nor is this to be wondered at. The Gospels record the life and labours of Jesus among his own people only, as stated by himself: 'I am not sent but to the lost sheep of the house of Israel:' therefore when one section of the people is alluded to, it is to distinguish them from the other section, not from men of other nations; just as in a history of the English people the constant repetition of the word 'English' might signify the exclusion of Scotch and Welsh, without thought or reference to Continental nations. Unfortunately Mr. Matthew Arnold, taking up the popular and not the evangelist's sense of the term 'Jews,' has thence drawn the conclusion that John's Gospel could not have been written by John, nor by a Jew. Here is his argument.* 'Now, a plain reader will certainly, when his attention is called to the matter, be struck with the extraordinary way in which the writer of the Fourth Gospel, whom we suppose a Jew, speaks of his brother Jews. We do not mean that he speaks of them with blame and detestation; this we could quite understand. But he speaks as if they and their usages belonged to another race from himself,—to another world. The waterpots of Cana are set "after the manner of *the purifying of the Jews;*" "there arose a question between some of John's disciples *and a Jew about purifying;*" "now *the Jews' Passover* was nigh at hand;" "there they laid Jesus, because of *the Preparation of the Jews.*" No other Evangelist speaks in this manner. It seems almost impossible to think that a Jew born and bred,—a man like the Apostle John,— could ever have come to speak so. Granted that he was settled at Ephesus when he produced his Gospel, granted that he wrote in Greek, wrote for Greeks; still he could never, surely, have brought

* "God and the Bible. The fourth Gospel from without."

himself to speak of the Jews and of Jewish things in this fashion! His lips and his pen would have refused to form such strange expressions, in whatever disposition he may have written ; nature and habit would have been too much for him. A Jew talking of *the Jews' Passover*, and of a dispute of some of John's disciples *with a Jew about purifying?* It is like an Englishman writing of the Derby as *the English people's Derby*, or talking of a dispute between some of Mr. Cobden's disciples *and an Englishman about free-trade*. An Englishman would never speak so.' Mr. Matthew Arnold is not quite correct in saying, ' No other Evangelist speaks in this manner,' as will be seen on referring to 7 Mark 1—3. No other Evangelist needed to speak in that manner, inasmuch as only John sought to bring out so prominently and methodically the fact, that the whole opposition to Jesus, from first to last, was not national but local, had no existence in Galilee, but sprang from Judaea, and was confined to those who were distinguished by their own countrymen as ' Jews.'

The examination of the parents confirmed the account previously given. They identified their son, and attested the fact that he was born blind. ' His parents answered and said, We know that this is our son, and that he was born blind.' Beyond this they could say nothing. ' But how he now seeth, we know not ; or who opened his eyes, we know not.' That information could be obtained from the son himself, who was of an age competent to give reliable testimony ; ' Ask him : he is of age ; he shall speak for himself.' From this it is to be inferred that he was of youthful appearance. The boon Jesus had conferred upon him was all the more to be appreciated because he stood only upon the threshold of manhood, and the gift of sight would prove a life-long blessing. The parents were the more reticent because they stood in fear of the consequences which might result from any acknowledgment of the supernatural power of Jesus. It was known that any confession of him as Messiah involved the penalty of excommunication. ' These things said his parents, because they feared the Jews: for the Jews had agreed already that if any man should confess him *to be* Christ, he should be put out of the synagogue. Therefore said his parents, He is of age ; ask him.' The man had already owned to a belief in Jesus as a prophet. Even that conception of him these Jews would not let pass without a protest and a warning. So they summoned the man again to their presence, and urged him to attribute his recovery from blindness to God alone, and to take it from them that his visible Benefactor was the very reverse of a prophet,—actually a breaker of the divine law. ' So they called a second time the man that was blind, and said unto him, Give glory to God : we know that this man is a sinner.' We are left to suppose that the dissentients from that opinion had retired from the council, leaving the bigots to take their own course. As to the character of Jesus the man could not profess to know anything ; but one thing he did know for certain,—that he had been blind and now could see. ' He therefore answered, Whether he be a sinner, I know not : one thing I know, that, whereas I was blind, now I see.' They reminded him, in reply, that the bare fact was not enough, but that the method of performing the miracle had to be taken into account. ' They said therefore unto him, What did he to thee ? how opened he thine eyes ?' The man seemed to miss the drift of their insinuation; the idea that the act involved the sin of sabbath-breaking was not in his mind; probably he was ignorant of the discussion which had taken place on that question, and only knew that as soon as he had mentioned the fact about the clay they paid no more attention to his words, and would listen to no further details.

v. John 27 'He answered them, I told you even now, and ye did not hear.' The man seems to have been fairly puzzled, and expressed his astonishment, asking why they wanted him to go over the matter again, having heard him with impatience and comparative inattention before, and suggesting, apparently, that no amount of repetition

" 27 would be likely to convert them into disciples of Jesus. 'Wherefore would ye hear it again? would ye also become his disciples?' Alford observes: 'This latter clause is of course ironical.' The tone and tenor of the man's replies and criticisms indicate that absence of conventional respect for the council, the place, the dress and rank of the Pharisees, which would be natural and excusable in one who looked upon such things for the first time. It is an unconscious touch of truthfulness in the narrative. The very idea of the Pharisees becoming disciples of Jesus was dismissed with scorn. They replied disdainfully that the man himself appeared to be a disciple, but

" 28 they owned allegiance to none but Moses. 'And they reviled him, and said, Thou art his disciple, but we are disciples of Moses.' About his divine inspiration there could be no question, but Jesus

29 was an utter stranger to them. 'We know that God hath spoken by Moses: but as for this man, we know not whence he is.' The Revisers have softened the Authorised Version by putting 'this man' instead of 'this fellow,' therein agreeing with Alford. Tischendorf and Young render 'this one.' That itself deserved to be called a miracle.

30 'The man answered and said unto them, Why, herein is the marvel, that ye know not whence he is, and yet he opened mine eyes.' It was an axiom of their faith that no sinner could gain the ear of Deity:

31 for that, it was imperative to adore God and to obey his will. 'We know that God heareth not sinners: but if any man be a worshipper of God, and do his will, him he heareth.' The miracle performed was altogether without precedent, and taken by itself was an irrefragable testimony that Jesus was divinely taught and authorised.

32, 33 'Since the world began it was never heard that any one opened the eyes of a man born blind. If this man were not from God, he could do nothing.' The common-sense, the logic, the religious sentiment of the argument, were beyond refutation. But the man, ignorant, owing to his infirmity, of many social customs and deferences, had yet to learn that the Pharisaic spirit was too proud to brook contradiction, and that the power of authority was greater than any force of argument. All at once, the evil spirit within these men broke bounds. They resented as an insult the attempt to convince them, and scrupled not to pronounce his past blindness a brand of infamy.

34 'They answered and said unto him, Thou wast altogether born in sins, and dost thou teach us?' Alford quotes the following from Trench: 'They forget that the two charges,—one that he had never been born blind, and so was an impostor,—the other, that he bore the mark of God's anger in a blindness that reached back to his birth,—will not agree together.' This comment goes beyond the narrative. The evangelist says only that they did not believe he had

been born blind *until* they called the parents. We must not charge them with deliberate prevarication. The fact of blindness had been proved: they accepted the proof, and then presumed to regard the infirmity as a divine judgment. They seem even to have construed his vindication of Jesus as a proof of discipleship deserving the threatened penalty of excommunication, which they proceeded to inflict upon him. 'And they cast him out.' Alford explains: 'Probably the first of the three stages of Jewish excommunication,—the being shut out from the synagogue and household for thirty days, but without any anathema. The other two, the repetition of the above, accompanied by a curse,—and final exclusion, would be too harsh, and perhaps were not in use so early.' The sentence of exclusion passed upon the blind man was infamous and cruel. The report of it reached the ears of Jesus, who sought him out, for the purpose of giving him an opportunity of that discipleship with which he had been charged, and for which he was now bearing punishment. 'Jesus heard that they had cast him out, and finding him, he said, Dost thou believe on the Son of God?' The expression of the Revisers, 'finding him,' must not be taken to denote an accidental meeting. The Authorised version stands, 'when he had found him;' Tischendorf and Alford have, 'he found him;' Young has 'having found him,'—all of which denote a set purpose of seeking. The Revisers have inserted the note, 'Many ancient authorities read *the Son of man*.' Tischendorf does so, following the two oldest MSS. It matters little which we take, 'Son of God' or 'Son of man,' for the stress of the question lay upon the man's faith rather than upon the nature of him who was the object of it. On this latter point the man was absolutely ignorant, for he did not even understand who was alluded to. 'He answered and said, And who is he, Lord (Sir—Young), that I may believe on him?' The question had no relation to any article of doctrine or creed, but to a living Person on whom the man could rely: 'believe on him' must needs mean that, and not merely 'believe something about him.' Jesus replied that the person to whom he alluded had been actually seen by the man, this man born blind!—and heard by him, and was, indeed, the very person now speaking with him. 'Jesus said unto him, Thou hast both seen him, and he it is that speaketh with thee.' What a revelation was that! What adoring gratitude must have gleamed in those eyes which had been so long sightless, as they now gazed for the first time on him who had opened them to the light and glory of the world! And to learn from his own lips that he was the Messiah, and be invited to believe on him, having already realized his divine power and beneficence! Without a moment's hesitation came the answer and the homage. 'And he said, Lord, I believe. And he worshipped him,' rendered by Young: 'And he said, I believe, Sir, and bowed before him.' What a contrast that to the spirit and demeanour of the Pharisees! Jesus in a very solemn sentence expressed his sense of it. 'And Jesus said, For judgement came I into this world, that they which see not may see; and that they which see may become blind.' He was not only light to some, but darkness to others. None could escape his influence, and those who opposed his work and doctrine must needs have the eyes of their understanding darkened. Some of the Pharisees were present when the discourse containing these words was delivered. 'Those of the Pharisees which were with him heard these things, and said unto him, Are we also blind?' The expression 'these things,' rendered in the Authorised Version 'these words,' seems to refer to some special remarks made by Jesus on the subject. In reply to their question, he assured them that blindness in itself was no mark of sin, but that the power of vision, misused and perverted, was an evidence of sin unrepented of and unremoved. 'Jesus said unto them, If ye were blind, ye would have no sin: but now ye say, We see: your sin remaineth.' This was a most emphatic protest against their false ideas and prejudices. Jesus utterly repudiates their expressed opinion that the blind man was necessarily born in sin, and asserts, on the contrary, that guilt attached itself to them who could see, but who shut their eyes wilfully against truth and righteousness.

There is no very obvious connection, to say the least, between what precedes and the following discourses of Jesus. As was usual with him when uttering some solemn and important truth, he gave emphasis to it by beginning with the words, Verily, verily. He pictured a man entering into a fold of sheep, not by the proper entrance, but by climbing over at some other place: the act itself was sufficient proof that he must needs be bent on robbery. 'Verily, verily, I say unto you, he that entereth not by the door into the fold of the sheep, but climbeth up some other way, the same is a thief and a robber.' Evidently Jesus was designedly bringing a heavy charge against somebody. On the other hand, the man who was seen to enter the sheepfold by the door, could be no other than the shepherd. 'But he that entereth in by the door is the (or, a) shepherd of the sheep.' The Revisers seem doubtful whether the article should be definite or indefinite. Tischendorf and Young omit it altogether: 'is shepherd of the sheep.' The doorkeeper knows him and admits him, and the sheep recognise his voice. 'To him the porter openeth; and the sheep hear his voice.' He has a peculiar call, which his own sheep are accustomed to listen for and follow. 'And he calleth his own sheep by name, and leadeth them out.' It seems to be assumed that the enclosure contains various flocks, taken care of by different shepherds, all of whom of course would be known to the doorkeeper. First of all, the shepherd has to assemble the sheep which are under his own charge: then he walks in front, and the flock follows, guided by his voice. 'When he hath put forth all his own, he goeth before them, and the sheep follow him: for they know his voice.' They are safe therefore from being led astray. If a stranger should approach, they instinctively avoid him, and the sound of his unaccustomed voice, far from enticing them, would but add to their terror. 'And a stranger will they not follow, but will flee from him: for they know not the voice of strangers.'

As usual, Jesus offered no explanation of the similitude he had put forward. Doubtless it enfolded important truths, but the hearers were without a clue to them. 'This parable (or, proverb) spake Jesus unto them: but they understood not what things they were which he spake unto them.' Perceiving their lack of comprehension, Jesus illustrated his meaning. He took up three points of the allegory: the door, the thief, the shepherd, disregarding as immaterial the fold itself and the porter, but introducing the additional metaphors of a hireling and a wolf. He explained that the door of the sheep represented himself. 'Jesus therefore said unto them again, Verily, verily, I say unto you, I am the door of the sheep.' Luther renders —freely—' I am the door to (zu) the sheep.' The only access to the sheep, the assembly, the flock, the church,—call it what we will—of Jesus, is Jesus himself. No man having any legitimate purpose can attempt to approach them otherwise. Whoever would assume the office of a teacher and guide of men in matters pertaining to the gospel, must go to them in the spirit of Jesus, preaching the truth as it is in him. Doctrines, creeds, hopes, fears, modes of worship, schemes of government, not prescribed by him, cannot constitute his gate of entrance. The Authorised Version continues: 'All that ever came before me are thieves and robbers.' The word 'ever' is omitted in the Revised Version: 'All that came before me are thieves and robbers.' Young renders, 'All, as many as came before me.' Alford says: 'I believe that the right sense of these words, *All that ever came before me*, has not been apprehended by any of the Commentators. First, they can only be honestly understood of *time*: all who came *before* me (not, *without regard to me*, nor *passing by me as the door*, nor *instead of me*: nor *pressing before me*, ch. v. 7, which would have been *come*, not *came*: nor *before taking the trouble to find me, the door*: nor any other of the numerous shifts which have been adopted).' Alford considers the reference to be to the Devil 'and all his followers:' 'His was the first attempt to lead human nature *before* Christ came.' Tischendorf, following the oldest MS., omits the words 'before me:' 'All that ever came are thieves and robbers.' Jesus here, as often elsewhere, speaks not of himself as an ordinary man, but as charged with a divine mission, possessing powers of attraction and protection which none else could claim to exercise. His object was to found a society, a church, an assembly, a flock, upon his own principles, under his own guidance. All previous attempts to dominate large masses of mankind had been dictated by selfish motives, by love of pomp and power, by earthly ambitions, and pre-eminence had been sought and gained through strife, war, bloodshed, in contempt of personal liberty and disregard of individual interests. Nations of warriors, slaves, serfs, swayed by kings and conquerors: the people existed for their rulers: they fainted and were as sheep without a shepherd; no leader had risen up in whom they could confide: 'All that came before me are thieves and robbers; but the sheep did not hear them.' Jesus presents himself to suffering humanity as 'the door,' the entrance to a place of refuge, rest and safety. 'I am the door: by me if any man enter in, he shall be saved.' Each sheep of his fold is secure of freedom, under due restraints of time and prudence, every natural impulse and aspiration being realised to the utmost: 'And shall go in and out, and shall find pasture.'

There have ever been those who are ready and anxious to disturb the peace and assail the liberties of mankind. They use and consume the flock for their own base purposes; disdaining to herd with them, they seek to live upon them, and in the pursuit of wealth, luxury, supremacy, are careless of the social wrongs they inflict and the misery and destruction which their policy entails. Political and dynastic ambitions, perpetuated from generation to generation, have deluged the world with blood. The race for wealth has engendered the grinding competition of commerce, and transformed the logic of political economy into a godless and inhuman system of oppression, reducing the wages of some operatives to starvation point, and leaving the toiling masses to sink into a slough of mental, moral and physical degradation. To the authors of such wrongs and miseries the words of Jesus apply : 'The thief cometh not, but that he may steal, and kill, and destroy.' The frightful persecutions which have sprung from false theology have been occasional, intermittent : but the warlike spirit has been a constant scourge, and the worship of Mammon has deteriorated the life blood of the community. Any exposition of the words of Jesus which overlooks these evils, fails thereby to grasp his spirit and apply his warning. The mission of Jesus to mankind had the very opposite tendency and object. 'I came that they may have life, and may have it abundantly (or, have abundance).' He brings no new gift to men except the gift of his Spirit. The heavenly Father has supplied, in the constitution of our nature and by the arrangements of the physical universe, all that is needful for his children's welfare. 'Life age-during :' the promise of Jesus could go no further. The regulation and preservation of our lives—that was the declared purpose of his coming. God's world overflows with blessings to mankind. There is enough for all, and to spare, if only covetousness be abolished, and replaced by the spirit of Christian equity.

The metaphor is now changed. Jesus is no longer the 'door,' but the 'shepherd.' He presents himself under a different figure, the new aspect showing his willingness and ability to meet the needs of humanity. 'I am the good shepherd.' In that capacity he was prepared not only to labour and watch, but to sacrifice his life for the safety of the flock. 'The good shepherd layeth down his life for the sheep.' That extreme of unselfish devotion could exist only through a conscious identity of interest. A hired servant would do his duty faithfully up to the point of a due regard for his own safety, but at the approach of danger he would think of himself rather than of the sheep, esteeming his own life as more precious than theirs. 'He that is a hireling, and not a shepherd, whose own the sheep are not, beholdeth the wolf coming, and leaveth the sheep, and fleeth.' He escapes, but the flock suffers, some being devoured and all scattered. 'And the wolf snatcheth them, and scattereth *them*.' The result might have been foreseen. The hireling cannot have the same instinct of self-sacrifice as the shepherd who owns the sheep. '*He fleeth* because he is a hireling, and careth not for the sheep.' Tischendorf, without any loss of clearness, omits the italicised words 'them' and 'he fleeth,' inserted by the Revisers. 'The sheep' stands in the Authorised Version after 'scattereth,' but not in the two oldest MSS.; and 'the hireling fleeth' stands before 'because,' but is not in the three oldest MSS., having been erased from the Vatican MS. by a later hand.

Jesus reverts to the intimacy subsisting between a devoted, careful shepherd and the flock he guides and guards. 'I am the good shepherd : and I know mine own, and mine own know me.' The simile does not admit the idea of equal knowledge on both sides. The sheep-know the shepherd by his voice, but his powers of discernment are of a higher order. Between Jesus and his own, however, there is a knowledge based upon intellect and will : 'even as the Father knoweth me, and I know the Father.' Alford notes : ' Beware of rendering the former clause of verse 15, as in the Authorised Version, as an independent sentence, *As my Father knoweth me, even so know I the Father*: it is merely the sequel to verse 14.' Tischendorf agrees with the Revisers, who have adopted Alford's view, which corresponds also with Luther's version. Jesus knew well that the tragic end of the faithful shepherd was appointed for himself. 'And I lay down my life for the sheep.' Yet in spite of premature death he looked forward to an extension of his influence. 'And other sheep I have, which are not of this fold : them also I must bring (or, lead), and they shall hear my voice.' Alford observes : 'The *other sheep* are the *Gentiles*; not the dispersion of the Jews, who were already in God's *fold*.' That interpretation is corroborated by the vision subsequently sent to Peter, by the mission of the apostle Paul to the heathen world, and by the reverential enthusiasm with which he and Barnabas announce the fact that God ' had opened a door of faith unto the Gentiles.' It is to be observed that Jesus reverts to the words of the original simile, 'them also I must lead, and they shall hear my voice,' but he does not repeat, 'even as the Father knoweth me, and I know the Father.' His mode of guidance now is indirect ; he is in the heavens ; we hear his voice as of one who towers above us, and whose nature and attributes we cannot attain to. His earthly flock is held together rather by the instinct of gregariousness than by the guidance of himself and his Spirit; we have a knowledge of his voice, of his call, rather than of his words ; some have professed to reveal him through the subtleties of the Athanasian creed ; some have attained to the conceptions of him embodied in the Nicene creed ; for most of us the simple, historical facts of the Apostles' creed suffice : we hear his voice and are to a certain extent led by it,—he himself did not say that we should understand it,— and how little his words and their spirit are comprehended throughout Christendom, let our standing armies, our daily records of crime, our social evils in their multitudinous forms, attest. He has told us earthly things, and we believe not : how shall we believe when he tells us of heavenly things ? The first and foremost aim of Jesus was to give pasture to his flock,—to satisfy the needs of our common humanity ; and till the Church accomplishes that work, by moulding the framework of Christian society after the pattern of the Sermon on the mount and the other hints which Jesus gave respecting the principles and regulations of his 'assembly,' no realisation will have been attained, or properly attempted, of that kingdom of heaven which he came to establish on earth. It was the purpose of Jesus to unite all of mankind who would accept his supremacy into one companionship and fellowship. 'And they shall become one flock (or, there shall be one flock), one shepherd.' Alford observes : 'The *one flock* is remarkable—not *one fold*, as characteristically, but erroneously rendered in the Authorised Version : not *one fold*, but *one flock* ; no one exclusive enclosure of an outward church, but one flock, all knowing the one Shepherd and known of Him.'

In the pursuit of his self-sacrificing plan on behalf of mankind,

Jesus felt himself to be working out the divine will. 'Therefore doth the Father love me, because I lay down my life.' In the same breath he added: 'that I may take it again.' This was the characteristic of Jesus. No instance is recorded of his ever having spoken of his death except in connection with life. 'They shall condemn him to death . . . . and the third day he shall be raised up.' 'They shall scourge and kill him : and the third day he shall rise again.' His idea of death involved resurrection and fuller life : ' Verily, verily, I say unto you, Except a grain of wheat fall into the earth and die, it abideth by itself alone ; but if it die, it beareth much fruit. He that loveth his life loseth it ; and he that hateth his life in this world shall keep it unto life eternal.' "And I, if I be lifted up from the earth, will draw all men unto myself. But this he said, signifying by what manner of death he should die.' Jesus encountered death of his own free will ; his adversaries had not rushed against him, but he against them ; just as the wolf, attacking only the sheep, was resisted by the shepherd, who sacrificed himself for them. 'No one taketh it away from me ; but I lay it down of myself.' The Revisers note : ' Some ancient authorities read *took it away.*' The Sinaitic and Vatican MSS. first and second in point of age, read, 'No man hath taken it,' although Tischendorf has not followed them. That reading points to a higher and altogether different sense attaching to this saying of Jesus, for it cannot be said, with absolute, literal truth, that no man took his earthly life. The apostle Peter asserted the contrary : 'Him . . . ye by the hand of lawless men did crucify and slay.' 'The God of our fathers raised up Jesus, whom ye slew, hanging him on a tree.' The form of the expressions, 'No man took it away,' or, 'No man hath taken it away,' Jesus being yet alive, does not denote a future act. The oldest readings harmonise with and are indicative of the true meaning, which must not be set aside because later copyists, failing to discern the reason and bearing of so exceptional and peculiar an expression, altered it from 'hath taken it away' to 'taketh it away.' One result of the alteration has been to set commentators upon a search for wrong inferences from this and other passages. Alford appears to take a view the very opposite of that of Peter, and does not scruple to say of the death of Jesus : 'It was *his own act.*' The arguments upon which that astounding assertion is based are strained and far-fetched : 'The truth of this voluntary rendering up was shewn by his whole sufferings, from the falling of his enemies to the ground in the garden (ch. xviii. 6) to the last words, '*I* commend (render up) my spirit, Luke xxiii. 46.' Could anything be weaker in the way of argument ? The evangelist records, 'They went backward and fell to the ground.' Alford assumes that they were struck down by the power of Jesus : ergo, no man put him to death ! Jesus said : 'Father, into thy hands I commend my spirit :' and that also is taken to prove that no human power killed him ; in fact, that crucifixion and the draining away of his life blood would never have resulted in death but for the voluntary determination of Jesus ! The dying cry of Stephen, 'Lord Jesus, receive my spirit,' has never been so perverted, nor would the equivalent last utterance of Jesus have been so, were it not for a foregone and erroneous conclusion. Anything within reach is laid hold of in support of it : 'None of the Evangelists say He *died :*—but it is, *yielded up the spirit*, Matthew; *breathed his last*, Mark, Luke: *delivered up his spirit*, John.' Were not all these customary modes of expression, applied constantly to the deaths of ordinary men? The life which Jesus had laid down, and which he would resume, was a life prior to that he led on earth, and of that former life he said : ' I have power (or, right) to lay it down, and I have power (or, right) to take it again. This commandment received I from my Father.' In exposing himself to the hostility of his foes, in abating no jot of his pretensions before their prejudices and criticisms, in carrying on his work despite their malice and threats, and with the inevitable end of scorn, scoffs, scourging, crucifixion plainly revealed and ever before his eyes, Jesus went forward, upheld by the consciousness that such was the will of God concerning him.

[19 John 18]

The criticisms of Mr. Matthew Arnold on this part of John's gospel are based on the assumption that an obviously wrong arrangement of the words of Jesus has been adopted. He says : * ' Who can doubt that here, again, we have two separate sets of *logia* of Jesus ; one set which have *I am the good shepherd* for their centre, and another set which have for their centre *I am the door* ; and that our Evangelist has thrown the two together and confused them ? Beautiful as the sayings are even when thus mixed up together, they are far more beautiful when disentangled. But the Evangelist had a doorkeeper and a door and sheep in his first parable ; and he had another parable in which was a "door of the sheep." Catching again at an apparent connection, he could not resist joining the two parables together, and making one serve as the explanation of the other.' That statement is made in a very cool and positive way, but it has no better foundation than the critical acumen of a scholar dealing with a narrative of remote antiquity. Mr. Matthew Arnold assumes that two similar parables were spoken by Jesus, the one not overlapping or repeating the similes of the other,—that the evangelist had them before him in proper form, but was so obtuse that he did not appreciate their simplicity and symmetry,—that, failing to do so, he was misled by 'an apparent connexion,' and 'could not resist joining the two parables together.' Now, that is done by verse 6, which stands as follows : 'This parable spake Jesus unto them : but they understood not what things they were which he spake unto them. Jesus therefore said unto them again...' Did the evangelist invent that connexion ? Mr. Arnold seems to say so, for he proceeds as follows : ' To explain the first parable, and to go on all fours with it, the second ought to run as follows : " I am the door of the sheep. All that *climb up some other way* are thieves and robbers ; but the sheep *do not hear* them. I am the door ; by me if any man enter, *he is the shepherd of the sheep*." The words in italics must be substituted for the words now in the text of our Gospel ; and Jesus must stand, not as the door of salvation in general, but as the door by which to enter is the sign of the true teacher. There can be no doubt, however, that the words now in the text are right, and that what is wrong is the connexion imposed on them.' That very serious charge against the compiler of the narrative amounts to this : He did not know, and did not much care, what he was about ; he fancied

* "God and the Bible. The Fourth Gospel from Within."

there was 'a connexion which did not exist': he therefore joined 'the two parables together,' and made 'one serve as the explanation of the other': but when he had done that, the second parable did not 'explain the first,' or 'go on all fours with it'! Was there ever such a bungler as this meddlesome, not very scrupulous evangelist? Mr. Matthew Arnold, after all these centuries, steps forward to put him and us right; and he does so in this way. 'The seventh and ninth verses are a *logion* quite distinct from what precedes and follows, and ought to be entirely separated from it. Their *logion* is: "I am the door of the sheep. I am the door; by me if a man enter he shall be saved, and shall go in and out and find pasture." The eighth verse belongs to the first parable, the parable of the shepherd: not to the parable of the door. It should follow the fifth verse, and be followed by the tenth. Jesus says of the sheep: "A stranger will they not follow, but will flee from him, for they know not the voice of strangers. All that ever came before me are thieves and robbers; but the sheep did not hear them. The thief cometh not but to steal and to kill and to destroy; I am come that they might have life, and that they might have it more abundantly. I am the good shepherd."' That is how Mr. Arnold would remedy what he terms 'the artistic failure at the beginning of the tenth chapter.' But there is no evidence, outside Mr. Arnold's own mind, that any such failure is chargeable against the compiler of the narrative. Surely he could have discerned,—a child could have discerned the fact,—that it would be simpler to combine all that was said about a door in one parable, and to make a separate parable about the shepherd. The evangelist, with the original records before him, would not, could not, do that. Mr. Arnold is bolder: he not only does it, but imputes stupidity, 'an artistic failure,' to the evangelist for not having done it,—charges him with imagining and actually 'imposing a connexion which did not exist,' and blandly condescends to argue thence that we must needs have the actual words of Jesus, although in a wrong sequence, because the evangelist has shewn such an utter incompetency: he could not even arrange them properly,—how much less could he have invented them! 'A consummate artist, inventing for Jesus, could not have been satisfied with such a merely seeming and verbal connexion.' Not by such criticisms, erudite and honest though they be, can the gospel narratives be properly gauged, set aside, or upheld.

This discourse of Jesus produced opposite feelings in those who listened to it. Many affected to regard him as a kind of inspired lunatic, to whose rhapsodies it was not worth while to pay attention. 'There arose a division again among the Jews because of these words. [20] And many of them said, He hath a devil (Gr. demon) and is mad: why hear ye him?' The Revisers, on the authority of the two oldest MSS., have omitted the word 'therefore' before the word 'again.' This contemptuous criticism was not suffered to pass unchallenged. Words so solemn, so cogent, so touching as those of Jesus, had never been, and could never be uttered by one labouring under [21] any kind of mental aberration. 'Others said, These are not the sayings of one possessed with a devil (Gr. demon).' His words must be taken in conjunction with his works, and it would be impossible to attribute to demoniacal influence the miraculous restoration of sight to the blind. 'Can a devil (Gr. demon) open the eyes of the blind?'

The narrative proceeds as follows: 'And it was the feast of the dedication at Jerusalem: and it was winter; and Jesus was walking in the temple in Solomon's porch.' There is here an impression of consecutiveness. The Vatican MS. begins with the words, 'It was then'; and the Revisers note: 'Some ancient authorities read *At that time was the feast.*' Alford explains: 'This feast had become usual since the time when Judas Maccabæus purified the temple from the profanations of Antiochus. It was held on Chisleu (December) 25, and seven following days: see 1 Macc. iv. 41—59: 2 Macc. x. 1—8.' An attempt was made on this occasion to extract from Jesus a positive declaration of his Messiahship. His countrymen surrounded him, reproached him with the ambiguousness attaching to his claims and position, and desired a plain answer to the question whether he was the Christ. 'The Jews therefore came round about him, and said unto him, How long dost thou hold us in suspense? If thou art the Christ, tell us plainly.' The expression in the Authorised Version is, 'How long dost thou make us to doubt?' Young renders literally: 'Till when our soul dost thou hold in suspense?' The reply of Jesus was peculiar: 'Jesus answered them, I told you, and ye believe not.' To the Samaritan woman Jesus had said: 'I that spake unto thee am *he*.' If he had said the same to these Jews, they would not now have been putting their question. There must have been some good reason which withheld Jesus from answering by a simple 'yes' or 'no'; the latter he could not, and the former he would not say. We know that 'the Jews had agreed already that if any man should confess him *to be* Christ, he should be put out of the synagogue.' There were many who had believed in him without waiting for any fuller declaration on his part. A word from Jesus might have doomed his disciples to the threatened penalty of excommunication: all of them would have had to decide at once between recantation and martyrdom. If the Teacher himself claimed to be Christ, they would either have been forced to own him such, and suffer, or to disown him. That was a dilemma which these unbelieving questioners would have rejoiced to bring about. By 'Jews' here we understand the Judæans, to whom the title properly applied, and who were hostile to Jesus from first to last, ever seeking to kill him, and compelling him to carry on his labours outside the sphere of their jurisdiction and influence. By returning to Jerusalem and teaching in their midst, he was now defying their animosity. They were on the watch to entrap him, and it behoved him, for the sake of others as well as of himself, to answer warily. The popular notion of the Christ was out of harmony with the true vocation of Jesus: men had yet to learn that the Messiah was simply a moral reformer, a spiritual guide, that he was no king or conqueror after the recognised earthly fashion. Who he was, and what his office was, could be manifested only by his own words and works. It would have been misleading and dangerous to adopt to himself a title sure to be misunderstood. His claim to Messiahship must follow his teaching, not precede it or be extolled apart from it. After his spiritual discourse at the well, and when the Samaritan woman had expressed her conviction that Messiah was a Teacher of such truths, Jesus could safely present himself to her in that character. But he manifested intense anxiety not to be proclaimed publicly. It was well that Peter should recognise and own the fact, 'Thou art the Christ,' but it must nevertheless be held back from the world's knowledge: 'Then charged he the disciples that they should tell no man that he was the Christ.' This reticence on the part of Jesus was not understood by John the Baptist, who 'heard in the prison the works of the Christ,' and 'sent by his disciples, and said unto him, Art thou he that cometh, or look we for another?' Even to them Jesus gave no direct reply, but 'answered and said unto them, Go your way and tell John the things which ye do hear and see,' thereby intimating that his personality and office were to be disclosed only by his course of action, that it was enough to know that he did 'the works of the Christ,' without bringing the title itself into notoriety. But for this cautious reserve, it is probable that the popular enthusiasm with respect to Jesus would have taken some undesirable form of development, thereby interfering with his plan of teaching, bringing him into collision with the ecclesiastical and civil rulers, and precipitating that catastrophe which overtook him at the last. On one occasion Jesus perceived that the multitude 'were about to come and take him by force, to make him king': he knew, moreover, that his adversaries were ever on the watch to formulate an accusation against him; he would have been simply playing into their hands had he allowed them to extort from him an unqualified admission of his Messiahship. His answer to them was identical with that he had formerly given to the Baptist: 'The works that I do in my Father's name, these bear witness of me.' His works of mercy were sufficient attestation of his spirit and power. He claimed no title, nor would he suffer one to be put forward, which might serve as a rallying cry for the populace to lay hold of and pervert. He had no quarrel with the ruling powers; he preached no crusade; the followers he sought were not fighting volunteers, nationalists, resolute partisans, but had been described by him as 'sheep'; the only title that Jesus chose was that of 'shepherd': in that character it was for men to reject him or follow him. 'But ye believe not, because ye are not of my sheep. My sheep hear my voice, and I know them, and they follow me.' The Revisers have omitted the concluding words of verse 26, 'as I said unto you,' on the authority of the two oldest MSS. All that Jesus offered them was that which they had already—life, but life prolonged to its utmost limit: 'And I give unto them eternal life; and they shall never perish.' This is rendered by Young: 'And life age-during I give to them, and they shall not perish—to the age.' Jesus does not say that he will immortalise his sheep, but he promises to safeguard them: 'and no one shall snatch them out of my hand.' The Authorised Version continues: 'My Father, which gave them to me, is greater than all; and no man is able to pluck them out of my Father's hand.' The Revised Version stands: 'My Father, which hath given *them* unto me, is greater than all; and no one is able to snatch *them* (or, *aught*) out of the Father's hand.' The Revisers have inserted the note: 'Some ancient authorities read, *That which my Father hath given unto me*.' Alford states that to be the reading of 'most of our ancient copies.' The three oldest MSS., however, give no hint of that reading; yet Tischendorf adopted it, the alteration being included among the 'errata.' The passage as it thus stands harmonises with the preceding idea : 'That which my Father hath given unto me is greater than all'; the guidance and safe-keeping of the sheep entrusted to me are greater than all besides: the word *meizōn*, greater, judging from the 44 passages in which it occurs, does not denote 'stronger,' but *more important*. And the life which the Father gives through the Son, and desires to perpetuate, is beyond the reach of any adverse power : 'and no one is able to snatch out of the Father's hand.' Alford explains that the italicised word 'them' or 'aught' is 'not in the original.' Then Jesus added : 'I and the Father are one.' Alford explains : 'Notice, *One* is *neuter* in gender, not masculine : the Father and the Son are not *personally* one, but *essentially*.' The meaning of the expression is clear from its use elsewhere by Jesus. 'Holy Father, keep them in thy name which thou hast given me, that they may be one, even as we are.' Again : 'That they may be one, even as we *are* one ; I in them, and thou in me, that they may be perfected into one.' The unity existing among Christians is spoken of in the same breath and as being of the same character, with that existing between Jesus and his Father. Yet so incensed and scandalised were the Jews by this saying of Jesus, that they prepared to stone him. 'The Jews took up stones again to stone him.' Not on the impulse of the moment, as though first one had stooped down to lift a stone, and then another had followed his example. Tischendorf brings out the deliberateness of the purpose by rendering, 'The Jews again bore stones to stone him.' In the 26 other instances in which the verb *bastazō*, here rendered 'take up,' occurs, it is translated in the A. V. 'bear' or 'carry.' It was a moment of grave peril. Jesus could not fail to perceive their design, and he calmly expostulated with them. 'Jesus answered them, Many good works have I shewed you from the Father ; for which of those works do ye stone me ?' They replied that it was not for any of his works, but for his words : that has ever been the cry of persecutors. 'The Jews answered him, For a good work we stone thee not, but for blasphemy.' Young, here and elsewhere, renders the word 'blasphemy' by 'evil speaking.' They added : 'and because that thou, being a man, makest thyself God.' Their idea is still current, and prevails : that the term 'God' is necessarily restricted to the one Supreme Being. Jesus repudiated that idea. He reminded them that in Scripture the title was used in a much wider sense, and had been applied, under revelation from God himself, to certain of mankind. 'Jesus answered them, Is it not written in your law, I said, Ye are gods ?' The reference is evidently to one of the Psalms of Asaph :

> 'God standeth in the congregation of God ;
> He judgeth among the gods.
> How long will ye judge unjustly.
> And respect the persons of the wicked ?
> I said, Ye are gods,
> And all of you sons of the Most High.
> Nevertheless ye shall die like men,
> And fall like one of the princes.
> Arise, O God, judge the earth.'

Alford observes : 'The Psalm is directed against the injustice and tyranny of judges (not the *Gentile rulers* of the world, nor, the *angels*) in Israel. And in the Psalm reference is made by *I have said* to previous places in Scripture where judges are so called, viz. Exod. xxi. 6; xxii. 9, 28.' The passages here referred to stand in Young's version as follows: 'Then hath his lord brought him nigh unto God.' 'Unto God cometh the matter of them both; he whom God doth condemn he repayeth double to his neighbour.' 'God thou dost not revile, and the prince among thy people thou dost not curse.' In the Authorised Version these passages stand: 'Then his master shall bring him unto the judges.' 'The cause of both parties shall come before the judges; *and* whom the judges shall condemn, he shall pay double unto his neighbour.' 'Thou shalt not revile the gods (or, judges), nor curse the ruler of thy people.' Evidently the translators deemed the term 'god' synonymous with 'judge,' and did not scruple on occasion so to render it. The Revisers have followed Young by inserting 'God' in the text, and the Authorised Version by putting 'judges' in the margin. On this obvious and undeniable application of the word 'God' in the Scriptures, Jesus founded an argument. 'If he called them gods, unto whom the word of God came (and the scripture cannot be broken), say ye of him, whom the Father sanctified (or, consecrated) and sent into the world, Thou blasphemest; because I said, I am *the* Son of God?' Jesus admits that he had claimed the title, not of 'God,' but of 'Son of God.' In the true, old, recognised Scriptural sense of the word, there was nothing to forbid the application to himself of the title 'God'; he could not disclaim it, but he claimed it only as bestowed and derivative, as one consecrated by the Father and sent into the world, as being Son of God. Jesus was willing that his assumptions should be brought to the test of fact. Did he, or did he not exercise powers which, being superhuman, stamped themselves as God-given, divine? 'If I do not the works of my Father, believe me not.' It were enough to make them the sole criterion of judgment. Let his own assertions about himself be set aside, let his teachings and his miracles be regarded by themselves: they proved sufficiently their character and origin, 'But if I do them, though ye believe not me, believe the works: that ye may know and understand that the Father is in me, and I in the Father.' The Authorised Version has: 'that ye may know and believe;' the Revisers have followed the Vatican MS. by putting 'understand' for 'believe.' The last word, 'Father,' stands in the Authorised Version 'him,' which has been altered on the authority of the two oldest MSS.

The argument of Jesus could not be refuted, but in spite of it, and of his appeal in connection with it, an attempt was made to apprehend him. If they could not venture to stone him uncondemned, they were anxious at least to put him on his trial for blasphemy. 'They sought again to take him.' The Authorised Version adds: 'But he escaped out of their hand.' Instead of 'escaped,' Alford renders 'passed,' and Young 'went forth.' The latter is adopted by Tischendorf and the Revisers. 'And he went forth out of their hand.' The expression 'out of their hand' indicates the imminence of the peril, if not an actual 'escape.'

Jesus retired for safety to the other side of the river Jordan, and chose as his abode the place where the Baptist had commenced his ministry. 'And he went away again beyond Jordan into the place where John was at first baptizing; and there he abode.' There hearers flocked to him. The memory of the Baptist's work was still fresh, and comparison was naturally made between Jesus and his forerunner. Miracles were now witnessed which John never attempted, and all that he had foretold of Jesus was admitted to be fully realised. 'And many came unto him; and they said, John indeed did no sign: but all things whatsoever John spake of this man were true.' The result was a large accession, if not of disciples, at least of convinced listeners and beholders. 'And many believed on him there.'

While Jesus was engaged in that safer and more encouraging field of labour, the brother of the two ladies who had formerly shown him hospitality was attacked by illness. 'Now a certain man was sick, Lazarus of Bethany, of the village of Mary and her sister Martha.' The evangelist, or a subsequent compiler, has here thrown in an observation which anticipates a later incident in the narrative. 'And it was that Mary which anointed the Lord with ointment, and wiped his feet with her hair, whose brother Lazarus was sick.' The sisters sent a special message to Jesus acquainting him with the fact. The wording of the message indicates that Jesus had formed a close intimacy and friendship with Lazarus. 'The sisters therefore sent unto him, saying, Lord (Sir—Young), behold, he whom thou lovest is sick.' On receiving the news, Jesus remarked that the illness would not be fatal, but would redound to the glory of God, and of himself as the Son of God. 'But when Jesus heard it, he said, This sickness is not unto death, but for the glory of God, that the Son of God may be glorified thereby.' We have already seen that Jesus claimed that title. The evangelist explains that the whole family was very dear to Jesus. 'Now Jesus loved Martha, and her sister, and Lazarus.' Two days passed before he gave any indication of his intention to respond to the call of the sisters. 'When therefore he heard that he was sick, he abode at that time two days in the place where he was.' Then he startled his disciples by proposing that they should revisit Judæa. 'Then after this he saith to the disciples, Let us go into Judæa again.' The suggestion filled them with consternation; they trembled for his safety, reminded him that his life had been but lately put in peril there, and expressed astonishment at his design. 'The disciples say unto him, Rabbi, the Jews were but now seeking to stone thee: and goest thou thither again?' The reply of Jesus indicated that there was nothing rash or hazardous in the step he proposed to take. He had due regard to time and opportunity. When the night of persecution had settled down upon him, during which he had felt that there was no work possible for him in Jerusalem except under conditions of danger and anxiety which it would have been unwise to face, he had remained quiescent. Now it was again day: there was light in him and around him, and he could see his course straight and clear before him. 'Jesus answered, Are there not twelve hours in the day? If a man walk in the day, he stumbleth not, because he seeth the light of this world. But if a man walk in the night, he stumbleth, because the light is not in him.' That assurance of Jesus gave them no clue to the purpose which was in his mind; but presently he disclosed to them the fact that his journey was undertaken on account of their common friend Lazarus. 'These things spake he: and after this he saith unto them, Our friend Lazarus is fallen asleep; but I go, that I may awake him out of sleep.' The saying sounded enigmatical. The disciples construed the mention of sleep in connection with the idea of repose, as an augury of speedy recovery. 'The disciples therefore said unto him, Lord (Sir—Young), if he is fallen asleep he will recover (Gr. be saved).' Young and Tischendorf adopt the Greek expression 'be saved.' The Authorised Version has instead, 'do well,' which is altered by the Revisers and Alford to 'recover.' If the Greek form, 'be saved,' had been adhered to here and wherever else it occurs, the word 'salvation' would probably never have been so restricted and perverted in meaning as it is now in its popular acceptation.

The disciples had not grasped the meaning of Jesus, nor was it possible for them to do so without clear explanation. 'Now Jesus had spoken of his death: but they thought that he spake of taking rest in sleep.' Jesus now spoke in plainest terms. 'Then Jesus therefore said unto them plainly, Lazarus is dead.' Here is, apparently, another instance of supernatural perception on the part of Jesus. We can venture no positive opinion as to how such knowledge was arrived at, whether by intuition or by direct revelation from superior Beings, through visions, as is recorded to have been the case with Zacharias, the mother of Jesus, and the shepherds, or through dreams, as in the case of the Magi and of Joseph the husband of Mary. Not only was Jesus assured of the death of Lazarus, but he rejoiced that he himself had been away during the illness and at the final crisis. 'And I am glad for your sakes that I was not there.' That circumstance, instead of being regrettable, would prove a means of confirming their confidence in Jesus, for he added: 'to the intent ye may believe.' Notwithstanding the fact that Lazarus was already dead, probably even buried, Jesus proposed that he and his disciples should visit him! 'Nevertheless let us go unto him.' To make the journey at that time, with his disciples about him, seemed like courting death; yet one of them used his influence with the rest to persuade them all to comply with the desire of Jesus: rather than refuse to do so, leaving him to carry out his intention alone, let them be ready to face death out of loyalty to him and in companionship with him. 'Thomas therefore, who is called Didymus (that is, Twin), said unto his fellow-disciples, Let us also go, that we may die with him.' Alford explains: 'The meaning of *Thomas*, in the Aramaic, which was the dialect of the country, is the same as that of the Latin *Didymus*, viz., a *twin*.'

On reaching their destination it was ascertained that the burial of Lazarus had taken place four days previously. 'So when Jesus came, he found that he had been in the tomb four days already.' The wording of this would lead to the inference that Jesus himself made enquiry as to the time, and must therefore have been ignorant of it exactly. But this does not follow from Young's literal rendering: 'Jesus therefore having come, found him four days already in the tomb.' Not only was Jesus now close to Jerusalem, but his arrival must necessarily soon be known to his enemies, many of the Jews having come to condole with the bereaved sisters. 'Now Bethany was nigh unto Jerusalem, about fifteen furlongs off; and many of the Jews had come to Martha and Mary, to console them concerning their brother.' The approach of Jesus was notified to Martha, who went out to meet him, leaving her sister seated in the house. 'Martha therefore, when she heard that Jesus was coming, went and met him: but Mary still sat in the house.' The rendering of Young, 'but Mary kept sitting in the house,' and of Tischendorf, 'but Mary continued sitting in the house,' may be taken to denote a deliberate purpose. Consider the circumstances. Jesus had but lately fled from Jerusalem. The sisters, when their brother was overtaken by illness, could not venture to ask that Jesus should again expose himself to danger by returning: they simply acquainted him with the fact, 'He whom thou lovest is sick.' When they found that Jesus had dared everything for their sake, their first impulse would naturally be to conceal, if possible, his coming: Martha must go quietly to meet him, whilst Mary kept at home, giving no indication of the proximity of Jesus. In her greeting of Jesus, Martha's regret at his absence burst forth unchecked. 'Martha therefore said unto Jesus, Lord (Sir—Young), if thou hadst been here, my brother had not died.' The cruel persecutors of Jesus had indirectly brought about the death of Lazarus. Yet Martha's faith in the power of Jesus was still unshaken, although her brother had passed away while he was not at hand to save. 'And even now I know that, whatsoever thou shalt ask of God, God will give thee.' Jesus replied in one pregnant sentence. 'Jesus saith unto her, Thy brother shall rise again.' Martha perceived no specific promise in the assurance, but took it simply as a confirmation of her faith in an ultimate resurrection. 'Martha said unto him, I know that he shall rise again in the resurrection at the last day,' rendered by Young with tautological exactness, 'I know that he will rise again, in the rising again at the last day.' Whether consciously or unconsciously Martha here laid hold upon a doctrine and form of expression which had been previously enunciated by Jesus in the words, 'I will raise him up at the last day.' Did she grasp the true import of the saying? Did she understand 'the last day' to apply to some far distant day when there would come to pass a simultaneous resurrection of all mankind? If so, her notions were about on a par with those still generally prevalent, their crudeness, strangeness, inconceivableness, covered over and made up for by a verbal positiveness of assertion miscalled 'faith.' It is a very easy thing to take up the words of the Athanasian Creed: 'At whose coming all men shall rise again with their bodies:' multitudes who have never given five minutes' consecutive thought to the subject have been wont to repeat them glibly, as with a sacred unction, and as though they held a truth clear as the noonday sun, and a hope sufficient to live and die by. 'I know,' said Martha, but it is a matter on which none of us have knowledge. The words of our divine Teacher need to be pondered deeply, reverentially, with all humility, and apart from the dogmas which have grown up round them. Jesus did not endorse Martha's unfaltering declaration, but proceeded to put the subject in his own way. Resurrection and life were his indwelling attributes. 'Jesus said unto her, I am the resurrection and the life.' And those attributes would be possessed by all his followers. 'He that believeth on me, though he die, yet shall he live: and whosoever liveth and believeth on me shall never die.' We cannot be too careful to get at the true sense of these words. The Authorised Version has: 'He that believeth in me, though he were dead, yet shall he live.' Tischendorf renders: 'though he die, yet will he live.' Young: 'even if he may die, shall live:' Alford: 'though he have died, yet shall he live:' Samuel Sharpe: 'even though he die, will live:' the 'Englishman's Greek New Testament': 'though he die, he shall live.' By using 'will' instead of 'shall,' Tischendorf and Sharpe obviate the idea of a special exercise of power in the case of every believer: Jesus asserts simply what 'will' happen,—the divinely-appointed law of resurrection from death. His promise is not completed by this utterance: having before us but one sentence, the two members of which are connected by the word 'and,' we must not divide the saying into two sentences, as though Jesus gave two separate promises. Resurrection and life were his, and would also be the lot of his followers,—the life, that is, which follows upon resurrection, there being obviously no reference to the life which precedes it : 'and whosoever liveth and believeth on me shall never die.' Tischendorf renders: 'shall never die;' Alford: 'shall not die for evermore:' the 'Englishman's Greek New Testament': 'in no wise shall die for ever:' Sharpe: 'will not die till the end of the age.' The entire passage in Young's version is as follows: 'He who is believing in me, even if he may die, shall live; and no one who is living and believing in me shall die unto the age.' To make the sense clear, Young renders *pas . . . ou mē apothanēi* = 'every-one . . . in no wise shall die,' by 'no one . . . shall die.' In other respects his translation is strictly literal : *eis ton aiōna* is undoubtedly 'unto the age,' *eis* signifying, in connection with time, 'until' or 'up to.' The life is 'age-during,' not endless: its term will be fixed by the constitution of our nature, by the decree of God, and Jesus assures us that, we being under his guidance, it will not be cut short as in the case of the life inherited from Adam. This promise of Jesus may be regarded under two aspects. It seems to be generally assumed that the life here spoken of is an arbitrary gift, to be bestowed or withheld by Jesus according to the possession or non-possession of faith in him. This is to individualise and narrow the promise, instead of to generalise and broaden it: the gift thus becomes in each case a miraculous endowment, an exercise of super-natural power. But why should the declaration of Jesus be taken in that sense? He does but unfold the divine will and purposes. He steps forth as the leader, the prince, the Messiah of mankind, discloses the fact of human resurrection, and assures to believers in him the prolongation to its utmost limit of the life which lies beyond. If we ask—How? surely it must be by his guiding and protective influence, by regulating the lives of his followers, and bringing them into harmony with the laws of God, of nature and of society. That is the aspect under which Jesus himself has presented the matter. 'My sheep hear my voice, and I know them, and they follow me: and (Young) life age-during I give to them, and they shall not perish—to the age, and no one shall pluck them out of my hand.' A promise going beyond this was once given by Jesus, when he said, 'This is the will of Him who sent me, that every one who is beholding the Son, and believing in him, may have life age-during, and I will raise him up in the last day.' Taking those words in the order in which they stand, the resurrection 'in the last day' by the power of Jesus, is subsequent to the 'life age-during:' a second resurrection is here foretold. But in the discourse with Martha, it was she, not Jesus, who spoke about Lazarus rising again 'in the resurrection at the last day.' Jesus called her mind away from that high mystery; enough for her to be assured of the lower doctrine of an age-during life beyond the grave, and her positive 'I know' must take the simpler form of 'I believe:' 'Believest thou this?' was the enquiry with which Jesus closed. The reply of Martha indicated rather a confidence in his words than a full comprehension of them. 'She saith unto him, Yea, Lord (Sir—Young): I have believed that thou art the Christ, the Son of God, *even* he that cometh into the world.' Alford quotes Enthymius as follows: 'That He spoke great things about Himself she knew: but in what sense He spoke them, she did not know: and therefore when asked one thing, she replies another.'

Martha now hastened to inform her sister of the arrival of Jesus, and of the fact that he had expressed a wish to see her. But she did this warily, doubtless out of regard to his safety, knowing that his enemies were round about. 'And when she had said this, she went away, and called Mary her sister secretly, saying (or, her sister, saying secretly), The Master (or, Teacher) is here, and calleth thee.' This is quite consistent with the previous notification to Mary of the approach of Jesus. Martha had gone to meet him on the first news of his coming, and now not only confirms the report but announces that he is actually at hand. Young renders: 'The Teacher is present, and calleth for thee.' Not an instant did Mary lose in obeying the call. 'And she, when she heard it, arose quickly, and went unto him.' Even then Jesus had not reached the village, having remained outside it in the place whither Martha had hastened to meet him. '(Now Jesus was not yet come into the village, but was still in the place where Martha met him).' Everything indicates the caution and secrecy which naturally sprang out of their anxiety for the safety of Jesus. But the precautions taken did not avail. The hasty departure of Mary was noticed by the Jews, who were acting the part of comforters: they guessed that she had gone to the grave, there to indulge in an outburst of grief, and therefore they resolved to follow her. 'The Jews then which were with her in the house, and were comforting her, when they saw Mary, that she rose up quickly and went out, followed her, supposing that she was going unto the tomb to weep (Gr. wail) there.' Their notion of comfort in bereavement appears to have been the very opposite of ours. We are accustomed to repress, assuage, check, reprove even, any violent demonstration of grief; but the Jewish habit was to weep with them that wept, minstrels being engaged to add their sorrowful melodies to the lamentations of the mourners.

When Mary reached the presence of Jesus she fell prostrate at his feet,—it may have been as a mark of reverence, or that her faltering strength could no longer uphold her. The only words she could find were those with which Martha had first greeted him, and which must have formed the burden of the two sisters' reflections throughout the last few days. 'Mary therefore, when she came where Jesus was, and saw him, fell down at his feet, saying unto him, Lord (Sir—Young) if thou hadst been here, my brother had not died.' It was a trying scene, and its effect upon Jesus was very marked and peculiar. 'When Jesus therefore saw her weeping (Gr. wailing), and the Jews *also* weeping (Gr. wailing) which came with her, he groaned in the spirit (or, was moved with indignation in the spirit), and was troubled (Gr. troubled himself), and said, Where have ye laid him?' Alford explains: 'The word rendered by the A. V. *groaned* can bear but one meaning,—the expression of *indignation* and *rebuke, not of sorrow*. This has been acknowledged by all the expositors who have paid any attention to the usage of the word.' It is clear therefore that the marginal reading introduced by the Revisers must be adopted as correct, 'was moved with indignation in the spirit.' Alford modifies his own assertion of 'indignation' and 'rebuke' by saying, 'I think the meaning to be, that Jesus, with the tears of sympathy already rising and overcoming His speech, *checked them, so as to be able to speak the words following* . . . Thus Bengel: "Jesus for the present austerely repressed his tears."' That conjecture is not satisfactory, and does not seem to meet the case : the mere repression of emotion is not to be confounded with indignation or rebuke. The intense, heartfelt wail of Mary, and the conventional, perfunctory, hypocritical wail of the Jews were well calculated to arouse opposite feelings in the breast of Jesus. Alford admits : 'Meyer's explanation deserves mention : that our Lord was indignant at seeing the Jews, his bitter enemies, mingling their hypocritical tears with the true ones of the bereaved sisters.' That was like Jesus, and worthy of him. Nothing ever stirred his indignation so much as hypocrisy, whether conscious or unconscious, or so repeatedly drew forth the expression of his measureless abhorrence. In reply to his question, 'Where have ye laid him?' 'They say unto him, Lord (Sir—Young), come and see.' The trouble which had manifested itself in the demeanour of Jesus now reached its climax, and found vent in an outburst of tears. 'Jesus wept.' Even on the way to the grave the Jews could not abstain from criticism of Jesus. 'The Jews therefore said, Behold how he loved him! But some of them said, Could not this man, which opened the eyes of him that was blind, have caused that this man also should not die?' At these uncalled for and unseemly comments, the signs of unspoken, repressed, indignation again showed themselves in Jesus. 'Jesus therefore again groaning in himself (or, being moved with indignation in himself) cometh to the tomb.' It was a cave, and against the entrance, which was probably horizontal (Alford), a stone had been placed. 'Now it was a cave, and a stone lay against (or, upon) it.' Jesus requested that the stone might be removed. 'Jesus saith, Take ye away the stone.' Martha, always impulsive and foremost, ventured to expostulate. Four days having passed, the work of corruption must have set in. 'Martha, the sister of him that was dead, saith unto him, Lord (Sir—Young), by this time he stinketh : for he hath been *dead* four days.' Tischendorf and Young do not insert the italicised word 'dead.' The former has : 'he is four days gone ;' the latter, literally, 'it is four days.' Jesus reminded Martha of an assurance he had previously given her. It was for him to act, and for her to have confidence in him. 'Jesus [11 John 40] saith unto her, Said I not unto thee, that, if thou believedst, thou shouldest see the glory of God?' Then the request of Jesus was complied with. 'So they took away the stone.' The revisers and [41] Tischendorf, following the two oldest MSS., have omitted, 'from the place where the dead was laid.' How strange and solemn must have been the scene! What an awe-struck hush of wonder and expectation, while Jesus stood before the opened tomb! Turning his eyes heavenwards, he lifted up his voice in thanksgiving. 'And Jesus lifted up [41, 42] his eyes, and said, Father, I thank thee that thou heardest me.' Alford notes: '*When* he prayed, does not appear. Probably in Peræa, before the declaration in verse 4.' Having uttered those few words to his heavenly Father, Jesus instantly expressed his reason for doing so. Neither the prayer nor the hearing were exceptional. 'And I knew that thou hearest me always.' But for the sake of all [42] now standing about him, that they might be convinced of his divine mission, Jesus had prefaced the miracle he was about to perform by this reverential acknowledgment of the divine power vouchsafed to him: 'but because of the multitude which standeth around I said it, [42] that they may believe that thou didst send me.' Then, raising his voice, so that it rang out sharp and clear enough to pierce into the cave and rouse one simply sleeping there, Jesus commanded Lazarus to come forth. 'And when he had thus spoken, he cried with a loud [43] voice, Lazarus, come forth.' What a word was that! And what a marvel followed on its utterance! The body of the dead and buried man was seen to issue from the tomb, not free and unimpeded, but the hands and feet still circled with their bandages, and the face with the napkin which had been wrapped round it. 'He that was dead [44] (*literally*, had been dead) came forth, bound hand and foot with grave-clothes (or, grave-bands); and his face was bound about with a napkin.' Alford notes: 'The word rendered *grave-clothes* is explained to mean a sort of band of rush or tow, used to swathe infants, and to bind up the dead. It does not appear whether the bands were wound about each limb, as in the Egyptian mummies, so as merely to *impede* motion,—or were loosely wrapped round both feet and both hands, so as to hinder any free movement altogether. The latter seems most probable, and has been supposed by many. Basil speaks of the *bound man coming forth* from the sepulchre, as *a miracle in a miracle*: and ancient pictures represent Lazarus gliding forth from the tomb, not stepping: which apparently is right. The napkin, or handkerchief, appears to have tied up his chin.' As the awe-struck beholders gazed upon the apparition, the voice of Jesus was again heard. 'Jesus saith unto them, Loose him, and let [44] him go.'

The evangelist makes not a word of comment on this astounding miracle. Jesus himself alluded to it as 'the glory of God,' and as [40] 'for the glory of God, that the Son of God may be glorified thereby.' [4] The evolvement and manifestation of life, the triumph over death, the arrest of decay, the reorganisation of materialism,—we can conceive no higher powers of Deity. Life, Rulership: these constitute the very essence of the true idea of GOD. What does the miracle of the resurrection of Lazarus amount to? His earthly life had closed. Had he then ceased to be? In the ordinary course of nature his body could never again become reanimated, but would have turned to earth. No Lazarus would then have walked visibly again among men, known and recognised of them. Jesus called his death a sleep, but that was foreseeing what would happen, knowing that he would 'awake him out of sleep.' Yet he literally and really died : 'Jesus therefore said unto them plainly, Lazarus is dead.' Nevertheless there still existed a Lazarus to whom Jesus lifted up his voice and cried aloud, 'Come forth.' That was a true call : it would not have been uttered without need or reason. How Jesus shrank from useless words was shown the very instant previously, when he explained his thanksgiving to have been spoken for the sake of those standing by. That Lazarus was there, within reach of the voice, we may be sure. How he came to be there, must remain a mystery : as also whether in the same body, or in some other invisible form, or altogether formless. We know nothing about the 'disembodied spirit,' of which men sometimes speak as a matter of course. There were, in fact, two miracles : the bringing back of Lazarus to the living, and the snatching of him from the dead. In order that the earthly life might be renewed, the continuity of the heavenly life was broken. The appointed mode of existence after death was interfered with equally, whether we suppose the 'unclothed' soul of Lazarus to have been restored to his former body, or his 'spiritual body' to have been forsaken, dissolved, or merged, when his fleshly tabernacle was re-entered and reanimated.

'When Lazarus left his charnel-cave,
And home to Mary's house return'd,
Was this demanded—if he yearn'd
To hear her weeping by his grave?

'"Where wert thou, brother, those four days?"
There lives no record of reply,
Which telling what it is to die,
Had surely added praise to praise.

'From every house the neighbours met,
The streets were filled with joyful sound,
A solemn gladness even crown'd
The purple brows of Olivet.

'Behold a man raised up by Christ!
The rest remaineth unreveal'd ;
He told it not ; or something seal'd
The lips of that Evangelist.' *

'Where wert thou, brother, those four days?' is a question to which our existence in this world forbids the answer. 'Except a man be born of water and the Spirit, he cannot enter into the kingdom of God.' 'Flesh and blood cannot inherit the kingdom of God.' The new life demands a new incarnation. The faith of the apostle Paul enabled him to grasp and elucidate this mystery. 'For we know that if the earthly house of our tabernacle (or, bodily frame) be dissolved, we have a building from God, a house not made with

* Tennyson's "In Memoriam."

hands, eternal (age-during—Young), in the heavens. For verily in this we groan, longing to be clothed upon with our habitation which is from heaven : if so be that being clothed we shall not be found naked.' The resurrection of Lazarus had been foreseen by Jesus, and we make no visionary supposition in assuming that invisible agents had anticipated and arranged with respect to it, as about the birth of Jesus and his own uprising from the tomb. The idea of Martha that putrefaction must necessarily have set in, may have been contrary to the fact, it being more reasonable to believe that the body was preserved from decay, than that all traces of it were instantaneously and miraculously obliterated. Nor is it fanciful to bear in mind the fact that the performance of the miracle had been intentionally timed by Jesus. He had deliberately delayed his departure ,, John 6 two days : it was no mere chance that he arrived when three full days had elapsed since the decease. There must have been some reason, hidden from us, why Jesus, whenever he foretold his own resurrection, prognosticated that it would happen 'after three days,' some occult reason why it did take place after that interval. The second birth, like the first birth, must have its appointed sequences and period ; there must be a graduated development into the heavenly life, as there was into the earthly life ; the incarnation of ' water and spirit ' is doubtless as natural a process as the incarnation of 'flesh and blood.' The knowledge of Jesus with respect to these matters was more than human ; the laws of life and death were within his cognizance ; he knew when and how to seize the right moment for the working of his power; he could call back at once the soul of the damsel newly-departed, but in the case of Lazarus he saw fit to delay three days, and he was aware from the first that the same lapse of time would have to occur in the resurrection of himself. These facts are neither arbitrary nor meaningless, and we do well to ponder the hints afforded us with respect to the extension and perpetuation in supermundane matters of that regularity and spontaneity in the laws of growth and change which prevail throughout the only world with which we are as yet familiar.

On many of the Jews who beheld the miracle its effect was immediate and unmistakable : they could not but express their faith in Jesus. 'Many therefore of the Jews, which came to Mary and ,, 45 beheld that which he did, believed in him.' The Revisers have followed the Vatican and Alexandrine MSS., by inserting 'that which' instead of 'the things which,' but Tischendorf retains the latter, which is the reading of the oldest MS., the Sinaitic.

Reports of the miracle could not fail to be carried to the enemies of Jesus. 'But some of them went away to the Pharisees, and told ,, 46 them the things which Jesus had done.' Alford observes : 'We must take care rightly to understand this. In the last verse, it is not *many of the Jews which had come*, but *many of the Jews*, viz., *those which had come*, "many .... to wit .... *these that came*." All these believed on Him. Then *some of them*, viz., of those which had come, and believed, went, &c.' Alford adds : 'The evangelist is very simple, and at the same time very consistent, in his use of *particles :* almost throughout his Gospel, the great subject, the manifestation of the Glory of Christ, is carried onward by 'then,' or 'therefore,' whereas 'but' as generally prefaces the development of the antagonist manifestation of hatred and rejection of him.' Without undervaluing the importance of such minute criticisms, Alford seems to carry his deduction too far where he says: 'The *but* certainly shews that this was done with a hostile intent.' We may consider the 'but' to refer to the result, not to the intent; this will still agree with Alford's note on verse 27: 'St. John seldom uses *but* as a mere copula, but generally as expressing a contrast.' On receiving an account of the miracle, the Jewish rulers called a council to consider what steps they should take with respect to Jesus and his works. 'The chief priests therefore and the Pharisees gathered a council, and said, What do we? for this man doeth many signs.' The growing influence of Jesus must be counteracted in some way. But why? What was to be dreaded from it? This was their argument, their ground of action. 'If we leave him thus alone, all men will believe on him: and the Romans will come and take away both our place and our nation.' Luther renders the closing words 'Land und Leute,' 'land and people.' Could any idea be more visionary, more baseless, more utterly contrary to the fact? The doctrine of Jesus was for the salvation of the people. We know that to its rejection he attributed the woe and destruction which impended over Jerusalem. 'He saw the city and wept over it, saying, If thou hadst known in this thy day, even thou, the things which belong unto peace! but now they are hid from thine eyes. For the days shall come upon thee, when thine enemies shall cast up a bank about thee, and compass thee round, and keep thee in on every side, and shall dash thee to the ground, and thy children within thee; and they shall not leave in thee one stone upon another: because thou knewest not the time of thy visitation.' Jesus foresaw the very same evils which were apprehended by these Jewish rulers, but he and they attributed them to precisely opposite causes. They dreaded any radical change, any interference with the existing order of things, any Reform which was not inaugurated and directed by themselves. Alford observes: 'The word *our* (our place and nation) is emphatic, detecting the real cause of their anxiety. Respecting this man's pretensions, they do not pretend to decide: all they know is that if he is to go on thus, their standing is gone.' One of them, and he the most eminent, disparaged the opinion which had been expressed, which was not founded upon any actual knowledge. 'But a certain one of them, Caiaphas, being high priest that year, said unto them, Ye know nothing at all.' And in speculating on contingencies and probabilities, they overlooked the fact that it would be better the Romans should find one popular leader whom they could hold responsible and put to death, than that the whole nation should be visited with the consequences of rebellion. Apart from any subsequent explanation, that might seem to be the import of the words: 'nor do ye take account that it is expedient for you that one man should die for the people, and that the whole nation perish not.' The Authorised Version has 'for us,' which is altered by the Revisers and Tischendorf into 'for you,' agreeing with the Vatican MS. The Sinaitic MS. omits both words. But the evangelist, or the compiler, has inserted an explanation, which places the passage outside the rules of ordinary interpretation. 'Now this he said not of himself: but being high priest that year, he prophesied.' . . . The words 'not of himself,' imply some influence over-ruling the speaker. Alford observes : ' There certainly was a belief, probably arising originally from the use of the Urim and Thummim, that the High Priest, and indeed every priest, had some knowledge of dreams and utterance of prophecy. Philo the Jew says, "A true priest is *ipso facto* a prophet." That this belief existed, may account for the expression here ; which however does not confirm it in all cases, but asserts the fact that the Spirit *in this case* made use of him as High Priest, for this purpose.' The prophecy of Caiaphas is thus described : 'that Jesus should die for the nation ; and not for the nation only, but that he might also gather together into one the children of God that are scattered abroad.' The word 'prophecy' does not necessarily denote the foretelling of future events, but may stand for any kind of high spiritual teaching. It is not stated that Caiaphas delivered his prophecy before the council : it seems rather to be implied that in his official capacity as high priest he had broached the doctrine that the death of Jesus would be for the welfare of the nation, and would lead to the unification of the dispersed Israelites. 'This said he not of himself :' the deep meaning of his saying was hidden from him, and the evangelist, or the compiler, elucidates it for us. The opinion expressed by Caiaphas appears to have been regarded as a counsel, if not a justification of the death of Jesus, for the result is summed up thus : 'So from that day forth they took counsel that they might put him to death.'[11 John 51. 52]

An expression used in verses 49 and 51 of this chapter has led Mr. Matthew Arnold to express the following opinion.[*] 'Twice the fourth Gospel speaks of Caiaphas as "high-priest of that year," as if the Jewish high-priesthood had been at that time a yearly office, which it was not. It is a mistake a foreigner might perfectly well have made, but hardly a Jew. It is like talking of an American President as " President of that year," as if the American Presidency were a yearly office. An American could never adopt, one thinks, such a way of speaking.' The conclusion drawn by Mr. Matthew Arnold from this supposed error, is that the Gospel was not written by the Apostle John : ' St. John cannot have written it for the same reason that he cannot have . . . made the high-priesthood of Caiaphas a yearly office.' Let us examine this objection. Alford's note on the passage is as follows : ' In the words *that year*, there is no intimation conveyed that the High Priesthood was changed every year, which it was not : but we must understand the words as directing attention to *that* (remarkable) *year*, without any reference to time past or to come. *That year* of *great events* had Caiaphas as its High Priest.' That idea seems weak and forced, so we will reject it. Still it does not follow that the expression ' high priest that year,' which is the reading of the Revised Version, denotes a yearly change in the office : it may simply indicate that the change had occurred that year,—that Caiaphas had that year entered upon his term of office. But Mr. Arnold obviates that solution by introducing the word ' of : ' ' high-priest of that year.' And we are bound to admit that he is right, on the authority of Tischendorf and Young, both of whom insert the word ' of.' That being admitted, we can

---

[*] "God and the Bible. The fourth Gospel from Without."

now fairly raise and face the question. Does the writer of the Gospel show ignorance upon the point? Had he less knowledge about it than Mr. Arnold has? Before deciding in favour of the latter, we must refer to other allusions to the subject in John's Gospel. Its author, having previously stated that Caiaphas was 'high-priest of that year,' nevertheless tells us that when Jesus had been seized and bound, the officers of the Jews 'led him to Annas first.' And he explains their reason for doing so: 'for he was father-in-law to Caiaphas, which was high priest that year,' rendered again by Tischendorf and Young, 'high priest of that year.' The expression deemed so inapplicable is here for the third time repeated, but so far is the writer from being ignorant, that he shows the most minute knowledge of the subject, actually stating the relationship between the two men. Afterwards he tells us: 'Annas therefore sent him bound unto Caiaphas the high priest.' All this indicates a contemporaneous familiarity with the facts, which were not a little remarkable. Why should Jesus have been sent to Annas first? What could the father-in-law of the high priest have to do with the matter? By what right did Annas send back the prisoner bound? The evangelist did not care to explain. He could not anticipate that eighteen centuries later a scholarly critic would rise up, and argue that he did not understand what he was writing about. He told the circumstance simply and naturally, and what he stated has been confirmed and elucidated by another evangelist. Luke mentions, as a well-known historical fact, 'the high-priesthood of Annas and Caiaphas.' Obviously the office at that time was held conjointly, which was quite as much out of the ordinary course as that it should be yearly. What more likely than that the two high priests should have acted alternately, year by year? That simple and probable conjecture makes everything clear: Luke's narrative agrees with John's, and the deference shown to Annas, and his interference, Caiaphas nevertheless having to adjudicate, as well as the expression 'high priest of that year,'—all these things agree together and corroborate the accuracy and fulness of the writer's knowledge. The assumption of Mr. Matthew Arnold is as hasty as it is positive; however plausible at first sight, the tenor of the narrative is opposed to it.

In consequence of the determined hostility of the chief priests and Pharisees, Jesus again withdrew from open intercourse with the inhabitants of Judæa. He retired to a city in the country bordering the wilderness, and there continued with his disciples. 'Jesus therefore walked no more openly among the Jews, but departed thence into the country near to the wilderness, into a city called Ephraim; and there he tarried with the disciples.' The Authorised Version has 'his disciples,' which is now altered to 'the disciples,' to accord with the two oldest MSS.

The Sermon on the mount, as recorded in Matthew's narrative, is much fuller than in Luke's account of it; and among the portions contained in the former, but omitted from the latter, is the Lord's prayer. Luke introduces that subsequently, and he obviously refers to a different occasion, when the prayer was repeated by Jesus in an abridged form. 'And it came to pass as he was praying in a certain place, that when he ceased, one of his disciples said unto him, Lord (Sir—Young), teach us to pray, even as John also taught his disciples. And he said unto them, When ye pray, say ...' The closing doxology which stands in the Authorised Version of Matthew, is omitted by the Revisers, not being in the two oldest MSS., and it is not in Luke. Let us compare, clause by clause, the forms given by the two evangelists.

6 Matthew 9—13.	11 Luke 2—4.
(1) Our Father.	Father.
(2) Which art in heaven.	Omitted.
(3) Hallowed be thy name.	The same.
(4) Thy kingdom come.	The same.
(5) Thy will be done, as in heaven, so on earth.	Omitted.
(6) Give us this day our daily bread (Gr. our bread for the coming day).	Give us day by day our daily bread (Gr. our bread for the coming day).
(7) And forgive us our debts, as we also have forgiven our debtors.	And forgive us our sins; for we ourselves also forgive every one that is indebted to us.
(8) And bring us not into temptation.	The same.
(9) But deliver us from the evil one (or, evil).	Omitted.

Tischendorf agrees with the above Revised Version. To the clauses numbered 1, 2, 5 and 9, the Revisers attach in Luke the note, 'Many ancient authorities read,' &c., to correspond with Matthew. Alford considers that these clauses 'could hardly by any possibility have been *omitted* by any, had they ever formed a part of' Luke's text. He adds: 'The shorter form, found in the Vatican ... and in the recently published Sinaitic MS., was the original one: then the copyists inserted the clauses which were not found here, taking them from St. Matthew. That this, and not the converse process, must have been the one followed, is evident to any one who considers the matter. Stier's argument, that our text has not been conformed to Matthew, because the doxology has never been inserted here, seems to me to tend in quite another direction: the doxology was inserted *there*, because *that was the form in general liturgical use*, and *not here*, because *that was never used liturgically.*'

Consider the simplicity and brevity of the form of prayer bequeathed to us by Jesus. At its first delivery he connected with it a warning against all ostentation and 'vain repetitions' in prayer. He never broached the doctrine, so fondly held and zealously propagated by some, that prayer is to be regarded as a test of character, that God loves him best who prays best, or most, or always: that idea is as irrational as it would be to insist upon our children asking us constantly, repeatedly, as a matter of duty and privilege and of moral obligation, to watch over them and supply their wants. They are sure we shall do that, without the asking: their petitions are occasional only, and naturally and properly confined to those things of which they feel the want. What is prayer but the effort, either to bring the divine will into harmony with our will, or our will into harmony with the divine will? Whenever they are felt to coincide, there is no need of prayer. The higher our advancement towards perfection of character, the less our impulse towards prayer on our own account. It becomes transformed into praise, and that not of necessity verbal and formal, but deep-seated, the silent, reverential, adoring gratitude of a soul redeemed, at peace, and hopeful of futurity. The cry is no longer, 'I pray thee to hear me,' but, 'I thank thee that thou hast heard me;' and even that utterance is checked by the thought, 'I know that thou hearest me always.'

When the disciples asked Jesus to teach them to pray, he was content to refer them to the brief form he had previously delivered, and even that he further simplified and shortened. Nothing could be more condensed than this: 'Father, Hallowed be thy name. Thy kingdom come. Give us day by day our daily bread. And forgive us our sins; for we ourselves also forgive every one that is indebted to us. And bring us not into temptation.' The wants and aspirations of humanity summed up into those six petitions! There is our model. Are we content to copy it? Or do we prefer to amplify it, as though God could be better pleased with a stilted style and flowery language?

In the following parable Jesus represents prayer as the natural and necessary outcome of a sudden and unexpected emergency, and great as was the importunity he described, it was wholly unselfish, the intercession being on behalf of another. He supposed the case of a man venturing to trouble his friend, in the depth of night, not in consequence of any grave calamity, but merely for the purpose of borrowing a little bread. 'And he said unto them, Which of you shall have a friend, and shall go unto him at midnight, and say to him, Friend, lend me three loaves;' the sole justification for the request being that a traveller had unexpectedly arrived, and there was no food in the house: 'for a friend of mine is come from a journey, and I have nothing to set before him.' The applicant was met with expostulation and rebuff. Why should a person be disturbed at so unseemly an hour, and expected to get up and furnish a meal for the friend of his friend? He positively refused to be troubled with the matter; it was preposterous to ask him to get out of bed, and disturb his sleeping family, for such a purpose. 'And he from within shall answer and say, Trouble me not: the door is now shut, and my children are with me in bed; I cannot rise and give thee?' His friendship was not great enough for that. But necessity knows no law: the man outside continued knocking, asking, pestering him; the clamour could not be stopped, or endured; the trouble of repeatedly refusing was more than the trouble involved in complying: this persistent fellow must needs have what he wants; it will be better to give him anything, everything, for the sake of quiet and repose. 'I say unto you, Though he will not rise and give him because he is his friend, yet because of his importunity he will arise and give him as many (or, whatsoever things) he needeth.'

The harshness of colouring in this picture was undoubtedly intentional. There is nothing lovely or amiable about either of the men. The one was coldly indifferent, a friend in name, who shrank from the trouble entailed by a friendly action; the other was overbearing in purpose, rough, rude, bent on gaining his wish by sheer force of will. The very opposite of all that was to be attached to the true notion of prayer. Jesus here teaches not by similarity but by contrast. He knows nothing of unwillingness on the one side, or of importunity on the other. He teaches that to ask is to have, to seek is to obtain, to knock is to gain access. 'And I say unto you, Ask, and it shall be given you; seek, and ye shall find; knock, and it shall be opened unto you.' There is no restriction on the divine bounty, no favouritism on the part of God; he is the universal friend, whose ear is ever open, who is never weary of giving, and whose store is unlimited. None need ask him twice, and though often the eagerness of our desire impels us to beseech him thrice, it is not that his grace is insufficient, but that our faith is weak, or our self-will strong. Jesus repeats his assurance, and applies it without exception. 'For every one that asketh receiveth; and he that seeketh findeth; and to him that knocketh it shall be opened.' His way of putting the matter is opposed to the notion commonly entertained of Prayer. The general idea and definition of the word needs to be changed and broadened. It is not a mere asking: that is only one of its aspects; nor is it merely 'the soul's desire, uttered or unexpressed:' that is but the foundation on which it rests. It comprises asking, seeking, knocking: it is the human will in action, anxious and energetic in whatever direction may have been clearly prescribed by the divine will. Effort is as much a part of prayer as are words and wishes; let us not mistake the part for the whole. There are moments when our energies are exhausted, when we can no longer be seeking and knocking, and can only say, in sheer weariness and resignation, Father, not my will, but thine be done. Only the murmured wish is then within our power; but at other times, what we pray for we must seek for, or prayer degenerates into formalism and hypocrisy. Jesus insisted upon that truth in the very point where it might seem most difficult of application. We pray for forgiveness: what can we do towards it? Nay; even that is not to be divorced from our own free-will and effort. 'For if ye forgive men their trespasses, your heavenly Father will also forgive you. But if ye forgive not men their trespasses, neither will your Father forgive your trespasses.'

Prayer is the cry of a child to its father. That is its true and best illustration. The parental instinct forbids indifference. Callousness on the part of a father is inconceivable, contrary to nature. 'And of which of you that is a father shall his son ask a loaf, and he give him a stone? Or a fish, and he for a fish give him a serpent? Or if he shall ask an egg, will he give him a scorpion?' The son's request is supposed to be confined to necessary and wholesome food,— a loaf, a fish, an egg. That, and only that, will be supplied: nothing useless, nothing hurtful. However degraded the condition of mankind, the law prevails universally, that the knowledge and experience of the father will be used for the son's welfare. How much more, then, must that be the case with the heavenly Father? 'If ye, then, being evil, know how to give good gifts unto your children, how much more shall *your* heavenly Father give the Holy Spirit to them that ask him?' Alford notes that the italicised word 'your' is 'not expressed at all;' the literal translation is, 'the Father the from heaven.' Young renders: 'the Father who is from heaven;' Tischendorf, 'your Father from heaven.' Samuel Sharpe renders: 'How much more will the father from heaven give holy spirit to them that ask him.' It cannot be denied that translators, by beginning the two words 'holy' and 'spirit' with capital letters, have thereby conveyed to ordinary readers the idea of a Person. Even Dr. Young has followed suit in that respect. But where the words occur in the Old Testament the Revisers have not used capitals. 'Take not thy holy spirit from me.' 'They rebelled and grieved his holy spirit.' 'Where is he that put his holy spirit in the midst of them?' In the Authorised Version the passage from the Psalm agrees with the Revised Version; and in the other two verses a capital is used for the word 'Spirit' only; whereas in the three passages Young has deferred to 'orthodox' ideas by using capitals for both words. Why, unless for the same reason, do the Revisers always introduce capitals when the same words occur in the New Testament? To obtain an unprejudiced view of the matter, let us turn to a translation which was uninfluenced by the generally received doctrine of the Trinity. Samuel Sharpe agrees with the Revisers as to the three passages in the Old Testament, and, with some exceptions, adheres to the same plan throughout the New Testament. His exceptions are the following.

3 'With child of the Holy Spirit.' 3 'Is of the Holy Spirit.' 2 'Whosoever speaketh against the Holy Spirit.' 5 'He that shall blaspheme against the Holy Spirit.' 4 'Him that blasphemeth against the Holy Spirit.' 4 'The Holy Spirit will teach you.' 5 'The Comforter, the Holy Spirit.' 5 'Well spake the Holy Spirit through Isaiah.' 5 'As the Holy Spirit saith.' 5 'The Holy Spirit signifying this.' These ten passages are the only ones in which Sharpe introduces capitals. In those numbered 3 the original has *pneuma hagion*, 'spirit holy;' in those numbered 4, *to hagion pneuma*, 'the holy spirit;' in those numbered 5, *to pneuma to hagion*, 'the spirit the holy;' number 2, *to pneuma*, 'the spirit.'

In the following 28 passages Sharpe omits the article before 'holy spirit,' because all of them come under number 3 and are without an article in the original. 'In holy spirit and fire.' 'He will baptize you in holy spirit.' 'He will baptize you in holy spirit and fire.' 'He that baptizeth in holy spirit.' 'Ye will be baptized in holy spirit.' 'David himself in holy spirit, said.' 'Holy spirit will come upon thee.' 'Elisabeth was filled with holy spirit.' 'Zacharias was filled with holy spirit.' 'Jesus being full of holy spirit.' 'Give holy spirit to them that ask him.' 'They were all filled with holy spirit.' 'They were all filled with holy spirit.' 'Peter, filled with holy spirit.' 'A man full of faith and holy spirit.' 'Being full of holy spirit.' 'And be filled with holy spirit.' 'God anointed him with holy spirit and power.' 'Ye shall be baptized in holy spirit.' 'Full of holy spirit and faith.' 'Being filled with holy spirit.' 'Filled with joy and holy spirit.' 'Righteousness and peace, and joy with holy spirit.' 'In power, and in holy spirit and in much assurance.' 'With joy of holy spirit.' 'Gifts of holy spirit.' 'With holy spirit sent from heaven.' 'Praying with holy spirit.'

In the following two passages Sharpe inserts the indefinite article, although there is no article in the original. 'No man can say that [1 i. Cor. 3] Jesus is the Lord but by a holy spirit.' 'By a holy spirit.' In both [6 ii. Cor. 6] passages the Authorised Version, Young and Tischendorf insert the definite article and capitalise the words.

In the Authorised Version one passage stands: 'full of the Holy [6 Acts 3] Ghost and wisdom,' there being no article in the original. The Revisers have altered that to, 'full of the Spirit and of wisdom.' The Sinaitic MS. has, 'full of the spirit of wisdom,' and the translation from Tischendorf's critical text is, 'full of the spirit and wisdom.' The Revisers, by capitalising the word 'spirit,' convey the same meaning as 'Holy Ghost' has in the Authorised Version.

Here is a similar instance. The Authorised Version stands, 'which [2 i. Cor. 13] the Holy Ghost teacheth,' although there is no article in the original. The three oldest MSS. omit 'holy.' The Revisers capitalise the word 'spirit.' Sharpe agrees with Tischendorf: 'taught by the spirit.'

In the following passage the Revisers have capitalised the word 'spirit,' contrary to the Authorised Version, which stands: 'the [5 i. John 5] spirit, and the water, and the blood.' Tischendorf, Young and Sharpe adopt the small *s* in spirit.

In the following passage Sharpe agrees with the Revisers in capitalising the word 'Spirit.' 'The blasphemy against the Spirit shall not [12 Mat. 31] be forgiven.'

The last passage which needs to be referred to is: 'And the Holy [10 Heb. 15] Ghost also beareth witness to us,' which is rendered by Sharpe, 'And the Spirit also witnesseth for us:' he capitalises the word 'Spirit,' but there is nothing to indicate why he omits the word 'holy.'

There are 50 other passages in addition to the foregoing, in which the words 'holy spirit' occur, in all of which Sharpe has discarded capitals.

It must be admitted that he is not altogether consistent. Probably he could have given reasons, more or less satisfactory, for the 10 instances in which he has followed the plan adopted throughout by other translators. But the explanation is not forthcoming, and one is certainly required. If, however, we are unable to see why he in those exceptional cases capitalises the words, how much less can the justification be imagined for doing so in every case! The habit indicates a foregone conclusion, a settled doctrine, just as much as the writing of the word 'God' with a capital denotes the supreme Being: when that is not signified by the translators they omit the capital, which is done in a multitude of passages, notably in the following: 'For though there be that are called gods, whether in [8 i. Cor. 5, 6] heaven or on earth: as there are gods many, and lords many: yet to us there is one God, the Father, of whom are all things, and we unto him, and one Lord, Jesus Christ, through whom are all things, and we through him.' The context must in every instance fix the sense, equally as regards the word 'god' and the word 'spirit.' No translator, and no sufficiently intelligent reader, can escape the responsibility of exercising his own judgment in the matter. Unfortunately our translations and retranslations have been undertaken by theologians deeply committed to Trinitarian doctrines,—men who could not, owing to their previous training, or who would not if they could, owing to their clerical status and surroundings, refrain from bringing out, by such an easy method, their own way of understanding the repeated allusions in Scripture to the 'spirit' and the 'holy spirit.' Even Dr. Robert Young, in the preface to his independent, literal and idiomatic translation, thought it well to say of his alterations: 'While they affect very considerably the outward *form* of the translation, it is a matter of thankfulness that they do not touch the *truth* of a single Scripture doctrine,—*not even one.*' That betrays a theological bias, sufficient by itself to explain why he has so submissively followed the Authorised Version in this matter of capitalising. If we are to claim and use the freedom of judgment which the apostle Paul urged in the words, 'Brethren, be not children in mind . . . in mind be men (Gr. of full age),' it becomes an absolute necessity, either that the translation of these crucial texts should stand uncapitalised, or that we should deal with them as though they were. Thereby we shall show a readiness of mind to receive truth, let it come from or incline to whichever side it will; which certainly was not the case with the Revisers, who regarded the presence of the one acknowledged Unitarian among them as a scandal, and so necessitated his withdrawal from the work to which he had been called in conjunction with themselves. The use of capitals is arbitrary, and may easily grow into an abuse; and their disuse entails no risk of misconception. That must be obvious, when we remember that in the German Version there is and could be nothing answering to the plan resorted to by our translators, every substantive in that language being capitalised. German readers are on this point compelled to judge of the sense by the context, which is the only safe rule in studying Scripture. Luther did not capitalise the adjective 'holy' before 'Spirit,' as our translators have done. The translation of Samuel Sharpe has the merit, with very few exceptions, of being faithful to the original, which is more than can be said of those versions in which the definite article is inserted where it does not appear in the text. No unprejudiced, unshackled searcher for the truth will be content to regard the doctrine involved, as settled for him by his forefathers, and therefore incontrovertible. It must be faced, and argued out honestly and impartially, in calm defiance of ecclesiastical censures and time-honoured assertions and denunciations. Happily the days are past when theologians could excommunicate, imprison, burn those whose views seemed to them heretical.

The foregoing remarks are not made in any spirit of opposition to the prevailing doctrine of the Trinity, nor with any leaning in favour of Unitarianism. Before a step can be taken towards a thorough investigation, it is essential thus to clear the way, by ascertaining to what extent the dogma may have been affected by the idiosyncrasies of translators.

We turn now to the 13th chapter of Luke. 'And he went on his way through cities and villages, teaching, and journeying on unto Jerusalem.' There is no connection traceable between that statement of the evangelist and the portion of the narrative immediately preceding. The author of 'Gospel Difficulties'* has arrived at the

---

* "Gospel Difficulties, or the Displaced Section of S. Luke." By J. J. Halcombe, M.A.

conclusion that here 'a section of S. Luke's Gospel has been placed after a section which it originally preceded, and that a new and utterly confusing order of events has been created at three points: (a) where the section was taken from its right place, (b) where it was inserted in the wrong place, (c) where a fictitious connection was established between the reversed sections.' Accordingly he places between verses 21 and 22 of chapter 8, the portion of chapter 11 from verses 14 to 54, the whole of chapter 12, and chapter 13 up to verse 2; and he asserts 'that the above displacement being rectified, the general arrangement of the Gospels is perfectly simple throughout, S. Luke's restored order at once explaining both the exact plan of of S. Matthew's Gospel and the rare and very slight departures from a chronological arrangement observable in S. Mark.' Without entering upon the argument relating to Matthew and Mark, it is no small gain to have effected by this one simple alteration an obvious consistency and consecutiveness throughout the Gospel according to Luke. That evangelist, having mentioned the course of teaching from place to place undertaken by Jesus, proceeds in this and the five following chapters to give examples of his teaching.

A question was put to Jesus. 'And one said unto him, Lord (Sir—Young) are they few that be saved?' Young renders: 'Are those saved few?' Tischendorf: 'Are there few to be saved?' The former simply indicates a fact; the latter denotes a purpose. An examination of the multitude of scriptural passages in which the words 'save' and 'saved' occur, makes it evident that the term 'saved' had the same breadth of meaning and application as it now bears in ordinary language. The one sense which cannot be justified, is that restricted theological one which somehow has come to be attached to it,—the idea of deliverance hereafter from the penalty of sin, escape at the day of judgment from endless misery, and admission to the happiness of heaven. The word 'saved' signifies deliverance from evil, actual or threatened, without reference to any specific event or period.

The reply of Jesus intimated that personal safety must depend upon personal effort, and upon the due use of the right way and fitting opportunity. 'And he said unto them, Strive to enter in by the narrow door.' An easier, broader entrance is here suggested, which must be avoided with a view to safety; many will be lost through choosing either the wrong way or the wrong time. 'For many, I say unto you, shall seek to enter in, and shall not be able.' The figure of admission by a narrow entrance is now enlarged into a parable. Jesus represents a householder as rising up, shutting the door, and excluding later comers. 'When once the master of the house is risen up, and hath shut to the door . . .' The Revisers indicate by a note a doubt whether the full stop between 'able' and 'when' should not be replaced by a comma. That arises from the change in verse 24 of 'strait gate' to 'narrow door,' in accordance with the two oldest MSS. It seems right to keep the ideas distinct, the 'narrow gate' in 7 Matthew 13 denoting a safe *pathway*, and the *house* in this parable having, as a matter of course, only one recognised 'door' for entrance, quite irrespective of its breadth or narrowness. Finding the door closed, the late comers would crowd round and knock, but be denied admission: 'and ye begin to stand without,

13 Luke 23

,, 23, 24

,, 24

,, 25

,, 25

and to knock at the door, saying, Lord, lord, open to us; and he shall answer and say to you, I know you not whence ye are.' The cry 'Lord, lord' may signify that they came not as guests, but as servants desiring a place in the household, and the answer, 'I know you not whence ye are,' imports that inasmuch as they had not presented themselves previously, their character and fitness could not be recognised. Then they claim some prior knowledge of the householder, but it is casual and distant at the best. 'Then shall ye begin to say, We did eat and drink in thy presence, and thou didst teach in our streets.' But what could it avail that some of them had met him in society, and others had known him by report as their city missionary? That could only prove how negligent they had been to cultivate his acquaintance, how indifferent and averse to his teachings. His social intercourse, his repeated pleadings, had not attracted them to his cause and person. Those worthy of him had followed him: 'Where I am, there shall also my servant be.' Their delay in obeying his call sufficed to prove their true character. They were not fit for his work, nor could they be admitted to a place in his household: 'and he shall say, I know not whence ye are: depart from me, all ye workers of iniquity.' Alford renders: 'ye workmen of iniquity.' These are they who have not been saved—from their sins. Deep will be their grief, and bitter their disappointment, to find themselves excluded on that account from God's kingdom hereafter. Jesus drops the parable of the house and householder, and bids them contemplate the future life, when they will hold communion with the dead, the age-during existence of the Jewish patriarchs enabling them to clasp hands with their remote descendants. 'There shall be the weeping and gnashing of teeth, when ye shall see Abraham, and Isaac, and Jacob, and all the prophets, in the kingdom of God, and yourselves cast forth without.' Jesus surely was not deluding us with visionary hopes, when he so calmly and assuredly spoke about realities such as these in the world to come. He only could disclose these things. 'No man hath ascended into heaven, but he that descended out of heaven, *even* the Son of man.' While in this world he held converse with departed saints. Moses and Elijah came to him on the mountain-top, the fact being witnessed by three, and very positively and solemnly attested in writing by two of his disciples. However little we ponder and are influenced by these revelations, they are absolutely, literally true, having a basis as real and substantial as any established scientific fact relating to the earth or its inhabitants. In proportion as we yield ourselves to the teachings of Jesus on other matters, our minds will become able to grasp and realise his declarations respecting the future life and the heavenly world. His scheme of teaching is based upon his knowledge of both worlds, and is designed to make the present life homogeneous with that which is to come. That is the secret of his divine philosophy, and that our faith may reach the highest round of that ladder which he has raised between earth and heaven, we must begin our climbing at the bottom, and ascend patiently and carefully step by step. 'If I told you earthly things, and ye believe not, how shall ye believe, if I tell you heavenly things?' The words of Jesus applied to the actual hearers: 'when YE shall see Abraham, and Isaac, and Jacob, and all the prophets in the kingdom of God, and YOURSELVES cast out.' Though the Jewish nation be intended, that will not exclude individuals, nor were those then living excepted because their posterity were included in the warning. And there will be no exclusion on account of nationality in God's kingdom : ' And they shall come from the east and west, and from the north and south, and shall sit down (Gr. recline) in the kingdom of God.' Tischendorf renders : ' will sit down at table :' under the figure of a social feast, Jesus foretells the friendly welcome and intimacy which will prevail in the company of the redeemed. The picture he draws is one of universal physical and moral happiness, the wicked banished and the righteous rejoicing. That is his ideal of the 'salvation' of humanity. And this renovation of society will involve not only the separation of the bad from the good, but in many instances among the redeemed themselves a reversal of their previous relative positions as regards rank, honour and influence. 'And behold, there are last which shall be first, and there are first which shall be last.' The law of advancement in God's kingdom will be vastly different from that which prevails on earth. That reflection was often in the mind of Jesus, for he repeated more than once his saying with respect to it. Of course the pride and pomp which are now dependent upon wealth will cease, and the glory of the warrior will find no place in that kingdom which triumphs in righteousness, peace and joy. Science, art, intellect, refinement, moral worth, and the spirit of brotherhood, —these will be held in everlasting honour. Social status will depend on social worth. The spiritual hierarchy, from the pope downwards, archbishops, bishops, archdeacons, deans, vicars, rectors, deacons, who have claimed to be ministers of Christ, successors of the apostles, dispensers of sacramental gifts, or at the very least instructors in the things of Christ and guides to the heavenly world : how far will their pretensions hold good hereafter ? Will the round they now prescribe and practise of prayer, praise, penance, and the mystical communion through the eating of bread and drinking of wine duly consecrated, be found indeed to accord with the mind of Christ, and to have helped forward his kingdom ? Or will these men generally find their occupation gone, many of their assumptions to have been unwarranted, many of their dogmas exploded and rejected as erroneous, and the church of Christ a different organisation altogether from what they had been taught and had taught others to believe ? We are all fallible, probably they most so whose teaching is most positive. How astounded must the scribes and Pharisees have been to hear Jesus express the opinion that they were shutting up the kingdom of heaven against men : that their zeal in compassing heaven and earth to make one proselyte, ended in their making him twofold more the child of hell than themselves ! The rank now assigned to men is quite as much the outcome of class as of character : none can rise in 'the Church' who either fall below a recognised standard of orthodoxy or rise above the spirit and doctrine of the age in which they live. 'Ye know not what manner of spirit ye are of,' said Jesus to his apostles. When all things come to be ruled according to his will, and all men to be placed according to his judgment, great and surprising will be the reversals in their respective positions : 'There are last which shall be first, and there are first which shall be last.'

The incident next related by the evangelist begins in the Authorised Version with the words, 'The same day.' Following the three oldest MSS., the Revisers have altered this to, 'In that very hour,' and Tischendorf to 'In that same hour.' Certain Pharisees urged Jesus to stop his course of teaching, and to hasten his departure from the place, on the ground that Herod was seeking his life. 'In that very hour there came certain Pharisees, saying to him, Get thee out, and go hence: for Herod would fain kill thee.' The last four words are clearer than 'will kill thee' in the Authorised Version. Alford renders, 'is minded to:' Tischendorf, 'desires to;' Young, 'wisheth to.' Alford observes: 'These Pharisees appear to have been sent by Herod for the purpose of getting rid of Jesus out of his jurisdiction. Considering his character, it is hardly possible that he should really have wished to kill *one who was so popular*; he refused to do so when Jesus was in his power afterwards in Jerusalem; but, as great multitudes were now following him about, and superstitious fears, as we know, agitated Herod, he wished to be quit of him, and took this means of doing so. I think this view is necessary to justify the epithet applied to Herod, which certainly implies *cunning on his part*.' The reply of Jesus was couched in a tone of dignified reprobation and remonstrance. 'And he said unto them, Go and say to that fox . .' We are accustomed to regard the prominent characteristic of a fox to be that of cunning, but it by no means follows that the idea was familiar to the Jews. In a country where foxes abounded, the damage done by the animals, and their habit of attacking and destroying things on which the husbandman had expended much care and labour, would naturally be the foremost thought in connection with them.

'Take us the foxes, the little foxes, that spoil the vineyards;
For our vineyards are in blossom.'

Herod had stopped the career of John the Baptist by first imprisoning and at last beheading him. Therein he had acted the part of a fox, and he now showed an inclination to interfere with Jesus and mar his work in the same way. Jesus met the threat by explaining that he meant to carry on his labour of exorcising and healing during three days only. 'Behold, I cast out devils (Gr. demons) and perform cures to-day and to-morrow, and the third *day* I am perfected.' Tischendorf renders, 'the third day I finish;' Sharpe, 'the third day I shall have ended.' The verb *teleioō*, is the same as in the passage: 'and when they had fulfilled the days.' And although during those three days Jesus must needs carry out his work, yet he would at the same time be complying with the desire of Herod by journeying onwards. 'Howbeit I must go on my way to-day and to-morrow and the *day* following.' Tischendorf renders: 'I must go about;' Young: 'go on;' the Authorised Version has: 'I must walk;' Alford renders: 'I must journey,' and he explains: 'In the original it is the very word in which they had addressed him, *Depart* (journey) *hence*.' All this seems very clear; but to Alford it seemed quite incomprehensible. He says: 'The interpretation of this answer is difficult, for two reasons—(1) that the signification of the *to-day, to-morrow*, and *the third day* is doubtful—(2) that the meaning of *I am perfected* is also doubtful.' He begins by assuming that the words used have some mysterious meaning; he rejects the natural interpretation of Meyer and Bleek: 'In three days (literal days) the Lord's working of miracles in Galilee would be ended, which had excited the apprehension of Herod; and that He would leave the territory, not for fear of Herod, but because he was going to Jerusalem to die:' and after vainly searching for some satisfactory mystical sense, he ends by saying: 'I own that neither of the above interpretations satisfy me, and still less the various modifications of them which have been proposed. Nor can I suggest one less open to objection.' No wonder: for he started with the conviction 'that *perfected* is used in the solemn sense elsewhere attached to the word,' and he refers to eleven passages in which the word occurs. Other translators saw no such reason for doubt and uncertainty here. The sense of the expression must be fixed by the context. It is most unreasonable to suppose that Jesus returned an answer to Herod in the form of an enigma, so difficult of solution that a luminary of the Church in the nineteenth century found himself unable to elucidate it.

Jesus being on his way towards Jerusalem, there was no necessity for Herod to urge his moving forward; and that he, a prophet, should be killed anywhere outside of Jerusalem would be indeed a new event in history. 'For it cannot be that a prophet perish out of Jerusalem.' That city stood foremost in the work of persecution and bloodshed. Luke here inserts the apostrophe beginning, 'O Jerusalem, Jerusalem,' which Alford considers to be 'in too close connexion with the preceding to allow of the supposition that' it was 'inserted unchronologically, as many suppose.' If, however, Luke had only the saying, with nothing to guide him as to its proper place, he would naturally insert it in connection with the word Jerusalem. It tallies so closely with 23 Matthew 37—39, that it will be best to take the passages together. Here in Luke the apostrophe seems out of place: 'your house is left unto you,' could only be spoken appropriately to dwellers in Jerusalem; and 'ye shall not see me,' would be a strange expression to apply to them at a time when Jesus was actually journeying towards Jerusalem.

The party hostile to Jesus appears to have maintained everywhere and always a watch over his actions. On a sabbath day (it would seem to have been during this journey), he entered the house of a Pharisee who stood in high repute, to partake of his hospitality. There, as usual, the eyes and ears of critics were on the alert. 'And it came to pass, when he went into the house of one of the rulers of the Pharisees on a sabbath to eat bread, that they were watching him.' Immediately facing Jesus was a man suffering from dropsy. 'And behold, there was before him a certain man which had the dropsy.' It is not said that he was one of the guests, nor must it necessarily be assumed that he was inside the Pharisee's house. Young's version points the other way: 'On his going into the house ... there was a certain dropsical man before him,'—placed at the entrance, right in the way of Jesus, obviously with a desire and expectation of a cure. Thereupon Jesus turned to the lawyers and Pharisees surrounding him, and asked their opinion. 'And Jesus answering spake unto the lawyers and Pharisees, saying, Is it lawful to heal on the sabbath, or not?' The words 'or not' have been added by the Revisers, being in the two oldest MSS. No answer was given to the question. 'But they held their peace.' They could not venture a plain 'yes' or 'no.' No one of them had the courage of his convictions; probably they halted between two opinions, afraid to break God's law, yet by no means sure about their accustomed rigid interpretation of it. Jesus was not troubled with any such doubts or scruples. 'And he took him, and healed him, and let him go.' Tischendorf renders: 'And he took hold of and cured him, and sent him away.' Young: 'And having taken hold of *him*, he healed him, and sent *him* away.' Then, to those who had refrained from answering his former question, he put another. 'And he said unto them, Which of you shall have an ass or an ox fallen into a well, and will not straightway draw him up on a sabbath day?' The Revisers have altered 'pit' in the Authorised Version to 'well.' The word, *phrear*, is rendered 'well' in the passage, 'the well is deep ... which gave us the well,' and it is defined: 'a well: or more commonly a water tank, cistern, reservoir.' The idea conveyed is an impending death by water, and an analogy may have been intended to the disease from which the man suffered: he was 'dropsical,' *hudrōpikos*, which is derived from *hudōr*, 'water.' Instead of 'ass' Tischendorf renders 'son,' on the authority of the Vatican and Alexandrine MS., but the older Sinaitic MS. has 'ass.' The Revisers note that 'many ancient authorities read *a son*.' Alford observes: 'This reading, which, from the weight of ancient testimony in its favour, evidently was the original, seemed incompatible with the supposed argument *from the less to the greater: son* was therefore altered to 'ass' (as in ch. xiii. 15) or *sheep*, as one of our ancient MSS. has it.' The argument of Jesus was a crushing one. Who could deny that the instinct of humanity was a sufficient guide? When danger threatened, and help could be given, who would stop to debate nice questions of Sabbatarian ritualism? Once more, those addressed were dumb. 'And they could not answer again unto these things.'

If others were watching Jesus, he also was watching them, though in a very different spirit. His observation and criticism were directed to their benefit, and led him to deliver a short parable. 'And he spake a parable unto those which were bidden, when he marked how they chose out the chief seats.' The Revisers, agreeing with Tischendorf, have altered 'rooms' to 'seats;' Alford to 'places.' Young renders: 'And he spake a simile to those called, marking how they were choosing out the first couches.' Tischendorf inserted a special note, that the proper translation is, 'how they were choosing out.' Not to offend needlessly the susceptibilities of his hearers, yet at the same time to make the application of the parable sufficiently obvious, Jesus, whilst alluding to a feast, specified one of a different kind: 'Saying unto them, When thou art bidden of any man to a marriage-feast, sit not down (Gr. recline not) in the chief seat.' Young renders: 'When thou mayest be called by any one to marriage feasts, thou mayest not recline on the first couch.' By using the plural, 'marriage feasts,' the parable was still more generalised, and therefore less liable to give offence. The same remark applies to the rendering, 'thou mayest not recline on the first couch:' there is a touch of delicate feeling in thus assuming that ordinary courtesy and self-respect dictated this as a matter of course. If, perchance, a person should forget, in caring for himself, what was due to others, he would run the risk of being unpleasantly reminded of his selfish breach of etiquette: 'lest haply a more honourable man than thou be bidden of him, and he that bade thee and him shall come and say to thee, Give this man place: and then thou shalt begin with shame to take the lowest place.' Nothing beyond a passing discomfort, an admission of error, a feeling of mortification, a sense of one's own dignity being lessened by contrast with that of a superior, would ensue. But it would be wiser and pleasanter to anticipate and avoid such a result, and to form the habit of erring, if at all, on the safe side in a point of precedence. Rather than run the risk of claiming too much, it would be better to keep quite in the background. 'But when thou art bidden, go and sit down in the lowest place.' The duty of seating the guests properly devolves upon the host, and he must needs fulfil the responsibilities of his position. If there should have been an unseemly scramble for places, he will quietly and courteously see to its rectification, and will take care that each guest at his table is treated with the respect due to his acknowledged rank and character: 'that when he that hath bidden thee cometh, he may say to thee, Friend, go up higher.' Such an experience would be pleasant and honourable, the reverse in all respects of the other. 'Then shalt thou have glory in the presence of all that sit at meat with thee.' The Revisers have altered 'worship' to 'glory,' agreeing with Tischendorf and Young. They have also, on the authority of the three oldest MSS., inserted the word 'all.'

Had Jesus added nothing to the parable by way of explanation, it would have been scarcely safe and wise for us to enlarge its application. In this instance, we are specially told that he was rebuking a fault of disposition and conduct which had just come under his observation. Why should we take upon ourselves to extend the parable? Alford assumes much when he says: 'The whole of this has, besides its plain reference, a *deeper one*, linked into it by the important word *wedding*, carrying with it all that meaning which it always has when *relating to the kingdom of God*. Both senses are obvious.' This means that the words, 'When thou art bidden of any man to a marriage feast,' must of necessity signify the invitation to enter the kingdom of heaven, the 'host' representing either God or Jesus. Such a mode of interpretation being adopted, theologians are free to exercise their fancies and air their favourite dogmas to their hearts' content. In this case, however, difficulties arise in attempting to unravel this 'deeper reference.' No sooner does Alford say, 'Both senses are obvious,' than he feels bound to qualify the assertion, adding: 'and only one remark needed.' Here it is: 'That all that *false* humility, by which men put themselves lowest and dispraise themselves *of set purpose to be placed higher*, is, by the very nature of our Lord's parable, *excluded*: for that is not bonâ fide abasing one's self. The exaltation at the hands of the Host is not to be a *purposed end* to the guests, but will follow true humility.' The parable standing in its simplicity, and the application which Jesus makes from it, are free from such entanglements, and require no such cautions against misapprehension. Why should it be considered beneath the dignity of so great a Teacher to seize the occasion for reproving the vice of self-esteem and eulogising the opposite virtue, even were that his only object? True, Luke calls the discourse 'a parable,' but it was spoken not of set purpose, as a simile deliberately chosen to illustrate the kingdom of heaven, like many other parables, but casually, on witnessing the behaviour of some of the guests, to whom it conveyed a necessary lesson of good manners and right feeling. Jesus did, however, see fit to deduce from the parable a particular conclusion, and to the application which he himself has made we shall do well to restrict ourselves. The inference he drew stands out clearly. 'For every one that exalteth himself shall be humbled, and he that humbleth himself shall be exalted.' Young, by putting the present tense in a different form, indicates a habit of mind and action: 'For every one who is exalting himself shall be humbled, and he who is humbling himself shall be exalted.' The human aspect in the parable is most prominent. The guests are fellow-men, and the placing of each is in accordance with his recognised social status. Nor is 'he that bade thee and him' necessarily to be interpreted as representing God. Jesus avoids giving any mark of distinction or superiority to the host. He is not described as a king, nor is there anything to indicate that he was superior in rank to any of the guests. We are simply led to contemplate society as it exists, each individual entitled to occupy a certain position, the majority falling naturally into their appropriate places, but some over-estimating their own importance, ambitious of distinction, not caring whose may be the place they seize if only it be within their reach and sufficiently conspicuous. That is an outrage which Society will not long endure. The imposter is detected, and the man of real worth is welcomed. The shame of rejection may be more personal than public, but the chorus of approval when true merit is advanced to the front is loud and universal: 'then shalt thou have glory in the presence of all.' Jesus traces to its source the law of degradation and elevation. The former springs from self-exaltation, the latter from humility. At all times, and on every side, we may see this law at work; and as human society advances towards the ideal of Christianity, the process of selection will become more refined, accurate and discriminating, the Church will be purged from the curse of selfish ambition, and through the docility which becomes us as 'sons of God, through faith, in Christ Jesus,' we shall pass onwards from our humble infancy to the perfection of his glorious manhood. 'For every one that exalteth himself shall be humbled, and he that humbleth himself shall be exalted.' The law is universal: 'every one.'

Jesus addressed to his host a few words of friendly counsel, conceived in the highest spirit of charity. Such entertainments as he was accustomed to give were not, as was evident on this occasion, without their drawbacks. A desire for precedence was observable among the guests, with respect to which it might be necessary for the host to interfere. Why should he not, for once at least, resolve to change his company? Instead of inviting a distinguished assembly, let him throw open his doors and extend his hospitality to the poorest and most miserable. As it was, there was a constant round of visiting and feasting, every man of high position deeming it a duty to return the invitation. No benefit was conferred, no sentiment of gratitude evoked: the host to-day became the guest to-morrow. There was no scope in that ceaseless pursuit of mutual pleasure for the blessing which attaches to pure, unselfish benevolence. Something better ought to be attempted. 'And he said to him also that [11 Luke 12] had bidden him, When thou makest a dinner or a supper, call not thy friends, nor thy brethren, nor thy kinsmen, nor rich neighbours: less haply they also bid thee again, and a recompense be made thee.' But setting aside conventionalities, let him issue invitations to a class with whom he had hitherto contracted no friendships, among whom he had no relatives, and who could boast of nothing in the shape of wealth or social status. Let him welcome the poor, and those of them especially who through accident or infirmity were unable to help or raise themselves, as others might. 'But when thou makest a feast, bid the poor, the maimed, the lame, the blind.' Such a social innovation, however it might be criticised, would have a happy effect upon himself: 'and thou shalt be blessed (happy—Young).' The very impossibility of any return being made to him would constitute the charm and sweetness of his hospitality: 'because they have not *wherewith* to recompense thee.' Not here, but in the next life, when the distinctions between mankind will be reduced to the one point of character, two classes only being recognised, the just and the unjust, his neighbourly and compassionate liberality would be reciprocated. 'For thou shalt be recompensed in the resurrection of the just.' Sharpe uses the words 'repayment, repaid,' instead of 'recompense, recompensed'; and certainly a repayment in kind seems to be intended. We have here a hint or two with respect to the arrangement of society in the future life: the poor in this world may become rich in the next, and the remembrance of past kindnesses will survive the shock of death and flight of time. Jesus holds out to 'the just' a pleasant prospect of life in the world to come. Alford's note on the words, 'the resurrection of the just,' is as follows: 'The *first* resurrection, here distinctly asserted by our Lord: otherwise the words *of the just* would be vapid and unmeaning. See 1 Cor. xv. 22: 1 Thess. iv. 16: Rev. xx. 4, 5.' This blending together of Scriptural passages with the view of establishing a doctrine not clearly revealed in any one of them, is a practice which needs cautious watching, and is always open to suspicion, so much depending upon the tone of the commentator's mind and on the ease with which a word or form of speech in the original may be misapprehended and unintentionally perverted. The apostle Paul touched on this matter: 'Having hope towards [24 Acts 15] God, which these also themselves look for (or, accept), that there shall be a resurrection both of the just and unjust.' From this it is evident that it was a settled article of belief among the orthodox Jews that there would be a universal resurrection, and in connection therewith a division of mankind into two classes, the just and the unjust. Alford's argument that the mention of the resurrection of the just indicates that there will not only be a distinction into two classes, but a separation in point of time in the resurrection of the two, is scarcely consistent with the idea conveyed by Paul's expression, 'a resurrection of the just and of the unjust:' he speaks not of two resurrections, but of one. Let us examine the passages alluded to. 'But now hath Christ been raised from the dead, the firstfruits [15 i. Cor. 20–23] of them that are asleep. For since by man *came* death, by man *came*

also the resurrection of the dead. For as in Adam all die, so also in Christ (Gr. the Christ) shall all be made alive. But each in his own order: Christ the firstfruits; then they are Christ's, at his coming (Gr. presence).' Observe: it is not said that Christ was raised from death, but 'from the dead.' It is important to bear the distinction in mind. The German version shows 'the dead' as a plural substantive, equivalent to 'dead persons': 'auferstanden von den Todten,' 'risen up from those who are dead.' Dead persons had been raised before Christ died, as is evident from the appearing of Moses and Elijah, and by the argument of Jesus that the mention of Abraham,
_{20 Luke 37} Isaac and Jacob, living after death, was proof that 'the dead are raised.' Obviously, the sense in which the apostle alludes to Christ as 'the firstfruits of them that are asleep,' is that of the presentation of the firstfruits to God under the Mosaic law. Jesus has gone, first
_{7 Acts 56} and foremost of mankind, to the divine presence, 'the Son of man standing on the right hand of God.' Pursuing that idea, the apostle, having spoken of 'the dead,' not as extinct but as 'them that are asleep,' tells how all in Christ shall be 'made alive,' quickened into
_{3 Col. 3} active vitality; as elsewhere: 'Your life is hid with Christ in God.' Then he adds: 'But each in his own order (rank—Englishman's Greek New Testament)': not each of the two classes, but each individual. And that this means an order in rank or place, not in time, is evident from what follows: 'Christ the firstfruits,' the foremost, honoured, accepted representative of humanity; 'then they that are Christ's at his presence.' All this has no bearing on the question
_{4 i. Thess. 15-17} of two resurrections. Take the next passage: 'We that are alive, that are left unto the coming (Gr. presence) of the Lord, shall in no wise precede them that are fallen asleep. For the Lord himself shall descend from heaven with a shout, with the voice of the archangel, and with the trump of God: and the dead in Christ shall rise first; then we that are alive, that are left, shall together with them be caught up in the clouds, to meet the Lord in the air, and so shall we ever be with the Lord.' The apostle begins by asserting that the living will have no precedence over the dead. He represents the arrival of a moment of crisis and culmination. Jesus descending from heaven, as the great Captain of our salvation, a shout of triumph raised, a word of command uttered by a 'chief messenger' (Young), and God's trumpet sounded as a signal understood, expected and to be obeyed. The language is highly figurative. 'The dead in Christ shall rise first.' Whence? We know not. Whither? 'To meet the Lord in the air,' the living also being 'caught away in clouds' (Young). That is the rising, or uprising, here spoken of. Those 'asleep' are not described as raised from death at that instant, for in the previous verse it is said that Jesus will bring them with him, so that they in fact will rise first to meet him, taking precedence of the living. The rising 'first' has no reference to the idea of two resurrections, that of the just prior to that of the unjust.

The last passage to which Dean Alford referred is one of deepest
_{20 Rev. 4-6} mystery. 'And I saw thrones, and they sat upon them, and judgement was given unto them: and *I saw* the souls of them that had been beheaded for the testimony of Jesus, and for the word of God, and such as worshipped not the beast, neither his image, and received not the mark upon their forehead and upon their hand; and they

lived and reigned with Christ a thousand years. The rest of the dead lived not until the thousand years should be finished. This is the first resurrection. Blessed and holy is he that hath part in the first resurrection: over these the second death hath no power (or, authority); but they shall be priests of God and of Christ, and shall reign with him a thousand years.' One is soon lost and bewildered in wandering through the marvellous symbolism and imagery of the Book of the Revelation. Probably this passage is the origin of the idea that the resurrection to life of all mankind will be deferred to some remote period; that all of a certain character will be raised first; and after a further period all the rest of mankind; and as the expression 'a resurrection of the just and of the unjust' happens to fit in with this conclusion, it has been assumed that the passages may be taken together, as embodying the same doctrine. Nothing of the kind can be inferred safely, to say the least. 'Thrones, and they sat upon them'; who are 'they'? Again: 'The souls of them that had been beheaded . . . and such as worshipped not the beast.' To apply a passage thus hedged round with restrictions, doubts and uncertainty, to the destiny of the human race in general, is most unwise. Looking to the context, the expression 'the rest of the dead lived not,' apparently refers back to the last verse of the preceding chapter: 'the rest were killed with the sword of him that sat upon the horse,' that is, 'them that had received the mark of the beast, and them that worshipped his image.' The events thus darkly foretold in connection with the millennium, can have no bearing on any doctrine touching the ultimate fate of the innumerable generations of mankind.

The idea broached by Jesus of the possibility of a return being made in the next world for kindness shown in this, was taken up by one of the guests, who ventured to address to him an observation naturally suggested by the subject. 'And when one of them that sat at meat with him heard these things, he said unto him, Blessed is he that shall eat bread in the kingdom of God.' We are so accustomed to restrict the term 'blessed' to the divine blessing, that Young's constant rendering of the word as 'happy' is preferable. The happiness alluded to is not that of the future, but of the present: it is not 'happy shall he be,' but literally, 'happy he that shall eat,' denoting a condition of mind and being which can afford to overlook the present, be it joyous or grievous, in the assurance of the future. But Jesus at once started a parable which plainly intimated that the generality of men did not so prize the heavenly banquet, but were immersed in other and nearer ambitions and enjoyments. 'But he said unto him, A certain man made a great supper; and he bade many.' Those invited showed, however, so little inclination to attend, that when the time arrived he sent his servant round to the guests to urge their coming, everything being now in readiness for their reception. 'And he sent forth his servant (Gr. bondservant) at supper time to say to them that were bidden, Come: for *all* things are now ready.' Alford omits 'all,' and explains that it is 'omitted by several ancient authorities.' It is not in the oldest MS. The Revisers have retained the word, but have italicised it. The message-bearer was dismissed with a series of excuses. One and all of those invited offered an apology, more or less plausible, for his refusal.

'And they all with one *consent* began to make excuse.' The word 'consent' not being in the original, the expression must not be taken to mean that a combined refusal had been previously resolved upon: the passage is literally: 'And began with one to excuse themselves all.' The first explained, courteously, that he was on the point of starting to inspect a field he had just purchased. 'The first said unto him, I have bought a field, and I must needs go and see to it: I pray thee have me excused.' Another was anxious to test the working of a fresh purchase of oxen, and therefore, with the same courteous formality, refused the invitation. 'And another said, I have bought five yoke of oxen, and I go to prove them: I pray thee have me excused.' Another gave as a reason, so obvious and insuperable as to dispense with the need of any apology, the fact that he was bound to be present at the festivities attendant upon his wedding. 'And another said, I have married a wife, and therefore I cannot come.' On receiving the report of these evasive replies, the householder was naturally moved with indignation. His supper was prepared, but the guests were wanting. Still, there were many to be found who would appreciate the banquet. So he desired his servant to hasten to the city, and out of its streets and lanes to assemble the poor, and among them those whose bodily infirmities had reduced them to utter helplessness and destitution. 'Then the master of the house being angry said to his servant (Gr. bondservant), Go out quickly into the streets and lanes of the city, and bring in hither the poor and maimed and blind and lame.' Having done this, the servant reported that the guests were still small in number compared with the extent of the house and banquet. 'And the servant (Gr. bondservant) said, Lord, what thou didst command is done, and yet there is room.' Then a wider circuit must be made, country roads and byways searched, and pressure must be put upon the wayfarers to accept the invitation, the householder being determined to see his house filled with guests. 'And the lord said unto the servant (Gr. bondservant), Go out into the highways and hedges, and compel *them* to come in, that my house may be filled.' To understand the bearing of the next sentence a little consideration is required. 'For I say unto you, that none of those men which were bidden shall taste of my supper.' Why should this have been said by the householder? All expectation of those first invited being present, had been relinquished. After it was known that they *would* not come, it would be strange indeed for the offended host to say that they *should* not come. And why should this be said to the servant, who knew all the circumstances, and could not possibly suppose that those originally selected would make an effort now to claim admission? But it is by no means clear, and must not be assumed, that the householder addressed these words to his servant. It is not, 'I say unto thee,' but 'I say unto you.' Alford observes: 'I think with Stier, that our Lord here speaks *in his own Person: unto you* will fit no circumstance in the parable: for the householder and his servant are alone: the guests are not present. He speaks with his usual *For I say unto you, to the company present:* and half continuing the parable, half expanding it, substitutes Himself for the master of the feast, leaving it hardly doubtful who *those men which were bidden* are.' This remark must be taken subject to a slight but important difference of rendering introduced by Tischendorf; instead of: 'none of those men which were bidden shall taste of my supper,' he renders: 'none of those men who have been called will taste of my supper.' There is a great difference between *shall* and *will*, which unfortunately is not brought out distinctly by ordinary grammatical construction, and this defect of language is apt to cause uncertainty and mistake. As translated by Tischendorf the expression has a tone of regret, 'none ... will taste,' none are willing to taste, 'of my supper'; whereas 'none ... shall taste' conveys the idea of a threat and forbiddal. No doubt the former is correct, the latter incorrect. Jesus having finished his parable, reduced its application to this one sentence. He was like the householder: his invitation to the kingdom of God was not accepted by those whose social position required that they should be foremost, and his efforts were therefore of necessity directed to the gaining of an influence over the lower class, between whom and the rulers and Pharisees the gulf was as wide as that between prosperous men of business and the poorest of the poor. There is nothing to indicate that Jesus ever gained a single professed convert or follower from the higher ranks of society. The common people heard him gladly, but his enemies could exclaim in triumph, 'Hath any of the rulers believed on him, or of the Pharisees?' How true and sorrowful his saying: 'None of those men who have been called will taste of my supper!' 7 John 48

While Jesus was thus despondent with respect to some, he deemed it necessary to repress the hasty, inconsiderate ardour of others. Large numbers not only heard him, but followed him, rendered by Young, 'were going on with him.' Jesus turned round, faced the crowd, and assured them that this keeping by him, watching him, listening to him, did not and could not amount to discipleship. His idea of a disciple was a man prepared to go to the very extreme of sacrifice and self renunciation. 'Now there went with him great multitudes, and he turned, and said unto them, If any man cometh unto me, and hateth not his own father, and mother, and wife, and children, and brethren, and sisters, yea, and his own life also, he cannot be my disciple.' The dedication of one's self to the cause of Jesus would necessitate the snapping of every earthly tie, the abandonment of all other duties and relationships, however close and sacred, and the sacrifice of life itself. Even that strong language was not enough, for Jesus added: 'Whosoever doth not bear his own cross and come after me, cannot be my disciple.' We know that Jesus anticipated,—for he foretold,—his own death by crucifixion. His mention of a cross for his followers meant nothing less than that. The sight, in those days of stern Roman justice, must have been a common one, of a malefactor led out to death bearing his own cross. That was the end to which Jesus would have his disciples look forward; and he desired those about him to weigh the matter well, to count the cost fully, before committing themselves to his enterprise. In his usual way, he illustrated the subject by a parable. In entering upon any costly undertaking, it was wise and necessary to forecast the extent of the probable requirements and resources. 'For which of you, desiring to build a tower, doth not first sit down and count the cost, whether he have *wherewith* to complete it.' To leave the work unfinished for want of funds, would be a folly so egregious as to expose the builder to derision. 'Lest haply, when he hath laid 14 Luke 25, 26

14 Luke 27

,, 28

,, 29, 30

a foundation, and is not able to finish, all that behold begin to mock him, saying, This man began to build, and was not able to finish.' As though that simile were not strong enough, Jesus put forward another. He pictured a king compelled to face the stern arbitrament of war; and on very unequal terms, having at his command only one half of the forces likely to be arrayed against him. The certainty of utter ruin in the event of defeat, would impel to the gravest and most careful counsel beforehand: the question would be earnestly pondered whether the deficiency in numbers could be counterbalanced by superiority in valour, skill, or otherwise. If not, an ambassador would be forthwith despatched to arrange terms of peace. 'Or what king, as he goeth to encounter another king in war, will not sit down first and take counsel whether he is able with ten thousand to meet him that cometh against him with twenty thousand? Or else, while the other is yet a great way off, he sendeth an ambassage, and asketh conditions of peace.' The question of fighting or capitulating might depend, however, not upon the most probable issue, but upon the spirit of the king and his people, if they were prepared to face all risks rather than to submit to a hateful foreign sway. Such were the difficulties to be faced and the problems to be solved by those who contemplated discipleship to Jesus. They were called to an undertaking which would swallow up the whole of their fortune, to a war to be waged at heavy odds, which gave no hope of victory, but must be fought out for the sake of Jesus and of conscience. 'So therefore whosoever he be of you that renounceth not all that he hath, he cannot be my disciple.' All this, we may be sure, was not said without a serious and definite purpose. The disciples of Jesus were not mere investigators and adherents of a system of philosophy or religion, but followers of himself, destined to go forth as he did on the work of evangelisation. It was of the utmost importance to his cause that it should not be undertaken by the wavering and half-hearted. He had warned his twelve apostles of the persecution which would surely overtake them, and he desired that none should join them who were not animated by enthusiasm, ready to suffer the loss of all things, and even to lay down their lives for the truth's sake. So far was Jesus from inviting all to become his disciples, that he repelled all who were not cast in the strongest mould, resolute men, intensely earnest, prepared to spend and be spent in his service. It is important to recognise and emphasise this fact, for many readers and expounders of the gospels are apt to assume that every saying of Jesus is of universal application. It behoves us to study his words closely, carefully, exercising common sense and discrimination. Those he sought to keep back from a profession of discipleship were none the less able, on that account, to rejoice in the gospel he preached and the truths he taught, to take him as their shepherd, their life-guide, their Saviour, laying hold of the promise of age-during life through him. Jesus never called all men to relinquish everything and to follow him. Still less does he do so now. High-flown exhortations to that effect, however much they may seem to accord with his commands, are misplaced, misleading, irrational. We do not, we will not, we cannot act upon them. The error of judgment which leads to them cannot be too strongly deprecated, for it tends to the wounding of weak consciences, and to the perpetuation of the pernicious idea that obedience to Christ's precepts is beyond our reach. The great dread of Jesus was lest men should profess and attempt too much, hastily and only nominally enrolling themselves as his disciples, whom he had previously designated as 'the salt of the earth.' The simile was aptly chosen, the quantity of salt required being out of all proportion to the enormous mass of food consumed. So, the disciples of Jesus, few in number, destined to exert a widespread influence, must be selected with the utmost care, the qualities and character of each individual severely tested beforehand, in view of the important trust committed to him and the severe strain and trial to which he would be exposed. If these disciples wavered in their career, failed in their duty, there would be none who could supply their place. Jesus reverted to his former simile. 'Salt therefore is good: but if even the salt have lost its savour, wherewith shall it be seasoned?' If they failed to retain unimpaired their principles, their spirit of self-sacrifice, their unconquerable determination to suffer all things for Christ's sake, they would become utterly worthless to mankind, fit for no heavenly or earthly use, like salt grown insipid, which could be turned to no advantage in any way. 'It is fit neither for the land nor for the dunghill: men cast it out.' Jesus deemed it so important that this should be fully understood, that he urged every individual present to hear his warning, that they might act accordingly. 'He that hath ears to hear, let him hear.'

At this time there was a large attendance of the lowest class of the people at the discourses of Jesus. 'Now all the publicans and sinners were drawing near unto him for to hear him.' The Pharisees and the scribes were much scandalised at seeing him encourage intimacy with the despised tax-gatherers and with persons of notoriously evil lives. 'And both the Pharisees and the scribes murmured, saying, This man receiveth sinners, and eateth with them.' The Revisers and Tischendorf have introduced the word 'both' as the best reading. Those whose profession it was to expound the Mosaic law, agreed in opinion with the strait-laced Pharisees as to the unseemliness of the conduct of Jesus. Not satisfied with simply preaching to the people, he consorted with them. The expression, 'receiveth sinners, and eateth with them,' indicates that Jesus received them as guests and sat at the table with them; and as it was their object to hear him, and his to talk to them, doubtless the meal was made use of, as it had been by him in the Pharisee's house, as an opportunity of addressing them. It was the habit of Jesus to lead the conversation at such social gatherings, and never was religious teaching presented under a more charming aspect. The sense of friendliness and nearness to the great Teacher, his affability, his warm-heartedness, the simple, touching eloquence and self-evident appropriateness of his parables, the rational, pleasurable excitement of the mind naturally connected with the taking of meat and drink together,—all these were adjuncts to his influence, bridging over the gulf which separated class from class, and bringing home to the souls of the listeners the feeling of a common brotherhood, and an impulse, a hope, a resolution towards self-amendment and self-elevation. The scribes and Pharisees betrayed the prejudices and exclusiveness of the spirit of class and caste. Jesus refused to be bound by their rules of propriety. Their sanctimonious punctiliousness and their love of precedence were obnoxious to him, and he scrupled not, when occasion offered, to expose and reprove them. He now repelled their ill-natured and offensive criticism, and justified his own conduct, by delivering in their hearing the following parables. 'And he spake unto them this parable, saying, What man of you, having a hundred sheep, and having lost one of them, doth not leave the ninety and nine in the wilderness, and go after that which is lost, until he find it?' Each sheep is equally precious in the eyes of the shepherd, and the sense of responsibility impels him to seek the erring one. He scruples not to leave his flock, safe in their gregariousness, for a time; and his search takes him to strange, difficult, dangerous places, into which no shepherd would think of leading his flock. And when he has found the lost sheep, he carries it on his back exultingly. 'And when he hath found it, he layeth it on his shoulders, rejoicing.' The loss of one sheep out of a hundred was not a thing to be borne with equanimity, and its recovery is hailed with satisfaction. It is assumed that the fact of one of the flock being missed was matter of notoriety, of consternation, of condolence, so that when the shepherd returns, all his fellows are ready to congratulate him, and he, in the joy of his heart, summons them to a feast, to signalise the happy issue. 'And when he cometh home, he calleth together his friends and his neighbours, saying unto them, Rejoice with me, for I have found my sheep which was lost.'

The primary application of the parable was obvious. Jesus had been going about among those who, to use his own words, 'were distressed and scattered, as sheep not having a shepherd.' Among that class his mission had been most successful, and the festive meal at which his flock and disciples were present, and which gave such umbrage to Pharisees and scribes, might be deemed his calling 'together his friends and his neighbours, saying unto them, Rejoice with me, for I have found my sheep which was lost.'

But Jesus gave to the parable a fuller, deeper meaning. His conduct and labours, however much they might be criticised and blamed, were in harmony with the spirit and practice of heavenly Beings. Their interest was engaged and concentrated on the reformation of society, and to them it was a matter of rejoicing when one sinner was restored to the paths of virtue and safety. The evil thereby prevented, the advance thereby gained, were more considered than all previous attainments towards the perfecting of the social state. The well-being of any and every individual is to be desired, not only and entirely out of regard to his own personal happiness, but because he is a living unit in the vast total of humanity. As the spirit of philanthropy widens, there is developed an intense interest in the moral state of the least, the lowest, the worst among mankind. 'I say unto you, that even so there shall be joy in heaven over one sinner that repenteth, *more* than over ninety and nine righteous persons, which need no repentance.'

Jesus gave another illustration of the matter. 'Or what woman having ten pieces of silver, if she lose one piece, doth not light a lamp, and sweep the house, and seek diligently until she find it?' The Revisers note that the Greek word used, *drachma*, was a coin worth about eight pence. The intrinsic value of the lost drachma, as of the lost sheep, was not great; but stress is laid upon the fact that the shepherd had but a hundred sheep and the woman only ten drachmas. The illustrations are chosen from humble life, the object being to bring out in each case the value in the eyes of the owner of that which was lost, without which there would have been no earnest search for it. The woman is represented as extremely anxious and energetic, lighting the lamp, sweeping the whole house, and carefully examining every nook and crevice, until the missing coin is discovered. Again it is assumed that the fact of the loss, and her trouble over it, had been made known to those about her, and when her search has proved successful she is overjoyed, and calls her women friends together to celebrate the happy finding. 'And when she hath found it, she calleth together her friends (female friends—Young) and neighbours, saying, Rejoice with me, for I have found the piece which I had lost.'

All this might be taken as apposite to the occasion. Jesus had been searching out among persons and in places which the Pharisees and scribes scorned to visit. He had called together the waifs and strays of humanity, whom he made his friends and neighbours, and had celebrated the success of his mission by a friendly entertainment. And his supercilious critics look on disdainfully, lifting up their voices in pious amazement: 'This man receiveth sinners, and eateth with them!' How mean, how low, how destitute of self-respect he is! Nay: but it was they who failed to realise the importance of the work in which he was engaged. The sweet balm of social intercourse never poured forth its fragrance more worthily than on such an occasion as this, when repentant sinners yielded to truth and righteousness, and sought the company of the Son of man, who had come to seek and to save that which was lost. Beings higher than mankind were watching this work of Jesus, and rejoicing in its results. 'Even so, I say unto you, there is joy in the presence of the angels of God over one sinner that repenteth.'

Had this statement been uttered by an ordinary mortal, we might receive it as an inspiration of faith, a sublime flight of poetical imagination. But from the lips of Jesus it is much more than this. The heavenly world, with all its mysteries, lay open to his gaze. No other man could have presumed to teach the prayer 'Thy will be done on earth *as it is in heaven*.' Angels ministered to him on earth: a voice from heaven proclaimed his divine sonship; Moses and Elijah held converse with him on the mountain-top; the departed spirit of one dead and buried heard his voice at the tomb, and came forth in the body at his call; he foresaw and foretold his own death and resurrection; angels sat watching by his grave, and joyously proclaimed its emptiness.—'He is not here: for he is risen, even as he said:' and when his mission to mankind had been fully accomplished, his resurrection-body soared above the earth, became enfolded in a cloud, and was seen no more. 'two men . . . in white apparel' standing below to predict the return of 'this same Jesus which is taken up from you into heaven.' He it is who tells us that 'there is joy in the presence of the angels of God over one sinner that repenteth.' The inhabitants of earth and heaven are linked together by bonds of sympathy and mutual interest, none the less real because to us invisible and incomprehensible. 'Hereafter ye shall see heaven open, and the angels of God ascending and descending upon the Son of man.' [1 John 51]

Surely these parables, thus viewed, are full of instruction and interest; yet theological commentators, not satisfied with their primary, self-evident import, coupled with the momentous truth which Jesus brought out in connection therewith, have set themselves to the task of allegorizing, amplifying, decorating the parables with touches, glosses and fanciful interpretations of their own devising. Here is Alford's attempt in that direction : '*The lost piece of money.* In the following wonderful parable, we have the next class of sinners set before us, sought for and found by the power and work of the Spirit in the Church of Christ. It will be seen, as we proceed, how perfectly this interpretation comes out, not as a fancy, but as the *very kernel and sense* of the parable.' What an assumption! He takes it for granted that Jesus did not bring out 'the very kernel and sense of the parable,' but that 'the interpretation comes out,' that is, Dean Alford's interpretation. He assumes that each of the things mentioned in the parable is itself a parable or simile : the woman, the house, the coin, the lamp. But that there is room for difference of opinion as to their significance is evident from his first remark : 'The *woman* cannot be *the Church absolutely*, for the Church herself is a lost sheep at first, sought and found by the Shepherd.' Observe the expressions, 'absolutely,' and 'the Church *herself*,' and the mention of 'a lost sheep' in elucidating the parable of a lost coin. This haziness of thought and diction is not a good beginning of the exposition. Alford is 'rather' of opinion that the 'house' is the Church, and therefore he considers that the 'woman' must be—but let us take his own words. ' Rather is the *house* here the Church—as will come out by and by ' (how it comes out by and by is by no means clear), 'and the *woman* the *indwelling Spirit* working in it.' That is very bold, the woman having 'friends and neighbours,' who of course must be equal to her in rank and familiar in intercourse. Next : ' All men belong to this Creator-Spirit ; all have been *stamped with the image of God.*' This is an addition if not an improvement to the parable, which referred to the coin but not to its image and superscription. Not satisfied with that touch of his own, Dean Alford adds another : the dust in the house, which somehow was omitted to be mentioned, represents ' sin and death and corruption.' These are his words : ' But the sinner lies in the dust of sin and death and corruption—"wholly unconscious."' These last two words constitute an additional touch of ornamentation : this lack of vitality in the coin did not come to the front in the parable itself. Alford puts those words in inverted commas, probably because he took the idea from Bengel, whom he had before quoted as follows : ' Bengel, in distinguishing the three, says, "The sheep, the drachma, the prodigal son,—signify respectively, (1) the stupid sinner, (2) the sinner wholly unconscious of the fact and of himself, (3) the sinner conscious and of purpose."' Ordinary readers, without the guidance of theologians, could have no idea that Jesus intended to describe three different classes of sinners. Alford proceeds : ' Then the Spirit, lighting the candle of the Lord (Prov. xx. 27 ; Zeph. i. 12), searching every corner and sweeping every unseen place, *finds out* the sinner; restores him to his true value as made for God's glory.' Alford's choice of texts to support his argument is a very strange one. That from Proverbs runs: 'The spirit of man is the lamp of the Lord;' that from Zephaniah: 'And it shall come to pass at that time, that I will search Jerusalem with candles (Heb. lamps).' In no way do these quotations bear out or bear upon the assertion that the 'woman' is to be taken as representing the 'Creator-Spirit.' But now Alford drags in 'the Church,' not in the high, Scriptural sense of 'assembly,' but in the low, common, ritualistic sense of an ecclesiastical intitution: 'This lighting and sweeping are to be understood of the office of the Spirit in the Church, in its various ways of seeking the sinner—by the preaching of repentance, by the Word of God, read, &c. Then comes the joy again.' So the lighting of the lamp and the sweeping, are symbolical of the duties of the ministerial office! What might the woman's broom represent? Why is not that introduced as an additional metaphor, as the 'dust' was? But now something is *brought in* by way of corroboration, simply on the ground that it is *left out* of the parable! 'Her (female) friends and her neighbours are invited — but there is *no return home* now—nor in the explanation, ver. 10, is there any *in heaven*.' Simply, one would naturally think, because the woman, being at home, could not be spoken or thought of as returning home, because the parable did not admit or need the idea. Not so, says Alford, but 'because the Spirit *abides in the Church*— because *the angels are present in the Church*, see 1 Cor. xi. 10.' That is the passage which contains the puzzling words, 'because of the angels.' Alford continues: 'nor is it *shall be* (as in ver. 7, at the return of the Redeemer then future), but *is*—the ministering spirits rejoice over every soul that is brought out of the dust of death into God's treasure-house by the searching of the blessed Spirit.' Here is a new parable, founded upon the original parable by introducing two new metaphors, 'the dust of death' and 'God's treasure-house.' Not by such additions and verbal trivialities as these can we grasp the broad, open lessons designed to be conveyed by the parables. They were spoken not only to but for those who heard them, and who could have no conception of the elaborately wrought out and recondite meanings which, in the course of centuries, have overgrown them, marred their charm, force, freshness, and more or less distorted the truths they were designed to illustrate.

It has seemed right and necessary to criticise thus fully and unreservedly this tissue of explanations and arguments, which may serve as a specimen of the style of thought and method prevalent amongst professed theologians. No one doubts the learning, the honesty, the reverence, the earnestness, the good intentions of this class of men. But we are all subject to the same laws and limits of development, and none can rise above the level of the doctrine he has been taught from childhood upwards, except by a long training in the direction of unfettered, original, independent thought. It is hard and rare indeed for those who have bound themselves solemnly and unreservedly to the acceptance of authorised creeds and articles of religion, to emancipate themselves from that thraldom. Everything is against their doing so. At the best, they can but kick against the pricks in some things, and the opposition and persecution thence ensuing warn them and their fellows against further encroachments in the same direction. The young clergyman begins his career with a stock of inherited theological beliefs, which he no more thinks of questioning and replacing by others, than he would of criticising grammatical rules and framing a new language for himself and the world. He preaches 'the truth' as he has been taught it, and his mind revolves continuously round the subjects with which he deals, always in the same direction. The longer he preaches, the more does this habit and mode of thought become to him as a second nature. At first he was the obedient, humble recipient of dogmatic teaching; now he has become himself a teacher and 'defender of the faith.' So long as the clergy are not left wholly free from the first to believe and preach whatever their own minds and consciences dictate, so long will their numbness of individual thought, their dumbness of enlarged ideas, their narrowness of theological views, cling to them and mar their influence. One who had escaped the trammels of orthodox theology, and whose works are full of a spirit and wisdom rising high above the common standard, J. E. Channing, said truly: 'The consistency of great error with great virtue, is one of the lessons of universal history. But error is not made harmless by such associations.' For that reason, it behoves us to be on our guard against error, and to oppose it whenever and wherever it may be found. The responsibility of an author, dealing with the momentous subjects of religion and morality, would be too overwhelming, apart from full and free criticism. However honest and earnest our searchings after truth, we are all liable to error, and sometimes the more erroneous a doctrine, the more emphatic is its expression, and the more tenacious one's hold of it. Thereby an evil influence has often proceeded from the works of good and thoughtful men, who would be the first to repudiate their wrong conclusions and fallacious arguments, in the light of a more perfect knowledge and wisdom. Take, as an example, the late Dean Alford, whose life was spent in intellectual toil, and who sought in all he wrote to set forth and help forward what he believed to be the true doctrine of Christ. Not one jot or tittle of his writings can be modified now. May it not be, that in that world where we all hope to find more light and truth, he will welcome as a friend any man, be he who he may, who dealt boldly with whatever seemed wrong in his books, however remorseless the exposure of their underlying fallacies? How unwise, how antagonistic to truth and progress, have been the efforts made in past times to stereotype the theological ideas of one generation with the object of imposing them on the next! And how faulty must have been the spirit in the Church which has bowed submissively to such a yoke during many successive generations!

Jesus delivered a third parable, having an obvious bearing on the subject illustrated by the two preceding ones. 'And he said, A certain man had two sons: and the younger of them said to his father, Father, give me the portion of *thy* (Gr. the) substance that falleth to me.' The word 'thy' is introduced in italics by the Revisers, the correct word, 'the,' being banished to the margin. Why should they have gone out of their way to insert a wrong word by the side of the right word? The Authorised Version has neither 'the' nor 'thy.'

15 Luke 11, 12

Young and Tischendorf use 'the,' the rendering of the latter being, 'Father, give me the portion of the property that falls to me.' Alford explains: 'Such a request as this is shewn by Orientalists to have been known in the East, though not among the Jews. The firstborn had *two thirds* of the property, see Deut. xxi. 17.' Young, agreeing with the Authorised Version, has italicised the words 'to me,' which the Revisers have omitted to do.

The father apportioned the property as desired. 'And he divided unto them his living.' The Revisers have not italicised 'his,' which was done in the Authorised Version. Young, following the original, uses the definite article in place of 'his.' Alford observes: 'The father, as implied in the parable, reserves to himself the power during his life over the portion of the firstborn, see ver. 31.'

The intention of the younger son was soon manifested. He realised the property, and emigrated to a distant land. 'And not many days after the younger son gathered all together, and took his journey into a far country.' Not covetousness, but extravagant self-indulgence was his predominant vice. Removed from home influence and restraint, he 'scattered his property' (Tischendorf) recklessly and riotously: 'and there he wasted his substance with riotous living.' So far did he carry his excesses, that absolutely nothing remained to him. Then there came a time of great scarcity and privation throughout the land. 'And when he had spent all, there arose a mighty famine in that country.' In proportion to the scarcity of the necessaries of life was the difficulty of obtaining help or employment. A foreigner, however willing to work, stood but a poor chance when all felt the pressure of the times. The spendthrift found himself reduced to a very low level: 'and he began to be in want.' In this strait he was forced to seek a refuge anywhere. He deliberately bound himself to menial service in a foreign household. 'And he went and joined himself to one of the citizens of that country.' A stranger and an outcast, the lowest drudgery was imposed upon him: 'and he sent him into his field to feed swine.' What a repulsive occupation that, for a man who had scorned to labour at home, and who, rather than do so abroad, had lived in folly and idleness until his last coin was spent. To Jewish ears, the very mention of his present occupation would be abhorrent, swine being classed in their law as unclean animals. So ill paid was his labour, that he lived habitually in a state of semi-starvation, and could have begrudged the swine the food with which he fed them, a full meal being now a luxury beyond his reach. 'And he would fain have been filled with the husks (Gr. the pods of the carob tree) that the swine did eat.' Whether he stooped to beg, may be in doubt; but not a hand was stretched out to relieve his wants: 'and no man gave unto him.' His life of enjoyment had vanished like a dream: homeless, friendless, helpless now, he could but look back upon his past career as a period of insanity, a chaos of self-delusion, vanity, neglected duties, lost opportunities, a fitful delirious fever which had run its course, and left him weak, worn, weary, but, thank God, sound in mind at last. He could realise now the value of the home he had forsaken, and think once more of the father he had neglected. The scenes familiar to him from childhood rose up before him,—the labours of the well-ordered household, all the hired servants there rejoicing in plenty. 'But when he came to himself he said. How many hired servants of my father's have bread enough and to spare.' And here was he, who might have been honoured as a master over them, on the verge of starvation : 'and I perish here with hunger.' Reduced now to the last extremity, no longer deaf to self-reproach, he resolves to take the course which had been open to him from the first. His proud and obstinate self-will has melted away in the fiery trial, his faults are patent to himself, nor will he seek to hide them from others, or shrink even from open acknowledgment. 'I will arise and go to my father, and will say unto him, Father, I have sinned against heaven, and in thy sight.' He had fondly deemed himself above the common lot, and despised the humdrum life of daily toil, had lived for to-day, forgetting the morrow, for pleasure, and not for duty, and now the retributive decree of divine Providence had scourged and avenged his folly. He sees and owns it all, taking shame to himself for the unblushing effrontery with which he had pursued his mad career : he had been fighting against heaven, before his father's face ! It rises up before him now, reproachful, amazed, sorrowful, as when he first decided upon his proudly independent course. He will own himself unworthy of his parentage : 'I am no more worthy to be called thy son.' He will crave only some place of servitude in the paternal home, wherein to atone for the past, as far as may be, by docility and assiduity: 'Make me as one of thy hired servants.' A long course of misery had been needed to bring him to this resolution : but once taken, there was no delay in executing it. 'And he arose, and came to his father.' In how terrible a plight must he have been, as he neared his journey's end ! And with what mingled feelings of hope, doubt, joy, dread, must he have entered upon its last stage ! But while he was still 'a great way off' (Authorised Version), 'yet far distant' (Young), his coming was perceived. Along the road by which, if ever, he must return, the father's eye was gazing, and as, at last—at last, his son's well remembered form appeared, the father's heart rushed forth to meet him. But as he drew near enough to be clearly recognized, what a wreck, what a shadow, what a parody of his former self ! Emaciated, footsore, travel-stained, a humbled spirit in an abject form,—oh ! he must not be left thus one moment longer. The father ran to meet him, his loving arms once more encircled the neck of his erring child, and with a shower of kisses he welcomed his return. 'But while he was yet afar off, his father saw him, and was moved with compassion, and ran, and fell on his neck, and kissed him (Gr. kissed him much) : kissed him tenderly' (Tischendorf). Then, in that first burst of greeting, on the open road, the prodigal made his humble confession. 'And the son said unto him, Father, I have sinned against heaven, and in thy sight : I am no more worthy to be called thy son.' The Revisers note : 'Some ancient authorities add *make me as one of thy hired servants*.' That is not in the Authorised Verson, nor is it adopted by Tischendorf, although it stands in the two oldest MSS. Either, at a very early date, it was introduced from verse 19, or omitted from this verse. It is just such an error as would be likely to arise in copying, and the balance of probability is on the side of its accidental insertion, it being easy for the eye of the copyist to fix on verse 19. No doubt transcribers were chosen for their superior skill in writing, and it would be too much to assume that every one of the class was intelligent and punctiliously honest. The detection of an error of this kind would depend upon the way in which the original MS. was compared with the copy. If the supervisor read out to the copyist, it was in the power of the latter to omit calling attention to what he might consider unimportant discrepancies; and there would be a temptation in that direction, because the accidental omission or insertion of several words together might necessitate the re-writing of a sheet or more of MS. We know how easily printers' errors creep in, despite every precaution. The original 'proof' is now destroyed, and the printed book alone circulated; but in those days the original MS. remained extant, as well as the copies. These trifling variations among the ancient versions handed down to us are not to be wondered at. They are certainly very numerous. The frequent alterations in the oldest MSS., made 'by a later hand,' indicate that the existence of errors was recognised from the first, and the task of rectification undertaken. That task must have been almost, if not quite, as difficult then as it is now.

Whether or not the son actually made the request he had intended, it was at once felt to be an impossibility that his father should treat him as a servant. On reaching home, the domestics were bidden instantly to attend to all the wanderer's needs. The best robe was selected for his wear, a jewel sparkled on his hand, and the weary feet were fitted with shoes. 'But his father said to his servants (Gr. bondservants), Bring forth quickly the best robe, and put it on him; and put a ring on his hand, and shoes on his feet.' What a transformation! What a blessed change from squalor and degradation to luxury, refinement, and deferential service! The father's heart overflowed with joy. He must needs arrange a feast to celebrate his son's return. The stalled calf was ordered to be killed, and preparations made for a merry banquet. 'And bring the fatted calf, and kill it, and let us eat, and make merry.' No greater cause could there be for grateful rejoicing: his son had risen up suddenly, unexpectedly, as one from the dead, or like a straying child found after long and anxious search. 'For this my son was dead, and is alive again; he was lost and is found.' A joyous feast indeed it was: 'And they began to be merry.'

What could the Pharisees and scribes say now against Jesus? What reproach was it to him that he had feasted with sinners, even as this father with his returned prodigal? But Jesus enlarged his parable, picturing therein the evil spirit and temper which these cavillers had displayed.

The elder son as yet knew nothing of his brother's return, and when he came to hear the news it was with undisguised feelings of envy and ill-will. He was away at the time, about the farm, engaged in his routine of duty. As he drew near to the house, what was his astonishment to hear sounds of revelry, music playing and dancing going on! What craze was this which had come over his old father, —to make a feast, and say nothing about it to him? 'Now his elder son was in the field; and as he came and drew nigh to the house, he heard music and dancing.' Unable to divine the mystery, he called one of the servants, and asked what it all meant? 'And he called to him one of the servants (Gr. bondservants), and inquired what these things might be.' Then he learnt the news, over which natural affection should have prompted him to rejoice. 'And he said unto him, Thy brother is come; and thy father hath killed the fatted calf, because he hath received him safe and sound.' The elder thought more about himself at that moment, than about his younger brother. A wave of ill-will and jealousy swept over his soul. His dignity was hurt; his egotism, pride, self-conceit, perverted his judgment, and quenched alike filial respect and brotherly love. In sullen anger, he refused to give a welcome to his brother, to share in the festivities, or even to enter the house. 'But he was angry, and would not go in.' Thus, in the midst of joy, came a sudden, sharp trial to the father's heart. It was a sad presage for the future; it would be a terrible thing for him and them, if these brothers should not shake hands now, should refuse to bury in oblivion faults and animosities, and so mar the peace of the home for ever. All his influence must be exerted to reconcile these two: 'and his father came out, and intreated him.' But the hot-headed son began to complain equally of his father and his brother. He was mightily offended at the slight which had been put upon him. He considered that he had been treated with gross injustice. He had lived for many years a laborious and blameless life, but never once had the father proposed a feast for him and friends of his. 'But he answered and said to his father, Lo, these many years do I serve thee, and I never transgressed a commandment of thine: and *yet* thou never gavest me a kid, that I might make merry with my friends.' But the instant this spendthrift and debauchee returns, a sumptuous entertainment is prepared in honour of the event, no prior notice being sent to the elder son, and no heed given to his absence. 'But when this thy son came, which hath devoured thy living with harlots, thou killedst for him the fatted calf.' The father's answer was grave, passionless, argumentative. There was no thought of putting a slight upon the elder son, who had spent his life by his father's side, and was now heir to all his property. And it was very natural that there should be this outburst of rejoicing on the sudden arrival of him who had been as one dead and lost to them for many years. 'And he said unto him, Son (Gr. child), thou art ever with me, and all that is mine is thine. But it was meet to make merry and be glad: for this thy brother was dead, and is alive *again;* and *was* lost, and is found.'

The parable was sketched with consummate tact and delicacy. None could take offence at it: but how must the career of the prodigal have come home to some of those 'sinners' whom Jesus had not scrupled to receive and welcome! And how accurately did the captiousness and envy of the elder brother portray the spirit by which the Pharisees and scribes were animated! The first and foremost application of the parable lies in that direction: but as every parable is susceptible of a variety of interpretations, it is but natural that commentators should differ widely from each other in their attempts at elucidation. Alford gives his own views, and combats those of others. He says: '*A certain man,*—our heavenly Father, the Creator and Possessor of all: not Christ, who ever represents himself *as a Son.* . . *Two sons,* not, in any direct and primary sense of the Parable, *the Jews and the Gentiles,*' and so on. All such interpretations are of men's own devising, excrescences to the pure and simple teaching of Jesus, glosses, inventions, which can only be profitable when held in check wisely and reverently, and can scarcely fail to be hurtful when pressed in the shape of dogmatic theology. How comes it to be assumed that Jesus intended his parables to be taken as illustrations of truths or doctrines which he himself was not teaching at their first delivery?

The last three parables were spoken to the Pharisees and scribes; the one which follows was delivered to the disciples: 'And he said also unto the disciples'.. It is important to note this distinction whenever it occurs. The word 'disciple' signifies a person who has deliberately placed himself under the instruction and guidance of his Teacher. Not all who attended the discourses of Jesus were disciples, but only such as offered themselves to him and were accepted by him. We have seen how Jesus bade men count the cost before they took upon themselves his discipline, and what trials he foretold for them, even to the loss of all things. Would it not at the time have been a palpable absurdity to say that, nevertheless, every one was called to be his disciple; that none who believed in him could refuse the title, with its accompanying obligations? Is it not equally absurd now to assume that every Christian is, by simple baptism, either infant or adult, enrolled as a disciple? John baptised whole multitudes, but his 'disciples' were alluded to as a body by themselves. It was the very essence of discipleship that the disciple should be, for a time at least, with his Teacher, should 'come after' him, 'follow' him, learn and accept his doctrines, and devote himself to his cause. We read of no female disciples: the work of evangelisation was not suited for them, nor they for it. Mention is made of only one woman, Tabitha, under that designation,—the only instance in which the Greek word is in the feminine form, *mathētria*, —and she had evidently devoted herself entirely to a life apart from worldly interests: 'this woman was full of good works and almsdeeds which she did:' her sphere of action was the making of garments for the poor. In the proper sense of the word, only a living Teacher can have 'disciples,' who, after their Master's death, raise up 'disciples' of their own. We may fondly deem ourselves disciples of Jesus, but in reality we have dwindled down to a very different discipleship, and not one of us in a million dreams of attempting to carry out every commandment which Jesus laid upon his disciples. Nor is it incumbent upon us to do so. He would have all believe in him, but he chose, even while he lived on earth, few to be his disciples. In the four Gospels the word 'disciple,' *mathētēs*, occurs 230 times. In every instance the use of the term indicates a clear, sharp distinction between 'disciples' and others. One passage only might seem, at first sight, of somewhat doubtful meaning: when the Pharisees said, 'We are disciples of Moses;' but no doubt they claimed the title exclusively, for Jesus said of them, 'The scribes and the Pharisees sit on Moses' seat:' their lives were devoted to the promulgation and enforcement of his law. The true sense of the word comes out in the passage: 'Upon this many of his disciples went back, and WALKED NO MORE WITH HIM. Jesus said therefore unto the twelve, Would ye also go AWAY?' And again the statement that 'Jesus was making and baptizing more disciples than John (although Jesus himself baptized not, but his disciples).' Jesus certainly did not baptize more persons than John, but 'more disciples,' the disciples he had made already being, it would seem, employed in administering baptism to those who were anxious to join them. Accordingly we find that Jesus was able at one time to appoint 'seventy others,' whom he sent 'two and two before his face into every city and place whither he himself was about to come.' Subsequently to the Gospels the word 'disciple' occurs in the New Testament 30 times. Let us examine those passages. 'When the number of the disciples was multiplied .... the twelve called the multitude of the disciples unto them.' It must not be assumed that 'disciples' here is synonymous with 'believers.' The contrary appears to be the fact, for the question was as to whether a certain work should be undertaken by the twelve or by other disciples. Seven of the latter were appointed 'over this business,' among whom was Stephen, whose life seems to have been entirely devoted to the work of evangelisation, for we are told that he 'wrought great wonders and signs among the people,' and was occupied in disputations, until he was brought to a public trial on account of his preaching, and suffered for it the penalty of death. 'The number of the disciples multiplied in Jerusalem exceedingly: and a great company of the priests were obedient to the faith.' It is not said that the priests became disciples: they could not, their lives being devoted to the performance of their priestly functions. The title applied to those who were 'obedient to the faith,' although not 'disciples,' was 'believers.' 'And believers were the more added to the Lord, multitudes both of men and women.' And Timothy was exhorted: 'Be thou an ensample to them that believe.' Again: 'Thou seest, brother, how many thousands (Gr. myriads) there are among the Jews of them which have believed.' 'As touching the Gentiles which have believed.' Those myriads of Jews and Gentiles are not styled disciples: they constituted the churches or assemblies, for whose formation and edification the multitude of disciples was required. 'Why tempt ye God, that ye should put a yoke upon the neck of the disciples, which neither our fathers nor we were able to bear?' Peter's argument was against compelling the 'disciples' to teach the Gentiles that they must be circumcised: that doctrine would have been a yoke on the teachers' necks. We read that Paul 'assayed to join himself to the disciples: and they were all afraid of him, not believing that he was a disciple.' Obviously Paul's object was to associate himself with the disciples in their work: none would have been afraid at his simply professing his faith in Christ. 'Saul, yet breathing threatening and slaughter against the disciples of the Lord,' that is, against those who were engaged in the work of promulgating the hated doctrine. 'That if he found any that were of the Way, whether men or women, he might bring them bound to Jerusalem.' To make sure of getting at the disciples, he desired to bring every professed believer to Jerusalem for examination. In short, all the passages lead to the same conclusion: discipleship to Jesus, or to his doctrine, involves entire dedication to his cause and work. 'Believers' generally should be content with that humbler title; and we should ever bear in mind that directions given by Jesus specially to his 'disciples' are not to be deemed of universal application. Misapprehension on this point has led to much error. Finding that some of the commands of Jesus are unsuited for, and, in truth, impossible of general adoption, and failing to understand that they were addressed to disciples, and not to all believers, many thoughtful, earnest-minded men have looked upon Christianity as a thing too high for them; whilst those who profess to have devoted themselves to the work of Jesus, and who, as his 'disciples,' teachers of his truth, devotees to his cause, should have taken up and carried out *all* his maxims, have made no attempt to do so, but have swum with the tide of ordinary humanity. The evil takes two directions: the religion of Jesus is deemed by some an ideal system, too lofty and refined for the grasp of common men and women; and those who have made profession of discipleship, claiming the rank and title of ministers and ambassadors of Christ, have never even aimed at that ideal which Jesus desired that his disciples should exhibit to the world. We are here treading on difficult ground: so much the more need is there for bold, free, careful, honest thought and speech. Jesus did not call all men, but he did call some, to lead a life conformable to his ideal. Once, to a young man whom he had looked upon and loved, he said: 'If thou wouldest be perfect, go, sell that thou hast, and give to the poor, and thou shalt have treasure in heaven: and come, follow me.' It is open to question whether the doctrine of the cross is not preached both too high and too low. The sheep and their shepherds cannot stand upon the same level. The 'perfect' life must be entirely consistent with the precepts of Jesus, in the fulness of their breadth and depth. Count Tolstoi has lately raised and grappled with this puzzling question. He carries to its literal and logical extreme Christ's doctrine of non-resistance. Unfortunately he starts with a wrong assumption, when he says:* 'In the Sermon on the Mount, addressed to all men, He (Jesus) says: "And if anybody sue thee at the law for thy coat, let him have thy cloak also." Therefore He forbids our going to law.' But the sermon on the mount was not 'addressed to all men,' but to the disciples: 'And seeing the multitudes, he went up into the mountain: and when he had sat down, his disciples came unto him: and he opened his mouth and taught them.' Count Tolstoi continues: 'But perhaps this applies only to the relations between private individuals and public courts of law; yet Christ does not deny justice itself, and admits in Christian societies the existence of persons chosen for the purpose of administering justice. I see that this hypothesis is likewise inadmissible. In His prayer Christ enjoins all men, without any exception, to forgive, as they hope to be forgiven. We find the same precept repeated many times. Each man must forgive his brother when he prays, and before bringing his gift. Then how can a man judge and condemn another when, according to the faith he professes, he is bound to forgive? Thus I see that, according to the doctrine of Christ, a judge who condemns his fellow-creature to death is no Christian.' The argument and conclusion are pertinent, only Count Tolstoi has overlooked the fact that the Lord's prayer was for disciples. Matthew gives it as part of the Sermon on the Mount,

_{10 Mark 21}

_{5 Mat. 2}

---

* "What I believe." Translated from the Russian. Page 26. Elliot Stock, 62, Paternoster Row.

and Luke introduces it as follows: 'And it came to pass, as he was praying in a certain place, that when he ceased, one of his disciples said unto him, Lord, teach us to pray, even as John also taught his disciples.' In dealing with this difficult question, it is important not to start with a false assumption. Nevertheless Tolstoi's book supplies much food for thought. He says: 'Each of us gives the doctrine of Christ an interpretation of his own, but it is never the direct and simple one which flows out of his words. We have grounded the conduct of our lives on a principle which He rejects; and we do not choose to understand His teaching in its simple and direct sense. Those who call themselves "believers" believe that Christ-God, the second person of the Trinity, made Himself man in order to set us an example how to live, and they strictly fulfil the most complicated duties, such as preparing for the sacraments, building churches, sending out missionaries, naming pastors for parochial administration, etc.: they forget only one trifling circumstance—to do as He tells them.' Again: 'Christ says that the law of resistance by violence, which you have made the basis of your lives, is unnatural and wrong; and He gives us instead the law of non-resistance, which, He tells us, can alone deliver us from evil. He says: "You think to eradicate evil by your human laws of violence; they only increase it. During thousands and thousands of years you have tried to annihilate evil by evil, and you have not annihilated it; you have but increased it. Follow the teaching I give you by word and deed, and you will prove its practical power." Not only does He speaks thus, but He remains true to His own doctrine not to resist evil in His life and in His death. Believers take all this in with their ears, hear it read in churches, calling it the Word of God. They call Him God, and then they say, "His doctrine is sublime, but the organization of our lives renders its observance impossible: it would change the whole course of our lives, to which we are so used and with which we are so satisfied. Therefore, we believe in His doctrine, only as an ideal which man must strive after—an ideal which is to be obtained by prayer, by believing in the sacraments, in redemption, and in the resurrection of the dead."'

Everything which Jesus commanded his 'disciples,' they were bound to obey. At the same time, counsels given to them may be followed, more or less, by others also. Of his disciples Jesus said: 'They are not of the world, even as I am not of the world.' 'I have given them thy word: and the world hated them, because they are not of the world, even as I am not of the world.' The selection of disciples out of the world did not imply the condemnation of other men, but the contrary: 'For God sent not the Son into the world to judge the world, but that the world should be saved through him.' And his plan of saving men was through the disciples, to whom he said: 'Ye are the salt of the earth . . . Ye are the light of the world.' The disciples of Jesus were as much out of, apart from the world, as afterwards were anchorites of the desert, monks and nuns, as much a class by themselves, only with very different duties laid upon them than those of making prayers, chanting hymns, readings of Scripture, and frequent communion, coupled with a worship more or less idolatrous of the sacramental bread and wine. All baptised Christians are no more 'disciples' of Jesus, in the proper sense of the word, than they are monks or nuns. The note of Christian obligation has been pitched too high for ordinary men and women. The ideal Jesus set before the world was a real and visible one: a body of men living on earth according to his own heavenly maxims. The Church of England has, instead of holding forth that reality, assumed that all, without exception, are called to lead the ideal life. Jesus warned all not to profess discipleship who were not resolutely determined to take up his cross and follow him: but over every baptised infant the minister utters the words: 'We receive this child into the congregation of Christ's flock;' that should have been enough, but he must add: 'and do sign *him* with the sign of the Cross, in token that hereafter *he* shall not be ashamed to fight under his banner, against sin, the world, and the devil; and to continue Christ's faithful soldier and servant unto *his* life's end.' Brave words these: but nothing more! In how many cases must they be, if sober truth be spoken, a solemn farce! The child, perchance, grows up in the slums, picks up the language of the gutter; until the last few years it might have been left without the merest rudimentary intellectual teaching: even at the best, it will lead only an average, common-place life, labouring perforce for the meat which perisheth, caring and knowing nothing about Christ's cross, or any soldiership under his banner. And most of us, except the comparatively few who come within the charmed circle of sacerdotal influence, make but feeble attempts and faint profession of active service in the cause of Jesus. It cannot be right to apply indiscriminately, to every infant, words of momentous import such as would suit the consecration of a Bishop. Precisely the opposite plan was adopted by Jesus. Not only did he restrict the call to discipleship, but he was ever careful not to impose on the multitudes any doctrines which might be above their capacities. He spoke constantly to them in similes. 'With many such parables [4 Mark iv. 34] spake he the word unto them, as they were able to hear it: and without a parable spake he not unto them: but privately to his own disciples he expounded all things.' And when the disciples asked the reason for his reticence towards others, he explained that it was not given to the multitudes to comprehend the mysteries of the kingdom of heaven, their vision, hearing, and understanding being imperfect. 'And the disciples came, and said unto him, Why speakest thou unto [12 Mat. 10, 11, 13] them in parables? And he answered and said unto them, Unto you it is given to know the mysteries of the kingdom of heaven, but to them it is not given . . Therefore speak I to them in parables: because seeing they see not, and hearing they hear not, neither do they understand.' Why should we be afraid of a principle thus sanctioned by Jesus? If discipleship, involving implicit, unreserved obedience, was not laid by him upon all who heard him preach the gospel, how much less can such an obligation be insisted on universally now? We profess too much; and having done so, we minimise and explain away certain plain directions of Jesus, the simple truth being that they are too high for us, that we do not choose to adopt them. It were better to say so boldly: to confess ourselves 'believers' but not 'disciples.' 'Resist not him that is evil: but whosoever [5 Mat. 39, 40] smiteth thee on thy right cheek, turn to him the other also. And if any man would go to law with thee, and take away thy coat, let him have thy cloke also.' Did the apostle Paul hold it obligatory upon all believers to assert no right by legal means? No: on the contrary, he urged that the 'assembly' itself should constitute a legal tribunal, to whose decisions believers should bow, rather than resort to adjudication by the 'unrighteous.' 'Dare any of you, having a matter against his neighbour, go to law before the unrighteous, and not before the saints?... Are ye unworthy to judge the smallest matters?... Is it so, that there cannot be *found* among you one wise man, who shall be able to decide between his brethren, but brother goeth to law with brother, and that before unbelievers?' That suggestion of the apostle was in conformity with the plan laid down by Jesus for the submission of all trespasses and faults to the judgment of the assembly. But Paul urged at the same time that there was a higher standard lost sight of by them in thus resorting to lawsuits in any shape. 'Nay, already it is altogether a defect in you (or, a loss to you), that ye have lawsuits one with another. Why not rather take wrong? why not rather be defrauded?' That would be a following out of Christ's counsel of perfection, thereby making themselves in that respect his disciples indeed. What shall be said then about war and bloodshed? Is not the profession of a soldier diametrically opposed to the teaching of Jesus? John did not refuse baptism to soldiers on service, but surely they could never be called his 'disciples,' much less 'disciples' of Jesus. And yet we read of Cornelius, a centurion of the Italian cohort, 'a devout man, and one that feared God with all his house, who gave much alms to the people, and prayed to God alway.' He was assured by an angel of the approval of God, and was baptised into the faith of Jesus: yet without relinquishing his trade of arms, he could never presume to call himself a 'disciple' of Jesus, being simply a believer in him, saved indeed through him, but not wholly conformed to his life and doctrine, a servant still of the Roman Emperor, and not of him who said, 'Put up again thy sword into its place: for all they that take the sword shall perish with the sword.' In modern phraseology, we might say he was a Christian although not a disciple: but we read that 'the DISCIPLES were called Christians first in Antioch,' doubtless from their strict adherence to the tenets of Jesus, which marked them out as his followers, their new principles of action and mode of life giving rise to a new title. Count Tolstoi does not use the term 'Christians' in its primitive sense; but if it be restricted to 'disciples,' his argument is logical, and his conclusions, however startling, beyond dispute.

The parable which Jesus delivered to his disciples is as follows,— 'There was a certain rich man, which had a steward; and the same was accused unto him that he was wasting his goods.' The master called his servant, challenged him to refute the accusation if he could, decided that he was unfit to retain his office, and required him to make up his accounts. 'And he called him, and said unto him, What is this that I hear of thee? render the account of thy stewardship: for thou canst be no longer steward.' The loss of his office gave occasion for serious reflection: not by way of self-accusation or regret for any past misdoings, but as to the best method of 'feathering his nest' for the future. If not unfit, he was certainly indisposed for manual labour, and he scorned the idea of asking loans or favours.

'And the steward said within himself, What shall I do, seeing that my lord taketh away the stewardship from me? I have not strength to dig; to beg I am ashamed.' The 'I cannot' of the Authorised Version is replaced by 'I have not strength to:' other translators do not go so far: Young and Tischendorf have simply 'I am not able,' and Luther, 'graben mag ich nicht,' 'dig I may not.' Being in this dilemma, he set his wits to work, and devised a scheme which was as clever and far-sighted as it was unprincipled and immoral. 'I am resolved what to do, that, when I am put out of the stewardship, they may receive me into their houses.' He could yet manage, at his master's cost, to ingratiate himself with the tenants or debtors of the estate. He knew human nature well enough to rely upon their covetousness and self-interest, without much risk of being foiled by any conscientious scruples on their part. By virtue of his office he would naturally have great power over these men, for it rested with him to drive a hard bargain or the reverse, to press for payment or to do them a good turn. This latter was his cue now. 'And calling to him each one of his lord's debtors, he said to the first, How much owest thou unto my lord?' Not a pleasant question at any time, and one likely to awaken anxiety if it were known that the steward was about to close his accounts. 'And he said, A hundred measures (Gr. baths) of oil.' Tischendorf renders, 'pipes of oil,' and Samuel Sharpe inserts, '(or seven hundred gallons).' It was a large quantity: too much by half, said this generous steward. Here is your account; sit down at once, and alter it yourself by that amount. 'And he said unto him, Take thy bond (Gr. writings), and sit down quickly and write fifty.' It was all regular and legal enough to pass muster: the steward was yet in office, authorised to act, master of the situation. If he pronounced the sum excessive, and suggested the amendment of the document, it was not for the debtor to say him nay. 'Then said he to another, And how much owest thou?' The word 'and' before 'how' sufficiently indicates either that all the debtors were assembled together, or at least that no concealment was attempted. Each would hope to be treated as his neighbour had been, and thenceforth they would have common cause to shield and justify each other, and maintain, if questioned, the spontaneousness and validity of the transaction. The second was dealt with in the same liberal manner as the first. 'And he said, A hundred measures (Gr. cors) of wheat. He said unto him, Take thy bond (Gr. writings), and write fourscore.' Young renders 'homers,' Tischendorf 'quarters;' Sharpe has, 'a hundred Cors (or seven thousand gallons).' The value in each case was considerable. Yet these were only two instances out of many. Nothing was said to any one of the debtors about a division of the spoil. As one after another fell into the trap laid by the wily steward, his power over each and all of them became so much the more. Each knew himself to be implicated with others in a transaction which would scarcely bear investigation, and which it would be best for all to hush up for ever. He had made himself a friend, a benefactor to every one of them. He could claim henceforth, as it suited him, some return at their hands. He having freely given them so much capital, might justly set up a claim to so much interest. He had put them on the best terms with himself, and would take care to give them the opportunity of reciprocating his good offices. Thenceforth they would undoubtedly, one and all, be willing to receive him into their houses; he need not be a permanent guest anywhere, having free choice of all. The plan, however unprincipled, was cleverly conceived and skilfully carried out. So large a deduction from the revenue of the estate was necessarily detected, but the owner seems to have felt himself helpless either to remedy or resent the loss, and is represented as simply expressing his admiration at the consummate audacity, ability and foresight of the steward. 'And his lord commended the unrighteous steward (Gr. the steward of unrighteousness) because he had done wisely.' There is no approval of the man's character, which is sufficiently condemned by the title given him, 'the steward of unrighteousness.' Dean Alford took upon himself to render 'the lord' by 'his lord,' and observed: 'The A. V. ought to have been thus expressed, and not *the lord*, and there would have been no ambiguity.' The Revisers have made the alteration; but Tischendorf, Young and Luther, following the original, render 'the lord.' Sharpe throughout the parable has 'the master,' which removes all doubt. It is well to be clear on the point, although the next sentence shows that Jesus himself endorsed the opinion of the master.

Commentators, as usual, have assumed the parable to contain hidden meanings not brought out or indicated by Jesus. Accordingly their interpretations are various and contradictory. Alford says: 'In the interpretation, the rich man is *the Almighty Possessor of all things*. This is the *only tenable view*. Meyer, who supposes him to be mammon (defending it by the consideration that *dismissal from his service* is equivalent to *being received into everlasting habitations*, which it *is not*), is involved in inextricable difficulties further on. Olshausen's view, that he represents the *Devil*, the *prince of this world*, will be found equally untenable. Schleiermacher's, that the *Romans* are intended, whose stewards the Publicans were, and that the debtors are the Jews, hardly needs refuting: certainly not *more* refuting than any consistent exposition will of itself furnish.' We are not here compelled to choose between God and the Devil. Why should expounders of the parables introduce such ideas, which are but arbitrary guesses after all, and which keep out of view those *human* lessons which Jesus sought to inculcate. This parable is of so peculiar a character that we might well stand in doubt as to the true interpretation, had not Jesus himself undertaken to guide us. He drew seven lessons from the parable.

1. The wise and thrifty use of opportunities.
2. The use which his disciples should make of wealth.
3. The inseparable connection between character and conduct.
4. And between conduct and destiny.
5. And between responsibility and freedom.
6. The need for singleness of mind and purpose.
7. The choice between discipleship and money-making.

(1). Here is the foremost lesson. 'For the sons of this world (or, age) are for their own generation wiser than the sons of the light.' Those whose aims and hopes are bounded by the present life, display greater prudence in regard to their future welfare than do those who are enlightened by higher principles and are called to a nobler destiny. Instead of simply drifting on towards futurity, bewailing what is past and dreading what is to come, it behoves us to take account of what is left to us of life and energy, anticipating the fast approaching day when our present stewardship must be resigned, and a new stage of being entered upon.

(2). Jesus urged his disciples to anticipate and prepare for that, by rightly using the wealth of this world. 'And I say unto you, Make to yourselves friends by means of (Gr. out of) the mammon of unrighteousness; that, when it shall fail, they may receive you into the eternal tabernacles.' Tischendorf renders 'mammon of unrighteousness' as 'mammon of injustice.' Wealth is so unevenly and unfairly apportioned among men as to justify the appropriateness of this title. The Authorised Version has 'when ye fail,' which is changed by the Revisers and Tischendorf to 'when it shall fail.' The Alexandrine MS. stood so from the first, and it is the altered reading of the Vatican MS. Young renders 'eternal' as 'age-during.'

This application of the parable is very direct and peculiar. Dropping all thought of the want of honest principle on the part of the steward, Jesus held up as an example his friendly and munificent spirit. And inasmuch as all must deal with money, the 'unrighteous mammon' which has no connection with moral rectitude, he counselled his disciples to turn it social uses, cementing thereby the bonds of mutual friendship. And as the views of the steward reached beyond his term of office, so must their views reach beyond the present life. As his emoluments were bound to cease, so must their hold on earthly possessions; and as his object was to provide for himself a home for the future among friends, so they should look forward to a welcome, by those who have been made friends here, into a far more enduring home. The expression 'age-during tabernacles' sufficiently indicates the unworldliness of the exhortation. Jesus brings out the fact of a continuity of existence, the friendships formed in this life being perpetuated in the next. His words imply, moreover, a condition of existence analogous to the present, under the same necessities for mutual help and comfort, the lot of each individual there as dependent as it is here on the dispositions and actions of his fellows. Our relative positions may be reversed, but the grand law of retribution will continue to work through human instrumentality. Jesus does not say, Give, and God will recompense you; but, Make to yourselves friends by giving, and they will repay you. This parable will not bear close pressing—To attempt that, eads to its distortion in one direction or another. All thought of the rascality of the steward has to be dropped: there is nothing imitable in that. His purely selfish motive must not be ours; and yet it is true that as we sow in social matters, so we shall reap. Neither can it be imagined that benefactors must survive the friends they have made, and who will of necessity have gone before and be in a position to offer helpful ministrations; nor is to be assumed that the poor in this world will be transformed into the rich of the next: nor that those whose motives and lives have been highest on earth will hereafter need the help of those they befriended. Nor must the fact be overlooked that the parable was spoken to 'disciples,' whose choice of following Jesus involved the relinquishment of worldly affairs, hopes, position,—to the 'little flock' who from the first had been exhorted, 'Sell that ye have, and give alms; make for yourselves purses which wax not old, a treasure in the heavens that faileth not. For where your treasure is, there will your heart be also.' To apply such directions to all alike would be absurd: Christian society cannot be founded on the basis of all giving up everything, and Jesus never propounded so monstrous and mischievous a doctrine. If maxims intended for comparatively few are sought to be made of universal application, the only result must be, as it has been, to fritter away the sense of the wise and necessary counsels given by Jesus to his disciples, and to perpetuate the false notion that none can comply literally and fully with his commands. He never laid upon all men's shoulders the burden of discipleship: and we wrong his spirit and pervert his words by mistaking the former and explaining away the latter. It behoves every Christian to act up to his profession. If he professes himself a disciple, let him truly and completely carry out every instruction given to disciples; and let the sober, solemn truth be recognised, that a 'minister' of Christ and a 'disciple' of Christ are synonymous terms. As it is, in this matter of the giving away of property, we seem to think that the man who gives, not all but most, comes nearest to the ideal of a Christian. Such a conception is mean and paltry. If a man gave up all he had, but not himself to the work of evangelisation, he would still be no 'disciple.' Aye! and the thought is worth our pondering, whether any 'disciple' of Jesus is justified in holding property, seeing he must live for heaven, and lay up his only treasure there? Let us take our stand on lower ground. The command has not been addressed to us, as it was to the young man who wanted to be 'perfect': 'Sell that thou hast, and give to the poor, and thou shalt have treasure in heaven: and come, follow me.' Still, the spirit of discipleship may be ours, more or less, as we are able to receive it; and inasmuch as the parable of the unjust steward was obviously designed to elucidate rather principles of action than any particular form of action, we may lay hold, to our comfort and profit, on the truths deducible therefrom. 'Make to yourselves friends . . . that they may receive you into the eternal tabernacles.' The words of Jesus convey a charming picture of the life to come: to rejoin those we have known and loved on earth, to receive from them a hearty welcome, to enter their heavenly homes, to renew, under better auspices, all friendly intimacies, and share in common our far more enduring inheritance, all mutual offices of tender love and sweet fellowship still existent and interchanged: the hope is more than all we could desire, and the reality beyond our powers of conception. God be thanked for such a revelation! The clay and dross of earth are transmutable, by a heavenly alchemy, into the spirit and life of the world to come; our earthly homes have their antitypes in heaven. Jesus sets before us the duty, not of promiscuous almsgiving, but of social charities. Our best and truest friends must be those of our own household and the comparatively few who come within the circle of our personal influence. To do our utmost, wisely and liberally, for all about us, is to uncoil a chain of love which will join earth and heaven, and circle round eternity.

(3). The third deduction drawn by Jesus from the parable is in the words: 'He that is faithful in a very little is faithful also in much; and he that is unrighteous in a very little is unrighteous also in much.' The steward's negligence of oversight which led to the simple 'wasting' of his master's goods, was at once, under the pressure of temptation, replaced by a deliberate scheme of robbery. Punctiliousness with respect to small duties is a good augury of fidelity in general, and the rule reversed is equally true. Every trust is a test of character, and the qualities displayed in one condition of existence are sure to act under all circumstances.

(4). From this consideration Jesus drew the inference: 'If therefore ye have not been faithful in the unrighteous mammon, who will commit to your trust the true *riches?*' Alford notes that the italicised word 'riches' is 'not expressed in the original.' Tischendorf renders: 'who will commit to your trust the true good?' Young's rendering is no doubt preferable: 'If, then, in the unrighteous riches ye were not faithful—the true who will entrust to you?' The contrast is between 'true' and 'unrighteous,' both words referring to 'riches.' The words are used in the same way elsewhere: 'The same is true, and no unrighteousness is in him.' There is a form of wealth to which no injustice clings, which is attainable only in conjunction with moral rectitude, and the distribution of which is impartial and unselfish. Jesus does not further specify its nature; but probably we shall not err in interpreting it to mean that miraculous power over diseases and over hostile spirits which was constantly exhibited by Jesus, and which he imparted, as they were able to receive it, to his disciples, making it an essential preliminary that before going forth to exercise it, they should strip themselves of all money and everything superfluous, and determine to take no recompense beyond food and lodging. Suppose one of those seventy whom Jesus thus sent forth, had filled his purse, and tried to sell his miraculous gifts: where would have been the faith on which alone his power depended? 'Thy silver perish with thee,' said Peter to Simon the sorcerer, 'because thou hast thought to obtain the gift of God with money.' Spiritual gifts and worldly wealth lie very far apart: they are, in truth, inimical. So Jesus taught, and on that principle his disciples acted. But the right use of wealth is a test of character. The first followers of Jesus were called upon to give it up, and gave it up altogether, that they might secure to themselves a more enduring treasure. The proper spending of money requires soundness of judgment, liberality of mind, unselfishness of motive. The getting and the keeping of it are hard enough, and at that point the efforts of many terminate: the method and habit of disbursing it wisely and freely are harder still. Self-denial may be coupled with rapacity, parsimony with covetousness, profusion with recklessness and self-indulgence. If our minds and hearts lead us astray in dealing with the current coin of the world, which not only symbolises but actually embodies effort, power, influence, how can we be fit for higher gifts, for a wider and more unfettered sphere of action, for the 'true riches' which the Son of man shall give unto us?

(5.) Jesus dwelt on this idea, adding: 'And if ye have not been faithful in that which is another's, who will give you that which is your own?' The Revisers note that 'some ancient authorities read *our own.*' That is not the reading of the three oldest MSS. It is incongruous, and may be dismissed as erroneous. The words of Jesus import that our earthly duties constitute a training for a higher stage of existence. The unfaithfulness of the steward deprived him of all opportunity of rising in the world, and kept him in a state of utter dependence upon others. The due fulfilment of one trust certifies our fitness for another; and to fall short of our duty in any assigned responsibility, must prevent our advancement to a position involving unfettered powers of action. The connection here indicated by Jesus between temporal and spiritual gifts deserves to be more deeply pondered than it is. The fact gives significance and dignity alike to the lowest and the highest earthly occupations. This world is our school: labour our taskmaster; our home lies elsewhere, and our life to come is hid with Christ in God. The earning of a livelihood, the acquirement, employment, and distribution of wealth, call forth the exercise of moral qualities, and serve as stepping-stones to a higher platform of thought and energy. All the concerns of this life, rightly viewed and utilised, tend heavenwards. In proportion to our sense of responsibility, and our earnest devotion to the duties of this life, will be our fitness for heavenly and spiritual things, when the time shall come for us to enter upon them.

(6). From the steward's breach of trust in preferring the interest of his friends to that of his master, Jesus drew another lesson. 'No servant (Gr. household-servant) can serve two masters: for either he will hate the one, and love the other; or else he will hold to one, and despise the other.' The maxim must not be misread, as though it were impossible to undertake the management of conflicting interests. It is a matter of daily experience that upright men can and do act independently of favour or self-interest. The reference is to a 'household-servant,' the rendering of Young and Tischendorf being 'domestic.' There must not be two masters in one house; a servant must not owe a divided allegiance. Not only will the two controlling powers clash, but the servant must needs incline to the one or the other. Professing equal devotion to both, either he will obey one willingly and the other unwillingly, or deliberately refuse obedience to one of the two. A double rule may be so harmonised as to become practically one mastership; but Jesus had in mind two opposing powers, putting forth diverse claims impossible to reconcile, so utterly different in character and purpose, that if love be felt for the one, antipathy must exist to the other, and submission to one involve disobedience to the other.

¹⁶ Luke 13

(7). This parable lies within the previous parable, and is applied by Jesus in the same direction: 'Ye cannot serve God and mammon.' The choice lay between discipleship and money-making. Jesus does not hint at anything wrong or degrading in the latter. Young simply renders 'mammon' by the word 'riches.' The entire time, energy, and devotion of a domestic are claimed by his master: the service of God to which Jesus here alludes is of that kind. The man who had professed discipleship was not free for the ordinary business of the world. The disciples, to whom the parable was addressed, must disentangle themselves from their former avocations: they could not attend as before, and as other men, to the concerns of this life; they professed to have accepted the call of Jesus, and must devote themselves unreservedly to his cause. To regard this statement of Jesus as applicable to every baptised Christian is to mistake its bearing, to involve our ideas of duty in inextricable confusion, and to encourage that mild, unconscious hypocrisy which grows out of half truths and wrong notions. The majority of mankind throughout their lives do, perforce or willingly, 'serve riches.' It is incumbent upon most to labour for daily bread, for family requirements, for the education and advancement of children, for the accumulation before our death of property for those we love and must leave behind. It were absurd to argue against this as being contrary to the law of Christ : it is the teaching of nature ; it is the decree of Providence ; it is an instinct of humanity to make the best of this earthly life which God has given us. The manufacturer who invests his capital in buildings and machinery, the merchant who ventures on the importation or exportation of goods, the agent who undertakes their disposal, the banker who provides the requisite coin and credit, the tradesman who distributes according to the requirements of the community: all these are engrossed, six days out of seven, in the work of 'serving riches.' Not for them is there any command to forsake houses, lands, brethren, wife, children, for Christ's sake. Let us face this question honestly, and clear our minds of cant with respect to it. Away with the folly of imagining ourselves 'disciples' and 'followers' of Jesus, when we are not such in reality, and have no intention of making an effort to become such. The teaching and exhortations of Jesus must be applied with judgment. They deserve an amount of thought and study which they have not received. Ministers of the gospel start with the idea that they know all about the matter: have they not studied 'theology?' Yes: and what they have been taught, that they will teach. The errors attaching to gospel truth are propagated the more easily, owing to the fetters which our well-meaning forefathers unwisely imposed upon freedom of opinion in religious matters. Under pains and penalties, what they fondly and falsely deemed 'the truth, the whole truth, and nothing but the truth,' has been taken for granted, upheld, proclaimed by their most obedient followers. At the same time, the doctrine of Scriptural inspiration has had the effect of making it an orthodox opinion that every syllable of the Bible comes direct from God, and hence that every command therein is his, and that all his commands are obligatory upon all. Accepting generalisations such as these, the faculty of discrimination has been well nigh lost for want of exercise ; the maxims of Jesus have been taken all together, blended into a hotchpot, and then equally apportioned out to the whole body of Christians, share and share alike, or so much to each as each may care to appropriate. A clergyman, a bishop, an archbishop, is no more a 'disciple,' forsooth, than the school child who is able to learn the catechism ! And so the solemn call of Jesus to his 'followers' is taken to have no special application to our spiritual pastors; they, although claiming to be representatives of Christ, are as free to make a purse for themselves as other men are ! On the other hand, in some mysterious way apart from the ordinary process of reasoning, the commands not to serve riches, not to lay up treasure upon the earth, to forsake all for Christ's sake, to take up his cross and follow him, never to return a blow, never to bring an action at law, are held to be within the pale of ordinary Christian duties, incumbent upon all alike, either capable of fulfilment generally, or not capable of fulfilment at all ! What a farce is this ! How can we ever learn the mind of Christ, whilst such confusion of thought and prevarication of judgment remain unchecked, unreproved, undetected?

The remarks of Jesus to his disciples were listened to by the Pharisees. They were a money-loving class, and openly expressed their contempt for such teaching. 'And the Pharisees, who were lovers of money, heard all these things; and they scoffed at him.' Jesus solemnly reproved their unjust levity. Nothing easier than to mock at any earnest teacher, to turn the laugh against him, gaining applause themselves whilst bringing him into contempt. 'And he said unto them, Ye are they that justify yourselves in the sight of men.' But their conduct and their principles were subject to Divine scrutiny, and that which was highly esteemed by men was hateful to God. 'But God knoweth your hearts: for that which is exalted among men is an abomination in the sight of God.' Jesus specified two conspicuous instances of repugnance to the will of God: 1. The persistent opposition to the introduction of the gospel. 2. The operation of the law of divorce.

(1). The time had come for the introduction of a higher system of morality, based on a new religious teaching. John the Baptist had come as the harbinger of that better state of things. 'The law and the prophets *were* until John: from that time the gospel of the kingdom of God is preached.' In the Authorised Version the words 'the gospel of' are omitted. Tischendorf agrees with the Revised Version; Luther rendered: 'das Reich Gottes durchs Evangelium gepredigt'; Young's version stands: 'since then the reign of God is proclaimed as good news.' The verb in the original, *euangelizō*, signifies to preach or announce good news. Yet no free acceptance of the proffered boon was allowed to men: whoever wished to enter the kingdom of God had to force his way through obstacles: 'and every man entereth violently into it.' The Authorised Version has: 'and every man presseth into it'; Young adopted that wording, but Tischendorf strengthened the expression as the Revisers have done: 'and every one enters into it with violence'; Luther has: 'und jedermann dringet mit Gewalt hinein, 'and every one presses in with force.' The spirit of religious intolerance prevailed, and it was diametrically opposed to the divine purposes designed for the advancement of humanity.

(2). Simultaneously with this active hostility to the gospel, there was a lack of regard to that divine law which is as immutable and irrefragable as the universe itself. 'But it is easier for heaven and earth to pass away than for one tittle of the law to fall.' Against the deliberate, constant, recognised infraction of that law in the most sacred relationship of life, Jesus emphatically protested. He asserted that the Mosaic law of divorce was an infraction of the divine law— 'Thou shalt not commit adultery.' The argument was as unwelcome as it was bold and uncompromising. It involved a distinction between one part of the canon of Scripture and another part of it. Moses permitted divorce: God did not. 'Every one that putteth away his wife, and marrieth another, committeth adultery: and he that marrieth one that is put away from a husband committeth adultery.' This declaration of Jesus was so startlingly at variance with the recognised law and practice of the Jews, that the Pharisees some time afterwards reverted to the subject, hoping either to entangle him into an argument demonstrably fallacious, or to charge him with bringing the law of Moses into disrepute. Their attack on Jesus, and his reply thereto, are recorded by Mark and Matthew. 'And there came unto him Pharisees, and asked him, Is it lawful for a man to put away *his* wife? tempting him.' Matthew represents something more to have been added to the question. 'And there came unto him Pharisees, tempting him, and saying, Is it lawful *for a man* to put away his wife for every cause?' The two oldest MSS. omit the words 'for a man,' which the Revisers have italicised. They have also omitted from this verse the words 'unto him,' and from the next verse the words 'unto them,' which do not appear in those two MSS. They have also omitted 'the' before 'Pharisees,' inserting the note: 'Many authorities, some ancient, insert *the*.' Tischendorf does so, following the two oldest MSS. Jesus, in reply, referred his questioners to the account they were accustomed to read of the creation of man. 'And he answered and said, Have ye not read, that he which made *them* from the beginning made them male and female'? The reference is to the first chapter of Genesis: 'male and female created he them.' Then Jesus added: 'and said, For this cause shall a man leave his father and mother, and shall cleave to his wife; and the twain shall become one flesh.' Alford observes: 'He quotes as *spoken by the Creator* the words in Gen. ii. 24, which were actually said by Adam,' and: 'He cites both from the first and second chapters of Genesis; and in immediate connexion; thus shewing them to be consecutive parts of a continuous narrative, which, from their different diction, and apparent repetition, they have sometimes been supposed not to be.' Both these statements of Alford are open to question. Verses 24 and 25 of the second chapter of Genesis appear to be explanatory, not spoken by Adam. Assuming the words in verse 24 to be Adam's, Alford was forced to qualify them thus: 'They must therefore be understood as said in prophecy, by divine inspiration which indeed the terms made use of in them would require, since the relations alluded to by those terms did not yet exist. As Augustine says, "God said by man that which man foretold."' On the contrary, the fact that Jesus attributed the words to God and not to Adam, should be taken as confirming that interpretation of the passage. The suggestion about 'prophecy' is really made to get over a difficulty otherwise insuperable. As regards the assumed connection and continuity between the first and second chapters of Genesis, there is a mystery which has yet to be solved. Not only is there a difference in diction, but the repetition is only 'apparent,' as stated by Alford. The first chapter starts from a state of chaos, and describes the gradual uprising and ordering of all things, including grass, herbs and fruit trees, flying fowls, beasts of the earth and cattle, ending with the creation of man, male and female simultaneously, after which there was a cessation of creative power during a period, 'a seventh day,' equal in duration to one of the 'days' preceding. The arbitrary division into chapters is misleading, for it is obvious that the narrative is continuous up to and including verse 3 of the second chapter. Verse 4 is the opening of a separate document, beginning with the words: 'These are the generations of the heaven and of the earth, when they were created, in the day' (not days) 'when the Lord (Jehovah) God made earth and heaven.' Young renders: 'These are the genealogies of the heavens and of the earth in their being framed, in the day of the Lord God's making the earth and the heavens.' Samuel Sharpe commences verse 4 with capitals, 'to mark the beginning of new matter,' as follows: 'THIS IS THE BIRTH-BOOK of the heavens and of the earth when they were created, in the day that Jehovah God made the earth and the heavens.' There is now neither a chaos nor a habitable world: no plant, no herb, no man to till the ground,—

2 Gen. 5, 6   nothing but a misty atmosphere and the damp earth. 'And no plant of the field was yet in the earth, and no herb of the field had yet sprung up: for the Lord God had not caused it to rain upon the earth, and there was not a man to till the ground: but there went up a mist from the earth, and watered the whole face of the ground.' Then man was formed 'of the dust of the ground,'—nothing said as in the former account about his being 'in the image of God,'—not male and female as before, but a solitary man. Then a portion of the earth was redeemed from barrenness, and planted as a garden for man's dwelling-place. Later on, the woman was created out of the man. It is not possible to combine the first chapter with the second, nor to make the latter a mere supplement to the former: neither can they be considered as different accounts of the same creation: the discrepancies between the two, if that view be taken, amount to contradictions. The two chapters record two distinct exercises of creative power, separated by some vast interval of time, God's sabbath 'day' intervening between them. The argument of Jesus fits in with this idea. He quotes from the first chapter, to show that 'from the beginning' God created 'male and female,' a living pair. From the second chapter he quotes the statement about the unity of nature in the man and the woman, so that throughout all time the marriage tie must take precedence of every other relation-

19 Mat. 6   ship, being essentially indissoluble: 'So that they are no more twain, but one flesh.' On that, Jesus based his argument. The constitution of human nature, the ordinance of God, decreed the inseparableness of husband and wife. Man's wandering desires must

,, 6   not be suffered to override the will of the all-wise Creator. 'What therefore God hath joined together, let not man put asunder.'

10 Mark 6-9   Mark's report is somewhat more succinct. 'But from the beginning of the creation, Male and female made he them. For this cause shall a man leave his father and mother, and shall cleave to his wife; and the twain shall become one flesh; so that they are no more twain, but one flesh. What therefore God hath joined together, let not man put asunder.' The two oldest MSS. omit, 'and shall cleave to his wife.' Let it be observed that the opening words of Luke, 'Have ye not read,' and also the expression 'and said,' are omitted by Mark. This discrepancy shows on how uncertain a foundation Alford rested his argument that the words 'and said' indicated that Jesus quoted 'as spoken by the Creator the words which were actually said by Adam.' We cannot tell whether Mark's or Luke's narrative approaches most nearly to verbal accuracy. There is a further difference between the two narratives. They both start with the question put by the Pharisees, but only Mark represents Jesus as replying

10 Mark 3   thereto by the following question: 'And he answered and said unto

them, What did Moses command you?' To this they replied unhesitatingly. 'And they said, Moses suffered to write a bill of divorcement, and to put her away.' Jesus characterised that permission as a policy necessitated by obdurate self-will, opposed to the divine will and to the true interests of humanity. 'But Jesus said unto them, For your hardness of heart he wrote you this commandment.' Then followed the observations respecting the original institution of marriage, and the recognition of its indissolubleness from the first. Jesus had only asked about the command of Moses for the purpose of repudiating it. It was therefore very natural to enquire why Moses gave a command more honoured in the breach than in the observance. 'They say unto him, Why then did Moses command to give a bill of divorcement, and to put *her* away?' If, piecing the two narratives together, we suppose the allusion to Moses to have occurred twice, Jesus on the second occasion simply repeated his previous statement. 'He saith unto them, Moses for your hardness of heart suffered you to put away your wives: but from the beginning it hath not been so.' Alford notes the distinction between the word 'command' used by the Pharisees in verse 7 and the word 'suffered' used by Jesus in verse 8, and says: 'The Pharisees imagine that they have overthrown our Lord's decision by a *permission* of the law, which they call a *command*.' That idea, however natural, is displaced by Mark's account, for he represents Jesus to have used the word 'command,' and the Pharisees the word 'suffered.' The permission was, in fact, a prohibition against unconditional divorce, a command not to divorce without first writing the bill of divorcement. There is no escape from the conclusion that Jesus declared the command or permission of Moses to be contrary to the command and will of God. The assertion of Jesus involves a distinction between the law of Moses and the divine law; and on looking carefully we find that such a distinction is obvious enough. The law of divorce is laid down in the first four verses of the 24th chapter of Deuteronomy. It is embedded among a large number of directions and ordinances beginning with the 12th chapter, and prefaced by the words: 'Ye shall observe to do the statutes and the judgments which I set before you this day.' The words are the words of Moses: again and again that fact is brought out prominently. 'In the place which the Lord shall choose in one of thy tribes, there thou shalt offer thy burnt offerings, and there shalt thou do all that I command thee.' 'What thing soever I command you, that shall ye observe to do.' 'Wherefore I command thee, saying, Thou shalt separate three cities for thee.' 'Do according to all that the priests the Levites shall teach you: as I commanded them, so shall ye observe to do.' 'The Lord thy God redeemed thee thence: therefore I command thee to do this thing.' 'And Moses and the elders of Israel commanded the people, saying, Keep all the commandment which I command you this day.' Here the elders are represented as endorsing the law laid down by Moses. He himself claimed a divine authority for it: 'When thou shalt hearken to the voice of the Lord thy God, to keep all his commandments which I command thee this day, to do that which is right in the eyes of the Lord thy God.' 'If thou shalt hearken unto the commandments of the Lord thy God, which I command thee this day, to observe and to do *them*, and shalt not turn aside from any of the words which I command you this day.' As a divinely-appointed legislator Moses issued his edicts, but throughout their delivery his own personality stands out clearly and unmistakably. The voice is human; at the most, all that can be asserted is that the speaker has God's authority, and that there was a blending of the divine with the human. That the latter preponderated over the former is sufficiently indicated by the frequent repetition of the personal pronoun 'I.' Knowing well the people with whom he had to deal, Moses deemed it wise and right to allow a liberty of divorce, fencing it round with certain formalities and restrictions, so that it might at least be a deliberate, public, and irrevocable act. Alas! that the state of so-called 'Christendom' should necessitate the perpetuation in our own time of the permission granted by Moses to a nation but lately redeemed from slavery, with its accompanying degradation and lack of intellectual and moral culture. How far off are we still from the mind and rule of Christ! In his eyes the marriage bond was divine, too sacred for man to sever: 'What therefore God hath joined together, let not man put asunder.' He now repeats the law which, according to Matthew, he laid down

19 Mat. 9   in the sermon on the mount: 'Whosoever shall put away his wife, except for fornication, and shall marry another, committeth adultery; and he that marrieth her when she is put away committeth adultery.' Jesus is not speaking of the guilt, but of the nature of the act: however customary or legalised, the fact of promiscuous sexual intercourse was patent and undeniable. The disruption of the old tie and the recognition of the new, are both equally illegal and dishonourable in the eye of God. The perfection of manhood and womanhood is marred, when husband and wife are sundered: divorce is as it were an act of amputation, and a second marriage, under such circumstances, is like putting on another person's limb, disfiguring and monstrous to human nature, the severance and the misplacement being alike unnatural and revolting.

There is some uncertainty as to the proper rendering of verse 9. The Revisers note that 'some ancient authorities' adopt the reading of 5 Mat. 32, namely 'saving for the cause of' instead of 'except for,' and with the addition, 'maketh her an adulteress.' Of the three oldest MSS. only the Vatican has this addition. The Revisers note further that the following words 'are omitted by some ancient authorities:' 'and he that marrieth her when she is put away committeth adultery.' This sentence appears to have been inserted to correspond with 5 Mat. 32. It is not in the oldest MS., and Tischendorf omits it. Count Leon Tolstoi asserts that there has been a mistranslation.

5 Mat. 32   He takes the original Greek words seriatim:* '*parektos*, besides; *logou*, the matter; *porneias*, of lewdness; *poiei*, causes; *autēn*, her; *moichasthai*, to commit adultery.' In the lexicon *parektos* is defined: 'out of, without, besides;' and *porneia* is defined: 'fornication, prostitution.' Tolstoi says:† '*porneia*, which is, in all translations except the English, rendered as "adultery," in the same way as *moichasthai*, is, in reality, quite another word.' To make clear the distinction, he chooses the word 'lewdness,' as equivalent to 'debauchery' or 'fornication,' and as 'expressing not an action, but a

* "What I Believe," p. 82.   † "What I Believe," p. 81.

quality or state.' He does not scruple to say: 'Every Greek scholar will construe the passage thus . . . Therefore the text stands word for word thus: He who divorces his wife, besides the sin of lewdness, causes her to commit adultery.' That refers to the 5th chapter. Tolstoi adds: 'We find exactly the same in the 19th chapter. No sooner is the incorrect translation of the word *porneia* amended, as well as that of the preposition *epi*, which has been translated "for;" no sooner is the word "lewdness" placed instead of "adultery," and the preposition "by" instead of "for," than it grows perfectly clear that the words *ei mē epi porneia* can have no reference to the wife. And as the words *parektos logou porneias* can have no other meaning than "besides the sin of lewdness of the husband," so the words *ei mē epi porneia*, which we find in the 19th chapter, can have no reference to anything except the lewdness of the husband. It is said, *ei mē epi porneia*, which, being translated literally, is, "if not by lewdness." "if not out of lewdness." And thus the meaning is clear that Christ in this passage refutes the notions of the Pharisees that a man who put away his wife, not out of lewdness, but in order to live matrimonially with another woman, did not commit adultery; Christ says that the repudiation of a wife, even if it be not done out of lewdness, but in order to be joined in bonds of matrimony to another woman, is adultery.' Much in favour of Tolstoi's argument is the fact, that the word *ei*, 'if,' is omitted by Griesbach, Lachmann, Tischendorf, Tregelles, Alford and Wordsworth, as not being in accordance with the best readings; and also the fact that whether *epi* be rendered 'by' or 'for,' his argument is equally strong. The question is both novel and important, and calls for close investigation, the intense earnestness and honesty of Tolstoi giving weight to his opinion.

Jesus declared that to be wrong in the sight of God which was justified and legalised among men. So rigid did his doctrine appear to the disciples, that they exclaimed that it would be inexpedient for a man to marry under such conditions. 'The disciples say unto him, If the case of the man is so with his wife, it is not expedient to marry.' That conclusion Jesus repudiated. The leading of a single life must be exceptional, and for those only having a peculiarity of constitution or temperament. 'And he said unto them, All men cannot receive this saying, but they to whom it is given.' 'This saying' appears to refer to the opinion just expressed by the disciples, not to what Jesus had previously said. A similar instance occurred when Jesus replied to the Canaanitish woman, 'For this saying go thy way.' Jesus went on to explain that an unmarried life was abnormal: some were born without the natural instinct towards marriage; some were compelled by position or circumstances to renounce it; some, devoting themselves to a higher and heavenly destiny, deliberately avoided it. 'For there are eunuchs which were so born from their mother's womb; and there are eunuchs which were made eunuchs by men; and there are eunuchs which made themselves eunuchs for the kingdom of heaven's sake.' Such a maxim, advocating a solitary life, was not for general adoption, but for those who were exceptionally disposed towards it. 'He that is able to receive it, let him receive it.'

The teaching of Jesus respecting divorce was so startling to the disciples, that in the privacy of their common home they again questioned him on the subject. 'And in the house the disciples asked him again of this matter.' Jesus reiterated his former dictum: he had nothing to retract, nothing to modify. 'And he saith unto them, Whosoever shall put away his wife, and marry another, committeth adultery against her: and if she herself shall put away her husband, and marry another, she committeth adultery.' Be it observed that there is here nothing which can be construed into an exception. Mark's narrative gives no hint of any such saving clause. This is in favour of Tolstoi's argument that there has been a mistranslation and misconception: the account handed down to Mark, and by him to us, would surely have alluded to an exception, if Jesus had been understood to have made one.

The following parable, recorded by Luke, is placed immediately after that of the unjust steward, and continues the train of thought with respect to the right employment of wealth, and the possible contrasts in men's relative positions here and hereafter. Jesus pictures a man at the very summit of prosperity and luxury. 'Now there was a certain rich man, and he was clothed in purple and fine linen, faring sumptuously every day (or, living in mirth and splendour every day).' In contrast to this man, Jesus describes a man in direst poverty, reduced to the utmost extremity of want and misery. He names him Lazarus, 'God is my help,' as indicating that he had no hope of human succour. His place was at the outer porch of that abode of magnificence and revelry. 'And a certain beggar named Lazarus was laid at his gate.' He was altogether in a deplorable condition, his body being covered with sores, and hunger impelling him to long for the broken victuals which came from the well-spread table of the rich man: 'full of sores, and desiring to be fed with the *crumbs* that fell from the rich man's table.' The Revisers have italicised the word 'crumbs,' and Tischendorf, following the two oldest MSS., omits it, rendering 'what fell.' The only companions of the poor man were the dogs, probably attracted to the gate by the same motive as himself, and these dumb creatures showed their sympathy by licking his sores, as though they were their own. 'Yea, even the dogs came and licked his sores.' Tischendorf renders, 'usually licked,' and Young's literal rendering conveys the same idea: 'yea, even the dogs, coming, were licking his sores.' So much only of the history of these two men in this world. Jesus now shows them to us transported to another. The poor man died first, as well he might from semi-starvation and disease. 'And it came to pass that the beggar died.' The Revisers have retained the word 'beggar,' which is discarded from the parable by Young and Tischendorf, who adopt instead the term 'poor man.' Luther also has 'Armer,' 'poor man.' The primary sense of the word, *ptōchos*, is 'one who crouches or cringes,' from *ptōssō*, to crouch or cower. It will be well for us to drop the idea of his being a recognised 'beggar,' and to take the parable as that of the 'rich man' and 'the poor man.' Thus viewed, it has a far wider application than otherwise. The next sentence stands in the Authorised Version: 'and was carried by the angels into Abraham's bosom,' but is altered by the Revisers to: 'and that he was carried away by the angels into Abraham's bosom,' Young's literal rendering being: 'And that he was carried away by the messengers into the bosom of Abraham.' We have here, to say the least, the view which Jesus entertained of those 'angels' or 'messengers' of whom we read: 'Are they not all ministering spirits, sent forth to do service for the sake of them that shall inherit salvation?' On the expression 'Abraham's bosom,' Alford observes: 'This, as a form of speech among the Jews, was not even by themselves understood in its strict literal sense; and though the *purposes of the parable* require this, ver. 23, no one would think of pressing it into a truth, but all would see in it the graphic filling up of a state which in itself is strictly actual.' The expression seems to have been a proverbial one, indicating nearness and dearness, and the Jewish custom of reclining at meals was in itself sufficient to make this meaning obvious. 'There was at the table reclining in Jesus' bosom one of his disciples, whom Jesus loved.' The fourth evangelist used the expression as one recognised and conveying a definite meaning: 'The only begotten Son, which is in the bosom of the Father.' The figure of speech had been familiar from the time of Moses, who used it: 'Have I conceived all this people? have I brought them forth, that thou shouldest say unto me, Carry them in thy bosom, as a nursing-father carrieth the sucking child, unto the land which thou swarest unto their fathers?' The translation of Lazarus to Abraham's bosom may be taken to denote his entrance upon a career under the patronage and guardianship of the venerated father of the Israelitish nation. The teaching of Jesus is throughout intensely human. He does not represent the departed spirit as summoned before a divine tribunal, but he reveals another world with relationships between men analogous to and founded upon those of the present life. The departed may be nearer to us even on earth than we are accustomed to suppose. Who would have imagined, when Jesus took his three disciples to the mountain-top, that it was for the purpose of meeting and conferring with Moses and Elijah? How profoundly interesting is the prospect of futurity opened out to us by these hints and glimpses of the spiritual world!

After a time the rich man's life came also to its close. 'And the rich man also died, and was buried.' Through the grave and gate of death he passed on to far other experiences than those of this world. Jesus represents him in a condition of grievous suffering. 'And in Hades he lifted up his eyes, being in torments.' The Revisers have done good service towards removing popular misconceptions by altering 'hell' to 'Hades.' Here is Alford's comment. 'Hades, in Hebrew Sheöl, is the abode of *all disembodied spirits* till the resurrection, not, the place of torment,—much less 'hell,' as understood commonly, in the A. V. Lazarus was *also in Hades*, but separate from Dives; one on the blissful, the other on the baleful side. It is the *gates of Hades, the imprisonment of death*, which shall not prevail against the Church (Matt. xvi. 18); the Lord holds the *key of Hades*. (Rev. i. 18). Himself went into the same Hades, of which Paradise is a part.' In face of the parable itself, the conception of Dives and Lazarus as 'disembodied spirits' is a strange one; the words 'till the resurrection,' and the reference to another 'place of torment,' are thrown in glibly, as part and parcel of an accepted creed, but such ideas are not the teaching of Jesus, and a careful investigation is needed to detect and expose the misconceptions of Scriptural passages on which such erroneous doctrines are based. In the next life the relative positions of the two men were reversed. Their lots still lay wide apart: but Lazarus was in comfort and honour, and the man of pomp and luxury was reduced to a state of anguish. We must not, however, exaggerate the import of the expression, 'being in torments.' The Greek word is *basanos*, from *basanizō*, and both noun and verb were employed to denote afflictions and labours of an ordinary kind, as in the following passages.

<small>4 Mat. 24</small> 'Holden with divers diseases and torments (*basanois*).' 'Seeing <small>6 Mark 48</small> them distressed (*basanizomenos*) in rowing.' 'Vexed (*ebasanizen*) <small>2 3. Pet. 8</small> his righteous soul.' Enough, that heavy toil or discomfort of some kind were now the portion of the man once rich in this world, and <small>16 Luke 23</small> that above him, in the distance, was a region of bliss: 'and seeth Abraham afar off, and Lazarus in his bosom.' He could no more hope to enter that bright abode than Lazarus, when they both lived on this earth, could have gained admission to his palace of feasting. But he prayed that some assuagement of his misery might be vouchsafed, and that Lazarus might be sent to moisten, were it but with <small>24</small> a drop of water, his fevered tongue. 'And he cried and said, Father Abraham, have mercy on me, and send Lazarus, that he may dip the tip of his finger in water, and cool my tongue; for I am in anguish in this flame.' Young renders: 'I am sorrowing in this flame,' the 'Englishman's Greek New Testament,' 'I am suffering;' the Authorised Version has: 'I am tormented.' The Greek verb is *odunaomai*, which was in common use to signify any great mental <small>2 Luke 48</small> distress. It occurs in the passages: 'Thy father and I sought thee <small>20 Acts 38</small> sorrowing (*odunōmenoi*).' 'Sorrowing (*odunōmenoi*) most of all for the word which he had spoken.' In the answer of the patriarch there was a tone of compassionate sadness. He began by reminding this, his unhappy descendant, of the mutability of human destiny, how enjoyment led on to suffering, and suffering was a discipline <small>16 Luke 25</small> preparatory to joy. 'But Abraham said, Son (Gr. Child), remember that thou in thy lifetime receivedst thy good things, and Lazarus in like manner evil things: but now here he is comforted, and thou art in anguish.' Tischendorf and the Revisers have introduced the word 'here,' on the authority of the three oldest MSS. Young renders 'in anguish' by 'sorrowing:' it is the same word, *odunasai*. Small as was the boon now craved, there stood a physical impossibility in the <small>26</small> way of its accomplishment. 'And besides all this (Or, in all these things) between us and you there is a great gulf fixed.' Young renders, 'And besides all these things.' The line of demarcation between class and class is more insuperable in hades than it is on <small>26</small> earth: 'that they which would pass from hence to you may not be able, and that none may cross over from thence to us.' The rendering of the Authorised Version is: 'so that they which would pass from hence to you cannot; neither can they pass to us, that *would come* from thence.' The Revised translation is stronger, as indicating not simply the existence of such an obstacle, but the fact it was designedly set up to prevent closer intercourse. Tischendorf's rendering conveys the same idea: 'that they who desire to pass hence to you may not be able, nor those cross over to us thence.' Young does not render 'may not be able,' but the form he adopts implies an insuperable law: 'so that they who are wishing to go

over from hence to you are unable, nor do they from hence to us pass through.' Forced now to recognise the fact that any immediate alleviation of his own sufferings was hopeless, the suppliant turned his thoughts to those who had been near and dear to him on earth, and out of his dread lest they should come also to the same terrible experience of suffering, he ventured to ask that Lazarus might be sent to them. 'And he said, I pray thee, therefore, father, that thou wouldest send him to my father's house ; for I have five brethren.' The expression 'my father's house' obviously does not signify 'my father's abode,' but is equivalent to 'my family,' the word 'house' being similarly joined to the word father's, in that sense, in about 50 passages of Scripture. It was a request that Lazarus might go to the various members of the family, and reveal to them the penalties attaching hereafter to lives misled on earth : 'that he may testify unto them, lest they also come into this place of torment.' The word rendered torment is *basanon*. Young renders, 'thoroughly testify ;' the Englishman's G. N. T., 'earnestly testify.' The idea did not commend itself to the judgment of the patriarch. The law and the prophets were enough for the teaching of mankind. 'But Abraham saith, They have Moses and the prophets ; let them hear them.' Not so, it was argued : but a messenger direct from the world beyond the grave would startle them into a reformation of life. 'And he said, Nay, father Abraham : but if one go to them from the dead, they will repent. Young, as usual, renders 'repent' by 'reform.' However plausible the suggestion, it was based on an error of judgment. Abraham held a contrary opinion. 'And he said unto him, If they hear not Moses and the prophets, neither will they be persuaded if one rise from the dead.'

To this marvellous parable not a word was added by way of comment or explanation: we are left to interpret and apply it as we will. If it had been uttered by any one except Jesus himself, it would have been worth no more to us than one of Æsop's fables. The value of any moral teaching contained in it would have been more than counterbalanced by our uncertainty as to the truthfulness and reality of the groundwork on which the narrative rests. If its revelations of a future life were purely imaginary, they would be not only unreliable, but misleading. Only our confidence in Jesus can induce us to attach importance to his teaching on matters beyond the reach of ordinary human knowledge. We know of his miraculous birth, his superhuman words and works, his converse with Moses and Elijah when he was transfigured on the mount, his resurrection from the dead, and his ascension into heaven : and our belief in all these things impels us to receive with reverence this parable of the rich man and Lazarus. Every parable delivered by Jesus on earthly matters within our cognizance, is true to nature, and consistent with actual experience : and we may be confident that he is equally accurate and reliable when revealing to us the laws and conditions of 'heavenly things.' The following deductions are inseparable from the parable, and are therefore stamped with the authority of Jesus.

1. The life of each individual on earth is but the prelude to life in another world.

2. Angelic ministrations are needed and granted in the world to come.

3. Human destinies differ there, as here, class being separate from class; and acute suffering may be experienced by one individual, and perfect enjoyment by another.

4. In the future life there will be a clear recollection of the former life, and the grouping of society there is on the earthly pattern, so that neighbours will recognise each other, and there will be a consciousness and acknowledgment of previous social and family relationships.

5. The introduction of Abraham into the parable involves the doctrine of a perpetuity of existence: not necessarily an unchangeable, inextinguishable existence, for there may be other deaths and other resurrections analogous to the first death and the first resurrection. The 'age-during life,' of which Jesus so often spoke, embodies the idea of an appointed term: the revivification which comes after the close of the present life, may it not be granted also at the culmination and crisis of the next stage of being, life and death alternating, life ever triumphing over death, the tendency deathward declining, and the tendency lifeward augmenting, until, like our Lord Jesus, we are made 'after the power of an endless (Gr. indissoluble) life?'[7 Heb. 16] That is the conception of human destiny which seems best to elucidate, combine and harmonise the promises of our Redeemer and all other revelations of Scripture.

6. The next state of being is revealed to us subject to laws, physical and moral, as immutable as those which encompass us on earth. The line of demarcation between class and class is represented as rigid in the extreme. Divine Providence has fixed certain boundaries which none, though urged by the most charitable motives, may seek to overpass. The more perfect the condition of society, the more imperative does it become to remove the evil from the proximity of the good. The two principles of good and evil must, if brought into contact, involve ceaseless strife; the ethics of Christianity require for their free, unchecked development a complete immunity from the hostile powers of unrighteousness. That is the condition of humanity hereafter, as sketched out by Jesus. Punishment by way of penalty and retribution is not hinted at, but conduct and destiny are revealed linked together as cause and effect. And there is a recognised continuity of being,—no hiatus between the concerns of this life and the next,—but the one leading up naturally and inevitably to the other: that was the ground of anxiety with respect to the five brethren still living upon earth.

7. The closing words of the parable, 'if one rise from the dead,' indicate what is meant in other passages by a similar form of expression: not, that is, the resurrection from death to life, but the revisiting of the living by the dead.

In this parable it is clear, beyond the possibility of doubt or gainsaying, that Jesus taught the doctrine of an individual, personal resurrection of—not from—the dead. In face of this, and of the plain teaching of Paul and other apostles, it is a marvel and mystery how that earnest searcher after truth, Count Leon Tolstoi, could have been led to form and express the following opinion: 'And strange as it may seem to say so of Christ, who Himself rose from the dead, and who promised to raise all men, He never by a single word, confirmed the belief in individual resurrection, in individual immortality beyond the grave, but He even attached to the raising up of the dead in the kingdom of the Messiah, as taught by the Pharisees, a meaning which excluded the idea of individual resurrection.'* Again: 'Christ could never have supposed so strange an idea among His followers. He supposes all men to understand that individual life must inevitably perish; and he reveals a life which cannot perish.' Again: 'The whole purport of Christ's doctrine is to teach His disciples that individual life being but a delusion they should renounce it, and transfer their individual lives into the lives of all humanity, into the life of the son of man.' Tolstoi has been misled by his own imagination. Let it suffice to say that his misconceptions are based upon a misapprehension of the meaning of the words he quotes, namely, 'With God all are living,' from which he hastily draws the conclusion, as though it were the only conceivable one : ' And therefore, if there be a living God, the man who is one with God lives too.' The mind of Tolstoi is, as it were, microscopic : his earnest gaze on some particular passages may reveal depths of truth and reality which, for want of such a power of concentration, have been passed over by others ; but when his focus of vision is disarranged, a truth becomes distorted, and an error magnified. Take, as an example of his self-deceptive reasoning, the following explanation on another subject : ' It was necessary to feed several thousand men. One of the disciples said to Christ that a boy there had a few fishes. The disciples had also a few loaves. Christ knew that some of those who had come from a distance had brought food with them and others had not. That many had brought provisions with them is evident from there being twelve basketfuls gathered of what remained, as we read in all the four Gospels. (If nobody had had anything except the boy, there would not have been twelve baskets in the field.) Had Christ not done what he did, that is, the " miracle " of feeding thousands with five loaves, what now takes place in the world would have taken place then. Those who had provisions with them would have eaten all they had, would have overeaten themselves rather than that anything should have been left. Misers would perhaps have taken the remainder home. Those who had nothing would have remained hungry, looking on with wicked envy at those who ate, and some would very likely have stolen from those who had provisions. Quarrelling and fighting would have ensued, and some would have gone home satisfied, the others hungry and cross ; exactly what takes place in our present lives would have happened then. But Christ knew what he meant to do ; He told them all to sit in a circle, and enjoined his disciples to offer a part of what they had to those next them, and to tell others to do the same. The result was, that when all those who had brought provisions with them followed the example set them by the disciples, and offered a share of their provisions to others, there was enough for all. All were satisfied, and so much remained that twelve baskets were filled.'

It is a beautiful conception of Tolstoi's, and admirably worked out. At first one is inclined to rub one's eyes, and wonder why so simple an explanation of the 'miracle' has never presented itself before. But how came it to pass that not one of the four evangelists presented it

* " What I Believe," pp. 135, 147, 146.

in that light? Any one of them, by introducing a sentence or simply turning a phrase, could have made the matter as clear to us as Tolstoi has done. Not a hint of his interpretation is conveyed by the narratives; not a word about the multitude having food left of their own; no such expression as he uses, 'tell others to do the same;' nothing to lead to the conclusion that 'those who had brought provisions with them followed the example set them by the disciples.' On the contrary, Mark ends with the words, 'And they that ate the loaves were five thousand men,' and John says that 'they filled twelve baskets with broken pieces from the five barley loaves.' When Jesus alludes to the miracle, it is in the same strain: 'Ye seek me, not because ye saw signs, but because ye ate of the loaves, and were filled.' In the similar miracle, when four thousand were fed with seven loaves and a few fishes, there is nothing mentioned consistent with the idea of Tolstoi, nothing about the people bringing out their own stores of food, but on the contrary, Matthew and Mark agree as to the exact words of Jesus: 'I have compassion on the multitude, because they continue with me now three days and have nothing to eat.' And when Jesus referred to both miracles, the number of loaves he specifies as divided among the multitude is five and seven. 'Do ye not yet perceive, neither remember the five loaves of the five thousand, and how many baskets ye took up? Neither the seven loaves of the four thousand, and how many baskets ye took up?' Count Tolstoi seems incapable of extending his range of vision outside his own argument: he is blind to the facts which tell against it. In the same way, in framing his theory about the resurrection, he overlooks the parable of the rich man and Lazarus, the revelation of Moses and Elijah on the mount, and the sublime reasoning of Paul in the fifteenth chapter of the first epistle to the Corinthians. The errors of Christianity have ever arisen from the mistakes of its friends, and it behoves us to be on our guard against them, thankful for any fresh light, yet watchful against mistakes of judgment, seeking to sift the true from the false, and following no man blindly.

Holding fast to the doctrine of a resurrection of the dead, it must prove rather a curse than a blessing if it leads to a neglect of the obligations resting upon Christians in the present life. This is wisely and forcibly insisted on by Mr. J. A. Froude. He says: * 'The Egyptians, in the midst of their corruptions, had inherited the doctrine from their fathers which is considered the foundation of all religion. They believed in a life beyond the grave—in the judgment bar of Osiris, at which they were to stand on leaving their bodies, and in a future of happiness or misery as they had lived well or ill upon earth. It was not a speculation of philosophers—it was the popular creed; and it was held with exactly the same kind of belief with which it has been held by the Western nations since their conversion to Christianity. But what was the practical effect of their belief? There is no doctrine, however true, which works mechanically on the soul like a charm. The expectation of a future state may be a motive for the noblest exertion, or it may be an excuse for acquiescence in evil, and serve to conceal and perpetuate the most enormous iniquities. The magnate of Thebes or Memphis, with his huge estates, his town and

---

* "On Progress."

country palaces, his retinue of eunuchs, and his slaves whom he counted by thousands, was able to say to himself, if he thought at all, "True enough, there are inequalities of fortune, but it is only for a *time* after all; they have immortal souls, poor devils! and their wretched existence here is but a drop of water in the ocean of their being. They have as good a chance of Paradise as I have— perhaps better. Osiris will set all right hereafter; and for the present rich and poor are an ordinance of Providence, and there is no occasion to disturb established institutions. For myself, I have drawn a prize in the lottery, and I hope I am grateful. I subscribe handsomely to the temple services. I am myself punctual in my religious duties. The priests, who are wiser than I am, pray for me, and they tell me I may set my mind at rest." Under this theory of things the Israelites had been ground to powder. They broke away. They too were to become a nation. A revelation of the true God was bestowed on them, from which, as from a fountain, a deeper knowledge of the Divine nature was to flow out over the earth; and the central thought of it was the realization of the Divine government—not in a vague hereafter, but in the living present. The unpractical prospective justice which had become an excuse for tyranny, was superseded by an immediate justice in time. They were to reap the harvest of their deeds, not in heaven, but on earth. There was no life in the grave whither they were going. The future state was withdrawn from their sight till the mischief which it had wrought was forgotten. It was not denied, but it was veiled in a cloud. It was left to private opinion to hope or to fear; but it was no longer held out either as an excitement to piety, or a terror to evil doers. The God of Israel was a living God, and His power was displayed visibly and immediately in rewarding the good and punishing the wicked while they remained in the flesh. It would be unbecoming to press the parallel, but phenomena are showing themselves which indicate that an analogous suspension of belief provoked by the same causes may possibly be awaiting ourselves. The relations between man and man are now supposed to be governed by natural laws which enact themselves independent of considerations of justice. Political economy is erected into a science, and the shock to our moral nature is relieved by the reflection that it refers only to earth, and that justice may take effect hereafter. Science, however, is an inexorable master. The evidence for a hereafter depends on considerations which science declines to entertain. To piety and conscientiousness it appears inherently probable; but to the calm, unprejudiced student of realities, piety and conscientiousness are insufficient witnesses to matters of fact. The religious passions have made too many mistakes to be accepted as of conclusive authority. Scientific habits of thought, which are more and more controlling us, demand external proofs which are difficult to find. It may be that we require once more to have the living certainties of the Divine government brought home to us more palpably; that a doctrine which has been the consolation of the heavyladen for eighteen hundred years may have generated once more a practical infidelity, and that by natural and intelligent agencies, in the furtherance of the everlasting purposes of our Father in heaven, the belief in a life beyond the grave may again be about to be withdrawn.'

This voice of warning is not lifted up without a cause. They are not fit for the hope of a life to come, who make no effort to realise the Christ-like life on earth.

Immediately following the parable of the rich man and Lazarus is placed a discourse of Jesus to his disciples. 'And he said unto his disciples, It is impossible but that occasions of stumbling should come.' This corresponds with Young's word 'stumbling-blocks,' in place of 'offences' in the Authorised Version. The term 'stumbling-block' conveys the idea of something laid in the way of social progress, something which is detrimental to the general welfare, a cause of danger to many and of injury to some. The condition of society excludes the hope of immunity from such evils: they 'come' inevitably, generated out of the imperfections of humanity. If they who fall and suffer by them are to be pitied, much more miserable and condemnable are the men by whom they are originated and perpetuated. Jesus added: 'but woe unto him, through whom they come.' Sharpe renders: 'but alas for him,' which throws a tone of compassion into the threat. A premature and ignominious death would be preferable to a life prolonged to exercise an obstructive influence. 'It were well for him if a millstone were hanged about his neck, and he were thrown into the sea, rather than that he should cause one of these little ones to stumble.' The original is stronger than the translation. Sharpe renders, 'an upper millstone'; Young 'a mighty millstone'; the 'Englishman's Greek New Testament,' 'a millstone turned by an ass.' The expression, 'these little ones' must refer to the disciples, to whom the discourse was addressed. Jesus was accustomed to allude to them under that designation. 'Whosoever shall give to drink unto one of these little ones a cup of cold water only, in the name of a disciple . . .' 'One of these little ones which believe on me.' Jesus was ever mindful of the fact that those who followed his teaching and example were shorn of the powers of resistance and self-defence. So much the worse for them, from the point of view of this world. So much the worse for their oppressors, when the rulership of Jesus is established. Meantime, he counsels his disciples to be vigilant over themselves, allowing no sin in their midst to pass without rebuke. 'Take heed to yourselves: if thy brother sin, rebuke him.' Not punishment, threats or litigation, but argument, expostulation, rebuke must be resorted to. Should that prove effectual, the matter must end with amendment on the one side and forgiveness on the other. The offence must be condoned, not avenged: 'and if he repent, forgive him.' Young here, as elsewhere, renders 'repent' as 'reform'; but the definition of the verb *metanoeō* is: 'to perceive afterwards or too late. 2 to change one's mind or opinion. 3 to repent,' and the noun *metanoia*, rendered by Young 'reformation,' is defined: 'afterthought: change of mind on reflection, repentance.' Of course change of thought or purpose must take a practical form; but the will is the mainspring of conduct, and as soon as mind and heart begin to move aright, rebuke should cease. No matter how often the offence might be renewed: human nature is most weak when most erring, and the spirit of forgiveness must not be less persistent than the evil which calls for its exercise. 'And if he sin against thee seven times in the day, and seven times turn again to thee, saying, I repent; thou shalt forgive him.' Following the two oldest MSS. the Revisers do not repeat 'in a day' before 'turn.' The precept aims at the maintenance of a spirit of watchfulness and of healthy criticism. The word 'brother' indicates that the Christian community is referred to, not the outside world. Between the followers of Jesus no wrong must be suffered, and no tame submission to wrong doing is inculcated. Brother should rebuke brother, and a discipline of virtue and rectitude be encouraged and upheld: not, however, by punishment meted out under the idea of retributive justice, the penalty being proportioned to the offence; but by the development of a proper spirit and right judgment: immediately the offender is conscious of his fault and desirous to amend it, no further rebuke is required. Reformation can only proceed from within, through a change in the mind of the offender himself, and the instant that becomes evident, the end of reproof is gained, and no further pressure should be applied. It must not be assumed that the habit of repeated forgiveness is inculcated merely with reference to the perfecting of the character of the offended person, that he may become more Christ-like. Jesus had at heart the welfare of all, and if he advises the acceptance of an express desire and intention of amendment, it is because that is the most efficacious method of dealing with wrong-doers, the course best calculated to promote not only the peace but the perfection of the Christian community. The counsels of Jesus with respect to Church government have not been recognised or adopted: that 'force is no remedy' is a maxim of the highest wisdom, constituting the very essence of Christian judicature; the object is not to punish criminals, but to reform them. Jesus gave his followers power to remit sins, but not to avenge them. His strongest weapon is 'rebuke'; if the sinner 'turn again,' nothing more could be desired; if not, Jesus has elsewhere laid down a course of procedure which has been strangely, sadly overlooked, a scheme of Church discipline which has yet to be urged, tested, established, before it can be asserted that Christianity has been even tried, much less found wanting. The existence, for example, of wars between so called Christian nations, is of itself a proof that there is no such thing as national Christianity: all fightings are contrary to the spirit of its Founder, whose 'kingdom is not of this world,' and who laid down as a maxim of belief and practice that 'all they that take the sword shall perish with the sword.' [18 Mat. 15-17] [26 Mat. 52]

The Evangelist proceeds: 'And the apostles said unto the Lord, Increase our faith.' The introduction of the words 'the Lord,' instead of 'him,' seems to indicate that this was not a continuation of the preceding subject: there is certainly no apparent connection between forgiveness and faith. To the request of the disciples Jesus gave a very remarkable answer. He seems not to admit the idea of any need for the increase of faith, declaring, on the contrary, that the minutest imaginable quantity was sufficient to work the greatest conceivable miracle. 'And the Lord said, If ye have faith as a grain of mustard seed, ye would say unto this sycamine tree, Be thou rooted up, and be thou planted in the sea; and it would have obeyed you.' A very strong hyperbole, this! But is it anything more than [17 Luke 5] [,, 6] an exaggerated figure of speech? Having regard to the Speaker, it may carry a meaning which it could not bear had it fallen from the lips of an ordinary man. It raises the question of the power of mind over matter. There are subtle influences at work in nature, acting invisibly and even independently of volition, which are as certain and mighty in operation as they are inscrutable and astounding. Magnetic attraction is a mystery and marvel. Who can explain why the compass points invariably to the north? What is the occult property in the loadstone, which causes a piece of iron to fly to it through space, and then adhere so firmly? There dwells in the magnet an inexplicable force; give it a name: call it attraction: the mystery remains as great as ever. Is it, then, a thing incredible, that there should emanate from the human mind a power analogous to that which we know can exist in a piece of metal? Give that power a name: call it faith: you do not thereby elucidate the marvel: you simply define the existence of an inherent quality and force in mind, that is, in a certain combination of spirit with matter. Jesus asserts the possibility of what we, in our blind ignorance, would declare to be impossible. This question reaches to the very basis of our belief in Deity. Either the order of the universe was self-generated, or it has been arranged by a supreme Spirit working upon unconscious matter. That was the belief of the Psalmist:

³³ Psa. 6

'By the word of the LORD were the heavens made;
And all the host of them by the breath of his mouth.

,, 9

For he spake, and it was done;
He commanded, and it stood fast.'

Jesus bade his disciples recognise the rudiments of a similar God-like power in themselves. What is faith but assurance,—confidence,—the conviction that what we will to do is ensured by the act of willing? I will to move my finger, and it is done: I had the faith that I could move it, and the result corresponded to the conviction. I have no faith, not one grain of faith, that I can uproot a tree: but if I had that faith, the act would lie within the compass of my power. The infant unfolds day by day new attributes, the child develops new capacities, the adult puts forth new energies; and as with the individual, so with the race. Out of the gloom of barbarism the nations have gradually emerged into the light of commerce and civilisation, through them to rise to a yet higher culture and purer morality. Each age has its own degree of faith, corresponding to the scale of advancement to which it has attained: to desire an increase of faith, is to seek that which lies beyond our present grasp; to grant it, would be to disturb the order of nature and providence. Faith must needs be the spontaneous outcome of the human soul: it is the certainty of conviction, the consciousness of power, the limit of our own ability to will and do; nothing is impossible to it; it is a quality, not a quantity; to crave for more, is as though we were to ask that the brightest light should be altogether dazzling, for two suns instead of one, that we may scorch ourselves and die. No: we must be content to bide our time, to circle in our little round of duty, passing through our appointed probation of servitude, and gradually rising to a higher range of faith and action. What the disciples wanted was not more faith, but more obedience. Jesus at

17 Luke 7, 8

once turned their thoughts in that direction. 'But who is there of you, having a servant (Gr. bond-servant) plowing or keeping sheep, that will say unto him, when he is come in from the field, Come straightway and sit down to meat; and will not rather say unto him, Make ready wherewith I may sup, and gird thyself, and serve me, till I have eaten and drunken; and afterward thou shalt eat and drink?' Rules of rank and gradation must be recognised and adhered to; the master must needs take precedence of the servant. The lesson conveyed by the parable amounts to this: be content to work in your allotted sphere of duty; do not expect things which are above you, and too high for you; seek no increase of faith in the hope of display of power and a sudden elevation; that which is necessary and desirable for your Master is equally so for you, and will in due time be granted you. Be content to do his bidding and wait his time. Your position and prospects are your sufficient and only recompense. Aim not at anything beyond, for you can claim nothing and receive nothing more. 'Doth he thank the servant (Gr. bond-servant) because he did the things which were commanded?' The Revisers and Tischendorf omit the words, 'I trow not.' Alford notes that they are 'omitted by several ancient authorities,' but no indication is given of their absence from any of the three oldest MSS. In such a spirit let the disciples simply endeavour to perform their duty. Enough for them, instead of asking for higher gifts of faith, to obey every command laid upon them, dismissing the idea of any works of supererogation, and indulging no ambition outside their proper sphere of action. 'Even so ye also, when ye shall have done all the things that are commanded you, say, We are unprofitable servants (Gr. bond-servants); we have done that which it was our duty to do.' The word 'unprofitable' needs consideration. Alford says: 'In the case of *men* this is different; a good servant is *profitable*, not *useless*.' But to represent such servants as unprofitable to their Master is contrary to the parable, for they were either ploughing or keeping sheep, and afterwards waiting at table; and in another parable Jesus describes a heavy punishment to be due to an unprofitable servant. Alford quotes Bengel, who gets over the difficulty in this way: 'Wretched is he whom the Lord calls an unprofitable servant: happy he who calls himself so.' But as the word 'unprofitable' does not apply to the servants in respect of their master, it must in respect of themselves: their labour was profitable to him, being justly due to him; it brought no profit to them, they being bound to render him service. That the application of the word may be twofold is shown in the passage: 'That they may do this with joy, and not with grief: for this *were* unprofitable for you.' It might have stood 'for them': had the writer omitted the last two words, we should have had to judge for ourselves whether he meant 'for you' or 'for them,' or 'for you and them.' In the case before us, the context sufficiently indicates that the application of the word 'unprofitable' is not to the master but to the servants: it was for them to do their duty, without expectation of profit in the shape of thanks or special emoluments.

In recording the miracles of Jesus, Luke is careful to supply such particulars of time and place as were within his knowledge. The following incident occurred in a journey towards Jerusalem, somewhere near the boundary-line between Galilee and Samaria. 'And it came to pass, as they were (or, as he was) on the way to Jerusalem, that he was passing through the midst of (or, between) Samaria and Galilee.' No record was handed down of the exact spot: the 'certain village' alluded to was probably too little known to have been generally recognised by name. At the entrance to the village Jesus was met by ten lepers. 'And as he entered into a certain village, there met him ten men that were lepers, which stood afar off.' This isolation from others was obligatory on account of their disease. The expression 'there met him' coupled with 'which stood afar off,' may be taken to indicate that the meeting was intentional on their part: the fame of Jesus had long been spread abroad, and wherever he went with his disciples the news of his coming would be likely to precede him. The lepers with one accord besought the compassion of the great Teacher: 'and they lifted up their voices, saying, Jesus, Master, have mercy on us.' Probably Jesus was surrounded by a crowd eager to see and hear him, outside which the ten lepers were constrained to keep at some considerable distance, endeavouring to attract his attention by crying aloud. This is implied by the words: 'And when he saw them, he said unto them.' It is not said that he called back to them: probably one of the disciples conveyed to them his message, which was as follows: 'Go and shew yourselves unto the priests.' They were justified in regarding that as a favourable answer: the only object of undergoing inspection by the priest was that he might pronounce the leprosy either diminished or cured. They went as Jesus bade them. 'And it came to pass, as they went, they were cleansed.' One of them, when he became conscious of the marvellous change which had come over him, returned to Jesus, proclaiming loudly as he went his thankfulness to God. 'And one of them, when he saw that he was healed, turned back, with a loud voice glorifying God.' The uplifting of the voice was no needless demonstration: none would approach a leper, and to shout out, 'God be thanked for my cure!' was natural, and, under the circumstances, not unbecoming. On reaching the presence of Jesus, he fell prostrate, pouring forth his thanks. 'And he fell upon his face at his feet, giving him thanks.' The nationality of the man was discernible: 'and he was a Samaritan.' But why, Jesus asked, had one only out of ten returned? 'And Jesus answering said, Were not the ten cleansed? but where are the nine?' The feeling of gratitude was strongest in this alien from the commonwealth of Israel. 'Were there (or, There were) none found that returned to give glory to God, save this stranger (or, alien).' This may be accounted for on the supposition that the rest were Jews, who might consider it enough to comply with the observance laid down by Moses on the cleansing of leprosy. The spirit of Jesus appears in his observation: he valued much, if not most, the immediate recognition of a benefit; and the acknowledgment to a benefactor was, in his eyes, consistent with, if not equivalent to, a thanksgiving to God. Moreover, he would not have the man leave him under the idea that only to God alone, or to Jesus in conjunction with God, the cure was to be attributed. The man's faith had been a means in the working of the miracle. 'And he said unto him, Arise, and go thy way: thy faith hath made thee whole (or, saved thee).' Young and Tischendorf render 'saved thee;' the 'Englishman's Greek New Testament,' 'cured thee.' The expression, however translated, is obviously restricted to the healing of the leprosy. Unfortunately, the training and traditions of theologians embolden them to discover meanings which are not disclosed or suggested by the narrative. Dean Alford's comment is as follows: '*Hath made thee whole*—in a higher sense than the mere cleansing of his leprosy—*theirs* was merely the beholding of the brazen serpent with the outward eyes,—but his, with the eye of inward faith; and this faith saved him;—not only healed his body, but his soul.' What a lamentable overstepping of the narrative is that! How can the simple but momentous truths which Jesus sought to teach be realised, when his words are thus stretched beyond their natural and proper meaning?

Jesus was once questioned by the Pharisees as to the time when God's kingdom, which we know had been proclaimed since the days of John the Baptist, would come. Jesus replied that no outward signs marked its advent. 'And being asked by the Pharisees, when the kingdom of God cometh, he answered them and said, The kingdom of God cometh not with observation.' There were no external symbols of that rulership; it was not a thing to be localised and gazed at. 'Neither shall they say, Lo, here! or, There! for lo, the kingdom of God is within you (or, in the midst of you).' The Revisers have retained the word 'within,' but the sense of the marginal reading is expressly given by Tischendorf's note: 'translate *is among you*.' Alford says: 'The misunderstanding which rendered these words *within you*, meaning this in a spiritual sense, *in your hearts*, should have been prevented by reflecting that they are addressed to the Pharisees, in whose hearts it certainly was not.' Young renders 'within,' not necessarily intending it in a spiritual sense. Yet his translation of 'kingdom of God' by 'reign of God,' includes that sense: God's 'reign' can only be 'among' men in proportion to their obedience to his will.

What follows was spoken to the disciples, not to the Pharisees, and must not be assumed to be a continuation of the same subject. 'And he said unto the disciples, The days will come, when ye shall desire to see one of the days of the Son of man, and ye shall not see it.' The earthly career of Jesus must draw on to its close; and when his daily round of teaching and healing should be ended, there would spring up in the hearts of his disciples, a longing for his presence and instruction. Then rumours of his return to earth would be promulgated, some saying he would be found in one place, some in another. All such visionary expectations must be set aside. 'And they shall say to you, Lo, there! Lo, here! go not away, nor follow after *them*.' Tischendorf renders: 'Go not away and pursue not.' Such reports would not be worth their heeding and investigating. When the day of his manifestation should come, there would be no need to seek him in a particular spot: the whole world would know of his coming, which would be as open and unmistakable as the lightning which flashes at opposite points of the horizon. 'For as the lightning, when it lighteneth out of the one part under the heaven, shineth unto the other part under the heaven; so shall the

Son of man be in his day.' The Revisers note that 'Some ancient authorities omit *in his day*.' Of the three oldest MSS. the Vatican only omits those words; Tischendorf retains them. But before the day of his manifestation, Jesus must pass through much suffering and be rejected by his contemporaries. 'But first must he suffer many things and be rejected of this generation.' Foreseeing all that, he looked far beyond, even to a time when he would be the supreme arbiter of the world's destiny. Jesus had previously foretold as much, when expounding his parable of the tares of the field. 'So shall it be in the consummation of the age. The Son of man shall send forth his angels, and they shall gather out of his kingdom all things that cause stumbling, and them that do iniquity.' Meantime all the affairs of the world are left to go on after their accustomed fashion, the long-deferred crisis coming suddenly at its appointed time. 'And as it came to pass in the days of Noah, even so shall it be also in the days of the Son of man. They ate, they drank, they married, they were given in marriage, until the day that Noah entered into the ark, and the flood came, and destroyed them all. Likewise even as it came to pass in the days of Lot; they ate, they drank, they bought, they sold, they planted, they builded; but in the day that Lot went out from Sodom it rained fire and brimstone from heaven, and destroyed them all.' The rendering of Tischendorf, Young, and the 'Englishman's Greek New Testament,' 'they were eating, they were drinking,' &c., is preferable. These two illustrations point to some catastrophe, a universal judgment, a special and irresistible interference with the course of nature: 'after the same manner shall it be in the day that the Son of man is revealed.' So sudden will be the emergency that not an instant must be lost by those who would escape destruction. 'In that day, he which shall be on the housetop, and his goods in the house, let him not go down to take them away: and let him that is in the field likewise not return back. Remember Lot's wife.' As this represents imminent danger to life, the significance of the following verse is not obvious, and seems at first sight contradictory. 'Whosoever shall seek to gain his life (or, soul) shall lose it: but whosoever shall lose *his life* (or, *soul*) shall preserve it (Gr. save it alive).' Alford translates the verse thus: 'Whosoever shall have sought his life shall lose it: and whosoever shall have lost it shall quicken it;' and he adds the note: '*whosoever shall have sought*, i.e. during his preceding life, *shall lose it* then: *whosoever shall have lost it*, by self-sacrifice during this life, shall quicken it then'; and he quotes Wordsworth as follows: 'The verb in the original is an expressive word, derived from animal parturition, bringing forth to air and life what was before concealed in the womb.' Tischendorf's rendering is: 'Whosoever shall seek to possess his life, will lose it; and whosoever shall lose it will preserve it'; Young: 'Whoever may seek to save his life, shall lose it; and whoever may lose his life, shall preserve it.' Nothing can ward off death, and nothing can hinder life after death. The axiom was one which Jesus impressed on his disciples at various times, and which he sought to make them realise as their rule of life and action. And the coming of the Son of man will be in connection with the final change and crisis of our present existence, and will involve a process of selection and separation altogether irrespective of worldly conditions and surroundings.

'I say unto you, In that night there shall be two men in one bed, the one shall be taken, and the other shall be left. There shall be two women grinding together: the one shall be taken, and the other shall be left.' The Revisers, following the three oldest MSS., have omitted the following verse: 'There shall be two men in the field; the one shall be taken, and the other shall be left.' Alford suggests that 'it was probably inserted here from Matt. xxiv. 40.'

There has been nothing in the world's history answering to this description of the coming of the Son of man. It represents not only a general, overwhelming catastrophe, but simultaneously or antecedently the deliverance of certain persons. Jesus dwells especially on this last circumstance, telling us that the discrimination of character will be so close and unerring that men and women living, resting, working together will be separated from each other, some taken from the evil to come and others left to meet their doom. It is the story of Dives and Lazarus in another form, the same truth, but without a metaphor, as is revealed in the parables of the tares of the field and the drag-net, both of which had reference to 'the consummation of the age.' The disciples asked Jesus where this stupendous manifestation of the Son of man was destined to take place. 'And they answering say unto him, Where, Lord (Sir—Young)?' The reply of Jesus was metaphorical: 'And he said unto them, Where the body *is*, thither will the eagles (or, vultures) also be gathered together.' Divine judgment will be executed, not with reference to particular localities, but as it may be necessitated by the course of events: as the vultures swoop to their prey, attracted thither by the miasma of the carcase, so the advent of the Son of man, and the work of separation assigned to his messengers, will come to pass where and when the state of society may demand such an interference.

Of the parable of the unjust judge which immediately follows, Alford says: 'This parable, though not perhaps spoken in immediate unbroken sequence after the last discourse, evidently arose out of it.' The opening words imply, at least, that it was spoken to the same persons: 'And he spake a parable unto them,' that is, to 'the disciples' (see verse 22 of the last chapter): 'to the end that they ought always to pray, and not to faint, saying, There was in a city a judge, which feared not God, and regarded not man.' Young renders literally: 'A certain judge was in a certain city, God not fearing, and man not regarding.' A man without conscience and without principle, setting at naught all laws, divine and human. To his judgment seat there came a lonely, persecuted woman. 'And there was a widow in that city, and she came oft unto him, saying, Avenge me (or, do me justice) of mine adversary.' That, for some time, he refused to do; but, later on, he altered his mind, and resolved to do her justice. Not willingly, however, nor from any sense of rectitude, but simply to save himself the annoyance caused by her repeated applications. 'And he would not for a while: but afterward he said within himself, Though I fear not God, nor regard man, yet because this widow troubleth me, I will avenge her, lest she wear me out ((Gr. bruise me) by her continual coming.' Persistent entreaty was a sufficient lever wherewith to overcome his conscienceless immobility. On that point of the parable Jesus seized, emphasising the lesson it conveyed. 'And the Lord said, Hear what the unrighteous judge (Gr. the judge of unrighteousness) saith.' If he was moved by the widow's importunity to vindicate her cause, how much more will God exercise his judicial power in favour of those whom he has chosen out of the world, and whose cry, under the wrongs and persecutions of the world, sounds unceasingly in his ears ? 'And shall not God avenge his elect, which cry to him day and night, and he is longsuffering over them ?' The Authorised Version has : 'though he bear long with them,' but the wording of the Revisers agrees with Tischendorf and Alford. The latter explains : 'He is long-suffering to those who oppose them ;' but surely the word 'them' must refer back to the elect. So Peter applied the term : 'long-suffering to you-ward.' The word 'though,' in the Authorised Version, is not in the original. The long-suffering or patience of God to the cry of his chosen, is put in contrast with the impatience of the unjust judge to the complaint of the widow ; the divine long-suffering is in the direction of a willing, continuous attention, which was the quality lacking in the unjust judge, who would not suffer the woman's importunity. The reverse of that holds good with respect to God and his elect : 'I say unto you, that he will avenge them speedily.' From this it follows that the drift of the parable, that 'they ought always to pray and not to faint,' is not to be understood as referring to the reiteration of prayer, for there can be no need of that to One who answers 'speedily.' The expression, 'which cry to him day and night,' denotes the incessant wrong-doing which is committed in the world, so that an unbroken chorus of supplication is ever rising to God in appeal against man's injustice. Generation after generation, by day and night, that goes on : yet 'the Lord is not slack concerning his promise ;' the warning of Jesus never ceases to apply : 'Agree with thine adversary quickly, whiles thou art with him in the way ; lest haply the adversary deliver thee to the judge.' That will be the lot of every oppressor. Our earthly life soon ends, and how speedily after death come judgment and the rectification, even to reversal, of this world's inequalities, let the parable of the rich man and Lazarus,—whose name signifies 'God is my help,'—testify. All this, however, is a matter of faith, unbacked by any evidence : the 'I say unto you' of Jesus is the only basis for our hope to rest upon. And as time goes on, century after century passing without any visible divine interference, the anticipation of a judgment to come grows fainter, so that even 'in the last days' the question will be asked, 'Where is the promise of his coming ? for, from the day that the fathers fell asleep, all things continue as they were from the beginning of the creation.' Foreseeing this, Jesus added : 'Howbeit, when the Son of man cometh, shall he find faith (or, the faith) on the earth ?' Young, Tischendorf, and Alford render 'the faith,' the latter considering it to be 'faith *in reference to the object of the parable.*'

Although the Revisers have not dropped from verses 3, 5, 7, and 8 the word 'avenge,' they have given as its equivalent, 'do me justice of.' Alford suggests, 'deliver me from ;' Young has 'do me justice' .. 'do her justice' .. 'execute the justice'; Luther uses in each instance the word 'retten,' 'save.' The alteration is important, because in modern language the words 'avenge' and 'vengeance' have come to signify more than impartial 'justice,' and convey the idea either of actual vindictiveness or of punishment inflicted with extremest rigour. It is clear that in this parable the term 'avenge' applies rather to the benefit conferred on the oppressed than to any penalty inflicted upon the oppressor; and throughout the Scriptures by the words 'avenge, avenger, vengeance,' should be understood simply the execution of 'justice.' In that, its true sense, the doctrine of divine 'vengeance' is a grand, ennobling, consolatory truth. Thus viewed, passages in the Psalms and elsewhere, which otherwise must be regarded as revolting or inexplicable, assume solemnity and pathos. Vengeance or avengement must never be dissociated from or go beyond the idea of justice; retaliation is not synonymous with vindictiveness. On 'the avenger of blood' in Israel devolved the duty of slaying every murderer, without trial, without delay; he was the exponent of the divine law, 'Whoso shedded man's blood, by 9 Gen. 6 man shall his blood be shed.' Flight to one of the cities of refuge was the only way of avoiding immediate destruction, and of claiming the right of trial; and even if the charge were reduced to manslaughter, the manslayer was not safe from the avenger outside the city of refuge. Only the avenger was justified in executing vengeance, 35 Num. and he was commissioned to act unhesitatingly, unvaryingly, like a passionless law of nature, as surely, as swiftly, as remorselessly, on meeting a murderer, as a flame of fire consumes the stubble within its reach. Consider the effect which such an office, always existing among the Israelites, must have had on the popular conception: the idea of 'vengeance' was connected with the exercise of a strictly judicial function, an unsparing severity against bloodguiltiness, established for the protection of the community. 'Vengeance' was declared to be an attribute of the God of Israel, and is spoken of in connection with his prerogative of supreme judgment. 'Vengeance is mine, and 32 Deut. 35 recompence.'

'O Lord, thou God to whom vengeance belongeth, 94 Ps. 1-3
Thou God to whom vengeance belongeth, shine forth.
Lift up thyself, thou judge of the earth:
Render to the proud *their* desert.
Lord, how long shall the wicked,
How long shall the wicked triumph?'

Not cruelty, but mercy, and a sublime love of justice, were in the soul of David when he sang:

'The righteous shall rejoice when he seeth the vengeance: 58 Psa. 10, 11
He shall wash his feet in the blood of the wicked.
So that men shall say, Verily there is a reward for the righteous:
Verily there is a God that judgeth in the earth.'

In the mind of Paul also vengeance and judgment seem to have been synonymous, for he asks: '*Is* God unrighteous who taketh ven- 3 Rom. 5, 6 geance?' and answers: 'God forbid: for then how shall God judge the world?'

Luke next records another parable, which was not addressed to the disciples, but to certain persons who showed a spirit of self-laudation, and at the same time held others in contempt. 'And he spake also 18 Luke 9 this parable unto certain which trusted in themselves that they were righteous, and set all others (Gr. the rest) at nought.' Possibly some unrecorded incident revealed that trait of character and called forth this reproof from Jesus. Young's rendering points that way: 'And he spake also to certain who were trusting in themselves that they were righteous, and despising the rest, this simile.' Tischendorf, however, renders: 'certain who trust in themselves that they are righteous, and set at nought the rest.' Alford also adopts that rendering. Jesus describes two men, one at the top, the other at the bottom of the social scale, both going to pray in the temple. 'Two men went up into the temple to pray; the one a Pharisee, and the other a publican.' The Authorised and Revised Versions continue: 'The Pharisee stood and prayed thus with himself.' The words 'with himself' are omitted by Tischendorf, and by Young who renders: 'The Pharisee having stationed himself, thus prayed:' the recognized formality of posture was punctiliously observed. And his prayer turns out to be a thanksgiving—on behalf of himself, all about himself, his integrity, his morality. 'God, I thank thee, that I am not as the rest of men, extortioners, unjust, adulterers. Ah! how thankful he ought to be, not only on account of his freedom from such gross immoralities, but for his honourable position in society: how different his lot from that of this tax-gatherer, whose calling was deemed, if not infamous, certainly not respectable; so he adds: 'or even as this publican.' What a privilege to have a strict sense of religious duty, involving constant, voluntary self-denial in food and money! 'I fast twice in the week; I give tithes of all that I get.' The Revisers have altered 'possess' to 'get;' Tischendorf and Alford render the word 'acquire;' the 'Englishman's Greek New Testament' 'gain.' He gave a tenth part of his income. The heart of the Pharisee stands revealed to us: nothing he said can be assumed to be hypocritical or untrue. He is represented as simply trusting in himself that he was righteous, and looking down upon the publican. The tax-gatherer was humble in demeanour, and would not even lift his eyes heavenwards, a custom which we know that Jesus himself observed in prayer. 'But the publican, standing afar off, would not lift up so much as his eyes unto heaven.' That his soul was filled with compunction was evident from his gesture, his intensity of self-reproach impelling him to smite his breast, as he confessed his sinfulness and craved forgiveness: 'but smote his breast, saying, God, be merciful (or, be propitiated) to me a (or, the) sinner.' What a contrast between these two men, the one esteeming himself as best among the best, the other as worst among the worst: the one full of thankful self-congratulation, airing his virtuousness of heart and life in the sight of heaven, the other a self-accused criminal, anxious only to deprecate the wrath of God due to his misdeeds! As they left the house of prayer for their respective homes, which of the two was the more acceptable in the sight of God? Jesus tells us: I say unto you, This man went down to his house justified rather than the other.' And this by the working of an inflexible law: 'For every one that exalteth himself shall be humbled, but he that humbleth himself shall be exalted.' That is the point of the parable; the one lesson which Jesus bids us draw from it. He impressed this truth on his disciples on two other occasions also. 'But he that is greatest among you shall be your servant. And whosoever shall exalt himself shall be humbled; and whosoever shall humble himself shall be exalted.' Again: 'Then shalt thou have glory in the presence of all that sit at meat with thee. For every one that exalteth himself shall be humbled; and he that humbleth himself shall be exalted.' The three instances in which Jesus enforced this argument applied to matters of social conduct and demeanour: he would have us take it as a rule of life, with respect to claims of precedence in society and in the church. The apostle Paul laid hold upon this truth, and acted in accordance with it: 'For we are not bold to [10 ii. Cor. 12] number or compare ourselves with certain of them that commend themselves; but they themselves, measuring themselves by themselves, and comparing themselves with themselves, are without understanding.' Accepting this as sound philosophy and a doctrine of Christian ethics, surely that educational system must be unwise and wrong, which is based upon emulation, the standard of a boy's progress being his position in a class, claims to distinction arising out of a comparison of the scholars with each other, so that they are taught to be 'measuring themselves by themselves, and comparing themselves with themselves.' 'Every one when he is perfected shall be [6 Luke 40] as his teacher.' Whatever is thoroughly learnt by all ceases to be a subject of competitive examination: comparison in degrees of attainment is but the badge of imperfection; the custom of prize-giving and of 'honours' in our educational system is an evidence either of the fact that the effort to teach thoroughly has not been successful with the majority, or that the scholars generally have been exercised beyond their mental powers. Distinctions granted to the few are, in truth, reproaches chargeable against the teacher for his failure with the many. A wiser method should be adopted. Instead of the artificial system of prize-giving, and the detestable custom of sending periodical 'reports,' with the names and 'marks' of respective scholars, which too much resembles an attempt to shift the responsibility from the schoolmaster upon the parents, who desire that their children may be taught, not simply classified as more or less unsuccessful scholars, why should not certificates of competency be issued? That could easily be arranged for all subjects: certificates, for instance, of having become perfect in the first four rules of arithmetic, in practice, in simple and compound proportion, in decimals; certificates of thorough attainment in specific grades of geometry, of languages, grammatically, by translation, and colloquially, of geography, of writing and drawing in their several stages, and so on. Such certificates would be reliable evidences of progress, and would obviate the objectionable system of 'cramming' for examinations. Such a plan has been adopted with satisfactory results by Mr. Isaac Pitman. He issues certificates for phonography: that a speed of so many words per minute has been attained. Every student should perform his work for the work's sake, apart from the stimulus and strain of competition. Why should he be induced to compare himself with his fellows, and measure his own attainments by those of others? So far as the spirit of emulation is instinctive and spontaneous, it will find its natural outcome in games of strength and skill, which are undertaken for the play's sake, just as studies should be for the work's sake. There is no need to encourage in the young a yearning for distinction and pre-eminence. Jesus detected too much of such a spirit in his days, and he counsels us to hold aloof from it, to act upon the contrary principle, to accept as a truth and life-maxim his assurance : 'Every one that exalteth himself shall be humbled, but he that humbleth himself shall be exalted.'

Luke's narrative now again falls in with Matthew and Mark. The three evangelists record the bringing of infants to Jesus. 'Then were there brought unto him little children, that he should lay his hands on them, and pray.' Luke says nothing about praying, but uses a word which denotes the earliest age. 'And they brought unto him also their babes, that he should touch them.' Mark : 'And they brought unto him little children, that he should touch them.' Matthew and Mark state : 'and the disciples rebuked them.' Luke says : 'But when the disciples saw it, they rebuked them.' The Revisers have substituted in Mark 'them' for 'those that brought them,' on the authority of the two oldest MSS. The rebuke could scarcely fail to be reflected upon such of the children as were old enough to understand the prohibition. Possibly it seemed to the disciples derogatory to the character and office of their Teacher that he should be importuned in this way : that his touch, which had so constantly worked miracles of healing should be sought when no infirmity required it, perchance even with a superstitious notion. But the interference of the disciples was hotly resented by Jesus. 'But when Jesus saw it, he was moved with indignation.' Luke represents him as summoning the disciples to give them his opinion of the matter. 'But Jesus called them unto him, saying, Suffer the little children to come unto me, and forbid them not : for of such is the kingdom of God.' Mark : 'and said unto them, Suffer the little children to come unto me : forbid them not : for of such is the kingdom of God.' Matthew : 'But Jesus said, Suffer the little children, and forbid them not, to come unto me : for of such is the kingdom of heaven.' In Matthew and Luke the Authorised Version omits the word 'the' before 'little children,' thereby making the words apply generally ; but Tischendorf, Young and Alford agree with the Revisers. Tischendorf in the three places uses the expression : 'Leave the little children to come unto me : ' the force is on the word 'come ; ' the children, invited by the gesture of Jesus, were to be left free to follow their natural impulse, no man forbidding them. The saying of Jesus must not be stretched beyond the occasion, as though it applied in any way, except by analogy, to the question of infant baptism. The calling together of the disciples indicated a purpose of stating an important truth, and the lesson conveyed by Jesus was in the opposite direction : not that children were to be admitted to the rite of baptism, not that they needed to be brought into the kingdom of heaven, but that their characteristic innocency and helplessness were the pattern of the heavenly disposition : 'for of such is the kingdom of heaven.' Instead of depreciating children, Jesus would have his disciples imitate them. God's kingdom was not for the independent and self-confident ; men must receive it in a childlike spirit, put away the sense of self-confidence and self-esteem, unlearn their previous teaching, begin life afresh, starting with new maxims, new aims, new hopes : ' Verily I say unto you, Whosoever shall not receive the kingdom of God as a little child, he shall in no wise enter therein.' Young renders, 'the reign of God :' what is that but implicit submission to the divine will ? Jesus was the guide to that new state of being, the teacher of the heavenly doctrine, the alphabet of which could only be acquired by childlike docility. Once within the kingdom, heavenly lessons would be learned, spiritual powers unfolded, a nobler career of duty opened out, the higher life inaugurated. But only through humility, passive, unquestioning, reverential submission to the heaven-sent doctrine, could entrance be gained. Jesus had previously taught that truth, enforcing it by calling to himself a little child, and assuring his disciples, 'Except ye turn, and become as little children, ye shall in no wise enter into the kingdom of heaven.' No wonder his indignation was roused, when he found them rebuking and driving away children from his presence. He scrupled not to comply with the wish of those who brought them, embracing the little ones, blessing them, laying his hands on each. 'And he took them in his arms, and blessed them, laying his hands upon them.' Matthew explains that it was a parting benediction, the last act of Jesus in the place where he had been teaching. 'And he laid his hands on them, and departed thence.'

[side: 18 Mat. 2, 3]
[side: 10 Mark 16]
[side: 19 Mat. 15]

The compilers of the 'Ministration of Public Baptism of Infants to be used in the Church,' availed themselves of this incident with consummate judgment and tact. After reading the account given by Mark, the Minister comments as follows: 'Beloved, ye hear in this Gospel the words of our Saviour Christ, that he commanded the children to be brought unto him; how he blamed those that would have kept them from him; how he exhorteth all men to follow their innocency. Ye perceive how by his outward gesture and deed he declared his good-will toward them; for he embraced them in his arms, he laid his hands upon them, and blessed them. Doubt ye not, therefore, but earnestly believe, that he will likewise favourably receive this present Infant; that he will embrace him with the arms of his mercy; that he will give unto him the blessing of eternal life, and make him partaker of his everlasting kingdom. Wherefore we being thus persuaded of the good-will of our heavenly Father towards this Infant, declared by his Son Jesus Christ; and nothing doubting but that he favourably alloweth this charitable work of ours in bringing this Infant to his holy Baptism: let us faithfully and devoutly give thanks unto him.' That, in truth, is the only foundation on which the theory and practice of infant baptism can be upheld: and it is a weak foundation at the best. For the good-will of Jesus was shown towards children as children, simply in their natural condition, apart from any doctrine of regeneration: whereas the Minister deals with children from an opposite point of view, saying: 'Forasmuch as all men are conceived and born in sin, and that our Saviour Christ saith, None can enter into the kingdom of God, except he be regenerate and born anew of Water and of the holy Ghost: I beseech you to call upon God the Father, through our Lord Jesus Christ, that of his bounteous mercy he will grant to this Child that thing which by nature he cannot have.' How different is this, in tone and spirit, from the words of Jesus, 'of such is the kingdom of God.' Infant baptism is held to be much more than a mere emblematic and figurative rite, as the prayers by which it is accompanied plainly indicate. Something supernatural is besought from God, and is declared to have been bestowed by him: for the priest says, 'We yield thee hearty thanks, most merciful Father, that it hath pleased thee to regenerate this Infant with thy holy Spirit.' That supernatural gift is assumed to be granted at the font, the prayers used putting God foremost and the Priest somewhat in the background. But in urgent cases of private baptism, only 'so many of the Collects appointed to be said before in the Form of Public Baptism, as the time and present exigence will suffer,' are to be used; and as soon as the water is poured upon the child, and the words uttered, 'I baptize thee In the name of the Father, and of the Son, and of the Holy Ghost,' God is thanked as before: 'We yield thee hearty thanks, most merciful Father, that it hath pleased thee to regenerate this Infant with thy holy Spirit.' The change is believed to have been wrought through the magic of those few priestly words! And in order that the people may rely unhesitatingly on the efficacy of the rite, both in this world and the next, this note is added: 'It is certain by God's Word, that Children which are baptized, dying before they commit actual sin, are undoubtedly saved.' Our Lord Jesus never claimed for his touch and blessing any such power as that. Infant baptism, with the doctrines thereto attached, is no part of his gospel, but an invention of theologians. They have not only sought to justify the practice by referring to his kindly and eulogistic words spoken with respect to children, but in another Church ceremony devised by them they have imitated his laying on of hands. Having claimed the mystic power of regenerating infants through water and the holy Spirit, allowing sponsors to promise and vow repentance and faith, in the name and on behalf of the unconscious child, they thought it advisable, and from their point of view it might well be deemed absolutely necessary, that some twelve years or more afterwards these children should 'themselves with their own mouth and consent, openly before the Church, ratify and confirm what their Godfathers and Godmothers promised for them in Baptism.' That, by itself, would have constituted a very simple, touching ceremony: but that also was elaborated in accordance with assumptions of priestly influence and power. 'The Order of Confirmation, or laying on of hands upon those that are baptized and come to years of discretion,' does not put forward any claim to the effect that grace and virtue flow from the touch of the Bishop's hands. On the contrary, that action is left altogether vague and undefined: it may be taken to mean little or much, anything, nothing, or everything, according to the ideas and teaching which may have been impressed upon the candidates for Confirmation. But it is a most natural question, Why should the laying on of hands have been instituted, and why should it have been restricted to one holding highest office in the Church? and it is an equally natural inference, that when the Bishop lays 'his hands upon the heads of every one severally,' some benefit is claimed, or intended, or believed, or hoped, to be conveyed thereby. If not, why is the laying on of hands by the apostles thus imitated, and in connection with solemn prayers for the outpouring of 'the holy Ghost?' The only guidance vouchsafed on this point is that the Bishop, in the Collect, says, 'upon whom (after the example of thy holy Apostles) we have now laid our hands, to certify them (by this sign) of thy favour and gracious goodness towards them.' The individual Bishop assumes the recognised style of royalty, speaking of himself as 'we,' 'we have now laid our hands.' When the apostles laid on their hands, some visible, oral, or other manifestation of the Holy Spirit's presence followed: the Bishop claims only that he gives a 'sign,' not even of some inward and spiritual grace, but simply of God's 'favour and gracious goodness.' If that is all, why this punctiliousness of ceremony and gesture? We do not need the touch of a Bishop's hand to assure us of the well-known truth that our heavenly Father is loving unto every man. Infant Baptism, the Catechism, and the Order of Confirmation constitute an artificial system of Church membership, and cry aloud for honest criticism and revision. The intention was good: to christianise every child from birth, to lay down a recognised form of religious teaching, and in due time to impress upon every young person the solemn obligations of Christianity. No provision was made, however, for any changes which might become necessary by the advancement of religious thought and the modification of existing creeds: the compilers of the Prayer Book assumed the absolute perfection and incontrovertibility of every doctrine they laid down, and demanded an unquestioning submission to the forms and ceremonies they prescribed. How little influence such clerical teaching has had upon adults generally is evidenced by the constant failure of multitudes to attend, except at rare intervals of their own choosing, the Lord's supper. In vain do the clergy invite, implore, insist upon spiritual benefits to be derived from frequent participation, and danger to the soul from neglect of the ordinance: the majority of the congregation habitually turn their backs upon it, and treat the exhortations of the Minister with silent contempt, albeit in every other point of divine worship and Christian living they may be as devout and blameless as the comparatively few regular communicants. Does not that prove the existence of a widespread unbelief with respect to the sacramental dogmas insisted on by the clergy? Men and women are not afraid to disregard their teaching and injunctions, and face the threatened penalties. But their children they are still careful to bring to baptism, and would not withhold them from confirmation. This state of things might go on for an indefinite period, were it not that the number of those who think for themselves on religious matters, or are led by other teachers, is ever on the increase. Some there are, none can say how many or how few, who deem the clergy generally unsafe and unwise guides, and who are anxious to keep their children's minds free from clerical dogmatic teaching; who dare not take the responsibility of imposing upon their children a catechism, to be learnt by rote, which is altogether out of harmony with their own convictions and feelings; and who could not conscientiously urge them to submit themselves to examination by a clergyman to be prepared after his fashion as candidates for confirmation. The next step in advance must needs be that the catechism and rite of confirmation will fall more and more into desuetude, and unless that should lead to an utter disregard of the Lord's supper,—which God forbid, though one sees not how, under present circumstances, it can permanently hold its ground,—there must be a deliberate setting aside of the rule originally laid down: 'And there shall none be admitted to the holy Communion, until such time as he be confirmed, or be ready and desirous to be confirmed.' The clergy themselves must needs be leavened with the spirit of the age in which they live. As a body they have already ceased from making any vigorous protest ; some of them are sure to imbibe or to sympathise with the new opinions embraced by the intelligent among the laity. There are old penalties and antiquated laws still upon the statute-book, which no man now would think of enforcing: the same gradual process of neglect and oblivion will render obsolete the Catechism and the Confirmation ceremony, and then, to save Baptism and Holy Communion from a similar fate, they will have to be freed from the superstition, errors and false assumptions with which they are interwoven, and remodelled in a form to harmonise with the light of reason and the simplicity which led men to welcome them when first instituted. Meantime, until that or some other devoutly to be wished for consummation is arrived at, the breach between clergy and laity must widen, the influence of the former continue to decline, and some of the best minds and purest hearts among the latter be content to bear, silently or with an occasional protest, the false charge of indifference, irreverence, atheism, or whatever other brand denoting a fundamental difference of opinion may be imposed upon them. Not the clergy of the present day, but their predecessors, who fondly persuaded themselves that they held the truth, the whole truth, and nothing but the truth in theology, and vainly hoped to stereotype their own ideas upon the members of the Church of England for all time, are responsible for this entanglement. There are two things the heaven-sent doctrine will not bear: the pressure of the human hand, moulding it into a particular form ; and the admixture of human inventions.

In the account of the following incident the discrepancies between the ancient MSS. indicate that commentators in early times had set themselves to the task of revising and altering the original documents. In the Revised Version Matthew begins as follows : 'And behold, one came to him and said, Master (or, Teacher), what good thing shall I do, that I may have eternal life ? ' The Revisers note that ' some ancient authorities read *Good Master*.' It so stands in the Authorised Version, but the two oldest MSS. omit 'good.' The Authorised Version continues : ' And he said unto him, Why callest thou me good ? ' The Revisers, following the two oldest MSS., render : ' And he said unto him, ' Why asketh thou me concerning that which is good ? ' This refers, not to any appellation bestowed on Jesus, but to the question, ' What good thing shall I do ? ' The Authorised Version, agreeing with ' some ancient authorities,' adds : ' *There is none good but one, that is* God.' The Revised Version stands : ' One there is who is good.' Tischendorf's Tauchnitz Edition gives the reading of the two oldest MSS. thus : ' Why askest thou me concerning what is good ? He who is good is One.' But Dr. Samuel Davidson's translation of Tischendorf's critical text is as follows : ' Why askest thou me concerning the good ? One is the good.' There seems to be uncertainty about the translation as well as about the reading. Mark describes how the man ran to Jesus and knelt before him ; and the question put differs somewhat, and the answer entirely. ' And as he was going forth into the way (or, on his way), there ran one to him, and kneeled to him, and asked him, Good Master (or, Teacher), what shall I do that I may inherit eternal life ?

And Jesus said unto him, Why callest thou me good? none is good save one, *even* God.' Luke adds that the man was a ruler. 'And a certain ruler asked him, saying, Good Master (or, Teacher), what shall I do to inherit eternal life? And Jesus said unto him, Why callest thou me good? none is good, save one, *even* God.' The reading of the Sinaitic and Vatican MSS. proves that the passage in Matthew had been altered to harmonise with Mark and Luke. Alford says : 'This passage furnishes one of the most instructive and palpable cases of the smoothing down of apparent discrepancies by correcting the Gospels out of one another and thus reducing them to conformity.' Let us consider first the words as they stand in Mark and Luke. The point of the reply turns upon the word 'good' in the question. 'Good Master ... Why callest thou me good?' It seems to have been assumed, as though it were a matter of course, that Jesus thereby reproved the questioner for applying to him the term 'good,' and afterwards proceeded to answer the question. But that is a mere guess, without a foundation, and it is more reasonable to take the words as forming part of the answer to the question. 'Why?' is properly equivalent to 'wherefore?' 'on what account?' 'for what reason?' The questioner is bidden to ask himself that question. What induced him to come to Jesus, and to consider him a 'good Teacher?' Was it not because of his work, his life, his teaching? He was engaged in God's work : his life was devoted to God's cause, the establishment of 'the kingdom of God ;' he taught men to obey the will of God. God was the sole fountain of good ; 'none is good save one—God ;' that must be the doctrine of every good teacher. Therefore the question, 'What shall I do?' admitted only of one answer : 'Thou knowest God's commandments:' do them. This harmonises perfectly with the original reading of Matthew's gospel as now accepted by the Revisers. He also makes the point of the answer turn upon the word 'good' in the question : but in quite a different way. He omits mention of the title 'good' which was applied to Jesus as a Teacher, and he brings out the fact that the questioner asked, 'What good thing shall I do?' There is no inconsistency between the evangelists so far. Then Matthew omits the sentence which the others record 'Why callest thou me good?' and he introduces a sentence which they omit : 'Why askest thou me concerning that which is good?' Still there is no inconsistency, and if only we do not presume to introduce without warrant the extraneous idea that Jesus wished to convey a reproof and to repudiate any claim to a customary title of respect, the evangelists are in harmony as to the sense : 'Why callest thou me good?' and 'Why askest thou me concerning that which is good?' are sentences which might naturally be spoken in conjunction, the 'good Teacher' being applied to 'concerning that which is good.' Any ambiguity attaching to the words, 'Why callest thou me good?' is removed, and the true sense of that expression shown, by the additional sentence, 'Why askest thou me concerning that which is good?' Instead of assuming a discrepancy between the evangelists, read the accounts together, and all difficulty of interpretation disappears. The attempt to reconcile them by partially suppressing and transforming the original account of Matthew, proceeded from error of judgment and want of insight The question, 'Why askest thou me concerning that which is good?';

[18 Luke 18. 19]

would surely not be assumed to indicate reproof, as though the man deserved blame for making such an enquiry of Jesus: there is no more reason for such a supposition with respect to the words, 'Why callest thou me good?' The drift of the two questions is in the same direction: whoever regarded Jesus as a good teacher concerning that which is good, must be prepared to believe that God was the only good, for the life and life-work of Jesus began, continued, and ended in God.

Here as elsewhere Young renders 'eternal life' by 'age-during life:' a most important distinction: for 'age-during' life denotes the natural continuance of being, whereas 'eternal life' seems to be regarded as a new, exceptional, or special gift, even when it is not explained away into something different, as equivalent to eternal happiness. There can be but one way of reaching the utmost span of life, either now in this world or hereafter in another. God's laws must be observed, not only in view of their constitutional, individual influence on mind and body, but of their indirect effects, socially as well as personally. The life of each depends upon his neighbour's observance of the law, 'Thou shalt not kill,' and the law of heredity, working retributively in silence, lays upon children the sins, wilful or ignorant, of parents, sapping the health and shortening the lives of the entire community. Jesus could only give one answer to the enquiry. 'But if thou wouldest enter into life, keep the commandments.' Here again Mark and Luke are more condensed than Matthew, their record of the words being simply, 'Thou knowest the commandments.' Matthew tells us that another question was here put. 'He saith unto him, Which?' Jesus in reply quoted the commandments relating to the duties of man to man. 'And Jesus said, Thou shalt not kill, Thou shalt not commit adultery, Thou shalt not steal, Thou shalt not bear false witness, Honour thy father and thy mother: and, Thou shalt love thy neighbour as thyself.' Mark omits the closing summary, and introduces, 'Do not defraud.' 'Thou knowest the commandments, Do not kill, Do not commit adultery, Do not steal, Do not bear false witness, Do not defraud, Honour thy father and thy mother.' Luke reverses the order of the first two. 'Thou knowest the commandments, Do not commit adultery, Do not kill, Do not steal, Do not bear false witness, Honour thy father and mother.' The answer of Jesus amounts to this: that an 'inheritance' of age-during life is only attainable through the due observance of every social duty. But as a matter of course the greater includes the less: personal virtue and self-control are indispensable to every man; nature itself teaches that intemperance must destroy health, and cut short life, and that proper care must be taken to preserve the body from dangers, from undue heat and cold, and from accidents. These things are necessarily foremost in our own minds, but Jesus does not even mention them. The question proposed was purely personal,—selfish: 'What shall I do that I may inherit age-during life?' That is a boon which can never come through individual self-seeking; never to any except through fulfilment of the duties due from each to all. Apart from that consummation of social life, and until it shall be reached, there can be no age-during life for any. That good gift of God will never be ours until, through the teaching and grace of Jesus, the Church, that is the assembly of believers, the community of

Christians, shall have learnt to live by his precept, 'Thou shalt love thy neighbour as thyself.'

Probably the enquirer was disappointed at the reply. Instead of the 'good thing' he had desired to learn about, Jesus had simply thrown him back upon old, well known duties. 'And he said, All these things have I observed from my youth up.' Mark notes that he still addressed Jesus as 'Teacher.' 'And he said unto him, Master (or, Teacher), all these things have I observed from my youth.' Matthew, as before, is a little fuller, telling us that the man was young, and that he propounded another question. 'The young man saith unto him, All these things have I observed : what lack I yet'? The answer to that was very plain and startling. 'And when Jesus heard it, he said unto him, One thing thou lackest yet : sell all that thou hast, and distribute unto the poor.' The expression, 'when Jesus heard it,' seems to denote that he was struck by the observation. Mark adds that he gazed upon the speaker, and at once manifested an affection towards him. 'And Jesus looking upon him loved him, and said unto him, One thing thou lackest : go, sell whatsoever thou hast, and give to the poor.' Matthew again adds a sentence : 'Jesus said unto him, If thou wouldest be perfect, go, sell that thou hast, and give to the poor.' That was indeed a counsel of perfection, a demand wholly unexpected. Yet it would be but another step in the same direction : he who claims to have fulfilled all duties, up to the point of loving his neighbour as himself, and then asks what more he can do, must needs be called upon to prove that he loves his neighbour better than himself. That involved discipleship to Jesus, self-sacrifice for the world's sake being the very essence of his call. He wanted men as followers who would forsake all things for his cause, who accepted his axiom that where the treasure is there is the heart also, and who would be content to have no tie to earth, laying up treasure in heaven. That hope he held out to the young man, inviting him to share the same lot as himself : 'and thou shalt have treasure in heaven : and come, follow me.' The Authorised Version of Mark has after 'come' the words 'take up the cross,' which the Revisers have omitted on the authority of the two oldest MSS. It was a magnificient opportunity, this invitation to place himself by the side of the good Teacher, and to help forward his plans for the establishment of God's kingdom. But the young man was unable to rise to the occasion. His demeanour changed at once ; a great sorrow took possession of him, for he could not bring himself to accept the call, involving as it did the loss of property and position, and he must needs turn his back upon Jesus, whose advice he had sought with such enthusiasm. 'But his countenance fell at the saying, and he went away sorrowful : for he was one that had great possessions.' 'But when the young man heard the saying, he went away sorrowful : for he was one that had great possessions.' 'But when he heard these things, he became exceeding sorrowful ; for he was very rich.' Must not Jesus himself have felt sorrowful at this failure of his effort to gain a disciple ? He could not abate his terms, but he knew well how hard it was to comply with them. 'And Jesus seeing him said, How hardly shall they that have riches enter into the kingdom of God !' The observation was addressed to the disciples. 'And Jesus said unto his disciples, Verily I say unto you,

It is hard for a rich man to enter into the kingdom of heaven.' Mark notes that he surveyed his disciples, as though realising the fact that they were all of another class than this young ruler. 'And Jesus looked round about, and saith unto his disciples, How hardly shall they that have riches enter into the kingdom of God!' It is added: 'And the disciples were amazed at his words.' That he should make the forsaking of all things a condition of discipleship, was no new doctrine to their ears; for he had previously laid down the rule, 'Whosoever he be of you that renounceth not all that he hath, he cannot be my disciple.' But this saying about the incompatibility of wealth and godliness seemed to extend the rule beyond professed discipleship. Jesus however, repeated the assertion. 'But Jesus answereth again, and saith unto them, Children, how hard is it for them that trust in riches to enter into the kingdom of God!' The words, 'for them that trust in riches,' seem to tone down somewhat the previous remark; but they are not found in the two oldest MSS., and the Revisers have noted that 'some ancient authorities omit' them. Jesus reiterated the truth in a strikingly emphatic form. 'And again I say unto you, It is easier for a camel to go through a needle's eye, than for a rich man to enter into the kingdom of God.' The words stand precisely the same in Mark, and in Luke the only difference is 'enter in through' instead of 'go through.' The hyperbole denotes an absolute impossibility. We must not venture to explain away or diminish the force of a declaration which Jesus saw fit to make so solemnly. It looks as if some early commentator had sought to do that, by inserting in Mark the words 'for them that trust in riches.' Nothing can qualify the simile, which enforces the moral impossibility under the figure of a physical impossibility. 'The kingdom of God,' rendered by Young, 'the reign of God,' obviously denotes a state of life in which everything is ruled after the divine will. 'The law and the prophets *were* until John: from that time the gospel of the kingdom of God is preached.' Men were invited to enter into a higher sphere of spiritual activity, to throw aside all worldly maxims, to inaugurate the life of heaven on earth, taking the precepts of Jesus for their rule of duty. There is no favouritism in God's kingdom; there must be no selfishness among God's children. Between Christian brethren there must be no sharp contrasts of wealth and poverty, no superfluity of riches restricted to a few, whilst many suffer abject poverty. That is Christ's ideal of a Christian community; that is God's ideal of his kingdom: not all that is meant by 'the reign of God,' but an important part thereof, so that it was impossible for a rich man to enter in. If words have meaning, Jesus meant that. If we say: under the present state of society that cannot be,—that is simply asserting that God's kingdom cannot be. In truth, it is a vision which has never yet been realised on earth. One fact alone is enough to prove that much: the existence of armies and navies, the perpetuation throughout nineteen centuries after the coming of Christ of the spirit and habit of war, with the multiplied and inevitable horrors attendant upon destruction and carnage. There is no approach to the reign of God whilst the kingdoms of the world are ruled after such a fashion. The inequalities of social life, the highest class revelling in splendid luxury, the lowest class, generation after generation, born to want and misery : are not these contrasts equally contrary to the spirit and teaching of Jesus ? He declared that before a rich man could take the first step into the kingdom of God, he must part with his wealth. All the first disciples, undertaking as they did to devote themselves to the establishment of the kingdom of God were urged to renounce all they had for the cause of Jesus. Only by coming within the circle of discipleship could men enter the kingdom of God. The two terms, a 'disciple' and a 'member of the kingdom of God,' are synonymous. The rich ruler's refusal of the call, 'Come, follow me,' is instantly spoken of by Jesus as a refusal to 'enter into the kingdom of God,' the one being identical with the other. And as but few became disciples, not many being invited by Jesus, and all men being dissuaded by him unless they first counted the cost, so there were but few who entered the kingdom of God, Jesus declaring it to be a very hard thing to do so, especially for the rich. But no condemnation was involved on the multitudes who were not disciples, and who did not enter into the kingdom of God. That kingdom was not even preached until the coming of the Baptist, and then only the strong-minded could take it as by force. 'The law and the prophets 16 Luke 16 *were* until John : from that time the gospel of the kingdom of God is preached, and every man entereth violently into it.' For weaker men there was room enough to live in peace and safety outside, taking 'the law and the prophets' for their rule of conduct. Their loss was a loss of privilege, not of the life, not of the soul. To be outside God's kingdom involved no threat of divine judgment : exclusion and regret were the penalties pressed home to the minds of the Jews by Jesus : 'There shall be the weeping and gnashing of teeth, when ye 13 Luke 28 shall see Abraham, and Isaac, and Jacob, and all the prophets in the kingdom of God, and yourselves cast forth without.' Not individual salvation, but the regeneration of society, was the sum and scope of the 'gospel of the kingdom' which Jesus preached ; the word 'kingdom' sufficiently denotes that the coming reformation was to be not simply individual and personal but socialistic and communal, termed by Jude ' our common salvation.' So far off are we from such a Jude 3 realization of God's kingdom, that the work of its establishment has to be begun afresh. Not until those who claim to be Ministers, representatives, disciples, followers,—no matter what title be chosen, —of Jesus, adopt his maxims and requirements absolutely without an exception, renouncing all things for his sake, thereby giving to the world the strange spectacle of a body of believers prepared not to resist evil, not to claim legal rights, not to fight under any circumstances, not to accumulate property, but to live entirely for the kingdom of heaven,—not until we are taught by such living examples the true doctrine of Jesus, will his spirit begin again to permeate society. Count Leon Tolstoi has boldly thought out that truth ; we must not let it go, neither must we assume such a rule of life to be binding upon all men. Discipleship to Jesus must be voluntary and exceptional still, as it was at first. The idea that all are called to discipleship is an absurdity. Ministers of the Church of England sign any and every child 'with the sign of the cross, in token that hereafter he shall not be ashamed to confess the faith of Christ crucified, and manfully to fight under his banner, against sin, the world, and the devil ; and to continue Christ's faithful soldier and servant unto his life's end.' Words, words, nothing but words! The ideal is pitched too high : such a 'high calling of God in Christ Jesus' was never meant to be universal, still less to be imposed upon unconscious infants. It is as utterly out of place and wide of truth, as it would be to devote every babe to a soldier's life and duties, knowing well that in nearly every case a different profession would be followed. Fictions such as these, passed on as an inheritance from age to age, have dimmed our spiritual eyesight ; and until they are put aside, and the plain truth, which is always and alone God's truth, faced, our perceptive faculties will not be equal to the comprehension of 'the things that are freely given us by God.' Before Christ's precepts can be acted upon, men must rise to the level of them. In the present state of society any general adoption of them would be impossible, and, if suddenly attempted, injurious. That many rich men should sell their possessions and give to the poor, would be quite as much to the loss and detriment of the poor as of the rich. Almsgiving tests the character of those who receive as well as of those who give ; indiscriminate charity quenches energy and self-reliance, and tends to pauperise, that is, to render perpetually poor those who rely upon it. The trustees of the Peabody fund could find no better way of benefiting the poor of London than that of building better dwellings, at moderate rentals, for the working class. Hospitals, infirmaries, refuges, reformatories, workhouses,—we must needs have them still, but the less the better : for they are evidences either of under-payment for labour or of improvidence among labourers. The masters who are careful to pay their workmen fairly, do more for the poor and promote more the kingdom of God, than those who accumulate huge fortunes, keeping down wages under cast-iron laws of supply and demand as decreed by 'Political Economy,' and who then disgorge a portion of the ill-gotten superfluity to help workmen in ways wherein, if the profits on labour were fairly divided, they should be able and would be willing to help themselves. Preachers boast of what Christianity has done in the shape of charitable institutions : but all that paraphernalia of charity is really an evidence that the 'kingdom of God' has not yet come, that the spirit and scheme of Christianity have not yet been realised.

The disciples heard the declaration of Jesus with the utmost amazement. If it was impossible for a rich man to enter God's kingdom, who would be found ready to accept salvation at such a cost ? This rich ruler might be taken as an example of others in like circumstances. 'And when the disciples heard it, they were astonished exceedingly, saying, Who then can be saved ?' The Authorised Version of Mark represents them as enquiring this 'among themselves,' but the Revisers, following the two oldest MSS., take the question to have been addressed to Jesus. 'And they were astonished exceedingly, saying unto him, Then who can be saved ?' Luke is briefer and vaguer. 'And they that heard it said, Then who can be saved ?' Obviously the word 'who' signifies, 'who among such persons,' only the wealthy being alluded to. The sense of the word 'saved' must be fixed by the context : saved out of the world, and admitted into the kingdom of God. There is no fixed meaning attachable to the word 'saved,' albeit theologians are in the habit of defining it in one particular way. The apostle Peter speaks of 'salvation' as a term of such wide and doubtful meaning that those who used it had been uncertain as to its import: 'Receiving the end [1 i. Pet. 9–11] of your faith, *even* the salvation of *your* souls. Concerning which salvation the prophets sought and searched diligently, who prophesied of the grace that *should come* unto you: searching what *time* or what manner of time the Spirit of Christ which was in them did point unto.' Salvation relates to a time or manner of time, that is, the establishment of the kingdom of God.

Luke gives the reply of Jesus thus: 'But he said, The things [18 Luke 27] which are impossible with men are possible with God.' Matthew is more definite: 'and looking upon *them* said to them, With men this [19 Mat. 26] is impossible; but with God all things are possible.' Mark: 'Jesus [10 Mark 27] looking upon them saith, With men it is impossible, but not with God: for all things are possible with God.' The habitual manner of Jesus must have been as impressive as his words. Occasionally it was so striking that special mention was made of it. Here his earnest gaze, 'Jesus looking upon them,' is noted. Words which we often read, or hear read, coldly and carelessly, fell from the lips of Jesus with solemn emphasis, change of voice, of attitude, of countenance, adding force and dignity to what he said. Did Jesus assert that what he had just pronounced impossible was not absolutely so, but only humanly impossible, and that God, although a man clung to his riches, could nevertheless enable him to enter into the kingdom of heaven? That would simply have been to contradict and explain away the statement he had just before deliberately corroborated by a strong hyperbole. The import of the passage depends upon the sense given to the expressions 'with men . . with God.' By taking them as equivalent to, 'to men . . to God,' we introduce a contradiction. But 'to' and 'with' are not synonymous. Luther renders the word 'bey:' 'bey den Menschen . . . bey Gott,' which conveys the idea of association with men . . with God. The Greek word is *para*, which is rendered in the Authorised Version 24 different ways, but never as 'to.' When it governs the dative, as it does in these three passages, it is frequently rendered 'with,' in the sense of Luther's 'bey,' as in the following examples. 'There were *with* us [22 Mat. 25] seven brethren.' 'To be guest *with* a man that is a sinner.' 'That [19 Luke 7] he would tarry *with* them.' Following human maxims, customs, [4 John 40] counsels, it is impossible; but with God, led by him, it is not impossible to enter his kingdom in this way of his appointment, leaving earthly wealth outside. That truth flashed upon the mind of Peter. He and his fellow apostles had indeed entered in that way the kingdom of God. 'Peter began to say unto him, Lo, we have [10 Mark 28] left all, and have followed thee.' Luke varies the words: 'And Peter [18 Luke 28] said, Lo, we have left our own (or, our own *homes*), and followed thee.' The oldest MS. adds, in Mark, the additional words, 'What shall we have therefore?' They may have been inserted from Matthew, which stands as follows: 'Then answered Peter and said [19 Mat. 27] unto him, Lo, we have left all, and followed thee, what then shall we have?' Earthly wealth being excluded, what kind of riches were to be gained in God's kingdom? Jesus prefaced his reply with his accustomed solemn, 'Verily.' He would have them believe that the words he was about to utter were spoken with deliberation and certainty. 'And Jesus said unto them, Verily I say unto you, that [,, 28] ye which have followed me, in the regeneration when the Son of man

shall sit on the throne of his glory, ye also shall sit upon twelve thrones, judging the twelve tribes of Israel.' The words, 'ye which have followed me,' must be taken in their fullest, deepest sense, not as denoting a simple profession and badge of discipleship, but an actual, lifelong imitation of the career of Jesus, the forsaking of all things, the taking up of his cross, the hating of their own lives for his name's sake. Thereby they would become fitted for pre-eminence hereafter, taking part with Jesus in the judicial responsibilities of the kingdom of God which he came to proclaim and found. A state of society has to be attained so intrinsically different from that now existing as to amount to a 'regeneration;' Young renders the word 'renovation.' Then the 'Son of man,' Jesus as the head and representative of redeemed humanity, will 'sit on the throne of his glory.' No more scorning of his truth and person, no false charges of blasphemy and sedition, no plotting, betrayal, or crucifixion, but an acknowledged supremacy, a reverential homage, with all that appertains to regal power and majesty. Jesus not only foretold his sufferings and death on earth, but looked beyond all that to the glory which should be given him. His cause would surely triumph; the kingdom of God would be established, and then the twelve apostles he had chosen, having been its pioneers, would have earned a high position, ranking next to Jesus, and holding office under him. When redeemed humanity has come beneath the sway of Jesus, the changed conditions of existence will still admit of conflicting interests, which will have to be settled, not on the old lines of physical strife and murder legalised by the name of war, but by the judgment of those whom Jesus shall appoint, who have submitted themselves unreservedly to his guidance, and may therefore be trusted as fit exponents of his mind and will. The mention of 'the twelve tribes of Israel' was full of meaning. At that time the nationality of Israel, as regarded ten of the tribes, was a thing of the past. The land was ruled by strangers, and there was no king over Israel or Judah. The epistle of James is addressed 'to the twelve tribes which are of the Dispersion.' Yet Jesus asserted that the twelve tribes of Israel would come under the rule of himself and his apostles. The problem of Israel's restoration is dealt with by Paul, and he arrived at this conclusion: 'And so all Israel shall be saved; even as it is written,
There shall come out of Zion the Deliverer:
He shall turn away ungodliness from Jacob:
And this is my covenant unto them,
When I shall take away their sins.'

That is a spiritual deliverance, from ungodliness and sins. The apostle argued: 'For they are not all Israel which are of Israel:' he insists upon the proper sense of the word 'Israel,' which is, 'contender or soldier of God.' He proceeds: 'Neither, because they are Abraham's seed, are they all children: but, In Isaac shall thy seed be called.' Elsewhere he says: 'Now we, brethren, as Isaac was, are children of promise:' that is, Gentiles with Jews, redeemed by Jesus, constitute the Israel of God. 'The twelve tribes of Israel' is an expression which, in the mouth of Jesus, of James, and of Paul, has a breadth of meaning beyond that which they would have given it who cried, 'Our Father is Abraham,' to whom Jesus answered, 'If ye were Abraham's children, ye would do the works of Abraham.'

Not only to the apostles, but to all who followed in their steps, Jesus held out an assurance of recompense. 'And every one that hath left houses, or brethren, or sisters, or father, or mother, or children, or lands, for my name's sake, shall receive a hundredfold, and shall inherit eternal life.' The Authorised Version has after 'mother,' 'or wife,' which is the reading of the Vatican MS. The Sinaitic MS. originally had 'houses' where it stands above, but the word there had been erased and inserted by a later hand after 'lands,' so as to stand last instead of first. Instead of 'hundredfold' the Vatican MS. has 'manifold.' Luke now stands as follows: 'And he said unto them, Verily I say unto you, There is no man that hath left house, or wife, or brethren, or parents, or children, for the kingdom of God's sake, who shall not receive manifold more in this time, and in the world (or, age) to come eternal life.' Here the Revisers have altered the order of the words, making them agree with the Sinaitic MS. The word *aiōn*, rendered 'world (or, age),' is the root of the word *aiōnios*. To be consistent, it should be rendered, not 'eternal,' but 'age-during,' as it is by Young. Mark's record is fuller: 'Jesus said, Verily I say unto you, There is no man that hath left house, or brethren, or sisters, or mother, or father, or children, or lands, for my sake, and for the gospel's sake, but he shall receive a hundredfold now in this time, houses, and brethren, and sisters, and mothers, and children, and lands, with persecutions; and in the world (or, age) to come, eternal life.' Here the Revisers, following the two oldest MSS., have omitted 'or wife,' which is in the Authorised Version, and they have reversed the order of 'mother, father,' according to the Vatican MS. The original reading of the Sinaitic MS. omitted the thirteen words from 'houses' to 'persecutions,' and also 'for my sake and' before 'for the gospel's sake.' These frequent erasures and insertions by a later hand in the old MSS. indicate great care in revising and collating. The evangelists themselves often differ, as here, in the form of the expressions attributed to Jesus. Mark has, 'for my sake, and for the gospel's sake;' Luke, 'for the kingdom of God's sake;' Matthew, 'for my name's sake.' We have to choose between two probable explanations: either the exact words of Jesus were not caught or remembered by all alike, those who reported them caring more to convey the obvious sense than the precise form of expression; or Jesus may have used different terms, all having a similar meaning: 'for my sake, for the kingdom of God's sake, for my name's sake, for the gospel's sake.' Possibly Jesus was in the habit of reiterating those portions of a discourse which he wished specially to emphasise, and in doing so varied his words; he may even have combined different modes of expression, either to show that each of them bore the same meaning, as those above quoted, or to amplify the sense and deepen the impression, as by first saying 'manifold' and then 'a hundredfold.' Young renders Luke as follows: 'who may not receive back manifold more in this time, and in the coming age age-during life.' These words of Jesus import that his promise of 'age-during life' is reserved for 'the coming age;' it does not take effect 'in this time.' Here is a corroboration of the conclusions previously deduced from the words of Jesus. Wherein the 'manifold more in this time' consists, we are not told. Jesus simply assures us that devotion to his cause is more to our advantage, immediately as well as remotely, than all else which gives to life its comfort and its charm. The apostle Paul emphatically and rejoicingly testified to that effect. Mark throws in two words omitted by the other evangelists : 'with persecutions.' Paul had his full share of them, and triumphed in spite of them. To Timothy he wrote : 'But thou didst follow my teaching, conduct, purpose, faith, longsuffering, love, patience, persecutions, sufferings ; what things befell me at Antioch, at Iconium, at Lystra ; what persecutions I endured : and out of them all the Lord delivered me. Yea, and all that would live godly in Christ Jesus shall suffer persecution.' He does not say that believers in Jesus will necessarily suffer persecution : the expression, 'all that would live godly in Christ Jesus' denotes the entire dedication of the life to the cause of Jesus. The persecution arose in consequence, not of holding, but of preaching a particular doctrine. 'If I still preach circumcision, why am I still persecuted ? then hath the stumblingblock of the cross been done away.' To avoid persecution, it was only necessary to cease preaching, or to preach differently. 'Through many tribulations we must enter into the kingdom of God :' those words were addressed, not to believers generally, but to 'the disciples,' and the expression 'enter into the kingdom of God' is identical with that used by Jesus when he called the rich ruler to follow him, first giving up his property. To 'enter into the kingdom of God,' to 'follow' Jesus, to 'leave all' for 'the kingdom of God's sake, for the gospel's sake, for Christ's name's sake :' these seem to have been but different forms of expression, all denoting the entire dedication of the life to the cause of Jesus. In following out that career, there would not only be differences between one and another, but often an absolute reversal of men's relative positions. 'But many shall be last *that are* first ; and first *that are* last.' The Authorised Version stands : 'But many *that are* first shall be last ; and the last *shall be* first.' The Revisers have adopted the reading of the oldest MS. Mark has : 'But many *that are* first shall be last ; and the last first.' It is not, many that are esteemed first, or placed first, or claim to be first : the meaning goes deeper, and relates to the actual character and conduct. The course of duty involves self-development ; not only can there be no equality between one and another, but there can be no fixed status for any individual. The saying holds good if the italicised words are omitted. The literal rendering of Matthew, and of Mark also according to the reading of Griesbach, Lachmann, and Wordsworth, is : 'Many shall be first last, and last first.' The progress is onward and upward with all and each ; all may run well, but some better, and the best will of necessity stand foremost. Every man also must wait for his call and opportunity : our tasks are varied, and there are appointed times for doing them. This Jesus illustrated by a parable. He compared the life of activity in his cause, which he had been speaking of as an entrance into the kingdom of God or of heaven, to the hiring of labourers for vineyard work. 'For the kingdom of heaven is like unto a man that is a householder, which went out early in the morning to hire labourers into his vineyard.' The amount of wages was agreed, and the work entered upon. 'And when he had agreed with the labourers for a penny a day, he sent them into his vineyard.' Some time after he again went out, found other labourers unemployed, and engaged them, not fixing the wages, but telling them that he would pay them fairly. 'And he went out about the third hour, and saw others standing in the marketplace idle; and to them he said, Go ye also into the vineyard, and whatsoever is right I will give you. And they went their way.' Three hours later, and also six hours later, he did the same. 'Again he went out about the sixth and the ninth hour, and did likewise.' Once more, two hours later, when there remained only one hour for labour, he went to the marketplace. 'And about the eleventh hour he went out, and found others standing; and he saith unto them, Why stand ye here all the day idle?' The two oldest MSS. omit the word 'idle,' but it is retained by Tischendorf as well as by the Revisers. The labourers replied that no employment has been offered to them, whereupon they also were sent into the vineyard. 'They say unto him, Because no man hath hired us. He saith unto them, Go ye also into the vineyard.' The Authorised Version adds: 'and whatsoever is right, *that* shall ye receive.' This is not in the two oldest MSS., and is omitted by the Revisers. At the close of the day the proprietor of the vineyard bade his 'overseer,' so Tischendorf renders the word, summon the labourers and pay them, beginning with those last engaged. 'And when the even was come, the lord of the vineyard saith unto his steward, Call the labourers, and pay them their hire, beginning from the last unto the first.' A full day's pay was given to those who had done only one hour's work. 'And when they came that *were hired* about the eleventh hour, they received every man a penny.' Seeing how liberally these had been dealt with, the men who had laboured from early morning flattered themselves with the hope that they also would be overpaid. 'And when the first came, they supposed that they would receive more.' Not so: nothing beyond the agreed amount was paid to them. 'And they likewise received every man a penny.' Disappointed and discontented, they complained that they were not treated fairly. Why should those who had done an hour's work in the cool of the evening, be put on an equality with those who had done a hard day's work under a scorching sun? 'And when they received it, they murmured against the householder, saying, These last have spent *but* one hour, and thou hast made them equal unto us, which have borne the burden of the day and the scorching heat (or, hot wind).' To one of these murmurers the employer gave an answer: no injustice had been done to those who complained; an agreement had been made and it had been adhered to. The contract having been completed on both sides, the labourer had simply to take up his money and depart. 'But he answered and said to one of them, Friend, I do thee no wrong: didst not thou agree with me for a penny? Take up that which is thine, and go thy way.' The proprietor of the vineyard had no intention of raising the standard price of labour. He had simply decided to put those last engaged on an equality with the first. The difference between the amount earned and the payment made, was so much out of the employer's pocket, a free gift which he chose to make, and which no one had the right to gainsay. 'It is my will to give unto this last, even as unto thee. Is it not lawful for me to do what I will with mine own?' Did not the complaint proceed from envy, rather than from a sentiment of justice? 'Or is thine eye evil, because I am good?' Jesus would have the parable pondered as illustrating the saying with which he prefaced it,

20 Mat. 16   for he added: 'So the last shall be first, and the first last.' The Authorised Version continues: 'for many be called, but few chosen.' That sentence is not in the two oldest MSS., and it is omitted by Tischendorf as well as by the Revisers. Alford notes that it is 'omitted in several of the oldest authorities.' The insertion cannot be attributed to a copyist's error, for the two sentences are not found in conjunction elsewhere. Possibly some early commentator thought he discerned in the allusion to a free gift, the principle expressed by Jesus in the words 'many be called, but few chosen,' and inserted that sentence as explanatory of 'so the last shall be first, and the first last.' How frequently do preachers and commentators, without venturing upon an actual addition or misplacement, read different passages of Scripture into each other, as though they stood side by side, instead of being widely separated, and thereby lose the special application of each, and misinterpret both!

'So the last shall be first, and the first last.' That is the only clue which Jesus gave towards the interpretation of the parable. We shall best arrive at its proper application by keeping close to the text and context. It was delivered as an illustration of what must occur in 'the reign of the heavens,' which expression, as is obvious from what precedes, denotes the condition of society when brought under the sway of Jesus. Only his disciples and followers can enter 'the reign of the heavens.' To them, and with reference to them, he spoke the parable, which followed immediately upon the answer which he had given to the question put by Peter, 'Lo, we have left all, and followed thee; what then shall we have?' Jesus made no distinction between one apostle and another, but placed all upon an equality: the twelve should sit upon twelve thrones, judging twelve tribes. And all who devoted themselves to the same cause would share the same lot, would be recompensed to the same extent, 'manifold more' or 'a hundredfold,' and would attain to the same perfection of existence, 'in the age to come age-during life.' This raising of all to one level involves of necessity the readjustment of men's relative positions. The status of society generally can be improved only through a process of equalisation; in other words, 'Many first shall be last, and the last first.' The parable was spoken to illustrate that truth. There is absolutely nothing to favour the idea that the first became last through their own fault or conduct, or the last first on account of any superiority of character. On the contrary, the first laboured throughout the day, and Jesus was careful to state that the last had been idle only because no man had hired them. The central point of the parable is the 'penny,' which represents the amount required for the proper maintenance and comfort of a labourer. That, neither more nor less, was given to all. A similar process of adjustment goes on in 'the reign of God.' Every man is called to exercise his functions to the uttermost: and at the close of the gospel dispensation, as its final result, that which was the object of its establishment, all within the kingdom of God and of Christ will stand on an equal footing, the perfect life being secured to each and all alike. Socialism and not individualism, the general welfare and not personal ambition, a higher standard for all and no sharp contrast between wealth and poverty: that is the lesson deducible from the parable, the very spirit and essence of Christ's gospel. We must be content to accept the kingdom of God in that shape, or not at all. 'He hath put down princes from *their* thrones, and hath exalted them of low degree.' 'The last shall be first, and the first last.' That, in truth, is the triumph-shout of Christianity. 1 Luke 52

> 'Every valley shall be filled,
> And every mountain and hill shall be brought low ;
> And the crooked shall become straight,
> And the rough ways smooth ;
> And all flesh shall see the salvation of God.'   3 Luke 5, 6

The salvation of humanity, not of individuals, is 'the salvation of God.' In face of this great work of the regeneration of society, how mournful is the question, 'Why stand ye here all the day idle?' And how pathetic is the answer: 'Because no man hath hired us'! Many stand waiting in the marketplace, ready and anxious to do their share in Christ's work, but hearing no special call, and knowing of no vineyard in which to labour. From doctrinal religion, as by law established, and as preached by those who deem themselves Christ's ministers, they turn away. What a blessing would it be, to themselves and others, to find some opening into the kingdom of God, some sphere of duty lying parallel with that of the apostles and first disciples, whose sublime act of self-devotion and renunciation not one of us in ten thousand professing Christians feels himself called to imitate. Still, in lowlier ways, the great cause may be helped forward; and when truer, clearer perceptions of the nature and character of Christian work begin to dawn upon men's minds, they will be found willing to sow seed in gospel furrows, albeit they may not profess to put their hands to the gospel plough. What a work for Christ and for the poor, has that noble-hearted writer of fiction, Walter Besant, been able through his novels to accomplish! What a strange, unexpected, marvellous development and sign of the times is the 'Salvation army,' raised out of the working classes! What a hopeful augury for the future! Give to the leaders of these men, and to the men themselves, a purer and more rational theology, a more accurate perception of the real nature of Christ's teaching, and of that kingdom of God into which they seek to enter, and what a stride will then be made in the right direction! Christianity has ever been a motive-power. Only free it from the mass of errors and superstitions which have encrusted, disfigured, hampered it, and it will yet change, rule and save the world.

When last in Jerusalem the life of Jesus had been threatened, and knowing that the chief-priests and Pharisees were bent on putting him to death, he had retired from Judæa, staying at Ephraim, near the wilderness, with his disciples. Now, for some time past, he has been again 'on the way to Jerusalem.' As they drew nearer to the metropolis, Jesus showed no sign of halting, but kept in advance of his disciples, as though anxious to avoid delay and indifferent to the risk he ran. The disciples were astonished at this, and although they followed, it was with fear and trembling. 'And they were in the way going up to Jerusalem; and Jesus was going before them: and they were amazed; and they that followed were afraid (or, but some as they followed were afraid).' Then he repeated to the apostles that prophecy of his coming sufferings, death and resurrection, which 11 John 5: 17 Luke 11 10 Mark 32

twice before he had delivered to them. 'And he took again the
twelve, and began to tell them the things that were to happen unto
him.' Luke uses a similar expression, denoting that the information
was restricted to the apostles. 'And he took unto him the twelve,
and said unto them . . .' Matthew explains that he arranged for
the twelve only to accompany him, and in the course of his journey
with them he told them what it would result in to himself. 'And as
Jesus was going up to Jerusalem, he took the twelve disciples apart,
and in the way he said unto them, Behold, we go up to Jerusalem;
and the Son of man shall be delivered unto the chief priests and
scribes; and they shall condemn him to death, and shall deliver him
unto the Gentiles to mock, and to scourge, and to crucify: and the
third day he shall be raised up.' Mark adds 'shall spit upon him;'
instead of 'crucify' he has 'kill;' instead of 'the third day,' 'after
three days;' and instead of 'raised up.' 'rise again:' the last-named
difference arises from an alteration in the reading of Matthew. 'Behold, we go up to Jerusalem: and the Son of man shall be delivered
unto the chief priests and the scribes; and they shall condemn him
to death, and shall deliver him unto the Gentiles: and they shall
mock him, and shall spit upon him, and shall scourge him, and shall
kill him; and after three days he shall rise again.' Luke inserts an
allusion to the prophecies, and he adds the words 'shamefully entreated.' 'Behold, we go up to Jerusalem, and all the things that
are written by (or, through) the prophets shall be accomplished unto
the Son of man. For he shall be delivered up unto the Gentiles, and
shall be mocked, and shamefully entreated, and spit upon: and they
shall scourge and kill him: and the third day he shall rise again.'
This was but a repetition and amplification of what Jesus had previously told his disciples generally, not to the twelve only, for it is
stated, 'And he spake the saying openly.' Some time afterwards
Jesus had again touched upon the same topic. Although it is now
mentioned for the third time, it is with a repetition of the statement
that the declaration of Jesus was incomprehensible: 'And they
understood none of these things; and this saying was hid from them,
and they perceived not the things that were said.' On the second
occasion a similar observation was made both by Mark and Luke:
the former: 'But they understood not the saying, and were afraid to
ask him;' the latter: 'But they understood not this saying, and it
was concealed from them, that they should not perceive it: and they
were afraid to ask him about that saying.' Had this referred to the
saying in Mark: 'after three days he shall rise again,' it might well
be that the prodigy of a bodily resurrection could not be anticipated;
but Luke had not quoted those words, and the saying on which he
commented is simply, 'The Son of man shall be delivered up into the
hands of men.' That saying the disciples did understand sufficiently
to be made thereby, as Matthew tells us, 'exceeding sorry.' And
on the first occasion also the meaning of what Jesus said was so
evident that 'Peter took him, and began to rebuke him, saying, Be
it far from thee, Lord: this shall never be unto thee.' Jesus could
not have used clearer language; so anxious was he to make the
matter plain, that he told it thrice; so unmistakable was the sense
of his words, that one of the apostles tried to silence him, and all of
them were grieved. The varied expressions in Luke seem to indicate

a difficulty as to the choice of words whereby to convey the sense accurately. Luke was but a compiler: either he had before him three recorded observations, or one record combining the three sentences which he has handed down to us. No matter which: in either case the reiteration indicates that no one of the three sentences is by itself sufficiently elucidatory. First we have, 'They understood none of these things:' this is modified or explained by, 'this saying was hid from them;' that does not convey the sense with perfect accuracy, so a third explanation is added: 'they perceived not the things that were said.' On the previous occasion also Luke's narrative shows the same hesitation as to the choice of words proper to explain the meaning. 'But they understood not this saying—it was concealed from them—that they should not perceive it.' They did not understand the saying, not because it was not plain, but because it was concealed from them, not through any supernatural influence, for nothing of the kind is hinted at, but through a lack of perception on their part. The failure to comprehend arose within themselves, was owing to something in their own minds, some preconceived notion to which they clung, which this declaration shocked and threatened, which they dreaded might be extinguished if the matter were further inquired into, so that they were afraid to ask him for fuller information. The disciples regarded Jesus as the Christ, that is, the Messiah. He had justified that belief in him, at the same time charging them 'that they should tell no man that he was the Christ.' In that capacity they expected, as a matter of course, 'that it was he which should redeem Israel.' If, instead of doing so, he should be put to death by his enemies, their hope was vain, their faith in himself misplaced. They dared not face the thought; they could not reconcile the prophecy of Jesus with his claim to the Messiahship; his words were enigmatical; there must be some mystery connected with them which they could not solve; such a saying was to them utterly incomprehensible, in its literal sense incredible; it might be a figure of speech, a parable, or be susceptible of modication in some unexplained way: anything rather than admit the possibility of his leaving the world without having restored the kingdom to Israel, or wrought any visible redemption of his people.

We are told that Jesus 'learned obedience by the things which he suffered:' that statement is made in connection with the mention of his death. On that point he had received supernatural instruction, Moses and Elijah having spoken with him 'of his decease which he was about to accomplish at Jerusalem.' Jesus never courted death, but shrunk from it instinctively. If in his three years' ministry he did so much, what might he not have accomplished had he been permitted to labour in the world for another thirty or forty years, up to the age of seventy! His enemies were bent on preventing that, and it was not the will of his Father to interfere by a miracle to save him from a premature death. All that Jesus could do, he did. He raised up a band of disciples, to whom he communicated, as far as they were able to receive it, his scheme for the establishment of the kingdom of God. He chose them 'out of the world,' and left them 'in the world,' to follow out his precepts. Had his life been prolonged, he would have been persecuted to the end of it, even as his apostles were after him. That probably was the thought in the mind of Paul, when he said, 'I rejoice in my sufferings for your sake, and fill up on my part that which is lacking of the afflictions of Christ in my flesh.' Jesus himself was the first martyr in his cause; he carried out to the bitter end his doctrine of patient, non-resisting sufferance; no exception was made in his favour; he left an example that others might follow; his 'followers,' in the true sense of the term, must live, as he did, a life on earth based on maxims of the heavenly world, and be content, as he was, to take the consequences. All that, as yet, was very far from the minds of the disciples. The ideas prevalent with respect to his coming 'kingdom,' led them to entertain hopes of honour and aggrandisement. At the very time Jesus was foretelling his inevitable doom of suffering and death, some about him were coveting for themselves the highest and most dignified positions in his kingdom. Two of his disciples, accompanied by their mother, approached him, with the utmost respect, bowing to him, and begging of him a certain boon. 'Then came to him the mother of the sons of Zebedee with her sons, worshipping *him* (bowing—Young), and asking a certain thing of him.' The woman obviously was foremost in the matter, and Jesus, before saying yea or nay, naturally requested her to state what she wanted. 'And he said unto her, What wouldest thou?' The blessing she craved was not for herself, but for her children. They had perfect faith in him, and in the triumph of his cause, and forestalling in imagination the time when he would sit on his glorious throne, they were ambitious of the honour of being seated next to him. 'She saith unto him, Command that these my two sons may sit, one on thy right hand, and one on thy left hand, in thy kingdom.' The three must have consulted together, before venturing to make the suggestion. The request was based upon their faith in Jesus, their reverence for his character, their attachment to his person. From the first he had shown his appreciation of the two brothers, for 'them he surnamed Boanerges, which is, Sons of thunder.' Simon also he had surnamed Peter—Rock; and to these three Jesus had given, and continued up to the last, special opportunities of being with him: he chose them to witness his transfiguration, and to accompany him in the garden of Gethsemane; they are mentioned as taking the lead in expressing their opinions, and the three, with Andrew, once questioned Jesus privately on the mount of Olives. These facts, as well as their surnames, indicate that they possessed in a conspicuous degree firmness and energy, and received from Jesus peculiar marks of confidence. James and John entertained so high an opinion of their Master's dignity, that on one occasion they wished to call down fire from heaven to consume those who treated him with disrespect. Having cast in their lot with him ever since the day when, at his call, they unhesitatingly left their fishing boat in sole charge of their father and followed Jesus, they may have considered that they were fairly entitled to secure for themselves whatever future advantages might be attainable. Would they not be so much the more devoted to him now, if they could be assured of reaching the highest possible position under him hereafter? Their father had been left to carry on their former business without the assistance of his sons; their mother now was urgent on their behalf, fondly deeming them superior to others, and firing them with ambitious hopes. Matthew describes her as foremost in making the application; but the three were at one on the point. Mark says nothing about the mother, but represents the two disciples as making the request themselves. 'And there come near unto him James and John, the sons of Zebedee, saying unto him, Master (or, Teacher), we would that thou shouldest do for us whatsoever we shall ask of thee. And he said unto them, What would ye that I should do for you? And they said unto him, Grant unto us that we may sit, one on thy right hand, and one on *thy* left hand, in thy glory.' Both evangelists agree that an effort was made to extract a promise from Jesus without first disclosing the nature of the request: Matthew says, 'asking a certain thing of him'; Mark: 'do for us whatsoever we shall ask of thee.' They should have known Jesus too well for that; he, at least, knew well what was due to himself and them, and refused to promise blindly. And when they had made known their wish he assured them that they did not understand what it amounted to and involved. 'But Jesus answered and said, Ye know not what ye ask.' It was not a mere question of granting them a favour, and of their accepting it, but of their power of endurance in his cause. Were they able to undergo the same sufferings as himself? 'Are ye able to drink the cup that I am about to drink?' The alteration by the Revisers of 'I shall drink of,' into 'I am about to drink,' agrees with the rendering of Tischendorf and Young. The Authorised Version continues: 'and to be baptized with the baptism that I am baptized with?' which is now omitted, not being in the two oldest MSS. Those words were probably inserted from Mark, which stands as follows: 'But Jesus said unto them, Ye know not what ye ask. Are ye able to drink the cup that I drink? or to be baptized with the baptism that I am baptized with?' The drinking from a cup and submission to baptism are voluntary actions: the reference was unmistakably to the bitter and overwhelming sorrows which Jesus was about to experience, as he had been explaining to his disciples. Yes: these two were even prepared to face shame, suffering and death. 'They say unto him, We are able.' And he knew they were destined for that. 'He saith unto them, My cup indeed ye shall drink.' Here again the Revisers, following the two oldest MSS., have omitted the words, 'and be baptized with the baptism that I am baptized with.' That is in Mark: 'And they said unto him, We are able. And Jesus said unto them, The cup that I drink ye shall drink; and with the baptism that I am baptized withal shall ye be baptized!' Beyond that, Jesus could give them no assurance. Positions of nearness to himself were not matters of favour and arbitrary bestowment: he had no power to promise and grant them; they must be earned, not forestalled; they were reserved for those who best could fill them. 'But to sit on my right hand or on *my* left hand is not mine to give: but *it is for them* for whom it hath been prepared.' Matthew adds the words, 'of my Father.' 'But to sit on my right hand, and on *my* left hand, is not mine to give, but *it is for them* for whom it hath been prepared of my Father.' The insertion of the italicised words, 'it is for them,' may be deemed unnecessary. The Authorised Version has in italics, 'it shall be given to them.' Luther makes no such addition to the text, nor does Dr. Young, who renders: 'is not mine to give, but to those for whom it hath been prepared by my

Father.' The effect of the addition is to prevent the reading of the word 'but' as equivalent to 'except,' which Alford, with Chrysostom and others, admits not to be contrary to the sense of the original. Alford says: 'If however we understand after *but* "it shall be given *by Me*," the two interpretations come to the same:' that is, if two more words are inserted without authority, then the previous unauthorised insertion will not obviate the probable sense of the original apart from any addition whatever.

When the other apostles heard of the application which had been privately made by James and John, they seem to have regarded it as an underhand and selfish action, and they manifested indignation against the two brothers. 'And when the ten heard it, they were moved with indignation concerning the two brethren.' 'And when the ten heard it, they began to be moved with indignation concerning James and John.' They certainly had not raised themselves in the estimation of Jesus, who had told them, 'Ye know not what ye ask,' as once before he had occasion to rebuke them, saying, 'Ye know not what manner of spirit ye are of.' Now they had also drawn down upon themselves the deserved reproaches of their fellow labourers. Jesus took the opportunity of assuring the twelve that the mode, method and surroundings of earthly rulership could have no counterparts in his kingdom. Power, pre-eminence, lordship, authority,— these constituted the very essence of human government, and a *great man* was held to be synonymous with an *arbitrary ruler*. 'But Jesus called them unto him, and said, Ye know that the rulers of the Gentiles lord it over them, and their great ones exercise authority over them.' According to Mark's wording, Jesus spoke of that as only a show, a mockery of true rulership: 'And Jesus called them to him, and saith unto them, Ye know that they which are accounted to rule over the Gentiles lord it over them; and their great ones exercise authority over them.' Alford notes: 'They which are accounted to rule,—who have the title of rulers: literally, they which seem to rule, or, think that they rule.' By introducing the word 'Gentiles' the translators lead English readers to assume that the reference is to heathen nations only. That is not so. The Greek word *ethnos* is rendered in four ways: 'Gentile, heathen, nation, people.' The lexicon defines it: 'a company, body of men. 2 a race, tribe. 3 a nation, people; plural, the Gentiles, *i.e.*, all except Jews and Christians.' The last and subsidiary signification is the term generally used in the Authorised Version, but Dr. Young adopts the term 'nation, nations.' That it is equally applicable to the Jews is clear from various passages, as: 'he loveth our nation (*ethnos*); that Jesus should die for the nation (*ethnous*); and not for the nation (*ethnous*) only.' Luther renders the passage under consideration: 'die weltlichen Fürsten herrschen,' 'the worldly princes rule.' No such domination must exist among the disciples of Jesus: 'Not so shall it be among you.' Mark has it: 'But it is not so among you.' Freedom of thought and action was the privilege of each, and their notion of superiority must be the reverse of that prevalent in the world. Voluntary service must be their badge of distinction, the spirit of humility and self-sacrifice their token of nobility. 'But whosoever would become great among you shall be your minister (or, servant); and whosoever would be first among you shall be your servant (Gr. bondservant).' Mark agrees exactly, except that instead of 'your servant' he has 'servant (Gr. bondservant) of all.' Greatness with them must be synonymous with usefulness, and pre-eminence consist in an entire devotion to the general welfare. That was the lot of Jesus himself, his sole ambition: 'even as the Son of man came not to be ministered unto, but to minister, and to give his life a ransom for many.' Here Mark is in exact agreement, except as to the first two words, 'even as,' which are now replaced by 'for verily.' In the Authorised Version they stand 'for even' which agrees with Young and Tischendorf. Alford suggests rendering 'even' by 'also,' which corresponds with Luther's 'auch.' There is nothing to indicate why the Revisers introduce the word 'verily.' Alford has the following note: '*A ransom for many*, is a plain declaration of the sacrificial and vicarious nature of the death of our Lord. The principal usages (in the Greek Scriptures) of the word rendered *ransom* are the following; (1) a payment as equivalent for a life destroyed; (2) the price of redemption of a slave; (3) a propitiation for.' Jesus was not then directing the minds of the apostles to the doctrine of 'the sacrifical and vicarious nature' of his death, and to imagine that, is to take away the force of the words 'even as' or 'for even' or 'for also,' which indicate a possible correspondence between his own life and death and the life and death of each one of them. Taking the words apart from any particular dogma, thus much, at least, is clear from them: that Jesus believed that the sacrifice of his life would result in the ransom of many of mankind. It is not said, as a ransom for many *other lives*: we should not be justified in adding those last two words; and if we assume that to be the sense, the question arises: Did the death of Jesus prevent the death of many others? On the contrary, had he not told his disciples that they would have to give up their lives for his name's sake? The death of Jesus was the price he paid in carrying out his scheme for the ransom or redemption of mankind, that is, for the establishment of the kingdom of God among men. Is it not equally true that some of his apostles and first followers gave up their lives in the same cause? And is it not equally reasonable to say that they, as well as he, gave their lives a ransom for many? That is but equivalent to the well-known saying that 'the blood of the martyrs was the seed of the Church.' Only one of two senses is to be attached to the words of Jesus: either that in which they must have been understood at the time, or that in which he obviously intended that they should be understood. Here there is nothing to warrant the idea that the disciples could have interpreted the saying as Alford does; nothing to justify the inference that Jesus taught that his own death was 'sacrificial and vicarious' in any other way than the death of his followers might be so termed. Let it be understood that no question is here raised as to the truth of the doctrine alluded to by Alford, but simply a protest against importing it into this passage. The words of Jesus must be held too sacred and inviolable to admit of any other ideas than his own being mixed up with them. What he designed to teach at the time of uttering them, that only can we admit to be their true, full and proper meaning.

Still pursuing his journey towards Jerusalem, Jesus drew near to

18 Luke 35 — Jericho. By the roadside a blind man was seated. 'And it came to pass, as he drew nigh unto Jericho, a certain blind man sat by the way side begging.' Is it not strange that after eighteen centuries of Christian teaching, the same pitiable spectacle of men and women incapacitated from work by blindness, and begging in the streets, should still be seen? Surely it is time that some plan should be devised for maintaining, at the cost of the community, those who are so totally unable to engage in the battle of life. It would not be difficult to provide shelter, food and raiment for all the helpless, friendless blind and cripples who now are left to depend upon casual almsgiving, the hands of many willing to help being held back through fear of the deceptions practised by professional and sham beggars. We build prisons, and keep our criminals at a heavy cost, and lunatic asylums for those who are dangerous to us in other ways. Surely we ought to go further than that. The blind, the lame and the mute should not be suffered to beg; refuges should be provided at the public charge, with proper supervision, and arrangements for the profitable employment, according to their various capabilities, of those who are shut out by blindness, lameness or dumbness from the ordinary avocations of life. We cannot cure these unfortunates, as Jesus did; for that reason it is our duty to succour them. But as long as such works of charity are left to private individuals, so long will they be performed inadequately, sufficient funds not being forthcoming for the work. What is admitted to be everyone's business is undertaken by no one in particular, and amid the multitude of claims for help the most pressing are sometimes the least urged. The want of our age is precisely the want of the age in which Jesus lived, and which he sought to supply by proclaiming and inaugurating 'the kingdom of God,' that is, a *kingdom of Christians*. Not yet can

11 R. v. 15 — it be said: 'The kingdom of the world is become *the kingdom* of our Lord, and of his Christ.' They are not founded on the basis of his teaching, but make their boast in principles and modes of action the very reverse of his. The preponderance of national force is determined by war, and commercial rivalry rests on the maxims of a science of political economy as hard and merciless as the warrior's sword. The need of the world is the same as ever, the times cry out

2 Tit. 14 (A. V.) — for 'a peculiar people, zealous of good works.' That was the ideal of a Christian community in the eyes of the apostle Peter: 'But ye *are*

2 i. Pet. 9 (A. V.) — a chosen generation, a royal priesthood, an holy nation, a peculiar people; that ye should shew forth the praises of him who hath called you out of darkness into his marvellous light.' The Church, that is, the assembly of believers in Jesus, should present the aspect of a select family, bearing the stamp of royalty and saintliness, a nation within a nation, a people distinct from the surrounding world, a body animated by the indwelling spirit of Jesus, moved by one sacred impulse, and living as an organic whole the life of Jesus among mankind. In the formation of such a society, the nucleus must needs consist of disciples round whom believers can gather; such disciples must take all the precepts of Jesus, not a choice or modification of them, as their rule of life and action: thereby only can they become the heart, the central moving impulse of the whole body. Is not the existing system of Christianity defective in that, its initial point? We have no separate class of disciples living, not apart from the

world but in the midst of the world, in contempt of all worldly ambitions, maxims, policies, and in unfeigned, entire subjection to the teaching, mind and will of Jesus. The men recognised as ministers of Christ are not of that stamp, nor do they profess or really strive to be so. Ask any one of them whether he does not consider that every member of his flock is as much bound as himself to obey every precept and counsel of Jesus, and he will unhesitatingly answer, Yes. The shepherds have placed themselves and the sheep on the same level of duty. Christianity was not founded upon that principle: Jesus chose but few disciples, taught them to make special sacrifices, to expect special trials. They went forth in his name and spirit, and gathered round them multitudes of believers, both men and women, who certainly were not called to discipleship: 'Are all apostles? are all prophets? are all teachers?' If those who have claimed to be successors of the apostles had been so in reality, discipleship to Jesus would have assumed a very different phase in the eyes of all men, and the universal Church would have been taught by the pattern of a heavenly life as designed by Jesus. Under the existing system of Church doctrine and discipline, his kingdom comes not. We have agreed to expect salvation in the next world, not on earth, and to regard it as an individual concern rather than a social question. When the jailer at Philippi asked, trembling for fear, 'What must I do to be saved?' Paul and Silas answered, 'Believe on the Lord Jesus, and thou shalt be saved, thou and thy house.' This need of a 'common salvation' was learnt by Dives in the next life, and led him to desire it for his 'father's house.' Religion ceases to be a merely personal matter, when we come to realise it as the establishment of 'the kingdom of God.' Not through prayers, praises, creeds, sacraments, can we be saved, but only through social progress, for 'we, who are many, are one body in Christ, and severally members one of another.' The Christian community needs to be defined, restricted, that it may assume a bodily shape and perform the functions of a living organism. At present it is formless, a vague monstrosity, supposed to be here, there, everywhere, each individual in the nation having an equal claim to membership. Thence it comes to pass that the national career is held to be identical with the career of Christianity, the earthly is blended with the heavenly, the State with the Church, the precepts of Jesus with the maxims of the world, the spirit of war and aggrandisement with the gospel of peace and self-sacrifice. This worthless and deceptive amalgam of the human with the divine is not Christianity, and is altogether out of harmony with the scheme of its Founder. Let us go back to that. If those who profess to be our heavenly guides become truly 'apostolic,' disciples of Jesus as separate from the world and as hostile to its spirit as were the twelve who first proclaimed the gospel of peace, what a transformation of society may be brought about by their example and their teaching! The ideal of an apostolic life is not too high for Ministers generally. The Church of Rome has gone beyond it, requiring every priest to be a celibate. Jesus never made that an indispensable condition of discipleship, but the relinquishment of property and the laying up instead of treasure in the heavens, he did. Possibly it was the vow of poverty which led to the enforced relinquishment of marriage: for it might be deemed better not to marry than to leave wife and children without adequate means of support. At least it must be assumed that the decree of celibacy must have originated in some high and good motive. But it was none the less an error of judgment, a mistaken attempt (how many such have there been!) to improve on the method of Jesus. He desired that his followers should rely upon the sense of justice and obligation in those to whom they ministered. He taught them that 'the labourer is worthy of his hire,' and he appealed to them as to whether their experience had not justified the spirit of reliance he had inculcated : ' When I sent you forth without purse, and wallet, and shoes, lacked ye anything ? and they said, Nothing.' The apostle Paul laid down the maxim : ' The husbandman that laboureth must be the first to partake of the fruits ;' and he declared : ' Even so did the Lord ordain that they which proclaim the gospel should live of the gospel.' That did not prevent him from insisting that a bishop must be, not only 'without reproach,' but also 'the husband of one wife ;' and that those to be appointed 'elders' should be family men : 'If any man is blameless, the husband of one wife, having children that believe.' It may be a question open to discussion, whether the Church of Christ will always require a body of 'apostles,' 'disciples,' 'bishops,' 'elders,' 'overseers,' or by whatever other name those who take the foremost places are designated ; but so long as they exist, and claim to be ministers of Christ, descendants of the apostles, they are tied down to these rules of life, and are no true shepherds of the sheep whilst they infringe them. There is nothing in the New Testament to justify the holding of wealth by the professed 'disciples' of Jesus. It might be well for archbishops and bishops to take the huge incomes they inherit, if only they would spend the whole of them in the cause to which they have professedly devoted themselves, and let the world know and see that they are doing so. It might be well to retain the services of men of learning, as preachers or otherwise, endowing them liberally without requiring them to give up all for Christ's sake, if only they would abate their pretensions of apostolical descent, and take their place among laymen. In the rank and file of the ministry there are comparatively few overpaid, and the majority are sadly underpaid. It would be no sacrifice to them, were they to profess openly their adherence to the apostolic system of living 'from hand to mouth.' That they do perforce, every day of their lives. What is wanting is, that all who claim office as leaders of men to Jesus should from the first, deliberately, in the sight of all men, renounce worldly possessions and ambitions, and throw themselves upon the charity of those to whom they minister, 'eating and drinking such things as they give.' A strange counsel that ! Undoubtedly : yet not more strange now than when Jesus first gave it. It was his plan, deliberately formed and earnestly insisted upon by him, and carried out to the letter by those whom he sent forth. True, he empowered them to 'heal the sick,' but that was in conjunction with and subsidiary to their preaching, 'the kingdom of God is come nigh unto you.' To men animated by such a spirit and living such a life, an influence would attach which otherwise is lacking. It would be now, as then, a question either of receiving them or rejecting them ; and over those receiving them they would exercise a power of direction, of guidance, of leadership, which would suffice to bind together churches, that is, assemblies of believers, not nominally as at present, but in reality. Infant baptism, which is too much a myth, a superstition, a fetish, would either be abolished, or regarded as a simple emblematic ceremony, the distinction between the church and the world becoming as evident as the difference between their respective leaders, far too wide to be bridged over by a sacramental form which makes all Christians in name, but cannot make them Christians in deed. When the pastors stand out separate from the world, the sheep who rally round them will be distinguishable from others, and a true church will be constituted, instead of a professed one. The organisation will assume definiteness, compactness, homogeneity, as naturally and easily as did that new and strange outcome of our times—the Salvation Army. Is not the marvellous success attaching to that movement an evidence of what can be accomplished when men work on the lines of self-sacrifice and brotherhood which were laid down by Jesus? He trusted not his cause to priests, Levites, pharisees or religious doctors; one only of the pharisaic rulers, Joseph of Arimathea, became his 'disciple,' and he 'secretly, for fear of the Jews.' Must that experience be repeated after eighteen centuries? Be that as it may, not until the leaders in Christianity stand aloof from and above the world, bearing in their hands the standard not of doctrinal theology, apostolical succession and sacramental theories, but of an earthly life woven to the exact pattern of the precepts given by Jesus to his disciples, will 'the kingdom of heaven' be established upon earth; and when that comes to pass, the Church—the Christian community—will become a recognised brotherhood, seen and known of all men, 'a peculiar people, zealous of good works.' Then it will be understood that for the propagation of the gospel men are needed, and money avails nothing, the first requirement of every ambassador of Christ being that he should relinquish property, and throw himself unreservedly on the liberality of those among whom he labours. The apostle Paul, who was the first missionary to the heathen, acted on that principle, and even went beyond it. Having 'suffered the loss of all things' for Christ's sake, he speaks of himself as moneyless. We find him labouring at Corinth together with Aquila and Priscilla: 'because he was of the same trade, he abode with them, and they wrought: for by their trade they were tentmakers.' Writing of himself and, it would seem, of Sosthenes and Apollos, to the Corinthians, he says: 'Even unto this present hour we both hunger, and thirst, and are naked, and are buffeted, and have no certain dwellingplace; and we toil, working with our own hands.' Further on, in the same epistle, he laid down the law of Jesus: 'Even so did the Lord ordain that they which proclaim the gospel should live of the gospel,' adding: 'But I have used none of these things; and I write not these things that it may be so done in my case: for *it were* good for me rather to die than that any man should make my glorying void . . . What then is my reward? That, when I preach the gospel, I may make the gospel without charge, so as not to use to the full my right in the gospel.' From the Philippians only did he receive any payment, and that was in the shape of a purely voluntary gift: 'And ye yourselves also know, ye Philippians, that in the beginning of the gospel, when I departed from Macedonia, no church had fellowship with me in the matter of giving and receiving, but ye only; for even in Thessalonica ye sent once and again unto my need ... But I have all things and abound: I am filled, having received from Epaphroditus the things *that came* from you, an odour of a sweet smell, a sacrifice acceptable, well-pleasing to God.' For some reason, Paul refused to receive help from the Corinthians. In his second epistle to them he wrote: 'Or did I commit a sin in debasing myself that ye might be exalted, because I preached to you the gospel of God for nought? I robbed other churches, taking wages *of them*, that I might minister unto you; and when I was present with you and was in want, I was not a burden on any man: for the brethren, when they came from Macedonia, supplied the measure of my want; and in everything I kept myself from being burdensome unto you, and *so* will I keep *myself*.' Paul gives his reason for that departure on his part from the rule laid down by Jesus: 'But what I do, that I will do, that I may cut off occasion from them which desire an occasion: that wherein they glory, they may be found even as we.' He was determined to make the impecuniosity of preachers of the gospel generally, a test of their sincerity. He admits that it was not quite fair on his part to relieve the Corinthians at the cost of other churches, and that in so doing he was not carrying out the ordinance of Jesus, and might be charged with injustice. 'For what is there wherein ye were made inferior to the rest of the churches, except *it be* that I myself was not a burden to you? forgive me this wrong.' What Paul did, others could do. And if the voluntary impoverishment of Christ's ambassadors is possible and obligatory when they go forth as missionaries to foreign countries, how much easier would it be to adopt the same course of action among their own countrymen! The scheme of Jesus was based on human effort and human sympathy, and no advance in Christianity has ever been made, or will be made, apart from them. They are the only reliable bond of union between the clergy and the laity, and between individuals constituting the Christian community. The crying want of the Church is unity of interest and purpose among all its members. Some great and fundamental change is required, some plan of reorganisation, which will give form, character, definiteness to the Church. The method insisted upon by Jesus, and acted upon by his first disciples, would be as effectual now as it proved then. The Master's servants will fight best with the weapon which he placed in their hands. Unless they wield it, and trust in it, they cannot conquer in his cause. The spirit of unworldliness and heavenly-mindedness, carried to its extreme in the shape of voluntary poverty and self-sacrifice, is demanded of those who claim to be our spiritual guides: demanded not by the flock, but by the chief shepherd of the flock—Jesus himself. That truth seems to have been lost sight of. The clergy do not regard it as their special duty and privilege, a condition attached to their 'high calling of God in Christ Jesus.' Poverty they are content to accept, if need be, as an accident of their lives, but not as a ruling principle of their conduct. The laity, immersed in worldly affairs as the prime necessity of their existence, must needs feel that such precepts are not for them. For whom then? For all in general, and no one in particular? For each individual Christian, as far as he may choose to apply them and act upon them, and no further? That is what our want of perception and looseness of thought have led to. These solemn and reiterated exhortations of Jesus to his disciples have come to be held nugatory, ineffective, visionary, well nigh obsolete, altogether impracticable; they are regarded as counsels of a perfection which is unattainable, undesirable in this life, principles of action too high for ordinary mortals, and not specially binding upon any class. Why then did Jesus utter them? Was he a mere dreamer of dreams, an enthusiast counselling the impossible? Not so, surely! These rules of life were laid down in all sober seriousness, and only a careful and discriminating study of the gospels and epistles is needed to make evident their application. They are the heritage of professed disciples, men willing to throw away their fortunes and hazard their lives for the name of the Lord Jesus. With such men for leaders, and not without them, the Church of Christ will grow and prosper. They will possess a power of organisation, control, direction, which can be enforced by no statutes and maintained by no formal creeds: the wealth of the—then—visible Church will flow forth at their bidding, and will supply every need. Not more willingness to give, but more system and unanimity in giving, is required; and not by almsgiving alone can the inequalities of society be redressed, but by the ceaseless overflowing of that stream of sympathy with which the spirit of Jesus must needs flood his true Church, making the welfare of each the concern of all, and uplifting, by just and fair dealing, the degraded masses now forming the lower stratum of society to the dignity of Christian brotherhood. The lesser works of charity are bound up with that greater one, in comparison with which it will be a small thing to obviate for ever the sad spectacle of blind men sitting by the wayside begging.

Upon the ears of this blind man there fell the sound of the passing crowd, leading him to enquire the cause of such an unusual gathering. 'And hearing a multitude going by, he inquired what this meant?' 18 Luke 36 On learning that the well-known Teacher was about to pass, he instantly cried out, addressing him by name, as the expected Messiah, and beseeching his compassion. 'And they told him, that Jesus of ,, 37, 8 Nazareth passed by. And he cried, saying, Jesus, thou son of David, have mercy on me.' Those foremost in the procession reproved the clamouring man, hoping to silence him. 'And they that went before 39 rebuked him, that he should hold his peace.' This effort of theirs may be taken as an indication that Jesus showed an aversion to all needless commotion, and that those about him were aware of the importance of making his progress from place to place as quiet and undemonstrative as possible. Wherever there is a crowd, not much is wanted to create disturbance. Jesus was now performing a journey which involved considerable hazard to himself and his disciples, so much so, that at its commencement 'they that followed were afraid.' 10 Mark 32 The nearer they drew to Jerusalem, the greater became the peril. Openly to hail him in the way as 'the Son of David,' was to play into the hands of his enemies, whose emissaries might even now be among them, watching for anything on which to found an accusation against him. But the effort to subdue the enthusiastic outcry of the blind man was futile: 'But he cried out the more a great deal, Thou 18 Luke 39 Son of David, have mercy on me.' It reached the ears of Jesus, who

at once halted, and desired that the man should be conducted to him.
'And Jesus stood, and commanded him to be brought unto him.'
Then the kindly voice of this to him invisible benefactor entered
the blind man's ears: 'and when he was come near, he asked him,
What wilt thou that I should do unto thee?' The man's brief
answer proved that he doubted not the power of Jesus, marvellous as
was the boon he craved. 'And he said, Lord (Sir—Young), that I
may receive my sight.' Nothing was needed now but the mighty
word of Jesus. 'And Jesus said unto him, Receive thy sight.'
But he added, as he was wont to do: 'thy faith hath made thee
whole (or, saved thee),' and we must not venture to overlook or
explain away those words. They signify that the faith of the man
was quite as necessary, to say the least, to the performance of the
miracle, as was the volition of Jesus: indeed, he attributes the cure
entirely to the faith. All the instances of healing by Jesus, or by
those to whom he communicated a similar gift, were obviously performed under certain conditions; they were not scattered broadcast:
special application had always to be made, either by the afflicted
person or by some one on his behalf; as a general rule, but not
without exception, physical contact occurred, and was essential,
between the healer and the healed. Jesus touched, or he was touched,
and sometimes much more than a touch appears to have been needed,
as when he anointed the eyes of the blind man with clay mixed with his
saliva, and when he placed his fingers in the ears of the deaf, the
sufferer was brought somehow into relation with his benefactor: a few
words exchanged between them, or even a look, might suffice; and
Jesus occasionally impressed upon those he healed the fact that their
own faith had much, if not everything, to do with the working of the
miracle. The same law acted subsequently, and was so widely recognised that 'they even carried out the sick into the streets, and laid
them on beds and couches, that, as Peter came by, at the least his
shadow might overshadow some of them.' We are told that 'God
wrought special miracles by the hands of Paul: insomuch that unto
the sick were carried away from his body handkerchiefs or aprons,
and the diseases departed from them, and the evil spirits went out.'
Not without a reason did Peter, before curing the cripple, fasten his
eyes upon him, with John, and say, 'Look on us;' and when Paul
healed a similar case of lameness, we read of his 'fastening his eyes
upon him, and seeing that he had faith to be made whole, said with a
loud voice, Stand upright on thy feet.' Such facts indicate the
existence of some occult law of our being, some blending of the
spiritual with the bodily powers, some kind of animal magnetism, subtle
electric force, or whatever else it may be—we know not—which can
be brought into action under certain circumstances, conditions,
limitations, but which being altogether unusual and as yet undefined
by science, we term miraculous.

The cure of the blind man was instantaneous and complete. No
longer compelled to remain helplessly inactive, to be led like a child,
or grope his slow, uncertain way in doubt, dread and darkness, he was
able to enter the surging crowd and take his place in the procession
which he had heard, indeed, but had never hoped to see and join.
'And immediately he received his sight, and followed him.' With
joy and thankfulness, yet not in silence: still his voice uprose, no

longer in pitiful entreaty, but in devout thanksgiving: 'glorifying ⁴³ Luke ⁴³
God.' The enthusiastic admiration of the crowd rose to the same
level: as they marched forward a chant of praise was sounded out, a
triumph-shout of adoring gratitude for this manifestation of God-like
power and mercy. 'And all the people, when they saw it, gave praise ,, ⁴³
unto God.' Here was Jesus of Nazareth in their midst, who had thus
repeatedly transformed into an actual reality of life the figurative
language of the prophet: 'Then the eyes of the blind shall be opened, ³⁵ Isa. 5, 6
and the ears of the deaf shall be unstopped. Then shall the lame
man leap as an hart, and the tongue of the dumb shall sing.' If any
one of the multitude remembered such a passage, and uttered it aloud,
it may well have been passed from mouth to mouth, and shouted out
in solemn chorus.

Luke distinctly states that this miracle was performed as Jesus
was approaching Jericho: 'as he drew nigh unto Jericho.' Either ¹⁸ Luke ³⁵
the same or a similar miracle is described by Mark as happening on
the departure of Jesus from Jericho: 'And they come to Jericho. ¹⁰ Mark ⁴⁶
And as he went out from Jericho, with his disciples and a great
multitude, the son of Timæus, Bartimæus, a blind beggar, was sitting
by the way side.' This account was evidently obtained at first hand,
from one who had full knowledge of the circumstances, and who knew
the place and its inhabitants. Except as regards the locality, the two
accounts agree perfectly. Mark stands as follows: 'And when he ,, ⁴⁷-⁵²
heard that it was Jesus of Nazareth, he began to cry out and say,
Jesus, thou son of David, have mercy on me. And many rebuked
him, that he should hold his peace: but he cried out the more a great
deal, Thou son of David, have mercy on me. And Jesus stood still,
and said, Call ye him. And they call the blind man, saying unto
him, Be of good cheer: rise, he calleth thee. And he, casting away
his garment, sprang up, and came to Jesus. And Jesus answered him,
and said, What wilt thou that I should do unto thee? And the
blind man said unto him, Rabboni, that I may receive my sight. And
Jesus said unto him, Go thy way; thy faith hath made thee whole (or,
saved thee). And straightway he received his sight, and followed him
in the way.' Here are several graphic touches, which must have been
thrown in by an eye-witness. Instead of saying that Jesus 'commanded him to be brought unto him,' the actual words of Jesus are
given, 'Call ye him.' The encouragement thereupon offered by the
bystanders is noted: 'Be of good cheer: rise, he calleth thee:' and
the impulsive eagerness and alacrity of the blind man: 'And he,
casting away his garment, sprang up, and came to Jesus.' The
somewhat unusual term 'Rabboni,' which he used, is given. Alford
observes: 'Rabboni, *i.e.*, Master, or My Master, see John xx. 16. It
was said to be a more respectful form than *Rabbi* mercly.' These
variations may be taken to denote greater accuracy of detail, rather
than any inconsistency between the two narratives. We should unhesitatingly assume that to be the case, if it were not for the
discrepancy of time and place, which seems to involve the existence of
an error either in Mark or Luke. To an unbiased mind there is
nothing shocking in the idea that either of these honest compilers
should unintentionally misplace a fact. There may have been many
occasions when either Mark or Luke may have had to exercise an
independent judgment in grouping the materials placed in their

hands. Imagine the diary of a traveller to consist of scattered notes: if edited long after his death by another hand, what more likely than that an occasional mistake should occur in the sequence of the incidents detailed, or even arise from defect of memory on the part of the original recorder? To suppose that supernatural assistance was given for the preparation of their respective histories to Mark and Luke, although they themselves never claimed to have received it, is nothing more than a wild freak of the imagination, however much it may be disguised under the solemn term of Inspiration, and worked into certain passages of Scripture supposed to justify the doctrine. But in this instance it is quite possible that both these evangelists are correct, and are relating two different miracles. Matthew records the departure of Jesus from Jericho: 'And as they went out from Jericho, a great multitude followed him.' That is a statement by itself. Then it is added, without reference to time or place: 'And behold, two blind men sitting by the way side, when they heard that Jesus was passing by, cried out, saying, Lord, have mercy on us, thou son of David.' It would be too much to infer that the word 'and' before 'behold' of necessity means that this happened as they went out from Jericho. Matthew continues: 'And the multitude rebuked them, that they should hold their peace: but they cried out the more, saying, Lord, have mercy on us, thou son of David. And Jesus stood still, and called them, and said, What will ye that I should do unto you? They say unto him, Lord, that our eyes may be opened. And Jesus, being moved with compassion, touched their eyes: and straightway they received their sight, and followed him.' Matthew does not say that these two blind men were sitting together and were healed together. Blindness was so common, and every wayside so suitable for begging, that it may well have happened that Jesus passed one blind man on entering and another on leaving Jericho. The conditions being precisely similar, the results would be equally so. Men unable to see would naturally raise their voices. If one had sight restored on the entrance to Jericho, there would be ample time, before Jesus left the place, for the news to be carried to the blind man at the other end of the town. What more natural than that he should adopt the same form of address and method of attracting the attention of Jesus, which had been successful previously? Those who wanted such outcries stopped before, would be as anxious on that point now: if Jesus were to be constantly hailed as 'Son of David,' Jerusalem might be in an uproar before he reached it, and his enemies find good ground for apprehending him. That Jesus should stand still, call the man, question him, and cure him, would come as naturally to pass now as on the first occasion. Nothing more probable than that two such miracles should happen, and the one be almost a counterpart of the other. The similarity between them would naturally prevent a reporter from giving details of both: he would either choose one of them, or combine the salient features of the two. Luke found and preserved the account of the first; Mark was able to record the second; Matthew related the chief points of the two. On that view, the differences between Mark and Luke are noteworthy: the latter describes the man as 'brought' to Jesus, adding 'and when he was come near,' as though the approach was slow; the former represents the crowd as anticipating the miracle: 'Be of good cheer: rise, he calleth thee;' and the man as extremely active and hopeful, so sure of a cure now, that he cares nothing about leaving his robe behind, jumps up on the instant, and makes his way, unaided, boldly and alone, in the direction of the voice of Jesus: 'And he casting away his garment, sprang up, and came to Jesus.' That is in favour of the idea that the news of the first miracle had travelled, and led to the performance of the second. The words of Jesus, 'Call ye him,' are not quite synonymous with the expression, 'commanded him to be brought,' and would seem rather to have been spoken of another man; and whereas the one addressed Jesus as *Kurios*, 'Lord' the other is represented as using the word *Rabboni*, 'Master.' Such differences may be owing to greater facility and accuracy of observation and a more reliable memory, possessed by one of the reporters; or they may be, as seems on the whole most probable, equally true to fact, and descriptive of two different miracles. Dean Alford did not admit that. His note is as follows: 'He must be indeed a slave to the *letter*, who would stumble at such discrepancies, and not rather see in them the corroborating coincidence of testimonies to the fact itself. Yet some strangely suppose our Lord to have healed *one blind man* (as in Luke) *on entering Jericho*, and *another* (Bartimæus, as in Mark) *on leaving it*, and St. Matthew to have "with his characteristic brevity in relating miracles," *combined both these in one*. But then, what becomes of St. Matthew's assertion, "*as they departed from Jericho?*" Can we possibly imagine, that the Evangelist, having *both facts* before him, could combine them and preface them with what he *must know to be inaccurate?*' Of course not: no one would make such an assumption. It is Alford himself who assumes, without warrant, that Matthew must be understood to mean that the facts recorded happened after leaving Jericho, which he certainly does not say. Something would have to be added to the narrative to make that clear: if it ran, 'And, behold, two blind men *who were then* sitting by the way side,' Alford's argument would hold good; but without some such additional words, it does not, and he is not justified in insisting that the sentence must be read as though they had been inserted. Alford was not careful to search for any possible way of reconciling the three evangelists; he saw how others were constantly at work toning down and explaining away, in a very injudicious fashion, every discrepancy met with in the sacred narratives, and against such a task he resolutely set his face, and uttered a strong protest. Without troubling himself to investigate the probabilities of the case, he jumped to the conclusion that of course Matthew was wrong in stating that there were two blind men, and he made this startling assertion: 'The supposition that they were two miracles is perfectly monstrous; and would at once destroy the credit of St. Matthew as a truthful narrator.' He adds: ' It is just thus that the Harmonists utterly destroy the credibility of the Scripture narrative. Accumulate upon this the absurd improbability involved in two men, under the same circumstances, addressing our Lord in the same words at so very short an interval,—and we may be thankful that Biblical criticism is at length being emancipated from "forcing narratives into accordance."' In a 'Harmony of the Gospels' contained in 'Helps to the study of the Bible,' issued from the Oxford

University Press, the accounts of Matthew and Mark are given under the head 'Healing blind Bartimæus,' Luke's account being entirely ignored. That seems to be an instance of what Alford called 'forcing narratives into accordance.' Those who are free from the trammels of the Inspiration theory have, on the one hand, no temptation to do that, and on the other hand, are not afraid to consider the various ways in which apparent discrepancies lying on the surface of the narratives may admit of reconcilement.

Matthew alone records the fact that Jesus touched the eyes of the blind men; from which it may be inferred that the habit of healing by the touch was then so well known, that the recorders did not always specially mention it.

The three evangelists agree in stating that the blind men 'followed' Jesus. That expression means much, although it may or may not have been intended here to denote a profession of discipleship. We know that Jesus on one occasion turned and faced the crowd, and pointed out to them what the true following of him involved. Every one cured by his power and joining the procession, thereby offered a kind of homage to him, just as in our own day those who walk with the Salvation Army are assumed to ally themselves with the cause.

14 Luke 25, 35

Jesus halted, for some hours at least, in Jericho. Luke relates an incident which took place there. One of the inhabitants, a wealthy tax-gatherer, was anxious to catch sight of Jesus. 'And he entered and was passing through Jericho. And behold, a man called by name Zacchæus; and he was a chief publican, and he was rich. And he sought to see Jesus who he was.' It might have been the natural curiosity to see what manner of man the great Teacher was; but the expression is peculiar: 'who he was,' rendered literally by Young 'who he is,' seems to signify that he had some expectation of being able to identify Jesus; it is possible, for instance, that Zacchæus might have met years before and remembered, the young carpenter of Galilee, in whom there were discernible mysterious presages of future greatness, or they might have met on some occasion when Jesus was travelling incognito, 'and would have no man know it,' and Zacchæus have been so struck with his demeanour and conversation as to wonder, afterwards, whether he had not been privileged to associate with the great Teacher whose fame was in all men's mouths. But Jesus was shut out from sight by the crowd, and the diminutive stature of Zacchæus made it hopeless for him to get a view of him in the same way as others. Knowing the course which Jesus would necessarily take, he ran on in advance, and climbed a tree, from which position he would be able to look down on everything: 'and could not for the crowd, because he was little of stature. And he ran on before, and climbed up into a sycamore tree to see him: for he was to pass that way.' It was by no means a dignified position, but it answered the purpose. We are not told whether Zacchæus recognised Jesus as one he had met before, but Jesus certainly identified him, and addressed him familiarly by name. More than that, he bade him come down instantly, and welcome him to his house, where Jesus intended to stay, as though they were old friends. 'And when Jesus came to the place, he looked up, and said unto him, Zacchæus, make haste, and come down; for to-day I must abide at thy house.' All

19 Luke 1-3

,, 3, 4

,, 5

that reads very naturally, and the evangelist leaves us to draw our own inferences. He does not add a word which might lead us to suppose that the knowledge exhibited by Jesus was supernatural, and it is not for us to assert that which Luke refrained from saying. After 'looked up' the Authorised Version has, 'and saw him,' which is omitted by the Revisers and Tischendorf, not being in the two oldest MSS. That the quick eye of Jesus should light upon the man whose position was so conspicuous, is not to be wondered at. Alford observes: 'The *probability* is, that our Lord's supernatural knowledge of man (see John i. 48–50) is intended to be understood as the means of his knowing Zacchæus: but the narrative does not absolutely exclude the supposition of a personal knowledge of Zacchæus on the part of some around him.' No: nor on the part of Jesus, whose mode of address decidedly indicated a prior mutual acquaintance. Zacchæus was of the class with whom Jesus had been in the habit of consorting; the expression 'who he is,' indicates that Zacchæus was bent upon ascertaining whether he might not be able to recognise him, and there is no reason why Jesus should have feigned a recognition and assumed a tone of friendly familiarity with an utter stranger. Let the narrative be taken in its entirety, and interpreted naturally and rationally. That the evangelist gives no hint of anything supernatural or extraordinary, is by itself good evidence that he did not intend us to view the account in that light. Zacchæus is not represented as being astounded or awed when thus familiarly addressed by Jesus. On the contrary, the following words read like the description of a renewal of intimacy between persons who have been long separated, and who rejoice to meet again. 'And he made haste, and came down, and received him joyfully.' That Jesus should have thus deliberately chosen to associate with one whose hated calling was of itself enough to bring his character into disrepute, excited much comment and ill-natured criticism. 'And when they saw it, they all murmured, saying, He is gone in to lodge with a man that is a sinner.' Zacchæus stood forward, and repelled the taunt. So far from deserving it, he had given half of his property away to the poor, and if any wrongful exaction had been made by him in his business of tax-collector, he was anxious to offer the amplest compensation. 'And Zacchæus stood, and said unto the Lord, Behold, Lord (Sir—Young), the half of my goods I give to the poor; and if I have wrongfully exacted aught of any man, I restore fourfold.' Jesus accorded to him the fullest credence and sympathy. Whatever the past career of Zacchæus might have been, and whatever others might think and say of him now, Jesus recognised in this declaration an honest heart and purpose, an augury and evidence of moral rectitude. That was the true salvation of personal, family and social life, the genuine sign of a descent from Abraham. 'And Jesus said unto him, To-day is salvation come to this house, forasmuch as he also is a son of Abraham.' The contempt poured upon the class to which Zacchæus belonged, was the attracting power which drew Jesus to his side. 'For the son of man came to seek and to save that which was lost.'

This justification of Zacchæus was spoken in presence of his accusers, who, it seems, were believers in Jesus, for he seized the opportunity to address to them a warning on another subject on which also they held erroneous views. They were indulging an expectation that the approaching visit of Jesus to Jerusalem would result in some open manifestation of God's kingdom. The parable now delivered disclosed the faulty basis and inherent evils of a kingdom founded on an earthly pattern. 'And as they heard these things, he added and spake a parable, because he was nigh to Jerusalem, and *because* they supposed that the kingdom of God was immediately to appear.' Jesus sketched a vivid picture of an earthly potentate, of kingdoms taken, held, ruled, after the fashion of this world, of social anarchy, of the high-handedness, selfishness, and favouritism of governors, no man able to call anything his own, and every aspiration after political freedom and representative government ruthlessly suppressed and quenched in blood. 'He said therefore, A certain nobleman went into a far country, to receive for himself a kingdom, and to return.' Young renders : 'A certain man of birth proceeded into a distant region to take to himself a kingdom, and to return.' Whether to 'receive for himself,' as a family heritage, or 'to take to himself,' by force of arms, matters little : he was an aristocrat, born to hold sway over men, and claiming to exercise dominion even in a far distant land. It was his intention, after taking possession of the colony, to leave its administration to others, he himself returning to rule over his native country. Before departing he summoned ten of his slaves, and entrusted them with ten minæ, bidding them trade with the money on his behalf during his absence. 'And he called ten servants (Gr. bondservants) of his, and gave them ten pounds, and said unto them, Trade ye *herewith* till I come.' Alford explains : 'The sums given are here all the *same*, and all *very small*. The (Attic) mina is $\frac{1}{60}$ of a talent, and equal to about £3 of our money.' The transaction does not disclose a spark of liberality, or the least discernment of character : the same miserable pittance is placed in the hands of each, and an intimation is given that the trust will end on their lord's return. He is represented as a man held in universal detestation : his slaves were not free to express an opinion, but his subjects hated him, and the popular indignation against him rose to such a height that after his departure a deputation from the citizens was sent after him to announce their determination to submit no longer to his rule. 'But his citizens hated him, and sent an ambassage after him, saying, We will not that this man reign over us.' But it proved easier to frame a declaration of independence in his absence, than to free themselves from his tyranny and escape his vengeance. The picture was not over-coloured. Alford observes : 'The groundwork of this part of the parable seems to have been derived from the history of Archelaus, son of Herod the Great. The kings of the Herodian family made journeys to Rome, to receive their " kingdom." On Archelaus's doing so, the Jews sent after him a protest, which however was not listened to by Augustus. The situation was appropriate ; for at Jericho was the royal palace which Archelaus had built with great magnificence.' If that piece of contemporaneous history be fitted into the parable, the circumstances are not improved. In either case, we have a system of arbitrary and irresponsible government, the wishes, interests and aspirations of the people being held as of no account by their rulers. The monarch, having accomplished the object of his journey, on his return summoned his slaves to account to him for the money he had advanced and the profit resulting from its employment. 'And it came to pass, when he was come back again, having received the kingdom, that he commanded those servants (Gr. bondservants) unto whom he had given the money, to be called to him, that he might know what they had gained by trading.' Alford notes that the closing words should be read and rendered, 'what business they had carried on.' Young's translation is, 'that he might know what each had done in business :' the result in each case would prove their aptitude for affairs, and to what extent they could be trusted to look after their master's interests. The first had succeeded in increasing the small fund tenfold. 'And the first came before him, saying, Lord (Sir—Young), thy pound hath made ten pounds more.' That showed energy, shrewdness, fidelity ; the man could be relied upon to make the most of opportunities, to add wealth to the royal coffers. 'And he said unto him, Well done, thou good servant (Gr. bondservant).' His capacities in that direction marked him out for far larger responsibilities : ' because thou wast found faithful in a very little, have thou authority over ten cities.' That indeed was a huge trust : the successful money-maker is at a stroke transformed into a governor of men. What connection between the two offices there might be, it were difficult to say. The driver of hard bargains is scarcely the man whom a wise ruler would prefer to entrust with the lives, liberties, physical and moral welfare of vast multitudes. 'He that ruleth over men *must be* just, ruling in the fear of God.' Those were 'the last words' of David. No such requirement is made of this governor of ten cities. The smallness of the amount he had to deal with is a striking feature of the parable, and that point is emphasised by the king's admission that it was 'a very little.' No matter how trifling the concerns in which royal favourites minister to their master's selfishness : that has too often been the surest road to promotion, the welfare of the people being sacrificed and their destinies committed to men whose only claim to consideration was the title and the influence conferred upon them by an arbitrary monarch. As mankind progress, these things slowly mend. But in the days of Jesus that system was in full force ; and knowing that the people were looking to him to inaugurate a new kingdom, he brought vividly before them in this parable the inherent evils of those then existing in the world. The second of the ten slaves had increased his capital only half as much as the first, but the ability to make five hundred per cent. pointed him out as a fit man to rule over five cities. 'And the second came, saying, Thy pound, Lord (Sir—Young), hath made five pounds. And he said unto him also, Be thou also over five cities.' These two instances indicate sufficiently the rule of promotion in king's courts. The aggrandisement of the monarch was the primary concern ; devotion to his interests the only road to elevation ; high principles of action and earnest labour on behalf of the people committed to their charge,—these things were well-nigh out of sight and out of mind among kings and nobles. One of the ten slaves, however, did not choose to swim with the stream ; despotic rule was an abomination to his mind, and he had determined not to spend his life in labours the fruits of which would go to his master, not to himself. 'And another (Gr. the other) came, saying, Lord (Sir—Young), behold, *here is* thy pound, which I kept laid up in a napkin : for I feared thee, because thou art an austere man: thou takest up that thou layedst not down, and reapest that thou didst not sow.' That might be true: but he was a bondservant, bound to labour for his lord, and blamable if he did not. He ought either to have dealt faithfully with the trust, or have handed it over to others, the one thing needful being that the royal wealth should constantly go on accumulating. 'He saith unto him, Out of thine own mouth will I judge thee, thou wicked servant (Gr. bondservant). Thou knewest that I am an austere man, taking up that I laid not down, and reaping that I did not sow; then wherefore gavest thou not my money into the bank, and I at my coming should have required (or, I should have gone and required) it with interest?' Responsibilities and advancement were not for such as he. Let the money be taken from him, and handed over to him who could make the best use of it. 'And he said unto them that stood by, Take away from him the pound, and give it unto him that hath the ten pounds.' Against that the instinctive sense of justice rose in protest. 'And they said unto him, Lord (Sir—Young), he hath ten pounds.' Alford observes that this 'is parenthetical, spoken by *the standers-by in the parable*, in surprise at such a decision.' This additional touch of nature was not thrown into the parable without a motive. It is of the same tone and colour as the surrounding incidents, the object being apparently to represent this pattern of earthly rulership in an unfavourable light. From first to last it presents a scene of disorder, of enforced subjection, of imperiousness on the one side and a tendency to rebellion on the other. The citizens muttered discontent, and would have shaken off, if they could, the hated yoke of sovereignty. One of the slaves of the household deliberately neglected to labour for his lord's advantage, would not even take the trouble to place out his money where it would bear interest, and when called to account, boldly denounced his master's character and conduct to his face. And now, when the command is given to transfer the pound to the man who least needed it, having already more to deal with than any of the others, dissatisfaction is excited in the minds of his fellows, and an attempt at expostulation made. No one, outside the circle of a few reigning favourites, is contented in that kingdom; the autocrat rules by fear, not by love; his will and his interest are the only things to be considered; the people's wishes are treated with contempt; no man's time or energy can be claimed for himself; and the system is upheld by favouritism, those most subservient to the royal will and pleasure being elevated to positions in which they can aid and imitate their lord's despotic rule: 'Have thou authority over ten cities ... Be thou also over five cities.' Success to the successful, was the inexorable rule: for them all the honours, emoluments and opportunities of distinction, which the despot might choose to apportion out as the reward of obsequious fidelity. But woe to the unprofitable servant: whoever failed to increase the royal revenue, was adjudged incompetent, and unworthy to hold office. 'I say unto you, that unto every one that hath shall be given; but from him that hath not, even that which he hath shall be taken away from him.' The vigour and rigour thus exercised by the monarch within his court, were as nothing compared with the sternness shown towards those outside who had presumed to seek deliverance from his rule. No hint is given that they had taken up arms against the government; it was enough that they had formulated the resolution, 'We will not that this man reign over us.' That constituted them, in his eyes, rebels of the deepest dye; such citizens he regarded not as subjects, but as enemies, with whom he would hold no parley, to whom he would show no mercy. 'Howbeit these mine enemies, which would not that I should reign over them, bring hither, and slay them before me.' It was a terrible picture of arbitrary rule, its basis, its working, its results, which Jesus placed before the minds of his hearers. That was the kind of 'kingdom' with which mankind had become familiar. Could they desire that the world's history should continue to be written after such a fashion? Whenever 'the kingdom of God' should 'appear,' it would surely be something altogether different from this. We are not told that Jesus added a single word of comment or explanation: he left the parable to speak for itself; it is not prefaced, as many are, with the words, 'the kingdom of heaven is like unto . . . ,' nor had he been discoursing previously on the subject. It was because those about him were expecting God's kingdom, that he sketched out this one after the world's model. Touch after touch added to the sombreness and unloveliness of its characteristics and surroundings, and the closing catastrophe was an awful scene of revengeful slaughter. The kingdom of a despot, or the kingdom of the devil, it may be: anything rather than a picture of 'the kingdom of God!' Yet that is the light in which men have come to view it. Here is Dean Alford's interpretation: 'The nobleman, son of a king, literally *one high born*, is the Lord Jesus; the kingdom is that over his own citizens, the Jews. They sent a message after Him; their cry went up to heaven, in the persecutions of His servants, &c.; *we will not have this man to reign over us*.' The ideas are as frightful as they are fanciful. Once on that wrong track of thought, there is no stopping: on the words, 'These mine enemies, which would not that I should reign over them, bring hither, and slay them before me,' Alford's comment is, 'This command brings out both comings of the Lord,—at the destruction of Jerusalem, and at the end of the world.' Away, once and for ever, with the monstrous, horrible notion of theologians, that the destruction of Jerusalem by the Romans was, in any sense, the 'coming' of the Lord Jesus! He foresaw it, indeed, and foretold it, pitying the helpless sufferers, and bidding his disciples, 'pray ye that your flight be not in the winter.' It was one of those episodes in human history brought upon mankind by themselves, the natural and inevitable outcome of that system of rulership on which the kingdoms of the world were founded, the selfish wielding of irresponsible power, the rebellious spirit thereby generated, the arbitrament of the sword, the triumph of might over right. The kingdom and the coming of Jesus are the very opposite of that: 'the Son of man came not to destroy men's lives, but to save *them*.'

Whilst Jesus was travelling towards Jerusalem many others also were proceeding thither from various points to keep the annual festival of the passover. 'Now the passover of the Jews was at hand: and many went up to Jerusalem out of the country before the passover, to purify themselves.' They were anxious to see Jesus, and were not without hope of finding him in Jerusalem, although it was notorious that he could only go there at peril of his life. Would he venture to come up to the feast? 'They sought therefore for Jesus, and spake one with another, as they stood in the temple, What think ye? That he will not come to the feast?' After his last visit he had found it necessary to withdraw with his disciples to a retired spot, 'a country near to the wilderness,' and a decree of the Jewish rulers was still in force, making it incumbent upon any one who knew his whereabouts to disclose it. 'Now the chief priests and the Pharisees had given commandment, that, if any man knew where he was, he should shew it, that they might take him.' Jesus was now on the point of putting himself again within reach of their power, although he knew full well that they would exercise it to his destruction. Six days before the passover he appeared in Bethany, sure of a welcome from the family of Lazarus. 'Jesus therefore six days before the passover came to Bethany, where Lazarus was, whom Jesus raised from the dead.' Following the two oldest MSS., the Revisers have omitted the words, 'which had been dead.' Very hearty was the greeting he received. An entertainment was prepared to celebrate his arrival, Martha busying herself with serving, and Lazarus being one of the guests. 'So they made him a supper there: and Martha served; but Lazarus was one of them that sat at meat with him.' This was not, as might have been inferred, in Martha's house, for Matthew's account begins: 'Now, when Jesus was in Bethany, in the house of Simon the leper;' and Mark's: 'And while he was in Bethany in the house of Simon the leper, as he sat at meat.' There the following incident occurred. 'There came unto him a woman, having an alabaster cruse (or, a flask) of exceeding precious ointment, and she poured it upon his head, as he sat at meat.' In the Authorised Version the word is 'box,' not 'cruse.' Young and Tischendorf retain the word 'box.' Mark describes the kind of ointment: 'there came a woman having an alabaster cruse of ointment of spikenard very costly; *and* she brake the cruse, and poured it over his head.' The Revisers' note is: 'Gr. *pistic nard*, pistic being perhaps a local name. Others take it to mean *genuine*; others *liquid*.' Young renders it 'myrrh' in Matthew, and 'spikenard' in Mark. Luther renders Matthew: 'ein Glas mit köstlichem Wasser,' 'a glass with costly water,' and Mark, 'ein Glas mit ungefälschtem und köstlichem Nardenwasser,' 'a glass with unadulterated and costly nardwater.' John does not allude to the vessel which contained it, but states its weight, and identifies the woman as Mary, the sister of Lazarus. 'Mary therefore took a pound of ointment of spikenard, very precious, and anointed the feet of Jesus, and wiped his feet with her hair.' The act has been previously alluded to by John as that of Mary: 'And it was that Mary which anointed the Lord with ointment, and wiped his feet with her hair, whose brother Lazarus was sick.' John does not mention the pouring of the ointment over the head, and the two other records do not allude to the anointing of the feet, nor to the use of Mary's hair in drying them. It may be that the account of John is that of an eye-witness, and the other accounts made up from hearsay evidence, which did not give the woman's name, or state more than the current report that the ointment was poured upon the head. Although very costly, it was applied profusely, lavishly, even 'wastefully' in the opinion of certain critical observers. There is in John's narrative an additional touch, which indicates that it was derived from one who was present at the entertainment: 'and the house was filled with the odour of the ointment.' Some of those present were scandalized at beholding such extravagance; they estimated the cost of the ointment, and thought how large an amount of comfort the expenditure of so much money might have brought to the poor. 'But there were some that had indignation among themselves, *saying*, To what purpose hath this waste of the ointment been made? For this ointment might have been sold for above three hundred pence, and given to the poor.' As the denary was the common day's wage of a labourer, the three hundred denaries would be equivalent to about £50 in our time. Matthew informs us that this question was raised by the disciples of Jesus. 'But when the disciples saw it, they had indignation, saying, To what purpose is this waste? For this *ointment* might have been sold for much, and given to the poor.' John was able to state with whom the idea, which was thus taken up by the disciples, originated. 'But Judas Iscariot, one of his disciples, which should betray him, saith, Why was not this ointment sold for three hundred pence, and given to the poor?' The evangelist does not scruple to assert that the suggestion was simple hypocrisy on the part of Judas, that he cared nothing about the poor, but watched for an opportunity of purloining money from the poorbox, which was entrusted to his keeping. How well does that suit the character of the man who sold his Master! 'Now this he said, not because he cared for the poor, but because he was a thief, and having the bag (or, box) took away (or, carried) what was put therein.' The criticism of the disciples was directed against Mary: 'And they murmured against her.' Jesus, becoming conscious of all this, expostulated with his disciples on the woman's behalf. 'But Jesus perceiving it said unto them, Why trouble ye the woman?' 'But Jesus, said, Let her alone; why trouble ye her?' Jesus was as poor as anybody, and he regarded the action as a good deed rendered to himself: 'She hath wrought a good work upon me.' 'For she hath wrought a good work upon me.' The poor would be always present among them, but not Jesus. 'For ye have the poor always with you; but me ye have not always.' Mark is fuller: 'For ye have the poor always with you, and whensoever ye will ye can do them good: but me ye have not always.' Death was very near to him, and this office of womanly love might be regarded as performed in anticipation of his burial. 'She hath done what she could: she hath anointed my body aforehand for the burying.' The form of the expression is given somewhat differently by Matthew: 'For in that she poured (Gr. cast) this ointment upon my body, she did it to prepare me for burial.' John is to the same effect, but he reverses the sayings: 'Jesus therefore said, Suffer her to keep it (or, Let her alone: *it was* that she might keep it) against the day of my burying. For the poor ye have always with you, but me ye have not always.' It was hard for Mary to be blamed and shamed for her good action. That must not be. It was a deed worthy to be recorded, and it should be held in world-wide remembrance. 'Verily I say unto you, Wheresoever this gospel (or, these good tidings) shall be preached in the whole world, that also which this woman hath done shall be spoken of for a memorial of her.' Mark records that saying word for word, simply putting 'and' before 'verily,' according to the two oldest MSS., which have been followed by the Revisers in this point; on the same authority they have here altered 'this gospel' to 'the gospel,' as Tischendorf has done. Alford has the following note: 'We cannot but be struck with the majesty of this prophetic announcement: introduced with the peculiar and weighty *verily I say unto you*, conveying, by implication, the whole mystery of the *gospel* which should go forth from His Death as its source,—looking forward to the end of time, when it shall have been preached in the whole world,—and specifying the fact that this deed should be recorded wherever it is preached. We may notice (1) that the announcement is a distinct prophetic recognition by our Lord of the existence of *written records*, in which the deed should be related; for in no other conceivable way could the universality of mention be brought about: (2) that we have here (if indeed we needed it) a convincing argument against that view of our three first Gospels which supposes them to have been compiled from an original document, for if there had been such a document, it must have contained this narrative, and no one using such a Gospel could have failed to insert this narrative, accompanied by such a promise, in his own work,—which St. Luke has not done: (3) that the same consideration is equally decisive against St. Luke having used, or even seen, our present Gospels of Matthew and Mark.' Sections (2) and (3) constitute a very strong argument, which may be commended to the consideration of those who might be disposed to accept the contrary idea, which has been put forward by the Rev. J. J. Halcombe in 'Gospel Difficulties,' (page lxxxiv), as follows: 'S. Luke's object was to remove an uncertainty, or suspicion of untruthfulness, which had affected certain Gospels (Logoi) which, he states, had been handed over to the Church by those whose authority for writing them consisted in their having been either "eye-witnesses or ministers of the word;" this uncertainty, or suspicion, having been engendered by certain unsuccessful attempts which many had previously made to rearrange, or harmonize, these Gospels. That these Logoi were in fact the Gospels of S. Matthew, S. Mark, and S. John, we gather (1) from the use which S. Luke makes of the word *Logos* in his Preface to the Acts, where he styles his own Gospel a *Logos*, (2) from his definition of the writers, and (3) from the fact that from the very commencement to the end of his Gospel, he traverses the same ground, and deals with the same incidents, as those Evangelists; and that, not only in the same general order, but in such a manner as to elucidate on every occasion . . .' and so on. This chain of reasoning hangs on a very fragile thread. *If* Theophilus had the Gospels of Matthew, Mark and John, the word *Logoi* might represent them: but that is a mere assumption, advanced without a shred of evidence, and improbable on the face of it.

Section (1) of Alford's argument is overstrained, and open to question. He takes the expression, 'Wheresoever these good tidings shall be preached in the whole world,' as proof positive that the good tidings were to take the shape of *written records*. That no more follows from this passage than from another passage: 'Go ye into all the world, and preach the gospel to the whole creation.' Who would understand that to signify that the apostles would issue written records, and that 'in no other conceivable way could the universality of mention be brought about?' The application of the word 'gospel' to written or printed documents was the outcome of later times. The words 'this gospel,' uttered by Jesus, could only refer to something which was at that moment in the mind and mouth of the Speaker, and equally present to the minds of his hearers. In Young's literal version the word is always rendered 'good news' or 'good tidings:' whenever and wherever it occurs it is necessarily in connection with a particular idea, the revelation of a fact or truth, in the same way as 'news' is understood and grasped in reference to any topic of the day. The sense of the word 'gospel' was invariably fixed by the context, the 'good news' being presented now in one shape and now in another. Take a few passages, using Young's version. 'The good news of Jesus Christ:' obviously, about Jesus Christ. 'Believe in the good news:' that is, that 'the reign of God hath come near.' 'Whoever may lose his life for my sake and for the good news:' in promulgating what Jesus preached. 'To all the nations it behoveth first to proclaim the good news:' which they had been assisting Jesus, and would continue, to proclaim. 'As he is teaching the people in the temple, and proclaiming the good news:' the teaching being the aspect under which the good news was presented. 'God among us made choice, through my mouth, for the Gentiles to hear the word of the good news:' which is to the same effect. 'The good news of the grace of God.' 'The good news of God .. concerning His Son.' 'The good news of Christ.' 'According to my good news:' Paul's doctrine of a judgment of the secrets of men 'through Jesus Christ.' 'They were not all obedient to the good tidings:' that is, 'good tidings of peace, good tidings of the good things.' 'As regards, indeed, the good tidings, *they are* enemies on your account:' the good tidings referring to the coming of a deliverer out of Zion, 'who should turn away ungodliness from Jacob.' 'The good news of God.' It is not necessary to go through the other passages in which the term 'gospel' or 'good news' occurs: these are sufficient to show, at least, that written records of the sayings and doings of Jesus do not properly come under that designation. Luke gives two titles to his so-called 'Gospel:' 'a narrative,' and 'a treatise concerning all that Jesus began both to do and to teach.' The naming of each of the four histories 'the gospel,' and the failure to give the literal translation, 'good news,' have led to some confusion of thought, approaching sometimes to misapprehension. Let anyone disposed to doubt this take the pains to read in Dr. Young's literal version the passages, about 70, in which the expression 'good news' occurs. A clearer insight will thereby be gained of the nature and definiteness of the apostolic teaching: the proclamation of 'good news,' as such, raises naturally and instantaneously in the mind the conception both of a Sender and of an authorized Messenger, which the word 'gospel' does not, unless a special mental effort is made by the reader.

Reverting to the words of Jesus, it will be observed that they appear in Matthew as 'this gospel' or 'these good tidings.' 'This' or 'these' must refer to something spoken at the time. He may have been discoursing at the meal, as was his custom, of 'the good news of the reign of God;' or the reference may have been to the context, 'to prepare me for burial.' That climax of his career was 'good news' for the world, however distressing at the time to himself and his disciples. Alford seems to assume that connection, for he speaks of 'the *gospel* which should go forth from his Death as its source.'

John does not record the prediction of Jesus concerning Mary's action, but he mentions a fact omitted by the other evangelists. The presence of Jesus at Bethany had been noised abroad, and many of the populace were attracted thither by the expectation of seeing not only Jesus but Lazarus also, whom he was known to have raised from the tomb to life. 'The common people therefore of the Jews learned that he was there: and they came, not for Jesus' sake only, but that they might see Lazarus also, whom he had raised from the dead.' The Revisers have altered 'much people' to 'the common people.' Tischendorf renders, 'the great multitude;' 'Young, 'a great multitude;' Luther, 'viel Volks,' 'much people.' The expression chosen by the Revisers is not a happy one.

The clerical party were so incensed against Jesus, that they determined to let nothing stand in the way of their attempt to counteract his influence. Lazarus was now obnoxious to them, and they decided that it would be necessary for their purpose to put him to death as well as Jesus. 'But the chief priests took counsel that they might put Lazarus also to death.' He had become so conspicuous, and was saying or doing so much in favour of Jesus, that many converts were being made, who turned their backs upon the chief priests and professed their faith in Jesus : 'because that by reason of him many of the Jews went away, and believed on Jesus.' Alford observes as follows : 'Remember here, as elsewhere in John, the *Jews* are not *the people*, but the rulers, and persons of repute : the representatives of the Jewish *opposition* to Jesus.' How can that be, when it is said that 'the great multitude of the Jews' went to see Jesus and Lazarus, and that many of them believed?' The term 'Jews' appears to denote the men of Jewry, inhabitants of Judæa, whose only opportunity of seeing and hearing Jesus was when he came into their neighbourhood. The evangelist gives, without comment, a bare statement of the fact, but it is, by itself, a frightful example of clerical bigotry and persecution. What detestable, sanguinary principles of action have cloaked themselves under the garb of Religion, and made the professed ministers of God the bitterest opponents of human progress, and the enemies of mankind!

Luke seems to intimate that the parable of the nobleman who was hated by his citizens, feared by his servants, and who exterminated his enemies, was the last discourse delivered by Jesus on his journey : for it is said : 'And when he had thus spoken, he went on before, going up to Jerusalem.' We have seen that he reached Bethany six days before the passover, and was received into the house of Simon the leper. On approaching the place, Jesus had given to two of his disciples directions of a very remarkable kind. He told them to go into the neighbouring village, where they would find an ass tethered and a colt by her side. 'And when they drew nigh unto Jerusalem, and came unto Bethphage, unto the mount of Olives, then Jesus sent two disciples, saying unto them, Go into the village that is over against you, and straightway ye shall find an ass tied, and a colt with her.' Mark adds the fact that the colt was unbroken : 'And when they drew nigh unto Jerusalem, unto Bethphage and Bethany, at the mount of Olives, he sendeth two of his disciples, and saith unto them, Go your way into the village that is over against you : and straightway as ye enter into it, ye shall find a colt tied, whereon no man ever yet sat.' Luke uses very nearly the same words : 'And it came to pass, when he drew nigh unto Bethphage and Bethany, at the mount that is called *the mount* of Olives, he sent two of the disciples, saying, Go your way into the village over against *you*; in the which as ye enter, ye shall find a colt tied, whereon no man ever yet sat.' Such similarities of diction between three historians are indications that they borrowed from a common narrative, the merely verbal differences arising from the amplification of the original, which would probably be in the form of condensed notes. In this instance, there may have been two, and could have been no more than two independent sources of information. Matthew states the instruction given by Jesus in these words : 'Loose *them*, and bring *them* unto me.' Young renders literally : 'Having loosed, bring to me.' Only Matthew alludes to the ass being with the colt. Mark and Luke, having spoken of the colt only, use the same expression : 'Loose him and bring him.' Thus to appropriate another person's property would seem extraordinary, and required some warrant. Jesus admitted as much, and instructed his disciples how to meet the difficulty. 'And if any one say aught unto you, ye shall say, the Lord hath need of them ; and straightway he will send them.' Here the word 'them' is no insertion. Combining the evangelists, it would seem that the colt only was required, but the she-ass was sent with him, it being unadvisable to separate the mother from her foal. Mark and Luke still allude to the latter only. 'And if any one say unto you, Why do ye this? say ye, The Lord hath need of him : and straightway he will send (Gr. sendeth) him back (or, again) hither.' The word 'back' (or, again) has been introduced from the two oldest MS. Luke says merely, 'And if any one ask you, Why do ye loose him ? thus shall ye say, The Lord hath need of him.' The omission by Luke of the assurance given by Jesus may be accounted for by supposing it to have been absent from the manuscript from which Luke compiled this portion of the history. The greater the demand for these early records, the greater also would be the difficulty of meeting it with promptitude, the copying of manuscripts being a slow process. Thence it might well happen that the deficiency was supplied by the best means available, and that abstracts of the facts might be compiled from memory, or attempts made to follow in writing the reading of some original document. This would sufficiently account for variations and omissions which do not amount to discrepancies.

Matthew, as was his custom, traced in the event a fulfilment of prophecy. 'Now this is come to pass, that it might be fulfilled which was spoken by (or, through) the prophet, saying,

    Tell ye the daughter of Zion,
    Behold, thy king cometh unto thee,
    Meek, and riding upon an ass,
    And upon a colt the foal of an ass.'

The original passage stands as follows: 'Rejoice greatly, O daughter of Zion ; shout, O daughter of Jerusalem : behold, thy king cometh unto thee ; he is just, and having salvation, lowly, and riding upon an ass, even upon a colt the foal of an ass.' Alford observes : 'That this riding and entry were *intentional* on the part of our Lord, is clear : and also that He did not thereby mean to give any countenance to the temporal ideas of His Messiahship, but solemnly to fulfil the Scriptures respecting Him, and to prepare the way for His sufferings, by a public avowal of His mission.' Jesus seized upon this Scriptural picture as illustrating the nature of the kingdom he desired to found. The homage paid to him must be natural and spontaneous : justice, salvation, meekness, constituted the basis of his power and influence ; he resolved to make himself conspicuous in this particular way to his enthusiastic followers, and, knowing that his death was very near, to bequeath to the world this pattern of what a king's triumphal entry ought to be. It is not to be supposed that Jesus would have been any less the Messiah of mankind, if he had not thus literally accomplished the terms of this prophecy ; the incident by itself proved nothing, convinced nobody ; a false Christ might have assumed the same position ; it was no evidence in his favour at the time, for we are expressly told that his disciples had no recollection of such a prophecy : but the character, the doctrine, the aims of Jesus were entirely in harmony with it, and he would let the world know what kind of sovereignty he claimed, and see, once for all, a true pattern of regal dignity.

The two disciples found it easy to accomplish the task which Jesus had laid upon them. Everything happened as he had foretold, and when they delivered his message the animal was at once given over for his use. 'And they that were sent went away, and found even as he had said unto them. And as they were loosing the colt, the owners thereof said unto them, Why loose ye the colt ? And they said, the Lord hath need of him. And they brought him to Jesus.' Mark is somewhat more precise. 'And they went away, and found a colt tied at the door without in the open street, and they loose him. And certain of them that stood there said unto them, What do ye, loosing the colt ? And they said unto them even as Jesus had said : and they let them go. And they bring the colt unto Jesus.' In the Authorised Version the locality is described as 'in a place where two ways met,' which is rendered by 'Tischendorf ' on the crossway,' and by Young 'by the two ways.' The Revisers have altered it to ' in the open street.' Alford explains : ' The word rendered *a place where two ways met*, only means, *a road leading round a place*, and probably imports simply *the street*. Wordsworth interprets it, *the back way, which led round the house*. But there does not appear to be any reason for supposing the word *round* to refer to the *house*, rather than to the whole block, or neighbourhood, of houses, round about which the street led. Dean Trench would render it *a way round, a crooked lane*.' Matthew's account is far more concise. 'And the disciples went, and did even as Jesus appointed them, and brought the ass, and the colt.'

As the message of Jesus induced the owners to lend their property for his use, it is natural to consider in what sense they must have understood the words, ' The Lord hath need of him.' Alford's note on Matthew is as follows : ' *The Lord*, here, *the* LORD, *Jehovah :* most probably a general intimation to the owners, that they were wanted *for the service of God*. I cannot see how this interpretation errs against decorum, as Stier asserts. The meanest animals might be wanted for the service of the Lord Jehovah. And after all, what difference is there as to *decorum*, if we understand with him the *Lord* to signify the *King Messiah?* That there has been a general tendency towards straining the sense of the word 'Lord' is evident from the repeated instances in which Dr. Young, alone among translators, renders it by the word 'Sir.' There are passages, of which this is one, in which "Sir" cannot be used; but it by no means follows that the term is therefore to be taken in such cases as applying to the Deity. Probably the term in the original was equivalent to the German word 'Herr,' and used in the same manner, either in speaking to or of a person recognised as a superior, a Master or Teacher. That is the import which Jesus himself attached to the word : ' Ye call me Master (or, Teacher), and, Lord : and ye say well ; for so I am.' And again : 'A servant (Gr. bondservant) is not greater than his lord.' That form of expression was in general use between man and man ; it was also used, in the same sense of supremacy, when speaking of God. The context in writing, and the circumstances in speaking, are a sufficient guide as to the intended significance, limitation, or extension, of the title. In the case before us, there could be small room, or none at all, for uncertainty. Jesus had come into the neighbourhood accompanied by a crowd of followers : his disciples were recognisable as such, and when two of them went together, loosed the colt, and explained that they did it in obedience to the directions of the lord or master, either the owners must have at once understood the reference to be to Jesus, or the disciples would make it clear that it was he who had sent them and who required the animal. If, on the contrary, it be supposed that Jesus was kept out of sight in the transaction, and that two strangers simply stated that they were taking the ass because Jehovah, the God of Israel, had need of him, there is much force in the objection of Stier, that the request would have appeared indecorous, and would not have been instantly and unhesitatingly complied with. This argument is all the stronger, when it is remembered that there was no idea in the mind of any one that the fulfilment of a prophecy was in question.

The disciples simply carried out the instructions of Jesus, and everything happened just as he had led them to expect. Was this a display of supernatural prescience on the part of Jesus ? That may be inferred from the narrative : but the evangelists themselves have not touched upon the question. We can easily believe that one who displayed such miraculous powers, and applied them in such various ways, might possess such a gift of foresight, and might even exercise a controlling influence on others by his own force of will. Or it may be that invisible Beings, heavenly messengers, were superintending and directing his career, revealing to him, as they had done to Mary and to Joseph, the things which were about to happen. In this instance, however, we are not tied down to that conclusion. The message, 'the Lord hath need of him,' may, perchance, have referred to some previous conference between Jesus and the owners. It is not to be supposed that he was never was out of sight and hearing of his disciples, that he never conversed with anyone except in their presence, that he was not free to take an independent course and arrange a plan for himself. The wording of Mark's narrative, as altered by the Revisers on the authority of the two oldest MSS., seems to indicate that the colt had lately been to the place where Jesus was. The Authorised Version has 'straightway he will send him hither;' the word 'back (or, again)' is now placed before 'hither.' The three evangelists agree that Jesus told his disciples they would discover the colt immediately upon entering the village : 'straightway ye shall find,' 'straightway as ye enter into it,' 'in the which as ye enter.' Therefore the colt had but lately passed Jesus on its way to the village. Moreover, Jesus was no stranger in Bethany; he had visited the place before; he may have known the abode of the owners, and where they took the colt on its customary round, and he seems to have relied upon their knowledge of himself as a sufficient inducement to comply unhesitatingly with his expressed desire : 'straightway he will send them.' Wherever Jesus went he healed many, and thereby, as well as through his teachings, must have gained many friends, all glad to serve him in anything within their power. The apparent mystery is capable of solution in a perfectly natural manner : the evangelists have not hinted at anything supernatural, and it would ill become us to assert the existence of a marvel with respect to which they maintained entire silence.

11 Mark 7
19 Luke 35
The colt being without a saddle, one was extemporised out of the garments of the disciples, and then Jesus mounted : 'and cast on him their garments; and he sat upon him.' 'And they threw their garments upon the colt, and set Jesus thereon.' Matthew adheres to the
21 Mat. 7
plural : 'and put on them their garments; and he sat thereon.' Then ensued a scene of enthusiastic exultation. The example set by the disciples was imitated by the multitude, who stripped off their
„ 8
robes and laid them on the ground over which he was to pass. 'And the most part of the multitude spread their garments in the way.'
11 Mark 8
19 Luke 36
21 Mat. 8
'And many spread their garments upon the way.' 'And as he went, they spread their garments in the way.' Others supplemented this with a carpet of leafy boughs, cut off from the trees. 'And others cut branches from the trees, and spread them in the way.' Young
11 Mark 8
renders literally, 'were cutting.' 'And others branches (Gr. layers of leaves), which they had cut from the fields.' The Revisers, following the two oldest MSS., have omitted from Mark the words 'and strawed *them* in the way,' which were probably inserted at an early date from Matthew. Alford notes that they are 'omitted in many ancient authorities,' and explains : 'the word signifies not merely branches, but branches cut *for the purpose of being littered to walk on :* and this *implies* the *strawing in the way*, which has been unskilfully supplied.' The expression used by the Revisers in Mark, 'which they had cut from the fields,' agrees with Tischendorf's, 'having cut them out of the fields,' and with Alford's statement that they had been 'cut for the purpose.' This is corroborated by the fourth evangelist, who stated, before mentioning the riding upon the ass, that the multitude
12 John 12
had taken branches of palm trees and gone out to meet Jesus. 'On the morrow a great multitude that had come to the feast, when they heard that Jesus was coming to Jerusalem, took the branches of the palm trees, and went forth to meet him.' To the words, 'a great multitude,' the Revisers have affixed the note : 'Some ancient autho-

rities read *the common people.*' Not the three oldest MSS., however: that form of speech looks like the gloss of some commentator. The coming of this multitude with palms in their hands was not without a meaning. They were bent on honouring Jesus as the Messiah, the expected king of Israel, and with loud shouts they hailed him under that title: 'and cried out, Hosanna: Blessed *is* he that cometh in the name of the Lord, even the King of Israel.' When the ass arrived, and Jesus had been placed thereon, the prophetic picture was complete. Here was just such a king as Zechariah had foretold, entering Jerusalem in just such a way as he described, no troops, no courtiers by his side, no insignia of royalty upon his person, nothing in his favour except the two things which alone give real dignity to a king, —his character, and the willing homage of his people. 'And Jesus, having found a young ass, sat thereon, as it is written, Fear not, daughter of Zion: behold, thy King cometh, sitting on an ass's colt.' The evangelist summarises the sense of the passage without adhering to the actual words. 'Fear not' is not in the original, but the context clearly conveyed the idea of protection and safety. The evangelist explains that there was no thought at the time in the minds of any of the disciples, of the prophecy which they unconsciously fulfilled. 'These things understood not his disciples at the first: but when Jesus was glorified then remembered they that these things were written of him, and that they had done these things unto him.' The gathering of so great and enthusiastic a multitude on this occasion was due to two causes: (1) they 'had come to the feast,' and therefore would be under the influence of religious ideas, and at leisure to seek out and honour the great Teacher whose probable coming to Jerusalem had been eagerly anticipated; (2) many among them had been present when Jesus had called Lazarus out of the grave, and the account given by these eye-witnesses of that miracle excited the popular imagination in favour of Jesus, and resulted in this form of public ovation. 'The multitude therefore that was with him when he called Lazarus out of the tomb, and raised him from the dead, bare witness. For this cause also the multitude went and met him, for that they heard that he had done this sign.' There is no inconsistency between the narratives; indeed, they throw light upon each other: John says nothing about the sending forth of the two disciples in search of the ass, but states simply that one was found by Jesus, which implies that some means were taken by him to obtain it. Matthew, Mark and Luke say nothing about the coming of the multitude with palms and singing, which explains the otherwise unaccountable outburst of enthusiasm, which the mere fact of seeing Jesus riding was not calculated to evoke. The bearing of the palms harmonises with the statement of Luke, that layers of leaves had been cut from the fields; and the strewing of them upon the road would naturally lead others to cut branches from the trees with the same object, as described by Matthew. In the same way, the stripping off of their garments by the disciples to improvise a saddle, was imitated by the most part of 'the multitude,' the laying down and constant replacing of the garments supplying the gaps between the carpet of greenery. From first to last it was a scene of tumultuous gladness. The multitude divided into two bands, one preceding and the other following, Jesus being in the midst. After a time, when they were nearing Jerusalem and had reached the downward slope of the mount of Olives, the song with which he had been hailed at starting was taken up and added to by his disciples. 'And as he was now drawing nigh, *even* at the descent of the mount of Olives, the whole multitude of the disciples began to rejoice and praise God with a loud voice for all the mighty works (Gr. powers) which they had seen: saying, Blessed *is* the King that cometh in the name of the Lord : peace in heaven, and glory in the highest.' That was well suited to the mouths of professed disciples, and was, as Luke intimates, rather an acknowledgment of the work which Jesus had done than a claim for his future supremacy: the words 'peace in heaven and glory in the highest' sufficiently indicated that no earthly kingship was in the minds of these his followers when they greeted him as 'the King that cometh in the name of the Lord.' The expression 'King of Israel' is dropped by the disciples, and also the word 'Hosanna,' which might be open to misconstruction by the enemies of Jesus. Alford explains : 'Hosanna —from Psalm cxviii. 25 = save now.' The Psalm runs : 'Save now, we beseech thee, O Lord.' The crowd composed of visitors to the feast had started that cry, and however discreet some of his disciples may have been, knowing how he had once charged them to tell no man that he was the Christ, the multitude were enamoured with that idea, and took it up enthusiastically. 'And the multitudes that went before him, and that followed, cried, saying, Hosanna to the son of David : Blessed *is* he that cometh in the name of the Lord ; Hosanna in the highest.' 'And they that went before, and they that followed, cried, Hosanna ; Blessed *is* he that cometh in the name of the Lord : Blessed *is* the kingdom that cometh, *the kingdom* of our father David : Hosanna in the highest.' It could not be helped : the conception of a temporal sovereign, and of a kingdom, not ' of God,' not ' of heaven,' but ' of David,' was ever uppermost in men's minds.

Not all among the multitude participated in these demonstrations. There was a sprinkling of Pharisees, who had come to watch and criticise. There was much that a hostile and fastidious observer might object to. Not every man in those days, any more than now, would strip off his coat in the open air, without caring about conventional etiquette. The social status of the class composing the crowd might be judged thereby. It was all very well for fishermen and others whose daily toil made such an action habitual, to be thus enthusiastic and demonstrative, but well-bred, cultured onlookers, who were careful to make broad their phylacteries and enlarge the borders of their garments, were little likely to use their robes for such a purpose or in such a fashion. The fact repeatedly stares us in the face, and here is another evidence of it, that the bulk of the disciples and welcomers of Jesus consisted of what would now be designated by the supercilious term, 'the lower orders,' or more correctly 'the working classes.' The men and women who, chiefly, came under the influence of Jesus resembled those composing the 'Salvation Army,' who of late years have been sought out and gained by 'General' Booth and his coadjutors. The very chiefest of the apostles, Peter and John, in the full tide of their spiritual gifts and successful preaching, were classed by the priestly rulers of the Jews as 'unlearned and ignorant men.' There were Pharisees who looked scornfully and disapprovingly on this scene of which Jesus was so conspicuously the central figure, and as the cavalcade swept onwards they expostulated with him on the unseemliness of such proceedings, and urged him to check his disciples in their singing. 'And some of the Pharisees from the multitude said unto him, Master (or, Teacher), rebuke thy disciples.' Their chant of praise, as recorded by Luke, had nothing in it about 'the king of Israel,' or 'the kingdom of David.' Whatever the multitudes might shout, the disciples, trained and taught by Jesus, were not likely to give expression to such ideas. The chosen apostles were careful, perhaps were directed by him, to lead the thoughts and voices of the multitude into a higher, holier channel, 'to rejoice and praise God with a loud voice for all the mighty works which they had seen;' and their salutation of Jesus as 'the King that cometh in the name of the Lord,' coupled with the refrain 'peace in heaven, and glory in the highest,' conveyed no thought of an earthly throne and kingdom. Jesus replied that the eulogy well beseemed his life-work and his teaching, and if the good works he had showed them from the Father were forbidden to be mentioned by the tongues of his disciples, the very stones might be expected to proclaim them. 'And he answered and said, I tell you that, if these shall hold their peace, the stones will cry out.' By selecting so strong an hyperbole Jesus, in the most emphatic way possible, justified his disciples and condemned the Pharisees. Not long ago they had banished him from Judæa, and they were now surprised and angered to find him setting at naught their decree, and actually about to enter Jerusalem amid the enthusiastic acclamations of the populace. 'The Pharisees therefore said among themselves, Behold (or, Ye behold) how ye prevail nothing: lo, the world is gone after him.' But there was no triumph, only sorrow, in the heart of Jesus. He knew well what would be the fatal result to himself of this his last visit, and he foresaw also the certain ruin of Jerusalem in days not far distant. As he approached the city his soul grew sad, and when he saw it stretched out before him, his emotions of grief and pity found vent in tears. In short, sobbing sentences, he bewailed the coming evils, all of which might have been prevented if only the citizens had known what was the true basis of peace and prosperity. 'And when he drew nigh, he saw the city and wept over it, saying, If thou (or, O that thou) hadst known in this day, even thou, the things, which belong unto peace! but now they are hid from thine eyes.' The national policy and the temper of the people would culminate in rebellion, a trial of strength and endurance between them and their enemies, bringing on the city the horrors of a weary siege, cruel, relentless carnage, and resulting finally in utter defeat and devastation. 'For the days shall come upon thee, when thine enemies will cast up a bank (Gr. palisade) about thee, and compass thee round, and keep thee in on every side, and shall dash thee to the ground, and thy children within thee; and they shall not leave in thee one stone upon another.' In all human history, national as well as individual, the Present is ever the father of the Future. 'If thou hadst known in this day,' said Jesus; (that is the reading of the two oldest MSS., omitting the word 'thy' before day): his teaching was meant to be the salvation of the people, but being thwarted and repudiated the opportunity was lost, and another chapter must be added to the bloodstained page of history, another attempt to conquer

^{19 Luke 44} force by force, another triumph of might over right: 'Because thou knewest not the time of thy visitation.' This was not the only occasion when Jesus gave expression to these thoughts, in conjunction with a lamentation over Jerusalem. The records of the Past were ominous in the extreme. 'It cannot be,' he once said, 'that a prophet perish out of Jerusalem.' And then he uttered an apostrophe, very similar to the foregoing, conceived in the same spirit and conveying the same ideas. 'O Jerusalem, Jerusalem, which killeth the prophets, and stoneth them that are sent unto her! how often would I have gathered thy children together, even as a hen *gathereth* her own brood under her wings, and ye would not! Behold, your house is left unto you *desolate:* and I say unto you, Ye shall not see me, until ye shall say, Blessed *is* he that cometh in the name of the Lord.' Taking the passages together, they elucidate each other. In the first place, however, a few technical points have to be considered. The Revisers have altered 'sent unto thee' to 'sent unto her' which is the rendering of Young and Tischendorf. The italicised word 'gathereth' is omitted by Young, not being in the original. The Revisers have omitted to italicise 'her' before wings; Young and Tischendorf render 'the wings.' The Revisers have italicised the word 'desolate,' which is not in the three oldest MSS. and is omitted by Young, Tischendorf and Alford. The Authorised Version has 'until *the time* come when ye shall say,' which is rendered by Young, 'till it come when ye may say,' altered by the Revisers in accordance with the two oldest MSS. to 'till ye shall say.' It is probable, as is supposed by many, that these verses have been inserted unchronologically by Luke. If he were in doubt where they ought properly to be placed, it would be natural for him to bring them in, as he has done, immediately after the mention of Jerusalem. In Matthew they occupy a different position, being introduced immediately after ^{23 Mat. 37-39} the condemnation of the Pharisees. 'O Jerusalem, Jerusalem, which killeth the prophets, and stoneth them that are sent unto her! how often would I have gathered thy children together, even as a hen gathereth her chickens under her wings, and ye would not! Behold, your house is left unto you desolate. For I say unto you, Ye shall not see me henceforth till ye shall say, Blessed *is* he that cometh in the name of the Lord.' The chief point of difference is the introduction in Matthew of the word 'henceforth.' There is some doubt as to the word 'desolate,' which the Revisers note is 'omitted by some ancient authorities.' It does not appear in the Vatican MS.

The import of the expression, 'Because thou knewest not the time of thy visitation,' now becomes clear. Jesus had often sought to draw Jerusalem to himself, but his efforts had failed. The simile he chose was striking and peculiar: 'How often did I desire to gather thy children together, even as a hen gathers her chickens under the wing, and ye desired not' (Tischendorf). The dread of a coming danger was in his mind, and he knew that only the protection he offered could save them from it. Yet his mode of defence was not after the fashion of the world: he urged no resistance, he uttered no rallying cry, he wielded no weapon of defence, but simply tried to attract men to himself, induce them to lay aside every thought of violence, and keep their souls in charity and peace. If his kingdom had been of this world, then would his servants have fought; but

his only effort and aim was to save others by sacrificing himself:
'If therefore ye seek me, let these go their way: that the word might   18 John 8, 9
be fulfilled which he spake, Of those whom thou hast given me, I
lost not one.' The spirit and teaching of Jesus forbade any resort to
violence and bloodshed, and led all who came to him to seek the
rectification of wrong and evil by other means, to overcome the
world by peace, and antidote its tribulations by the hope and foretaste
of the kingdom of God and heaven. 'Peace I leave with you; my   14 John 27
peace I give unto you: not as the world giveth, give I unto you.
Let not your heart be troubled, neither let it be fearful.' That
was his panacea for the trials of the time then present. True, his
wisdom then, as now, seemed folly to the world; only his disciples
could receive and comprehend his saying: 'These things have I   16 John 33
spoken unto you, that in me ye may have peace. In the world ye
have tribulation: but be of good cheer; I have overcome the world.'
Few indeed were they who embraced that doctrine, and thence his
lamentation over Jerusalem: 'O that thou hadst known in this day,
even thou, the things which belong unto peace.' The old, old
warlike spirit must needs revive, the cry of patriotism uprise, instead
of that nobler aspiration after a heavenly inheritance to which Jesus
called his followers, swords must clash, and blood must flow, and
brute force triumph as of yore. The tears of Jesus were shed over
his own lost cause in Jerusalem. It was appointed to him that he
should die for the people, and if he could only have drawn them
to himself, the nation would have been saved, and the ultimate
triumph of Christianity antedated by many, none can say how many,
centuries. To the high priest alone was given a prophetic insight of
this truth: 'A certain one of them, Caiaphas, being high priest that   11 John 49-52
year, said unto them, Ye know nothing at all, nor do ye take account
that it is expedient for you that one man should die for the people,
and that the whole nation perish not. Now this he said not of
himself: but being high priest that year, he prophesied that Jesus
should die for the nation; and not for the nation only, but that he
might also gather together into one the children of God that are
scattered abroad.' Not until the whole body of Christians are thus
gathered together into one united heavenly-minded phalanx, taking
all the precepts of Jesus for their creed and heritage, and suffering no
admixture of earthly elements with his pure, unworldly doctrine, can
Christianity assume the form which its founder sought to give it, and
bless mankind with the salvation which he offered them.

The omission of the word 'desolate' from the three oldest MSS. in
Luke, and from the Vatican and other ancient authorities in Matthew,
may be taken to indicate either that the word was first introduced by
Commentators to suit their view of the sense intended, or at the
least, that no stress is to be laid upon the word in interpreting
the passage. The expression, 'Behold, your house is left unto you,'
conveys the idea of the withdrawal of any attempt at guidance or
interference on the part of Jesus. It was their own house, 'your
house,' and it must now be 'left unto' them, to manage and rule as
they thought fit. This seems to be admitted by Alford, although he
at the same time thought there was an allusion to the temple. He
says: 'No more *God's* but *your house*—said primarily of the
temple,—then of Jerusalem,—and then of the whole land in which ye

dwell!' The efforts of Jesus to guide and save them having been repulsed, the people must be left to their own devices. This interpretation of the passage harmonises with what precedes, and also with the words which follow : 'Ye shall not see me henceforth, till ye shall say, Blessed is he that cometh in the name of the Lord.' Jesus could attempt no more ; he must leave them to themselves, and wait until they were prepared to welcome him as the divinely-commissioned Saviour. We see that the words of the carol sung by the disciples on the occasion of his triumphal approach to Jerusalem not only met his approval but were adopted by Jesus himself.

When the procession of disciples and others entered the city, the inhabitants naturally manifested considerable excitement and curiosity. 'And when he was come into Jerusalem, all the city was stirred, saying, Who is this?' The visits of Jesus to the metropolis being only occasional, he was not so well known there as in Galilee. 'And the multitudes said, This is the prophet, Jesus, from Nazareth of Galilee.' The distance between the two places being considerably over 50 miles, the career of Jesus did not come within the cognizance of dwellers at Jerusalem. His visits were at festival times, when there was a large influx of strangers ; probably most of those who sought him out at Jerusalem and attended his preaching there, had become acquainted with him in Galilee or elsewhere.

Jesus at once proceeded to the temple, and manifested much interest in what he saw going on about him. The night was approaching, he had freed himself from the presence of the clamorous multitude, keeping with him only the twelve apostles, and with them he retired to Bethany, which was about a mile and a half from Jerusalem. 'And he entered into Jerusalem, into the temple ; and when he had looked round about upon all things, it being now eventide, he went out unto Bethany with the twelve.' The next morning they returned to Jerusalem, and Jesus, ever more anxious about his work than about his food, began to suffer from hunger. 'And on the morrow, when they were come out from Bethany, he hungered.' Matthew adds that it was in the morning. 'Now in the morning as he returned to the city, he hungered.' The expression 'as he returned,' may be taken to indicate that he had started without breakfasting, and felt exhausted on the journey. On the road he saw a solitary fig tree, and made his way towards it. 'And seeing a (or, a single) fig tree by the way side, he came to it.' Mark explains that it was at some distance, and was seen to be in leaf, so that it was possible, though by no means certain, that fruit also might be found on it. 'And seeing a fig tree afar off having leaves, he came, if haply he might find anything thereon.' The word 'haply' implies that it was a mere chance, and the slender hope was doomed to disappointment ; 'and found nothing thereon, but leaves only.' Mark explains that the season was not sufficiently advanced to justify the expectation of fruit being found as a matter of course : 'and when he came to it, he found nothing but leaves ; for it was not the season of figs.' Having ascertained the fact, Jesus uttered some very remarkable words, not to his companions, but to the tree itself. 'And he saith unto it, Let there be no fruit from thee henceforward for ever.' Mark is to the same effect : 'And he answered and said unto it, No man eat fruit from thee henceforward.

for ever. And his disciples heard it.' It was a strange thing to say. Why did Jesus say it? Was it a mere expression dropped in haste, anger, disappointment, vindictiveness? That would be contrary to all we know of Jesus. No question appears to have been asked, no comment made. They went on their way, spent the day in Jerusalem, returned to Bethany, and the next morning passed the spot again. Then the incident was recalled to their minds. There stood the tree : but what had happened to it? Its foliage was fading, and a close examination showed that it had withered from the root upwards. 'And as they passed by in the morning, they saw the fig tree withered away from the roots.' Matthew condenses the account, saying nothing about the intervening day, but simply, 'And immediately the fig tree withered away.' The word 'immediately' stands in the Authorised Version as 'presently;' Young renders : 'And forthwith the fig tree withered.' The disciples were astounded at so inexplicable a phenomenon. The Anthorised Version puts their words in the form of an exclamation of surprise. 'And when the disciples saw it, they marvelled, saying, How soon is the fig tree withered away !' Tischendorf agrees with that, but Young renders it as a question : 'And the disciples having seen, wondered, saying, How did the fig-tree forthwith wither?' and the Revisers have done the same. 'And when the disciples saw it, they marvelled, saying, How did the fig tree immediately wither away?' One of the disciples called the attention of Jesus to the circumstance. 'And Peter calling to remembrance saith unto him, Rabbi, behold, the fig tree which thou cursedst is withered away.' The Revisers have altered 'Master' to 'Rabbi,' therein agreeing with Tischendorf, Young and Alford. The term was equivalent to 'Teacher,' and was by itself a mark of distinction, and on that account coveted by the Pharisees, for Jesus once described them as loving ' to be called of men Rabbi,' and added, 'But be not ye called Rabbi, for one is your teacher, and all ye are brethren.' The companionship between Jesus and his disciples, however intimate, was not, could not be of an ordinary kind. They had always a becoming sense of his superiority, and the esteem and honour in which they held him appear frequently in their mode of addressing him.

In the opinion of the disciples the utterance of Jesus was a malediction : Peter did not scruple to say, 'the fig tree which thou cursedst.' The miracle can be regarded in no other light. For this once, the power of Jesus was put forth to blight and destroy, instead of to bless and heal. Such an act could benefit no one : to kill a fruit-producing tree because it did not bear prematurely, offends our notions of wisdom and benevolence. That Jesus did this thing, can make no difference in the judgment we pass upon it. In some mysterious way, he had thwarted the operation of the laws of nature with respect to this tree, so that it ceased to draw nourishment out of the earth and the elements, and was transformed into a barren, useless stock. Once he had spoken a parable about a fig-tree, representing it to have been fruitless for three years together, and yet when the owner decided to cut it down, the experienced vinedresser pleaded for a fourth year's trial, to see the effect of increased care and culture. That parable harmonised with the mind and teaching of Jesus ; but now his own deed runs counter to it ; he goes out of his way, to seek for figs out of season, and failing to find them, he anathematises the tree and withers its root. Again the question presses: Why did he do this? Doubtless he had a motive. He himself gave the clue thereto, and explained the significance of his action. 'And Jesus answering saith unto them, Have faith in God.' That is the key note of the explanation. To blast the fig tree by a word, was the very reverse of faith in God: it was an interference with the divinely-arranged system of the universe, a transgression against the beneficent laws of nature, an exercise of human influence in opposition to the will of God, by whose providence the fruit tree bears fruit after its kind and in its proper season. The tongue and will of man are potent, aye! omnipotent, in the direction of such evils. Jesus asserted that fact: 'Verily I say unto you, Whosoever shall say unto this mountain, Be thou taken up and cast into the sea; and shall not doubt in his heart, but shall believe that what he saith cometh to pass; he shall have it.' The Sinaitic MS. begins: 'If you have faith in God, verily I say unto you . . ,' but that reading, although indicated by Tischendorf was not adopted by him. In the Authorised Version the verse ends with the words, 'he shall have whatsoever he saith,' which is now altered to, 'he shall have it,' in accordance with the two oldest MSS. Matthew's fuller record of the words of Jesus places the uprooting of the mountain and the withering of the fig tree in the same category. 'And Jesus answered and said unto them, Verily I say unto you, If ye have faith, and doubt not, ye shall not only do what is done to the fig tree, but even if ye shall say unto this mountain, Be thou taken up and cast into the sea, it shall be done.' The Authorised Version stands: 'ye shall not only do this *which is done* to the fig tree;' omitting the italicised words 'which is done,' the sentence would stand, 'ye shall not only do this to the fig tree.' This brings out the character of the action itself, as does also Young's literal rendering: 'not only this of the fig tree shall ye do.' The acts are of the same kind: both abnormal, needless, destructive, interfering with the settled order of the universe, bringing no advantage to mankind, but the reverse, introducing confusion into the harmony of nature, the human will, selfish, passionate, reckless, setting itself against physical arrangements and sequences ordained from of old by the will of God. Jesus was hungry, sought fruit, found none, and instantly cursed the tree appointed to bear it. There was none to say him nay: he had the power, a faith in his own word sufficient for the purpose, and he spoke the word and exercised the power. What he had done, others also could do: there is no limit to the operation of man's will up to the point in which he has confidence in himself. True, no man save Jesus knew the secret of working that mighty spiritual influence; but in the direction of beneficence he had imparted it to some extent to his disciples, and when they on one occasion had failed in their attempt to imitate him, he had attributed their want of success to a lack of faith, which faith he now declares to be an influence more subtile than the process of vegetable life, and mightier than the force of gravitation. Jesus is asserting the existence of a common attribute of humanity: 'Whosoever shall say . . shall not doubt in his heart . . shall believe that what he saith cometh to pass . . ye shall not only do what is done . . but even if ye shall say . . it shall be done.' It is all personal to man, a pure act of volition on his part: in fact and in a word—man's faith in himself. What Jesus urged them to aim at and cultivate was precisely the reverse of that. Instead of saying, Have faith in yourselves, he says: 'Have faith in God,' which Young renders, 'Have God's faith,' in opposition to man's faith. a faith submissive to the divine will and satisfied to rest upon the divine working. This unwonted, strange act of Jesus carried and proclaimed its own moral; it was as though he said to them, You see what mischief I am able to do. You will be able to do the same. I would have you fully conscious of that power, and draw from it a lesson, not of self-confidence and self-will, but of submissiveness and prayer. Let your faith work in that direction only. If you can do mischief, God can do all things; be persuaded that he doeth all things well, and strong in that faith, be passive, and make your requests known unto him. 'Therefore I say unto you, All [11 Mark 24] things whatsoever ye pray and ask for, believe that ye have received them, and ye shall have them.' The Authorised Version has: 'Whatsoever things ye desire, when ye pray,' which stands in the two oldest MSS, thus: 'What things soever ye pray and desire.' The Revised Version, 'whatsoever ye pray and ask for,' does not quite correspond with that, nor does Dr. Davidson's rendering of Tischendorf as, 'whatsoever ye pray for and ask.' In all three versions a formal petition is implied, whereas the words 'what things soever ye pray and desire,' may include both actual prayer and desire unspoken. The Authorised Version has, 'believe that ye receive,' now altered to 'believe that ye have received,' which Alford states is the reading of 'most ancient authorities;' it is adopted by Tischendorf, although not noted by him as the reading of either of the three oldest MSS. The sense appears to be this: Let your faith have reference to God. Whatever you ask, let it always be something which has already been vouchsafed by God, and which cannot therefore be contrary to his will; let it never be anything which lies outside the scope of his gifts, or is opposed to his providential arrangements, as to blight a tree or overturn a mountain. Matthew's account is condensed. He simply records the saying thus: 'And all things, what- [21 Mat. 22] soever ye shall ask in prayer, believing, ye shall receive.' So much of the discourses of Jesus as those who first reported them were able to record, has been handed down to us. In this instance Matthew's narrative is imperfect. Even when the sayings of Jesus are noted, however correctly and fully, it does not follow that the evangelists always grasped their meaning. To elucidate that, to get, as it were, behind the mind of Jesus, it is necessary to compare the records and exercise a careful and independent judgment. Mark has here brought out in the discourse of Jesus, a connecting link. 'Therefore I say unto you,' which Matthew seems to have missed. Jesus brings into close connection two things which we are apt to view apart: the power of man, and the power of prayer. He argues: because you are able of yourselves to exercise unbounded supremacy over nature, therefore be sure that whatever you confidently ask or wish, you will receive; therefore ask and wish nothing which you ought not. Jesus willed the destruction of the fig tree: he brought to bear upon it, we know not how, some mysterious power, we know not what, and his desire was accomplished. If a man wills to overturn a mountain, it is because he knows that the act lies within the compass of his power; if not, his professed will would be an imposture upon himself. Addressing his disciples generally, not individually, Jesus added that if they desired anything, they must believe that it was a thing granted them to have, and their wish would be fulfilled. The answer to prayer, 'uttered or unexpressed,' is through human instrumentality. We pray for daily bread. There is no need for the formal utterance of the petition, except that it is well for us to look up to God, and when we do so to recognise the fact that the supply of our necessities is in harmony with and dependent upon his will. The life of every creature is in itself a prayer for the nourishment needed for its preservation.

<small>104 Psa. 27</small>

'These wait all upon thee,
That thou mayest give them their meat in due season.'

But the skies do not rain down upon man unground corn or flour or wheat: he must sow, reap, grind, and prepare the food; not each individual for himself, but some for all: the community as a whole thus bringing to pass the universal prayer, 'Give us this day our daily bread.' It is so with everything we need, pray for and desire: all things vouchsafed to mankind must come to us through men, in connection with that power of self-help and mastery over the material world with which it has pleased God to endow us. 'Therefore I say unto you, All things whatsoever ye pray and ask for, believe that ye have received them, and ye shall have them.' That is the law of God's giving and of man's asking and receiving.

And the law of forgiveness runs parallel therewith. Jesus touched upon that also. 'And whensoever ye stand praying, forgive, if ye have aught against any one; that your Father also which is in heaven may forgive you your trespasses.' The Jewish doctors held that none but God could forgive sins, and that it was rank blasphemy for men to profess to do so. Jesus taught, on the contrary, that the forgiveness of sins was the privilege of humanity, and that the prerogative of divine forgiveness would not, could not, be exercised independently thereof. Not only did he class them together, but he declared plainly that they must act in conjunction. 'For if ye forgive men their trespasses, your heavenly Father will also forgive you. But if ye forgive not men their trespasses, neither will your Father forgive your trespasses.' The disciples of Jesus are bound to pray in these terms: 'Forgive us our sins; for we ourselves also forgive every one that is indebted to us.' Every law of God is for man's benefit, and every infraction of his law a sin against humanity. So long as man continues to call man to account for wrongs committed, forgiveness is an impossibility. To suppose that God forgives when man does not, or that man can forgive when God does not, is to take away reality from forgiveness, making it not a fact, but a form of words, a mere sentiment or emotion of the mind. Jesus did not take that surface view of the question. His teaching went deeper far, down to the very root of the matter. He saw, and tried to make his disciples see, that God's forgiveness was contingent upon man's, the latter being the antecedent and earnest, if not the form and embodiment of the former. This doctrine is too important to be passed without a thorough investigation of the Scriptural meaning of the word forgiveness. According to Cruden's Concordance the words 'forgive, forgiven, forgiveth, forgiveness, forgivenesses,' occur in the Old Testament 44 times. Three of those passages relate to human forgiveness, and 41 to divine forgiveness, and in every instance the actual remission of a punishment is connected with the word. Only with respect to two passages could there be a moment's hesitation in arriving at that conclusion : the first relates to the forgiveness of a woman's vow, and the context there (verse 15), declares that the husband 'shall bear her iniquity ; ' the second is : 'Thou, Lord, art good and ready to forgive,' and there the context alludes to a prayer for help in a day of trouble. Some of the passages in Leviticus and Numbers relate to offerings, ending with the words, 'they shall be forgiven . . he shall be forgiven :' to such instances the statement applies, that under the law 'every transgression and disobedience received a just recompense of reward.' In the Gospels forgiveness is alluded to 32 times. The passages may be classified as follows : [30 Num. 5, 8, 12] [86 Ps. 5] [2 Heb. 2]

(a) By the Son of man, 12 times ; (b) divine, conditional on human, 8 times ; (c) of a brother, 3 times ; (d) of a sinful woman, twice ; (e) of all sins except blasphemy against the Holy Spirit, 5 times ; (f) Father, forgive them, once; (g) it should be forgiven them, once. There is nothing in these passages inconsistent with the previous conclusion that forgiveness signifies the remission of a punishment, an actual deliverance from a condition brought about by wrong conduct. [4 Mark 12]

In the Acts and Epistles forgiveness is alluded to 16 times. The passages may be classified as follows : (a) Of offences, sins, trespasses, and avoidance of punishment, 12 times ; (b) mutual, 3 times ; (c) 'Forgive me this wrong,' once. There is still nothing to alter the previous conclusion. The idea of absolution or forgiveness apart from an actual, evident remission of punishment, has no foundation in Scripture. If the penalty due to an offence is exacted by man, it cannot truly be declared forgiven by God : 'Forgive . . that your Father also which is in heaven may forgive :' that was the doctrine of Jesus, the aspect of divine in conjunction with human forgiveness which he repeatedly and earnestly impressed upon his disciples. Let us honestly and boldly face the truth in this matter. Take the case of a thief or a murderer, the one condemned to penal servitude, the other to death. Unless the sentence be revoked it would be absurd to say that either of the criminals was forgiven : they are left to bear the punishment of their iniquity, and death to the manslayer was ordained by God himself. The accusers, the witnesses, the jury, the judge, the jailer, the executioner, all combine to punish the transgression, not to forgive it. Suppose Jesus were to revisit the world, and were to say, Forgive those men. That could have but one meaning : remit the penalty. Yet that would be precisely what he had said before. That earnest seeker after truth, Count Leon Tolstoi, has grappled with this difficult question among others. His reasonings, fearless, unsophisticated, luminous, are well worth our pondering. He says :* 'I was drawn away from the Church by various singularities in its dogmas ; by its approval of persecution, capital punishment, war ; and also by its intolerance of all other forms of worship than its own ; but my faith in the teaching of the Church was shaken still more by its indifference to what seemed to me the

---

* "What I Believe," pp. 6—25.

very basis of the teaching of Christ, and by its evident partiality for what I could not consider an essential part of that doctrine ... I turned away from the Church. For the precepts which were given me by the Church concerning belief in dogmas, observance of the sacraments, fast-days, prayers, I did not care ; and precepts really founded on the teachings of Christ were wanting ... What perplexed me most of all was, that all the evil things that men do, such as condemning private individuals, whole nations, or other religions ; and the inevitable results of these condemnations—executions and wars—were justified by the Church. I saw that the doctrine of Christ, which teaches us humility, tolerance, forgiveness, self-denial, and love, was extolled by the Church, but that at the same time she sanctioned what was incompatible with such teachings ... It was only after losing all faith in the explanations of learned theology and criticism, and after laying them all aside, in obedience to the words of Christ (Mark x. 15), that I began to understand what had till then seemed incomprehensible to me. It was not by deep thought only, or by skilfully comparing or commenting on the texts of the Gospel, that I came to understand the doctrine. On the contrary, all grew clear to me for the very reason that I had ceased to rest on mere interpretations. The text that gave me the key to the truth was the thirty-ninth verse of the fifth chapter of St. Matthew : " Ye have heard that it hath been said, An eye for an eye, and a tooth for a tooth. *But I say unto you, that ye resist not evil.*" The simple meaning of these words suddenly flashed full upon me ; I accepted the fact that Christ *meant* exactly what He *said;* and then, though I had found nothing new, all that had hitherto obscured the truth cleared away, and the truth itself arose before me in all its solemn importance ... Now I understood that the whole force of the teaching lay in the words, " resist not evil," and that all the context was but an application of that great precept. I saw that Christ does not require us to turn the other cheek, and to give away our cloak, in order to make us suffer ; but He teaches us not to resist evil, and warns us that so doing may involve personal suffering ... Christ meant to say, " Whatever men may do to you, bear, suffer, submit ; but never resist evil." What could be clearer, more intelligible, and more indubitable than this ? As soon as I understood the exact meaning of these simple words, all that had appeared confused to me in the doctrine of Christ grew intelligible ; what had seemed contradictory now became consistent, and what I had deemed superfluous became indispensable. All united in one whole, one part fitting into and supporting the other, like the pieces of a broken statue put together again in their proper places. This doctrine of " non-resistance " is commended again and again in the Gospels. In the " Sermon on the Mount " Christ represents his followers—*i.e.*, those who follow this law of non-resistance—as liable to be persecuted, stoned, and reduced to beggary. Elsewhere He tells us that the disciple who does not take up His cross, who is not willing to renounce all, cannot be His follower, and He thus describes the man who is ready to bear the consequences that may result from the practice of the doctrine of non-resistance. Christ says to His disciples : " Be poor, be ready to bear persecution, suffering, and even death, without resisting evil." He prepared for suffering and death

Himself without resisting evil ; reproved Peter who grieved over Him because He proposed thus to yield ; and he died, forbidding others to resist evil, remaining true to His own doctrine in His own example. All His first disciples obeyed the same law of non-resistance of evil ; and passed their lives in disability and persecution. We may bring forward as an objection, the difficulty of always obeying such a law ; we may even say, as multitudes do, that it is a foolish doctrine, that Christ was a dreamer, an idealist, who gave precepts which it is impossible to follow. But, whatever our objections may be, we cannot deny that Christ expresses His meaning most clearly and distinctly ; and His meaning is, that man must not *resist evil*; he who fully accepts His teaching cannot resist evil . . . If a man were to set all the faculties of his mind to the annulling of a given law, what more forcible argument could he use for its suppression than that it was an impracticable law, and that the legislator's own opinion of it was, that it could not be kept without supernatural aid ? And yet this was exactly what I had thought about the commandment " not to resist evil." I tried to remember when and how the strange idea had first come into my mind, that the doctrine of Christ was divine in authority, but impossible in practice. On reviewing my past life, I discovered that this idea had never been transmitted to me in all its nakedness, for then it would have repelled me ; but that I had imperceptibly imbibed it from my earliest childhood, and that the associations of my life had confirmed the strange error. I was taught from my childhood that Christ is God, and that His teaching is divine and authoritative ; while, on the other hand, I was also told to respect those institutions which, by means of violence, secured my safety from evil ; I was taught to honour those institutions as being sacred. I was taught to resist evil ; and it was instilled into me that it was humiliating and dishonourable to submit to evil, and to suffer from it ; and that it was praiseworthy to resist evil. I was taught to condemn and to execute. I was taught to make war, *i.e.*, to resist evil by murder. The army, a member of which I was, was called a "Christ-loving" army, and its mission was consecrated by the Church. I was taught to resist an offender by violence ; to avenge a private insult, or one against my native land, by violence. All this was never regarded as wrong, but, on the contrary, I was told that it was perfectly right, and in nowise contrary to Christ's doctrine. All surrounding interests, such as the peace and safety of myself and family, and of my property, were based on the law that was rejected by Christ—on the law of "a tooth for a tooth." Ecclesiastical teachers told me that the doctrine of Christ was divine, but that its observance was impossible on account of the weakness of human nature ; and that the grace of God alone could enable us to keep this law. Secular teachers told me, and the whole order of life proved, that the teaching of Christ was impracticable and ideal, and that we must, in fact, live *contrary* to His doctrine. Such a notion of the practical impossibility of following the divine doctrine was imbibed by me gradually and almost imperceptibly. I was so accustomed to it, it coincided so well with all my animal feelings, that I had never observed the contradiction in which I lived. I did not see that it was impossible to admit the Godhead of Christ—the basis of whose teaching is non-resistance of evil—and, at the same time, to work consciously and calmly for the institutions of property, courts of law, kingdoms, the army, and so on. It could not be consistent for us to regulate our lives *contrary* to the doctrine of Christ, and then pray to the same Christ that we might be enabled to keep His commandments—to "forgive," and not to "resist evil." . . . In *word* I acknowledged the teaching of Christ as sacred; but I did not carry out that teaching in *deed*, for I admitted, and respected, the unchristian institutions which surrounded me . . . To affirm that the Christian doctrine refers only to personal salvation, and has no bearing upon state affairs, is a great error. To say so, is but to assert an audacious, groundless, most evident untruth, which a moment's serious reflection suffices to destroy. Well, say I to myself, I will not resist evil; as a private man, I will let myself be smitten; but what am I to do if an enemy invade my native land, or other nations oppress it? I am called upon to take part in a struggle against evil—to go and kill. The question immediately arises: Which will be serving God, and which will be serving "toga" (vain things)? To go, or not to go? Suppose I am a peasant; I am chosen as the senior member of my village, as judge, as juryman. I am bound to take an oath, to judge, to punish. Fellow-creature, what am I to do? I have again to choose between the law of God and the law of man. Or let us say, I am a monk, and live in a monastery; the neighbouring peasants have taken possession of the hay we had mown for our own use. I am sent to take part in a struggle against evil—to prosecute these men. I have again to choose between the laws of God and the laws of man. None of us can evade the demand for such a decision. To say nothing of the class of society which I belong to—military men, judges, administrators, whose whole lives are passed in resisting evil —there is not a single private individual, be he ever so insignificant, who has not to choose between serving God by fulfilling His commandments, or serving the "toga" in the Government institutions of his country. Our private lives are interwoven with the organization of the State, and the latter requires unchristian duties of us, contrary to the commandment of Christ. At the present time, the military service, which is obligatory on all, and the participation of each, as jurymen, in the courts of law, place the dilemma with striking clearness before all. Each man is called upon to take up an instrument of murder—a gun, a sword—even if he do not kill a fellow creature; he loads the gun and sharpens the sword, *i.e.*, he is ready to commit murder. Each citizen is called upon to enter the courts of law, to take part in judging and punishing his fellow creature; *i.e.*, each must renounce the doctrine of Christ which teaches us not to resist evil . . . Christ says: "Resist not evil." The sole object of courts of law is—to resist evil. Christ enjoins us to return good for evil. Courts of law return evil for evil. Christ says: "Make no distinction between the just and the unjust." Courts of law do nothing else. Christ says: "Forgive all; forgive not once, not seven times, forgive without end. Love your enemies. Do good to them that hate you." Courts of law do not forgive, but they punish; they do not do good, but evil, to those whom they call the enemies of society."

The world and the Church, if they will but hearken, are indebted to Count Leon Tolstoi for his uncompromising logic. However startling and unconventional this disclosure of the naked truth. it is well for us to recognise the true form of Christianity, undraped by the garments woven by human hands after the fashion of the world. Like Luther, Tolstoi is bold enough to think and act for himself, and his voice and example are a trumpet call to the slumbering churches. Christ's doctrine is clear and incontrovertible. The maxims of worldly prudence by which it has been obscured, and the qualifications and exceptions devised by men, must needs be swept away. That being done, the only question is as to the limitations laid down by Christ himself. Did he impose his teachings upon all men, and call upon all to follow them? Assuredly he did not. That fact has been lost sight of by Tolstoi. What Jesus spake, he spake to his disciples, and he repelled from discipleship all who were not prepared to adopt his teaching, with all the suffering, self-denial, and self-sacrifice it entailed. Jesus drew a broad line of demarcation between his disciples and mankind in general. 'They are not of the world, even as I am not of the world.' They were separated from other men, called to live an unworldly life. There are precepts of universal obligation, but this is not one of them. God 'commandeth men that they should all everywhere repent:' not that they should all become disciples. 'God our Saviour; who willeth that all men should be saved, and come to the knowledge of the truth:' we must not presume to add: and profess themselves disciples of Jesus. The preaching of Jesus to men in general is thus summarised: 'Repent ye, and believe the gospel;' and his disciples 'went out, and preached that *men* should repent.' Not a word did Jesus say to the multitudes to this effect: 'Ye are the salt of the earth ... Ye are the light of the world:' such teaching, although in public, is addressed to his disciples, to whom he could say also: 'Blessed are ye when *men* shall reproach you, and persecute you, and say all manner of evil against you falsely, for my sake.' It excited the astonishment of the disciples that Jesus always taught the multitudes in parabolic form: 'Without a parable spake he nothing unto them.' And he explained that they were neither disposed nor able to receive from him any deeper teaching: 'Unto you it is given to know the mysteries of the kingdom of God: but to the rest in parables; that seeing they may not see, and hearing they may not understand.' There is no foundation for the idea that Jesus expected or desired that all men should follow the precepts given to his disciples. On one occasion Peter asked him: 'Speakest thou this parable unto us, or even unto all?' That question alone is sufficient proof that the disciples did not regard every doctrine of Jesus as of universal application. Such an assumption, however general, is as absurd as it would be to imagine the mysteries and duties of Freemasonry to be incumbent upon those who have never joined that fraternity. Jesus enlisted his disciples for no light enterprise. He had come to establish the rule of heaven upon earth, the kingdom of God among mankind. That involved the annulment of ancient and divinely-authorised laws, and the substitution of higher principles of action. It was a new departure; a fresh step onward in the progress of humanity. It was decreed, moreover, that Jesus himself must be the first martyr in his own cause; and it is a sublime fact, of vast significance, that a conference was held between himself, Moses and Elijah, on the mountain-top, wherein was discussed the subject of

^{9 Luke 31} 'his decease which he was about to accomplish at Jerusalem.' The first Jewish lawgiver approved and directed the course adopted by Jesus, sanctioning and welcoming his method of enlarging and altering the former code, Moses himself revisiting the earth, acknowledg-
^{5 Mat. 38, 39} ing Jesus, and thereby tacitly endorsing his command: 'Ye have heard that it was said, An eye for an eye, and a tooth for a tooth: but I say unto you, Resist not him that is evil.' That was but one of many precepts, all equally startling, connected therewith. The disciples were forbidden to take an oath, to go to law, to resent an outrage, to accumulate property, to perform the functions of a judge. Tolstoi writes: 'Now I understand what Christ meant when he said, "Ye have heard that it hath been said, An eye for an eye, and a tooth for a tooth. And I say unto you, that ye resist not evil." Christ means, "You have been taught to consider it right and rational to protect yourselves against evil by violence, to pluck out an eye for an eye, to institute courts of law for the punishment of criminals, to have a police, an army, to defend you against the attacks of an enemy; but I say to you, do no violence to any man, take no part in violence, never do evil to any man, not even to those whom ye call your enemies." I now understood that, in this doctrine of non-resistance, Christ not only tells us what the natural result of following this doctrine will be, but by placing the same doctrine in opposition to the Mosaic law, the Roman law, and the various codes of the present time, He clearly shows that it ought to be the basis of our social existence, and should deliver us from the evil we have brought on ourselves. He says: "You think to amend evil by your laws, but they only aggravate it. There is one way by which you can put a stop to evil; it is by indiscriminately returning good for evil. You have tried the other law for thousands of years; now try Mine, which is the very reverse."' In the early days of Christianity the disciples of Jesus acted up to his precepts. Justin Martyr (A.D. 140) says: 'We who were once slayers of one another, do not now fight against our enemies.' Irenæus, bishop of Lyons (A.D. 167) states that the followers of Jesus had disused their weapons of war, and no longer knew how to fight. Tertullian, later (A.D. 200), alludes to Christians who were engaged in military pursuits; but on another occasion informs us that many soldiers quitted those pursuits in consequence of their conversion to Christianity, and repeatedly expresses his opinion that any participation in war is unlawful for believers in Jesus, not only because of the idolatrous practices of the Roman armies, but because Christ has forbidden the use of the sword and the revenge of injuries. Origen (A.D. 230) in his work against Celsus says: 'We have become for the sake of Jesus the children of peace. By our prayers we fight for our king abundantly, but take no part in his wars, even though he urge us.' Is it wonderful that the law which regulates God's kingdom in heaven, should seem out of place and chimerical when introduced into man's kingdom, or rather the devil's kingdom, upon earth? The aim of Jesus was to introduce into human society that heavenly-mindedness by which alone it can be purified, regenerated, transformed. The new leaven must be put into the old lump, there to grow and spread until the whole should become leavened. It must needs be that the Founder of the new religion, and his first followers, should be martyrs in the cause; and

that others should rise up afterwards, and carry on the work in the same way and spirit. That is the true ministry of Christ, the true preaching of the cross. The need of the world cries out for the constant presence and example of a body of men prepared to live entirely in accordance with the rule of life laid down by Jesus, and to suffer gladly all the consequences. That ideal has been lost sight of, and instead thereof we have a Clergy claiming the right of administering sacraments of Baptism and Holy Communion, men who expound the Scriptures to us, or for us, christen us, indoctrinate us, marry us, visit us in sickness, bury us. Did Christ ever say one word about such a sphere of duty for his followers? That is not his work, his method, his scheme of action. One Tolstoi is worth an army of such evangelisers. Not that our clerical brethren are to be reproached for the position they occupy. They have not made it for themselves; they have simply inherited it; clergy and laity alike, we are all what our forefathers have made us. The so-called Christian community is full of unchristian notions; about salvation, war, law, the rights and duties of property. Society has never yet been organised upon the Christian basis. That is a consummation which can only be arrived at gradually; and the departure from the foundation which was laid by Jesus and his apostles has thrown it back many centuries. Only by reverting to his plan can the gospel have free course, run, and be glorified. The first step towards success is to discern what is lacking. There are multitudes willing to devote themselves to the cause of Jesus, and to do all that he commands, if only his requirements and the world's necessities be rightly apprehended. Mistakes of judgment and of principle in this matter are fatal to the progress of Christianity. The doctrine of Jesus must be disentangled from the parasitic growth of human maxims by which it has been covered and stifled. Let the professed followers of Jesus be called by what name they may: ministers of Christ, disciples, deacons, priests, pastors, bishops; only let it be understood that they are bound to frame their lives in exact accordance with the pattern of Christ's life and the spirit and letter of his teachings. Such men will be the salt of the earth, the light of the world, seen and known of all men, like a city set upon a hill which cannot be hid. With such leaders in light and love, the church will be constituted according to Christ's ideal. The profession of discipleship must be purely optional, as Jesus intended it to be, and all ordained thereto must take up the cross, relinquish wealth, scorn ambition, seek the honour which comes from God only, have their treasure in heaven, their hearts being there also, decline to take any oath by way of allegiance or otherwise, refrain from judicial proceedings, refuse to fight in any cause, either labour for a bare subsistence and distribute the overplus, or be content to give their time and labour to the church in exchange for food, raiment and shelter. Such men, and such men only, will be able to take up the apostle's words: 'Herein is love made perfect with us, that we may 4 i. John 17 have boldness in the day of judgement; because as he is, even so are we in this world.' They would be living sermons, epistles of Christ, seen and known of all men, 'written not with ink, but with the Spirit 3 ii. Cor. 3 of the living God.' What is wanted is a change, not of men, but of aim and system: that instead of simply hearing, year after year and generation after generation, the same doctrines inculcated, we should have ever before our eyes patterns and examples of men who, with like passions to ourselves, live the life ordained for them by Christ, each of them ready to say, if need be, with the apostle Paul: 'Now I rejoice in my sufferings for your sake, and fill up on my part that which is lacking of the afflictions of Christ in my flesh for his body's sake, which is the church.' In the strife for freedom and for truth, they must needs sometimes suffer who stand foremost; but the bitterness of the world's persecution is past, and an implicit adherence to the doctrine of non-resistance now, might not entail the frightful penalties endured by martyrs in darker ages. Be it remembered too, that the chief persecutors in bygone times were men who called and deemed themselves Christians, but who, in that matter at least, were as far off from the teaching and spirit of Christ as heaven is from earth, or from hell. If the true doctrine of Jesus had not been wholly obliterated from the minds of those who claimed to be descendants from him and his apostles, it would have been impossible for them to lift a hand against any man, far less against those they sought to influence and convert. When the church of Christ begins to adopt his policy, then Christianity will begin to flourish and bear its proper fruit of righteousness and peace. If the gospel of Jesus does not triumph, after all these centuries of preaching,—and who can dare to say it does?—it must be because some fundamental human error mars and hinders the heaven-sent gift. When that is recognised, the question of amendment will become practical, and not much will be wanted to ensure success. The commandments of Jesus involve self-denial, but they are not grievous. The pecuniary emoluments of most clergymen are so small already, that it would be no sacrifice to them were they formally to renounce, in Christ's name, all hope and desire of property. The great difficulty and trial in connection with that, was the necessity it laid upon men of abstaining from marriage, lest at their death those they loved should be left without provision. But the beneficent system of life assurance would now obviate that, so ameliorating the stern necessity of renouncing for Christ's sake wife and children as well as money and lands. Of course, under the system laid down by Jesus, pluralities and the huge incomes of our Bishops must be abolished: they are of the world, worldly, and befit not those who profess to be followers of a heavenly Master. But there is room in the Church for all, for men of wealth, culture, leisure, who could still devote themselves to preaching and other clerical offices, only taking second rank instead of first, renouncing the vain, pretentious claim of apostolical succession, in favour of those who in deed and in truth prove themselves imitators of Jesus and the apostles by life-long poverty and self-sacrifice, deliberately, voluntarily faced for the kingdom of heaven's sake. They alone can claim the title of soldiers of the Cross, and infinitely preferable would be their lot in this life, whatever persecutions and sufferings they might be called to endure, than is that of troops in a fighting army. Tolstoi draws the following graphic contrast between the soldiers of Christ and of the world :* 'Leaving their parents, their wives and children, they go in their buffoon attire, blindly submissive to some superior whom they hardly know; cold, hungry, worn out by a march above

---

* "What I Believe," p. 182.

their strength, they follow him like a herd of oxen to the slaughter. But they are not oxen, they are men! They cannot help knowing that they are driven to slaughter, with the unsolvable question, Why must I go? and with despair in their hearts they go on, many dying off through cold, hunger, and infectious diseases, till those that are left are placed under bullets and cannon-balls, and ordered to kill men whom they know nothing about. They kill and are at last killed themselves, and not one of those who kills his fellow-creature knows why he does so . . . And no sooner does anyone call than others go to the same dreadful suffering and to death. And nobody finds it hard. Neither do they themselves think it hard, nor do their fathers and mothers think so; the latter even advise their children to go. Not only do they think it necessary and unavoidable, but even perfectly right and moral. We might think the fulfilling of Christ's doctrine difficult if it were really an easy and pleasant thing to live according to the teaching of the world. But it is much more difficult, dangerous and painful to do so than it is to live up to the doctrine of Christ. It is said that formerly there were martyrs for Christianity, but these were exceptional cases; we reckon about three hundred and eighty thousand voluntary and involuntary martyrs for Christianity in the course of 1800 years. Now count those that have died for the teaching of the world, and for each martyr for Christianity you will find a thousand martyrs for the world's sake, whose sufferings were a hundredfold more dreadful. Thirty millions have been killed in war during the present century alone. Those were all martyrs for the world's sake. Had they but rejected the teaching of the world, even without following the doctrine of Christ, they would have escaped suffering and death . . . We need not be martyrs for Christ's sake; that is not what He requires of us. But he teaches us to cease martyrizing our own selves for the sake of the false teaching of the world. The doctrine of Christ has a deep metaphysical purport; it has a purport general to all humanity; the doctrine of Christ has the simplest, clearest, most practical purport for each of us. We may express this idea in a few words. Christ teaches men not to act foolishly. It this lies the simplest sense of Christ's doctrine, and it is one each has it in his power to understand.' There is a mine of philosophy in that simple sentence of Tolstoi: 'Christ teaches men not to act foolishly;' and also in the following: 'In order to secure an uncertain life, for an uncertain future, we resolutely ruin our real lives in the actual present.' The salvation designed by Christ is the salvation of mankind in this life. Losing sight of that truth, our spiritual guides teach us to acquiesce in its postponement to the next. Not aiming at Christ's pattern-life themselves, they have left the world to its own course, and instead of overcoming it have been overcome by it.

In the Authorised Version the following verse is added: 'But if ye do not forgive, neither will your Father which is in heaven forgive your trespasses.' This is not in the two oldest MSS., and the Revisers have banished it to the margin.

The expression, 'No man eat fruit from thee henceforward for ever' is rendered by Dr. Young literally, 'No more from thee—for the age—may any eat fruit.' Obviously the 'age' or natural duration of the tree is alluded to. In the same way, when Jesus promises men life 'to the age,' or 'age-during life,' the meaning is restricted to the full term of man's natural existence.

On returning to Jerusalem after spending a night in Bethany, Jesus entered the temple. He found it already occupied. It was transformed for the time being into a market place. Traffic and money changing were going on, and sellers of doves were comfortably seated. Not for such purposes had the temple been built, and to see its sacredness thus set at naught excited the indignation of Jesus. Unhesitatingly and alone he undertook the task of preventing such acts of desecration. 'And Jesus entered into the temple of God, and cast out all them that sold and bought in the temple, and overthrew the tables of the money-changers, and the seats of them that sold the doves.' The words 'of God' after 'temple' are not in the two oldest MSS., and the Revisers note that they are omitted in 'many ancient authorities.' Luke's account is very concise: 'And he entered into the temple, and began to cast out them that sold.' The words 'and them that bought' are omitted by the Revisers, not being in the two oldest MSS. Mark's account shows that Jesus not only ejected the trespassers but held possession, not even allowing those bearing vessels to pass through the building. 'And they come to Jerusalem: and he entered into the temple, and began to cast out them that sold and them that bought in the temple, and overthrew the tables of the money-changers, and the seats of them that sold the doves; and he would not suffer that any man should carry a vessel through the temple.' Luke continues: 'saying unto them, It is written, And my house shall be a house of prayer: but ye have made it a den of robbers.' The conciseness of the narrative might lead to the conclusion that these words were addressed to the traffickers, but Mark explains that they formed part of a subsequent discourse: 'And he taught, and said unto them, Is it not written, My house shall be called a house of prayer for all the nations? but ye have made it a den of robbers.' Matthew is as follows: 'And he saith unto them, It is written, My house shall be called a house of prayer: but ye make it a den of robbers.' Following the two oldest MSS., the Revisers have altered 'ye have made' to 'ye make,' rendered by Alford and Tischendorf 'ye are making.' The passage in Isaiah stands: 'Mine house shall be called an house of prayer for all peoples.' The second portion appears to be a quotation based upon the words of Jeremiah: 'Is this house which is called by my name, become a den of robbers in your eyes?' Having expelled the godless, grasping traders, Jesus is expostulating with the people for permitting such a scandalous misuse of the temple. The abuse was of long standing, and needed to be put down with a strong hand. The work of Jesus in the place was indeed sacred: he not only taught, but put forth his marvellous powers of healing. Blind men and cripples found their way to the temple, and received the blessing of restored sight and vigour. 'And the blind and the lame came to him in the temple: and he healed them.'

Very near the beginning of John's gospel stands the following record: 'And the passover of the Jews was at hand, and Jesus went up to Jerusalem. And he found in the temple those that sold oxen and sheep and doves, and the changers of money sitting · and he made a scourge of cords, and cast all out of the temple, both the sheep and the oxen; and he poured out the changers' money, and overthrew their tables; and to them that sold the doves he said, 'Take these things hence; make not my Father's house a house of merchandise.' This is so similar to the foregoing accounts that, apart from any apparent reason to the contrary, we should assume the incident to be one and the same. That idea is repudiated by Alford. He says: 'It is impossible to suppose that St. Matthew or St. John, or any one but moderately acquainted with the events which he undertook to relate, should have made such a gross error in chronology as must be laid to the charge of one or other of them, if these two occurrences were *the same*.' That argument would be valid enough on two assumptions: (1) that it was always the intention of the evangelists to write chronologically; (2) that the manuscript was bound together like a modern book, and so bound before it left the hands of its author. There is no evidence, no probability that such was the case. The original records of what Jesus did and said were most likely made at the time, as opportunity offered. This applies especially to John's gospel, which contains long discourses of Jesus, the recording of which was not attempted by any other evangelist. If the leaves were numbered at all, the numbering would most likely not be consecutive from first to last: each portion might be paged separately. In that case, the order of the events would depend upon the binder rather than the writer. The Rev. J. J. Halcombe claims to have made the important discovery that an entire section of Luke's narrative has been displaced from time immemorial, and that the portion from the 14th verse of the 12th chapter to the 21st verse of the 13th chapter should be inserted between verses 21 and 22 of the 8th chapter. The close agreement between John's account and that of the three other evangelists may be taken to indicate that it has been misplaced in the fourth gospel. Both this latter portion of the 2nd chapter and the whole of the 3rd chapter of John, relating the conversation with Nicodemus, probably belonged to a later period. It is not easily conceivable that Jesus would have commenced his career with such an action, or that he should have been visited by a ruler of the Pharisees so soon after his first miracle in Cana of Galilee, with the acknowledgment: 'Rabbi, we know that thou art a teacher come from God: 3 John 2 for no man can do these signs that thou doest, except God be with him.'

Whether Jesus twice in his life, or once only, took upon himself to purge the temple, is not a question of much importance. Only John makes mention of the oxen and sheep, and of the scourge of cords, which would be necessary in order to drive them out. Alford observes: 'That our Lord used the scourge on the beasts only, not on the sellers of them, is almost necessarily contained in the form of the sentence here: which, according to the grammar of the original, should be rendered, "He drove all out of the temple, both the sheep and the oxen."' The Revisers have adopted that rendering, instead of the Authorised Version, 'he drove them all out of the temple, and the sheep, and the oxen.' We may feel sure that Jesus never lifted his hand against any man. Luke says only, he 'began to cast out them that sold,' which seems to involve physical force, if not herculean strength. But the other evangelists explain the method by which he accomplished the object : when the sheep and oxen were driven away, the owners must of course follow ; when the bowls of coin were overturned together with the tables, the money-changers would be glad to collect their money and escape from the presence of Jesus ; and the dove-sellers were got rid of, with the doves, by throwing down their seats and stands, coupled with the expostulation, 'Take these things hence.' John attributes their departure to the expostulation only. When the cattle-dealers and bankers had gone, it would have been useless for others to remain. No market could be held, no bargaining go on, in face of such disturbance.

The disciples of Jesus must have regarded with astonishment a scene so strange and unexpected. Discussing the matter among themselves, they called to mind a passage in the Psalms,—which were probably as familiar to them as they are to members of the Church of England,—a passage which seemed to foretell just such an outburst of zeal in connection with the temple. 'His disciples remembered that it was written, The zeal of thine house shall eat me up.' In the Authorised Version it is, 'hath eaten me up.' Tischendorf notes that in the three oldest MSS. the words are 'eateth me up,' and in his version the quotation stands, 'Zeal for thine house consumes me.' In the Psalm the passage reads : 'For the zeal of thine house hath eaten me up.'

2 John 17

69 Ps. 9

It was but natural that after so high-handed a proceeding on the part of Jesus, he should be called upon to justify his conduct. 'The Jews therefore answered and said unto him, What sign shewest thou unto us, seeing that thou doest these things ?' The word 'therefore' may be taken to involve a connection not only with the act itself, but with the interpretation which his disciples were putting upon it. Probably their opinion agreed with that which Alford expresses as follows : 'This cleansing of the temple was in the direct course of His manifestation as the Messiah.' Jesus took up the challenge. He was prepared to give them such a sign, one which lay beyond the utmost conceivable range of merely human power. 'Jesus answered and said unto them, Destroy this temple (or, sanctuary), and in three days I will raise it up.' It was a deep saying, if not a hard one. The temple was for the worship and glory of God. They who desecrated it might carry their irreverence to the length of actually destroying it. In that event, which Jesus seems to speak of as a foregone conclusion, he would be able to repair the mischief done by them : not with difficulty, labour, or any long delay, but within a fixed term of three days. To them the assertion was an enigma, an inexplicable hyperbole. 'The Jews therefore said, Forty and six years was this temple (or, sanctuary) in building, and wilt thou raise it up in three days ?' But to us, as to the disciples when they had become witnesses of the resurrection of Jesus, his meaning is clear. 'But he spake of the temple (or, sanctuary) of his body.' When the true sense of the expression 'raise it up in three days,' dawned upon the disciples, they called to mind this occasion when he used it. 'When therefore he was raised from the dead, his disciples remembered that he spake this.' It is added : 'and they believed the scripture, and the word which Jesus had said.' Tischendorf renders, 'the word which Jesus spake,' and

2 John 18

19

20

21

22

22

Young, 'the word which Jesus said.' This is different from 'had said,' which seems to refer to something spoken long before. Tischendorf omits 'they' before 'believed,' thereby making one sentence only. It can scarcely be contended that the disciples 'believed the word which Jesus said,' if they waited until the event had proved its truth. Those who take that view are in a difficulty also with respect to the phrase 'believed the scripture.' What scripture? Alford says: 'At first sight it appears difficult to fix on any passage in which it is directly announced: but'—here peeps forth the conventionally-trained intellect of the theologian—'but with the deeper understanding of the Scriptures which the Holy Spirit gave the Apostles and still gives the Christian Church, such prophecies as that in Psalm xvi. are recognized as belonging to Him in whom alone they are properly fulfilled.' It is simpler to take the meaning thus: When Jesus was raised from the dead they remembered his saying and discussed its appropriateness; and at the time, although unable to grasp its import, they regarded him as the Messiah to whom the scripture they themselves had selected applied, and they were confident that the sign he promised would surely be given.

When alluding to his body as 'this temple,' Jesus uttered no mere figure of speech. The apostle Paul seized upon the idea, insisted upon it as a reality, and applied it to believers generally. 'Know ye not that ye are a temple (or, sanctuary) of God, and *that* the Spirit of God dwelleth in you? If any man destroyeth the temple (or, sanctuary) of God, him shall God destroy; for the temple (or, sanctuary) of God is holy, which *temple* ye are.' We read that Jesus was 'full of the Holy Spirit.' Where the Spirit of God dwells, there truly is His temple. Paul did not claim that title individually, but for the entire body of believers: 'ye are a temple,' not 'ye are temples;' 'the Spirit of God dwelleth in you,' collectively, not 'in each of you.' 'To each one is given,' not the Spirit in his fulness, but a certain measure and 'manifestation of the Spirit to profit withal;' so that 'in one Spirit were we all baptized into one body,' which body constitutes 'the temple of God.' The apostle's teaching is very clear on this point. He speaks of 'the church, which is his body, the fulness of him that filleth all in all;' and again: 'for his body's sake, which is the church.' And the apostle Peter, addressing 'the elect' says: 'ye also, as living stones, are built up a spiritual house.' There is a world of meaning in that phrase of Jude, 'our common salvation.' In proportion as our conception of salvation becomes individualized and personal, it falls short of the ideal of Christ and his apostles. 'None of us liveth to himself, and none dieth to himself.'

When Jesus alluded to his resurrection, it was in connection with an interval of 'three days.' Surely there must exist some reason for this, some law of development and reorganisation, which requires for its working that particular period of time. That is the case with every process of nature in respect of living organisms. Revivification, be it of a human soul or body, or of both combined, if it be universal, as we must needs believe, is not an exceptional, supernatural act of divine omnipotence, but comes as much within the ordinary dispensation of Providence as our birth and death. We cannot attempt to pierce the mystery which surrounds the grave and the afterlife; but the repeated mention of 'three days' by Jesus, and the fact that the interval between his death and his uprising coincided with what he had led his disciples to expect, may be taken to indicate rather a fixed relationship of cause and effect than an arbitrary decree apart therefrom.

Here, in verses 18 and 20, as so often in John's gospel, mention is made of 'the Jews:' 'the Jews therefore answered . . . the Jews therefore said,' obviously denoting the inhabitants of Jerusalem or of 'Jewry' generally. 'His disciples' (verse 17) took one side, 'the Jews' the other. It was a recognised fact that the disciples of Jesus were chiefly Galilæans, as distinguished from Jews. The distinction was sharp and clear. Jesus was known as 'Jesus the Galilæan,' and Peter was recognized as such: 'thou art a Galilæan.' And on the day of Pentecost it was observed, as a self-evident fact, 'Behold, are not all these which speak Galilæans?'

26 Mat. 69
14 Mark 70

2 Acts 7

Matthew describes the cures wrought by Jesus in the temple as 'wonderful,' and relates that the children within the building occupied themselves in chanting the words which had been uttered by the multitude the day before: 'Hosanna to the son of David.' We know how quickly a popular melody can be caught up by children, and it is not surprising that the words of the triumph-song should still have been re-echoed in this way. The chief priests and scribes watched the miracles, but with critical and jealous eyes, and they cast upon Jesus the responsibility for these childish outcries, which they seem to have considered a profanation. 'But when the chief priests and the scribes saw the wonderful things that he did, and the children that were crying in the temple and saying, Hosanna to the son of David, they were moved with indignation, and said unto him, Hearest thou what these are saying?' However erroneous the criticism, it was an honest one: 'they were moved with indignation.' The strength of men's convictions and feelings is no evidence of soundness of judgment in matters either political or religious; and very often those who are most positive and outspoken in their opinions and condemnations are utterly in the wrong. Regarded from different points of view, that which is offensive to one man may appear harmless and justifiable to another. Jesus was not disposed to reprove or to silence the children. They were far from understanding the deep import of the words they sang, but had not David declared that even the mouths of infants might be taught to praise God most perfectly? 'And Jesus said unto them, Yea: did ye never read, Out of the mouth of babes and sucklings thou hast perfected praise?' The original passage stands: 'Out of the mouth of babes and sucklings hast thou established strength.' Strength in utterance: that is, perfection of expression, which may be in the direction either of truth or praise, or both. The same combination of ideas is found in the passage: 'having offered up prayers and supplications with strong crying.' Nothing Jesus said or did was approved of by his enemies. Priests and scribes could not tamely brook his teaching of the people that the temple had become transformed into a robbers' den. That he should take upon himself to declare that trading in the temple to be a sacrilege, which they had suffered to exist as a necessary custom, was galling to their pride.

21 Mat. 15, 16

21 Mat. 16

8 Ps. 2

5 Heb. 7

Either their influence over the people would be lessened, or his voice must be silenced. They were bent upon proceeding to extremities. 'And the chief priests and the scribes heard it, and sought how they might destroy him.' The clerical party were the authors of the scheme, but Luke states that they were abetted by the leading citizens. 'And he was teaching daily in the temple. But the chief priests and the scribes and the principal men of the people sought to destroy him.' All they could possibly fear from him was a loss of prestige to themselves, the triumph of his arguments and teaching over theirs. But vanity and self-esteem are potent factors, especially in conjunction with self-interest, and the astounding popularity of Jesus was a sufficient explanation of their policy. 'For they feared him, for all the multitude was astonished at his teaching.' That, which was the chief motive of their action, rendered it very difficult of accomplishment. 'And they could not find what they might do, for the people all hung upon him, listening.' The Authorised Version stands, 'Were very attentive to hear him.' Alford notes: '*literally*, hung on him in hearing him.' Young has: 'were hanging on him, hearing him.' Tischendorf also agrees with the Revisers. To what an extent might not the history of the world have been changed, if Jesus had been suffered to go on unimpeded; if these priests and scribes had been otherwise disposed, or had possessed less power of doing evil; if the life of Jesus had been prolonged, and his personal ministry continued in the world, say thirty or forty years longer! The doctrine of human free will is a stern reality, a cardinal law of our being, as immutable in God's government of the moral world, as is the law of gravitation in the physical universe. God has never been known to annihilate either the one or the other. Man's history is of his own making. 'It was necessary that the word of God should first be spoken to you. Seeing ye thrust it from you, and judge yourselves unworthy of eternal life, lo, we turn to the Gentiles. For so hath the Lord commanded us.' That is the interpretation given by Paul and Barnabas to the divine plan of salvation of which Jesus is the appointed author and finisher. In how many things, since the apostles' time, have men, intentionally and unintentionally, through passion, blindness, error, ignorance, put away from them the doctrine of Jesus and the salvation he designs for mankind!

Unmoved by the opposition he encountered, and undeterred by the danger he ran, Jesus continued to teach daily in the temple, but never passing a night in the city. 'And every evening (Gr. whenever evening came) he went forth out of the city.' Probably that was done for safety, quite as much as for convenience.

The fourth evangelist, also, alludes to the growing popularity of Jesus at Jerusalem during the feast in which the cleansing of the temple occurred. 'Now when he was in Jerusalem at the passover, during the feast, many believed on his name, beholding his signs which he did.' Jesus showed no disposition to rely on the popular favour. 'But Jesus did not trust himself unto them.' The Authorised Version stands, 'But Jesus did not commit himself unto them.' The word 'commit' is changed to trust by Alford, Tischendorf and Young, as well as by the Revisers. Alford explains: 'In the original, the same word is used for *believed* in verse 23, and for trust in this verse.' That is a very important observation: whenever belief or faith is mentioned in Scripture, it is well for us to consider whether its proper equivalent in English is not trust or confidence. The Greek verb here is *pisteuō*, which is generally translated as 'believe,' and its derivitive *pistis* as 'faith.' A right apprehension of the true sense of both words will go far towards removing various erroneous doctrines which have arisen out of their misapplication. The confidence which the multitude were ready to place in Jesus, as their leader, he was not able to place in them as his followers. The evangelist adds that Jesus possessed a full, intuitive knowledge of men's characters : 'for that he knew all men.' This marvellous perceptive faculty placed him above the necessity of seeking the testimony of those whose judgment of others was based on intimacy and long observation : 'and because he needed not that any one should bear witness concerning man (or, a man).' His superior and unerring insight rendered him independent of the ordinary sources of information : 'for he himself knew what was in man (or, the man).' Alford renders 'of himself he knew,' but the word 'of' is not introduced by other translators, and the rendering in the 'Englishman's Greek New Testament' is simply, 'for he knew.' Alford certainly goes too far in saying : 'Nothing less than *divine knowledge* is here set forth . . . As the text now stands, it asserts an entire knowledge of all that is in all men.' Assuredly that is not the drift and intention of the evangelist. His assertion can only have value on the assumption that it is based upon his own observation, or upon some plain declaration of Jesus. The latter we have not ; and John is only referring to persons with whom Jesus came into contact, nor does he say, as Alford presumed to say, that Jesus knew all that was in all of them.

During one of the daily preachings in the temple, the declared enemies of Jesus came to him in a body, and demanded of him under what authority he acted, and from whom it emanated. 'And it came to pass, on one of the days, as he was teaching the people in the temple, and preaching the gospel, there came upon him the chief priests and the scribes with the elders ; and they spake, saying unto him, Tell us, by what authority doest thou these things ? or who is he that gave thee this authority ?' In Matthew's account the context makes it evident that this took place on the second morning of the preaching in the temple, after the discourse about the withered fig tree. 'And when he was come into the temple, the chief priests and the elders of the people came unto him as he was teaching, and said, By what authority doest thou these things ? and who gave thee this authority ?' In Mark also this follows immediately upon the incident of the fig tree. 'And they come again to Jerusalem : and as he was walking in the temple, there come to him the chief priests, and the scribes, and the elders ; and they said unto him, By what authority doest thou these things ? or who gave thee this authority to do these things ?' It may be assumed that 'these things' referred to his driving out the buyers and sellers from the temple three days before. It would have been useless to have done that, and then suffer the same traffic to recommence. The daily visits of Jesus to the temple, lasting from early morning to evening, enabled him to guard against and prevent any repetition of the scandal. Possibly the space formerly used as a market was now occupied by Jesus and the congregation of his hearers. As this altered state of things went on day after day, the buyers and sellers would naturally complain to the authorities, probably protest against interference with what they deemed a right of use and custom. It was not an easy question to deal with : it would be equally difficult to justify and insist upon the holding of the market as formerly, or to declare the presence of Jesus and his work of teaching and healing in the temple to be either illegal or improper. It behoved all parties to act warily, especially in view of the temper of the multitude which daily thronged to hear Jesus. That conjoint action was taken by priests, scribes and elders, indicates that there must have been previous discussion of the question, and arrangement as to the method to be adopted. The first step was to bring Jesus within the scope of their judicial powers. Alford explains that the three classes, chief priests, elders and scribes, ' make up the members of the Sanhedrim. It was an *official message*, sent with a view to make our Saviour declare Himself to be a prophet sent from God—in which case the Sanhedrim had power to take cognizance of his proceedings, as of a professed Teacher. Thus the Sanhedrim sent a deputation to John on his appearing as a Teacher, John i. 19. The question was *the result of a combination to destroy Jesus*, Luke xix. 47, 48.' Whether that be the correct explanation or not, Jesus saw fit to refrain from giving any direct answer to their question, but met it by putting another to them. ' And he answered and said unto them, I will also ask you a question (Gr. word) ; and tell me.' If they would answer him, he was ready to answer them. ' And Jesus answered and said unto them, I will ask you one question (Gr. word), which if ye tell me, I likewise will tell you by what authority I do these things.' ' And Jesus said unto them, I will ask you one question (Gr. word), and answer me, and I will tell you by what authority I do these things.' The question was simple and direct. ' The baptism of John, was it from heaven, or from men ?' They, as guides of the people, must have formed an opinion on that important matter, having sent priests and Levites from Jerusalem to investigate and report on it. ' The baptism of John, was it from heaven, or from men ? answer me.' ' The baptism of John, whence was it ? from heaven or from men ?' If they knew, why should they hesitate to say ? Why should they need to confer so mysteriously together ? Did they differ in opinion ? Alas ! they were not discussing as to what would be the right answer, but only the effect of giving a reply at all. With them, policy stood foremost, and truth in the background. The three evangelists coincide very closely, as though all quoted from the same record. Information as to this private conference and the motives which animated those who took part in it, must have been obtained later, and from one of them, probably some convert to the faith of Jesus. ' And they reasoned with themselves, saying, If we shall say, From heaven, he will say unto us, Why then did ye not believe him ? But if we shall say, From men ; we fear the multitude ; for all hold John as a prophet.' ' And they reasoned with themselves, saying, If we shall say from heaven ; he will say, Why then did ye not believe him ? But should we say from men (or, But shall we say, From men ?)—they feared the people : for all verily held John to be a prophet (or, for all held John to be a prophet indeed).' ' And they reasoned with themselves, saying, If we shall say, From heaven; he will say, Why did ye not believe him? But if we shall say, From men; all the people will stone us: for they be persuaded that John was a prophet.' They saw no way of extricating themselves from that dilemma. If they answered at all, they would either be constrained to admit that their opposition to Jesus was contrary to the will of heaven, or they would have to face the popular resentment, probably to suffer from it. They resolved not to commit themselves either way. 'And they answered Jesus, and said, We know not.' 'And they answered Jesus and say, We know not.' 'And they answered, that they knew not whence *it was*.' It was not that they did not know, but that they would not say. Alford expresses the opinion that these Jewish rulers had never believed in John as a heaven-sent prophet. He says: 'These "blind leaders of the blind" had so far made an insincere concession to the people's persuasion, as to allow John to pass for a prophet; but they shrank from the reproof which was sure to follow their acknowledging it now.' Having admitted themselves incapable of deciding as to the authority of the Baptist, it was obviously out of place for them to call in question that of Jesus, and useless for him to bring his claims before them. 'He also said unto them, Neither tell I you by what authority I do these things.' 'And Jesus saith unto them, Neither tell I you by what authority I do these things.' 'And Jesus said unto them, Neither tell I you by what authority I do these things.'

21 Mat. 27
11 Mark 33
20 Luke 7

21 Mat. 27
11 Mark 33
Luke 8

This account furnishes an interesting example of the 'Common Tradition of the Synoptic Gospels.' Taking Mark, verses 28 to 33, the words common to all three, Matthew, Mark and Luke, are as follows: 'Said—By what authority doest thou these things? who gave thee this authority?—And—said—them, I will ask of you—question—me. The baptism of John, was it from heaven, or from men?—Reasoned —themselves, saying, If we shall say from heaven; he will say, Why —did ye not believe him—Should we say from men—all—John—a prophet. And—answered—know—And—unto them, Neither tell I you by what authority I do these things.' Now, if Matthew, or another of the apostles, noted down at the time what took place, this is just the kind of memorandum one would expect to find. Care is taken to put down in full the question, the reply of Jesus, the reasonings of the questioners, and the closing observation of Jesus. In addition thereto, a word or two is thrown in here and there, serving sufficiently to guide the memory in subsequently enlarging the narrative. It is all very natural, and the only conceivable way by which anyone except a verbatim shorthand reporter could have recorded the incident in a reliable and satisfactory manner. The authors of the 'Common Tradition' assume that the *three* evangelists borrowed from one original document; but that raises a difficulty with respect to Matthew's gospel. Dean Alford states that its author 'has been universally believed to be the Apostle Matthew;' and that 'the testimony of the early Church is unanimous, that Matthew wrote *first* among the Evangelists.' In that case, he can hardly be supposed to have borrowed from the same original tradition as Mark and Luke. Is it not more probable that the condensed original tradition, the rough, apostolic note-book which is the basis of the first three gospels, was that of Matthew himself? Mark and Luke would naturally use that, as the oldest and most reliable record, comparing and supplementing it with any independent traditions handed down to them. The enlargement of Matthew's original memoirs, even by his own hand, would depend for its correctness to some extent on memory.

To the baffled questioners Jesus spoke a short parable. He began with the words, 'But what think ye?' However reticent they might be about the baptism of John, on this subject they could have no difficulty in forming an opinion. 'A man had two sons. And he came to the first, and said, Son (Gr. Child), go work to day in the vineyard.' Young and Tischendorf render literally 'son' as 'child' and 'two sons' as 'two children.' The request of the father was met by a point blank refusal. 'And he answered and said, I will not.' Subsequently he changed his mind, and did what he had been bidden : 'but afterward he repented himself, and went.' The father made the same demand upon the other son. 'And he came to the second, and said likewise.' The reply is given both in the Authorised and Revised Versions as follows : 'And he answered and said, I *go*, sir : and went not.' Young also inserts an italicised word, *will* instead of *go*: 'I will, sir.' Tischendorf renders, 'Yea, sir,' and Luther, 'Herr, ja. Sir, yes.' These are obviously given as supposed equivalents of the original, not as direct renderings. Alford puts the italicised word 'go' between brackets, adding the note, 'not expressed in the original.' The form of expression does not seem to have been colloquial, and if not, Jesus must have intentionally omitted to place any word between 'I' and 'Sir.' If a note of exclamation were added, the two words would signify a contemptuous refusal, as though the father had asked what was unreasonable ; a note of interrogation would give to the words a tone of expostulation. The sense of 'I—Sir' depends entirely on the emphasis of the voice and the manner of the speaker. It may be made to express either astonishment, doubt, hesitation, assent or dissent, combined with perfect courtesy or tacit reproof. But without introducing any idea of that kind, letting the two words stand by themselves, as they were left by Matthew, the meaning is altogether vague, which Jesus probably intended it to be, as fitly representing their mental attitude with respect to the Baptist. The 'Sir' was sufficient to show respect, the 'I' to indicate a consciousness of duty ; what intention was hidden under a form of reply so uncertain and equivocal remained to be seen, and was forthwith proved by the event : 'and went not.'

The parable, short and simple, was finished by the time they may have thought only the opening scene was reached, and sharp and clear rang out the question of Jesus : 'Whether of the twain did the will of his father?' There could be no doubt on that point. 'They say, The first.' Then Jesus took the unusual course of himself explaining and applying the parable. 'Jesus saith unto them, Verily I say unto you, that the publicans and the harlots go into the kingdom of God before you.' Those who had been openly, notoriously unjust and sinful were entering God's kingdom, whilst those who had made great professions of reverence and obedience were holding themselves aloof. The Baptist had come, an uncompromising teacher of moral rectitude, and what had been the result ? The despised tax-gatherers and erring women had believed and honoured him as a heaven-sent Teacher ; and these priests and scribes, whose solemn deputation and enquiries amounted to nothing more than a pretentious, hypocritical, formal 'I—Sir,' had seen the minds, hearts and lives of the populace touched, moved, changed, by the Baptist's call to reformation, yet themselves stood aloof from the inspired movement, and could not even yet say that they believed the Baptist to be what he had professed himself, the forerunner of One mightier than himself, who should baptize them 'with holy spirit and with fire.' 'For John came unto you in the way of righteousness, and ye believed him not; but the publicans and the harlots believed him: and ye, when ye saw it, did not even repent yourselves afterward, that ye might believe him.' This attitude of passive indifference was equivalent to rejection, and was so regarded generally, for we are elsewhere told: 'And all the people when they heard, and the publicans, justified God, being baptized with the baptism of John. But the Pharisees and the lawyers rejected for themselves the counsel of God, being not baptized of him.'

The expression 'go into the kingdom of God,' calls for consideration. The act is represented as purely voluntary. Men are not carried into God's kingdom by supernatural power, but enter into it of their own free will. If the 'kingdom of God' and the 'kingdom of heaven' be not strictly synonymous, so as to be used interchangeably, there is a close connection between them. The Lord's prayer indicates that the latter is bound up with the former, and must come as its perfect realization: 'Thy kingdom come. Thy will be done in earth as it is in heaven.' Preachers have been wont to talk much more about going 'to God' and going 'to heaven,' than about entering the 'kingdom of God' and the 'kingdom of heaven;' and that desired consummation, be it what it may, has been deemed altogether impossible of attainment on earth, and therefore relegated to another life in another world. So the gospel of Jesus has come to be represented as a scheme aiming at the salvation of individuals in heaven, apart from that of mankind in general both in earth and heaven. Dr. Young's literal renderings, 'reign of God,' 'reign of the heavens,' help to a better understanding of the matter. Individuals, one after another, may place themselves under the 'reign of God' by submitting to the commands which Jesus laid upon his disciples and followers; but the 'reign of the heavens' seems to refer to a state of existence in which all alike are living under the divine rulership.

The parable of the two sons was followed by another. Jesus said: 'Hear another parable.' Mark and Luke, not having recorded the previous parable, make no allusion to it. Mark says: 'And he began to speak unto them in parables.' Luke notes that he addressed himself to the people generally: 'And he began to speak unto the people this parable.' Luke states simply: 'A man planted a vineyard.' Mark: 'A man planted a vineyard, and set a hedge about it, and digged a pit for the wine-press, and built a tower.' Young renders, 'digged an under-wine-vat,' which stands in the Authorised Version 'digged *a place for* the winefat.' Instead of the italicised words 'a place for,' the Revisers have inserted 'a pit for,' which they have not italicised. Matthew describes the man as a householder. 'There was a man that was a householder, which planted a vineyard, and set a hedge about it, and digged a winepress in it, and built a tower.' The word here rendered 'winepress' is *lenon*; in Mark it is *hupolenion*. The planter of the vineyard being a 'householder,' not a cultivator, leased it to others; 'and let it out to husbandmen.' The three evangelists use that expression. According to the Authorised Version they also agree in stating, 'and went into a far country.' Alford notes: 'the original has only *left the country*;' Young and Tischendorf render, 'and went abroad;' the Revisers, 'and went into another country.' Luke adds the words: 'for a long time.' Mark continues: 'And at the season he sent to the husbandmen a servant (Gr. bondservant), that he might receive from the husbandmen of the fruits of the vineyard.' Luke: 'And at the season he sent unto the husbandmen a servant (Gr. bondservant), that they should give him of the fruit of the vineyard.' Matthew represents the despatch of 'servants,' not of 'a servant,' and this discrepancy between the evangelists continues throughout the parable. It can scarcely be considered a contradiction: probably, naturally, the chief servant would have assistants, but the negotiations would be between the tenants and himself, and against him, as well as those with him, their animosity would be directed. Matthew intimates that the mission was in ample time, before the actual commencement of the season. 'And when the season of the fruits drew near, he sent his servants (Gr. bondservants) to the husbandmen, to receive his fruits (or, the fruits of it).' Instead of meeting the just demands of their landlord, the occupiers assaulted his representatives, and sent them away without payment. 'And they took him, and beat him, and sent him away empty.' 'But the husbandmen beat him, and sent him away empty.' Matthew states that several servants were mentioned, and that they suffered in various ways. 'And the husbandmen took his servants (Gr. bondservants), and beat one, and killed another, and stoned another.' A larger number were then sent, but they met with no better treatment. 'Again, he sent other servants (Gr. bondservants) more than the first: and they did unto them in like manner.' Luke describes one servant only sent at a time. 'And he sent yet another servant (Gr. bondservant); and him also they beat, and handled him shamefully, and sent him away empty. And he sent yet a third: and him also they wounded, and cast him forth.' Mark also records the sending of a single servant on two other occasions, but he then adds that many others also were sent. 'And again he sent unto them another servant (Gr. bondservant); and him they wounded in the head, and handled shamefully. And he sent another; and him they killed: and many others; beating some, and killing some.' These last words, 'and many others; beating some, and killing some,' enable us to harmonise the evangelists. Luke states that one servant was sent alone on three several occasions; Mark agrees with that, adding the fact that the same thing happened subsequently and repeatedly. Matthew passes over in silence the sending of particular envoys, and contents himself with grouping all the messages and messengers together.

In verse 4 of Mark the Revisers have omitted the words 'and at him they cast stones,' and the word 'again' before 'he sent,' in verse 5, on the authority of the two oldest MSS.

Luke represents the proprietor of the vineyard deliberating with himself as to what further steps it was in his power to take, and resolving to send his son, whom he dearly loved, hoping that respect would be paid to him. 'And the lord of the vineyard said, What shall I do? I will send my beloved son: it may be they will reverence him.' The Authorised Version adds, 'when they see him,' which is omitted, not being in the two oldest MSS. Mark stands: 'He had yet one, a beloved son: he sent him last unto them, saying, They will reverence my son.' 'He had yet,' takes the place of 'having yet therefore,' and the word 'also' before 'last' is omitted, in accordance with the two oldest MSS. Here also Matthew is somewhat briefer. 'But afterward he sent unto them his son, saying, They will reverence my son.' The word 'afterward' here and in Young and Tischendorf takes the place of 'last of all' in the Authorised Version. Far from showing reverence to the son, the husbandmen conferred together, discussing the advantage they might gain by putting him to death and holding the vineyard as their own. 'But the husbandmen, when they saw the son, said among themselves, This is the heir: come, let us kill him, and take his inheritance.' In their wicked folly they thought that his death might be as good to them as a legal title to the estate. 'But when the husbandmen saw him, they reasoned one with another, saying, This is the heir: let us kill him, that the inheritance may be ours.' Mark represents them as having no doubt about that. 'But those husbandmen said among themselves, This is the heir; come, let us kill him, and the inheritance shall be ours.' Mark continues: 'And they took him, and killed him, and cast him forth out of the vineyard.' This seems to mean that the murder was committed inside the vineyard, and the dead body afterwards thrown outside. But the words are reversed in the other evangelists. 'And they took him, and cast him forth out of the vineyard, and killed him.' 'And they cast him forth out of the vineyard, and killed him.' Surely the bloody tragedy could not end there. The long-suffering and deeply-injured householder must needs take some further steps, unless he tamely submitted to the robbery and left the murderers unpunished. 'What therefore will the lord of the vineyard do? he will come and destroy the husbandmen, and will give the vineyard unto others.' Luke also: 'What therefore will the lord of the vineyard do unto them? He will come and destroy these husbandmen, and will give the vineyard unto others.' Both question and answer might be spoken by Jesus: but Matthew represents him as pausing, and the reply to have been given by the hearers. 'When therefore the lord of the vineyard shall come, what will he do unto those husbandmen? They say unto him, He will miserably destroy those miserable men, and will let out the vineyard unto other husbandmen, which shall render him the fruits in their seasons.' The question is not quite the same, the coming of the proprietor being included in it. We may imagine the reply to have been first, 'he will come,' and this to be a further question, 'When he shall come, what will he do?' The object of Jesus seems to have been to elicit the full and free opinions of the listeners, and Matthew records them, perhaps combines them. The infamy attaching to the robbers and murderers is emphasised. Alford observes: 'In the original the adverb rendered *miserably* is that belonging to the adjective rendered *wicked*. This could hardly be given in a *version* in English: it may be *represented* by some such expression as, '*He will destroy them wretchedly, wretches as they are.*' The Revisers and Tischendorf have brought out this peculiarity by altering, 'He will miserably destroy those wicked men' to 'he will miserably destroy those miserable men.' Young renders: 'Evil men—he will miserably destroy them.' Having regard to Alford's explanation it is obvious that a literal translation would be: 'Evil men—evilly he will destroy them,' and so Luther renders it: 'Er wird die Bösewichter übel umbringen.' It was the rendering of evil for evil, the principle on which men's ideas of justice, human and divine, had been founded, but which principle Jesus disavowed, teaching his disciples to 'render to no man evil for evil.' The vineyard being now freed from wrongful holders would be transferred to others. 'And will give the vineyard unto others.' Luke uses the same words. Matthew is fuller and more exact. 'And will let out the vineyard unto other husbandmen, which shall render him the fruits in their seasons.' An observation was here interposed which is recorded only by Luke. 'And when they heard it, they said, God forbid (Gr. Be it not so).' Alford says it is literally, 'Let it not be,' and Young so renders it. The exclamation must obviously be taken as a criticism upon the parable in its entirety, not as a deprecation of the vengeance inflicted upon the murderers, or as applying only to the closing words, 'and will give the vineyard unto others.' The hearers themselves had suggested the ending of the parable, which disclosed such a picture of injustice, cruelty, folly, and reckless wickedness, that they might well deem it too highly coloured, and expostulate against its being taken as representative of anything in the national history. 'Incredible! Impossible! God forbid! Let it not be!' Were they right? Was Jesus wrong? Had he drawn a fiction, or had he described a fact? He was terribly in earnest. He fixed his eyes upon them, and bade them explain, if they could, from their optimistic point of view, a certain passage in the Scriptures. 'But he looked upon them, and said, What then is this that is written,

The stone which the builders rejected,
The same was made the head of the corner?'

Did not that indicate an antagonism between the design of God and the ideas of those who claimed to be the appointed leaders in carrying out that design? The parable represented only too truly the injustice and inhumanity which have ever been disgraceful features in the development of religious intolerance and persecution. But putting all that aside, dismissing the simile which dealt with human nature thus perverted and brutalised, and taking up the figures of a stone and a building instead of a householder and husbandmen, the same lesson was conveyed. There must come to pass an utter reversal of human plans and purposes, the strength and beauty of the heavenly edifice being made to depend upon that corner-stone which the builders ignominiously rejected. Still keeping to the metaphor of a stone, Jesus added: 'Every one that falleth on that stone shall be broken to pieces; but on whomsoever it shall fall, it will scatter him as dust.' The Authorised Version stands: 'Whosoever shall fall upon that stone shall be broken; but on whomsoever it shall fall, it will grind him to powder.' The word 'broken' by itself might be taken to signify bruised, more or less injured, but the

Revisers have made it equivalent to 'dashed to pieces.' Tischendorf has : ' Every one that fell upon that stone will be broken ; but on whomsoever it shall fall, it will grind him to powder.' Young renders : ' Every one who hath fallen on that stone shall be broken, and on whom it may fall, it will crush him to pieces.' The prominent idea, brought out by Jesus with all the force of which language is capable, is the utter futility of human efforts and intentions when opposed to the divine will. Matthew and Mark represent an additional verse of the Psalm to have been quoted, leading our thoughts in the same direction. ' Have ye not read even this Scripture ;

12 Mark 10, 11

  The stone which the builders rejected,
  The same was made the head of the corner:
  This was from the Lord,
  And it was marvellous in our eyes?'

21 Mat. 42

  Matthew prefaces the quotation with the words : ' Jesus said unto them, Did ye never read in the Scriptures . . .' The original passage stands as follows :

118 Ps. 22, 23

  'The stone which the builders rejected
  Is become the head of the corner.
  This is the Lord's doing ;
  It is marvellous in our eyes.'

  Matthew alone records the following additional words of Jesus :

21 Mat. 43

' Therefore I say unto you, The kingdom of God shall be taken away from you, and shall be given to a nation bringing forth the fruits

44

thereof.' After which comes the verse : ' And he that falleth on this stone shall be broken to pieces : but on whomsoever it shall fall, it will scatter him as dust.' The Revisers note that ' some ancient authorities omit ' this last verse. Lachmann and Tischendorf omit it. It is enough that we have it standing unquestioned in Luke. From the parable of the vineyard Jesus drew an inference : that the kingdom of God should be taken from the unbelieving Jews, and given to others. From the simile of the stone he drew another inference : that opposition to the divine will must be hurtful or fatal to the opposers. These two lessons may be merged into one : the necessity of submitting to the will and purposes of God. Jesus was not careful what parable he took up to enforce that truth : the stone and the builders would do just as well as the vineyard and the husbandmen. To deduce from either parable any conclusion as to the mode and method of the divine judgments, is to overlook the spirit and misread the letter of the teaching of Jesus. None can be so foolish as to suppose that the final doom of the builders is to be mutilated or crushed to death in any literal sense. As little are we justified in rigorously interpreting the words 'he will miserably destroy those miserable men,' even were they the words of Jesus, which they are not. In another parable the catastrophe is thus

22 Mat. 7

described : ' But the king was wroth ; and he sent his armies, and destroyed those murderers, and burned their city.' Dean Alford scrupled not to add as an explanatory note : ' the *Roman* armies.' Here also he introduces the same idea, saying : ' We may observe that our Lord here makes *when the Lord therefore of the vineyard cometh* coincide with the destruction of Jerusalem, which is incontestably the overthrow of the wicked husbandmen. This passage forms therefore an important key to our Lord's prophecies, and a decisive justification for those who, like myself, firmly hold that *the coming of the Lord* is in many places to be identified, primarily, with that overthrow.' That is certainly a deduction from the parable which Jesus did not bring before his hearers. 'The kingdom of God shall be taken away from you:' did the Romans take away the kingdom of God from the Jews? 'And shall be given to a nation bringing forth the fruits thereof.' What had the destruction of Jerusalem to do with that? To call that frightful event the coming of the Lord Jesus, is to misconceive utterly the nature of his kingdom and the drift of his teachings.

The chief priests and the Pharisees could not fail to perceive that the wicked husbandmen and the foolish builders were designed to represent themselves. 'And when the chief priests and the Pharisees heard his parables, they perceived that he spake of them.' They decided to arrest him without any further delay. 'And the scribes and the chief priests sought to lay hands on him in that very hour.' But their dread of the populace caused them to defer their purpose. 'And when they sought to lay hold on him, they feared the multitudes, because they took him for a prophet.' Luke gives the same explanation. 'And they feared the people: for they perceived that he spake this parable against them.' Mark adds that they withdrew from the presence of Jesus. 'And they sought to lay hold on him; and they feared the multitude; for they perceived that he spake the parable against them: and they left him, and went away.' 21 Mat. 45 / 20 Luke 19 / 21 Mat. 46 / 20 Luke 19 / 12 Mark 12

It is interesting to consider the skeleton of the above narrative as it is disclosed by the authors of 'The Common Tradition.' In the fourth column are the words common to the three evangelists, and in the first, second and third columns the expansions of Matthew, Mark and Luke respectively.

Expansion of Matthew.	Expansion of Mark.	Expansion of Luke.	Common to the Three Evangelists.	
Hear another	And he began to speak unto them in	And he began to speak unto the people this	parable	1
There was			a man	2
that was a householder, which			planted a vineyard	3
and set a hedge about it, and digged a winepress in it, and built a tower	and set a hedge about it, and digged a pit for the winepress in it, and built a tower		and let it out to husbandmen, and went into another country	4
and when the	and at the	and at the	season	5
of the fruits drew near			he sent	6
his	a servant	a servant	servants to the husbandmen	7
to receive his	that he might receive from the husbandmen of	that they should give him of	fruits	8
and the husbandmen took his servants, and	of the vineyard. And they took him, and	of the vineyard; but the husbandmen	beat	9

Expansion of Matthew.	Expansion of Mark.	Expansion of Luke.	Common to the Three Evangelists.	
one, and killed another, and stoned another. Again he sent others	him, and sent him away empty. And again he sent unto them another	him, and sent him away empty. Again he sent other	servants	10
more than the first			and	11
they did unto them in like manner. But afterwards he sent unto them his son, saying	him they wounded in the head, and handled shamefully. And he sent another and him they killed: and many others, beating some, and killing some. He had yet one, a beloved son: he sent him last unto them, saying	him also they beat, and handled him shamefully, and sent him away empty. And he sent yet a third: and him also they wounded, and cast him forth. And the lord of the vineyard said, What shall I do? I will send my beloved son: it may be	they will reverence my son. But	12
		when	the husbandmen	
when they saw the son, said among themselves	said among themselves	saw him, they reasoned one with another, saying	this is the heir	13
come	come		let us kill him	14
and take his	and	that	inheritance	15
		may be ours	and they	16
took him, and	took him, and		cast him forth out of the vineyard	17
and	and	and	killed	18
him. When therefore	therefore	therefore	the lord of the vineyard	19
shall come			what will he do	20
unto those	the	these	husbandmen	21
The say unto him			he will	22
he will miserably	he will come and	he will come and	destroy	23
those miserable men			and will	24
let out	give	give	the vineyard unto other	25
husbandmen, which shall render him the fruits in their seasons. Jesus saith unto them, Did ye never read in	have ye not read even this	And when they heard it, they said, God forbid. But he looked upon them, and said, What then is this that is written	the scriptures	26
			The stone which the builders rejected the same was made the head of the corner	27

Expansion of Matthew.	Expansion of Mark.	Expansion of Luke.	Common to the Three Evangelists.	
This was from the Lord, and it is marvellous in our eyes. Therefore say I unto you, The kingdom of God shall be taken away from you, and shall be given to a {nation bringing forth the fruits thereof. And he that falleth on this stone shall be broken to pieces: but on whomsoever it shall fall, it will scatter him as dust.	This was from the Lord, and it is marvellous in our eyes.	Every one that falleth on that stone shall be broken to pieces; but on whomsoever it shall fall, it will scatter him as dust.		
And when the chief priests and the Pharisees heard his			parables they perceived that	28
he spake of	he spake against	he spake against	them	29
			and	30
when they	they	the scribes and the chief priests	sought	31
to lay hold on	to lay hold on	to lay hands on	him they feared	32
the multitudes, because they took him for a prophet.	the multitude	the people		33

The fourth column, which is common to the three evangelists, comprises the leading words of the discourse, as if they had been noted down hastily whilst it was delivered, for the purpose of aiding the memory in recording it subsequently. The suggestion is merely tentative, but assuming the original rough draft to have been Matthew's, the first column shows how he dealt with it, his recollection enabling him to fill up the slight sketch in that way.

The differences between the evangelists may be analysed as follows:

(a) Wordings in Mark and Luke differing from those in Matthew, but so similar in Mark and Luke as to indicate that they copied from a document common to both: 1, 10, 12.

(b) Phrases in Matthew only, indicating that he gives the actual words of Jesus: 1, 3, 11, 20, 23, 24.

(c) Verbal differences, insertions or omissions, apparently due to the compilers: 1 Matthew and Luke; 4 Matthew and Luke; 5, 6, Matthew and Luke; 8, 9, Matthew and Luke; 13, 14, Luke; 17, Luke; 25, Matthew and Luke; 29, 31, 32, Luke; 33.

(d) Verbal differences, additions, or omissions, indicating variations in the original records: 16 Luke; 23, 26 Mark and Luke; 28 Mark and Luke.

(e) Plural in Matthew, but singular in Mark or Luke, or in both, or vice versâ: servants, servant 7, 8, 9; also multitudes, multitude, 33.

The theory that Matthew's was the original record is only put forth suggestively. These comparisons tend, however, to confirm it. The above method of investigation is full of interest, and, in competent hands, would be fruitful of reliable conclusions. The doctrine of 'inspiration' has stood terribly in the way of any such independent study of the gospels. One hour's patient labour in this direction would suffice to dissipate erroneous ideas cherished by inspirationists; and a methodical and painstaking comparison of the evangelistic narratives on this basis, which is that adopted by the authors of 'The Common Tradition,' would be worth more than a multitude of 'Harmonies,' and do as much good as the doctrine of 'inspiration' has done harm.

22 Mat. 1   Jesus continued to address the people in parabolic form. 'And Jesus answered and spake again in parables unto them, saying . . ' His opening words indicate that he intended to illustrate something relating to that 'reign of the heavens,' the establishment of which was the object of his life. The ruler of a certain kingdom is repre-
2   sented as decreeing festivities on account of his son's marriage. 'The kingdom of heaven is likened unto a certain king, which made a marriage feast for his son.' Such an event lies outside the routine of daily life, and is an occasion for special rejoicing. Invitations to the banquet were issued, and in due time the chosen guests were sum-
3   moned to attend. 'And sent forth his servants (Gr. bondservants) to call them that were bidden to the marriage feast.' Strange to say, they cared nothing about the banquet, and showed not the least
3   respect to the king or the king's son. 'And they would not come.' Other servants were then despatched to repeat and enforce the former
4   message. 'Again he sent forth other servants (Gr. bondservants), saying, Tell them that are bidden, Behold, I have made ready my dinner: my oxen and my fatlings are killed, and all things are ready: come to the marriage feast.' In vain did they explain, invite, expostulate. Nobody paid the least attention to the message. The expected guests went off in various directions, and occupied themselves in different ways: they would go anywhere rather than to the king's
5   palace, and do anything rather than sit down at his banquet. 'But they made light of it, and went their ways, one to his own farm, another to his merchandise.' Instead of 'they made light of it,' Young renders, 'they having disregarded it,' Tischendorf, 'they neglected,' and 'The Englishman's Greek New Testament,' 'they being negligent of (it).' They were simply indifferent, wrapped up in thoughts of other things, preferring to follow their daily round of labour rather than break the monotony of the life to which they were accustomed, even for the sake of realising the brightness, the rejoicing, the refinement of a king's court. It does not appear that they had professed to accept the invitation, or ever for a moment intended to avail themselves of it. From first to last they held aloof, feeling no concern in the royal plans and purposes, and esteeming it no honour and no privilege to share therein. Some went beyond mere cool contempt and disrespect, and laid violent hands upon the king's
6   servants, maltreated them, even murdered them. 'And the rest laid hold on his servants (Gr. bondservants), and entreated them shamefully, and killed them.' It is altogether a strange story. Who could have expected that the good intentions of the king, his courteous

invitation, his costly preparations, his patient entreaties, would be met in such a spirit of utter indifference and hostility, and lead to so lamentable a result? The goodwill of the monarch being thus scorned, was replaced by indignation against the murderers. Justice demanded that his servants should be avenged, and stern retribution was forthwith exacted. 'But the king was wroth; and he sent his armies, and destroyed those murderers, and burned their city.' The Authorised Version has, after 'but,' 'when the king heard *thereof*;' these words are omitted by the Revisers, not being in the two oldest MSS. In verses 2, 3 and 4 Young uses the plural, 'marriage-feasts.' ^{22 Mat. 7}

In interpreting the parable the following points are to be noted: (1) The invitation was not universal. Certain persons were bidden to the wedding feast, and they only were called upon to attend. (2) Attendance involved the relinquishment for the time being of worldly affairs. (3) The bulk of the invited guests preferred their own business to the king's pleasure, and continued to conduct their affairs as though they had never been invited. (4) The rest of the invited guests were not simply indifferent to the invitation, but hostile to it, and took upon them to persecute the king's messengers. (5) Only these last, the murderers, are represented as being punished.

The parable is started as an illustration of 'the kingdom of heaven.' Only disciples of Jesus, true followers prepared to forsake all things for his cause, could enter therein. He could not soften his hard terms of admission, and when these were recognised many,—how many who can tell?—who heard his call and were ready enough to answer, 'Lord, Lord,' were not prepared to do the things he said. They kept on according to the course of this world, not less diligent in earthly business than before, or in any wise blameable therein. A call from above had come, which they had disregarded: it was their loss, the gospel's loss. The parable goes no further than that as regards these men. But there were others, who were not merely impassive to the call, but antagonistic to it, and to those by whom it was proclaimed. What moved them to this? Nothing but the invitation itself and the persistence with which it was urged. They were men so bent on having things go on in the old course, so determined to resent any new point of departure in thought and practice, that they scrupled not to treat as enemies and criminals those who called them and others to higher aims and nobler duties. The chief priests and Pharisees, who were even then taking counsel against Jesus to put him to death, stand in this category; so do they who afterwards persecuted and sought to kill his apostles; so do all who in bygone times have dragged to prison and the stake those who proclaimed religious opinions at variance with their own: so do they who now denounce pains and penalties for nonconformity, and in their poor, puny fashion rake up again the dying embers of religious intolerance and persecution. They are all of the same spirit, which leads up to murder as its extreme, and has various intermediate degrees of 'shameful handling.' Murder is murder, however much men may seek to justify it as a necessity in some cause which they deem sacred. 'Whosoever killeth you shall think that he offereth service unto God.' How often has that prophecy of Jesus come true! Taught by him, we may boldly apply to this matter the apostle's words: 'We know that the judgement of God is according ^{16 John 2} ^{2 Rom. 2}

to truth against them that practise such things.' Let us not restrict to one particular event that just judgment of God which Jesus indicated by the words: 'But the king was wroth; and he sent his armies, and destroyed those murderers, and burned their city.' It is here that Alford inserted his explanatory note: 'The *Roman* armies.' That narrows the application of the parable down to one specific incident in Jewish national history. True, armies did come, and Jerusalem was besieged and burnt, and so far there is a resemblance between that catastrophe and the climax of the parable. But that did not happen until nearly 40 years after the words were spoken, by which time many of the persecutors had died naturally. The theory of Alford is not without its difficulties. It assumes the king in the parable to be God; and as he sent forth his armies, it follows that the Romans were God's soldiers. That were hard to believe, if not incredible. Certainly they were not soldiers of Jesus, for the weapons of his warfare were not carnal but spiritual, and he foresaw and sought to avert the destruction of Jerusalem, and wept at the non-success of his efforts. There is a strange inconsistency in supposing, as Alford does, that the destruction of Jerusalem was the coming of Jesus. Moreover, the Romans spared none, so that the adoption of Alford's view leads to the conclusion that the neglecters of the invitation suffered together with the murderers, which is contrary to the parable. Jesus therein did not profess to foretell the nation's future, but to illustrate 'the kingdom of heaven,' and the application of the parable is general and universal, not individual and local. Destruction is the doom of persecutors who go to the length of murder, and not a trace will be left on earth of all their plans and labours. The armies of the Lord of hosts are invisible to mortal eyes; it is enough for us to know that their work of retribution is sure, irresistible, inevitable. Not once or twice, not here or there, but always and everywhere, the saying is fulfilled: 'He sent his armies, and destroyed those murderers, and burned their city.' The apostle Paul represented the judgment of God under the same figure of burning and destruction: 'Each man's work, of what sort it is, the fire shall prove it.... If any man destroyeth the temple of God, him shall God destroy; for the temple of God is holy, which *temple* ye are.' Human life is sacred, and woe to them who destroy it in their hatred of the truth of God enshrined therein. It is a remarkable fact that all the denunciations of Jesus were directed against hatred of truth and light. He did not attack the common vices of mankind, the grossness of immorality and wrong-doing in its multitudinous forms. His chief concern was about the promulgation of truth and the overthrow of error. With publicans and sinners he dealt lightly; not so with opposing scribes, priests and Pharisees. 'Woe unto you, scribes and Pharisees, hypocrites!' The same tone and direction of thought are observable in the parables. Jesus presented repentant sinners under the figures of the lost sheep recovered, the lost coin found, the prodigal returned and welcomed. Not blame, aversion, condemnation, but pity, hope, repentance, forgiveness and rejoicing, were prominent in his treatment of the frail and sinful. But the parables directed against the chief priests and Pharisees were reprobatory and threatening. 'He will come and destroy those husbandmen, and will give the vineyard to others.'

'He sent his armies, and destroyed those murderers, and burned their city.' Doubtless there were good reasons in the mind of Jesus for this difference of treatment. Sins of the body bring their own punishment, and stamp with degradation those who commit them. Society has taken upon itself the castigation of wickedness in a variety of forms. But against spiritual pride and rancour, opposition to light and truth, and the self-complacency which exalts itself and despises others, there is no appeal to any human tribunal. These are vices of the upper class, of those who have the making of laws and the wielding of judicial powers. Jesus came perforce into conflict with these men; they could not crush his spirit, but they took his life, and afterwards sought to crush his followers. The apostle Paul describes the nature of this strife: 'Our wrestling is not against flesh and blood, but against the principalities, against the powers, against the world-rulers of this darkness, against the spiritual hosts of wickedness in the heavenly *places*.' Young renders this: 'We have not the wrestling against blood and flesh, but against the principalities, against the powers' (authorities—Eng. G. N. T.), 'against the world-rulers of the darkness of this age, against the spiritual things of the evil in the heavenly places.' Luther's version carries the same meaning: 'Denn wir haben nicht mit Fleisch und Blut zu kämpfen, sondern mit Fürsten und Gewaltigen, nemlich mit den Herren der Welt, die in der Finsterniss dieser Welt herrschen, mit den bösen Geistern unter dem Himmel.' 'For we have not to fight with flesh and blood, but with the princes and mighty ones, namely with the lords of the world, who rule in the darkness of this world, with the evil spirits under heaven.' Take Count Leon Tolstoi's view of the Christian doctrine and warfare, and this passage will no longer be so inapplicable, so incomprehensible, or so vapid and well-nigh meaningless as it has hitherto seemed. The apostle's exhortation has a definite application, and if men fail to find it, it is because they mistake the nature and reality of the Christian warfare, and have wandered into a realm of unpractical imagination.

The parable does not end with the destruction of the murderers, but branches out in another direction. 'Then saith he to his servants (Gr. bondservants), The wedding is ready, but they that were bidden were not worthy.' Young and Tischendorf render 'wedding' as 'marriage feast:' the word in the original is the same as before. Unwillingness, as well as opposition, is represented as indicating unworthiness. The king now commands his servants to seek for guests, no matter of what class or from what quarter. 'Go ye therefore unto the partings of the highways, and as many as ye shall find, bid to the marriage feast.' The Revisers have altered 'highways' to 'partings of the highways,' which is rendered by Young and Tischendorf 'cross-ways,' and by the 'Englishman's Greek New Testament' 'thoroughfares of the highways.' The utmost publicity would thus be given to the invitation. This resulted, as was to be expected, in the collection of a very motley assemblage. No restrictions were imposed, all classes and characters being welcomed. 'And those servants (Gr. bondservants) went out into the highways, and gathered together all as many as they found, both bad and good.' The Authorised Version continues: 'and the wedding was furnished

22 Mat. 10. with guests,' which the Revisers have rendered, 'and the wedding was filled with guests,' Tischendorf, following another reading, renders, 'and the bride-chamber was filled with guests;' Young: 'and the marriage-feast apartment was filled with guests.' Luther also here drops the word 'Hochzeit,' 'wedding,' and chooses another word: 'und die Tische wurden alle voll,' 'and the tables were all filled.' From first to last the parable puts a limitation upon the number of the guests. Originally a certain selection was made: 'call them that were bidden to the marriage feast.' Now the room is represented as being filled up. This feature of the parable has its significance, and must not be disregarded. Alford assumes those first invited to be 'the Jewish people,' and he talks of 'the opening of the Feast to the Gentiles.' But the very structure of the parable forbids the idea of universality. To suppose a whole nation invited to assemble in a bridal-feast apartment is an absurdity. Such a mode of interpretation is wholly inconsistent with the aspect under which Jesus here presents 'the kingdom of heaven.' Only through discipleship to him is the kingdom of heaven attainable, and we know that he intentionally limited the number of disciples, and warned all men not to profess themselves as such, unless they had first counted the cost and resolved to hate all things else, even their own lives, for the gospel's sake. That every man should become a disciple was no more to be expected or desired, than that every house should become a church or chapel. 'Ye are the light of the world:' if all could claim that illuminating influence, there would be no world outside for them to enlighten. 'A city set on a hill cannot be hid:' city-crowned hills are exceptional; dwellers in the plains below must look and climb upwards to them. A sprinkle of leaven put in three bushels of meal, till the whole should become leavened; a tiny grain of mustard seed, which must be sown and grow up gradually into a tree; an assembly of wedding guests, favoured individuals, for each one of whom admitted, a thousand of their countrymen must have been, as a matter of course, excluded: such were the similes whereby Jesus represented the kingdom of heaven. At first the world received it but in embryo; poor and puny has been its development during eighteen centuries. Yet Christianity was no abortion: it was fairly born into the world in the first century. Where is it, what is it now? As an accepted creed, as a system of doctrine, it is everywhere, and professes itself everything. But as 'the kingdom of heaven' among mankind, it has no existence. There is no 'reign of the heavens' yet in this world, nor can it ever be established except through the method devised by Jesus. Not by an assumption on the part of the clergy that they have been commissioned and empowered to admit every infant into the kingdom of heaven by a supernatural act of grace in the sacrament of baptism, and then preaching the duty of everyone to live up to that high privilege and profession, can the kingdom of heaven be set up in our midst. That is a plan of human invention, an error, a fiction, a rotten foundation upholding a sham Christianity. The scheme of Jesus is the very reverse of that. To the world at large his call is, from its very nature, impracticable. Nevertheless he would have men follow it; not all—that cannot be—but those who deliberately resolve to become his disciples and to seek first the kingdom of God and his righteousness. That profession

entails a life of self-denial, the abnegation of this world, the sufferings incident to a career of protest against its errors and evils, coupled with an unequivocal acceptance of that doctrine of non-resistance which is the glory of the cross and the scorn of the world. Only such men can teach how to live and how to die after the example of Jesus and his apostles. If we had such soldiers of the cross among us, not standing aloof as ecclesiastical superiors, but simply bent on living in the midst of us the heavenly life, their example would surely be contagious. It would then be deemed a nobler thing to fight Christ's battle than to enter an army and be drilled to slaughter fellow creatures. Let us honestly state and face this truth : no disciple of Jesus may destroy a human life, or have recourse to violence. Whoever does that, is not his follower, however much he may deceive himself into that belief. Let every soldier take lower ground : he is of the world—opposed to the cause of Christ—by the nature of his calling. The rule extends in other directions also. No rich man is a follower of Jesus : the holding of superfluous wealth is contrary to his requirement. 'Follower, disciple, Christian :' the title itself matters not : the question is not about a name but about a reality. Let us be clear on the point. No condemnation is involved in non-discipleship ; but much harm results from laying claim to discipleship apart from obedience to Jesus and entire dedication to his cause. If the lump is mistaken for the leaven, called by its name, no sharp distinction being discernible between the two, the whole mass must continue unleavened. Either the gospel must fail of its purpose, or disciples must be found who will devote themselves to the cause, just as surely as the marriage feast would have been a failure if no guests had attended. Yet those most fitted for the work fail to recognise its claim upon them, so that it becomes necessary to hunt up recruits in all quarters. Jesus does not represent the mixture of classes at the marriage feast as a thing desirable in itself, but the occasion was of such urgency that no selection was possible ; they 'gathered together all as many as they found, both bad and good :' that touch was introduced into the parable deliberately and of set purpose. The apostle Paul recognised its truth and application. 'For behold your calling, brethren, how that not many wise after the flesh, not many mighty, not many noble : but God chose the foolish things of the world, that he might put to shame them that are wise ; and God chose the weak things of the world, that he might put to shame the things that are strong : and the base things of the world, and the things that are despised, did God choose, *yea* and the things that are not, that he he might bring to nought the things that are.' The closing words show the drift of the argument : the disciples were chosen ' to bring to nought the things that are,' that is, to annul the system of social life prevailing in the world, a system grounded upon selfishness and violence, and to replace it by the gospel of Christ Jesus, his ' wisdom from God, and righteousness and sanctification, and redemption.' Obviously, whoever undertakes such a work must rise to its level, however low and degraded his previous career. The way in which Jesus continues the parable brings out that fact. He describes the king as making an inspection of the guests, detecting one who was not clothed, as the others must have been, in the garment indispensable at such festivities, and calling him to account for the impropriety. 'But when the king came in to behold the guests, he saw there a man which had not on a wedding-garment: and he saith unto him, Friend, how camest thou in hither not having a wedding-garment?' The words 'to see' in the Authorised Version are replaced by the more emphatic words 'to behold.' Tischendorf renders, 'to look at the guests.' Young's version is as follows: 'And the king having come in to view the guests, saw there a man not clothed with clothing of the marriage-feast, and saith to him, Comrade, how camest thou in hither, not having the clothing of the marriage-feast?' By adding this to the parable Jesus obviated any idea that the kingdom of heaven required no change in those who accepted the invitation to enter it. Alford notes that the word 'Friend' is 'more properly *Comrade* or *Companion*.' Those who associate themselves with Jesus and his cause must conform their lives to his pattern. If not, sooner or later, in this age or the next, the enquiry will come home to them, 'Comrade, how camest thou in hither, not having the clothing of the marriage-feast?' The fashion of this world will not be recognised as suitable for the kingdom of heaven. It was no light offence which this man had committed. Of his own free will he had accepted the invitation, and he had no excuse to offer for neglecting the duty incumbent upon every guest to put on suitable apparel. 'And he was speechless.' It was necessary that he should be forthwith excluded. 'Then the king said to the servants (Gr. bond-servants), Bind him hand and foot, and cast him out into the outer darkness.' The words 'and take him away' after 'foot,' are omitted by the Revisers, not being in the two oldest MSS. The command, 'Bind him hand and foot,' suggests that the man would as a matter of course attempt to maintain his position by violence. Refusal to wear the prescribed raiment is indicative of an intention to follow the customs of the outer world. The practical rejection of Christ's doctrine of non-resistance is the fault most prominent and disastrous among those who assume a place in his kingdom without submitting to the guidance of his mind and will. Herein consists the gravest scandal upon our profession of Christianity. The warlike spirit has never been obliterated from the instincts of mankind. The strange, devilish notion still prevails, that War is a necessity of human existence upon earth. It is deemed paramount among the resources of civilization, and the professed ministers and representatives of Christ raise no protest in common against it, and not only suffer the curse to continue rampant and unreproved, but actually consecrate its banners and pray, by royal command, for its successful issue and the blessing of the God and Father of our Lord Jesus Christ upon those engaged in it. What a shameful parody of Christianity is this! It comes from our overlooking and forsaking one of the first principles of the gospel of Christ. All strife and bloodshedding are prohibited to the disciples of Jesus, and they who practise or approve such things have no part or lot in his kingdom, but must be cast out 'into the outer darkness.' The import of that phrase is clear, and must not be exaggerated. It simply denotes exclusion from the bright and festive joy inside: the man was thrust outside into the darkness of the night, as being unworthy and unfitted for the company within. That is the extent of the condemnation pronounced against those who are not in the kingdom of heaven, of which the marriage-feast is typical. Yet this is no light penalty, no trifling loss. It means the perpetuation of this world's miseries and crimes, the ceaseless round of wrong and suffering inseparable from a social system based upon selfishness and violence. The guilt of this man consisted in the fact that he introduced the habits and maxims of the world into the kingdom of heaven. Alas! that fatal mistake, that deadly sin, has grown into a widespread, crying evil, so that the professed Church of Christ has the form of godliness without the power thereof. There is no salvation for mankind under such a system. 'There shall be the weeping and gnashing of teeth.' How true, how applicable, that saying of Jesus to the existing condition of humanity! 22 Mat. 13

Jesus closed the parable with the words: 'For many are called, but few chosen.' That was a truth which pressed heavily upon his mind and heart. He represented all those first invited into the kingdom of heaven, as either neglecting or resenting the invitation. And when, after scouring the country, enough were found to start the gospel enterprise, the work of exclusion had to be undertaken. Jesus realised full well the difficulty of establishing the kingdom of heaven among mankind. Those to whom the duty of assisting naturally and of right belonged, held aloof from the enterprise. Men of light and leading preferred to devote themselves to the old, established routine, and not a few of them vehemently opposed the new scheme of life and doctrine. In spite of that, 'by men of strange tongues and by the lips of strangers' the gospel invitation was proclaimed, and the Church of Christ was founded. Then came another evil, foreseen by Jesus and figured in this parable: the blending of the world's teaching with his pure gospel. That evil grew monstrously and still prevails. Men boast of the spread of the gospel; but if the Church has overrun the world, the world has overrun the Church. The spirit of Christendom is not the spirit of Christ; the life of professed Christians is not the life of the kingdom of heaven. The freedom, the brightness, the joy and rejoicing of the gospel marriage feast are not our portion upon the earth. We are yet in the 'outer darkness;' and the state of society in general accords only too well with the sorrowful ejaculation, 'there is the weeping and gnashing of teeth.' The utmost possible peace, goodwill and happiness,—these are the characteristics of a marriage feast and of the kingdom of heaven. That conception of it may seem to most men too simple, too good to be true: but what higher, nobler, other object can the heavenly Father have than the prosperity of his children? The carol with which the angels welcomed the Saviour conveys the same idea: 'On earth peace, good pleasure among men.' This amelioration of the common lot of mankind on earth has been well nigh lost sight of as constituting the salvation of Jesus. The apostle Peter says that the 'precious blood' of Christ redeemed the elect 'from your vain manner of life handed down from your fathers.' Salvation, as preached and taught generally, is a very different kind of thing,—a system of intellectual beliefs, a scheme of justification, a method devised for the appeasement of divine justice without the sacrifice of transgressors. Saturated with such ideas, men interpret and work out the parables in such a way as to harmonise with their own notions. Here is Dean Alford's note on the wedding-garment.

'The guest was bound to provide himself with this proper habit, out of respect to the feast and its Author: *how* this was to be provided, does not *here* appear, but does *elsewhere*. The garment is *the imputed and inherent righteousness of the Lord Jesus*, put on *symbolically* in Baptism (Gal. iii. 27), and *really* by a true and living faith (ib. ver. 26), without which none can appear before God in His kingdom of glory; Heb. xii. 14: Phil. iii. 7, 8: Eph. iv. 24: Col. iii. 10: Rom. xiii. 14: which truth could not be put forward here, but at its subsequent manifestation threw its great light over this and other such similitudes and expressions.' Alford assumes that Jesus did not bring out this 'truth' in the parable, because he *could* not. Why? And it is taken for granted that scattered passages in the Pauline epistles are to be applied to the elucidation of a parable to which the apostle never referred. Again, why? And how could each man's particular wedding-garment represent the one robe of the king's son, whose robe is not even mentioned? And what connection is there between allusion to a garment and 'the imputed and inherent righteousness of the Lord Jesus'? Such an interpretation makes the robe the figure of a figure, not of a reality. That is a fallacy which pervades the whole doctrine of 'imputed righteousness.' Righteousness,—however much men may persuade themselves to the contrary,—is not, cannot be imputed to those who do not possess it. If Christ's righteousness is imputed to a man, it is because that man 'doeth righteousness,' and 'is righteous, even as he is righteous.' The word 'impute' is the pivot on which the popular doctrine of salvation rests and turns. Let us examine the passages in which the word occurs.

(a) 'And if any of the flesh of the sacrifice of his peace offerings be eaten on the third day, it shall not be accepted, neither shall it be imputed unto him that offereth it.' Young renders 'neither shall it be imputed' by 'it is not reckoned.'

(b) 'What man soever there be of the house of Israel, that killeth an ox, or lamb, or goat, in the camp, or that killeth it without the camp, and hath not brought it unto the door of the tent of meeting, to offer it as an oblation unto the Lord before the tabernacle of the Lord: blood shall be imputed unto that man; he hath shed blood.' Young renders, 'blood is reckoned to that man.'

(c) 'Let not the king impute anything unto his servant, nor to all the house of my father: for thy servant knoweth nothing of all this, less or more.' Instead of 'impute anything,' Young renders, 'lay anything.'

(d) 'Let not my lord impute iniquity unto me, neither do thou remember that which thy servant did perversely.'

(e) 'Blessed is he whose transgression is forgiven, whose sin is covered. Blessed is the man unto whom the Lord imputeth not iniquity, and in whose spirit there is no guile.'

(f) '*Imputing* this his power unto his god.' The Revisers render: '*Even* he whose might is his god.' Young renders: 'Ascribeth this his power to his god.'

In the New Testament there are two Greek verbs rendered in the Authorised Version 'impute:' *ellogeo*, 'to reckon in; to impute;' and *logizomai*, 'to count, reckon, calculate, compute; to take into

account, consider ; to calculate, reason.' The root of both words is *logos*, which is defined as 'the word by which the inward thought is expressed ; the inward thought or reason itself.' The verb *ellogeō* occurs only twice : 5 Rom. 13 (k) and Phile. 18 : ' PUT THAT to mine account.' The verb *logizomai* is rendered in the Authorised Version as ' impute ' 8 times, and in other passages as ' account, account of, conclude, count, despise, esteem, lay, number, reason, reckon, suppose, think, think on,' as for example : 'They REASONED with themselves.' [1 Mark 31]
' He was RECKONED with transgressors.' 'I THOUGHT as a child.' [15 Mark 28]
' Lest any man should ACCOUNT OF me above that which he seeth me.' [13 ii. Cor. 11]
[12 ii. Cor. 6]
' MAY it not BE LAID TO their ACCOUNT.' [4 ii. Tim. 16]

These examples, as well as the definitions and derivation of the word, sufficiently indicate that it denotes a conclusion founded upon facts, and is the very opposite of a merely supposititious, non-existent ideal. In Webster's Dictionary 'impute' is thus defined: ' 1. to charge ; to attribute ; to set to the account of. 2. to attribute ; to ascribe. 3. to reckon to one *what does not belong to him.*—Milton.' The last sense is that which has been introduced and generally held by theologians, as though to ' impute ' involved a pretence or make-believe. That idea does not properly appertain to the word, and it does not appear in Nuttall's Dictionary, where the definition is simply: ' to ascribe ; to reckon to ; to reckon.' The Revised Version obviates the danger of misapprehension by banishing the word 'impute' and supplying its place by ' reckon ', in all the passages except one in which it occurs in the Authorised Version. They are as follows :—

(g) 'Even as David also pronounceth blessing upon the man, unto [4 Rom. 6-8] whom God reckoneth righteousness apart from works, *saying*, Blessed are they whose iniquities are forgiven, And whose sins are covered. Blessed is the man to whom the Lord will not reckon sin '
(h) ' That righteousness might be reckoned unto them.' [,, 11]
(i) ' It was reckoned unto him for righteousness. Now it was not [,, 22 24] written for his sake alone, that it was reckoned unto him ; but for our sake also, unto whom it shall be reckoned.'
(k) ' Sin is not imputed when there is no law.' [5 Rom. 13]
(l) ' Not reckoning unto them their trespasses.' [5 ii. Cor. 19]
(m) ' Abraham believed God, and is was reckoned unto him for [2 James 23] righteousness.'

These are all the passages in which the word ' impute ' occurs. Let us summarise them.
(a) An offering not imputed as an offering.
(b) Slaughter of an animal not offered as an oblation, imputed as bloodshedding.
(c) A fault not to be imputed, because not committed.
(d) A fault not to be imputed, because repented of.
(e) and (l) A fault not imputed, because forgiven.
(f) Power imputed to a deity.
(g), (h) and (i) Righteousness imputed without works, after forgiveness.
(k) Sin not imputed when there is no law.
(m) Faith imputed as righteousness.
No difficulty can arise except in connection with the passages (g).

(h), (i), (k) and (m). Take first (k) : 'Sin is not imputed where there is no law.' Here is the apostle's argument. Sin entered into the world through the first man, Adam, and death through sin. Sin and death are inseparable from man's nature : ' Death passed unto all men, for that all sinned.' That was so before the law. Death was not a consequence of breaking the law given in the time of Moses : for in the absence of law there could be no transgression against it : ' For until the law sin was in the world : but sin is not imputed when there is no law.' Yet in the period between Adam and Moses death prevailed ; not because of the law, which then had not been given, nor because men repeated the first transgression of Adam, for that they did not : 'Nevertheless death reigned from Adam until Moses, even over them that had not sinned after the likeness of Adam's transgression.' The cause of death lies deeper down than any law,—in man's depraved nature and life. So the apostle teaches that sin is independent of the law, which after a time was 'added because of transgressions,' to reveal, denounce and prohibit them, 'that through the commandment sin might become exceeding sinful.' Another apostle defines sin as 'the transgression of the law.' That is true : but Paul argues that it is something more, a faulty condition of man's nature, tending inevitably to death, apart from the law which condemns it. The apostle John intimates as much by introducing the word 'also,' in the passage immediately preceding : ' Whosoever committeth sin transgresseth also the law.' The statement that 'sin is NOT imputed when there is no law,' implies the converse, that sin IS imputed when there is a law. Obviously the word ' imputed' here denotes, not the assumption of a state of being which does not actually exist, but the fact of its actual existence. Is it probable, or even possible, that the same word ' imputed' is not meant to carry the same meaning, when applied to the opposite condition of 'righteousness ?' To ascertain this, let us examine the passages (g), (h), (i) and (m), which relate to 'righteousness.' (g) ' Even as David also pronounceth blessing upon the man, unto whom God reckoneth righteousness apart from works, *saying*, Blessed are they whose iniquities are forgiven, and whose sins are covered. Blessed is the man unto whom the Lord will not reckon sin.' The law reckons sin, and declares its penalty : ' For as many as have sinned without law shall also perish without law : and as many as have sinned under law shall be judged by law.' The apostle places the Gentiles in the first class, and the Jews in the second class. To the latter the words of David apply, ' Blessed is the man to whom the Lord will not impute sin :' this signifies the withdrawal of the penalty against sin regarded as 'the transgression of the law ;' in other words, 'Blessed are they whose iniquities are forgiven, and whose sins are covered.' But forgiveness is a reality, not—as is too generally assumed—a kind of legal fiction, a simple change of disposition towards the sinner, a revocation of the curse of the law. If in that sense only iniquities were forgiven and sins covered, those 'under law' would simply revert to the position of those 'without law,' and would still ' perish.' The non-imputation of sin cannot alter its deadly effects : ' for the wages of sin is death.' Therefore when the apostle quotes the Psalmist's words, he regards them as a description of ' the blessedness of the man unto whom God imputeth righteousness without works.' To be clear as to the meaning of this we must have regard to the context. The apostle had asserted: 'By the works of the law shall no flesh be justified in his sight,' or, according to the marginal reading, 'out of works of law shall no flesh be accounted righteous in his sight.' Young renders: 'By works of law shall no flesh be declared righteous before Him.' If righteousness is attained, it cannot be through a law which has been disobeyed: 'For through the law *cometh* the knowledge of sin.' The apostle proceeds: 'But now apart from the law a righteousness of God hath been manifested; . . . even the righteousness of God through faith in Jesus Christ;' and he reaches this conclusion: 'We reckon therefore that a man is justified by faith apart from the works of the law.' Then he instances Abraham as justified not by works,—obedience to the law,—but by faith: 'Abraham believed God, and it was reckoned unto him for righteousness;' and then quotes David as pronouncing blessing 'upon the man unto whom God reckoneth righteousness apart from works.' 'God reckons,' 'imputes,' 'counts,' 'declares,' 'attributes,'—the words carry one and the same sense, both 'sin' and 'righteousness' to men, the former through his law against sin, the latter 'apart from the law.' Sin has been manifested through the law; but now righteousness through faith in Jesus Christ. Elsewhere the apostle proclaims the same doctrine: 'For we also were aforetime foolish, disobedient, deceived, serving divers lusts and pleasures, living in malice and envy, hateful, hating one another. But when the kindness of God our Saviour, and his love toward men, appeared, not by works *done* in righteousness, which we did ourselves, but according to his mercy he saved us, through the washing of regeneration and renewing of the Holy Ghost, which he poured out upon us richly, through Jesus Christ our Saviour; that, being justified by his grace, we might be made heirs according to the hope of eternal life.' Is it not obvious, indisputable, that the righteousness imputed through faith is as actual, real, visible, tangible, personal, as was the sin imputed through the law? Paul recognized in human nature two opposite conditions, 'sin,' and 'grace,' the one, condemned by the law, working misery and death, the other, arising out of faith in Jesus, tending to peace and life. 'Where sin abounded, grace did abound more exceedingly: that, as sin reigned in death, even so might grace reign through righteousness unto eternal life through Jesus Christ our Lord.' Introduce into any part of the impassioned arguments of Paul the idea of a merely substituted moral rectitude, the imaginative fiction about putting on the robe of 'the imputed and inherent righteousness of the Lord Jesus,' and you will thereby mar, distort, destroy, the force of the apostle's reasonings, and contradict scores of passages in which he asserts and glorifies the saving power of faith and grace.

Take now the passage (h): 'That righteousness might be reckoned unto them.' The word 'also,' after 'them,' has been omitted by the Revisers, not being in the three oldest MSS. The drift of the argument is clear. Abraham, whilst yet uncircumcised, was reckoned righteous by his faith in God; therefore he may be regarded as father of the uncircumcised Gentiles who have that same righteousness based on faith. That a real, active life of righteousness was in the apostle's mind, is evident from the context, when he says: 'who also walk in the steps of that faith of our father Abraham which he had in uncircumcision.'

Rom. 22–24   The passage (i) is as follows: 'It was reckoned unto him for righteousness. Now it was not written for his sake alone, that it was reckoned unto him; but for our sake also, unto whom it shall be reckoned, who believe on him that raised Jesus our Lord from the *20, 21* dead.' The faith of Abraham was perfect: 'Looking unto the promise of God, he wavered not through unbelief, but waxed strong through faith, giving glory to God, and being fully assured that, what he had promised, he was able also to perform.' The expression, 'waxed strong through faith,' indicates the effect of the faith upon Abraham,—on which account—'wherefore also—it was reckoned to him for righteousness.' As with him, so with us: our faith must produce its result, and will therefore be reckoned for righteousness. Young, instead of 'shall be reckoned,' renders literally, 'is about to be reckoned.' The faith of Abraham may be regarded in two ways: either as an instantaneous mental conviction, or as a continuous disposition of the mind. Those who assert most strongly and positively the apostle's doctrine of justification by faith, according to their own version of it, generally adopt the former view, which certainly was not that of Paul. For the scripture he quotes, *Gen. 6*   'Abraham believed God, and it was reckoned unto him for righteousness,' relates to the first giving of the promise. Years elapsed before *Rom. 18–21* it was fulfilled. Yet Abraham 'in hope believed against hope . . . and without being weakened in faith he considered his own body now as good as dead (he being about a hundred years old), and the deadness of Sarah's womb: yea, looking unto the promise of God, he wavered not through unbelief, but waxed strong through faith, giving glory to God, and being fully assured that, what he had promised, he was able also to perform.' The Revisers have omitted the word 'not' before 'his own body,' on the authority of the three oldest MSS., and have replaced 'neither yet' by 'and,' before 'the deadness,' which agrees with Young, the former being a mistranslation. The apostle Paul shows the patriarch's faith in active exercise from first to last. The apostle James goes farther in the same direction. In the last passage to be considered (m), he says: 'And the scripture was fulfilled which saith, And Abraham believed God, and it was reckoned unto him for righteousness.' He quotes that passage in connection with the offering up of Isaac, which was many years later *James 17* still; and his object was to prove that 'faith, if it have not works,   *20* is dead in itself.' He argues: 'But wilt thou know, O vain man,   *21* that faith apart from works is barren? Was not Abraham our father justified by works, in that he offered up Isaac his son upon the altar?   *22* Thou seest that faith wrought with his works, and by works was faith made perfect: and the scripture was fulfilled . . .' Paul and James are at one in their definition of faith, and they only who misunderstand the former imagine him to be in opposition to the latter. The marvellous breadth and fulness of Paul's intellect render his style difficult in some parts of comprehension, and careful study is required in order to grasp his meaning and avoid misconceptions. The apostle Peter recognised the value of Paul's epistles, but was also conscious of certain misconstructions put upon them from the first, *2 Pet. 15, 16* and uttered a caution with respect to them. He wrote: 'Even as our beloved brother Paul also, according to the wisdom given to him, wrote unto you; as also in all *his* epistles, speaking in them of these things; wherein are some things hard to be understood, which the ignorant and unsteadfast wrest, as *they do* also the other scriptures, unto their own destruction.' This warning is as much needed now as ever. Doctrines most startling and obnoxious have been deduced from the Pauline epistles. Theologians of past generations have founded sects and systems out of them, and some of their followers in the present day quote certain texts as conclusive arguments, knowing and caring little about the contexts, and never troubling to investigate for themselves the original meaning of passages 'hard to be understood' even by the best trained and most earnest minds, and the true sense of which is wholly obscured and lost to prejudiced or ignorant and self-confident readers.

When the enemies of Jesus left him and went their way, full of indignation at the obvious application of his parables to themselves, it was for the purpose of consulting as to the best means of silencing his voice for ever. They feared to arrest him themselves, and deemed it safer to bring him, if possible, under some criminal charge, within the clutches of the law. If they could ensnare him into some expression of an opinion which might be construed as treasonable, they could thereby ruin him with safety to themselves. 'Then went the Pharisees, and took counsel how they might ensnare him in *his* talk.' [22 Mat. 15] Luke discloses the plot in all its fulness. 'And they watched him, [20 Luke 20] and sent forth spies, which feigned themselves to be righteous, that they might take hold of his speech, so as to deliver him up to the rule and to the authority of the governor.' These emissaries were not common informers. Such men would have been ill-fitted for so delicate a mission. Men of high position in the religious and political world were not ashamed to become the acting agents in this detestable scheme. Mark records that fact. 'And they send unto him certain of the Pharisees and of the Herodians, that they might [12 Mark 13] catch him in talk.' Alford explains: 'The Herodians were more a political than a religious sect, the defendants and supporters of the dynasty of Herod, for the most part Sadducees in religious sentiment. These, though directly opposed to the Pharisees, were yet united with them in their persecution of our Lord, see Matt. xxii. 16: Mark iii. 6.' The teaching of Jesus was as hateful to the secularists as to the religionists. From the first, the world at large was opposed to his gospel: 'For of a truth in this city' (said the disciples) [4 Acts 27] 'against thy holy Servant Jesus, whom thou didst anoint, both Herod and Pontius Pilate, with the Gentiles and the peoples of Israel, were gathered together.' The doctrine of non-resistance to evil was enough, by itself, to rouse the opposition of military rulers. Their power is founded upon physical strength and justice—or injustice—by violence, war, bloodshed,—from all of which Jesus held back his followers. The following passage, from Count Leon Tolstoi's 'What I believe,' is well worth our consideration: 'Not one of the Apostles, not one of Christ's disciples, could have supposed it necessary to forbid a Christian's committing murder, which is miscalled war. See what Origen says in his answer to Celsus, chapter 63: "Celsus exhorts you to help the sovereign with all your strength, to take part in his duties, to take up arms for him, to serve under his banner, if necessary to lead out his army to battle. Moreover, we may say, in answer to those who, being ignorant of our faith, require the murder of men of us, that even their high-priests do not soil their hands in order that their God may accept their sacrifice. No more do we." And concluding by the explanation that Christians do more good by their peaceful lives than soldiers do, Origen says: "Thus we fight better than any for the safety of our sovereign. *We do not, it is true, serve under his banners, and* we should not, even were he to force us to do so." It was thus that the first Christians regarded war and thus their teacher spoke when addressing the great men of the world at the time when hundreds and thousands of martyrs were perishing for the Christian faith.' Here is a sufficient explanation of the hostility of rulers to the Christian faith. Whenever the head of the state authorises the persecution of a section of his subjects, it must be for some grave state reason, for the upholding of his supremacy against private opinions deemed antagonistic to national policy and welfare. The heathens had what we have and, alas! boast of having,—a state-religion, a system of faith and divine worship recognised as orthodox, an ecclesiastical organisation working harmoniously with the imperial policy, the State and the Church mutually supporting and strengthening each other. True, the persecutions under the Roman emperors took the form of upholding the recognised mode of divine worship. That came naturally about, because the divinities they honoured included such as Mars and Venus, whose cult was suited to a people which gloried in war and revelled in immorality.

10 i. Cor. 20
8 John 44
Paul asserted 'that the things which the Gentiles sacrifice, they sacrifice to devils, and not to God.' Jesus declared that the devil 'was a murderer from the beginning,' and told those who sought his life, 'Ye are of *your* father the devil, and the lusts of your father it is your will to do.' The apostle James thus criticised the warlike spirit :

4 James 1, 2
' Whence *come* wars and whence *come* fightings among you? *come they* not hence, *even* of your pleasures that war in your members? Ye lust, and have not; ye kill, and covet, and cannot obtain; ye fight and war.'

3 i. John 8
We are assured: 'To this end was the Son of God manifested, that he might destroy the works of the devil.' The apostle James

3 James 15
describes a wisdom 'that cometh not down from above, but is earthly, sensual (or natural, or animal), devilish.' That is the wisdom of the

„ 16
world, based on 'jealousy and faction,' and leading to 'confusion

„ 17
and every vile deed. But the wisdom that is from above is first pure, then peaceable, gentle, easy to be entreated, full of mercy and good fruits, without variance (uncontentions—Young), without hypocrisy.

„ 18
And the fruit of righteousness is sown in peace for (or, by) them that make peace.' The apostle Paul speaks in precisely the same terms:

2 i. Cor. 6
' We speak wisdom among the perfect : yet a wisdom not of this world (or, age), nor of the rulers of this world (or, age), which are

„ 7
coming to nought : but we speak God's wisdom in a mystery, *even* the *wisdom* that hath been hidden, which God foreordained before

„ 8
the worlds unto our glory : which none of the rulers of this world (or, age) knoweth : for had they known it, they would not have crucified the Lord of glory.' The method of Jesus is opposed to the

„ 5
method of the world, and our faith does 'not stand in the wisdom of

„ 2
men, but in the power of God,' in ' Jesus Christ, and him crucified : "

all strivings against evil relinquished, to make way for unlimited gentleness and patient, unresisting sufferance. That is the wisdom proclaimed 'among the perfect (or, full grown),' the strong 'meat' of the spiritual disciples of Christ, as contrasted with the 'milk' on which 'babes in Christ' must needs be fed, being 'yet carnal;'— 'for whereas,' says the apostle, 'there is among you jealousy and strife, are ye not carnal, and walk after the manner of men?' This conformity to the world in spirit and practice, robs the gospel of Christ of its most distinguishing characteristics, and accounts for the harmony prevailing between the Church and the world. Tolstoi continues: 'But in our times the question whether a Christian ought to take part in war never seems to occur to any. Youths brought up according to the Church law, go every autumn, at fixed periods, to the conscription halls, and, with the assistance of their spiritual pastors, there renounce the law of Christ.' Such facts give rise to very solemn reflections, and force upon us the conclusion that the spirit of the age is essentially anti-christian. It prevails, not in Russia only, but throughout Europe. Both in the last century and in the present it made France a desolating scourge, and threw her back, baffled, humiliated, defeated, to nurse again into activity, as soon as may be possible, the demon-spirit of revenge. Germany is a permanent camp of soldiery. The Continent seethes with the elements of disturbance, rebellion, anarchy. England rushes deliberately, light-heartedly, now and again, into wars supposed to be necessary for self-preservation or prestige. The lust for power, dominion, and military supremacy, is a national insanity, a delirium-tremens, resulting from an inherited habit and curse of blood-drinking. And all this goes on, generation after generation, side by side with a profession of Christianity! Not without reason did the apostle James connect the wisdom of the world, and its strifes, with 'hypocrisy.' Where are the 'disciples' of Jesus? Are they simply dumb, or are they non-existent? Assuredly they are not engaged in the work of bringing 'to nought the things that are.' Let any one of them, the very humblest, rise up in personal, practical protest, and he will be treated, as were the first disciples, as a fool, a fanatic, a rebel against social order. Tolstoi gives an instance: 'A short time ago a peasant refused to enter the military service, grounding his refusal on the words of the Gospel. The clergy all tried to persuade the man that his view of the matter was erroneous; and as the peasant still believed in Christ's words, and not in theirs, he was cast into prison, and kept there till he denied Christ. And this takes place although we, Christians, received 1800 years ago a perfectly clear and definite commandment from our God, which said, "Never consider men of another nation as thine enemies; look upon all men as brethren, and behave towards all men as thou dost towards thy fellow-countrymen; therefore shalt thou not kill those whom thou callest thine enemies; love all and do good to all."' The following fact, which is stated by the translator of Tolstoi's book, 'What I believe,' is equally suggestive: 'The work has unfortunately been forbidden in Russia, but the manuscripts pass from hand to hand, doing their silent work of regeneration in the hearts of those who long for the coming of the kingdom of God on earth.' The existing state of society has been brought about, and is maintained, by that same combination of religionists and secularists which schemed the death of Jesus and the overthrow of his teaching.

22 Mat. 16, 17 — Matthew's account is as follows. 'And they send to him their disciples, with the Herodians, saying, Master (or, Teacher), we know that thou art true, and teachest the way of God in truth, and carest not for any one: for thou regardest not the person of men. Tell us therefore, What thinkest thou? Is it lawful to give tribute unto Cæsar, or not?'

12 Mark 14, 15 — Mark stands as follows: 'And when they were come they say unto him, Master (or, Teacher), we know that thou art true, and carest not for any one: for thou regardest not the person of men, but of a truth teachest the way of God: Is it lawful to give tribute unto Cæsar, or not? Shall we give, or shall we not give?'

20 Luke 21, 22 — Luke's account is somewhat condensed. 'And they asked him, saying, Master (or, Teacher), we know that thou sayest and teachest rightly, and acceptest not the person *of any*, but of a truth teachest the way of God: Is it lawful for us to give tribute unto Cæsar, or not?' What a sudden change of tone! What an unexpected spirit of deference! What a flattering encomium of the Teacher they had hitherto hated and despised! What a subtle question, and how difficult to answer! Jesus saw through it and them, denounced their hypocrisy, and replied warily and wisely. Let them produce the coin which was payable as tribute. They did so. Whose was the likeness stamped upon it, and to whom did the

22 Mat. 18–20 — superscription refer? 'But Jesus perceived their wickedness, and said, Why tempt ye me, ye hypocrites? Shew me the tribute money. And they brought unto him a penny (denary—Young). And he saith unto them, Whose is this image and superscription? They

12 Mark 15, 16 — say unto him, Cæsar's.' Mark: 'But he, knowing their hypocrisy, said unto them, Why tempt ye me? bring me a penny, that I may see it. And they brought it. And he saith unto them, Whose is this image and superscription? And they say unto

20 Luke 23, 24 — him, Cæsar's.' Luke is briefer: 'But he perceived their craftiness, and said unto them, Shew me a penny. Whose image and superscription hath it? And they said, Cæsar's.' Obviously the coin had once been Cæsar's property, issued from his mint, and bore his name as subject to his control. As it was received from or through him, how could it be unlawful to restore it to him? The teaching of Jesus about 'the way of God' had no connection with Cæsar's property. Their claims must not be mingled, but kept distinct. Duty to God could not be paid in Cæsar's coin, and no question could properly arise as to whether it belonged to the Roman

22 Mat. 21 — emperor or to God. 'Then saith he unto them, Render therefore unto Cæsar the things that are Cæsar's, and unto God the things that

12 Mark 17 — are God's.' Mark: 'And Jesus said unto them, Render unto Cæsar the things that are Cæsar's, and unto God the things that are God's.'

20 Luke 25 — Luke: 'And he said unto them, Then render unto Cæsar the things that are Cæsar's, and unto God the things that are God's.' Jesus decided that tribute was lawfully payable; and the apostle Paul has

13 Rom. 6, 7 — expressed the same opinion: 'For this cause ye pay tribute also; for they are ministers of God's service, attending continually upon this very thing. Render to all their dues: tribute to whom tribute *is due*; custom to whom custom; fear to whom fear, honour to whom honour.' With equal clearness Jesus asserted that there were other

things which belonged to God, and which must be rendered to him, not to Cæsar. Need we ask, What things? 'Thou shalt love the Lord thy God from all thy heart, and from all thy soul, and from all thy mind, and from all thy strength.' Man himself, all his bodily and intellectual powers, must be yielded up to God. The command, 'Thou shalt love thy neighbour as thyself,' clashes not therewith, but is its necessary outcome: 'He that loveth his neighbour hath fulfilled the law.' That is the extent of human duty: 'Owe no man anything, save to love one another.' The question presented to Jesus was one of allegiance, not of neighbourly obligation, and his answer implied that some things no worldly monarch may claim. With the due payment of tribute, custom, fear, honour, the requirements of subjection and loyalty to an earthly ruler end, and Christian liberty lays hold upon the counsel of a free spirit, 'Owe no man anything, save to love one another.' 'Render unto God the things which are God's:' only that high rule of conscience makes discipleship to Jesus possible. When charged with disobedience to the commands of the ruling powers, religionists and secularists being again united in opposition to the doctrine of Jesus, 'Peter and the apostles answered and said, We must obey God rather than men.' There is a sharp distinction between the things of God and the things of Cæsar. The laws laid down by Jesus for the guidance of his disciples accord not with those on which human society has been constituted. They who were willing to present themselves 'a living sacrifice, holy, acceptable to God,' were exhorted to be altogether different from the world around: 'Be not fashioned according to this world (or, age): but be ye transformed by the renewing of your mind, that ye may prove what is the good and acceptable and perfect will of God.' Among the duties arising out of this transformation and renewal of the mind, the apostle includes these: 'Render to no man evil for evil ... Be at peace with all men ... Avenge not yourselves ... Overcome evil with good.' That is not the spirit of the world, neither are such maxims consistent with the office and duties of the world's rulers. Yet the apostle regarded the existing authorities as worthy of respect, and counselled subjection. Let us take Tischendorf's rendering, which harmonises with Young's: 'Let every soul be subject to the authorities that are over him. For there is no authority but from God: and those which are, have been ordained by God.' All government is of divine origin, for without it, society would fall into fatal anarchy: 'So that he who sets himself against the authority, resists the ordinance of God: and they that resist will receive to themselves judgement.' That is equally true, whether such resistance be justifiable or unjustifiable, tacit and passive or overt and active. Jesus told Pilate, 'Thou wouldest have no authority against me, except it were given thee from above: therefore he that delivered me unto thee hath greater sin.' The harmless Jesus ought never to have been dragged before the judgment-seat of Pilate. That was the act of the religionists of those days, and how often has it been repeated since! So common a thing was it from the first for Christians to be treated as their Master was, that the apostle Peter wrote as follows: 'Beloved, think it not strange concerning the fiery trial among you, which cometh upon you to prove you, as though a strange thing happened unto you: but inasmuch as ye are partakers of Christ's sufferings, rejoice ... For let none of you suffer as a murderer, or a thief, or an evil-doer, or as a meddler in other men's matters : but if *a man suffer* as a Christian, let him not be ashamed ; but let him glorify God in this name. For the time *is come* for judgement to begin at the house of God : and if *it begin* first at us, what *shall be* the end of them that obey not the gospel of God ?' There was no certainty of escape from arraignment before judicial tribunals ; all that could be said was, ' Is is better, if the will of God should so will, that ye suffer for well-doing than for evil-doing.' The experience was so general, that it seemed like a dispensation of Providence, and a somewhat puzzling one, even to the mind of Paul, who wrote, ' For, I think God hath set forth us the apostles last of all, as men doomed to death : for we are made a spectacle unto the world, and to angels, and to men.' Yet in truth, here was no new thing : always throughout human history the rectification of abuses has involved suffering, and the path of progress has had to be cut with difficulty, risk and loss through obstacles. That has been done by the banding of men together in a common cause, by taking up arms, resorting to violence, by strife, war, bloodshed. The method of Jesus is altogether different : there is the same concentration of energy, unity of purpose, spirit of opposition to existing evils ; but there is self-sacrifice without self-defence, arguments enforced without arms, freedom claimed and exercised, but not fought for, resistance to the utmost, if need be ' unto blood, striving against sin,' but always passive, never a sword in the hand, but often a cross on the shoulders, borne cheerfully even to the extremity of suffering and death. Only by regarding 'the things which are Cæsar's ' as separate and distinct from ' the things which are God's,' can the work of reformation go on, and the spirit of martyrdom prevail. Neither the judges who condemn, nor those who are condemned, being accused, with more or less truth, of seeking to turn ' the world upside down,' are to be blamed. The former are the representatives and exponents of the national mind and will, the latter, of the mind and will of Christ. That these are not in harmony, but contrary the one to the other, is a loss and grief to the whole community, all the heavier because not recognised and felt generally. Inherited opinions and habits of life must needs clash against new ideas, the earthly and the heavenly refuse to combine, and a struggle for mastery ensues. That is the penalty of past errors and evils, which the disciples of Jesus were called to endure. Paul suffered in that way more than did the other apostles : ' in prisons more abundantly, in stripes above measure, in deaths oft.' Yet he never railed against constituted authorities, but regarded them as ' ministers of God's service.' The world must needs take its own course, and Christians theirs. Police, judges, jailers, there must be, perchance even soldiers, though it is time that standing and invading armies should be abolished as inconsistent with modern enlightenment and civilization : but all these things appertain to Cæsar, not to Christ, and with them his true followers can have no concern. Neither Cæsar nor Cæsar's representatives are to be condemned : they are declared to be ministers of God, avengers 'for wrath to him that doeth evil ;' but they are not ministers of Christ, in the sense in which the apostles were, of whom Paul said, ' Let a man so account of us, as of ministers of Christ, and stewards of the mysteries of God.' Their offices, their function, their rule of life and action, are altogether different. Jesus chose his disciples out of the world, to be separate from the world, to the same extent and in the same way as he was. To call any man who wields a sword, returns a blow, sentences or executes criminals, goes to law, or accumulates property on earth, a disciple of Jesus, is to mistake the spirit of his calling and confer the title wrongly. Let us be content to take lower ground. It is enough that we are believers in Jesus, saved by faith in him; it is too much to arrogate to ourselves a position and status claimable only by such as devote themselves wholly to his cause. The first step towards clearness of view, accuracy of thought, and sound judgment on this important question, is to keep distinct in our minds the things of Cæsar and the things of Christ. The tendency of our spiritual guides has been in the opposite direction. Dean Alford's comment on this saying of Jesus is as follows: 'These weighty words, so much misunderstood, bind together, instead of separating, the political and religious duties of the followers of Christ.' Christ assumed no political duties: how then can his 'followers' do so?

The reply of Jesus astonished his questioners. 'And they marvelled greatly at him.' There was nothing in his words which they could condemn or dispute. Instead of being able to frame an accusation or argument against him, they were reduced to an ignominious silence. 'And they were not able to take hold of the saying before the people: and they marvelled at his answer, and held their peace.' They quitted his presence, foiled in their purpose and admiring his sagacity. 'And when they heard it, they marvelled, and left him, and went their way.' [12 Mark 17] [20 Luke 26] [22 Mat. 22]

Jesus was next questioned by the Sadducees with respect to their fundamental article of disbelief. 'And there come unto him Sadducees, which say that there is no resurrection.' Matthew states that it was on the same day. 'On that day there came to him Sadducees, which say (Gr. saying) that there is no resurrection.' Alford and Tischendorf adopt the reading 'saying,' which indicates that the Sadducees began a discussion about their peculiar doctrine. Luke's account implies that 'certain' of the sect had been selected for that purpose. 'And there came to him certain of the Sadducees, they which say that there is no resurrection.' The Authorised Version stands: 'which deny that there is any resurrection,' but the Revisers have followed the reading of the two oldest MSS. There is a substantial agreement between the evangelists as to the question propounded. Matthew: 'And they asked him, saying, Master (or, Teacher), Moses said, If a man die, having no children, his brother shall marry his wife (Gr. shall perform the duty of a husband's brother to his wife), and raise up seed unto his brother.' Mark: 'And they asked him, saying, Master (or, Teacher), Moses wrote unto us, If a man's brother die, and leave a wife behind him, and leave no child, that his brother should take his wife, and raise up seed unto his brother.' Luke: 'And they asked him, saying, Master (or, Teacher), Moses wrote unto us, that if a man's brother die, having a wife, and he be childless, his brother should take the wife, and raise up seed unto his brother.' A case was stated, which may [12 Mark 18] [22 Mat. 23] [20 Luke 27] [22 Mat. 24] [12 Mark 19] [20 Luke 28]

22 Mat. 25	have been real or imaginary, rising out of this custom. 'Now there
27	were with us seven brethren: and the first married and deceased, and having no seed left his wife unto his brother; in like manner the second also, and the third, unto the seventh (Gr. seven). And
12 Mark 20	after them all the woman died.' Mark: 'There were seven brethren:
22	and the first took a wife, and dying left no seed: and the second took her, and died, leaving no seed behind him; and the third likewise: and the seven left no seed. Last of all the woman also died.' The Revisers, following the two oldest MSS., have omitted the words 'had her, and' after 'seven.' In the Alexandrine MS. the additional word 'likewise' is introduced. In the constant copying and recopying of the manuscripts there seems to have been a temptation and tendency to improve occasionally upon the original. Luke:
20 Luke 29	'There were therefore seven brethren: and the first took a wife, and
32	died childless; and the second; and the third took her; and likewise the seven also left no children, and died. Afterward the woman also died.' That having been the state of things in this life, in what relation would the woman stand to these seven in the next? She had belonged to each: which one of them will be entitled to claim
22 Mat. 28	her? 'In the resurrection therefore whose wife shall she be of the
12 Mark 23	seven? for they all had her.' Mark: 'In the resurrection whose wife shall she be of them? for the seven had her to wife.' Luke:
20 Luke 33	'In the resurrection therefore whose wife of them shall she be? for the seven had her to wife.' The question was not an argument, but the answer might serve as a basis on which to raise one. Yet man's ignorance of the conditions of a future state of existence is no more a reason for denying it, than is the ignorance of an unborn child a disproof of all that appertains to the world into which it is destined to enter. Light and knowledge come with life, and human relationships in this world are modified by man's free will to suit with the necessities of his being. 'For this cause shall a man leave his father and mother, and shall cleave to his wife.' But death severs every
7 Rom. 2	bond: 'For the woman that hath a husband is bound by law to the husband while he liveth; but if the husband die, she is discharged from the law of the husband.' If these Sadducees meant to argue that the connections existing in this life must perforce continue in the next, that confusion and discord must thence ensue, and that there was no conceivable outlet from their supposed dilemma, they must have been shallow reasoners indeed. A bond of union first voluntarily entered into, and then by an overruling fate compulsorily and legally broken,—how can it be assumed to be binding and infrangible subsequently? Jesus told them that they were in error, their mistake proceeding from ignorance of the divine will and power.
22 Mat. 29	'But Jesus answered and said unto them, Ye do err, not knowing the scriptures, nor the power of God.' Mark represents this as a question, Jesus setting them to the task of self-scrutiny and enquiry.
12 Mark 24	'Jesus said unto them, Is it not for this cause that ye err, that ye know not the scriptures, nor the power of God?' Resurrection from death was not a marriage ceremony, but the entrance into an
22 Mat. 30	angelical and heavenly state of being. 'For in the resurrection they neither marry, nor are given in marriage, but are as angels in heaven.' It is not said, 'after the resurrection,' nor 'in the resurrection-life,' but simply 'in the resurrection,' that is, in the act and fact

of resurrection, which has nothing to do with marriage, but is a transformation to a more exalted condition of being. Mark is to the same effect. 'For when they shall rise from the dead, they neither marry, nor are given in marriage, but are as angels in heaven.' It is not, 'when they shall have risen,' but 'when they shall rise,' literally according to the 'Englishman's Greek New Testament,' 'when from among dead they rise:' it is not, 'they will neither marry, nor be given in marriage,' but, 'they neither marry, nor are given in marriage:' equivalent to: 'the rising from the dead is not marrying and giving in marriage, but the assumption of a heavenly life.' The argument resembles that of Paul, when he said: 'For the kingdom of God is not eating and drinking, but righteousness and peace and joy in the Holy Ghost.' Young renders 'angels' as 'messengers.' The idea of heavenly 'angels' or 'messengers' was familiar to the Jews: 'And of the angels he saith, Who maketh his angels winds (or, spirits), and his ministers a flame of fire.' The words of Jesus would naturally be taken in that sense, not as referring to any non-existence of marriage between angels: for what did the hearers know, what do we know, as to that? Such an interpretation of the saying makes it pointless, not an argument for conviction, but a statement beyond human apprehension. Is it not rather to be viewed as a waiver of the question the Sadducees had sought to discuss? The doctrine of the resurrection lies wholly apart therefrom, and has to be considered by itself, as little connected with marrying and giving in marriage, as with buying and selling, building and planting, or any other of the concerns of this life.

Luke's account of the words of Jesus is much fuller, and is evidently taken from a different record. 'And Jesus said unto them, The sons of this world (or, age) marry, and are given in marriage: but they that are accounted worthy to attain to that world (or, age), and the resurrection from the dead, neither marry, nor are given in marriage: for neither can they die any more: for they are equal unto the angels; and are sons of God, being sons of the resurrection.' This passage may be regarded from the same point of view. The institution of marriage is suited to man's necessities in this world: the attainment of a higher condition of existence and the resurrection from the dead, is not marrying or giving in marriage, for it is a state of immunity from death, of equality with angels, of divine sonship. Jesus puts aside the earthly, carnal question of the Sadducees, and dwells on the ideas properly arising in connection with the hope of a resurrection. There is another passage in which a reply of Jesus has to be applied and restricted in the same way. The disciples asked him, 'Rabbi, who did sin, this man, or his parents, that he should be born blind?' Jesus answered, Neither did this man sin, nor his parents.' Of course Jesus was not asserting that no sin had ever been committed by them, but simply that there was no sin to be thought of in connection with the blindness. Just so here: Jesus is asked, 'In the resurrection whose wife of them shall she be?' and he replies in effect, Neither wife of this man nor of that man: they neither marry nor are given in marriage; all thought of that must be dismissed in connection with the resurrection. Jesus turned the minds of the disciples into the proper channel by adding, 'but that the works of God should be made manifest in him,' and then went on to the truth, 'When I am in the world, I am the light of the world.' So here: having dismissed the idea about marriage, he explains, 'for neither can they die any more: for they are equal unto the angels; and are sons of God, being sons of the resurrection.' To adopt a scriptural phrase: 'He taketh away the first, that he may establish the second.' This interpretation is corroborated by the way in which the words of Jesus are understood and dealt with by Matthew and Mark. They are condensed into a single sentence: 'They neither marry nor are given in marriage, but are as angels in heaven,'—which corresponds in structure with: 'Neither did this man sin, nor his parents, but that the works of God should be made manifest in him.'

On the words: 'For neither can they die any more,' Alford makes this explanatory comment: *i.e.*, they will have 'no need of a succession and renewal, which is the main purpose of marriage.' That is as though we should argue that if Adam and Eve had not forfeited immortality they would have remained childless, having 'no need of a succession and renewal.' Not the simple perpetuation, but the increase of the species, has been the divine purpose from the beginning: 'Be fruitful, and multiply, and replenish the earth.' To reach the mind of Jesus, his meaning must not be thus guessed at, but pondered with earnest care. It is not enough to skim the narrative, and take for granted the inference which seems to lie upon the surface. Does the divine law, 'Be fruitful and multiply,' apply to this world only? Let those who infer as much from the saying of Jesus, 'they neither marry nor are given in marriage, but are as the angels in heaven,' at least take the pains to reconsider his words, and be quite sure about the doctrine before they promulgate it.

The words of Jesus as reported by Luke, 'they that are accounted worthy to attain to that world (or, age), and the resurrection from the dead,' are not consistent with the idea of a general resurrection and reunion of mankind. We are bound to give the same significance to the expression 'accounted worthy,' in Luke, as attaches to it elsewhere; and it must certainly be regarded as restrictive. 'Rejoicing that they were counted worthy to suffer dishonour for the Name.' 'To the end that ye may be accounted worthy of the kingdom of God, for which ye also suffer.' The attainment of 'that world (or, age)' in conjunction with 'the resurrection from the dead,' is not represented as a certainty for all men, but as a privilege dependent upon character. Such a conception of the resurrection was contrary to the popular notion, in accordance with which the Sadducees had argued. They assumed that there would be no exceptions, no selection, that the seven brethren and the woman, as a matter of course, would find themselves together hereafter under similar conditions to those existing in this world. Not so. The sons of this age do not all become sons of that age through the resurrection, which involves no resumption of former earthly ties, no marrying or giving in marriage. The Sadducees took the lowest and most carnal view of the resurrection; Jesus takes the highest and most spiritual, as did the apostle Paul, when he wrote, 'It is sown a natural body; it is raised a spiritual body.' They might with equal unreason have asked: In the resurrection whose servant shall he be, who bound himself to many masters, and was successively freed by each? Or, In the resurrection, who, out of a succession of Head Masters, will be

Head Master, the rights, duties, dignities and emoluments of the office being held for life, and then becoming vested in another? It might well be answered, In the resurrection they neither assume servitude nor mastership; in the resurrection they neither become teachers nor pupils: the meaning obviously being, not that there will be no servitude and no mastership, no teachers and no pupils in the resurrection-life, but that questions with respect to those matters can have no bearing on the primary question, Is there a resurrection? And then, having shown what the resurrection is not, in those respects, all that the resurrection really involves might be dwelt on in the precise way and words of Jesus when replying to the question which was actually propounded to him. He reveals an 'age,' a condition of existence, to be attained by those worthy of it, to whom the resurrection will be much more than the living over again of the former earthly life; they will become immortalised, etherialised, deified: 'for neither can they die any more: for they are equal unto the angels; and are sons of God, being sons of the resurrection.' The gift of immortality is promised, not to all, but to those worthy to attain to that 'age,' in which Jesus will bestow it upon those who behold him and believe in him: 'And this is the will of Him who sent me, that every one who is beholding the Son, and believing in him, may have life age-during, and I will raise him up in the last day.' On the words 'beholding the Son,' take this apostolic comment: 'But we all, with unveiled face reflecting as a mirror (or, beholding as in a mirror) the glory of the Lord, are transformed into the same image from glory to glory.' 6 John 40
3 ii. Cor. 18

Having disposed of the question of the Sadducees, Jesus proceeded to give a scriptural proof of the doctrine they disputed. 'But as touching the resurrection of the dead, have ye not read that which was spoken unto you by God, saying, I am the God of Abraham, and the God of Isaac, and the God of Jacob?' Mark is fuller. 'But as touching the dead, that they are raised; have ye not read in the book of Moses, in *the place concerning* the Bush, how God spake unto him, saying, I *am* the God of Abraham, and the God of Isaac, and the God of Jacob?' Luke is as follows: 'But that the dead are raised, even Moses shewed, in *the place concerning* the Bush, when he calleth the Lord the God of Abraham, and the God of Isaac, and the God of Jacob.' The italicised words, 'the place concerning,' in Mark and Luke, are rendered 'the history concerning,' by Alford, who observes: 'The words may in the original mean either "*in the chapter* concerning the history of God appearing in the Bush," or "*when he was at* the Bush." The former is the more probable.' From that passage Jesus drew this inference: 'God is not *the God* of the dead, but of the living.' The two oldest MSS. begin, 'He is not the God.' Tischendorf renders literally: 'He is not God of dead, but of living.' Mark: 'He is not the God of the dead, but of the living; ye do greatly err.' Luke: 'Now he is not the God of the dead, but of the living: for all live unto him.' Young translates the three passages thus: 'God is not a God of dead men, but of living.' 'He is not the God of dead men, but of living men.' 'He is not a God of dead men, but of living.' The argument is clear and conclusive, resting upon two foundations: (1) the essential relationship of God to man; (2) the declared continuance of that relationship centuries after the termination of the earthly lives of the patriarchs. Jesus takes the title 'God' in its natural and proper sense, as denoting rulership, oversight, protection. He asserts that, obviously and necessarily, 'He is not the God of dead men, but God of living men.' It is possible for men to imagine and worship false gods, as the apostle says: 'Not knowing God, ye were in bondage to them which by nature are no gods.' The term 'god' is synonymous with king, lord, judge: 'Hearken unto the voice of my cry, my King and my God.' 'The Lord is King for ever and ever.' 'God is the judge: He putteth down one and lifteth up another.' Any word will suit which denotes power, responsibility and loving care: 'A father of the fatherless, and a judge of the widows, is God in his holy habitation.' 'Wilt thou not from this time cry unto me, My father, thou art the guide (or, companion) of my youth?' 'For thy Maker is thine husband; the Lord of hosts is his name.' The title 'God' conveys the idea of absolute supremacy over living beings: 'all live unto him;' it cannot be applied in connection with those who have passed out of existence. Some four hundred years after the death of Abraham, God said to Moses, 'I am the God of Abraham, and the God of Isaac, and the God of Jacob.' That by itself was proof positive that those patriarchs were then alive. And inasmuch as they had died, they must as certainly have been 'raised,' resuscitated. Death and the resurrection are two parts, the one visible, the other invisible, of the same phenomenon. We can see the ending of the old and earthly life; we cannot see the beginning of the new and heavenly life. The course of the one is open to us, the course of the other is hidden from us. The latter is not, on that account, unnatural or incredible: are we not as sure of the existence of the wind which is invisible, as we are of the earth which is visible? God has revealed the one to mortal eyes, but not the other; true, we have evidences of the wind, through the senses of hearing and feeling, which we have not of departed yet still existent personalities: that is the only difference; the absence of physical certainty does not militate against a belief founded upon other testimony vouchsafed to us.

The word 'resurrection,' which is rendered by Young 'rising again,' obviously does not touch upon the question of corporeity or incorporeity: for the argument of Jesus is, that the mention of the patriarchs as living after they had died, is evidence of their 'resurrection' or 'rising again,' apart from any mention of a bodily form. The Sadducees assumed its existence hereafter, with all its parts and passions. Modern teachers have gone to the contrary extreme. Strange ideas have prevailed on this subject: as that the soul continues to exist, and will remain, in an unbodied condition, until a day of 'general resurrection,' when it will be reincorporated, some even have asserted with the identical particles of matter which were buried in the grave! That monstrous conception is fading away, as it needs must, before the light of Science and a more rational interpretation of the Scriptures. The words of the Athanasian Creed have a doubtful or double meaning: 'At whose coming, all men shall rise again with their bodies: and shall give account for their own works,' may be understood to signify a simultaneous uprising from tombs. That wrong notion involves another: either the intermediate 'sleep of the soul,' or its continuance until the day of judgment in a state of disembodiment. Both ideas are purely imaginary, not scriptural revelations, but mere logical inferences, the accuracy or inaccuracy of which depends on the truth or error of the premises on which they rest. Theologians dispute about them among themselves, as when Alford says, 'Stier remarks that this is a weighty testimony against the so-called "sleep of the soul" in the intermediate state.' The conception of a human soul or life without a body may be stated in words, as a supposition, but has no foundation in any fact within our cognizance, no analogy with anything in the world in which we live and move and have our being. Paul assumed that a doubt of the resurrection of the dead involved, as a matter of course, the question, 'With what manner of body do they come?' 15 i. Cor. 35 The resurrection of a man without any of the attributes of manhood, of a woman without any of the distinctions of womanhood, of the soul or mind without any reassumption of a material organism akin to the brain through which the intelligence works and the nervous system which conveys sensations: what kind of 'rising again' would that be? How conceive it, hope for it, long for it? It is as though you were to destroy a drum, and assert that the instrument still exists in the shapeless air which it once held, and which is now mingled with the surrounding atmosphere. They 'are as angels in heaven.' Angels are distinct personalities, possessing forms which have been rendered visible to mortal eyes, and organs of speech and touch which have enables them to hold intercourse with mankind.

There are two forms of expression: Mark: 'touching the dead, that they are raised;' Luke: 'but that the dead are raised.' That is one form; the other is, in Mark: 'when they shall rise from the dead;' in Luke: 'the resurrection from the dead.' It is the latter which is alluded to as a privilege, bestowed upon those who are accounted worthy to attain to it and to 'that age.' The 'resurrection OF the dead' is equivalent to the statement that 'the dead are raised,' that is, they are raised from death. The 'resurrection FROM the dead' carries a different meaning. The resurrection of the dead FROM DEATH, amounts simply to the fact that there is a 'rising again.' The resurrection of the dead FROM THE DEAD, denotes a pre-eminence granted to certain of the dead above others of the dead. This distinction is more easily caught through a language which gives the plural form to 'the dead,' as the French 'les morts' and the German 'die Todten.' In common language, when we speak of 'the dead' we mean those who have passed away from the earthly life, as though they no longer existed. But the instant we begin to speak in faith of the doctrine of a resurrection, they are no longer regarded as non-existent, and by 'the dead' is meant those who have entered upon the resurrection-life. Thus mankind are divided into two classes, 'the living' and 'the dead,' both equally alive, the former here, the latter elsewhere. A resurrection *from the living* is a thing unheard of, except in the cases of Enoch and Elijah, but we are taught to expect a resurrection 'from the dead,' which is alluded to as a similar translation to a higher existence, as when Paul exclaimed, 'if by any means I may attain unto the resurrection from 3 Phil. 11 the dead.' Jesus Christ is styled 'the firstborn from the dead:' in 1 Col. 18 what sense? Not, certainly, that he was the first who had been raised from death, for we have his own assurance that the three patriarchs had been so raised, and we are told that Moses and Elijah conversed with him on the mount. Neither is Jesus called 'the firstfruits of them that are asleep,' in the sense of being the first raised from death : for that he was not, as is proved by his own argument. In Jewish language, a 'firstborn' son was the one exalted by his father above his brethren : Isaac was deemed the 'firstborn,' the 'only son,' although born after Ishmael. The 'firstfruits' were the first-gathered portion of the harvest, rendered up as an offering to God : 'Thou shalt not delay to offer of the abundance of thy fruits, and of thy liquors. The firstborn of thy sons shalt thou give unto me.' Under both figures, Jesus stands forth as the representative of humanity. He 'is the beginning, the firstborn from the dead ;' 'Christ the firstfruits ; then they that are Christ's, at his coming (Gr. presence).' In his presence, 'beholding the Son, and believing on him,' the perfect 'will of God' in 'sending him' will be accomplished, in 'the resurrection from the dead' of those 'that are Christ's,' 'in the last day.' The doctrine of the resurrection, so easy either to deny or to profess, so hard to understand, demands a more careful and discriminating study than is generally bestowed upon it.

We are told that the teaching of Jesus excited general astonishment. 'And when the multitudes heard it, they were astonished at his teaching.' He had put the doctrine of the resurrection on a higher level of thought and certainty. The scribes also were struck by the novelty and cogency of his argument. 'And certain of the scribes answering said, Master (or, Teacher), thou hast well said.' His questioners felt that it would be useless to continue the discussion of a subject on which he had displayed such consummate knowledge. 'For they durst not any more ask him any question.'

The news of this intellectual encounter, and of its result, was carried to the Pharisees. Their opinions on the resurrection were diametrically opposed to those of the Sadducees. When Paul ' cried out in the council, Brethren, I am a Pharisee, a son of Pharisees : touching the hope and resurrection of the dead I am called in question,' there 'arose a dissension between the Pharisees and Sadducees : and the assembly was divided. For the Sadducees say that there is no resurrection, neither angel, nor spirit : but the Pharisees confess both.' It would naturally be felt by the Pharisees that for the Sadducees to discuss with the Teacher, who was equally obnoxious to both parties, their peculiar and false tenet, was to invite defeat and exalt the reputation of Jesus, which they were so anxious to depress. Therefore the Pharisees assembled themselves, doubtless still anxious to 'ensnare him in his talk.' 'But the Pharisees, when they heard that he had put the Sadducees to silence, gathered themselves together. And one of them, a lawyer, asked him a question, tempting him.' Mark does not allude to the Pharisees, but states the fact that this new questioner had been present at the previous discussion, and had heard the convincing answer which had been given by Jesus to the Sadducees. 'And one of the scribes came, and heard them questioning together, and knowing that he had answered them well, asked him . . .' Had we Mark's account only, we should take it for granted that the scribe had no bad motive in putting a further question. Had we Matthew's account only, we should naturally assume the contrary. Alford appears to suppose that one of the evangelists gives a wrong colour to the matter, and that we must choose which of their opposite views to take. He says: 'In the more detailed account of Mark, this question does not appear as that of one *maliciously* tempting our Lord: and his seems to me the view to be taken,—as there could not be any evil consequences to our Lord, whichever way he had answered the question.' And again: 'I should be disposed to take St. Mark's as the strictly accurate account, seeing that there is nothing in the question which indicates enmity, and our Lord's answer (ver. 34) plainly precludes it. The man, from hearing them disputing, came up, and formed one of the band who gathered together for the purpose of tempting Him. St. Mark's report . . . is that of some one who had taken accurate note of the circumstances and character of the man: St. Matthew's is more general . . .' There is no reason for setting aside either evangelist. Let us combine their accounts. It is plain from Mark that the scribe had listened to the former argument, and recognised the sagacity of Jesus. Probably his question was spontaneous, arising out of a desire to test the ability of Jesus further, and to elicit his opinion on a point much debated. That is to adopt the idea of Alford, that the question was not put maliciously, although Matthew describes it as 'tempting him.' The Greek verb here used, *peirazō*, is occasionally rendered as 'prove' and 'try:' 'This he said to prove him.' 'Try your own selves.' When the Pharisees who had *not* been present, but who, on receiving an account of what had passed, 'gathered themselves together,' as described by Matthew, this scribe, one of their own sect, without opportunity for previous consultation with them, put his question to Jesus. He anticipated them: and when he had been answered, convinced, almost converted, Mark tells us that any further questions they might have formulated were put aside: 'and no man after that durst ask him any question.' That observation indicates that there had been an evident intention of doing so, which was followed by an equally evident abandonment of the design. Thus viewed in conjunction, the narratives harmonise: Matthew discloses the purpose of the Pharisees, and Mark how it was thwarted. The test question of the scribe was innocent and harmless, for he had come under the influence of Jesus; and his fellow Pharisees could no more escape that influence than he had done. They had resolved to question, cavil and condemn, but were constrained to relinquish their purpose, and stood dumfounded in the presence of Jesus.

The question was this: 'Master (or, Teacher), which is the great commandment in the law?' Tischendorf renders: 'which commandment is great in the law?' Mark gives it thus: 'What commandment is the first of all?' In Matthew the reply of Jesus stands as follows: 'And he said unto him, Thou shalt love the Lord thy God with all thy heart, and with all thy soul, and with all thy mind. This is the great and first commandment.' The words 'great and first' possibly indicate that both were used by the questioner, although Matthew records only the former and Mark only the latter. In Mark the reply is fuller: 'Jesus answered, The first is, Hear, O Israel: the Lord our God, the Lord is one (or, The Lord *is* our God; the Lord is one): and thou shalt love the Lord thy God with (Gr. from) all thy heart, and with (Gr. from) all thy soul, and with (Gr.

from) all thy mind, and with (Gr. from) all thy strength.' The Greek rendered 'with' or 'from,' is *en* in Matthew and *ex* in Mark. Young and Tischendorf render the former as 'with ;' Young, the latter as 'out of' and Tischendorf as 'from.' In the Authorised Version, after the word 'first' are the words 'of all the commandments :' these are now omitted, on the authority of the two oldest MSS. Alford explains : 'St. Mark cites the passage entire :' that
6 Deu. 4, 5 is not quite accurate. The passage stands as follows : 'Hear, O Israel : the Lord our God is one Lord : and thou shalt love the Lord thy God with all thy heart, and with all thy soul, and with all thy might.' In Mark, the words 'and with all thy mind' are added.
10 Luke 27 The same addition is made on another occasion, the extra words being there placed last, and quoted by a lawyer. That first command was comprehensive in the extreme, and Jesus pointed out that there
22 Mat. 39 was another of the same character. 'And a second like *unto it* is this (or, And a second is like unto it), Thou shalt love thy neighbour
12 Mark 31 as thyself.' Mark : 'The second is this, Thou shalt love thy neighbour as thyself.' There was nothing original or novel in this
10 Luke 27 reply of Jesus : those two commands were likewise placed in conjunction by a lawyer, as containing a summary of human duties. Jesus heartily concurred in that view : when put forth by another,
„ 28 he said, 'Thou hast answered right,' and now he adopts it as his
22 Mat. 40 own, adding, 'On these two commandments hangeth the whole law, and the prophets.' Instead of that, Mark reports the following
12 Mark 31 words : 'There is no other commandment greater than these.' It may be safely assumed that both observations were made by Jesus. That we have two independent accounts, is evident from the fact that while Matthew ends at this point Mark proceeds. Jesus and
„ 32, 33 his questioner were at one on the matter. 'And the scribe said unto him, Of a truth, Master (or, Teacher), thou hast well said that he is one ; and there is none other but he : and to love him with all the heart, and with all the understanding, and with all the strength, and to love his neighbour as himself, is much more than all whole burnt offerings and sacrifices.' The Authorised Version has : 'for there is one God,' which is now altered to, 'that he is one,' on the authority of the three oldest MSS., but Tischendorf renders, 'that there is one,' the literal translation being 'that one is.' After 'understanding' the Authorised Version has, 'and with all thy soul,' which is now omitted in accordance with the two oldest MSS. The Revisers have inserted 'much' before 'more,' which is a reading adopted by Tischendorf and Tregelles. The word 'with,' *ex*, is rendered by Young 'out of' and by Tischendorf 'from.' Instead of 'all whole burnt offerings and sacrifices,' Young and Tischendorf render, literally, 'all the whole burnt offerings and the sacrifices,' which gives a definiteness wanting in the Authorised and Revised Versions, and brings out a contrast between the ceremonial and the moral requirements of the law. That was a splendid generalization, bold and wise, made by this scribe, and it afforded Jesus a favourable insight of his character. A mind of that stamp was well fitted to embrace the whole doctrine of Jesus, and the man stood upon the threshold
12 Mark 34 of God's kingdom. 'And when Jesus saw that he answered discreetly, he said unto him, Thou art not far from the kingdom of of God.'

According to Matthew, the reply of Jesus alluded to the heart, soul and mind; according to Mark, to the heart, soul, mind and strength; the word 'mind' not being found in the original command. The scribe spoke of the heart, understanding, and strength. These divergences are suggestive. Obviously not the bare words of the original, but the sense of them, was most cared for. In the course of centuries some words become changed in meaning; with the progress of thought shades of difference become noticeable which at first were overlooked; and sometimes two words may be required to convey the full import covered primarily by one word. This may have been the case with the word 'soul.' Originally the heart and soul may have been understood to comprehend all the moral and intellectual faculties, but gradually 'soul' became applied if not restricted to 'life,' the latter word standing as its equivalent in the New Testament. If such was the case, Jewish doctors did well to introduce the word 'mind,' thereby bringing out the full and proper sense of the commandment. Jesus himself followed that practice. In the same spirit the scribe preferred to use the word 'understanding,' instead of 'soul' and 'mind,' that term being inclusive of the two words. The object aimed at in such emendations was the complete and accurate rendering of the original passage. There is the same need in our own day for verbal additions and amendments, especially having regard to the translations from Hebrew and Greek into modern languages. Even with respect to our creeds the necessity is felt and acknowledged. The words 'hell,' 'quick' and 'catholic' carry other meanings than those current in ordinary speech. The terms 'substance,' 'incomprehensible,' 'begotten,' also need to be discriminated and explained. The same care is required in the interpretation of certain Scriptural expressions. Whoever would expound them rightly must be at the pains of retranslating or modifying them. The sense of the word 'church' is lost or perverted unless it be rendered 'assembly.' 'Eternal' and 'everlasting' are best represented by 'age-during.' 'Hell' involves a distinction between 'hades' and 'Gehenna.' 'Soul' is often interchangeable with 'life;' and the Hebrew expression 'only begotten Son' carries a meaning not generally borne in mind. Dr. Robert Young has done good service in this direction by his literal and idiomatic translation of the Bible. It would obviate error and promote the truth, if others would follow his example. The theory about verbal inspiration has stood in the way. Men have been afraid to touch a Bible-word, and the mistakes and imperfections of translators have been held as sacred as the book itself. How different this servile spirit from that of the Jews, who grasped the fact that the command to love God embraced man's whole nature, and who therefore did not scruple to insert the word 'mind,' or, having done so, to use the word 'understanding' as its equivalent. Accuracy of thought is not secured, but rather endangered, by a rigid adherence to set forms of speech. The recorders of our Lord's sayings seem to have been more careful to convey his meaning than his precise words, so that often we find them using different modes of expression, leaving us in doubt which of them, or whether both, actually fell from the lips of Jesus. There is an instance of this now before us. Matthew uses the word *en* where Mark uses the word *ex*. The Revisers merely point out this difference by a marginal note in Mark, indicating that the proper translation is 'from,' not 'with,' but Young and Tischendorf retain throughout the passage in Mark 'from' or 'out of.' One of the objects aimed at by Dr. Young in his version, was to avoid such different renderings of the same original word, and he gives in his 'General Preface to the New Translation' some striking examples of 'the lax renderings of king James' Revisers.' For instance: the Hebrew word *nathan*, 'to give,' is rendered by 84 English words and idioms; *asah*, 'to do,' by 74, and so on. The best translation is that which adheres most closely to the original and varies as little as possible the rendering of a particular word.

That the love of God enjoined by the commandment is much more than a mere sentiment, is evident from the expression 'from all thy heart, and from all thy soul, and from all thy mind, and from all thy strength.' We are too much accustomed to regard love to God as simply a mental, spiritual emotion, a feeling of devout veneration and affection. That is to mistake the foundation for the building, the seed for its fruit, the bare ground for the crop which grows upon it. Love is the active operation of every attribute and power we possess; it is the putting forth of all our moral, mental and physical energies towards and on behalf of the Being we adore. Be it observed also that the command is not merely, 'Thou shalt love Jehovah,' but 'Thou shalt love the LORD thy God,' bringing out that relationship between him and us, he our ruler, we his subjects. It is equivalent to, 'Thou shalt love thy sovereign Lord and King.' Loyal and submissive, having regard in all things to his supremacy, our faculties bent to his will, and our activities enlisted in his service: that is the love we owe to God. The name by which we know him cannot be dissociated from rulership, and our allegiance must wait upon his bidding. Again: the word 'thy' here denotes, not individualism but nationality, as is evident from the preface, 'Hear, O Israel, the Lord our God, the Lord is one: and thou shalt love the Lord thy God.' The intelligence and fortitude of the entire nation were demanded for the service and praise of that God who had chosen

14 Deu. 2 Israel 'to be a peculiar people unto himself, out of all peoples that are upon the face of the earth.' This divine command was addressed to the community, not to each man individually, promulgated to the people generally, yet not on that account less incumbent on all and each. The idea of duty restricted to individual obedience or disobedience, resulting in mere personal salvation or condemnation, is too narrow, too selfish, too egotistical. The apostle Paul insisted

14 Rom. 7, 8 upon that truth, asserting that 'none of us liveth to himself, and none dieth to himself. For whether we live, we live unto the Lord, or whether we die, we die unto the Lord; whether we live therefore, or die, we are the Lord's.' Is not that precisely the same obligation as was set forth in the words, 'Hear, O Israel, the Lord our God, the Lord is one: and thou shalt love the Lord thy God.' Devotion to God is not a mere personal concern, and the love he demands of us

Jude 3 has no scope for action apart from the grand cause of 'our common
2 Eph. 12 salvation.' Only as a member of 'the commonwealth of Israel' was a Jew bound or able to manifest his love to the Lord God of Israel; and only as we belong to the true 'Israel,'—the word denoting 'soldier or contender of God,'—can the heart, soul, mind and strength

of any one of us show forth love to our Lord God. The Scriptures define love as active and willing service: 'This is the love of God, that we keep his commandments: and his commandments are not grievous.' The love of God is more than morality, just as the love of our neighbour is more than common justice. Love stands on a higher platform of obligation than simple obedience and rectitude. It opens out a fuller, ampler life, a wider sphere of activity. It is one thing to say, 'All these things have I kept from my youth up;' it is quite another and loftier thing to say, 'The love of God hath been shed abroad in our hearts through the Holy Spirit which was given unto us.' The former carries us no further than the desponding question, 'What lack I yet?' The latter leads up to the joyous exclamation, 'The love of Christ constraineth us; because we thus judge, that one died for all, therefore all died; and he died for all, that they which live should no longer live unto themselves, but unto him who for their sakes died and rose again.' The utterance of love is not for every lip, the ambition and hope of love are not for every mind and heart. Love to God is the perfection of manhood, engaged in the service of humanity. It is 'the first commandment of all,' not meaning thereby the foremost in point of time, for we attain to it last of all, but first in rank and perfection,—'the great and first commandment.' It is easy to adopt the cant of religious phraseology, to talk and sing about our love to God, to persuade ourselves that it resides in our emotional faculties, and floats heavenwards in ecstasies of prayer and praise: it is something far more real and substantial; it involves the abnegation of self and the world, and devotion to Christ and the kingdom of heaven; and only in proportion as we have the Spirit of Christ can we possess the love of God. Who among us can lay claim to it? Not all, certainly: not many, probably. They are few who rise to the height of the 'great and first commandment;' but there are none of us who cannot, if we will, place our hands upon the second like unto it, 'Thou shalt love thy neighbour as thyself.' Only through the lower can we hope to reach the higher, 'for he that loveth not his brother whom he hath seen, cannot love God whom he hath not seen;' and when, climbing upwards on the love of man to the love of God, we have attained to the summit of Christian perfectness, it will be to realise the grand truth that the love of God is the love of Jesus, and the love of Jesus is the love of man, for 'this commandment have we from him, that he who loveth God love his brother also.'

The Pharisees who had assembled round Jesus showing no further inclination to question him, he took the opportunity of putting a question to them. 'Now while the Pharisees were gathered together, Jesus asked them a question, saying, What think ye of the Christ? whose son is he?' There was no hesitation or doubt about their reply. 'They say unto him, *The son* of David.' Jesus had been often greeted by that title, which carried with it more than the idea of mere descent, according to the popular notion. The Jews cherished the hope of a temporal Messiah, and were ready enough to hail Jesus as such, and to cry out, 'Blessed *is* the kingdom that cometh, *the kingdom* of our father David.' The expression 'our father,' not 'his father,' indicates that the terms 'father' and 'son' were taken generally in a broader sense than with us. We use the words 'fathers,' 'forefathers' in the same way, but the singular form, 'father' or 'forefather' is restricted by us to natural kinship. Those who welcomed Jesus as 'son of David' must have done so without any evidence of his pedigree; they did not wait or care to trace up his genealogy, before offering him their homage under that title.

Taking up the answer of the Pharisees, Jesus enquired how they would reconcile their conception of the Messiah's sonship to David, with that lordship of the Christ to which David had acknowledged himself to be subjected. 'He saith unto them, How then doth David in the Spirit call him, Lord, saying,

22 Mat. 43-45

> The Lord said unto my Lord,
> Sit thou on my right hand,
> Till I put thine enemies underneath thy feet?'

If David then calleth him Lord, how is he his son?'

The 'Psalm of David' begins in the Revised Version as follows:

110 Ps. 1

> 'The Lord saith unto my lord, Sit thou at my right hand,
> Until I make thine enemies thy footstool.'

A careful reader may observe that the second 'lord' is without a capital letter, therein differing from the Authorised Version; but a quick and critical eyesight is needed to take note of the fact that the first 'Lord' is in somewhat different type, all the letters being small capitals. A person hearing the verse read could not possibly imagine these differences existed; and those who are painstaking enough to detect them on perusal are left without a clue to their significance. If one happens to have read the Revisers' lengthy 'Preface,' and to remember the various explanations therein given, he will understand the reason and meaning of this capitalisation of the word 'Lord.' The Revisers explain: 'It has been thought advisable in regard to the word "Jehovah" to follow the usage of the Authorised Version, and not to insert it uniformly in place of "Lord" or "God," which when printed in small capitals represent the words substituted by Jewish custom for the ineffable Name according to the vowel points by which it is distinguished. It will be found therefore that in this respect the Authorised Version has been departed from only in a few passages, in which the introduction of a proper name seemed to be required.' That opens our eyes to the fact, doubtless new to most of us, that the same small capitalisation of the words 'Lord' and 'God' has always existed in the Authorised Version. If any ordinary reader ever observed it, he would find nothing whatever to indicate a connection with the word 'Jehovah,' for the Dedication to King James in the Authorised Version, beginning: 'Great and manifold were the blessings, most dread Sovereign, which Almighty God, the Father of all mercies, bestowed upon us the people of *England*, when first he sent Your Majesty's Royal Person to rule and reign over us,' —that Preface enters into no particulars as to the mode and method of the translation. Now if we turn to the Prayer Book Version of the Psalms, which is a still older translation, we find no capitalisation of the word 'Lord:' that was a step, half-hearted and ineffective, taken by King James' translators, not towards absolute accuracy, but towards an indication that a perfect and proper rendering had not been attempted either by their predecessors or themselves. And now, 270 years later, the Revisers frankly tell us that they deliberately decided to go no further in the direction of a true and literal rendering. 'It has been thought advisable' not to render the word 'Jehovah' as Jehovah, but instead thereof to put another word in small capitals; and for this no better reason is assigned than that others did so before them! In this passage Dr. Young's version stands:

> 'Jehovah * affirmeth to my Lord:
> Sit at my right hand,
> Till I make thine enemies thy footstool.'

But on this point even Dr. Young has been inconsistent, picking and choosing for himself, sometimes inserting Jehovah, but generally replacing that word, after the fashion of the Authorised Version, by 'Lord,' only in larger capitals, without a hint in his preface of what they signify. Considerations of expediency are out of place in the work of translating the Scriptures. We do not want to know what any theologian, or body of theologians, may consider 'advisable' in the way of adhering to former errors or imperfections of rendering, but to have placed before us the nearest possible approach to a literal translation. That no difficulty stands in the way of a scholar who is entirely free from the trammels of conventionality, with respect to the rendering of the word 'Jehovah,' is proved by Samuel Sharpe's translation of the Scriptures from Van der Hooght's edition of the Hebrew Bible printed in Amsterdam in 1705. The Preface states: 'The aim of the Translator has been to shew in the Text, by greater exactness, those peculiarities which others have been content to point out in Notes and Commentaries.' Accordingly, in Samuel Sharpe's Version there is no capitalisation of the words 'God' and 'Lord,' but a constant use of the name 'Jehovah.' Take this 110th Psalm as an example. Verse 1. 'Jehovah said to my Lord; 2. Jehovah will send the sceptre of thy power out of Zion; 4. Jehovah hath sworn;' but in verse 5 it is 'the Lord,' not 'Jehovah,' removing an obscurity needlessly introduced to the puzzlement of simple English readers. Turning page after page of Sharpe's translation, the word 'Jehovah' meets the eye, so that one can only wonder why it has been so systematically kept out by others. The exclusion begins with verse 4 of the 2nd chapter of Genesis, which Sharpe renders: 'This is the birth-book of the heavens and of the earth when they were created, in the day that Jehovah God made the earth and the heavens.' Up to the end of the 4th chapter the terms 'Jehovah God' and 'Jehovah' are used, whereas in the 1st chapter the word 'God' is used throughout. In the 5th chapter 'God' again recurs, but in the 29th verse 'Jehovah' is the word used. These distinctions in the original are by no means unimportant, and whoever would get at the true sense of these ancient records must resort to versions which bring out their variations clearly, rather than trust to a Version, however much 'Revised,' which persistently fails to do so. To print always a wrong word, but in different type, is not equivalent to giving the correct word. From the observation of the Revisers it appears that

---

* A careful and esteemed critic, on reading the author's MS., has called attention to the fact that the 'word "Jehovah"' itself is the result of combining the true consonants with false vowels, and therefore "a mongrel or fantastic word"—"a mere makeshift." Gesenius's Heb. Gram. tr. by Dr. B. Davies (Asher & Co.), pp. 52, 230, 356: cf. Spottiswoode's Variorum Bible, on Ex. iii. and vi.'

Jehovah 'stands in place of the ineffable Name,' a 'proper name' belonging to the Deity. Has the word a definable meaning? and if so, does it signify 'Lord' or 'God?' Nuttall's Dictionary gives the following definition: 'Jehovah. God as related to the Jew (literally, the self-existent and eternal, from Heb. *hayah*, to be).' The following passage in the Revised Version accords with this: 'And God said unto Moses, I AM THAT I AM (Or, I am, because I am, Or, I am who am, Or, I will be that I will be): and he said, Thus shalt thou say unto the children of Israel, I AM (Or, I will be, Heb. *Ehyeh*) hath sent me unto you. And God said moreover unto Moses, Thus shalt thou say unto the children of Israel, The Lord (Heb. Jehovah, from the same root as Ehyeh), the God of your fathers, the God of Abraham, the God of Isaac, and the God of Jacob, hath sent me unto you.' There is therefore a relationship between 'I am' and 'Jehovah' and the root of the latter word has reference to existence. 'The name Jehovah is formed from the Hebrew word which signifies *to be*, in its various inflections of *am* or *is*, *was* and *will be*.' It would seem, therefore, that if 'Jehovah' is translated it must be by some such equivalent as 'existing,' 'living,' or 'eternal.' To render it by 'Lord' or 'God' appears to be improper, and sometimes tautological. The expression 'Lord God' is tantamount to 'God God,' whereas 'Jehovah God' or 'living God' is correct in form and sense. This is borne out by the following passage: 'And God spake unto Moses, and said unto him, I am Jehovah: and I appeared unto Abraham, unto Isaac, and unto Jacob, as God Almighty (Heb. El Shaddai), but by (or, as to) my name Jehovah I was not known (or, made known) to them.' It is therefore obvious that 'God' and 'Jehovah' are not synonymous terms, and as 'God' and 'Lord' are synonymous, neither of them can properly be used in place of 'Jehovah.' Sharpe's rendering brings this out clearly: 'And God spake to Moses, and said to him, I am Jehovah. And I appeared to Abraham, to Isaac, and to Jacob, as El (or, God) Almighty, but by my name Jehovah was I not known to them.' There are passages which, as rendered by Sharpe, indicate a connection in Jewish minds between the word 'Jehovah' and the word 'living.' 'If we hear the voice of Jehovah our God any more, then we shall die. For who is there of all flesh, that hath heard the voice of the living God speaking out of the midst of the fire, as we have, and hath lived?' Again: 'Thy servant slew both the lion and the bear. And this uncircumcised Philistine shall be as one of them, seeing he hath defied the army of the living God. David said moreover, Jehovah, who delivered me out of the paw of the lion, and out of the paw of the bear, he will deliver me out of the hand of this Philistine. And Saul said to David, Go, and may Jehovah be with thee.' Many of the Psalms assume a different complexion when the word 'Jehovah' is introduced as the proper name of the Deity, and is not confused with the word 'God' or 'Lord.' Take as an example Sharpe's version of the following Psalm.

'I waited patiently for Jehovah.
And put into my mouth a new song of praise to our God.
Many will see it, and fear, and will trust in Jehovah.
Blessed is the man that maketh Jehovah his trust.
Many works hast thou done, O Jehovah, my God.
I delight to do thy will, O my God.

Lo, I have not closed my lips, O Jehovah, thou knowest.   40 Ps. 9
Withhold not, O Jehovah, thy tender mercies from me.   ,, 11
Be pleased, O Jehovah, to deliver me ;   ,, 13
O Jehovah, make haste to help me.
May Jehovah be magnified.   ,, 16
But I am poor and needy, yet the Lord thinketh on me.   ,, 17
Tarry not, O my God.'

The translation of Jehovah by 'Lord' is not confined to the English version. Luther habitually rendered it in the same way. For instance: in the 2nd chapter of Genesis Sharpe repeatedly introduces 'Jehovah God,' which is rendered by 'Gott der Herr, God the Lord,' and 'Jehovah' by itself is represented by 'Herr, Lord.' But then Luther is consistent, and avoids altogether the word 'Jehovah,' even in the crucial passage which has been considered, which he renders as follows: 'Und Gott redete mit Mose, und sprach zu ihm : 6 Ex. 2, 3 Ich bin der Herr. Und bin erschienen Abraham, Isaak und Jacob, dass ich ihr allmächtiger Gott sein wollte ; aber mein Name, Herr, ist ihnen nicht geoffenbaret worden :' 'And God spoke with Moses, and said to him, I am the Lord. And have appeared to Abraham, Isaac and Jacob, that I would be their almighty God ; but my name, Lord, was not revealed to them.' Obviously Luther made no attempt either to disclose the name 'Jehovah,' or to coin a word in place of it, but arbitrarily adopted as its representative, not as its equivalent, the word 'Herr,' which conveys the same meaning as 'Lord' in English. This imperfection in their own translation was recognised by King James' Revisers, who called attention to it, and indicated that there was something beyond the common meaning to be attached to the word 'Lord' wherever they caused it to be printed in small capitals. That is no sufficient guide to the sense of the original, and the constant use of a wrong word, however distinguished in type, can only mislead ordinary readers. The marginal notes now thrown in are important, and a careful student of the Scriptures must needs feel grateful for them; but it is much to be regretted that Dr. Robert Young and our Revisers did not go further in the way of correction, and that the bent of their minds led them to acquiesce in the mistake of former translators, and to perpetuate the banishment of the name 'Jehovah,' wherever possible, from the English Bible. The 'Appendix' placed at the end of the Revised Version of the Old Testament shows that the American Old Testament Revision Company protested against the omission of the word 'Jehovah.' Their note to that effect stands foremost, and is as follows : 'Substitute the Divine name "Jehovah" wherever it occurs in the Hebrew text, for "the LORD" and "GOD" and omit the marg. to "the LORD" at Gen. ii. 4, and "Heb. *Jehovah*" from the marg. at Ex. iii. 15, also substitute "Jehovah" for "the LORD" or "Jah" wherever the latter occurs in the Hebrew text, and retain or insert "Heb. *Jah*" in the marg.; where "Jehovah" immediately follows, viz., in Is. xii. 2, xxvi. 4, read "Jehovah *even* Jehovah" and omit "Jehovah" from the marg.'

The Pharisees were baffled by the question of Jesus, being unable to attempt any solution of the difficulty he had raised. Their discomfiture had a wholesome effect, and deterred all others thenceforth from interrupting his course of teaching by pestering him with hard

22 Mat. 46
"
"
12 Mark 35-
37

questions. 'And no one was able to answer him a word, neither durst any man from that day forth ask him any more questions.' Having failed to elicit an explanation from the Pharisees, Jesus referred the same enquiry to his hearers generally. 'And Jesus answered and said, as he taught in the temple, How say the scribes that Christ is the son of David? David himself said in the Holy Spirit,

> The Lord said unto my Lord,
> Sit thou on my right hand,
> Till I make thine enemies the footstool of thy feet.

David himself calleth him Lord; and whence is he his son?' Luke's

20 Luke 41-
44

account, also, implies that the question was put to the people. 'And he said unto them, How say they that the Christ is David's son? For David himself saith in the book of Psalms,

> 'The Lord said unto my Lord,
> Sit thou on my right hand,
> Till I make thine enemies the footstool of thy feet.'

David therefore calleth him Lord, and how is he his son?' In the Authorised Version the quotation in Matthew stands, 'Till I make thine enemies thy footstool,' which is altered by the Revisers to 'Till I put thine enemies underneath thy feet,' on the authority of the two oldest MSS. In Mark, the Vatican only out of the three oldest MSS. has a similar reading; the Revisers have not adopted it, but have inserted the note: 'Some ancient authorities read *underneath thy feet*.' In Mark and Luke the Revisers have altered 'footstool' to 'footstool of thy feet.' That is a difference of translation, not of readings, and Sharpe renders it in the same way as the Revisers, although Young and Tischendorf do not. The tautology of the expression sufficiently accounts for its not having been rendered literally. Luther agrees with the Revisers, but the German word for footstool being 'Schemel,' there is no tautophony between it and 'Füsse,' 'feet.'

By beginning the words 'Spirit' and 'Holy Spirit' with capitals, the translators have introduced the idea of a divine personality: at least, that is the sense which ordinary readers would give to words so distinguished. The Authorised Version renders Matthew, literally, 'in spirit,' uncapitalised, now altered by the Revisers to 'in the Spirit,' capitalised. Tischendorf agrees with the Authorised Version; Sharpe also; and the latter, in Mark, instead of 'in the Holy Spirit,' capitalised, has 'in holy spirit,' uncapitalised, a reading which was adopted by Griesbach and Wordsworth The introduction of capitals is obviously uncalled for, not warranted by the original, and scarcely fair towards English readers, who are accustomed to attach a certain significance to the use of them.

What would be the proper answer to the question which was left unanswered? Jesus did not deny, could not have intended to throw a doubt upon the fact, that Christ was actually descended from David. The apostle Paul announced that as an undoubted truth: 'Concerning his Son, who was born of the seed of David according to

1 Rom. 3
" 4

the flesh;' but he instantly went on to the higher truth: 'who was declared (Gr. determined) *to be* the Son of God with (or, in) power, according to the spirit of holiness, by the resurrection of the dead; *even* Jesus Christ our Lord.' It was that loftier relationship to which Jesus called attention, and the existence of which was clearly indicated when David himself owned personal allegiance to the Christ. There was obviously an aspect under which David contemplated the Messiah, which was incompatible with the ordinary ideas of mere natural descent and relationship. Writing under a spiritual influence, David reversed the recognised order of precedence, and spoke of Christ not as his son but as his lord. The word 'son' was equivalent to 'descendant,' one born in some distant age, and whose orbit of life and influence could at no point cross that of a long-departed ancestor; but the title 'lord' denotes a 'ruler,' one to whom David would look up for guidance, and to whose laws he would yield obedience. The promised son would be no mere follower of the father; there would be no repetition of the earthly career of David, no re-establishment of his kingdom founded upon force and cemented with blood. The spirit of prophecy had foretold a new order of things, under a new Lord, who would sit at Jehovah's right hand, 'from henceforth expecting till his enemies be made the footstool of his feet.' That attitude of non-interference and simple expectation accords with the Psalm, with the apostle's interpretation of it, and with the whole teaching and plan of Jesus. [10 Heb. 13]

'Jehovah will send the sceptre of thy power out of Zion;
Rule thou in the midst of thine enemies.'

To rule in the midst of enemies is surely a new development, and well describes the gospel scheme. Equally significant of the Christian warfare is the following verse:

'Thy people will be of willing heart in thy day of battle,
On the mountain of holiness
From the womb of the morning was the dew of thy youth.'

How well does that describe the voluntary discipleship demanded by Jesus, the earnest strife his people wage above and aloof from the world, so distinct from and high above its level, and the new and pure doctrine of Jesus, evolved out of the earth like dew by his uprising as a sun of righteousness. Then comes the verse:

'Jehovah hath sworn, and will not repent,
Thou art a priest for ever of the order of Melchizedek,'

which the same apostle applies to the high priesthood of Jesus. The Psalm throughout is Messianic in forecast and in spirit. The similes at the close are in the tone and language of the warlike David, but they must all be interpreted to accord with what precedes. The divine spirit of prophecy has breathed through human instruments, and the notes, although they make heavenly music, give evidence of the imperfection of the medium through which they are conveyed. This Psalm of David touches upon that 'salvation of souls' to which the apostle Peter alluded, and to it his words are applicable : 'Concerning which salvation the prophets sought and searched diligently, who prophesied of the grace that *should come* unto you : searching what *time* or what manner of time the spirit of Christ which was in them did point out, when it testified beforehand the sufferings of (Gr. unto) Christ, and the glories that should follow them. To whom it was revealed, that not unto themselves, but unto you, did they minister these things, which now have been announced unto you through them that preached the gospel unto you by (Gr. in) the Holy Spirit sent forth from heaven.' To call the attention of the Pharisees and of the people generally to the prophecy of David, was the best way of leading them to a conception of the spiritual [5 Heb. 5, 6] [1 i. Pet. 10-12] character of the reign of Christ. Their inability to solve the question was by itself a proof that there were heights and depths relating to the office and kingdom of the Christ, to which they had not attained, and which were not included in the popular expectation of a temporal Messiah. Alford observes: 'From the universally recognized title of the Messiah as the Son of David, which by His question He elicits from them, He takes occasion to shew them, who understood this title in a mere worldly political sense, the difficulty arising from David's own reverence for this his son: the solution lying in the incarnate Godhead of the Christ, of which they were ignorant.' That last sentence narrows down the explanation to one particular theological dogma, about which nothing was known. If that were the only possible solution, what would have been the use of putting the question? A knowledge of the miraculous incarnation of Jesus was not indispensable to the acknowledgment of him as Son of God. The import of the title rests not on that foundation only. When Jesus had calmed the tempest, 'they that were in the boat worshipped him, saying, Of a truth thou art the Son of God.' And we read that 'the centurion, and they that were with him watching Jesus, when they saw the earthquake, and the things that were done, feared exceedingly, saying, Truly this was the Son of God (or, a son of God).' The expression had a definite meaning altogether independent of the mystery of the incarnation, which is not once alluded to in the preaching of the apostles or in the epistles. Paul based the claim of Jesus to the title, not on his birth but on his resurrection: 'who was determined the Son of God in power, according to the spirit of holiness, by the resurrection of the dead,' rendered by Young: 'who is marked out Son of God in power, according to the Spirit of holiness, by the rising again from the dead.'

14 Mat. 33
27 Mat. 54

On the words, 'David in the Spirit,' in Matthew, and, 'David himself saith in the Holy Spirit,' in Mark, Alford makes the following note: 'This is a weighty declaration by our Lord of the inspiration of the prophetic Scriptures.' The remark is as natural as it is important. In proportion to our hostility to the theory of inspiration, when placed upon a wrong basis and carried to an extreme unwarranted by the Scriptures themselves and which is repugnant to common sense, must be our anxiety to admit the doctrine to the full extent to which it is justified by the divine revelation and does not offend our judgment or make unauthorised demands upon our credulity. We have here the belief of Jesus himself upon the matter, and it accords entirely with the statement of the apostle Peter, that 'men spake from God, being moved by the Holy Spirit.' The whole Bible, from the first verse of Genesis to the last of Revelation, is a declaration of divine power and influence exercised on behalf of mankind. That conviction uprose early in human history, and continued in full force during thousands of years. That is a fact which cannot be denied, the historical and prophetic books of the Old and New Testaments being in themselves a consecutive chain of evidence. We have not to deal with the primary beliefs of ignorant, uncivilized savages. The patriarch Abraham was not of that class, and the divine revelations and promises made to him either were realities, true in substance and fact, or fables invented by human genius. The same remark applies to the historical books which relate the deliverance of the Israelites from Egypt, the giving of the law, the institution of an elaborate

1 ii. Pet. 21

ritualism, the settlement in Canaan, the commencement of the monarchical system, the continuous stream of prophecy throughout the Psalms, Isaiah, Jeremiah, and all the prophets up to Malachi. It is easy enough for a solitary thinker to set aside the beliefs, and the outcome thereof, which have accumulated during past centuries, to treat them all as idle tales, to transfer the puerilities and unreliabilities attaching to the creeds of other nations to the history of the Jewish people, classing them all together, and waving them away as myths of olden times, unworthy of credence by a scholar of these enlightened days. The fashion sets that way. The solemn account of the raising of Lazarus is deemed, forsooth, a freak of the imagination, and the resurrection of Jesus is assumed to have no foundation in fact. All theories are possible and plausible to the minds which form them, and all alike must be established or crumble into nothingness at the touch of reality and truth. The Jews and their prophets, Jesus and his apostles, and the first and subsequent believers in Christianity, were neither fools nor children, but equal in capacity and power of judgment to the most enlightened scholars of the present day. The matters which the men of old believed in and placed on record were within the scope of their personal observation, and if they had not been true it is impossible to suppose such men would have accepted them, held fast to them at peril of suffering and death, and have devoted their lives to the promulgation of the gospel. We have to choose between two contrary propositions: (1) That God, the Jehovah of the Jews, has granted a revelation to mankind; (2) that no such revelation has been made. As a mere subject of scientific enquiry, the one is as credible and reasonable as the other. In support of the second we have the deductions, inferences, conclusions, of men who have investigated, more or less fully and carefully, the records of past times, and who express their opinion to the effect that the Scriptures of the Jews are worth no more than the sacred books of other nations, if so much; that the very idea of a miracle is offensive to a well-trained mind (the miracles of science always excepted), that it is a thing incredible that God should raise the dead, and that the whole human race, Jews and Gentiles alike, have been left from the first, whatever they may think to the contrary, without one law for guidance from above, or one spark of inspiration from a Supreme Intelligence. On the other hand, in favour of the first proposition, we have a mass of evidence handed down from earliest ages, carried on through successive generations, forming a consecutive narrative, one thread of purpose and design running through the whole. The mental calibre of the psalmists and prophets is not surpassed by that of their modern critics, and the mind of Jesus of Nazareth, as revealed to us through the gospels, apart from other evidence and claims, towers high above the intellects of those who would have us appraise him as a mere dreamer of dreams, an enthusiast who overrated himself and deluded his followers. The words of Jesus and the writings of the apostles survive them, amply demonstrating their powers of intelligence and soundness of judgment. It is enough for us that Jesus endorsed the belief current among his countrymen on the subject of inspiration. The extent to which that doctrine may be carried is still an open question. The apostle Peter was of opinion that the prophets themselves were not able to grasp the nature of that salvation to which the Messianic Spirit within them testified, although they were led to foretell a condition of mingled suffering and glory which should be realised in some distant future. The prophetic insight was not in all to the same extent, and it would seem that the visions of futurity necessarily took the form, character and words natural to the minds to which they were presented. It is quite conceivable that clearer and brighter views might be obtained at one time than at another, by the same individual, and that different men, speaking by the same Spirit, should realise in varying degrees the coming destinies of mankind, and describe them after the fashion of the ideas most prominent and habitual in their own minds. Take, for instance, the psalm to which Jesus referred. The first four verses accord with all we know of Messiah's spirit and kingdom, but then David proceeds to paint a picture in his own colours descriptive of the justice and triumph of the Christ.

110 Ps. 5, 6
'The Lord at thy right hand
Shall strike through kings in the day of his wrath.
He shall judge among the nations,
He shall fill *the places* with dead bodies;
He shall strike through the head in many countries.'

Taken as pure figures of speech, but in no other way, all this denotes the ultimate supremacy of the Messiah. The literal sense is utterly abhorrent to the aims and character of Jesus. In another Psalm, not of David, we have a clue to the true meaning of these 'desolations' which God will bring upon the earth.

46 Ps. 8-10
'Come, behold the works of the Lord,
What desolations he hath made in the earth.
He maketh wars to cease unto the end of the earth;
He breaketh the bow, and cutteth the spear in sunder;
He burneth the chariots in the fire.
Be still, and know that I am God:
I will be exalted among the nations,
I will be exalted in the earth.'

Take another Psalm, evidently prophetic.

72 Ps. 5-9
'They shall fear thee while the sun endureth,
And so long as the moon, throughout all generations.
He shall come down like rain upon the mown grass:
As showers that water the earth.
In his days shall the righteous flourish;
And abundance of peace, till the moon be no more.
He shall have dominion also from sea to sea,
And from the River unto the ends of the earth.
They that dwell in the wilderness shall bow before him;
And his enemies shall lick the dust.'

That last line is out of harmony with the rest, unless we take it in a figurative sense. The same remark applies to the closing words of verse 4, which stands as follows:

'He shall judge the poor of the people,
He shall save the children of the needy,
And shall break in pieces the oppressor.'

14 i. Cor. 32   Paul explained that 'the spirits of the prophets are subject to the prophets;' and when Peter expressed his conviction that the Spirit of
1 i. Pet. 10-12   Christ was in those who foretold gospel days, he claimed for them no

greater gift than that which every Christian must possess, for 'if any man hath not the Spirit of Christ, he is none of his.' There is no more justification for the assertion that the Spirit of God in the Old and New Testament writers conferred infallibility upon them, than there would be for claiming the same infallibility for all Christians now. 'To each one is given the manifestation of the Spirit to profit withal.' The test of true inspiration is profitableness: 'Every scripture inspired of God *is* also profitable.' Tischendorf, Sharpe and Luther render that passage in the same way, so that it really carries a meaning contrary to that deduced from the Authorised Version, which stands as follows: 'All scripture *is* given by inspiration of God, and *is* profitable.' To assume that there is nothing in the Bible purely human; that every sentence has been framed under divine guidance; that mistakes and misapprehensions were eliminated from the minds of the writers, when they wrote or dictated these records, however little that may have been the case with them at other moments: that is a proposition too monstrous and absurd to be upheld in all its nakedness. Yet the theory of Inspiration, long held and insisted on, amounts to neither more nor less than that. Let us distinguish between infallibility and spirituality, and between spirituality and omniscience. The saying of Jesus that David in the Holy Spirit called Christ Lord, testifies only to the spiritual insight of David. To that extent, at least, God had 'sent forth the Spirit of his Son,' into the heart of David, as he does now into our hearts: for 'no man can say, Jesus is Lord, but in the Holy Spirit.' Consider how unhesitatingly the apostle Paul asserted, not only the existence of a spiritual influence in believers, but its universality among them, and its varieties of operation. 'Now there are diversities of gifts, but the same Spirit. And there are diversities of ministrations, and the same Lord. And there are diversities of workings, but the same God, who worketh all things in all. But to each one is given the manifestation of the Spirit to profit withal. For to one is given through the Spirit the word of wisdom; and to another the word of knowledge, according to the same Spirit: to another faith, in the same Spirit; and to another gifts of healings, in the one Spirit; and to another workings of miracles (or, powers); and to another prophecy; and to another discernings of spirits: to another *divers* kinds of tongues; and to another the interpretation of tongues: but all these worketh the one and the same Spirit, dividing to each one severally even as he will.' The doctrine of inspiration cannot be rightly grasped by those who restrict it to the writers of the Old and New Testaments. That is the fundamental error to be guarded against. Inspiration has been held to signify, not spirituality, but infallible accuracy, not the natural, spontaneous outcome of that energy and intelligence which the Spirit of God has vouchsafed 'to each one severally, even as he will,' but a kind of religious ventriloquism, as though the lips of prophets were moved by a supernatural influence to utter words not of their own choosing. Except in the case of Balaam, what justification do the Scriptures afford for such an idea? The recognition by Jesus of the fact that David and other prophets spake 'in the Holy Spirit' must not be assumed to favour whatever views of inspiration happen to be current among theologians. His admission of the doctrine must not be confounded with their definition of it. Dean Alford, in the Introduction to his 'New Testament for English Readers' has defined his belief in inspiration: 'I regard the Canonical Books of the Old and New Testaments to have been given by inspiration of Almighty God, and in this respect to differ from all other books in the world. I rest this my belief on the consent of Christ's Holy Catholic Church, and on evidence furnished by these books themselves.' That phrase, 'the consent of Christ's Holy Catholic Church,' is sonorous and solemn, but put into plainer words it amounts to this: That the belief in inspiration is based upon the opinions of Christians in general, and that no one in particular is responsible for it. We are to accept it, because others accepted it before us. It is held to follow that, inasmuch as the four gospels have been consented to by the Church, their compilers are to be assumed to have been inspired,—Mark and Luke, who were not apostles, equally with Matthew and John who were. The successive steps of the argument are not disclosed, and consequently no attempt is made to examine and substantiate them. The 'consent of Christ's Holy Catholic Church' covers everything, and so, without enquiry and without scruple, Alford reaches the following conclusion: 'The two, three, or four, Gospel records of the same event are each of them separately true: written by men divinely guided into truth, and relating facts which happened, and *as* they happened.' This is another turning-point in the argument, it being taken for granted that inspiration and historical accuracy are either identical, or that the former includes the latter, and that inasmuch as the New Testament writers were inspired, they must been supernaturally guided in the task of compilation, and were enabled unerringly to sift the false from the true. So we are led on and on, from one assumption to another, only to find at last that the doctrine of inspiration, which is founded upon 'the consent of Christ's Holy Catholic Church,' is not consented to in the same sense by those who hold it, so that Alford has to argue against the theory of *verbal inspiration*, and to fall back upon *plenary inspiration*, saying, 'If I understand *plenary inspiration* rightly, I hold it to the utmost.' He arrives finally, however, at this conclusion: 'We must take our views of inspiration, not, as is too often done, from *à priori* considerations, but *entirely from the evidence furnished by the Scriptures themselves;*' with which, it may be added, the consent of the 'Church' has nothing to do.

Every attempt to bring the teaching of Jesus into contempt had failed ignominiously, and his discourses were now attended by crowds of eager listeners. 'And the common people (or, the great multitude) heard him gladly.' Alford notes that the expression 'common people' in the Authorised Version is 'literally *the great multitude*.' Young, Tischendorf and Luther so render it, and Sharpe and the 'Englishman's Greek New Testament,' 'the great crowd.' Jesus was addressing his disciples, but what he said to them was heard by others, and he did not scruple thus publicly to utter a warning against the scribes, their love of ostentation, their rapacity and hypocrisy. 'And in the hearing of all the people he said unto his disciples, Beware of the scribes, which desire to walk in long robes, and love salutations in the market-places, and chief seats in the synagogues, and chief places at feasts; which devour widows'

12 Mark 37

(?) Luke 45-47

houses, and for a pretence, make long prayers: these shall receive greater condemnation.' Mark is to the same effect: 'And in his teaching he said, Beware of the scribes, which desire to walk in long robes, and *to have* salutations in the market-places, and chief seats in the synagogues, and chief places at feasts: they which devour widows' houses, and for a pretence make (or, even while for a pretence they make) long prayers; these shall receive greater condemnation.' The Revisers have altered 'damnation' to 'condemnation.' Young renders, 'more notable judgment,' and Tischendorf, 'more abundant judgment.' In these few masterly words and touches Jesus thus summarised the lives and characters of this class of men: their love of dress and deference and precedence, always and everywhere, their grasping avarice, veneered over with sanctimonious observances. There was a world of cant in those days, as in ours, crying out for exposure, and meriting the contempt of every honest mind. Vices of that kind deserve, and will receive, a greater measure of reprobation than open transgressions: 'Some men's sins are evident, going before unto judgement: and some men also they follow after.' A poison disguised as fragrance and permeating the atmosphere, works more mischief than the open contamination of a dungheap. Jesus directed the full force of his eloquence, and that not once or twice only, against the miasma of hypocrisy. This condemnation of the scribes, related by Mark and Luke, was preliminary to a long and vehement discourse recorded by Matthew. Jesus began by bidding his hearers recognise the judicial position occupied by the scribes and Pharisees, whose counsels might be followed safely and in all good conscience. Their teaching by way of precept was right, but the example of their lives was pernicious. 'Then spake Jesus to the multitudes and to his disciples, saying, The scribes and the Pharisees sit on Moses' seat: all things therefore whatsoever they bid you, *these* do and observe: but do not ye after their works; for they say, and do not.' Tischendorf renders: 'sat on Moses' seat'; and Young literally: 'On the seat of Moses sat down the scribes and the Pharisees.' Alford notes: 'The verb rendered *sit* must not be pressed too strongly, as conveying blame,—*have seated themselves; it is merely stated here as a matter of fact.*' Their teaching was rigid and burdensome in the extreme, but their own lives were light and frivolous. 'Yea, they bind heavy burdens and grievous to be borne, and lay them on men's shoulders; but they themselves will not move them with their finger.' The Revisers note that 'many ancient authorities omit *and grievous to be borne.*' It is omitted by Tischendorf and Alford. The reading of the oldest MS. is, 'great heavy burdens, and lay.' The Authorised Version has, 'with one of their fingers,' but Young and Tischendorf agree with the Revisers in rendering, 'with their finger.' Their airy, fantastic finger-touch, which was all they cared to give, could not lay hold upon and grapple with the stern and solemn responsibilities they preached about. Their chosen sphere of action was in duties and customs which could be exhibited externally, making themselves conspicuous in the eyes of men. 'But all their works they do for to be seen of men: for they make broad their phylacteries, and enlarge the borders *of their garments*, and love the chief place at feasts, and the chief seats in the synagogues, and the salutations in the market-places, and to be called of men, Rabbi.' The two oldest MSS. omit ' of their garments,' which seems to be the reason why the Revisers italicised those words. The Authorised Version repeats the word 'Rabbi,' now omitted on the same authority. 'Uppermost rooms at feast' is now literally translated, 'chief places (couches—Young) at feasts.' Alford explains: 'Phylacteries, in the Hebrew, *Tephillin*, were strips of parchment with certain passages of Scripture, viz., Exod. xiii. 11—16 and 1—10: Deut. xi. 13—21; vi. 4—9, written on them, and worn on the forehead between the eyes, on the left side next the heart, and on the left arm.' On the title 'Rabbi,'

23 Mat. 8 Jesus observed: 'But be not ye called Rabbi: for one is your teacher, and all ye are brethren.' The words 'even Christ,' after 'teacher,' are now omitted, not being in the two oldest MSS. The word rendered 'Master' in the Authorised Version and 'director' by Young, is now replaced by 'teacher,' according to a different reading.

,, 9-12 Jesus continued: 'And call no man your father on the earth: for one is your Father, which is in heaven (Gr. the heavenly). Neither be ye called masters, for one is your master, *even* the Christ. But he that is greatest (Gr. greater) among you shall be your servant (or, minister). And whosoever shall exalt himself shall be humbled; and whosoever shall humble himself shall be exalted.' Tischendorf renders 'masters, master,' as 'leaders, leader,' and Young as 'directors, director.' Alford explains that 'call no man your father on the earth' is, 'literally, *name not any Father of you* on earth': the command is to the disciples collectively, not designed to touch upon personal and family relationships. Jesus strenuously insisted upon equality among his disciples. The collective title which best bescems them is 'brethren.' Freedom, absolute and entire, is their heritage. Much of the evil existing in the world has risen up and been perpetuated through the spirit of autocracy. Lordship on the one side, and servility on the other, have made the multitude obedient slaves to one absolute, imperious will, and have enabled monarchs and their coadjutors to deluge the world with blood, so that dynastic and national feuds, with all the accompanying horrors of war, have come to be regarded as the natural, justifiable, inevitable condition of humanity on earth. The aim of Jesus, the sum and substance of his gospel, was to introduce 'peace on earth'; and his repeated counsels to his disciples to eradicate from their minds the very idea of domination and direction by a recognised superior, to acknowledge no fealty except to one heavenly Father, and to own no Lord, no teacher, no leader, except Christ himself,—this was the best, the essential method of bringing to pass his gracious purposes of blessing to mankind. Let us not fall into the error of assuming that such exhortations have only a theological aspect and bearing, and relate simply to liberty of conscience and judgment in matters of faith and modes of divine worship. The precepts of Jesus touch the whole life and character. He bound his disciples to transfer their allegiance from others to himself. Absolute subjection to his rules of conduct constitutes the only reason and justification of this immunity from worldly claims and customs. The counsels of Jesus are for disciples of Jesus; what he speaks, he speaks to those who receive the law at his mouth and fashion their lives to his pattern. Emulations, distinctions, precedences, titles of honour,—these are badges of the world's system, and are contrary to the method and spirit of Jesus. To carry out his intentions, it was, and is, absolutely necessary that a Christian brotherhood should exist, owning no lord but the Christ, rejecting the world's maxims, holding aloof from all strife of law or arms, accumulating no surplus property, estranged from courtly rank, and allowing among its own members no titles of superiority or supremacy. The adoption of any lower standard of discipleship than this, is evidence of departure from the high ideal of the gospel, and of the blending of the church with the world. Alas! the very conception of such an organisation is now almost lost to mankind. No distinction is drawn, or even suggested, between simple 'believers' and professed 'disciples' of Jesus. The only difference now is between the clergy and the laity, and that not a difference between discipleship and non-discipleship, but of profession and of dress, all else that is lawful to a layman being equally lawful to a clergyman. There are two conceivable ways of bringing mankind under the rule of Christ, of establishing the kingdom of heaven upon earth. The first is, to introduce all into the church of Christ on easy terms, as a matter of course and of inherent right, adopting infant baptism, and then endeavouring, by means of Christian teaching, to persuade all men to live up to the precepts of Jesus, first toning them down somewhat, as though they were couched in figurative language which needs to be interpreted and modified to square with the established customs and recognised tone of society. That has been the system pursued through many centuries: the result being that dense masses of the population, in so-called Christian countries, are sunk in worse than heathen degradation, the worship of mammon prevails, and the warlike spirit among nations is as rampant as in the time of the Cæsars. The plan of Jesus is the very opposite of that which has been so long adopted and perseveringly adhered to. It consists in the enlistment and organisation of a band of 'disciples,' volunteers in the cause of Christ, who have pledged themselves not merely to aim at but actually to live the heavenly life on earth, having their hearts and their treasure in the heavens, taking all the counsels of Jesus, without exception or equivocation, as their rule of life, when reviled, reviling not again, but committing themselves to him who judgeth righteously, animated by the spirit of Jesus, devoting themselves as the apostles did, and able to take up the apostle's words: 'We are [4] made a spectacle unto the world, both to angels and to men. We are fools for Christ's sake, but ye are wise in Christ; we are weak, but ye are strong; ye have glory, but we have dishonour. Even unto this present hour, we both hunger, and thirst, and are naked, and are buffeted, and have no certain dwelling-place: and we toil, working with our own hands: being reviled, we bless; being persecuted, we endure; being defamed, we intreat: we are made as the refuse of the world, the offscouring of all things, even until now.' Such a body of disciples would teach by example, far more than by precept, and assemblies of believers watched over, taught and guided by such men, would imbibe the true spirit of Christianity, so alien from and antagonistic to that of the world, the flesh and the devil. thereby solving at a stroke all problems and oppositions of law and liberty, freedom and servitude, capital and labour, socialism and

[4] i. Cor. 9. 13

individualism, free trade and protection, peace and war, which now distract the minds and sever the interests of mankind. Christianity, rightly viewed, means emancipation from the false and narrow teachings, maxims and customs of the world: it aims at neither more nor less than the regeneration, purification and perfection,—physical, mental, moral,—of the whole human race. It is not a system of dogmas, a scheme of salvation offered for individual acceptance or rejection, but the establishment of a heavenly kingdom under the sway of Jesus.

72 Ps. 7
'In his days shall the righteous flourish:
And abundance of peace, till the moon be no more.'

There have always been men and women desirous of devoting themselves, their property and lives, unreservedly to Christ; but they have been encouraged to forsake the world, to enter monasteries and nunneries. Such a withdrawal from society, from the ordinary walks and avocations of life, is incompatible with discipleship to Jesus, and thwarts its very aim and object. To take vows of poverty, of celibacy, of obedience to ecclesiastical superiors, is contrary to the spirit of gospel freedom, and runs counter to the will of Jesus, who must be the only Rabbi, lord and master to his disciples. They must be left free to follow the leading of his Spirit. Nonconformity to the world and conformity to Jesus is the essence of discipleship. Any institution framed after the pattern of the world, which adopts badges of distinction, titles of pre-eminence, judicial powers, and claims the right of defining and restricting what is to be believed and preached, cannot be in unison with the mind of Jesus. He said: 'Be not ye called Rabbi, for one is your teacher, and all ye are brethren . . . Neither be ye called masters: for one is your master—the Christ.' There must be an absolute reversal of the system prevailing in the world without: 'He that is greater among you shall be your servant. And whosoever shall exalt himself shall be humbled; and whosoever shall humble himself shall be exalted.' How can the disciples of Jesus claim freedom from the world's teaching and behests, if they set up and bow down to a similar domination among themselves? Christianity could no more secure immunity from that gradual yet sure process of deterioration which attacks the loftiest ideals and aspirations of humanity, than could Judaism and the Mosaic dispensation. The scribes and Pharisees were the leaders and teachers of religious thought and practice, yet so far had they declined from the spirit of the divine law and of the prophets, that they scrupled not to seek the death of Jesus, and compelled him to aim at the weakening of their influence by exposing and denouncing the abominations of their principles and characters. They were the opponents of religious progress, hostile to Messiah's purposes, and doing all they could to hinder the establishment of his kingdom. 'But woe unto you, scribes and Pharisees, hypocrites! because ye shut the kingdom of heaven against (Gr. before) men: for ye enter not in yourselves, neither suffer ye them that are entering in to enter.' The verse which stands next in the Authorised Version is now omitted. It is not in the two oldest MSS. Alford says: 'It is wanting in almost all the oldest authorities. It appears to have been inserted here by the copyists from Mark xii. 40, or from Luke xx. 47.' The note inserted by the

23 Mat. 13

Revisers indicates that the position of the verse varies in the copies in which it stands.

It was no lack of energy which held these men aloof from the cause of Jesus. They had 'a zeal for God, but not according to knowledge.' They could be enthusiastic in the work of gaining converts to their own system of faith and practice. 'Woe unto you, scribes and Pharisees, hypocrites! for ye compass sea and land to make one proselyte.' Alas! for those who thus submitted to their influence: 'And when he is become so, ye make him twofold more a son of hell (Gr. Gehenna) than yourselves.' Of the word 'hell' the following explanation is given in 'Helps to the Study of the Bible.' 'Hell is from a root meaning "to hide," so that the original sense is "the hidden or unseen place" (Skeat). It serves as the translation of two words, viz. 1 *Sheól* (Heb.) or *Hades* (Gr.), the abode of departed spirits, as in the Apostles' Creed. 2 *Gehenna* (Heb.) the Valley of Hinnom, the dark gorge on the west side of Jerusalem, where was the furnace (Tophet) in which idolators offered human sacrifices, and "made their children to pass through the fire to Moloch;" and in which persons, convicted of aggravated wilful murder, were burnt to death; hence it was synonymous with a place of torment—"hell-fire" (Mat. v. 22).' That last statement, and the inference drawn from it, must not be accepted apart from proof. Where is the evidence that burning criminals to death was a Jewish custom? It could not have been in the days of Jesus, for the Jews said to Pilate, 'It is not lawful for us to put any man to death.' Mention is omitted to be made of the fact, stated by others, that the Gehenna fire was kept burning for the destruction of offal and garbage. Possibly the *dead* bodies of certain criminals may have been cast there to take their chance of putrefaction or cremation, for such a custom seems to be alluded to in the closing verse of Isaiah: 'And they shall go forth, and look upon the carcases of the men that have transgressed against me: for their worm shall not die, neither shall their fire be quenched; and they shall be an abhorring unto all flesh.' The idea of Gehenna in the minds of the hearers of Jesus, must have been connected with worthlessness, infamy, and corruption, the casting away and destruction of that which was vile and contaminating. It would be a frightful perversion of the meaning of Jesus to take his words, 'ye make him twofold more a son of Gehenna than yourselves,' as signifying that the scribes and Pharisees and their proselytes deserved to be and would be burnt to death. A still more hideous, revolting and absurd sense has been put upon them: that of being cast alive into fire, ever burning, yet never consumed.

The scribes and Pharisees played fast and loose with conscience, and had a systematised method of freeing men even from solemn obligations voluntarily entered into. Certain forms of words had been devised with that object, and on a former occasion Jesus showed that the effect of one of them was to abrogate a divine command: 'Ye say, If a man shall say to his father or his mother, That wherewith thou mightest have been profited by me is Corban, that is to say, Given *to God*; ye no longer suffer him to do aught for his father or his mother; making void the word of God by your tradition: and many such like things ye do.' Jesus now gives some further instances.

'Woe unto you, ye blind guides, which say, Whosoever shall swear by the temple (or, sanctuary), it is nothing; but whosoever shall swear by the gold of the temple (or, sanctuary), he is a debtor (or, bound *by his oath*).' Such casuistry was detestable; and it assumed the temple to be inferior to the metal which adorned it, which is as though one should argue that the dress is more than the wearer.

23 Mat. 17 'Ye fools and blind: for whether is greater, the gold or the temple (or, sanctuary) that hath sanctified the gold?' In the same way, they annulled an oath by the altar, and ratified an oath by the gift placed thereon: a fanciful and false distinction, making man's gift

„ 18, of more account than God's altar. 'And whosoever shall swear by
19 the altar, it is nothing; but whosoever shall swear by the gift that is upon it, he is a debtor (or, bound *by his oath*). Ye blind: for whether is greater, the gift, or the altar that sanctifieth the gift?' In truth, however, it was no question about less or greater, and an honest mind would brush aside such fine-spun theories, devised only as loopholes of escape for a guilty conscience. The greater includes

„ 20-22 the less, and the less involves the greater. 'He therefore that sweareth by the altar, sweareth by it, and by all things thereon. And he that sweareth by the temple (or, sanctuary), sweareth by it, and by him that dwelleth therein. And he that sweareth by the heaven, sweareth by the throne of God, and by him that sitteth thereon.'

It was the habit of these men's minds to regard the less more than
23 the greater. 'Woe unto you, scribes and Pharisees, hypocrites! for ye tithe mint, and anise (or, dill) and cummin, and have left undone the weightier matters of the law, judgement, and mercy, and faith: but these ye ought to have done, and not to have left the other undone.' Young renders: 'These it behoved *you* to do, and those not to neglect.' Tischendorf: 'These ought ye to have done, and not leave those,' which agrees with Luther's, 'Diess sollte man thun, und jenes nicht lassen.'

In the Authorised Version the next verse stands: 'Ye blind
„ 24 guides, which strain at a gnat, and swallow a camel,' rendered by the Revisers: 'Ye blind guides, which strain out the gnat, and swallow the camel,' and by Young: 'Blind guides! who are straining out the gnat, but the camel are swallowing.' As the straining out refers to drinking, so the swallowing would naturally be understood

11 Lev. 1 to refer to eating, the Jews being forbidden to eat camel. The use of the indefinite instead of the definite article in the Authorised Version has caused the passage to be regarded as a strong hyperbole, but there is no sufficient reason for assuming an interpretation so far-fetched and exaggerated. The idea of transgression in eating and

23 Mat. 25 drinking being thus laid hold of, it is carried on as follows: 'Woe unto you, scribes and Pharisees, hypocrites! for ye cleanse the outside of the cup and of the platter, but within they are full of extortion and excess.' Tischendorf renders, 'robbery and incontinence;' Young: 'rapine and incontinence;' Sharpe: 'rapine and injustice,' the last word being a different reading, adopted by Griesbach and Wordsworth, 'unrighteousness.' The meaning obviously is, 'full of that which proceeds from extortion and excess:' the livelihood of these men consisted not in the fruits of honest labour. It was a grave charge to make against a class, but Jesus accused them unhesitatingly and openly, asserting now that they devoured widows'

houses on religious pretexts, and once before : 'Now do ye Pharisees 11 Luke 39
cleanse the outside of the cup and of the platter; but your inward
part is full of extortion and wickedness.' Not all their punctilously
observed traditions about 'washings of cups, and pots, and brasen 7 Mark 4
vessels,' could purge away the taint of food acquired and eaten in
fraud and dishonour. Only an honest meal could be clean eating.
'Thou blind Pharisee, cleanse first the inside of the cup and of the 26 Mat. 26
platter, that the outside thereof may become clean also.'

Outward appearance was everything to them: they themselves
were like polished tombs, conspicuously fair outside and all foul and
corrupt within. 'Woe unto you, scribes and Pharisees, hypocrites! ,, 27
for ye are like unto whited sepulchres, which outwardly appear beautiful, but inwardly are full of dead men's bones, and of all uncleanness.' Jesus did not shrink from applying the simile, which was not
one whit too repulsive to describe their character. 'Even so ye also ,, 28
outwardly appear righteous unto men, but inwardly ye are full of
hypocrisy and iniquity.' Well might they take delight in building
sepulchres and adorning tombs. That was one of their forms of
ostentatious piety, to hold in reverence the names of martyred
prophets, and disclaim participation in the guilt of their murderers.
'Woe unto you, scribes and Pharisees, hypocrites! for ye build the 29, 30
sepulchres of the prophets, and garnish the tombs of the righteous,
and say, If we had been in the days of our fathers, we should not
have been partakers with them in the blood of the prophets.' There
was just one truth in that: the acknowledgment that they were sons
of persecutors and prophet-slayers. And it was equally true that
they were engaged now in the same course; and Jesus, whose life
they sought, challenges them to complete their fathers' deadly work.
He would not yield to them, and there was no outlet from the strife
between them, except the catastrophe from which neither he nor they
would shrink—his death. 'Wherefore ye witness to yourselves, that ,, 31, 32
ye are sons of them that slew the prophets. Fill ye up then the
measure of your fathers.' It was their very nature and training to
be inimical to the welfare of the community, treacherous, venomous,
and they must be left to work on towards and until their doom of
retribution. 'Ye serpents, ye offspring of vipers, how shall ye escape ,, 33
the judgement of hell (Gr. Gehenna)?' Three years had passed since
the Baptist applied to this class of men the same simile, 'offspring of 3 Mat. 7
vipers.' They were still unchanged; in the opinion of John and
Jesus they were, as a class, beyond hope of change. When such
religious teachers thus speak in the ears of all men, it must be
because the accused have been already tried and found guilty at the
bar of public opinion. The spirit of Pharisaism had infused itself
into the fountain-head of religious doctrine, poisoning the stream at
its source. No reform could be carried out except in opposition to
their influence and teaching; it was a question of life or death on
both sides: either the gospel must remain unpreached, the kingdom
of heaven shut up against men, or its opponents must be exposed,
impeached, defied and overcome. The career of Jesus was but the
beginning of the strife, which would be continued in his name by
men hostile to and ahead of the spirit of the times, as the prophets
were, teachers of a wisdom higher than the world, scribes of a new
class, apart from those who now stood up side by side with the

Pharisees. 'Therefore, behold, I send unto you prophets, and wise men, and scribes.' Like their Master they would be appointed to death, even as malefactors, to infamous punishment before the congregations they sought to influence, being hunted from place to place, and finding nowhere rest or peace. 'Some of them shall ye kill and crucify; and some of them shall ye scourge in your synagogues, and persecute from city to city.' The method of propagating the gospel on the one hand, and of opposing it on the other, differed not from that whereby advancing light and truth had been disseminated and resisted from the earliest times. The first martyr under the new dispensation proclaimed that fact: 'Ye stiffnecked and uncircumcised in heart and ears, ye do always resist the Holy Ghost: as your fathers did, so do ye. Which of the prophets did not your fathers persecute? and they killed them which shewed before of the coming of the Righteous One; of whom ye have now become betrayers and murderers.' These outrages upon humanity were all done in the name of religion, by those who had constituted themselves, and deemed themselves, spiritual guides and rulers of their countrymen. Civil magistrates take the lives of murderers and hardened criminals; conquerors slaughter all alike who stand in the way of their ambition; only theologians singled out for their attack the upright, the farseeing, those guiltless of aught save the love of truth and the spirit of enquiry and reform. The shedding of 'righteous blood' has been the speciality of religionists in all ages: the persecutors for conscience' sake can alone be held responsible for it; therefore Jesus added: 'That upon you may come all the righteous blood shed on the earth, from the blood of Abel the righteous unto the blood of Zachariah son of Barachiah, whom ye slew between the sanctuary (shrine—Tischendorf) and the altar.' The quarrel of Cain against Abel was a theological one, arising out of their different modes of worshipping Jehovah. It is not known who Zachariah son of Barachiah was: probably the victim last murdered in Jerusalem on account of his religious opinions and teaching.

But although a certain class was primarily and chiefly responsible for the perpetuation of the spirit and the carrying out of the system of persecution, the responsibility was not confined to them, and its consequences would fall upon the nation generally. The force of public opinion, that is, of the majority of their fellow citizens, must either have been in their favour, or utterly callous to their wrong doings. The high priest, the chief priests, the elders and the scribes, first laid their hands upon Jesus, 'and they all condemned him to be worthy of (Gr. liable to) death,' and 'delivered him up to Pilate.' We are told also that 'the chief priests stirred up the multitude, that he should rather release Barabbas unto them.' The high priest and his council said to the apostles, 'ye . . intend to bring this man's blood upon us.' Yet Peter charged the people generally with participation in the crime: 'But ye denied the Holy and Righteous One, and asked for a murderer to be granted unto you, and killed the Prince of life.' The guides and their followers were equally blind: 'And now, brethren, I wot that in ignorance ye did it, as did also your rulers.' Bigotry, ignorance, prejudice, indifference,—they all have a share in national crimes, serving to explain their origin, but they do not extenuate them, neither can the natural evil consequences of such wrong doing be averted, or confined to their authors and abettors. Jesus added : 'Verily I say unto you, 23 Mat. 36 All these things shall come upon this generation.' Hosea had prophesied : 'My people are destroyed for lack of knowledge : 4 Hos. 6 because thou hast rejected knowledge, I will also reject thee, that thou shalt be no priest to me: seeing thou hast forgotten the law of thy God, I also will forget thy children.' Things were now fast coming to that inevitable crisis. The moral tone of the nation was weakened and perverted under the influence of a false system of religious teaching. In vain had Jesus sought to stem the flowing current of corruption. His efforts had failed of success. In Galilee and elsewhere he was held in honour, but in the metropolis of Judæa the influence of the Pharisaic and clerical party was too strong for him, and the very centre of national life and policy remained under their guidance and control, its inhabitants generally either indifferent or hostile to his teaching. 'O Jerusalem, Jerusalem, which killeth 23 Mat. 37 the prophets, and stoneth them that are sent unto her! how often would I have gathered thy children together, even as a hen gathereth her chickens under her wings, and ye would not!' Luke recorded this apostrophe, but introduced it in another connection, and apparently out of place. 'O Jerusalem, Jerusalem, which killeth the 13 Luke 34 prophets, and stoneth them that are sent unto her! how often would I have gathered thy children together, even as a hen *gathereth* her own brood under her wings, and ye would not!' The simile is peculiar,—cast in a different mould of thought than that which bears the world's stamp. Jesus desired to become the Saviour of his countrymen. How? Not by inciting them to arms, infusing martial courage, bidding them stand upon their defence, and, if need be, resist their foes. He had a plan and purpose of his own, and would have them rest their confidence entirely upon himself. Had they done so, listened to his call, received his doctrine, heard his voice and followed him, as sheep their shepherd to the fold, or as a helpless brood nestles under the mother's wing, the war-storm would have passed over, leaving them unharmed. Jesus was no disturber of the world's peace, and would have brought the peace of heaven to his followers. The all-conquering Romans might have scorned his gospel, scoffed at the proclamation of a heavenly kingdom, but they would not have cared to oppose the Christian doctrine, or to exterminate its adherents. That was the work of the bigoted Jews, from whom the heathens had not yet learnt the art of religious persecution. The gospel of Jesus would have replaced patriotism by a nobler spirit, have quenched the animosities of creed and race, and made Jerusalem the source of glory and joy to the whole earth, instead of a heap of ruins. Jesus continued : 'Behold, your house 23 Mat. 38 is left unto you desolate.' The Revisers note : 'Some ancient authorities omit *desolate*.' It is not in the Vatican MS. In Luke the Revisers have italicised the word, which is omitted from the three oldest MSS. There was nothing to be expected for the country but utter ruin and devastation. Jesus could not stand forth as the Messiah of the people except in his proper character, nor save them otherwise than in his own way. False Christs might rise, holding out delusive hopes, but Jesus must retire from the scene, until

they were able to recognise the nature of his mission and hail him as
23 Mat. 39 the divinely-appointed Saviour. 'For I say unto you, Ye shall not see me henceforth, till ye shall say, Blessed is he that cometh in the name of the Lord.'

There is a great similarity between this denunciation of the scribes and Pharisees in Matthew and that recorded in the 11th chapter of Luke, but the two discourses appear to have been delivered on different occasions. That in Luke was addressed to a Pharisee and a lawyer (verses 38 and 45), others of their class being probably present; that in Matthew was spoken 'to the multitudes and to his disciples' (verse 1). Jesus had denounced the character and conduct of these men to their faces, before he launched out this attack upon them in public.

Samuel Sharpe has thrown a note of sorrowful pathos into the denunciations of Jesus, by rendering 'Woe unto you,' as 'Alas for you!' That certainly accords with all we know of the mind and heart of Jesus. The repeated utterances, 'Woe unto you,' are not to be taken as indicating any personal animosity or desire of inflicting retributive punishment.

Jesus had seated himself opposite the place where the gifts of the
12 Mark 41 people were deposited. 'And he sat down over against the treasury.' Alford explains: 'This is usually understood of *thirteen chests*, which stood in the court of the women, into which were thrown contributions for the temple, or the tribute (of Matt. xvii. 24). But it is hardly likely that *they* would have been called *the treasury*, and we hear of a *building* by this name in Josephus.' From the position Jesus occupied, he watched the givers throw in their offerings.
41 Many wealthy people came, and gave liberally: 'and beheld how the multitude cast money (Gr. brass) into the treasury: and many that were rich cast in much.' Luke's account indicates that rich
21 Luke 1 persons chiefly were the givers. 'And he looked up, and saw the rich men that were casting their gifts into the treasury (Or, And saw them that were casting their gifts into the treasury, and they were rich).' But among them there came one poor widow woman, who
12 Mark 42 put in two coins of the smallest value. 'And there came a (Gr. one) poor widow, and she cast in two mites, which make a farthing.' Sharpe renders literally: 'two Lepta, that is, a quadrantes.' Alford explains that a mite was the smallest Jewish coin, and its value about $\frac{1}{128}$ of a denarius. As the denarius represented the day wage of a vineyard labourer, which may be roughly taken as equivalent to five shillings, the two mites were equivalent to a gift of one penny of our money. From Mark's account it appears that only 'brass,' rendered by Young and Sharpe 'copper,' was deposited. Whatever the reason for that custom, it at all events made the giving of much needlessly conspicuous, and the giving of a trifle painfully prominent by comparison. This would naturally deter the poor in general from giving at all. The Authorised Version has in Mark, 'a certain poor widow,' which is rendered by Tischendorf as well as by the Revisers
21 Luke 2 marginally, 'one poor widow.' Luke says: 'And he saw a certain poor widow casting in thither two mites.' From the expressions 'one' and 'a certain,' it is obvious that not many of that class came to drop in with the fingers coin which others could throw in by

handfuls. The quick eye of Jesus observed both the giver and her gift, and his mind was so impressed thereby that he at once summoned his disciples to approach, that he might impart the lesson he would have them draw from the circumstance. 'And he called unto him his disciples,' rendered by Young literally, 'And having called up his disciples.' Being gathered round him, they found that he wished simply to explain to them that this one woman had given more than all the rest. 'And said unto them, Verily I say unto you, This poor widow cast in more than all they which are casting into the treasury.' Luke is to the same effect: 'And he said, Of a truth I say unto you, This poor widow cast in more than they all.' It is not 'more than any one of them:' so that the meaning may be, 'more than all of them together.' In either sense, that was an extraordinary assertion. Jesus proceeded to justify it by explaining his meaning. 'For they all did cast in of their superfluity; but she of her want did cast in all she had, *even* all her living.' Luke: 'For all these did of their superfluity cast in unto the gifts: but she of her want did cast in all the living that she had.' The words 'of God' after 'gifts,' are now omitted, not being in the two oldest MSS. How did Jesus know that this was 'all her living'? We need not assume the exercise of any supernatural prescience on his part. Alford gives no hint of any such suggestion by commentators. An open, empty purse in the woman's hand may have spoken volumes to the discerning eye of Jesus. In what sense are we to understand the statement that the woman gave 'more than they all'? Literally, as a bare matter of fact, that was not the case. Jesus was comparing the means of the givers, the poverty of the woman with the superfluity of the others. Her gift, so viewed, was out of all proportion to theirs. Alford's comment on the word 'more' is: 'more, *in God's reckoning*; more for *her own stewardship* of the goods entrusted to her care.' That is introducing two ideas which are not in the saying of Jesus. He made no allusion to Divine oversight and approval, or to responsibility towards God, with respect to giving. The woman had supplied a splendid example of liberality; Jesus drew the attention of the disciples to the generosity of the deed, but not a word did he add in commendation of it, or of exhortation to do likewise. He fixed their minds simply and entirely upon the fact, that the small donation of the woman was 'more' in his eyes than the much larger gifts of others. It is not likely that Jesus desired that people should impoverish themselves to supply funds for religious purposes, knowing as he did that the money would be applied under the direction of chief priests, Pharisees, scribes and leading men of the city, who were banded together in active opposition to himself and the preaching of the kingdom of God. If the money was set apart for the repair and decoration of the temple, how could he urge to liberality, knowing well that not one stone should be left upon another, which should not be thrown down? If the money went to the poor, why should the poorest of the poor contribute, thus bringing about the very destitution sought to be relieved? Is it reasonable to suppose that Jesus meant that the rich ought to strip themselves of all their wealth, leaving themselves penniless like this poor widow? Or that because they did not, and she gave her all, they were condemned, and she approved, in the sight of God and

Jesus? Nothing of the kind. Such ideas are not deducible from the words of Jesus. We shall fall into error, one way or another, if we attempt to press them beyond the point at which he aimed. Let us abide by the facts : he saw many rich, giving much, and one poor widow who gave her all,—a penny : and he said that her gift was 'more' than all the others put together. He brings into prominence, and sets a high value upon a small donation. There had been a grave fault, in his eyes, about this collection : it had been confined to rich men and large gifts, and the poor, with their trifles, had been conspicuous, to his mind, by their absence. He hailed the coming of this 'one poor widow' as a happy augury of that brotherhood of aim and effort which it was the purpose of his life to establish among mankind. With loving eyes he watched her in the act of giving, and was charmed to witness 'her deep poverty abounding unto the riches of her liberality.' He rejoiced, as Paul did subsequently over the Macedonians when he said : ' For according to their power . . . yea, and beyond their power, *they gave* of their own accord.' Some may think that Jesus called up his disciples merely for the purpose of pointing out the woman and eulogising her generous impulse. It is more probable that he had an intention of teaching something ; and if we are to draw a lesson for ourselves from his words, they are most naturally to be taken as pointing to : (1) The duty of combined effort, and (2) The value of small donations.

All great enterprises require for their performance, unity of purpose in many minds, and the hearty co-operation of a multitude of willing hearts and hands. The solitary thinker, with whom a great idea originates, doubtless does more for the world's advancement than the army of busy workers by whom it is subsequently carried out. But if the one is the soul of a grand work, the others constitute its body, and as the body without the soul is dead, so the soul without the body is powerless. Any plans for the common welfare call for the aid of the entire community. That is a general truth ; and the more clearly it is apprehended and acted upon, the more will social progress be accelerated. That has come to be recognised, late indeed in human history, as an article in the creed of advanced politicians. Democracy means, not merely self-government, but safe government : without the aid, the check, the combined judgment of the masses, class rulership degenerates into selfishness and tyranny. The gospel of Christ is a plan for ameliorating the condition of mankind, not in one particular direction only, that of theology, but in all directions. The church of Christ is simply an assembly of his followers and believers. He came to break down the barriers between Jew and Gentile, nation and nation, class and class, and to unite the entire human family in one organic whole. 'There can be neither Jew nor Greek, there can be neither bond nor free, there can be no male and female : for ye are all one *man* in Christ Jesus.' That was the idea and purpose in the mind of Jesus, as interpreted and realised by the apostle Paul, who regarded the entire Christian brotherhood as an instrument, specially designed by God, for the carrying out of good works. He wrote : 'For we are his workmanship, created in Christ Jesus for good works, which God afore prepared that we should walk in them.' These 'good works' have been too much restricted to one or two particular channels : the relief of poverty and sickness, and the propagation of the gospel in its theological conception as a scheme of individual salvation. The combined efforts of the Christian community should embrace a wider field of action. The depressed, degraded condition of the masses, is a scandal to our profession of Christianity. Generation after generation passes, with but small signs of improvement in that respect: the giving of money for the relief of destitution has been a salve to the consciences of the rich, but has only still further pauperised the poor, and will never lift them out of the mire. The labouring class, as a whole, has not received, and still does not receive, a fair share of the profits arising out of labour. To the recognition of this truth, and the solution of the problems connected with it, the thoughts and aims of Christians should be directed, rather than to the system of hand-to-mouth alleviation which can only serve to perpetuate the evil. Alas! this work, in which Christians should have been foremost, has been left to philosophers, socialists, secularists. These men are sufficiently emancipated from traditional errors of faith and practice to discern the truth of things about them, and have not shrunk from proclaiming existing wrongs and evils, from investigating their proximate causes, and seeking some method for their remedy. Shall they and their followers be left to find a solution for themselves? If so, it will probably be, ultimately, by force that society will be revolutionised. Let Christian philanthropists join hands with these men, who have often more of the spirit of Jesus than they have who denounce and defame them. The church of Christ should lay its hand to this plough, and not look back, until it has furrowed out a scheme of cooperation which will ensure to every honest, steady working man and woman sufficient for the decent upbringing of a family without recourse to alms in any shape. As workers rise, idlers must sink; as the labouring class claims and receives its fair recompense of reward, the making of huge fortunes will become difficult, if not impossible. Those who possess them have scarcely reason to be congratulated, at least in the judgment of the apostle James, who wrote: 'Go to now, ye rich, weep and howl for your miseries that are coming upon you. Your riches are corrupted, and your garments are moth-eaten. Your gold and silver are rusted; and their rust shall be for a testimony against you, and shall eat your flesh as fire.' Let us not, however, misunderstand or misapply those strong words. They were obviously dictated by a deep sense of wrong and injustice. If they were a bare denunciation of rich men simply as being rich, as well might James have denounced the increase of the fields and flocks, and the fruits hanging upon the trees. The apostle brings grave charges. He accuses the rich of letting their wealth lie idle. 'Your riches are corrupted, and your garments are moth-eaten.' It is the 'rust' of their treasures which testifies against the owners. And he reproaches them further for fraudulently keeping back the wages of their harvestmen, whilst living delicately on the earth and taking their pleasure, and for condemning and killing the righteous. With our full tides of commerce, the rich are not tempted to let their wealth lie idle: it is used to their profit and that of the community, either by themselves or those to whom they loan it. But the greed of profit-making has brought about a sad condition of affairs. Any shed which will hold machinery is deemed good enough for the workmen who tend it. Unlovely and unsanitary surroundings, from the cradle to the grave, are the lot of millions of our brother toilers. From the noise and grime of the workshop, they go to so-called 'homes,' squalid, filthy, unhealthy in the extreme. Wages are cut down to the lowest level of existence, rents are raised to the highest point, and the poor themselves have come to deem it cause for self-congratulation if only they can earn enough to keep body and soul together, utilising the early labours of their children, whom they had till lately no opportunity of educating. To remedy this state of things, Christians should join heart to heart and hand to hand. There are signs of improvement; but the dawn of hope for the oppressed, aye! the defrauded labourers, is as yet faint and flickering, and may die out altogether, or take many generations before it gathers light and strength enough to enable the community at large to recognise the causes of the evil and apply an effectual remedy. That remedy must come, sooner or later, either through Christianity or Socialism. The gospel of Jesus is all-sufficient, if only we understand and use it rightly. If every Christian employer will face his responsibility and do his part, adjuring 'the dismal science' of political economy, falsely so-called, and worshipping Christ as God, instead of Mammon, then society will indeed mount the hill of progress, and begin to breathe the free air of that heavenly kingdom which Jesus came to establish on the earth. If that is our ideal, we shall learn to look upon almsgiving, not as a meritorious offering to God and a benefit to mankind, but as a wretched palliative of the world's sores and wrongs, needful and acceptable only as a temporary expedient to supply the lack of that common justice which man owes to man.

As regards the propagation of the gospel, enormous sums are year after year collected and spent with that object. Home and foreign missions are pleaded for with earnest eloquence, and are set on foot and supported by a multitude of donations. To cast a doubt upon the value of this work, will seem to many little short of profanation, even blasphemy. But, at the utmost, what the preaching of the gospel has done for England and for Europe generally, it may be expected, in the course of time, to do for other parts of the world. Is the tone of so-called Christian society among ourselves, Christ-like or the reverse? According to our judgment on that question, will be our view of the value or worthlessness of missionary enterprises. If Christianity was intended by its Founder to be the establishment of the kingdom of heaven upon earth, then we have it not amongst us, nor can it come until war and mammon-worship shall have become things of the past. At present they are rampant in the nations which profess and believe themselves to be more or less christianised; and as these evils are promoted and perpetuated by those who hold front rank in society, and who are the highest exponents of our creed and practice, they may be taken, apart from the prevailing flood of immorality and injustice, as indexing our true, or false, position as followers of Jesus of Nazareth. If, however, the salvation of Christ is deemed a personal and individual rather than social matter, there is an easy way of escape from the terrible conclusion which otherwise cannot be gainsaid. And not only is that assumption made, proclaimed, insisted upon, but it is further urged that Christ offers us some mysterious kind of soul-salvation, to take effect hereafter, to save us in the world to come from the consequences of our earthly misdoings, and there, not here, to transform his people into his own likeness. Faith in Jesus as a Saviour is considered all sufficient, even though it be an instantaneous mental process, to make safe and happy everlastingly those who have it; and it is an unquestionable, undoubted fact that clergyman will and do preach that doctrine to vilest criminals, and do not shrink from holding out that hope, as the hope of the gospel, to the most hardened murderer, even when the rope is already round his neck. It is all with the best intentions, the highest motives, the most perfect conviction that God's word justifies the statements made. But the men who thus interpret it are, to say the least, fallible, and we all know, or have the means of knowing, that this is but one phase of the erroneous system of doctrinal teaching which has assumed to itself the name of Christianity. What good fruit can be expected from the promulgation of such a creed? What benefit could have accrued in bygone times from any missionary enterprise started under the auspices of Torquemada and the Holy Inquisition? The only gospel given us to preach is the 'gospel of [4] the kingdom;' and until that fundamental truth is recognised, it will avail little to go about preaching a personal salvation, the chief benefit of which will be realised hereafter, in the hour of death and in a day of judgment. Our missions to the heathen world cannot bear the test of impartial investigation, and the time is come for applying it. Canon Isaac Taylor has written an article in the *Fortnightly Review* of October, 1888, entitled, 'The great missionary failure.' What results can be shown for the men and money employed in the work? Here are some of the curiosities of the Mission Budget which Canon Taylor has collected. 'Last year in Ceylon 424 agents of the Church Missionary Society spent £11,003 15s. 7d. in making 190 adult converts out of a population of nearly three millions, but the relapses were more numerous than the converts, as there was a decrease of 143. in the native Christian adherents. In China 247 agents of the same society spent £14,875 3s. in making 167 converts out of a population of 382,000,000. In Northern India (Bengal, Bombay, and the North West Provinces), 715 agents made 173 converts at a cost of £34,186 2s. 5d.' And many of the so-called 'converts' would be dear at any price. Canon Taylor says: 'In the missions to Egypt, Persia, Palestine, and Arabia, where there are no heathen, the Church Missionary Society employs 119 agents, and has spent £23,545 4s. 7d. in the last two years. The net results are nil. In Egypt, last year, there were two "inquirers," one a negro and the other an Egyptian, but the inquiries did not lead to any further results. In Arabia a sick robber who was doctored by a missionary promised to abstain from robbing for ten days. In Palestine, the one Moslem convert of last year, a weak-minded orphan girl who required constant guidance, and for whom the prayers of all English Christians were invoked, has gone over to Rome, and is now immured in a nunnery. In the oldest of our West African possessions all the unrepentant Magdalens of the chief city are professing Christians, and the most notorious one in the place boasts that she " never missed going to Church on a Communion Sunday." Three years ago, in a nominally Christian village, a

[4] Mat. 23

quarrel broke out, and not a few were killed. The victors cooked and ate the bodies of the slain. As a punishment, the native pastor announced that they were "suspended from Church privileges." Cannibalism is punished by temporary exclusion from the Holy Communion!' As an instance of 'squabbles among the missionaries,' Canon Taylor relates the following : ' Mr. Squires, the local secretary of the Church Missionary Society in the Bombay Presidency, states that "one of the greatest hindrances to missionary effort is the existence of so many Christians who do not belong to any of the Protestant societies. Strange to say, the existence of so many Christians is a great hindrance to the spread of Christianity! Mr. Squires, with his 97 assistants, baptized last year 36 adults and 92 children, at a cost of £9441 7s. 1d., and the converts made by his society, after 66 years of labour, do not amount to 2000; while the devoted Roman priests are converting, educating, and consoling thousands upon thousands, at a nominal cost, which comes, not from any wealthy society, but mainly from the converts themselves. No wonder Mr. Squires is jealous of his successful rivals.'

Not much money is wanted, or can avail, for the conversion of the world. How much had the twelve apostles between them? Absolutely nothing: for Jesus insisted upon his disciples going forth with no money in their purses. The above hint about the Romanists indicates that the same policy would answer now. Christian men are the primary requisite, and they must be of the right stamp. It is not necessary to go back to Buddha or Saint Paul for types of the ideal missionary. There are, as Canon Taylor points out, plenty of modern instances. The 'Oxford Brethren' at Calcutta are one. The Salvation Army is another : ' Mr. Tucker, their leader, has given proof of his sincerity by surrendering a lucrative post in the Indian Civil Service. He heads a barefooted regiment of two hundred soldiers, who go for life, who give up everything they have, who receive no payment, but are content with a bare subsistence. They abstain from the flesh of animals, the slaughter of which is an abomination to the Hindu ; they touch no alcohol ; their food is a handful of rice and curry, which they beg from day to day from those to whom they minister. Like the natives they oil their bodies with colza oil, they go barefoot, with turbans to protect them from the sun, and their dress is a few yards of calico, costing about 5s. The whole maintenance of each missionary does not exceed 2s. a week, or £5 a year. Like the successful Moravian missionaries in South Africa or the West Indies their object is to become natives, to live among the natives exactly as the natives live, simply exhibiting a nobler life and higher aims. They never argue, or discuss doctrines, or go into the "evidences" of Christianity. They exhibit the ascetic life which appeals so strongly to the Hindu. They say, "See what our religion does for us, how happy it makes us, and how it enables us to despise poverty and conquer the troubles of the world, how it makes us contented and cheerful and free from sin" . . . As one of the greatest missionaries has said, The best preachers are not our words, but our lives ; and our deaths, if need be, are better preachers still. We must hold up the spectacle of devoted lives to enable the people to understand the first elements of the Christian faith. General Gordon, in one of his last letters, has told us the same hard truth. Writing from Khartoum, he says, in his trenchant style: "There is not the least doubt that there is an immense virgin field for *an apostle* in these countries among the black tribes. But where will you find an apostle? A man must give up everything, understand,—*everything, everything!* No half or three-quarter measures will do. He must be dead to the world, have no ties of any sort, and long for death when it may please God to take him. There are few, very few, such. And yet what a field!"

That a Canon of the Church of England should thus boldly recognise and expose the shortcomings and deceptiveness of her missionary system, is a happy augury for the future. The ceaseless cry for money, money, as the prime requisite for the extension of Christianity, is a degradation of the true ideal of the kingdom of God. If that is to be established, at home or abroad, the energies of believers must be directed into other and healthier channels. Many a good cause languishes for lack of the funds which are now expended in various enterprises assumed to be sacred, but which represent chiefly the theological conceptions or misconceptions of their founders and supporters. Societies were established by our forefathers—take the Religious Tract Society as a conspicuous example—for the purpose of disseminating their views of the plan of salvation, and of persuading the readers of their leaflets and books to accept their doctrines, that they might 'believe and be saved.' All the errors and crudities existent in the belief of a bygone generation have thus been, figuratively and literally, stereotyped, and handed down in their original form to the present day. It was a fundamental and inviolable rule of the Religious Tract Society to issue no book or tract which did not disclose the 'plan of salvation,' the mode and means of a sinner's justification in the sight of God, as interpreted by the founders and agents of the Society. The widening and ripening of Christian thought and judgment cannot avail to modify a system of theological ideas so pertinaciously insisted upon and widely disseminated. Much of the so-called 'religious' literature which has been gratuitously showered upon the masses appears to minds unwarped by dogmatic teaching, in some things foolish and in others revolting. It is thrust into the hands of those who may be intellectually incapable of thinking and judging for themselves: some swallow it, as they would a medicine vouched as beneficial, some openly reject it as a nauseous compound, the majority take no heed of it. But it is insisted upon as containing, multum in parvo, the Gospel, the whole Gospel, and nothing but the Gospel. There has been a deluge of tracts which are narrow-minded, damnatory, repulsive, which condemn innocent enjoyment as sinful 'worldliness,' describe 'faith' as though it were a magic process instantaneously 'saving' the vilest, paint 'hell' in frightful colours, proclaim abominable doctrines of 'endless torment,' and yield no higher notion of 'salvation' than that of being 'religious' on earth and 'happy for ever' in heaven. The only limit to the printing and dissemination of these dogmas is the amount of money subscribed for the purpose; as long as people continue to give, so long will such Societies go on publishing and distributing. It is time that better and more beneficent uses should be found for Christian generosity. The giving of money involves responsibility to the donors as well as to the distributors. Support should be withheld from the religious literature which is put, with the best intentions, but often with sad want of judgment and grave perversions of 'the gospel,' into the hands of the young and ignorant.

The claims upon Christian liberality are many, and the calls made upon it are innumerable. How to bestow alms without producing ultimate mischief as well as doing apparent present good, is a difficult problem. Probably Hospitals stand foremost, and deserve the largest amount of support. But it should rather be in maintaining those in existence than in building new ones. The upper and middle classes rarely resort to them, and when the working class rises to its proper level of remuneration and self-dependence, the need for gratuitous relief in sickness and accident will have passed away. That condition of things has been brought about with respect to education: the Board Schools have rendered Voluntary Schools, supported by private subscriptions, superfluous. Other institutions need assistance, not permanently, but as being 'good by reason of the present distress.' Reformatories, Refuges and Charity Organisations come under this category. Efforts on behalf of children deserve every encouragement, such as Dr. Barnardo's, and Infant and Orphan Asylums, though as society advances towards perfection they will cease to be required. Institutions for the Blind, Deaf and Dumb, Cripples and Idiots, demand sympathy and support. Yet there is no reason why our combined efforts for good should always take the form of charity. Probably the utmost amount of benefit to the labouring poor would be secured by a judicious investment of capital in Model Dwellings, the funds being provided by a multitude of small shareholders as well as by those more wealthy. The East End People's Palace in London marks a new departure: in such a work, Christians, Socialists, Democrats, Aristocrats, can join hands and efforts, and the gradual raising of the masses by that and other means will do more towards the realisation of 'the kingdom of heaven,' than all the preaching and mission-work in the world.

(2) The full benefit of combined effort cannot, however, be attained until some plan is devised for gathering in, methodically and continuously, the smallest contributions. Large donations are imperatively required; those that are rich must continue to give much, but the trifles of the multitude, if carefully collected, would probably amount to much more. This branch of charity is as yet an untilled field which would amply repay the labour of cultivation. The subscription lists of our most important institutions show sums of two guineas, one guinea, half a guinea, fewer of five shillings, and fewer still made up of yet smaller items, which are generally summarised into one comparatively insignificant total. In the 'Globe' newspaper of 8 October, 1888, there appeared a short article headed. 'Charitable Appeals. Many a mickle maks a muckle.' The following extracts bear on this subject. 'One of the latest developments of charity has been towards supplying poor town children with country holidays. In the pages of daily and weekly papers, and also in the magazines, there have been numerous appeals for funds for this object. The chief branch of this Country Holiday charity, which has its offices in Buckingham Street, Strand, and of which the Princess of Wales is patroness, has already boarded out over 13,000 children for a fortnight, at a charge of ten shillings a child. The

Fresh Air Mission has boarded out 1000 children; the Rev. A. Styleman Herring has boarded out 400; Miss Edith Woodworth's Buttercup and Daisy Fund provided a holiday for 300; and the Ragged School Union and numerous other societies or private individuals have worked in the same direction. Nor does this movement flourish in London only; there is a committee in Glasgow which has sent over 3000 children into the country, and Edinburgh has a holiday-house under the shadow of the purple Pentlands, which is entirely given up to poor children throughout the summer . . . Now, who supply the funds for all these holidays? Who are the people who answer the numerous appeals which are to be seen in every paper during the summer months? Doubtless these questions must have occurred to many who have hesitated to send their mite, or not thought it worth while to get a postal order for half-a-crown, though they have recognised the merits of the charity which advertised. Take the first 60 letters received in the course of a fortnight in answer to an appeal which appeared in a magazine.' A cheque for £10, another for £4, five postal orders for £1, and 10 shillings by nine people. ' But it was the small sums which swelled the fund . . . There were numerous five shilling, half-crown, and shilling orders, which, added to the cheques, yielded a total of over £50 . . . It certainly is a point worth remarking, that it is the small sums which mount up and send thousands of children away to breezy commons for healthy holidays. Only £19 out of the first £50 received for the charity in question came in sums over 10s., the other £31 came in small orders, more especially in half-crowns. There are plenty of people who would never miss half-a-crown, would indeed give it gladly were it not for the trouble of procuring an order and addressing an envelope. It is not meanness, nor want of sympathy, which keeps many of us from doing what we could; it is simply laziness, and an erroneous impression that it is not worth while to be at the trouble of sending small gifts.'

The facts here disclosed are very interesting and important. They illustrate the advantage of combined effort, and point to the necessity of concentration. The 'Country Holiday Charity,' for instance, might do all the advertising and collection, simply distributing the subscriptions among the half-dozen other organisation which carry out the same work. What an immense amount of useless expense would thereby be saved! Under the present system, our charities compete with one another, like rival tradesmen. For the sake of economy, there should be a system of combination, so that one small staff might take the place of a multitude of paid officials, one collector—if any collector should be found necessary—suffice for several charities, and one advertisement appeal simultaneously for all. But more important than this, and serving to lead up to this, would be the establishment of a few General Subscription Funds, one for each class of donations, ten shillings, five shillings, half a crown, one shilling, and one penny. These funds, having no specific objects, would not interfere with any charitable institution: they would simply advertise for and receive donations, to be apportioned, at the discretion of the committee, among existing charities. Each of the five classes, 10s., 5s., 2s. 6d., 1s., and 1d., might be superintended by a committee of twelve subscribers, and on the 1st of January or the

1st of July in each year, whether Sunday or weekday, at a fixed hour, and always at the same place, so that no expense of notification would be requisite, the subscribers might be invited to attend and elect another committee, comprising at least six new members. That would be a sufficient safeguard against partiality in the distribution of the funds, which might otherwise occur. Any persons willing to serve on the Committee, which would act gratuitously, should send in their names and addresses in the week preceeding the meeting of subscribers. Some such plan as that would open out new ground for charitable effort, and would doubtless result in a plenteous harvest, sown, reaped and gathered in without any needless expenditure of time or money. It is a matter of primary importance to avoid waste in our methods of giving, and also to evoke the personal interest of the givers. There are indications that the 'Half-crown Fund' would be at first the most popular and productive, but the 'Shilling Fund' and 'Penny Fund' would afford the poorest an opportunity of giving, and of controlling their own special Fund, in the same way as others. Possibly, aye! probably, the result would show that the poor had given more than all.

INDEX TO QUOTATIONS FROM THE GOSPELS.

The large Roman figures denote the Chapters. The first column shows the Verse, the second column the Series or Part, and the third column the Page.

MATTHEW.

I.			III.			V.			VI.			VII.			IX.			X.		
1	i.	46	1	i.	30	4	i.	115	4	i.	131	17	i.	148	1	i.	99	11	i.	214
2		46	2		31	5		116	5		132	18		148	2		99	12		214
3		46	3		31	6		116	6		132	19		148	3		100	13		214
4		46	4		31	7		116	7		132	20		148	4			14		214
5		46	5		32	8		117	8		132	21		149	5			15		216
6		46	6			9		117	9		134	22		149	6			16		216
7		47	7		32	10		119	10		134	23		149	7			17		216
8		47	8		33	11		119	11		134	24		149	8		103	18		216
9		47	9		33	12		119	12		134	25		149	9		103	19		216
10		47	10		33	13		121	13		134	26		150	10			20		216
11		47	11		34	14		122	14		135	27		150	11		104	21		218
12		47	12		114	15		122	15			28		150	12		104	22		218
13		47	13		37	16		122	16		136	29		150	13		104	23		218
14		47	14		38	17		122	17		136				14		104	24		218
15		47	15		38	18		122	18		136				15			25		219
16		47	16		38	19		122	19		137	VIII.			16		105	26		219
17		48	17		39	20		123	20		137				17		106	27		219
18		14				21		123	21		137	1	i.	96	18		201	28		219
19		14				22		123	22		137	2		96	19		201	29		220
20		14	IV.			23		125	23		138	3			20		201	30		
21		14				24		125	24		138	4			21		202	31		220
22		14	1	i.	49	25		125	25		138	5		151	22		203	32		220
23		14	2		49	26		125	26		139	6		151	23		204	33		221
24		15	3		49	27		126	27		139	7		151	24			34		221
25		15	4		50	28		126	28		139	8		151	25		205	35		222
			5		50	29		126	29		139	9			26		206	36		
			6		50	30		126	30		139	10			27		207	37		222
II.			7		50	31		126	31		140	11		153	28		207	38		222
			8		51	32		127	32		140	12		153	29		207	39		222
1	i.	21	9		51	33		127	33		140	13		153	30		207	40		223
2		21	10		52	34		128	34		142	14		65	31		207	41		223
3		22	11		53	35		128				15		199	32		208	42		224
4		22	12		58	36		128				16		65	33		208			
5		22	13		58	37		128	VII.			17		66	34		208			
6		22	14		59	38		128				18		192	35		212	XI.		
7		23	15		59	39		128	1	i.	143	19	ii.	82	36		212			
8		23	16		59	40		128	2		143	20		82	37		212	1	i.	227
9		23	17		84	41		129	3		145	21		82	38		212	2		157
10		23	18			42		129	4		145	22		82				3		
11		23	19		69	43		129	5		145	23	i.	192	X.			4		
12		24	20		69	44		130	6		145	24		192				5		
13		24	21		69	45		130	7		146	25		192	1	i.	213	6		
14		24	22		69	46		130	8		146	26		193	2			7		158
15		24	23		113	47		130	9		146	27		194	3			8		
16		24	24		113	48		131	10		146	28		197	4			9		
17		25	25		113				11		146	29		197	5		213	10		
18		25							12		146	30		197	6		213	11		160
19		25							13		147	31		197	7		213	12		160
20		25	V.			VI.			14		147	32		198	8		214	13		160
21		25	1	i. 115		1	i.	131	15		147	33		198	9			14		160
22		25	2		115	2		131	16		148	34		198	10		214	15		160
23		25	3		115	3		131												

INDEX TO QUOTATIONS FROM THE GOSPELS.

XI.		XIII.		XIV.		XVI.		XVIII.		XX.		XXI.	
16		1	i. 166	10	i. 226	1	i. 299	9	i. 313	7	ii. 221	40	ii. 286
17		2	166	11	226	2	299	10	315	8	221	41	286
18		3	166	12	227	3	299	11	315	9	221	42	288
19	i. 161	4	167	13	227	4	299	12	316	10	221	43	288
20	ii. 87	5	167	14	229	5	300	13	316	11	221	44	288
21	87	6	167	15	230	6	300	14	316	12	221	45	289
22	87	7	168	16		7	300	15	316	13	221	46	289
23	87	8	168	17	230	8	300	16	317	14	221		
24	87	9	168	18		9	300	17	317	15	221		
25	93	10	169	19	231	10	300	18	327	16	222	**XXII.**	
26	93	11	169	20	232	11	302	19	327	17	224		
27	93	12	169	21	231	12	302	20	327	18	224	1	ii. 292
28	94	13	170	22	235	13	255	21	327	19	224	2	292
29	94	14	170	23	236	14	256	22	328	20	226	3	292
30	94	15	170	24	236	15	256	23	328	21	226	4	292
		16	171	25	237	16	256	24	328	22	227	5	292
		17	171	26	237	17	256	25	328	23	227	6	292
		18	171	27	237	18	257	26	329	24	228	7	293
XII.		19	173	28	238	19	258	27	329	25	228	8	295
		20	175	29	238	20	258	28	329	26	228	9	295
1	i. 167	21	175	30	238	21	259	29	329	27	228	10	295
2	107	22	175	31	238	22	259	30	329	28	229	11	298
3		23	175	32	239	23	259	31	329	29	238	12	298
4		24	177	33	239	24	260	32	329	30	238	13	298
5	108	25	177	34	240	25	260	33	329	31	238	14	299
6	108	26	177	35	241	26	261	34	329	32	238	15	305
7	109	27	177	36	241	27	261	35	330	33	238	16	308
8		28	177			28	261			34	238	17	308
9		29	177									18	308
10		30	177									19	308
11	110	31	178	**XV.**		**XVII.**		**XIX.**				20	308
12	110	32	178					1	ii. 3	**XXI.**		21	308
13	110	33	179	1	i. 280	1	i. 262	2	3			22	311
14		34	180	2	280	2	262	3	181	1	ii. 250	23	311
15	111	35	180	3	281	3	262	4	181	2	250	24	311
16	111	36	180	4	285	4	263	5	181	3	251	25	312
17	111	37	181	5	285	5	263	6	182	4	251	26	312
18	111	38	181	6	285	6	264	7	183	5	251	27	312
19	111	39	181	7		7	264	8	183	6	252	28	312
20	111	40	183	8	285	8	264	9	184	7	254	29	312
21	111	41	184	9		9	267	10	185	8	254	30	312
22	ii. 40	42	184	10	286	10	268	11	185	9	256	31	315
23	40	43	185	11	286	11	268	12	185	10	260	32	315
24	40	44	185	12	287	12	268	13	206	11	260	33	318
25	41	45	186	13	287	13	268	14	206	12	274	34	318
26	41	46	186	14	287	14	270	15	207	13	274	35	318
27	41	47	187	15	287	15	270	16	210	14	274	36	319
28	42	48	188	16	288	16	271	17	210	15	278	37	319
29	42	49	188	17	288	17	271	18	212	16	278	38	
30	43	50	188	18	289	18	274	19		17		39	320
31	43	51	190	19	289	19	274	20	213	18	260	40	320
32	45	52	190	20	289	20	274	21	213	19	260	41	323
33	45	53	191	21	289	21	275	22	213	20	261	42	323
34	46	54	209	22	289	22	278	23	213	21	262	43	324
35	46	55	209	23	289	23	278	24	214	22	263	44	324
36	46	56	209	24	290	24	304	25	216	23	280	45	324
37	46	57		25	290	25	304	26	217	24	281	46	327
38	46	58	211	26		26	305	27	217	25	281		
39	47			27		27	306	28	217	26	281		
40	47			28	291			29	219	27	282		
41	47			29	291			30	220	28	283	**XXIII.**	
42	48	**XIV.**		30	293					29	283		
43	48			31	293	**XVIII.**				30	283	1	ii. 335
44	49	1	i. 227	32	295			**XX.**		31	283	2	335
45	49	2	227	33	296	1	i. 308			32	284	3	335
46	i. 191	3	226	34	296	2	308	1	ii. 220	33	284	4	335
47	191	4	226	35	296	3	308	2	220	34	285	5	335
48	191	5	226	36	296	4	309	3	221	35	285	6	335
49	191	6	226	37	297	5	309	36	285	36	285	7	
50	191	7	226	38	298	6	312	4	221	37	286	8	336
		8	226			7	312	5	221	38	286	9	336
		9	226	39	298	8	313	6	221	39	286	10	336

INDEX TO QUOTATIONS FROM THE GOSPELS. iii

XXIII.	XXIV.	XXV.	XXV.	XXVI.	XXVII.	XXVII.
11	12 iii. 8	1 iii. 40	45 iii. 60	40 iii. 183	5 iii. 206	49 iii. 243
12	13 8	2 40	46 61	41 183	6 206	50 244
13 ii. 338	14 11	3 40		42 183	7 207	51 245
14	15 14	4 40	XXVI.	43 183	8 207	52 246
15 339	16 15	5 40		44 183	9 210	53 246
16 339	17 15	6 40	1 iii. 65	45 185	10 210	54 247
17 340	18 15	7 40	2 65	46 186	11 215	55 250
18 340	19 15	8 40	3 65	47 186	12 217	56 250
19 340	20 16	9 40	4 65	48 186	13 217	57 254
20 340	21 16	10 41	5 65	49 187	14 218	58 254
21 340	22 25	11 41	6 ii. 246	50 187	15 220	59 255
22 340	23 26	12 41	7 246	51 190	16 220	60 256
23 340	24 26	13 41	8 247	52 191	17 220	61 256
24 340	25 26	14 41	9 247	53 191	18 220	62 256
25 340	26 26	15 42	10 247	54 192	19 221	63 256
26 341	27 27	16 42	11 247	55 192	20 221	64 257
27 341	28 27	17 42	12 247	56 192	21 221	65 257
28 341	29 27	18 42	13 247	57 197	22 221	66 258
29 341	30 28	19 43	14 iii. 66	58 197	23 222	
30 341	31 29	20 43	15 66	59 197	24 222	
31 341	32 30	21 44	16 66	60 198	25 223	XXVIII.
32 341	33 30	22 44	17 81	61 198	26 223	
33 341	34 30	23 44	18 82	62 198	27 223	1 iii. 258
34 342	35 34	24 44	19	63 198	28 223	2 266
35 342	36 34	25 44	20 84	64 199	29 223	3 266
36 343	37 35	26 44	21 87	65 200	30 223	4 266
37 258	38 35	27 44	22 87	66 200	31 227	5 273
38 258	39 35	28 44	23 87	67 201	32 227	6 273
39 258	40 36	29 44	24 206	68 201	33 229	7 273
	41 36	30 45	25 88	69 201	34 229	8 273
	42 37	31 46	26 88	70 202	35 230	9 274
XXIV.	43 39	32 48	27 90	71 202	36 232	10 274
	44 39	33 48	28 90	72 203	37 232	11 276
1 iii. 1	45 39	34 48	29 92	73 203	38 234	12 277
2 1	46 39	35 48	30 177	74 203	39 235	13 277
3 2	47 39	36 48	31 177	75 204	40 235	14 277
4 3	48 39	37 49	32 178		41 235	15 277
5 3	49 39	38 49	33 178		42 236	16 303
6 5	50 39	39 49	34 179	XXVII.	43 235	17 310
7 5	51 39	40 49	35 179		44 236	18 311
8 6		41 55	36 179	1 iii. 205	45 240	19 311
9 6		42 55	37	2 205	46 241	20 317
10 7		43 55	38 180	3 206	47 242	
11 7		44 60	39 180	4 206	48 243	

MARK.

I.	I.	I.	II.	III.	III.	IV.
1 i. 43	21 i. 62	41 i. 97	13 i. 103	2	22 ii. 40	4 i. 167
2 31	22 62	42 97	14 112	3	23 41	5 168
3	23	43 97	15 103	4 i. 110	24 41	6 168
4 30	24	44 97	16 104	5 110	25	7 168
5 32	25	45 97	17	6 111	26 41	8 168
6 31	26 63		18 104	7 113	27 42	9 168
7 34	27 63	II.	19 104	8 113	28 43	10 169
8	28 63		20 105	9 113	29 43	11 169
9 38	29 65	1 i. 99	21	10	30 43	12 170
10 39	30 65	2 99	22	11	31 i. 191	13 171
11 39	31	3 99	23 107	12	32	14 173
12 49	32 65	4 99	24 107	13	33	15 174
13 49	33 65	5	25 108	14 112	34 191	16 175
14 58	34 65	6 100	26 108	15 112	35	17 176
15 60	35 66	7 100	27 109	16		18
16 112	36 66	8 100	28 109	17 112	IV.	19
17 112	37 66	9 101		18		20
18 112	38 66	10 101	III.	19	1 i. 166	21 189
19 112	39 66	11 101		20 ii. 40	2 167	22 189
20	40 96	12 103	1	21 40	3 167	23 190

INDEX TO QUOTATIONS FROM THE GOSPELS.

IV.		VI.		VII.		IX.		X.		XII.		XIII.	
24	i. 190	5	i. 211	17	i. 288	7	i. 263	25	ii. 214	5	ii. 285	29	
25	190	6	212	18	288	8	264	26	216	6	286	30	iii. 30
26		7	213	19	288	9	267	27	217	7	286	31	34
27		8	214	20	288	10	267	28	217	8	286	32	34
28	180	9	214	21	289	11	268	29	219	9	286	33	37
29	180	10	215	22	289	12	268	30	219	10	288	34	37
30	178	11	215	23	289	13	268	31	220	11	288	35	37
31	178	12	225	24	289	14	270	32	223	12	289	36	37
32	178	13	225	25	290	15	270	33	224	13	305	37	38
33	184	14	227	26	290	16	270	34	224	14	308		
34	184	15	227	27	290	17	270	35	227	15	308		
35	191	16	227	28	291	18	271	36	227	16	308	**XIV.**	
36	191	17	226	29	291	19	271	37	227	17	308		
37	192	18	226	30	291	20	272	38	227	18	311	1	iii. 65
38	192	19	226	31	291	21	272	39	227	19	311	2	65
39	193	20	226	32	293	22	272	40	227	20	312	3	ii. 246
40	195	21	226	33	293	23	272	41	228	21	312	4	247
41	194	22	226	34	294	24	272	42	228	22	312	5	247
		23	226	35	294	25	273	43	228	23	312	6	247
		24	226	36	294	26	274	44	229	24	312	7	247
V.		25	226	37	294	27	274	45	229	25	313	8	247
		26	226			28	274	46	237	26	315	9	
1	i. 195	27	226			29	275	47	237	27	315	10	iii. 66
2	196	28	226	**VIII.**		30	278	48	237	28	318	11	66
3	196	29	226			31	278	49	237	29	319	12	81
4	196	30	227	1	i. 295	32	278	50	237	30	319	13	81
5	196	31	228	2	295	33	304	51	237	31	320	14	82
6	196	32	228	3	295	34	308	52	237	32	320	15	84
7	196	33	228	4	296	35	308			33	320	16	84
8	196	34	230	5	296	36	308			34	320	17	84
9	197	35	230	6	296	37	309	**XI.**		35	328	18	87
10	197	36	230	7	296	38	310			36	328	19	87
11	197	37	230	8	296	39	311	1	ii. 251	37	328	20	87
12	197	38	230	9	298	40	311	2	251	38	335	21	87
13	198	39	231	10	298	41	311	3		39	335	22	89
14	198	40	231	11	298	42	311	4	252	40	335	23	91
15	198	41	232	12	299	43	313	5	252	41	344	24	91
16	198	42		13	300	44		6	252	42	344	25	92
17	199	43	232	14	300	45	313	7	252	43	345	26	
18	199	44	231	15	300	46		8	254	44	345	27	
19	199	45	235	16	300	47	313	9	256			28	178
20	199	46	236	17	301	48	313	10	256			29	179
21	201	47	237	18	301	49	314	11	260	**XIII.**		30	179
22	201	48	237	19	301	50	314	12	260			31	179
23	201	49	237	20	301			13	260	1	iii. 1	32	180
24	201	50	237	21	302			14	260	2	1	33	180
25	201	51	239	22	302	**X.**		15	274	3	2	34	180
26	201	52	239	23	303			16	274	4	3	35	180
27	201	53	240	24	303	1	ii. 3	17	274	5	3	36	181
28	202	54	240	25	303	2	181	18	279	6	4	37	183
29	202	55	240	26	303	3	182	19	279	7	5	38	183
30	202	56	240	27	255	4	183	20	261	8	5	39	183
31	202			28	256	5	183	21	261	9	7	40	183
32	202			29	256	6	182	22	262	10	11	41	185
33	202			30	258	7	182	23	262	11	12	42	186
34	203	**VII.**		31	259	8	182	24	263	12	8	43	186
35	204	1	i. 279	32	259	9	182	25	264	13	8	44	187
36	204	2	279	33	259	10	186	26	273	14	14	45	187
37	204	3	280	34	260	11	186	27	280	15	15	46	190
38	204	4	280	35	260	12	186	28	280	16	15	47	190
39	204	5	280	36		13	206	29	281	17	16	48	192
40	204	6	280	37		14	206	30	281	18	16	49	192
41	205	7	280	38	261	15	206	31	281	19	16	50	193
42	205	8	280			16	207	32	281	20	25	51	193
43	205	9	281			17	210	33	282	21	26	52	193
		10	281	**IX.**		18	210			22		53	197
		11	281			19	212			23	26	54	197
VI.		12		1	i. 261	20	213	**XII.**		24	28	55	197
		13		2	262	21	213			25	28	56	198
1	i. 208	14	286	3	262	22		1	ii. 284	26	28	57	198
2	208	15	286	4	262	23	213	2	284	27	28	58	198
3	209	16		5	263	24	214	3	285	28	30	59	198
4	211			6	263			4	285				

INDEX TO QUOTATIONS FROM THE GOSPELS. v

XIV.		XIV.		XV.		XV.		XV.		XV.		XVI.	
60	iii. 198	72	iii. 203	10	iii. 220	22	iii. 228	34	iii. 241	46	iii. 255	9	iii. 271
61	198		XV.	11	221	23	228	35	242	47	256	10	274
62	199			12	221	24	230	36	243		XVI.	11	274
63	200	1	iii. 205	13	222	25	230	37	244			12	277
64	200	2	215	14	222	26	232	38	245	1	iii. 258	13	288
65	201	3	217	15	223	27	234	39	247	2	259	14	297
66	201	4	217	16	223	28	235	40	250	3	265	15	318
67	201	5	218	17	223	29	235	41	250	4	265	16	318
68	202	6	220	18	223	30	235	42	253	5	272	17	326
69	202	7	220	19	223	31	235	43	253	6	273	18	327
70	203	8	220	20	227	32	235	44	255	7	273	19	333
71	203	9	220	21	227	33	240	45	255	8	273	20	333

LUKE.

I.		I.		II.		III.		IV.		V.		VI.	
1	i. 3	53	i. 10	21	i. 18	17	i. 36	27	i. 61	31		40	i. 145
2	3	54	10	22	18	18	36	28	62	32		41	145
3	3	55	10	23	18	19	58	29	62	33	i. 104	42	145
4	4	56	11	24	19	20	58	30	62	34		43	
5	4	57	11	25	19	21	37	31	62	35		44	148
6	4	58	11	26	19	22	39	32	62	36	105	45	148
7	4	59	11	27	19	23	46	33	63	37		46	149
8	4	60	11	28	19	24	46	34	63	38		47	149
9	4	61	11	29	19	25	46	35	63	39	106	48	149
10	4	62	11	30	19	26	46	36				49	149
11	4	63	11	31	19	27	46	37					
12	4	64	11	32	19	28	46	38	65		VI.		
13	4	65	11	33	19	29	46	39	65				VII.
14	4	66	12	34	20	30	46	40	65	1	i. 107		
15	5	67	12	35	20	31	46	41	66	2	107	1	i. 151
16	5	68	13	36	20	32	46	42	66	3		2	151
17	5	69	13	37	20	33	46	43	66	4		3	151
18	5	70	13	38	21	34	46	44	66	5		4	151
19	5	71	13	39	21	35	46			6	109	5	151
20	6	72	13	40	28	36	46			7	109	6	151
21	6	73	13	41	28	37	46			8	109	7	152
22	6	74	13	42	28	38	46		V.	9	110	8	152
23	6	75	13	43	28			1	i. 67	10		9	153
24	6	76	13	44	28			2	67	11	111	10	153
25	6	77	13	45	28		IV.	3	67	12	111	11	154
26	6	78	13	46	28			4	67	13	111	12	154
27	6	79	13	47	28	1	i. 49	5	68	14	112	13	154
28	6	80	14	48	29	2	49	6	68	15	112	14	154
29	7			49	29	3	49	7	68	16	112	15	154
30	7			50	29	4	49	8	68	17	113	16	154
31	7		II.	51	29	5	51	9	68	18	114	17	154
32	7			52	30	6	51	10	68	19	114	18	157
33	7	1	i. 15			7	51	11	68	20	118	19	157
34	7	2	15			8	52	12	96	21	118	20	157
35	7	3	15			9	50	13	97	22	119	21	158
36	7	4	15		III.	10	50	14		23		22	158
37	7	5	15	1	i. 30	11	50	15	98	24	118	23	158
38	7	6	15	2	30	12	50	16	99	25	118	24	158
39	9	7	15	3	30	13	53	17	99	26	120	25	159
40	9	8	16	4	31	14	58	18	99	27	130	26	159
41	9	9	16	5	31	15	60	19	99	28	130	27	159
42	9	10	16	6	31	16	60	20		29		28	159
43	9	11	16	7	32	17	60	21	100	30	129	29	159
44	9	12	16	8	33	18	60	22		31	130	30	161
45	9	13	16	9		19	60	23		32	130	31	161
46	10	14	16	10	33	20	61	24		33	131	32	161
47	10	15	16	11	33	21	61	25	103	34	131	33	161
48	10	16	16	12	33	22	61	26	103	35	130	34	161
49	10	17	17	13	33	23	61	27	103	36	131	35	161
50	10	18	17	14	33	24	61	28	103	37	143	36	162
51	10	19	17	15	34	25	61	29	103	38	144	37	162
52	10	20	18	16	34	26	61	30	104	39	144	38	162

vi INDEX TO QUOTATIONS FROM THE GOSPELS.

VII.		IX.		X.		XI.		XII.		XIV.		XVI.	
39 i.	162	1 i.	213	7 ii.	85	33 ii.	51	47 ii.	71	16 ii.	153	12 ii.	177
40	162	2	8	8	85	34	51	48	72	17	153	13	178
41	162	3	214	9	86	35	52	49 i.	221	18	154	14	180
42	162	4	215	10	86	36	52	50	221	19	154	15	180
43	163	5	215	11	86	37	52	51	222	20	154	16	180
44	163	6	225	12	86	38	53	52	222	21	154	17	180
45	163	7	227	13	86	39	53	53	222	22	154	18	180
46	163	8	227	14	86	40	53	54 ii.	74	23	154	19	186
47	163	9	227	15	86	41	53	55	74	24	154	20	186
48	165	10	227	16		42	54	56	74	25	155	21	186
49	165	11	230	17	89	43	54	57	74	26	155	22	186
50	165	12	230	18	89	44	55	58	74	27	155	23	187
		13	230	19	90	45	55	59.	75	28	155	24	188
		14	231	20	91	46	55			29	155	25	188
VIII.		15	231	21	91	47	56			30	156	26	188
		16	232	22	91	48	57	XIII.		31	156	27	189
1 i.	165	17	232	23	93	49	57			32	156	28	189
2	166	18	256	24	93	50	57	1 ii.	75	33	156	29	189
3	166	19	256	25	97	51	57	2	76	34	157	30	189
4	166	20	256	26	97	52	58	3	76	35	157	31	189
5	167	21	258	27	97	53	59	4	76				
6	168	22	259	28	97	54	59	5	76				
7	168	23	260	29	98			6	77	XV.		XVII.	
8	168	24		30	98			7	77				
9	169	25	261	31	98	XII.		8	77	1 ii.	157	1 ii.	194
10	169	26		32	98			9	77	2	157	2	194
11	172	27	261	33	98	1 ii.	59	10	78	3	158	3	194
12		28	262	34	98	2 i.	219	11	78	4	158	4	194
13		29	262	35	99	3	219	12	78	5	158	5	195
14	175	30	262	36	99	4	219	13	79	6	158	6	195
15	176	31	262	37	99	5	219	14	79	7	158	7	196
16	176	32	263	38	100	6	220	15	79	8	158	8	196
17	189	33	263	39	100	7	220	16	80	9	159	9	197
18	190	34	263	40	100	8	221	17	80	10	159	10	197
19	191	35	263	41	101	9	221	18 i.	179	11	162	11	198
20		36	264	42	101	10 ii.	60	19	179	12	162	12	198
21	191	37	270			11		20	179	13	163	13	198
22	191	38	270			12		21	179	14	163	14	198
23	192	39	271	XI.		13	60	22 ii.	142	15	163	15	198
24	192	40	271			14	60	23	142	16	163	16	198
25	194	41	271	1 ii.	136	15	60	24	142	17	163	17	198
26	196	42	274	2	136	16	61	25	142	18	164	18	198
27	196	43	278	3	137	17	61	26	141	19	164	19	198
28	196	44	278	4	137	18	61	27	144	20	164	20	199
29	196	45	278	5	138	19	61	28	144	21	164	21	199
30	197	46	307	6	138	20	61	29	145	22	165	22	199
31	197	47	308	7	138	21	61	30	145	23	165	23	199
32	197	48	309	8	138	22	62	31	146	24	165	24	199
33	198	49	310	9	139	23		32	146	25	165	25	200
34	198	50	311	10	139	24 i.	139	33	146	26	165	26	200
35	198	51 ii.	80	11	139	25		34	258	27	166	27	200
36	198	52	81	12	139	26	139	35	258	28	166	28	200
37	199	53	81	13	139	27				29	166	29	200
38	199	54	81	14	140	28				30	166	30	200
39	199	55	81	15	140	29	140			31	166	31	200
40	201	56	81	16	140	30		XIV.		32	166	32	200
41	201	57	81	17	41	31						33	200
42	201	58	81	18	41	32 ii.	62	1 ii.	147			34	201
43	201	59	82	19		33	62	2	117			35	201
44	202	60	82	20	42	34	62	3	147	XVI.		36	201
45	202	61	82	21	42	35	62	4	148			37	201
46	202	62	83	22	42	36	62	5	148	1 ii.	167		
47	202			23		37	62	6	148	2	172		
48				24		38	64	7	148	3	173		
49	204	X.		25	49	39	64	8	148	4	173	XVIII.	
50	204			26	49	40	64	9	149	5	173		
51		1 ii.	84	27	49	41	64	10	149	6	173	1 ii.	201
52		2	84	28	50	42	65	11	150	7	173	2	201
53	204	3	84	29	47	43	70	12	151	8	174	3	201
54	205	4	85	30	47	44	70	13	151	9	175	4	201
55	205	5	85	31	48	45	70	14	151	10	176	5	201
56	205	6	85	32	48	46	70	15	153	11	177	6	201

INDEX TO QUOTATIONS FROM THE GOSPELS.

XVIII.	XIX.	XX.	XXI.	XXII.	XXIII.	XXIV.
7 ii. 202	13 ii. 242	14 ii. 286	16 iii. 8	27 iii. 126	4 iii. 218	1 iii. 259
8 202	14 242	15 286	17 8	28 126	5 218	2 266
9 203	15 243	16 286	18 8	29 126	6 218	3 273
10 204	16 243	17 287	19 8	30 126	7 218	4 273
11 204	17 243	18 287	20 14	31 127	8 218	5 273
12 204	18 243	19 289	21 15	32 128	9 219	6 273
13 204	19 243	20 305	22 16	33 128	10 219	7 273
14 204	20 243	21 308	23 16	34 128	11 219	8 273
15 206	21 243	22 308	24 16	35 130	12 219	9 273
16 206	22 244	23 308	25 28	36 130	13 219	10 274
17 206	23 244	24 308	26 28	37 132	14 219	11 275
18 211	24 244	25 308	27 28	38 133	15 219	12 275
19 211	25 244	26 311	28 30	39 179	16 219	13 277
20 212	26 244	27 311	29 30	40 179	17	14 277
21 213	27 245	28 311	30 30	41 180	18 222	15 277
22 213	28 250	29 312	31 30	42 180	19 222	16 277
23 213	29 251	30 312	32	43 184	20 222	17 278
24 213	30 251	31 312	33 34	44 184	21 222	18 278
25 214	31 251	32 312	34 36	45 185	22 222	19 278
26 216	32 252	33 312	35 36	46 185	23 222	20 278
27 217	33 252	34 313	36 37	47 186	24 223	21 278
28 217	34 252	35 313	37 65	48 187	25 223	22 278
29 219	35 252	36 313	38 65	49 190	26 227	23 278
30	36 254	37 315		50 190	27 228	24 279
31 224	37 256	38 315		51 192	28 228	25 279
32 224	38 256	39 318	XXII.	52 192	29 228	26 279
33 224	39 257	40 318		53 192	30 228	27 279
34 224	40 257	41 328	1 iii. 65	54 193	31 228	28 282
35 230	41 257	42 328	2 66	55 197	32 228	29 282
36 235	42 257	43 328	3 66	56 202	33 229	30 282
37 235	43 257	44 328	4 66	57 202	34 230	31 284
38 235	44 257	45 334	5 66	58 203	35 235	32 288
39 235	45 274	46 334	6 66	59 203	36 236	33 288
40 236	46 274	47 334	7 81	60 203	37 236	34 288
41 236	47 279		8 81	61 204	38 232	35 288
42 236	48 279		9 81	62	39 236	36 289
43 236			10 81	63 201	40 236	37 289
			11 82	64 201	41 236	38 289
		XX.	1 ii. 344	12 84	65 201	42 236	39 289
XIX.			2 344	13 84	66 197	43 239	40 289
	1 ii. 280	3 345	14 84	67 199	44 241	41 290
1 ii. 240	2 280	4 345	15 84	68 199	45 245	42
2 240	3 281	5 iii. 1	16 84	69 199	46 244	43
3 240	4 281	6 2	17 85	70 199	47 248	44 301
4 240	5 281	7 2	18 85	71 200	48 249	45 301
5 240	6 281	8 3	19 89		49 249	46 301
6 241	7 282	9 5	20 91		50 254	47 301
7 241	8 282	10 5	21 124		51 254	48 302
8 241	9 284	11 5	22 124	XXIII.	52 254	49 302
9 241	10 285	12 7	23 124		53 255	50 303
10 241	11 285	13 7	24 126	1 iii. 205	54 256	51 303
11 242	12 285	14 12	25 126	2 215	55 256	52 303
12 242	13 286	15 12	26 126	3 215	56 256	53 303

JOHN.

I.	I.	I.	I.	I.	II.	II.
1 i. 1	13 i. 41	25 i. 34	37 i. 43	49 i. 45	5 i. 55	17 ii. 276
2 2	14 26	34 38	43 50 46	6 56	18 276
3 2	15 42	27 34	39 43	51 46	7 56	19 276
4 2	16 42	28 37	40 44		8 56	20 276
5 2	17 42	29 37	41 44		9 56	21 276
6 13	18 43	30 37	42 44		10 56	22 276
7 13	19 34	31 37	43 44	II.	11 57	23 279
8 13	20 34	32 39	44 44		12 58	24 279
9 13	21 34	33 39	45 44	1 i. 55	13 ii. 274	25 280
10 40	22 34	34 39	46 45	2 55	14 274	
11 40	23 34	35 43	47 45	3 55	15 274	
12 40	24 34	36 43	48 45	4 55	16 274	

viii INDEX TO QUOTATIONS FROM THE GOSPELS.

III.	IV.	V.	VI.	VIII.	IX.	X.
1 ii. 11	32 i. 77	45 i. 95	65 i. 254	4 ii. 19	12 ii. 105	38 ii. 124
2 11	33 77	46 95	66 254	5 19	13 105	39 124
3 12	34 77	47 96	67 255	6 19	14 105	40 124
4 12	35 77		68 255	7 21	15 106	41 125
5 12	36 77		69 255	8 21	16 106	42 125
6 12	37 77		70 255	9 21	17 106	
7 13	38 77	VI.	71	10 21	18 106	
8 13	39 78			11 21	19 106	XI.
9 13	40 78	1 i. 228		12 22	20 111	
10 13	41 78	2 229		13 22	21 111	1 ii. 125
11 13	42 78	3 229	VII.	14 22	22 111	2 125
12 14	43 78	4 229		15 22	23 111	3 125
13 14	44 78	5 229	1 ii. 1	16 22	24 111	4 125
14 15	45 79	6 229	2 1	17 23	25 111	5 125
15	46 81	7 229	3 1	18 23	26 111	6 125
16 15	47 82	8 231	4 1	19 23	27 112	7 125
17 16	48 82	9 231	5 2	20 23	28 112	8 125
18 17	49 82	10 231	6 2	21 23	29 112	9 125
19 17	50 82	11 232	7 2	22 24	30 112	10 125
20 17	51 82	12 232	8 2	23 24	31 112	11 126
21 17	52 83	13 232	9 3	24 24	32 112	12 126
22 i. 67	53 83	14 236	10 3	25 24	33 112	13 126
23 67	54 83	15 236	11 3	26 25	34 112	14 126
24 67		16 236	12 3	27 25	35 113	15 126
25 69		17 236	13 4	28 25	36 113	16 126
26 70		18 236	14 4	29 26	37 113	17 126
27 70	V.	19 237	15 4	30 26	38 113	18 126
28 70		20 237	16 4	31 26	39 113	19 126
29 70	1 i. 84	21 238	17 4	32 26	40 114	20 127
30 70	2 84	22 241	18 4	33 26	41 114	21 127
31 70	3 84	23 242	19 4	34 26		22 127
32 71	4 85	24 242	20 5	35 26		23 127
33 71	5 84	25 243	21 5	36 27		24 127
34 71	6 84	26 243	22 5	37 27	X.	25 127
35 71	7 84	27 243	23 5	38 27		26 127
36 72	8 86	28 243	24 5	39 27	1 ii. 114	27 129
	9 86	29 243	25 6	40 27	2 114	28 129
	10 86	30 244	26 6	41 27	3 114	29 129
	11 86	31 244	27 6	42 28	4 114	30 129
IV.	12 86	32 244	28 6	43 28	5 114	31 129
	13 86	33 244	29 6	44 28	6 114	32 130
1 i. 72	14 87	34 245	30 6	45 30	7 115	33 130
2 72	15 87	35 245	31 6	46 30	8 115	34 130
3 72	16 87	36 245	32 7	47 30	9 115	35 130
4 73	17 87	37 245	33 7	48 30	10 116	36 130
5 73	18 87	38 245	34 7	49 30	11 116	37 130
6 73	19 88	39 247	35 7	50 30	12 116	38 130
7 73	20 88	40 247	36 7	51 31	13 116	39 130
8 73	21 88	41 248	37 7	52 33	14 116	40 131
9 73	22 88	42 248	38 7	53 33	15 117	41 131
10 73	23 88	43 248	39 8	54 33	16 117	42 131
11 74	24 88	44 249	40 8	55 34	17 118	43 131
12 74	25 89	45 249	41 9	56 35	18 118	44 131
13 74	26 90	46 249	42 9	57 36	19 120	45 133
14 74	27 90	47 250	43 9	58 36	20 120	46 133
15 74	28 90	48 250	44 9	59 36	21 130	47 134
16 74	29 92	49 250	45 9		22 121	48 134
17 74	30 94	50 250	46 9		23 121	49 134
18 74	31 94	51 250	47 9		24 121	50 134
19 74	32 94	52 250	48 9	IX.	25 121	51 134
20 75	33 94	53 250	49 10		26 122	52 135
21 75	34 94	54 251	50 10	1 ii. 102	27 122	53 135
22 75	35 94	55 251	51 10	2 102	28 122	54 136
23 75	36 94	56 251	52 10	3 103	29 122	55 245
24 75	37 94	57 251	53 10	4 103	30 123	56 246
25 76	38 94	58 251		5 103	31 123	57 246
26 76	39 95	59 253		6 104	32 123	
27 76	40 95	60 254	VIII.	7 104	33 123	
28 76	41 95	61 254		8 105	34 123	XII.
29 76	42 95	62 254	1 ii. 19	9 105	35 124	
30 77	43 95	63 254	2 19	10 105	36 124	1 ii. 246
	77 44	95 64	254 3	19 11	105 37	124 2 246

INDEX TO QUOTATIONS FROM THE GOSPELS.

XII.
3 ii. 246
4 247
5 247
6 247
7 247
8 247
9 250
10 250
11 250
12 254
13 255
14 255
15 255
16 255
17 255
18 255
19 257
20 iii. 67
21 67
22 67
23 67
24 67
25 68
26 68
27 69
28 70
29 70
30 71
31 72
32 73
33 73
34 73
35 74
36 75
37 75
38 75
39 75
40 75
41 76
42 76
43 77
44 77
45 77
46 77
47 77
48 78
49 78
50 78

XIII.
1 iii. 117
2 117
3 iii. 117
4 117
5 117
6 118
7 118
8 118
9 118
10 118
11 119
12 119
13 119
14 119
15 119
16 119
17 120
18 122
19 123
20 124
21 124
22 124
23 124
24 124
25 124
26 125
27 125
28 125
29 125
30 125
31 125
32 126
33 128
34 128
35 129
36 129
37 129
38 129

XIV.
1 iii. 133
2 133
3 134
4 134
5 135
6 135
7 135
8 135
9 135
10 136
11 136
12 136
13 137
14 138
15 iii. 138
16 139
17 140
18 141
19 142
20 142
21 142
22 142
23 142
24 142
25 142
26 143
27 144
28 144
29 145
30 145
31 146

XV.
1 iii. 148
2 148
3 148
4 148
5 148
6 148
7 149
8 149
9 149
10 149
11 150
12 150
13 151
14 151
15 151
16 151
17 151
18 152
19 153
20 153
21 153
22 153
23 153
24 153
25 154
26 154
27 154

XVI.
1 iii. 155
2 155
3 iii. 155
4 156
5 157
6 157
7 157
8 157
9 158
10 158
11 158
12 160
13 161
14 161
15 161
16 162
17 162
18 162
19 162
20 162
21 163
22 163
23 163
24 163
25 164
26 165
27 165
28 166
29 169
30 169
31 169
32 169
33 170

XVII.
1 iii. 170
2 171
3 172
4 173
5 173
6 173
7 173
8 174
9 174
10 174
11 175
12 175
13 175
14 175
15 175
16 176
17 176
18 176
19 iii. 176
20 176
21 176
22 176
23 177
24 177
25 177
26 177

XVIII.
1 iii. 179
2 179
3 186
4 187
5 187
6 188
7 190
8 190
9 190
10 191
11 191
12 193
13 194
14 194
15 194
16 194
17 194
18 195
19 195
20 195
21 195
22 195
23 196
24 196
25 202
26 203
27 203
28 205
29 215
30 215
31 215
32 215
33 216
34 216
35 216
36 216
37 216
38 217
39 220
40 222

XIX.
1 iii. 224
2 224
3 224
4 224
5 224
6 224
7 224
8 224
9 224
10 225
11 225
12 225
13 226
14 226
15 227
16 227
17 227
18 229
19 232
20 233
21 233
22 234
23 236
24 236
25 240
26 240
27 240
28 242
29 243
30 244
31 250
32 250
33 250
34 250
35 251
36 253
37 253
38 254
39 255
40 255
41 256
42 256

XX.
1 iii. 259
2 266
3 267
4 267
5 267
6 267
7 267
8 iii. 267
9 268
10 268
11 268
12 268
13 268
14 268
15 269
16 269
17 269
18 274
19 290
20 290
21 291
22 291
23 291
24 295
25 295
26 295
27 296
28 296
29 296
30 298
31 298

XXI.
1 iii. 304
2 304
3 304
4 304
5 304
6 304
7 304
8 305
9 305
10 305
11 305
12 305
13 305
14 305
15 305
16 307
17 307
18 307
19 308
20 308
21 308
22 308
23 308
24 309
25 310

INDEX TO VARIOUS SUBJECTS.

Age-during, I. 89, 251, 313; II. 15, 31, 122, 128, 212, 273; III. 172
Almsgiving, II. 344—354
Angels, I. 8, 183, 264, 315; II. 313; III. 50—55
Apostles, I. 112, 216
Arnold, Matthew, II. 110, 119, 135
Articles of Religion, II. 58
Athanasian Creed, I. 155, 221; III. 167
Baptism, I. 32, 273, 322; II. 18, 207; III. 313—315
Blasphemy, II. 43; III. 249
Church, I. 187, 257, 316—327; II. 230
Coming, III. 32, 33, 36, 47
Common Tradition, I. 106, 114, 167, 172, 241, 277, 301; II. 282, 289
Confirmation, II. 208
Demons, I. 63, 182, 200, 273; II. 49, 90
Disciples, I. 121, 129, 260; II. 62, 84, 117, 156, 167—172, 176, 179, 215, 231, 271, 296, 307; II. 311, 336—338; III. 6, 7, 49, 50—54, 68, 121, 150, 300, 312, 317, 321—326
Emulation, II. 205
Faith, I. 203, 207, 211, 274; II. 195
Fasting, I. 105
Forgiveness, I. 100—102, 134, 135, 163, 328—330; II. 44, 264; III. 292—294
Gehenna, I. 220, 313; II. 339
Glory, III. 280
God, I. 75, 155, 156; II. 316
Hell. *See* Gehenna.
Holy, I. 8, 40; II. 91
Holy Spirit, II. 8, 12, 91, 140, 328, 330; III. 13, 141, 143, 291
In my name, I. 316, 327; III. 4, 163, 313
Inspiration, I., 3, 12, 53, 56, 78, 232, 237, 281, 308; II. 240, 321, 330—334

Jehovah, II. 324—327
Jews, II. 3, 106—111, 250, 278
Last day, I. 247, 251; II. 127
Lord's Prayer, III. 78
Lord's Supper, I. 225, 252; III. 84—116
Miracles, I. 56—58, 193—195, 233, 239, 274, 297, 306; II. 236, 261; III. 298, 326
Mother of Jesus, I. 17, 209; II. 1, 50
Only-begotten, I. 42; II. 17
Parables, II. 160—162; III. 42
Political Economy, II. 65—72
Politics, III. 257
Prayer, I. 133; II. 55, 137—139, 263 III. 17—25
Preaching, II. 37, 56, 101, 348—352
Prophecies, I. 26, 66
Repentance, III. 302
Resurrection, I. 91; II. 127, 133, 151, 191, 277, 312—318; III. 8—10, 247
Revisers, I. 35
Righteousness, II. 300—305; III. 159
Sabbath, III. 261—265
Salvation. I. 174; II. 145, 223; III. 11, 58, 182, 254, 295, 319—326
Salvation Army, II. 256; III. 315
Scripture-reading, II. 34
Son of God, I. 40, 246, 255; II. 330; III. 249
Son of man, I. 101, 109, 120, 161, 218, 255; II. 64
Spirit, III. 140
Spiritual body, III. 285
Temptation, I. 49
Tongues, III. 327—332
Trinity, III. 167
Vengeance, II. 202
War, II. 272, 298, 305
Word, I. 1, 42
World, III. 3
Yoke, II. 94—96

INDEX TO MIRACLES.

	PAGE
Healing of demoniac	I. 63
" Simon's mother-in-law	65
" nobleman's son	82
" infirm man	84
" leper	96
" palsied man	99
" withered hand	109
" centurion's servant	151
" demoniac	196
" Jairus' daughter	201
" a woman	201
" two blind men	206
" a Gentile woman's daughter	289
" deaf, stuttering man	293
" blind man	305
" deformed woman	II. 78
" man born blind	102
" man with dropsy	147

	PAGE
Healing of ten lepers	II. 198
" two blind men	230
" Malchus' ear	III. 192
Casting out of dumb and deaf spirit	I. 273
" " demons into swine	198
Raising of widow's son	154
" Lazarus	II. 125
Turning water into wine	I. 55
Draught of fishes	68
" "	III. 304
Multiplication of loaves and fishes	I. 229
" " "	295
The fish and the stater	306
Stilling of the storm	193
Walking on the sea	237
Cursing of the fig-tree	II. 260

INDEX TO PARABLES.

	PAGE		PAGE
Marriage and fasting	I. 104	The wounded traveller	II. 98
Old and new cloth	105	Door, shepherd, sheep, thieves, and robbers	114
Wine and bottles	106		
Old and new wine	106	Shepherd and hireling	116
City on a hill	122	The friends and the traveller	138
Blind guides of the blind	144	The narrow door	143
Good and bad trees	148	Seekers of chief seats	148
" " treasure	148	The great supper	53
Wise and foolish builders	149	The builder of a tower	155
Two debtors	162	The king going to war	156
The sower and the seed	167	Savourless salt	I. 121
Good and bad seed	177		II. 57
Mustard seed	178	The lost sheep	II. 158
Leaven	179	" " coin	158
Growing seed	180	The father and his sons	162
Hidden treasure	185	The rich man and his steward	172
Merchant seeking pearls	186	" " Lazarus	186
Drag-net	187	The servant and his master	197
Lamp under a bushel	122, 189	The unjust judge	201
Householder and his treasures	190	The Pharisee and the publican	205
Shepherdless sheep	212	The camel and the needle's eye	214
Harvest and labourers	212	The householder and the labourers	220
Children and dogs	290		
Leaven of Pharisees and Herod	300	The cup and the baptism	227
Lost sheep	316	The nobleman and his kingdom	242
Two debtors	328		
Divided kingdom, city or house	II. 41	The withered fig-tree	260
The lighted lamp	51	The two sons	283
The rich fool	61	The vineyard and the husbandmen	284
Servants watching	62		
Unwatchful householder	64	The royal marriage	292
The faithful steward	65	Gnat and camel	340
The unfaithful servant	70	The budding trees	III. 30
Cloud and wind	74	The watchman	37
The slaughtered Galileans	75	The ten virgins	40
The tower in Siloam	76	The talents	42
The barren fig tree	77	The sheep and the goats	48
The dead	82	Vine, husbandman and branches	148
The ploughman	83		
Harvest labourers	84	The green tree and the dry	228

BRADBURY AGNEW, & CO. LD., PRINTERS, WHITEFRIARS

www.ingramcontent.com/pod-product-compliance
Lightning Source LLC
Chambersburg PA
CBHW020304240426
43673CB00039B/694